D0364550

100
Great Lives
of Antiquity

100
Great Lives
of Antiquity

EDITED BY
JOHN CANNING

GUILD PUBLISHING LONDON

This edition first published in 1985 by
Book Club Associates
by arrangement with
Methuen London Ltd
Copyright © 1985 Century Books Ltd
Printed in Great Britain

Contents

List of Illustrations   viii
Editor's Note   ix

Rulers and Warriors

Egypt
The Pharaohs: What the
    Mummies Reveal   Rosalie David   I
Thothmose III   M. L. Bierbrier   6
Ramesses II   M. L. Bierbrier   I I
Shoshenk I   M. L. Bierbrier   I 5
Ptolemy I (Soter)   Miriam Stead   20
Ptolemy II (Philadelphus) Miriam Stead   26

Babylonia, Assyria and Syria
Tiglath-Pileser I   Harry Saggs   31
Tiglath-Pileser III   Harry Saggs   37
Sargon II   Harry Saggs   42
Sennacherib   Harry Saggs   48
Ashurbanipal   Harry Saggs   54
Nebuchadnezzar   Harry Saggs   59
Seleucus I   Harry Saggs   65
Antiochus III   Harry Saggs   71

Palestine
David   David Bolt   78
Solomon   Geoffrey Parrinder   83
Herod I   Harry Saggs   87

Persia
Cyrus the Great   John Curtis   94
Cambyses   John Curtis   99
Darius the Great   John Curtis   103
Xerxes   John Curtis   108

Greece
Cleisthenes   R. A. Tomlinson   I 13
Themistocles   R. A. Tomlinson   I 20
Pericles   R. A. Tomlinson   I 26
Philip II of Macedon   R. A. Tomlinson   I 33
Alexander the Great   R. A. Tomlinson   I 39
Attalos I of Pergamon   R. A. Tomlinson   I 47

Carthage
Hannibal   Allan Massie   I 53

Rome
Scipio   Allan Massie   160
Marius   Allan Massie   164
Sulla   Allan Massie   170
Cicero   Allan Massie   176
Julius Caesar   Allan Massie   182
Julius Caesar and ⎱
    Shakespeare   ⎰   A. L. Rowse   189
Augustus   Allan Massie   197
Tiberius   Michael Hardwick   202
Claudius   Michael Hardwick   208
Nero   Michael Hardwick   213
Vespasian   Michael Hardwick   219
Trajan   Allan Massie   224
Hadrian   Michael Hardwick   229
Marcus Aurelius   Allan Massie   235
Diocletian   Allan Massie   239
Theodosius I (The Great)   Allan Massie   244

Writers and Sculptors

Homer   Richard Stoneman   249
Aeschylus   Richard Stoneman   253
Pindar   Richard Stoneman   257
Sophocles   Richard Stoneman   262
Pheidias   R. A. Tomlinson   266
Herodotus   Asa Briggs   271
Euripides   Richard Stoneman   277
Thucydides   Asa Briggs   282
Aristophanes   Richard Stoneman   288
Praxiteles   R. A. Tomlinson   293
Virgil   Michael Hardwick   299
Horace   Michael Hardwick   304
Livy   Richard Stoneman   310
Ovid   Michael Hardwick   314
Seneca   Allan Massie   321
Pliny the Elder   ⎱
Pliny the Younger ⎰   Richard Ormrod   324
Plutarch   Allan Massie   329
Josephus   Harry Saggs   333

Reformers

Hammurabi   Harry Saggs   339
Moses   Harry Saggs   344
Akhenaton   Geoffrey Parrinder 350
Solon   R. A. Tomlinson   354

Asoka   Geoffrey Parrinder   359
Tiberius Gracchus   Allan Massie   364
Constantine the Great   Allan Massie   369

Women of Power and Influence

Queen Hatshepsut   Mollie Hardwick   375
Sappho   Richard Stoneman   380
Olympias   R. A. Tomlinson   385
Aspasia of Miletus   R. A. Tomlinson   391
Artemisia of Halicarnassus   Richard Garrett   396
Cleopatra   Mollie Hardwick   400
Livia   Allan Massie   406
Boudicca   Mollie Hardwick   410
Zenobia   Harry Saggs   416
Hypatia of Alexandria   John Grant   422

Men of Science

Thales   R. A. Tomlinson   427
Democritus   John Grant   431
Hippocrates   John Grant   437
Euclid   John Grant   442
Herophilus   John Grant   447
Aristarchus of Samos   Patrick Moore   450
Erasistratus   John Grant   454
Archimedes   John Grant   458
Eratosthenes   R. A. Tomlinson   463
Pytheas   Kenneth Poolman   468
Hero of Alexandria   John Grant   473
Ptolemy   John Grant   477

Philosophers and Religious Leaders

Zoroaster   Geoffrey Parrinder   481
Lao Tzu   Geoffrey Parrinder   486
Confucius   Geoffrey Parrinder   490
Pythagoras   John Grant   495
Buddha   Geoffrey Parrinder   501
Plato   Geoffrey Parrinder   505
Aristotle   Geoffrey Parrinder   510
Saint Paul   Lord Soper   515
Mani   Geoffrey Parrinder   519
Saint Augustine of Hippo   Geoffrey Parrinder   524

Index   528

List of Illustrations

1a	Hammurabi praying	facing page 54
1b	The laws of Hammurabi	54
2a	The temple of Queen Hatshepsut at Deir el-Bahri	55
2b	The queen drinking from the udder of Hathor	55
2c	A black marble head of Queen Hatshepsut	55
3a	Sculpture of Akhenaton	86
3b	Akhenaton and his wife, Nefertiti	86
4a	The mummy of Ramesses II	87
4b	Colossal head of Ramesses II at Abu Simbel	87
5a	Assyrian bas-relief showing one of Tiglath-Pileser III's campaigns	150
5b	Ashurbanipal spearing a lion	150
6a	The tomb of Cyrus the Great at Pasargadae	151
6b	Darius the Great receiving tribute	151
7a	Homer	182
7b	Herodotus	182
7c	Thucydides	182
8a	Pericles	183
8b	The Parthenon	183
9	Statue of Buddha at Sarnath	342
10a	Sassanian rock-carving at Taq-i-Bustan, depicting royal investiture	343
10b	Lao Tzu	343
11a	Coin showing head of Philip II of Macedon	374
11b	Mosaic showing Plato with his pupils	374
12a	Mosaic at Pompeii showing Alexander the Great on horseback	375
12b	Darius III (from same mosaic)	375
13a	Alexander the Great depicted as divine Pharaoh with Amun-Re	438
13b	The Edict of Asoka	438
14a	Julius Caesar	439
14b	Cleopatra	439
14c	Wall-carving at Dendera showing Cleopatra with Caesarion	439
15a	Augustus Caesar	470
15b	Mosaic showing Virgil with Clio and Melpomone	470
16a	Trajan at a boar-hunt	471
16b	Marcus Aurelius addressing troops (both from the Arch of Constantine)	471

The photographs in this book are reproduced
by kind permission of the following:
Ronald Sheridan's Photo-Library, 1a, 2b, 3b, 4b, 6a, 8b, 13a, 14b;
the Mansell Collection, 1b, 3a, 5a, 5b, 6b, 8a, 9, 10b, 11b, 12a, 12b, 13b,
14a, 15a, 15b, 16a, 16b; BBC Hulton Picture Library, 2a, 2c, 11a, 14c;
Popperfoto, 4a, 7a, 7b, 7c, 10a

Editor's Note

The time-span I have taken to connote Antiquity is from earliest recorded history to the break-up of the Roman Empire. Translating this into significant individual lives of which we have sufficient knowledge to form an assessment, the earliest is Hammurabi (c. 1800 B.C.) and the latest Saint Augustine (died A.D. 430). The period covered therefore is over two thousand years. About the same time separates us today from Augustine as separates him from Solomon; nearly another millennium separates the latter from Hammurabi.

Traversing these immense periods of time through narrative histories is somewhat like flying at high altitudes. The main masses of the landscape are discernible, but the detailed topography often eludes the eye. To get a better picture of the territory it is necessary to make the occasional descent at well-chosen spots along the route. This is, in a sense, what I have attempted to do in this volume, alighting at a number of significant points along the historical road to look at the world as it appeared to people who also helped to mould it.

The contributions taken together will I hope provide a different focus on the past, and possibly an insight or two that might otherwise elude the reader interested in these times.

It is, for example, interesting to detect some of those qualities in a ruler that raised Babylon from a minor city to a renowned world capital. We are told that Hammurabi recognised the importance to his kingdom of canal-building, and spent most of his reign on this vital work. The vision which foresaw the increased power and security conferred by a controlled water supply was thus early apparent. An imaginative use of technology in warfare also paid dividends: 'By the wisdom given to him by the god Marduk, he destroyed (a certain city) with a great mass of water' – in other words he had inundated the city by contriving an artificial flood. To the visionary and warrior was added the wise statesman, as witnessed by his great code of laws.

Again, it is impossible to get a rounded perspective of the conquest of Gaul without a look at Caesar's motives and character. Nor is it possible to form even a sketchy view of life in

Periclean Athens without a look, in however brief detail, at the authors who had already put in place one of the greatest literatures of the world, embracing within its scope the sublimest lyric and epic poetry, drama which has only been surpassed by Shakespeare, philosophy which has never been surpassed, and history both entertaining and scrupulously researched.

Without the mighty proselytism of Saint Paul the development of Christianity – which at first seemed to the Romans no more than an obscure Jewish heresy – might have been very different. He more than anyone was responsible for transforming it into a great world religion. But in imparting to Christianity the impress of his powerful personality did he, as is controversially argued here, run counter to certain vital aspects of Christ's message?

The use of the word 'Great' in the title is intended to connote only historical importance; it has no ethical significance, as will readily be apparent from several of the Roman inclusions.

I have felt it worthwhile to include two additional chapters, though they are only contingent to the main subject matter. One deals with Egyptian mummification, the research into which makes it important today as a historical tool; the other with the impact of one of the greatest figures of the ancient world on the mind and art of the world's greatest dramatist.

John Canning

The Pharaohs:
What the Mummies Reveal

Along the banks of the Nile, some five thousand years ago, a civilisation developed which was to dominate all surrounding lands. A major feature of this civilisation was the concept of kingship. From *c.* 3100 B.C., when Narmer, the ruler of the southern kingdom, conquered the north and established a unified country, the role of the king became an essential element in creating a stable political, religious and social structure. From the beginning, it was the king who held together a land which, with its geographical background and its scattered tribal communities, was difficult to rule. Indeed, when the kings were weak or ineffectual rulers, the country once again became divided into regions which were each controlled by warring local chieftains who owed no allegiance to a central authority.

The Egyptians believed that their kings were partly divine. Each ruler was considered to be the offspring of the great state god and of a human mother – the Great Royal Wife of the previous king. With a status which was partly human and partly divine, the king was uniquely placed to act as a mediator between the gods and mankind. Some powers and duties were derived from his original role as a tribal chieftain but, as his responsibilities increased, the king delegated many of these to state officials. However, the fiction was maintained that, as the god's son, he alone could build and consecrate all the temples throughout Egypt, and he was also believed to perform the daily rituals in each one, presenting the gods' images with food and clothing. In practice, the priests who were the 'servants of the gods' undertook these duties on the king's behalf. Nevertheless, these rituals were regarded as essential to ensure the gods' favour, to give the king longevity, fame, and success over his enemies, and to obtain fertility for Egypt and its people.

When he died, the king was thought to join his father, the sun-god, in the sky where he would sail eternally in the sacred barque. He also became Osiris, the god who ruled the underworld. According to the famous myth, Osiris had been a human king who was murdered but eventually triumphed over death and was restored to life as the ruler and judge of the dead.

Thus, in death, the king was the embodiment of Osiris, but every living king was regarded as Horus, son of Osiris, who had avenged his father's death.

In the Old Kingdom (*c.* 2800–2100 B.C.), it was thought that only the king experienced a personal immortality, and his burial place – the pyramid – may have been regarded as a stone representation of a sun-ray by means of which he could ascend to join his father in the sky. All other Egyptians could only achieve a vicarious immortality through the king's bounty; thus, their contribution to his well-being, however humble, was believed to increase their chance of eternal life.

When the Old Kingdom finally collapsed, a more democratic attitude emerged, and all those who had led good and worthy lives were considered to be eligible for individual eternity. However, the king retained considerable power. In theory, he owned all the land, its resources and its people, although in practice he was advised and checked by his courtiers and state officials. He was in fact required to rule Egypt according to the principles of Ma'at. Personified as a goddess, Ma'at represented order, truth, righteousness, and justice, as well as the correct and continuing balance of the universe and of society. The kings were expected to follow convention and time-honoured traditions, although one king at least (Amenhotep IV) used his personal political power to impose an unacceptable political and religious system upon the country. In later times, the Ptolemaic conquerors and Roman emperors considered it expedient to adopt the role of Egyptian pharaoh to exercise widespread control over the country.

With only a few relatively brief interruptions, the kingship continued from the unification of Egypt in *c.* 3100 B.C. until the end of the Roman period. The line of descent in the royal family was not of course continuous during this time. There were usurpers who came from collateral branches of the royal family, and others who, although commoners, seized the throne and established new lines. There were also foreign rulers who seized power, such as the Hyksos, the Persians, the Greeks and the Romans, or Shoshenk I, the inaugurator of the 22nd Dynasty, who was a descendant of the Libyan mercenaries who had settled in Egypt. However, the foreigners also adopted the style and titles of the Egyptian pharaoh, and they continued to exercise the kingship in the Egyptian tradition, regarding themselves as the rightful heirs of the early rulers.

Despite an abundance of historical records regarding their exploits and a wealth of statuary and other artistic representation, it is difficult to glean much information about the kings as individuals. Scenes in tombs and temples which portray the kings give only the idealised view of their attributes and physique, for tradition required that all religious art should show the king, his family and even the nobility in this way; they are always in their youthful prime and without physical abnormality, for this is how they wished to appear in the afterlife. Because of the limitation of the written and artistic sources, it is particularly significant that, for one of the most important periods of Egypt's history, the mummified bodies of the kings and queens have been preserved. Two chance discoveries brought these to light, and enabled Egyptologists and other specialists to examine and study the physical condition, state of health and dietary patterns of the rulers of the New Kingdom (c. 1575–1087 B.C.).

Towards the end of the 20th Dynasty (c. 1120 B.C.), robbers plundered the tombs of the pharaohs in the Valley of the Kings at Thebes, as well as those belonging to queens and some nobles. The mummies were desecrated so that the robbers could steal the jewellery which adorned them. However, at the beginning of the reign of Shoshenk I, first king of the 22nd Dynasty, the royal mummies were collected by the priests and reburied in two caches. Some were hidden in an old tomb dating to the early 18th Dynasty at Deir el-Bahri, while others were laid in a chamber in the tomb of King Amenhotep II. Only in A.D. 1875 and 1898 were these caches rediscovered; their contents – some thirty-three royal and ten other mummies – have subsequently been the subject of several scientific investigations.

The mummies were transferred to the Cairo Museum before they were unwrapped and subjected to examination by Egyptologists and anatomists. In A.D. 1889 the French archaeologist, Maspero, examined them, and in 1912 Elliot Smith and his colleagues carried out a detailed study, the results of which were published in his book, *The Royal Mummies*, and in the *Catalogue of Egyptian Mummies in the Cairo Museum*. However, only the mummy of Thothmose IV was examined radiologically at that time, being taken for this purpose by taxi-cab to a private X-ray unit in Cairo. Many years later, the Michigan–Alexandria expedition was invited by the Egyptian Department of Antiquities to undertake a complete radiological study of the collection of royal mummies. This was started in 1967, and the results have since been published by James E. Harris and E. F. Wente in *An X-Ray Atlas of the Royal Mummies*. These mummies provide a unique source of information not only concerning the medical and social conditions at that time, but also about the technical procedures of mummification at a period when the embalmers had reached the highest levels of skill in their craft. The mummies show evidence of the most sophisticated techniques, involving evisceration of the abdomen, dehydration of the body tissues with natron (a salt compound), and, in many cases, extraction of the brain through the nose.

Study of these bodies adds to existing knowledge about the lives of the pharaohs. The radiological evidence supplies the information about Thothmose III that he had a straight profile and that his teeth did not protrude; it also indicates that he was aged between thirty-five and forty at the time of death. This age is at variance with the historical findings that his reign lasted for over fifty-three years, and highlights some of the problems which can be encountered when a radiological assessment of the age at the time of death of the mummies is attempted. His teeth show that he suffered from a moderate degree of attrition. This was the dental condition which most commonly afflicted adolescent and adult Egyptians, rather than caries which does not make a significant appearance before the period of Greek and Roman occupation. It has been shown that attrition was caused by the large quantities of sand and grit which were present in the bread that formed the staple diet in Egypt. Sand could enter the bread while it was being made, and fragments of quartz from the quern used to grind the flour were also introduced. However, unlike that of some of the pharaohs, Thothmose III's dental condition was otherwise moderately healthy.

Other findings include the presence of lesions on the skin surface which have not yet been specifically identified, and also of a diffuse increase in the density of the intervertebral discs of the spine. This condition has been noted in a number of mummies, some scholars maintaining that it was the result of the embalming process, while others considered it to be related to the disease ochronosis. However, recent studies presented at the 'Science in Egyptology' symposium in Manchester in 1984 have indicated that the former theory is almost certainly the correct interpretation of the evidence.

The radiological studies carried out on Thothmose III have also shown that the nasal septa are intact and that, from the density and outline of the cranial contents which can be interpreted as the remains of desiccated brain, it is unlikely that excerebration was carried out in this case.

Thothmose III, one of Egypt's greatest warriors, was found, together with many other mummies, in the same cache as another great empire-builder – Ramesses II. In terms of age at death, the radiological studies showed that Ramesses II was the oldest king amongst these royal mummies; the historical evidence suggests that his maximum age at death could have been ninety-two years. His mummy is well preserved, still conveying something of the haughty countenance of the imperious old man; there are the remains of his silky white hair, now yellowed by the mummification processes, and his features are dominated by a large and prominent nose. It is evident that there were few innovations in the techniques of preservation during the 19th Dynasty, for most of the procedures used in the 18th Dynasty are retained. In the mummy of Ramesses II, the brain was removed and the cranium filled with molten resin.

Ramesses II had a long life but one not entirely free from illness. He suffered from arteriosclerosis and from severe dental problems. In this mummy there is evidence of the dental and periodontal conditions which could and often did develop as the result of the attrition of the outer covering of the teeth. It is a good example of the pattern of dental disease in ancient Egypt, illustrating how, the longer a man lived and ate the gritty bread, the more he could expect to experience increasing dental discomfort. Here, there is not only marked wear of the teeth, but also exposure of the pulp chambers, loss of bony support of the teeth, and evidence of a periapical abscess.

Unfortunately, not all the kings of the New Kingdom have been positively identified with mummies from the Theban caches. One of the most fascinating and tantalising of all Egypt's kings is the man known as Amenhotep IV, who later changed his name to Akhenaton. The details of his political, religious and personal life are controversial and have provoked much scholarly debate. However, his medical history is even more obscure, since his body has never been found, and speculations regarding his physique must at present be based upon the strange statues and reliefs which show him with various physical abnormalities and apparently ambisexual features. Various explanations have been put forward for this: that this is an art-form which idealises him as a creator with both male and female attributes; or that these actually represent physical abnormalities occasioned by an illness from which he suffered. Again, various possible illnesses have been suggested, including acromegaly, hypogonadism due to a chromophobe adenoma, or liver cirrhosis with endocrine complications. One Egyptologist has theorised that Akhenaton may have suffered from a syndrome which rendered him incapable of begetting children, and that his official offspring may have been engendered by his own father, Amenhotep III.

Whatever the true cause of these strange representations,

during Akhenaton's reign it became customary to portray not only the king in this way, but also members of the royal family and the court entourage. In this instance, only the discovery and identification of the king's body would enable an accurate assessment to be made of the medical evidence.

It is clear therefore that, despite the importance of historical written accounts and of art representations, they provide only a limited and sometimes biased source. Evidence relating to disease and social patterns is often much more readily gained from first-hand examination of the mummified remains, and this is one reason why, although they represent merely one period of Egypt's long history, the royal mummies of the New Kingdom provide a unique insight into the lives and times of individual pharaohs.

Thothmose III

(*Ruled c.* 1479–1425 B.C.)

Thothmose III was one of the greatest military conquerors to rule Egypt, and one of its most successful monarchs. However, he found himself in his youth in a precarious position which belied the glory that was to come. The son of King Thothmose II by a minor concubine named Isis, his family's occupation of the throne of Egypt was relatively recent. His grandfather Thothmose I, the third ruler of the 18th Dynasty, had succeeded to the crown on the death of the childless Amenhotep I, to whom he was apparently distantly related. In accordance with Egyptian custom regarding marriage in the royal family, Thothmose I had married his sister, but this marriage produced only one surviving daughter, named Hatshepsut, so the king was succeeded by Thothmose II, his son by a minor wife.

A similar pattern followed in the next generation. Thothmose II had married his half-sister Hatshepsut, as she was the senior royal princess, but she produced apparently only one daughter. According to a later account, which cannot for that reason be regarded as utterly trustworthy, the future Thothmose III was placed as a young boy in the service of the god Amun in the temple of Karnak at Thebes. During a ceremonial procession of the divine image which was carried by the priests in the presence of the king and chief officials, the god is said to have promised the throne of Egypt to young Thothmose. If such a ceremony ever took place, it would seem that it must have been stage-managed by Thothmose II in order to recognise his only surviving son formally as his destined successor.

On his father's death, c. 1479 B.C., the succession of Thothmose III passed off smoothly with no hint of the trouble that was to come. He took the customary new throne-names 'Mighty Bull Shining in Thebes', 'Enduring in Kingship like Re in Heaven', 'Mighty in Strength, Splendid in Diadems', and, most important of all, his new royal name of Menkheperre. As he was still a child, it was inevitable that the high officials of his father's reign should continue to exert great influence.

The most important figure was his aunt and stepmother Queen Hatshepsut, who at first occupied her expected place in public in a subservient role to the new king, even though she actually wielded more power than he did behind the scenes. However, within a few years this ambitious lady managed to occupy the throne, and had herself crowned as 'king' of Egypt. She laid great stress on her position as the sole child of Thothmose I by his royal wife and, as such, heiress of Egypt. There is no evidence that prior to this discovery of hers the concept of heiress had played any role in Egyptian political thought, or would have led a legitimate daughter to be preferred to a son no matter who his mother was. By implying the illegality of the reign of Thothmose II, Hatshepsut was also attacking the legitimacy of the position of Thothmose III. There was even an alternate candidate available as heir in the person of her own daughter Neferu-Ra. However, Thothmose III had enough supporters to ensure that he remained nominally on the throne as Hatshepsut's co-regent. His regnal years continued to be used for dating, and he is occasionally mentioned in formal inscriptions.

The circumstances in which Thothmose III achieved sole power in Egypt are obscure. At some point between years 20–22 of his reign Hatshepsut disappears forever. She may have died a natural death or have been deposed by her now adult stepson. Thothmose III first appears in control at the head of his army marching into Palestine at the end of his 22nd year. And he began as he meant to carry on. Ever since Lower Egypt had been overrun by the Asiatic nomads known as the Hyksos, Egypt had viewed the neighbours to the north with deep suspicion. The Asiatics had been expelled from Egypt by the founder of the 18th Dynasty, and successive Egyptian monarchs had campaigned in Palestine and Syria, forcing the local kings to accept Egyptian suzerainty and to pay tribute. It is not entirely clear whether any formal Egyptian presence was left to ensure these demands, but probably previous campaigns had been *ad hoc* affairs with no permanent arrangements in the areas which had been overrun. Certainly by the end of the reign of Hatshepsut Egyptian influence had been weakened, while the power of the local rulers had revived. Behind them, however, loomed the growing power of the kingdom of Mitanni located in northern Iraq. Thothmose III was determined to restore and expand Egyptian power in this vital region.

The mobilisation of his army appears to have taken about two and a half months to arrange following his decision to attack. The king crossed the Egyptian frontier at Tjel near El-Qatara and reached Gaza ten days later. He then marched up the coastal road, receiving the submission *en route* of the cowed cities, except for the town of Jaffa which refused to surrender. Rather than delay the army, a small force was left behind under General Djehuty to besiege the city. Indeed, the story of the fall of Jaffa was later to become a popular folk-tale.

Meanwhile, the king marched on to confront the main forces of the local kings, led by the ruler of Kadesh. These had concentrated at Megiddo, which could be approached by a number of routes, although the quickest line of march lay through a narrow and dangerous pass. At a council of war the generals suggested one of the other routes, but the king insisted on attacking through the pass. He reasoned that the enemy would expect him to use one of the easier routes of approach and that he would have the advantage of surprise. It took a day for the whole army to clear the pass, but the manoeuvre was successfully accomplished without incident. The following day battle was joined before the walls of the city of Megiddo. The Egyptians were victorious and many local troops were trapped between the advancing Egyptian lines and the closed gates of the city. The kings of Kadesh and Megiddo had to be hauled up the walls to safety.

The city was besieged for seven months and eventually forced to surrender. The rebel kings were then obliged to swear allegiance to Egypt. An immense amount of booty was collected, notably numbers of war-horses and other livestock. During the course of the siege the Egyptians had increased their plunder by launching raids into the neighbouring countryside, and the king himself had led one such attack into the region of Galilee. The fall of Megiddo signalled the resurgence of Egyptian military might and power in the region. Even the king of distant Assyria sent presents of precious stones, mostly lapis lazuli, and fine woods. However, Thothmose III was determined to crush all possible resistance to his rule.

He had a large fleet prepared and sailed directly to northern
Lebanon in successive years to attack the important cities of
Tunip and Kadesh. In the 33rd year of his reign he determined to
raid the kingdom of Mitanni itself. The royal army crossed the
Euphrates and plundered towns down the river as far as Emar
before turning back. He does not appear to have aimed at
conquering Mitanni itself but only at weakening its interference in
what he regarded as Egypt's sphere of influence. Following this
success, the kings of Babylon and Hatti sent tribute to the new
regional power. Throughout the rest of the reign Egyptian control
was tightened in Palestine and Syria as Kadesh and Tunip were
finally subdued. The king was not content to accept oaths of
loyalty from the native dynasts as the sole guarantee of Egyptian
overlordship. Egyptian garrisons were installed in these areas
together with Egyptian political agents. The children of the local
rulers were taken to Egypt as hostages, and also to be educated as
Egyptians.

Thothmose III did not confine himself solely to campaigns in
the north. The land of Nubia had long been coveted by Egypt
because of its plentiful supply of gold. The early rulers of the 18th
Dynasty had pushed the frontier steadily south, but Thothmose
III enlarged the area of Egyptian control to its fullest extent up to
Napata, immediately below the fourth cataract. The Nubian
province was governed directly by an Egyptian official known as
the King's Son of Kush, although he was not a member of the
royal family. In the 50th year of his reign Thothmose III led a
punitive expedition into Nubia to put down unrest among the
tribes. In the course of his campaign he ordered the clearance of a
canal near the first cataract and directed that the fishermen of
elephantine be responsible for its upkeep in the future.

These conquests led to an enormous influx of wealth into Egypt
in the form of gold, slaves, and other booty. Some part of these
resources was, of course, used to reward the army for its services,
along with grants of land. The king also lavished much on the
temples of the gods, especially the god Amun, in recognition of his
divine help in the victories. Rich endowments were bestowed on
his temples, notably on his chief place of worship at Karnak. The
king also embarked on a programme of building works to enhance
the temple of Amun at Karnak. He had a hypostyle hall built
across the eastern end of the temple with a couple of chambers, in
one of which he had engraved a king-list naming his royal predecessors. He also erected two pylons near one of which two small
rooms were built supported by columns bearing the floral symbols
of Upper and Lower Egypt. A former chapel of Hatshepsut was

redesigned into a Hall of Annals on whose walls were inscribed the history of his conquests. Two pairs of obelisks were raised to celebrate his jubilees. Other gods were not disregarded. The Ptah-temple at Karnak was rebuilt, and work was carried on at the temple of Re-Harakhte at Heliopolis where further obelisks were set up, including the one now in London known as Cleopatra's Needle. Temples were built in Nubia at Semna and Buhen. The king did not intend to neglect his own cult. He built a splendid mortuary temple at Deir el-Bahri opposite Thebes with the intention of overshadowing the nearby temple of Hatshepsut, but it was later destroyed by an earthquake and has only recently been rediscovered. Naturally a royal tomb was made ready in the Valley of the Kings.

Very little is known of the internal politics of the reign and of the king's private personality. Towards the end of his life the dislike which he felt towards his stepmother Hatshepsut was expressed by an order to erase her name from every monument in Egypt and to expunge her reign from known history. In this end he was not successful. In his inscriptions the king is described as an outstanding bowman. He took great pride in his hunting abilities, describing his tally in elephant and lion hunts. It is interesting to note that, according to his mummy, he was only five feet four inches tall.

It has been speculated that he married his half-sister Nefrure, but there is no evidence for this. Indeed, her ultimate fate is unknown. He had three queens, presumably in succession: Satiah, Nebetiu, and Meryre Hatshepsut, none of whom is known to have been of royal birth. The last bore his ultimate successor Amenhotep II, so it is likely that there were other sons who predeceased their father. He also had several daughters. He may have created Amenhotep II co-regent in his own lifetime to ensure the succession. The king died in his 54th year on the throne, bequeathing a prosperous, well-governed country to his heir. His throne-name of Menkheperre became a charm for great good luck throughout the rest of Egyptian history.

Ramesses II

(*Ruled* 1279–1213 B.C.)

Ramesses II, one of the best known of ancient Egyptian
monarchs, was in fact born a commoner. His grandfather,
Paramesse son of Seti, was a military officer from the Delta of
Lower Egypt and an associate of General and later Pharaoh
Horemheb. When Horemheb succeeded to the throne as the
second ruler after Tutankhamun, he appointed Paramesse as his
vizier or prime minister. On the death of his childless sovereign,
Paramesse became king under the name of Ramesses I, founder of
a new dynasty now known as the 19th Dynasty (1295 B.C.). The
reign of Ramesses I was brief, barely two years, and he was
followed by his son Seti I.

Seti I had married Tuya, daughter of Raia, a lieutenant of
chariotry, and apparently had only one son, Ramesses, born
about ten years before his father's accession to the throne. During
the course of his reign, Seti sought to restore Egypt's power and
prestige. He engaged in a number of campaigns in Palestine and
Syria to try to revive the Egyptian empire in that area, in the face
of the growing might of the kingdom of Hatti, situated in modern
Turkey. His son Ramesses accompanied him on one of his
campaigns in Syria against the city of Kadesh, but Egypt's hold
here was short-lived as Hittite influence proved too strong.

About year 7 of his father's reign (*c.* 1288), Ramesses II was
installed as co-regent and joint sovereign, a common Egyptian
device to secure an untroubled succession. He adopted the regnal
name of Usimare, later to be corrupted into Ozymandias by the
Greeks. He was also furnished with wives and concubines as
befitted his new status. His two chief wives were Nefertari and
Isitnofret, both of unknown parentage. The former was to become
chief queen and mother of Ramesses II's eldest son and heir. The
court was generally located in the north at Memphis or Qantir
rather than at Thebes which had now become only the religious
capital.

The young king did not remain inactive at home. He led a
campaign into Nubia to put down a revolt and undertook the
suppression of pirates along Egypt's Mediterranean coast. He
doubtless acquired his taste for building during the reign of his

father when he supervised construction works at the royal temples at Karnak and Abydos. In the latter temple a list of the king's royal predecessors was carved before which Seti and his son are shown in veneration.

The length of the reign of Seti I is unclear, but he probably died about 1279 B.C. when his son was aged twenty-five at most. Apart from the full royal titulary which is now adopted, Ramesses II added the epithet 'Chosen of Re' to his throne name. The first act of the young king was to bury his father in a splendid tomb in the Valley of the Kings at Thebes, and at the same time to arrange for the construction of his own royal sepulchre. He also took the opportunity of his trip to Thebes to make an appointment to the vacant post of high priest of Amun at Karnak, the most important religious post in the land. New building works were put in hand at Luxor and Karnak. On his return journey north, the king stopped at Abydos and was shocked to discover that work had been abandoned on his father's temple there. He ordered that it be completed. In his year 3 he commanded that a well be excavated in the Nubian desert to open up new areas for Egyptian gold miners. Gold was becoming increasingly necessary to finance Ramesses's appetite for construction and for war.

Ramesses II was bent on restoring Egypt's position as the paramount world power and to reduce the Hittite sphere of influence in Syria and northern Palestine which had owed allegiance to Egypt in the days of Thothmose III. A first campaign in year 4 secured the Lebanese coast and forced the king of Amurru to renounce his allegiance to the Hittites and return to the Egyptian fold. The king of Hatti, Muwatallis, gathered his forces and marched into Syria to eject the Egyptians. In his year 5, about 1274 B.C., Ramesses II led his army north again to confront the Hittites. A month after leaving Egypt his forces had passed through the Beqa Valley and were just south of the city of Kadesh which was held by the enemy. The Egyptian army consisted of four main divisions as well as a force of auxiliaries which had been sent up the coastal road and were due to rendezvous with the main force at Kadesh.

Ramesses II at the head of the first division pressed on towards Kadesh, while the other divisions marched slowly behind him. As it neared the city, the royal party was approached by two deserters who informed the king that the main Hittite force was 120 miles away. The king was elated by this news and began to pitch his camp opposite the city which he intended to besiege. However, he had fallen into a cleverly laid Hittite trap. The Hittite king and his forces were in fact two miles away hidden behind Kadesh, and a full-scale attack was now launched on the disorganised and unprepared Egyptians. The second division which was nearing the Egyptian camp was cut to pieces and then the Hittites broke into the camp, spreading panic among the forces there. The Hittite advance was stalled as their soldiers began to loot the Egyptian camp.

Ramesses II rallied his forces and launched several counter-attacks, but he was saved from total defeat by the timely appearance of his force of auxiliaries which took the Hittites by surprise. The Hittites then retreated, leaving a badly mauled Egyptian force which was eventually joined by the third and fourth divisions of the army, who had missed the battle completely. A second battle the following day ended in stalemate. A truce was then agreed between the two parties and Ramesses II and his army withdrew south, abandoning any further attempt to recapture more territory. He later covered the walls of his temples with accounts of his 'victory'. He had no doubt salvaged a large part of his army by his personal bravery, but politically this campaign was a defeat. The Hittites were able to depose the king of Amurru, who had sided with the Egyptians, and occupied Egyptian territory south of Kadesh.

The weakness of the Egyptian position led to unrest in Palestine which was quickly put down, but the attempts of the king to improve his area of control in Syria in the next decade were inconclusive. The situation changed radically owing to internal developments in the kingdom of Hatti. Muwatallis, the opponent of Ramesses II at Kadesh, died and was succeeded by his son Urkhi-Teshub, who failed to consolidate his position against a powerful uncle, Hattusilis. Eventually after seven years Hattusilis deposed and exiled his nephew, but Urkhi-Teshub managed to escape from his captivity and seek political asylum in Egypt. To add to the difficulties of the new king, the kingdom of Assyria on his border was growing steadily more powerful. Under these circumstances, Hattusilis was prepared to try to negotiate a peace settlement with Egypt. Ramesses II, now no longer in the flush of youth, was also prepared to compromise. A formal treaty between the two powers was signed in year 21 of Ramesses II, c. 1259 B.C., and copies have been preserved both in Egypt and Turkey. The existing border in Syria was stabilised, and so Egypt recognised that Amurru and Kadesh were under Hittite suzerainty. Egypt's trade rights in the northern Syrian ports now under Hittite control were safeguarded. The two powers concluded a non-aggression pact and an alliance against attack from a third party. The treaty also included a clause concerning the extradition of criminals, although Urkhi-Teshub was apparently excluded as he appears to have remained permanently in Egypt.

Ramesses II is well known for his building activities, which covered the length of the country. The chief centre of construction was the old capital of Thebes, where he had erected the grand hypostyle hall in the temple of Karnak, a forecourt, pylon, and obelisks at the temple of Luxor, and a great mortuary temple now known as the Ramesseum on the west bank of the Nile. He also devoted a large part of his resources to beautifying the new capital of Pi-Ramesses in the Delta, which has not survived to this day. A series of temples was erected by him in Nubia, the most famous of which is at Abu Simbel. Apart from the main temple, there is a smaller temple there in honour of his favourite wife Queen Nefertari. A magnificent tomb for her was prepared in the Valley of the Queens. Although there is no actual Egyptian evidence for the use of the Israelites in these building projects, it has been speculated that they formed part of the conscripted labour customarily used in grandiose Egyptian construction works. The Exodus may have occurred in the first half of the reign of Ramesses II but if so it has left no trace in Egyptian historical records.

The royal court was diminished by the death of Queen Nefertari about year 25 and that of her successor Isitnofret about a decade later. Ramesses II had by custom also married his sister Henutmire, but her role at court appears to have been minimal and she bore no known children. The two queens were replaced by their daughters, Merytamun daughter of Nefertari and the more prominent Bintanath daughter of Isitnofret, who both bore the title of queen. It is uncertain whether this role was merely nominal or whether they were wives of their father in the fullest sense. Certainly Bintanath had a child, but it is not clear that Ramesses II was the father. Ramesses II also included a daughter of the king of Babylon and sundry foreign princesses in his harem.

In year 34 there arrived the daughter of King Hattusilis of Hatti, who was married to Ramesses II after much diplomatic wrangling. This alliance marked the final reconciliation of the two former enemies, Egypt and Hatti. The princess was renamed with the suitable Egyptian name of Maathornefrure. The marriage was such a political success that Ramesses II apparently married a second Hittite princess.

With his multitude of wives, Ramesses II engendered a large number of children, although not as many as some modern over-estimates suggest. He had about fifty sons and fifty daughters. His

eldest son by Nefertari appears to have been his destined successor, but he and most of her other sons died before their father so
the succession passed to the sons of Isitnofret. Prince Ramesses,
the second son, and Prince Khaemwese, the fourth son, held in
turn the rank of Crown Prince. The latter was high priest of Ptah
at Memphis and gained such a reputation for his knowledge that
later generations regarded him as a magician. These two also
predeceased their father, so it was his thirteenth son Merenptah
who eventually became the next pharaoh. Very little is known of
the careers of the younger sons of the king. Chance evidence has
preserved the fact that his twenty-third son was married to the
daughter of a Syrian ship's captain.

Ramesses II had an extremely long reign. It was customary for
an Egyptian ruler to celebrate his jubilee in his thirtieth year. The
jubilee was a religious ceremony in which the king was to be
magically rejuvenated to make him fit to continue his reign.
Thereafter a jubilee was celebrated at more frequent intervals.
Ramesses II celebrated thirteen and possibly fourteen jubilees in
the course of his reign. He ruled for sixty-six years and two months
and died at the age of approximately ninety, c. 1213 B.C. He was
buried in his tomb at Thebes; unlike many of his other monuments, this tomb is now in a poor state of preservation. In any
case, he did not sleep peacefully there for long since the royal
tombs were despoiled c. 1000 B.C. His mummified body was rescued by the local priests, reburied in secret, and only rediscovered
in the last century.

His dynasty did not long survive him as, after a series of civil
wars, it was replaced by the 20th Dynasty within twenty-five years
of his death. The kings of the 20th Dynasty, who may or may not
have been descended from Ramesses II, invariably used the name
of Ramesses which had by now become a synonym for kingship.

Shoshenk I

(*Ruled* 945–924 B.C.)

Shoshenk I, founder of the 22nd Dynasty, was the descendant of a
long line of Libyan chieftains settled in Egypt. Towards the end of
the 20th Dynasty, when central authority was breaking down,

bands of Libyans began to infiltrate into the Nile Valley and to disrupt the lives of the settled population. Some of these appear to have been employed as military auxiliaries by the authorities, but the degree of central control over the new Libyan settlements which were springing up in Egypt was probably very tenuous. One such group established itself at Bubastis under the chieftainship of the descendants of a Libyan named Buyuwawa. While the family evidently soon became completely Egyptianised in outlook, it retained its outlandish Libyan names.

During the 21st Dynasty the country was weak and divided, and the south centred on Thebes was virtually independent under the control of the high priests of Amun at Karnak. During this period a great-great-grandson of Buyuwawa, Osorkon son of Shoshenk, apparently had a position of some prominence in the country, probably in the military establishment. Indeed, Osorkon was able to ascend the throne of Egypt and to be nominally recognised by the authorities in Thebes. He ruled for about six years *c.* 984–978 B.C. However, his attempt to establish a Libyan line of pharaohs was premature since on his death the throne reverted to an Egyptian ruler.

The family of Osorkon continued to occupy positions of influence. No details are known of the career of his brother Nimlot, who bore the usual Libyan title of Great Chief of Foreigners. He had married Tentsepeh, described as a daughter of a Great Chief of Foreigners, so she was obviously a Libyan and probably a close relation. Their son Shoshenk was named after his paternal grandfather. During the reign of Psusennes II, who was to be the last king of the 21st Dynasty, Shoshenk too became a man of power and prestige. He was able to set up a mortuary statue of his deceased father Nimlot in the sacred temple of Abydos and to endow the statue with lands, servants, and gold and silver so that funerary offerings could be made before it in perpetuity. The importance of Nimlot and Shoshenk is emphasised by the fact that some of the silver was donated by the reigning king. The references to Shoshenk in the inscription recording this funerary endowment indicate that he had succeeded to his father's title of Great Chief and that he had military forces under his control. There can be no doubt that Shoshenk son of Nimlot was one of the principal military commanders in the kingdom. Moreover, he seems to have been allied by marriage with the very influential family of the high priests of Ptah at Memphis.

On the death or removal of Psusennes II, *c.* 945 B.C., Shoshenk obviously made use of his military position and links to the

Memphite priesthood to occupy the throne. In order to stress that he was intending to found a new dynasty, he adopted the throne name of Hedjkheperre Setepenre which had also been the throne name of the founder of the 21st Dynasty. His other royal names were also similar to the first ruler of the 21st Dynasty. He appears to have encountered no opposition to his accession in the north, and presumably set up his royal court in the northern capital of Tanis.

However, the southern part of the country around Thebes refused to acknowledge the new king. In his year 2 inscriptions from Thebes still referred to him only as the Great Chief of the Libyans. By year 5 Shoshenk seems to have overcome the last of the opposition to his rule, probably more by guile than by force. His son Iuput was installed as high priest of Amun at Karnak and also as military commander and governor of Upper Egypt. Other Libyans were placed in key positions, so that the independence of the south from the central government was ended. The local priests were placated with the hands of Libyan princesses and influential posts for those who proved loyal to the new régime. A daughter of the late King Psusennes II, who may have been of Theban origin, was married to Shoshenk's son and heir Osorkon so that the Egyptians could look forward to a king descended from both lines. In the event, no such succession took place as Osorkon was to be followed as king by a son from another wife. Control over Middle Egypt was effected in the same way. Another son Nimlot was created military commander at Heracleopolis and so was responsible for securing this region for his father's authority.

Shoshenk I was to rule for over twenty years, but details of events of his reign are very scanty indeed. His obvious intention was to revive the ancient glories of Egypt and to restore its power and influence in the world. Naturally his attention was attracted to Palestine and Syria, which had once owed allegiance to Egypt but were now divided into independent kingdoms which had grown up while Egypt was weak. According to the Bible, Jeroboam, a rebel against Solomon, found refuge in Egypt about this time. The existence of a strong Israelite kingdom on his border might be perceived as a threat and certainly as an obstacle to expansion by Shoshenk. His encouragement of Jeroboam can be seen as his attempt to weaken this neighbour, a policy which was ultimately successful on the death of Solomon when the united Israelite monarchy was broken up into the separate kingdoms of Israel and Judah.

An alliance of some sort, possibly only trade and diplomatic, was formed with the king of Byblos in Syria, to which a statue of

Shoshenk I was sent and installed in the temple of the main goddess of Byblos. Shoshenk I also appears to have launched a campaign into Nubia in the south and so re-established links with this area, which had slipped from Egyptian control at the end of the 20th Dynasty.

Shoshenk I is best known for his military expedition to Palestine, an event which is attested both in the Bible and in Egyptian sources. The division of Palestine into the kingdoms of Judah and Israel gave him an opportunity to reassert direct Egyptian control and to acquire new sources of wealth and booty to finance the activities of the Egyptian crown. Some time, probably not long before his 21st year, *c.* 925 B.C., the king led his army into Palestine, possibly on the specious excuse that raids by Bedouin tribesmen on Egyptian territory were the responsibility of the kingdom of Judah, which must be punished for attacking Egypt. Apart from the regular Egyptian forces, the army seems also to have included Libyan and Nubian contingents. The route of the king's march is not entirely clear and is the subject of much scholarly debate. He certainly began by overrunning the city of Gaza and then marched north through the kingdoms of Judah and Israel, exacting tribute or sacking recalcitrant towns *en route*. His most noteworthy victim was the city of Jerusalem, which was overawed by the approach of the Egyptian army. The king of Judah, Rehoboam son of Solomon, evidently decided that discretion was the better part of valour. All the treasures which had been accumulated by Solomon in the temple and other buildings in Jerusalem were collected together and handed over to the waiting Egyptians. In return, Jerusalem was spared the horrors of siege and pillage. The humbling of Judah was seen by some as punishment by the Lord for its pride and sins.

The rich haul from Jerusalem only encouraged the Egyptian king, who continued his march north to Megiddo seeking similar booty from the kingdom of Israel. The fact that King Jeroboam had once been a political refugee in Egypt and a protégé of the pharaoh was now no protection for him and his kingdom. Jeroboam seems to have fled into Jordan to avoid the Egyptian advance, leaving his kingdom to be ransacked by Shoshenk I and his army. Apart from looting the cities on the route of the royal army, various flying columns were sent off from the main force towards Jordan and the Negev as well as other locations, so that no sizeable settlement might be spared the unwelcome attentions of the Egyptian forces. However, even Shoshenk I realised that his resources were not to be compared with those of earlier rulers such as Thothmose III or Ramesses II. He confined his military action to the area of Palestine and made no attempt to venture north into the region of Syria.

The return of the victorious conqueror with the spoils of war was the signal for a massive building campaign to commemorate his great deeds. Little of his work has survived at Memphis. A new embalming-table for the mummification of the sacred Apis bulls was constructed there during his reign. His building works at the capital Tanis included additions to the main temple, which was enhanced by an avenue of sphinxes, although these were not newly built but older pieces reinscribed with the name of Shoshenk. Another temple was built at El-Hibeh. The bulk of the royal activities was directed at the temple of Amun at Karnak, since it was the god Amun who was credited with granting the king his victory in Palestine.

In year 21 the sandstone quarries at Gebel Silsila were opened up on the orders of the high priest Iuput to provide materials for the new works in Thebes. A new forecourt was built on to the front of the temple of Amun with new colonnades. This construction allowed the face of the old pylon, now at the back of the forecourt, to be inscribed with the king's triumphal deeds. A large formal scene was carved showing the king crushing his Asiatic foes in the presence of Amun. The names of the conquered cities were engraved in a series of name-rings, although not all names have survived to this day. This type of arrangement follows similar inscriptions of earlier kings. It is not a copy but a contemporary list of those towns which were subjugated. A new gateway was built at the side of the court and decorated with scenes of the king and his son the high priest of Amun Iuput. It is uncertain whether work on this gateway was ever completed. Its present unfinished state may be due to the abrupt cessation of construction or may possibly be the result of later demolition.

The length of the reign of Shoshenk I is a matter of debate. It is generally thought that he reigned a little over twenty-one years, and the unfinished work at Thebes reflects the king's death. However, there is some evidence to suggest that the king might have celebrated a jubilee, if the reference does not merely indicate wishful thinking on his part. If so, he must have reigned up to thirty years and possibly somewhat longer.

Very little is known of the personal life of Shoshenk I. His queen Karomat was the mother of his heir Osorkon, but nothing is known of her background. Presumably she was some relation of her husband. The mother of Prince Iuput is not named. Prince Nimlot, who was named after his grandfather and may have been the eldest son, was the son of a Libyan lady named Penreshnes who is described as the daughter of a Great Chief. She too may have been a relation of her husband. Two highly decorated gold bracelets inlaid with lapis lazuli and blue glass, made for Prince Nimlot, are now in the British Museum. One daughter of Shoshenk I, Tashepenbast, wife of a Theban priest, is also attested. Even the burial place of Shoshenk I is unknown. It would appear that he, like some of his descendants, ought to have been buried in the capital city Tanis, but no remains of his burial have been discovered.

The descendants of Shoshenk I were to rule Egypt for about two hundred and fifty years. Unfortunately, the policy of giving princes certain areas of the country to rule led eventually to the creation of petty principalities ruled by Libyan dynasts with no central authority. This weakened the country in the face of foreign aggression. Thus Egypt was only to be reunited by the successive invasions of the Nubians and Assyrians.

Ptolemy I (Soter)

(*Ruled* 323–283 B.C.)

In June, 323 B.C., Alexander the Great, having created an empire which stretched from Macedonia as far as India, died suddenly in Babylon. His early death revealed many weaknesses in the political structure of this vast kingdom, and worse yet, he left no heir competent to take the throne, nor did he clearly designate a strong successor among his followers. The empire was a rich prize for the boldest takers.

Following internal bickering within the army, a compromise was settled upon whereby a half-witted son of Philip of Macedon called Philip Arrhidaeus, half-brother to Alexander, should rule jointly with the posthumously born son of Alexander and his Persian wife Roxane. The child was known as Alexander IV. A council of the leading generals met to decide on the government of the empire during the minority of these boy-kings, and this amounted in effect to a division of the spoils. Uppermost in the minds of most of these generals was how to gain sufficient strategic territory from which later to launch a bid for the whole empire.

One of them, however, had a different plan. Some nine years earlier he had seen the territory he wanted and which would satisfy his ambition, an ancient land fabled for its wealth; a land whose populace was easy to master and whose borders were simple to defend against invaders, even erstwhile colleagues. The country was Egypt and the man Ptolemy, son of Lagus.

Ptolemy had grown up with Alexander at Pelca, a member of Philip of Macedon's corps of pages. Of his father Lagus nothing is known, although he was presumably a member of the Macedonian nobility. His obscurity later became a source of embarrassment to the dynasty which he fathered. Nevertheless, his son Ptolemy became a close friend of Alexander, sufficiently so that he was banished from the court with the prince when he quarrelled with his father Philip. The friendship continued when Alexander in due course became king.

When Alexander set out on his campaign in Asia Ptolemy accompanied him and rose steadily in rank, winning distinction as a commander, especially in India. He became one of the seven 'Companion Bodyguards' of the king, a high personal honour. Ptolemy emerges as a man of intelligence and sound common sense, one who knew his limits and who planned ahead for long-term, solid advantages; an able leader of men who could attract and lead an army, yet one who, as we shall see, was not without interest in culture and learning. He was to be the only one of the first Hellenistic kings to die in his bed after securing a peaceful succession to the throne.

Following the meeting of the Council in Babylon, Ptolemy left quickly for his chosen satrapy. Perdiccas, the most senior of the generals, commander of the army and head of the regency government, gave him only very little money and 2,000 men to take to Egypt. To ensure a welcome Ptolemy also took back with him the idols and sacred objects which had been looted from Egypt years before by the Persians.

Egypt at this time was under the governorship of Cleomenes, a Greek from Naucratis, who had been appointed by Alexander. He had used this position to his own advantage and for years had embezzled money collected for taxes, plundered the pay of the army, robbed temples and allowed the irrigation canals, on which agriculture depended, to fall into decay. The economy of Egypt was in ruins. Nevertheless, Cleomenes was a close ally of Perdiccas, and he was chosen to remain in high office as second in command to Ptolemy, with orders to keep a check on the new satrap.

Ptolemy, however, was a man with a plan and a streak of

independence. He soon rid himself of Cleomenes by placing him on trial for misplaced loyalties and other crimes. Cleomenes was found guilty and executed. The immense fortune amassed by Cleomenes, amounting to some 8,000 talents, fell to Ptolemy. This was of vital importance to him in order to build up a strong army and navy for defence against the threat he knew would come, and he made sure his forces were paid. Once word began to spread, large numbers of mercenaries began flocking to Egypt – and Ptolemy personally supervised their training into an efficient fighting force.

Ptolemy's next move was more spectacular. The next year, 322 B.C., he learned that the body of Alexander was being transported from Babylon to Macedonia for burial. He intercepted the *cortège* at Damascus and claimed that Alexander wished to be buried in Egypt, at the shrine of Zeus Ammon at Siwa in the western desert. Alexander's body was taken to Memphis to await construction of a tomb at Siwa. In the event this was never built, and Alexander was finally interred in a magnificent shrine at Alexandria.

This deed angered Perdiccas, already disturbed by the removal of his ally Cleomenes. Ptolemy's final break with the regent did not occur, however, until the next year (321 B.C.). Ptolemy was asked by the neighbouring Greeks in Cyrene to intervene in a civil war. This he did, but without asking permission from Perdiccas. When Ptolemy held on to the city of Cyrene as a prize this was too much for Perdiccas, who marched on Egypt with an army of 20,000 infantry and 5,000 cavalry. He successfully reached the Nile, but there fell foul of the great river. His vast number of troops, in attempting to cross, disturbed the sandy river-bed which broke up, and many were washed away. The rest were cut off. In what was to become true Hellenistic style, Perdiccas was betrayed and murdered by his three closest generals. They offered Ptolemy the regency and command of the army. The astute leader declined, preferring security in Egypt. Nevertheless, in declining this supreme position he left the way open for his ambitious rivals, and there ensued forty years of struggle for command of the empire, known as the 'Wars of the Successors'. Throughout this period Ptolemy's main aim was to consolidate his position. The territorial gains he made were mainly for Egypt's advantage and protection. Thus by the end of his reign Ptolemy held sway over Cyrene to the west, Palestine and part of Syria to the east, Cyprus and islands in the Cyclades.

One notable occurrence during the Wars of the Successors was Ptolemy's assumption of royal titles. For the first eighteen

years he had ruled Egypt as satrap in the name of the boy-kings
Philip Arrhidaeus and Alexander IV. The same was true of the
other warring generals who had carved up the empire of Alexander the Great. The fiction continued even after Arrhidaeus was
murdered in 317 B.C. and young Alexander in 311 B.C. The first of
the generals to assume a crown was Antigonus, with his son
Demetrius, following a victory over Ptolemy and other rivals. Not
to be outdone, Ptolemy and the others followed suit. It is interesting to note, however, that very quickly Ptolemy began to date his
reign from the time he first came to Egypt, 323 B.C.

The assumption of royal titles was of some importance to
Ptolemy, for in Egypt the anointed ruler was considered a god and
for Ptolemy to rule as a satrap was to lack divine authority in the
eyes of the natives. In this, however, he was fortunate to possess
the body of Alexander the Great, who had been accepted as
pharaoh by the Egyptians. Ptolemy could be seen to rule in his
name and, when he finally assumed the royal crown, to be the heir
of Alexander. An official state cult was established for the worship
of Alexander amongst the Greeks in Egypt, from which there
developed a cult of the ruling Ptolemaic house.

Within Egypt Ptolemy wrought many changes. Chief among
these was the creation of a new ruling élite which was almost
entirely Greek. Thousands of mercenary soldiers were granted
land in Egypt, to expand and improve the agriculture of the
country and to establish a bond between the settlers and their new
home. Ptolemy even founded a new, completely Greek city for the
immigrants in Upper Egypt, called Ptolemais. Centre and symbol
of the new order, however, was the capital city in the Delta,
Alexandria.

Alexandria had been founded by order of Alexander the Great,
and construction begun by Cleomenes, although it was under the
early Ptolemies that the city flourished and grew to be one of the
major centres of the Hellenistic world. It is difficult to distinguish
the exact contribution of Ptolemy I from that of his immediate
successors, but he is certainly accredited with building the city
walls and he was probably responsible for the construction of the
Pharos, which is noted as one of the seven wonders of the ancient
world. This lighthouse was polygonal in shape and built in three
stages; it tapered towards the top, and near the summit there
burnt a fire which shone far out to sea. The precise means of
magnification and projection of this light are not certain, but
evidently some form of mirror was employed.

The first Ptolemy was not simply a bluff soldier; he was also a
man of culture and some learning. In his later years he wrote a

history of the campaigns of Alexander the Great, which is now lost, although at the time it stimulated a number of historical writers and was used by later biographers of Alexander. He is most noted, however, for his patronage of scholars and the establishment of Alexandria as a centre of learning. He associated with philosophers of the peripatetic school of Aristotle, especially Demetrius of Phaleron, a former tyrant of Athens who came to Egypt when he was expelled from that city. Using his advice Ptolemy established a civil and legal code for the new city of Alexandria, based on elements from all over Greece. Ptolemy also instituted the practice of inviting leading intellectual figures to tutor the royal princes, a post later coupled with that of librarian.

The intellectual heart of Alexandria was the Museum, another creation of Ptolemy. The original *Mouseia* were cult centres for the Muses, but the Alexandrian *Mouseion* was designed as a base for the scientists and scholars attracted to Egypt by the king. It was probably both a research and teaching institution, although details are lacking. The best description of the Museum is provided by Strabo, who wrote at the time of Augustus, although probably little had changed since the early Ptolemaic period: 'The Museum is part of the royal quarter, and it has a cloister, an arcade and a large house in which is provided the common meal of the men of learning who share the Museum. And this community has common funds, and a priest in charge ... who was appointed previously by the kings, but now by Caesar.' Another important institution founded by Ptolemy was the Library, although this was developed by his son Ptolemy II Philadelphus.

The reign of Ptolemy I was marked by one new development destined to have an influence throughout the entire Greek world – the propagation of a new cult. A deity unknown to the mainland Greeks until this time became one of the great gods of late paganism – Serapis. The origins of Serapis lay in Memphis, the ancient religious capital of Egypt. There resided the cult of the bull god Apis, allied to that of the god of the Underworld, Osiris. Apis embodied the divinity and life-giving qualities of the Nile. Combined with Osiris, who was also a god of vegetation, they formed Osiris–Apis (Serapis), a deity who was capable of triumphing over death. Osiris–Apis was popular with the native Egyptians of the fourth century B.C., and also with Greeks who resided in Egypt before the arrival of Ptolemy.

By giving Greek immigrants a patron deity of native origin yet already recognised by the existing Greek population of Egypt, Ptolemy hoped to reinforce the ties with their adopted country. As advisers he had Timotheus, an Athenian authority on Greek religious practice, and Manetho, an Egyptian priest (more noted for his history of Egypt written in Greek). Serapis was given a Greek image and cult practices, and a temple was built at Alexandria. The statue of the god was created by the well-known fourth-century sculptor Bryaxis. It depicted an impressive figure wearing long flowing robe (*chiton*) and cloak (*himation*). The god had a flowing beard and locks, and on top of his head was a *kalathos* or corn measure. This symbolised the vegetal aspect of the god. The underworld element was demonstrated by the three-headed dog Cerberus lying at the god's feet. Serapis was essentially a patron deity of whom intercessions could be asked. He was also noted as a god of healing, linked with Asclepios, and there was a special shrine for this at Memphis.

During his life Ptolemy had a number of wives and concubines, by whom he had numerous children. His first recorded wife is the Persian princess Artacama whom he married at Susa in 324 B.C. at a mass wedding of Macedonian and Greek officers with Persian women organised by Alexander the Great. We never hear of Artacama again. Soon after Alexander's death, in about 321 B.C., Ptolemy made a political marriage with Eurydice, daughter of Antipater, who held Macedonia. She bore him two sons, one called Ptolemy, and at least two daughters. In about 316 B.C. he married a woman called Berenice, a Macedonian lady who had come to Egypt in Eurydice's retinue and who had three children already by a former husband. Her marriage to Ptolemy was a love-match. They had two children, a daughter Arsinoe, born about 315 B.C., and a son, Ptolemy, born on the island of Cos in 309 B.C. He probably had numerous mistresses besides his legitimate wives, the most noted being Thaïs of Athens, a star of the Greek *demi-monde*. Together they had three children.

In 285 B.C., having ruled as satrap and king of Egypt for thirty-eight years, Ptolemy made his elder son by Berenice, also called Ptolemy, co-ruler with himself. Two years later, having seen his successor securely established on the throne without bloodshed, he died peacefully at the age of eighty-two. The dynasty that succeeded him, all with the name Ptolemy, lasted until 31 B.C. when Octavian defeated the last ruler of the line, Cleopatra VII, and Egypt was incorporated into the Roman Empire.

After his death Ptolemy was deified by his son as Soter (Saviour), by which surname he has become known to history.

Ptolemy II (Philadelphus)

(309–246 B.C.)

Ptolemy, son of Ptolemy, known to history as Ptolemy Philadelphus, was born on the island of Cos in 309 B.C., during a campaign of his father, Ptolemy I. His mother was Berenice, the third wife of Ptolemy I, whom he had married in 316 B.C. This marriage had been a love-match and Ptolemy wished his son by Berenice to succeed him, rather than his eldest son, also called Ptolemy, by his second wife Eurydice. This Ptolemy, nicknamed Ceraunos (Thunderbolt), nevertheless had expectations of the throne. In this he was supported by the eminent scholar Demetrius of Phaleron, and possibly by a party among the Macedonian aristocracy resident in Egypt. Nevertheless in 285 B.C. it was the younger Ptolemy who was elevated to co-rulership with his father, two years before the old man's death. Ptolemy Ceraunos decided Egypt was no longer a safe place to be, and fled to the court of Lysimachus, king of Thrace and Macedonia.

In 283 B.C. Ptolemy I died, and Ptolemy II became sole ruler at the age of twenty-six. He was a man of very different temperament to his rugged, plain-living father. As a youth he had been tutored by noteworthy men of letters, including Philitas of Cos, a poet, and the scientist Strabo of Lampsacus. This upbringing encouraged in him a passion for learning, and he patronised scholars on an even greater scale than his father. Some constitutional weakness, according to Strabo, also encouraged his interest in sedentary activities, and he left the conduct of his wars to the generals. Physically he was of fair complexion and inclined to heaviness in later life.

In the early years of Ptolemy's reign events were occurring in Macedonia that were to have a profound influence on his future. At the court of Lysimachus Ceraunos found himself with two of his sisters, Arsinoe and Lysandra. Arsinoe, a half-sister, was married to Lysimachus; Lysandra, like Ceraunos a child of Ptolemy Soter and Eurydice, was married to Lysimachus's son Agathocles. Arsinoe conceived a violent passion for Agathocles, and on finding him unresponsive accused him of plotting against his father. Lysimachus, who doted on his young wife and was completely under the sway of her strong personality, had Agathocles arrested and imprisoned.

Impelled by a mixture of spite and ambition for her sons, Arsinoe conspired with Ceraunos to kill Agathocles. The murder of the king's son, attributed by all to Lysimachus, caused a wave of popular revulsion against the king. Ceraunos, sensing possible gain in the unstable situation, persuaded King Seleucus in Antioch to take action against Lysimachus. In the ensuing battle Lysimachus was killed; and as Seleucus prepared for a triumphal parade Ceraunos stabbed him to death. The way to the throne of Macedonia was open, and Ceraunos was acclaimed king.

Ceraunos now laid siege to the heart of Arsinoe, and succeeded in persuading her that he loved her and her two sons – his nephews. However, no sooner were they married than he killed the children. Arsinoe fled to Egypt. Some time later the Gauls invaded Macedonia, and the unspeakable Ceraunos was killed defending his kingdom.

In Egypt Arsinoe found Ptolemy married to another Arsinoe, the daughter of her late husband, Lysimachus. They had three children, Ptolemy, Lysimachus and Berenice. Notwithstanding this, Arsinoe the sister determined she would become queen in the house of her father. Well practised, she intrigued against her namesake, insinuating that she was guilty of plotting and disloyalty. The steady denigration combined with seduction of her brother resulted in poisoning Ptolemy's mind against his wife, and he banished her to Coptos in the deserts of the Thebaid. Ptolemy then married his full sister Arsinoe II.

This move may have been in accord with Egyptian royal tradition, but it certainly upset the Greeks. Such a degree of incest was considered outrageous and, what is more, it was thought to be a sell-out to the Egyptian element. Nevertheless Arsinoe soon won favour within the country. She was energetic in government and foreign policy, and adopted the three children of her brother by Arsinoe I. At her death seven years later she was deified by her brother Ptolemy, who sincerely mourned her loss; he never remarried.

The deification of Arsinoe was part of a pattern seen throughout the reign of Ptolemy II in the development of the dynastic cult, begun by his father with the deification of Alexander the Great. First, in about 280 B.C. he deified his father, Ptolemy I, and his mother Berenice. They were worshipped as the 'Saviour Gods'. A festival was established in honour of Soter called the Ptolemeia. This was held every five years and included gymnastic, musical and equestrian competitions.

In about 272 B.C. Ptolemy went further and established a cult for himself and Arsinoe II, in connexion with that of the founder Alexander. Various reasons may be suggested for this. He wished to continue and emphasise the link with Alexander, which was no longer direct, although his body was buried in Alexandria. Prestige was another factor. Similar cults were being established by other Hellenistic dynasties and appearances had to be kept up. Apart from this, in Egypt the pressure of native practice may have influenced his decision. Although the organisation of the ruler cult was essentially Greek, the pharaonic background created a favourable environment for its establishment. The pair were deified as the *Theoi Adelphoi* (Fraternal Gods) and on her death Arsinoe was called Philadelphus, as Ptolemy himself became on his death. This title, 'brother-loving' or 'sister-loving', although it emphasised their incestuous marriage, had also the more moral meaning of brotherly love, which softened the nature of their relationship and concentrated on the community of rule between the brother and sister.

Another characteristic of Ptolemy II's reign was his love of entertainment and splendour, in contrast to his thrifty father. This can best be illustrated by the *Pompe* or Grand Procession of Ptolemy Philadelphus. This procession seems to have been a vast parade of the gods of Alexandria in which were represented the cult of Soter and Berenice as well as those of the Olympian gods, with pre-eminence given to Dionysus, from whom the Ptolemies claimed descent. The procession is described by Kallixenos of Rhodes. 'A four-wheeled cart, 21 feet long by 12 feet wide, was drawn by 180 men; in it was a 15-foot statue of Dionysus pouring a libation from a golden vessel. ... Next came a carriage pulled by 600 men: on it was a wineskin made of leopard pelts which held 3,000 measures. As the wine was released little by little, it flowed over the whole street. ... On another immense vehicle was a deep cave profusely shaded with ivy and yew: all along the route there flew out from it pigeons, ring-doves and turtle-doves whose feet were fastened with ribbons so that they could easily be caught by the spectators. Two springs gushed from the cave, one of milk and one of wine. ... There were many striking effigies and images, a great number of beasts and horses and 24 extremely large lions. Upon other carriages were statues of kings and of gods. After these came a chorus of 600 men marching in procession, among whom were 300 harpists who had gilded harps and crowns of gold. Following them came 2,000 golden-horned bulls, all of the same colour, with golden frontlets, necklaces and aegises.'

Another aspect of his luxurious living was Ptolemy

Philadelphus's love of banquets, the preparations for which were very well organised. We hear that 'for as many states as there are which employ special usages in drink and food and mode of reclining, so many officials were assigned, and then whatever guests visited the king, preparations were made according to their customs, so that there should be nothing to discomfort them and they could pass the time in good cheer'.

Added to his extravagant habits, the second Ptolemy was also a lover of women. His mistresses are catalogued by a number of ancient writers including a descendant of his, Ptolemy Euergetes II. One was a native Egyptian with a Greek name, Didyme. Another, Myrton, came from the comic theatre, and her house became one of the finest in Alexandria after she captured the royal favour. Two others were flute players called Mnesis and Pothine, also noted for their fine dwellings. One by the name of Clino is found depicted in statues and statuettes as a goddess, clad in nothing but a chiton and carrying a cornucopia. Stratonice, another mistress, was remembered by an imposing sepulchre at the Egyptian town of Eleusis near Alexandria. The most celebrated of them all was Bilistiche, of whom it was said variously that she was a barbarian, a 'trull from the market place', or that she was of noble descent. In 268 B.C. she entered a team in the two-horse chariot race at Olympia, and won a prize. Ptolemy had her declared a goddess and she was worshipped under the name of Aphrodite Bilistiche.

So far Ptolemy Philadelphus has been presented as a somewhat decadent monarch, but this is by no means wholly the case. He had developed intellectual interests, actively encouraging scholars, and he was probably responsible for the main development of the Library of Alexandria, founded by his father. There appear to have been two libraries; one was probably housed in the temple of Serapis, and the main one possibly within the Museum. One source suggests that the libraries held as many as 42,000 and 490,000 books respectively. The main Library was presided over by a librarian appointed by the king, and it became the custom for the post to be held by the tutor to the royal children. Books, or rather scrolls, were acquired in a number of ways. Some were purchased in the major centres of Athens or Rhodes. Others, it seems, were confiscated from ships entering Alexandria. The scrolls were copied, and the copy given back to the owner. Once in the possession of the Library the book-rolls were placed in a store ready to be accessioned. They were labelled by their geographical origin, the editor of the copy or the name of the previous owner. They could then be catalogued for public use, usually by author, with the same subdivisions used in the original labelling. This would aid scholars in establishing the history of a given text, or the superiority of one over another. The aim of the Library was to have a complete corpus of Greek literature, plus works from other languages in translation. It is said that Ptolemy Philadelphus ordered the translation of the Septuagint into Greek for inclusion in the Library.

The establishment of the Library had a great influence on Alexandrian scholarship. Among the most notable scholars of the day were Apollonius and Callimachus. Apollonius was probably librarian from 270–245 B.C. He was a great expert on Greek literature, especially Homer. He also worked on the texts of poems by Hesiod and Archilochus, as well as writing literary criticism. Of greater influence and importance was the work of Apollonius's contemporary, Callimachus. His main work was the 'Tables of Persons Eminent in Every Branch of Learning, Together with a List of Their Writings'. This was a type of universal bibliography and biography in which authors and scholars were arranged according to subjects, alphabetically under each heading. Although not a catalogue of the Library, as was once supposed, it doubtless made use of early work on that catalogue.

Ptolemy Philadelphus had an especial interest in the natural sciences. This was presumably encouraged by his tutor Strato of Lampsacus, a physicist who developed theories regarding the nature of vacuum, and held the view that colours emanated from objects and imparted to the intervening air between object and observer the colours possessed by the original body. Philadelphus made a collection of rare animals and studied their habits. He created a zoo in the palace area of Alexandria. Diodorus Siculus tells us that Ptolemy 'brought to the knowledge of the Greeks different kinds of animals which had never before been seen and were objects of amazement'. He goes on to describe the capture of a huge snake in Ethiopia for the king, and its return to Alexandria where it was tamed and put on display.

The second Ptolemy also played an important role in the economic development of Egypt. One of his greatest works was the winning of large new tracts of land for cultivation and habitation in the Fayûm. This depression, some 40 by 30 miles across, to the south of modern Cairo, contains a large natural lake surrounded by fertile land. In the period before Philadelphus the lake filled most of the basin. By reducing the area of water new land was laid bare, and this was largely given over to the Greek and Macedonian settlers. The new territory was named after Queen Arsinoe, and a new town built there, Philadelphia, was also called after her.

There is evidence that Philadelphus also interested himself in the development of scientific agriculture to improve production. A letter in the Archive of Zenon states that: 'The king has ordered us to sow the land twice. As soon as you have reaped the early grain, water the land by hand, or if that is not possible, set up as many irrigation machines as you can and thus water the land. But do not keep the water on the land for more than five days. After letting the land dry, sow the three-months wheat immediately.' Such an idea, and the use of a wheat which matured in three months, were not native to Egypt. The order must have resulted from Ptolemy's interest in the sciences, and may have been inspired by a treatise on plants by the great scholar Theophrastus.

Another important economic measure of Ptolemy Philadelphus was the issuing of his so-called 'revenue laws' which, by establishing a government monopoly in the production of certain basic commodities and services, sought to increase and stabilise the royal revenues on which depended the safety and strength of the king himself and the kingdom.

Ptolemy Philadelphus died in 246 B.C. at the age of sixty-three. His reign had been a successful one. He had steadily increased the wealth and possessions of Egypt, but he must be more remembered as the creator of the golden age of Alexandria when the city became the economic and cultural centre of the Hellenistic world.

Babylonia, Assyria and Syria

Tiglath-Pileser I

(*Ruled* 1114–1076 B.C.)

It was not until the ninth century B.C. that the Assyrian empire as we meet it in the Bible rose to international supremacy, but there was an earlier period of expansion in the late second millennium which laid the foundations of subsequent greatness. The king most prominent in this development was Tiglath-Pileser I (1114–1076 B.C.).

The heartland of Assyria was a kingdom on the rich corn-plains

along the middle Tigris in what is now north Iraq. It was bounded
to the north by the foothills of the eastern Taurus beginning some
thirty miles north of Nineveh, and ended in the south at the
latitude where rainfall became too low for corn-growing, just
south of Ashur. A history of insecurity, from raiders coming in
from the desert or down from the hills to possess themselves of the
fruits of the labours of the hard-working Assyrian farmers, had
encouraged a philosophy of self-defence through the pre-emptive
strike.

Tiglath-Pileser I, the legitimate successor in an ancient dynasty
and a many-sided man of great energy, came to the throne at a
time when Assyria, after a period of considerable pressure which
had reduced it to its narrowest limits, was beginning to make a
recovery. We learn of the activities of Assyrian kings mainly from
their own cuneiform inscriptions. Earlier kings had left inscriptions, but Tiglath-Pileser introduced a new form which amplified
the royal information. This new development was Annals, in
which a detailed account of campaigns was given in chronological
order. The quantity of detail provided would make it possible to
give an account of Tiglath-Pileser's military activities full of
names of peoples and places, but this would not be very meaningful without an extended discussion of the geography, and the
following summary is therefore limited to the principal developments.

The capital of Assyria was Ashur, in the south of the country,
long unchallengeable because of its prestige as a venerable cult
centre. But in the conditions of the late second millennium B.C.,
Assyria was beginning to look northwards, and in consequence
the most northern city, Nineveh, had become at least the equal of
Ashur in military and economic importance. Tiglath-Pileser,
recognising it as the key to Assyrian security, built a palace there
and strengthened the city walls.

Tiglath-Pileser's attention had to be devoted to the north at the
very beginning of his reign. Racial movements in Asia Minor in
about 1200 B.C., reflected in the tradition of the Trojan War, had
brought a people called Mushki, the later Phrygians, into the
mountains south of the Tigris about 150 miles north-west of
Nineveh. At about the time of Tiglath-Pileser's accession they
moved down into nearer territory which was claimed by Assyria,
though not effectively held. Fearing invasion of Assyria itself,
Tiglath-Pileser attacked immediately and vigorously. He showed
his military leadership by defeating the invaders, but followed this
up with statesmanship. Instead of taking reprisals, he treated with
leniency those who submitted, settling them as Assyrian subjects.

This was the first step in what was to be a major and far-seeing policy of Tiglath-Pileser – land-settlement consciously aimed at increasing both the Assyrian population and also the area of cultivated land and thus total agricultural production. In the years that followed this was repeated many times, and Tiglath-Pileser sums up by saying: 'I added land to the land of Assyria and people to its people. I improved the lot of my people and made them dwell in peaceful habitations.' But farmers needed equipment to increase agricultural productivity, and Tiglath-Pileser took appropriate measures for this: 'I had ploughs teamed up throughout the whole of Assyria, and thereby heaped up more grain than my forefathers.'

North of the Tigris in the region where Tiglath-Pileser had settled the Mushki, there lived mountain peoples who had been involved in resisting the Assyrian claim to the area. Recognising these people as a threat to the stability of the region, he followed up with a series of campaigns, in which he compelled the small states in the area to accept at least nominal Assyrian suzerainty. These campaigns eventually took Tiglath-Pileser 300 miles north-west of Nineveh, 200 miles due north and as far east as the Lower Zab river, but despite these distances he still regarded them as defensive operations. At the conclusion of his account of his victories, he states as his achieved objective: 'I kept the feet of the enemy from my land.'

The results of Tiglath-Pileser's northern campaigns were twofold. Firstly, they brought substantial economic benefits to Assyria. These regions yielded several commodities vital to Assyria: they were major producers of copper and bronze, their forests provided good timber, and the people in some of these territories were breeders of cattle and horses. From this time onwards, metals, timber, cattle and horses came to Assyria in large quantities, either as booty extorted by the Assyrian army or as tribute sent by vassals. The metals, timber and cattle added to the general prosperity of Assyria, and the herds of horses allowed Tiglath-Pileser to build up a powerful chariotry force. The second result was cultural. Vassals were required to send hostages to reside at the Assyrian court as a guarantee of good conduct, and they would also periodically send embassies bearing tribute; contacts such as these would serve to accelerate the spread of Assyrian ideas and institutions into the northern areas. Tiglath-Pileser was quite conscious of this aspect of contacts with vassals and took active steps to develop them, for of one of the more important captured kings he records: 'I brought him bound as a prisoner to my city Ashur. I had mercy on him and let him go free

from my city with his life, to proclaim the glory of the great gods' –
in effect, to advertise Assyrian greatness.

Tiglath-Pileser also acted to advance Assyrian interests in the
south. In more favourable times the Assyrian kingdom reached
south-westwards as far as the middle Euphrates. Tiglath-Pileser
moved to reassert this boundary. Here he encountered the
problem of another racial movement, that of the Aramaeans, a
people whose origins and history were closely linked with those of
the biblical Hebrews. These Aramaeans were moving out of the
Syrian desert and crossing the middle Euphrates into Assyrian
territory, where their nomadic way of life came into conflict with
Assyrian agriculture. The problem was so serious that Tiglath-
Pileser had to make campaigns against them regularly twice a
year for fourteen years to bring them under control.

Tiglath-Pileser had a second problem in the south – the
prestigious kingdom of Babylonia, which less than a century
before had been in a position to intervene in Assyrian affairs.
Clashes over boundaries led Tiglath-Pileser to make a
demonstration of strength by capturing the cities of northern
Babylonia, including the capital Babylon, but after achieving
secure frontiers by this action he made no attempt at permanent
annexation.

The Aramaeans, spread out along the major route following the
Euphrates from Syria to Babylonia, played an important role in
international trade. When he had finally achieved security along
the middle Euphrates, Tiglath-Pileser followed the Aramaean
trade routes through to the Mediterranean coast, where he made
trading contacts with Phoenician cities as far south as Sidon. One
of his specifically stated objectives was to obtain timber from the
Lebanon for his building projects at home. But in his account he
went beyond this to show something of his own personality. This
was his first sight of the Mediterranean, and he chose to make a
long journey in a boat from one city to another. On the way he
tried his hand at harpooning, proudly recording that he killed, as
he put it, 'as an achievement of my own hand, a *nahiru*, which they
call a "sea-horse" ' – probably a dolphin. Tiglath-Pileser was so
fascinated by this animal that he subsequently made models of it
for the decoration of his palace entrance.

Hunting, of which harpooning was a specialised aspect, had
long been an activity of ancient Near Eastern rulers, but it was
Tiglath-Pileser who initiated the custom of including hunting
exploits in the Annals. He recorded how he slew the major fauna
still found between Assyria and the desert – wild bulls, elephants,
lions and other creatures, or, as he put it, 'every kind of wild beast

and winged bird of the heavens'. But his attitude to wild life was by no means exclusively destructive: for Tiglath-Pileser the other face of hunting was conservation. He records: 'I caught roe-deer, *ayalu*-deer, gazelles and ibex, which the gods who love me bestowed on me in high mountain ranges for hunting, and made herds of them. I counted them like flocks of sheep'. His interest in the fauna became recognised, and this resulted in his receiving as tribute such exotic animals as a crocodile, an ape, and an unidentified animal which has been taken very dubiously to be a yak. He also had two-humped camels imported into Assyria and attempted to breed them. The flora was equally of concern to him: he records introducing into Assyria new orchard fruits from abroad, and species of trees never before grown in Assyria. When he built his palace in Nineveh, he included with it a royal garden and had a canal excavated from a minor river to irrigate it.

In addition to his activities in military and economic affairs and the flora and fauna, he also took a creative interest in Assyrian literature. He was the first known royal founder of a library of cuneiform tablets, found at Ashur. Basically these texts, of which just over a hundred are extant, comprised on the one hand works relevant to religion and the state, and on the other hand works important for the scholars of the time, that is, the professional scribes. They included such various categories as court edicts; myths; incantations, hymns and other religious texts; recipes for ointment-making; lists of place-names, god-names, and names of plants and animals (all aspects of a scribal passion for classification); lists of archaic cuneiform signs (to help with the reading of ancient texts); vocabularies and lexical texts; and omens drawn from liver-divination. Many of these texts were copied from older examples, and for this purpose Tiglath-Pileser had a scribal staff, including one described as 'the royal scribe', who must have served as chief librarian, and junior scribes.

There was no rigid distinction between libraries and state archives, and some of the works listed above would, on our classification, belong to the latter category. Such were the harem decrees, a group of edicts regulating behaviour within the women's quarters of the palace. Some of these edicts stemmed directly from Tiglath-Pileser himself, but others originated with his predecessors over the previous two centuries and are preserved because Tiglath-Pileser and his scribes carefully collected and edited them. Basically these edicts were aimed at preventing impropriety or scandal within the palace. For example, the Assyrian king laid down that if palace women were singing or quarrelling and a royal eunuch, courtier or servant stopped to listen, he should receive a hundred lashes and have an ear cut off. No courtier who had occasion to speak to a woman was allowed to approach nearer to her than seven paces, and should the major-domo of the palace allow such an offence to go unpunished he himself would be punished.

Another major Assyrian literary compilation for which Tiglath-Pileser was responsible, showing the same concern for organisation as the court decrees and the library texts, was a collection of laws. Their origin was quite different from the laws of Hammurabi; they did not represent Tiglath-Pileser's own judicial decisions, but were a compilation, undertaken in Tiglath-Pileser's time, from laws which had originated several centuries earlier, as the language and contents indicate. They are systematically arranged by subject-matter, and so have a better claim than the laws of Hammurabi to the title 'code'. They fall into three groups, relating respectively to women, landed property, and property other than land. Their nature may be seen from a summary of the contents of the laws relating to women, which include such matters as: theft by a woman in various circumstances (from a temple, from her husband's estate); assault by or upon a woman; rape, adultery and fornication; financial arrangements for a woman at marriage; property of a widow; divorce and marriage; miscarriage from violence, and deliberate abortion; and rights of a husband to chastise his wife (he might flog her, pull her hair, and box – or perhaps mutilate – her ears). The laws were primitive and harsh, as the law relating to abortion demonstrates: 'If a woman has by her own will cast the fruit of her womb, and charge and proof have been brought against her, she shall be impaled and shall be left unburied. [Even] if she has died in casting the fruit of her womb, she shall be impaled and left unburied.'

Tiglath-Pileser died a natural death as an elderly man and was succeeded by his son. There was a swift decline, and it was another two centuries before an Assyrian king again reached the Mediterranean, after which a rapid expansion of empire took place. The extent to which later kings looked to Tiglath-Pileser I as their model is reflected in the fact that at many points their inscriptions contain themes or even whole passages verbatim, which first occur in the Annals of this king.

Tiglath-Pileser III

(*Ruled* 745–727 B.C.)

Tiglath-Pileser III was an Assyrian king mentioned in the Bible both by that name and as Pul. He played a pivotal part in the final rise of the Assyrian empire in the eighth century B.C., which at his death controlled the whole Fertile Crescent from the Egyptian border to the Persian Gulf.

In the half-century before his time there had been a gradual decline of Assyria. Several factors played a part in this. One was the rise of the kingdom of Urartu (Ararat), in the area later known as Armenia, near Lake Van in eastern Turkey. This kingdom, which grew out of a federation of petty states, had just before the time of Tiglath-Pileser become strong enough to expand westwards and compete with Assyria for control of the north Syria area between the Euphrates and the Mediterranean. Tiglath-Pileser's predecessor had attempted to check this by tying states to him by treaty, but without lasting success, and a whole bloc of states, which had hitherto been Assyrian vassals, had passed into the Urartian orbit. Even districts only seventy miles north of Nineveh had fallen to Urartu.

Problems were also developing with Assyria's southern neighbour, Babylonia. Here, alongside the ancient cities, were tribal peoples called the Chaldaeans who had settled in the southern marshlands some centuries before and gradually spread up the Euphrates. By the middle of the eighth century they were beginning to dominate some of the Babylonian cities, with adverse effects upon both security and trade, and thus secondarily upon Assyria which had vital trading links with the Babylonian cities.

A third problem was that a number of governors of provinces had become over-powerful, to the detriment of the central government.

These factors together produced tensions within Assyria, which culminated in a revolt in the capital, Calah (modern Nimrud). The previous weak king was overthrown, and a certain Pul, according to one inscription the son of an earlier king and so the brother of his predecessor, came to the throne. If the claim of the inscription is true, the date of death of his father would make him at least thirty-five at his accession, and there is other evidence that he was probably governor of Calah before his accession, so that he was already a mature and experienced administrator. He took Tiglath-Pileser as his throne-name; this was in effect a statement of programme, indicating that he proposed to emulate the achievements of the first bearer of that name, who had undertaken a vigorous expansion of the empire nearly four hundred years before.

Tiglath-Pileser III was evidently a man of great energy. He immediately took firm hold on the Assyrian empire. He first made demonstrations southwards to north Babylonia and then eastwards into the Zagros foothills, as a warning to disruptive elements in Babylonia and to potentially troublesome peoples in the eastern mountains, and then turned to his main problem, the conflict of interests with Urartu.

The bloc of north Syrian states which had thrown in their lot with Urartu stretched from Melid (present-day Malatya) to Arpad, north-west of Aleppo. Arpad controlled the main Assyrian route to the Mediterranean. In 743 B.C. Tiglath-Pileser took his army westwards to deal with the situation. He defeated the Urartian army in the area, and in 740 B.C. captured Arpad itself after a long siege: its fate is referred to in the Bible, in 2 Kings 19:13 (= Isaiah 37:13). Tiglath-Pileser now introduced an important new strategy. In the ninth century, Assyrian kings had already been expanding their control westwards, but had treated the Euphrates as the boundary for direct provincial rule: states west of that were allowed to remain nominally independent with vassal status. Tiglath-Pileser changed this. He turned the conquered north-Syrian region into a directly ruled Assyrian province, with Arpad as its capital. He then moved towards the Mediterranean via the northern end of the Orontes, and advanced along the coast. This resulted in the creation of further Assyrian provinces. Kings of other states hastened to pay tribute to preclude invasion: one of these was Menahem of Israel, whose payment of tribute to 'Pul the king of Assyria' 'that he might help him to confirm his hold of the royal power' is detailed in 2 Kings 15:19*f*.

In the intervals between his western campaigns, Tiglath-Pileser took action against Urartian influence elsewhere, in the mountains due north of Iraq, beyond the Zagros in north-west Iran, and eventually against Urartu itself south-east of Lake Van.

In 734 B.C. Tiglath-Pileser returned to the west to consolidate and extend his control of the Mediterranean area. There he marched down the coast, took Gaza, and reached Wadi el-Arish, known in the Bible as 'the Brook of Egypt', on the edge of the Sinai desert. This area was inhabited by Arabs, who were important for the part they played in the spice trade from south Arabia. Tiglath-Pileser made no attempt at extending Assyrian control over Egypt, but did enter into friendly relations with the Arab tribes of Sinai, northern Arabia and Transjordan to protect Assyrian interests in the buffer area and the southern approaches to Palestine and Syria.

Israel and Damascus had formerly benefited by the Arabian trade, and Assyrian influence over the Arabs now threatened this. They therefore organised an anti-Assyrian coalition, into which, as the Bible tells us, they tried to force Ahaz of Jerusalem (2 Kings 16:5–9). Ahaz, however, called for help from Tiglath-Pileser. This was given, and in campaigns of 733–32 B.C. Tiglath-Pileser defeated the coalition. The kingdom of Damascus and most of Israel were cut up into Assyrian provinces, a rump of Israel being left under a vassal king, Hoshea, appointed by Tiglath-Pileser.

Tiglath-Pileser's creation of Assyrian provinces was a matter of deliberate policy, but the objective was not mere imperial aggrandisement. Rather, it was in the interests of imperial security. Tiglath-Pileser did not make native kingdoms into provinces arbitrarily. On the contrary, those vassals who showed reliability towards Assyria were allowed – and, indeed, actively assisted – to retain their territories. Tiglath-Pileser's treatment of Ahaz of Jerusalem is a good case in point. Even in the case of the kingdom of Israel, the Bible shows that before taking more drastic action Tiglath-Pileser made attempts to reach an accommodation, and that even after strategic considerations compelled more drastic action, he still left a diminished vassal state of Israel in existence. Another vassal, in north Syria, left an Aramaic inscription testifying to the excellent relations between his dynasty and Tiglath-Pileser:

> My father grasped the hem of his lord, the great king of Assyria; then did he live and his kingdom lived. My father ran at the wheel of his lord Tiglath-Pileser, king of Assyria, in campaigns from east to west. My father died at the feet of his lord Tiglath-Pileser, on campaign, and all the camp of his lord the king of Assyria wept for him. And his lord, the king of Assyria, erected an image of him by the roadside, and brought my father across from Damascus. Then, because of my father's loyalty and my own loyalty, my lord Tiglath-Pileser set me on the throne.

The problem was that, with Urartu and a little later Egypt seeking support amongst the states from Palestine to north Syria, any minor state faced the likelihood that sooner or later it would enter into conspiracy against Assyria and so create the conditions for its own annexation.

There was a further consequence of Tiglath-Pileser's reduction of conquered territories to the status of provinces – the policy of deportation. It was not Tiglath-Pileser who initiated this, but he greatly extended it, and from his time it was a regular feature of Assyrian statecraft. The practice was that a proportion of a conquered population – normally the leading families of the community and craftsmen – would be moved from their homeland to another part of the empire, often chosen for an environment similar to that from which they originally came (2 Kings 18:32). Whilst deportation could to those who underwent it be tantamount to a punishment for rebellion, this was not the primary intention, since we know that, far from imposing rigorous conditions, Tiglath-Pileser and other Assyrian kings after him took steps to alleviate the hardships of deportation. A more important objective was to weaken centres of resistance by the removal of local leaders. At the same time deportation created new settlements in circumstances in which they would be likely to give active support to Assyrian interests; native populations would regard the deportees settled among them as intruders, creating an atmosphere of suspicion and hostility in which the deportees would see their security as tied up with maintenance of the imperial power. The total number of deportees moved by Tiglath-Pileser was very large, amounting, according to his inscriptions, to nearly half a million people.

Later in Tiglath-Pileser's reign he faced serious trouble in Babylonia, where the legitimate Babylonian king was killed and the throne seized by the chief of one of the great Chaldaean tribes. This brought to a head the long-standing conflict of interests between the ancient cities and the tribal Chaldaeans. In 732 B.C. Tiglath-Pileser sent an army into Babylonia to restore order, receiving the support of substantial parts of the urban population. The rebel leader was besieged in Babylon, and we possess some of the actual dispatches to Tiglath-Pileser by the general in charge of his siege. His report of his tactics is remarkably reminiscent of the biblical account of the siege of Jerusalem by the Assyrians in 701 B.C. (2 Kings 18:28*ff.*); just as at Jerusalem, so at Babylon the Assyrian general offered terms to those listening on the city walls, designed to highlight the differing interests of the ordinary citizens and those leading the anti-Assyrian movement, and so cause a split. Clearly Tiglath-Pileser had an efficient intelligence system, able to inform him of the local political situation and how it could be turned to Assyria's advantage. His agents were also able to negotiate secretly to buy the friendly neutrality of one of the

Chaldaean leaders, none other than the Merodach-baladan
known from the Bible as negotiating with Hezekiah of Judah some
twenty or more years later (2 Kings 20:12). In the end Babylon
was captured and the rebel Chaldaean leader fled to the southern
marshes. Tiglath-Pileser now made another innovation in Assyrian policy. Although Assyrian kings had frequently intervened in
Babylonian affairs and exercised indirect control, for four centuries and more they had always left that country its own native king.
Tiglath-Pileser in 729 B.C. took the new step of assuming in his
own person the kingship of Babylonia, which he held until his
death two years later.

The most important single factor in the rapid improvement in
Assyrian fortunes under Tiglath-Pileser III was his exceptional
administrative ability. When vassal kingdoms were made into
provinces with subsequent deportations, this demanded, if chaos
were not to ensue, a considerable amount of detailed planning
and the creation of a chain of command in which everyone knew
and performed his appropriate function. It was not sufficient
simply to install military garrisons. Organisation was needed for
deporting sections of the population; we have actual dispatches
showing that the king ensured that arrangements were made for
such details as footwear for the deportees and provisioning at
suitable stations *en route*. Resettlement of the new population
brought to a district would be even more complex: amongst other
things, there would be the need for land distribution, issue of
agricultural and building implements and of rations until the new
population became self-sufficient, the provision of priests to train
the people in the way of their new land (mentioned in 2 Kings
17:27f.), and arrangements for interpreters to facilitate communication between the new population and Assyrian officials.
There was also the need for a fiscal department in connexion with
taxation. Tiglath-Pileser set up an efficient organisation for all
this, involving a hierarchy of officials with a governor at the top.
There were organisational needs not only for the new provinces
but also for the older ones. There, under weak kings, the governors
had acquired a considerable measure of independence. Tiglath-
Pileser dealt with the resultant problems by reducing the size of
the territories, and the power and independence of the governors
correspondingly.

All governors were directly responsible to the king at the capital
and had to send him regular and prompt dispatches reporting on
their activities and ascertaining the king's wishes on matters
requiring high-level decision. The king kept a check on the governors themselves, not only through their reports to him, but by

the further means of an inspectorate of travelling officials whose duty was to visit governors and other officials in the provinces and report back to the king.

To facilitate communications between the provinces and the capital, Tiglath-Pileser established the beginnings of a network of staging posts along the main routes of the empire, by which relays of messengers could swiftly bring dispatches to the capital from any of the imperial territories. This was the first step in the posting system for which the Persians have usually received the credit, and which in essence continued to serve successive Near-Eastern empires until Ottoman times.

Sargon II

(*Ruled* 722–705 B.C.)

Sargon II was one of the first-millennium Assyrian kings known from the Bible. The name conveys the meaning 'True King'; it can hardly have been given at birth and must have been taken as a throne-name to bolster a doubtful claim to the throne when he succeeded Shalmaneser V (727–722 B.C.). Sargon tells us the background to his succession. The people of the venerable city Ashur, formerly the capital and of great religious prestige, had over the ages acquired certain privileges of freedom from taxation and forced labour. Shalmaneser had, contrary to precedent, challenged this, thereby sparking off an insurrection. The ensuing struggle brought Sargon to the throne, and the support he received from the anti-Shalmaneser faction obtained its reward in his confirming the traditional privileges both of the people of Ashur and of temples elsewhere in Assyria. In one inscription he claims to be a son of Tiglath-Pileser III; if true, this would make him a brother of the king he supplanted.

In the ancient Near East, a change of ruler was always potentially a source of widespread disturbance, especially if the change resulted from a coup. On this occasion there was immediate trouble both in Babylonia (south Iraq) and in Syria and Palestine. In Babylonia, the Chaldaean leader Merodach-baladan, mentioned in the Bible in 2 Kings 20:12, allied himself with Elam in south-west Iran, and seized the throne of Babylon, which Sargon's two predecessors had held and which he would have expected to assume in succession. Sargon's army moved south, but its advance was blocked by the Elamites, and he was unable to take any more effective action against Merodach-baladan for a decade.

All Syria and Palestine was by this time controlled by Assyria, some territories having become directly ruled Assyrian provinces during the preceding twenty years, whilst others remained as minor kingdoms with vassal status. One of the latter was Hamath, north of Damascus. In 721 B.C. its king attempted to benefit by Sargon's problems in Babylonia to organise a revolt of neighbouring territories recently made into provinces; these included Damascus and Samaria. Sargon acted decisively. He put down the revolt in 720 B.C., and captured the rebel leader and flayed him. Whilst this was a cruel punishment, it was not mere sadism. It was carried out only in the case of rebel leaders, and even amongst those only in isolated instances of the most heinous rebellion in which oaths by the gods were broken. This particular instance of punishment was depicted on a bas-relief in a palace of Sargon, where it might serve as a warning to other vassals paying ceremonial visits to their Assyrian overlord. Sargon and other Assyrian kings relied heavily on this and other forms of propaganda to maintain their authority.

Another aspect of royal propaganda was Sargon's rewriting of events. There had been two military incidents involving the Israelite capital, Samaria – the major one of its siege and capture in 722 B.C., by Shalmaneser, as 2 Kings 17:3–6 implies, and the minor one of its subsequent involvement in Hamath's revolt, put down by Sargon. In inscriptions later in his reign, Sargon conflated the two incidents, thereby giving himself unjustifiable credit for the earlier and major capture of Samaria.

A further factor in the situation in Palestine and Syria was Egypt. Over a very long period Egypt had intermittently controlled that area and was now attempting to regain its influence: it was the success of Egyptian diplomacy, in leading the king of Israel to transfer his allegiance from Assyria to Egypt, which had brought about the siege of Samaria in 724–722 B.C. There is no evidence that Egypt was behind the Hamathite revolt of 721 B.C., but certainly some of the Philistine city states on the south coast of Palestine responded to Egyptian overtures at this time. The centre of support for Egypt was Gaza. Sargon, after conquering Hamath, moved down the coast to that city, where he defeated an Egyptian army which had been sent for its defence, and recaptured Gaza. In an attempt to forestall further trouble from Egyptian interference he then established a military colony at Wadi el-Arish (the biblical 'Brook of Egypt'), which since the time of Tiglath-Pileser III had been regarded by Assyria as the boundary between Assyrian and Egyptian spheres of interest.

Sargon took a statesmanlike view of his relations with Egypt, and subject to a clear understanding on spheres of influence saw no reason to clash. He therefore deliberately worked to establish good trade relations with that country, and in his inscriptions explicitly mentioned this as an objective. There is no proof that Egypt was behind the attempt by another Philistine city, Ashdod, to form an anti-Assyrian coalition; action taken against Ashdod in 712 B.C. is mentioned in Isaiah 20:1.

A major problem Sargon had to face, unrelated to the circumstances of his accession, was the growth of the important kingdom of Urartu (Ararat) north of Assyria. Based on the region around Lake Van in eastern Turkey, this was spreading both south-eastwards into north-west Iran and westwards towards Asia Minor. Both areas were of considerable concern to Assyria, since they had strategic importance as the main sources of both horses and metals, essential for the Assyrian army.

In the north-west, Sargon used a combination of military measures and diplomacy in his attempts to protect Assyrian interests. He had considerable success there. Assyria held, subject to occasional setbacks, provinces and vassal states stretching from Cyprus and the south coast of Asia Minor to the area around present-day Malatya. Beyond this a new power was developing – Mita of Mushki, the original of the Midas of the Phrygians of Greek legend, whose proverbial golden touch reflected the wealth accruing to his kingdom from control of the trade routes between Europe and Asia. Initially Mita sided with Urartu and came into conflict with Assyria, but Sargon sent negotiators who succeeded in bringing Mita into a treaty with Assyria. This was a diplomatic success for Sargon and one which took the pressure off his north-western territories.

Further east, where Assyrian and Urartian territory touched, Sargon maintained frontier garrisons. Dispatches in the royal archives reporting frequent border clashes make it clear that Urartu was attempting to push southwards at this time. Assyrian vassals in north-west Iran had also gone over to Urartu. Assyrian interests were suffering and Sargon decided upon a major assault upon Urartu itself. This involved carefully balanced tactical decisions. There were obvious direct routes to Urartu, but these either passed through difficult mountain terrain or were heavily defended with fortresses. Other routes were much longer, involving considerable logistic problems. Sargon decided upon one of the longest routes, which demanded a high quality of generalship.

After crossing the Zagros with an army which included not only infantry and cavalry but also chariots, which must have needed manhandling along parts of the route, he first marched in a direction away from Urartu. This may have been a feint, but developed into a demonstration against peoples who might otherwise have come in as allies of Urartu. He then turned northwards, marching east of Lake Urmia, from the northern end of which he could approach Urartu on its lightly defended eastern side. On the way he was faced in a mountain pass by the main Urartian army and its allies. At this point he was three hundred miles from his home base, and his infantry, after an already long and arduous campaign of more than twice that distance, in which, as Sargon put it, 'they had crossed and recrossed sheer mountains innumerable, of great trouble for ascent and descent', was near to mutiny and not to be relied on. This is not speculation; Sargon explicitly states it. He resolved the problem of discipline by himself in his battle-chariot leading a cavalry charge on the opposing forces. The enemy line broke, and the Assyrian infantry took fresh heart and ploughed into the disordered enemy forces. The Urartian coalition evaporated and Sargon was able to lead his army deep into Urartian territory. There he took steps to make Urartu incapable of ever again challenging Assyria. His army ravaged the whole region, burning towns and growing crops, devastating gardens, orchards and forests, despoiling granaries, and smashing dams and canals so that their waters ran to waste in swamps. Urartu was a major centre of metal work, and the Assyrian army brought back a vast hoard of gold, silver and bronze objects. The booty included over three hundred thousand bronze daggers, as well as objects so unfamiliar in Assyria that they had no Assyrian name, or, as Sargon put it, 'bronze objects, the craftsmanship of their land, the names of which are not easy to write'.

The immediate result of this was to protect Assyria from any further threat from Urartu, but in the longer term it worked against Assyrian security. North of Urartu in south Russia were vigorous Indo-European tribes, some of them seeking new territories, and at this time one group, known as the Cimmerians (Gomer of the Bible) were thrusting southwards east of the Black Sea into Anatolia. Urartu was the civilised world's first line of defence against these invaders. With Urartu devastated and impotent, these tribes could now push in unhindered. The results for Sargon will be seen later.

Meanwhile, with Urartu no longer a problem, Sargon could

turn again to Babylonia. His operations there began in 710 B.C., with a march down the east side of the Tigris for its whole length to cut off Merodach-baladan in Babylon from his allies in Elam. The decade of Chaldaean rule in Babylonia had served to strengthen Sargon's hand. The tribesmen had imprisoned citizens of the great cities, appropriated their lands, and disrupted trade by robbing caravans. This ensured a strong pro-Assyrian faction amongst the Babylonian cities, and some of them, including Babylon itself, opened their gates to Sargon at his approach. Sargon now formally became king of Babylon. Merodach-baladan escaped to his tribal territories in the south, where Sargon besieged him, but after he had made submission Sargon confirmed him as chief of his tribe.

For much of his reign Sargon was occupied in building a new city. Two factors underlay this. One was political: capital cities tended to accumulate privileges which in the course of time produced considerable constraints upon the freedom of action of the king, as we have already seen in the circumstances of Sargon's accession. The other factor was strategic: Assyria needed defence against the north, and the site Sargon chose for his new capital, Dur-Sharrukin (meaning 'Fort Sargon', today Khorsabad, northwest of Mosul) well served this purpose, being further north than any other Assyrian capital and directly controlling the passes into the foothills of the eastern Taurus. The new city was defended with powerful walls and included a palace for Sargon. This palace was excavated by the French in the nineteenth century, and some of Sargon's treasures are now in the Louvre and other museums, with others at the bottom of the Tigris as the result of an unfortunate shipwreck on their journey to the sea.

We return to the Cimmerians. With Urartu impotent, these tribes flooded into eastern Anatolia and rapidly spread westwards towards the region of Assyrian provinces and vassal states. Sargon took his army against the Cimmerians in that area. What happened then is not wholly assured, but Sargon's reign ended in 705 B.C., and the most reasonable interpretation of obscure evidence is that he died in battle and was unburied. There may be an allusion to this in Isaiah 14:18*f*.; the passage certainly refers to a king of Babylon, and Sargon, though king of Assyria, also held that title:

> All the kings of the nations lie in glory, each in his own tomb;
> But you are cast out, away from your sepulchre, like a loathed
>   untimely birth,
> Clothed with the slain, those pierced by the sword.

There is seldom much evidence upon the personal characteristics of Assyrian kings. We have a wall painting showing Sargon in a religious scene, which represents him as a well-built man with a big black square Assyrian beard, but this was the conventional representation of an Assyrian king and not necessarily portraiture. One thing we can say about Sargon is that either he was a poet himself or from a taste for poetry he had a poet on his scribal staff; this appears from the fact that some of his inscriptions, notably the long one dealing with his main campaign against Urartu, are in poetical form. It also seems that he had high respect for the culture of Babylonia, the centre of civilisation of his time, to judge by the very favourable treatment he gave the people of the Babylonian cities after his defeat of Merodach-baladan and his tribal allies. Whilst he heavily despoiled the latter, he did everything possible to favour the citizens, releasing the imprisoned, returning confiscated lands, confirming their ancient privileges, bringing back captured gods to the cities, restoring temple revenues, and protecting the cities' trading caravans. Moreover, he claimed that he had actually been called and armed by Marduk, the great god of Babylon, to overthrow the Chaldaeans.

Sargon continued the Assyrian policy of mass deportation of populations, and in the course of his reign resettled nearly a quarter of a million people in this way. Some of these foreign peoples he used to populate his new capital. Sargon recognised the problems inherent in the different languages and backgrounds of his settlers, and deliberately worked to make them fit into their new environment. He says: 'Peoples of the four quarters of the earth, of different languages, dwelling in mountains and plains, I took as spoil. I made them of one purpose, I made them take up residence (inside Dur-Sharrukin). I sent competent natives of Assyria as overseers and supervisors, to train them in custom and in the service of the gods and the king.'

This indicates that Sargon was not a mere conqueror. He felt responsible for the millions under his control. We see this also in his attitude to agriculture, for which he had a development policy consciously intended to benefit the lot of his people. He tells us in an inscription that 'he set his mind to open up fallow land and plant orchards, to produce crops on steep rocky slopes which never before had produced vegetation; he set his heart on cutting furrows in waste land which under former kings had known no plough, to have people sing for joy, to save all mankind from hunger and want'.

Sennacherib

(*Ruled* 705–681 B.C.)

Sennacherib was an Assyrian king best known from the biblical account of his siege of Jerusalem (2 Kings 18–19, Isaiah 36–37), and from Byron's poem beginning 'The Assyrian came down like the wolf on the fold', based on that incident.

Despite his reputation as a warrior-king, Sennacherib had more important achievements outside the military sphere. He was essentially a practical man, interested in improved ways of doing things and in finding new resources. This was a rare gift in the ancient Near East, where the great obstacle to progress was the dead hand of tradition. The basis of Assyrian civilisation lay in Babylonia, and it was believed in Babylonia that the gods had given mankind all the knowledge they needed at the beginning of civilisation, and that nothing could be added to this. The whole system of Babylonian scribal education reinforced this attitude: learning was a matter of copying out ancient texts; any departure from tradition in any sphere was gravely suspect. Sennacherib shows traces of a different way of thinking. He was prepared to innovate, to seek for new sources of materials, to devise new ways of doing things. As an example of the novelty of his attitude we may instance the situation as to sources of timber. It was a matter of scribal knowledge that certain trees were associated with particular mountains, and this was set out in a traditional list. But the list was copied and recopied simply as a matter of scribal tradition, long after some of the mountains listed had become deforested and the identity of others forgotten. Sennacherib, however, when he needed large timber, actually sent surveyors out into the mountains to look for new sources of the various species needed. Similarly, he took deliberate steps to find new sources of various kinds of ornamental stone. He wanted to cast large bronze statues for a new palace but, he tells us, former kings had had great trouble in doing this. He himself, however, thought the problem over and devised a more efficient method. Similarly, when he wished to ensure an abundant supply of water for his new palace, he invented a system of beams and crosspieces over well-heads – presumably a type of winch – with an endless bronze chain with buckets attached.

It was Sennacherib who introduced cotton – 'the wool-bearing tree' – to Assyria. He personally took part in the search for suitable mountain springs to be tapped and led down by canals to Nineveh. In the canal system which he created to bring that water to Nineveh, he devised a means by which 'the sluice-gate of the canal opened by itself without the help of spade or shovel'. He prided himself upon these achievements as much as upon his military conquests, lauding himself as 'the one who digs canals, opens wells, makes the ditches murmur with running water, brings abundance and prosperity to the widespread ploughlands of Assyria, who furnishes irrigation waters for the fields of Assyria where no one had seen canals and mechanical irrigation in Assyria from days of old, and which none of those of former times had known or made'.

A particularly striking example of Sennacherib's creativity was his building of Nineveh in its final form. It was already ancient and famous, but it was he who planned and rebuilt it as an Assyrian capital in a park-like setting which must have made it one of the fairest of ancient cities, as well as, in terms of extent, one of the greatest.

The site of Nineveh was on the east bank of the Tigris, where a minor tributary, the Khosr, joins the main river. Sennacherib enlarged the site and provided it with a huge wall nearly eight miles long with fifteen named major gates. A classical author said that the walls of the city were wide enough for three chariots to be driven abreast on them, and this statement is confirmed by the extant remains, which are some forty feet thick. A further line of defence was provided by a curving outer wall running well east of the city from the Tigris upstream to the Tigris downstream. Within the inner walls, Sennacherib's city was an early example of town planning; there were new streets, enlarged squares, and splendid buildings. Sennacherib's principal building was a new palace, which he named 'Palace without a rival', to replace a smaller earlier one. Standing on a terrace 170 courses of bricks high above an old river bed, it covered an area of two and a half acres. It incorporated architectural features from Syrian buildings – another instance of Sennacherib's willingness to accept new ideas. Cedars and other great trees were brought in from the Amanus and Zagros mountains for use as beams, pillars and doors, and the place was adorned internally with alabaster, ivory and ornamental and scented woods, and on the external walls with coloured glazed bricks.

For the approach to his palace Sennacherib built a road of limestone slabs ninety feet wide. To encroach on this road by private buildings was an offence punishable by impalement. The possibility of such encroachment shows that private building must have taken place in some parts of the city, although Sennacherib gives no details of this. He does, however, state that upstream of the city he made plots of land available to citizens for planting orchards.

Reference has already been made to canals which Sennacherib had made to bring water to Nineveh. Although the Tigris ran alongside the city, it was too low in its bed to be used for irrigation for much of the year, and in the summer the Khosr tributary diminished to a trickle. Sennacherib therefore carried out major engineering works to feed waters from mountain streams, up to thirty miles away, into the Khosr. An elaborate system of canals, aqueducts, weirs and sluices controlled the flow; a three-hundred-yard stretch of an aqueduct, containing about two million stone blocks of a quarter of a ton each, still exists, and remains of some of the weirs, and of brick-lined sections of the canals, are still to be seen. The water irrigated what Sennacherib called 'a great park like Mount Amanus, in which there were all kinds of scented plants and fruit trees', a welcome amenity in a great city. The run-off water was not wasted, but was fed into an area allowed to develop into a swamp, where there was encouragement of colonisation by appropriate wild life, such as herons, wild pigs and water buffalo.

Sennacherib's ambitious building projects were of course made possible because he controlled vast imperial resources. He was the son and successor of Sargon, and as crown prince had been entrusted by his father with positions of responsibility in different parts of the empire. He thus came to the throne as an experienced administrator and soldier, and as legitimate successor was in a position to take firm hold of his inheritance, which extended from the Egyptian border to well inside Asia Minor and from north-west Iran to the Persian Gulf. In the course of his reign he campaigned in most parts of his domains, but his most significant exploits were in two areas, Palestine and Babylonia.

The events in Palestine are in large part known from the Bible. After the reduction of Israel to provincial status in 722 B.C., the most important remaining native kingdom in Palestine was Judah. At the beginning of Sennacherib's reign, Hezekiah of Judah joined with some of the city states of the Phoenician (Lebanese) and Philistine coasts in an anti-Assyrian league, backed by Egypt. Active rebellion broke out in 701 B.C. Sennacherib responded by bringing his army down the east Mediterranean coast. Most cities made immediate submission:

only Judah and two Philistine cities stood out, awaiting Egyptian support, which eventually came. But Sennacherib defeated the Egyptian army, and the remaining Philistine rebels submitted, leaving Hezekiah of Judah isolated. Sennacherib now proceeded to subjugate his country piecemeal, city by city. Bas-reliefs from Sennacherib's palace show scenes from the siege of Lachish, which is also mentioned in the biblical account (2 Kings 18:14, 17). From Lachish a detachment was sent to besiege Jerusalem, but withdrew without taking the city when Hezekiah made submission and paid a heavy tribute. The Bible saw the withdrawal of the Assyrian army as miraculous. From Sennacherib's point of view, the main objectives had been achieved by the elimination of all resistance in Palestine, and the army was needed in Babylonia.

It was in Babylonia that the greatest problems were, throughout the reign of Sennacherib. The handling of that country was a perennial problem for Assyrian kings. It was so closely linked with Assyria by culture, geography and trade that the situation in one inevitably affected the other. Assyria had the military power but Babylonia was held in high esteem as the homeland of the common culture; Assyrian kings, for example, including Sennacherib, wrote their inscriptions not in their own Assyrian dialect (used for their letters) but in Babylonian. Sargon had been very gentle with the Babylonian cities, and Sennacherib at first attempted the same policy.

There were two particular factors affecting good order in Babylonia – Chaldaean tribesmen, mainly in the south of the country, and the ancient kingdom of Elam to the east. In 703 B.C., one of the Chaldaean chiefs, Merodach-baladan of 2 Kings 20:12, rebelled, with support from Elam. Sennacherib acted against this with temporary success, devastating the Chaldaean areas, but the trouble recurred after his Palestinian campaign. He had formerly attempted to govern the country through a native Babylonian king as puppet; now he installed his own oldest son as king of Babylon, in an attempt to achieve Assyrian control with the minimum use of bare military force.

This was frustrated by the increasing involvement of Elam. Earlier it had provided Merodach-baladan with military assistance, and it was now giving the Chaldaean tribes a safe base east of the Persian Gulf, to which they could withdraw when pursued by Sennacherib. The security of the Babylonian cities could not be assured whilst Chaldaean tribes were able to raid with impunity. Sennacherib used his inventiveness to plan an elaborate amphibious operation to overcome this problem. He brought skilled shipwrights from the Mediterranean coast to build ships at Nineveh. From there they were sailed down the Tigris to near where Baghdad now stands, transported overland to a canal leading to the more easily navigable Euphrates, and then sailed down to the Persian Gulf. Sennacherib then shipped his cavalry and infantry to the other side of the Gulf, where they destroyed the Chaldaean bases and captured some Elamite cities.

This produced an escalation, and in 694 B.C. Elam made a counter-attack against Assyrian interests in Babylonia, taking Sennacherib's son prisoner and appointing an Elamite nominee to the throne of Babylon. This brought war between pro-Elamite and pro-Assyrian elements in Babylonia, with increasing chaos, which doubtless added to the unpopularity of the Assyrians as the occupying power. Even in the cities, traditionally pro-Assyrian, strong pro-Elamite factions developed, and eventually Babylon itself sent its temple treasures to buy Elamite military aid against Sennacherib. Elam responded, leading to a battle in 691 B.C. with appalling carnage on both sides. The Elamite army was broken and unable to oppose Sennacherib for the remainder of his reign, and Sennacherib himself had to return home to regroup.

The anti-Assyrian stance of Babylon had now convinced Sennacherib that to achieve a solution in Babylonia he must destroy the capital. In 689 B.C. he moved south with that objective. His operation was thorough. Sennacherib took Babylon by siege and 'overwhelmed it like a hurricane'. He filled the open spaces with corpses, shared out all valuables as booty for his troops, smashed statues of the gods and confiscated temple property, demolished houses, temples and city walls, and dug canals across the whole city to flood it. He even had the soil of the city thrown into the Euphrates to carry it down to the sea. Finally he set up memorial stelas to record what he had done. All this made an impression so widely that the people of Dilmun (Bahrein), in the Persian Gulf six hundred miles from Babylon, sent tribute as a token of submission.

Babylonian influence was so strong in Assyria that for centuries there had been pro-Babylonian elements in high places there. Sennacherib's sacrilegious sack of Babylon must have aroused opposition in Assyria as well as in Babylonia, and this may have been one factor behind a rebellion eight years later in which Sennacherib was murdered by two of his sons; a second possible factor is mentioned below. This murder is referred to in the Bible (2 Kings 19:37), and the name of one of the parricides has been recognised in a cuneiform text. An inscription marking Sennacherib's tomb was found at the city of Ashur.

Sennacherib left a very bad reputation in the biblical world because of his attack upon Jerusalem and in Babylonia for his sack of Babylon. But there was another side to him. In addition to his progressive attitudes already mentioned, he seems to have had a social conscience. He regarded himself as a protector of justice, and by ancient standards made good his claim: for instance, after he had put down a revolt in Ekron, he took steps to distinguish between actual rebels, who were executed, and citizens who had taken no active part, who were pardoned. He considered it his duty to defend the weak, and described himself as 'the one who renders assistance and comes to the help of the destitute'. It is difficult to get at the personality of an Assyrian king, but in the case of Sennacherib little glimpses come through from his inscriptions. We have already seen his concern to have trees and wild life around his capital. We also learn that he enjoyed campaigning, not just for the fighting but also for the opportunity it gave him to go mountaineering. Protocol demanded that on campaign he should normally be carried in a litter, but where the terrain became too difficult for this he was happy to scramble about on foot. He tells us: 'Where it was too difficult for my chair, I climbed up on foot. I went up the highest peaks like a mountain goat. When my knees got tired, I sat down on a mountain boulder and quenched my thirst with cold water from a water-skin.'

Little is known of Sennacherib's family life. Like many other oriental monarchs, he had concubines and quite a number of sons, and it is likely that the ambitions of sons of concubines were a factor in the power struggle which followed at Sennacherib's death. However, it was Esarhaddon, the son of his legitimate queen, who eventually succeeded to the throne. This queen was, to judge by her name, not an Assyrian lady but of Aramaean descent – a fact making it clear that Sennacherib, king of an empire of many races, had no racial prejudices.

Ashurbanipal

(*Ruled* 668–627 B.C.)

Ashurbanipal was the king under whom the Assyrian empire reached its widest extent, and was the main element in the Greek tradition of a king known as Sardanapalus. His father Esarhaddon, who had had to fight for his own succession, had made detailed arrangements for the succession after him, with his leading officers of state and vassals sworn to uphold it. The plan was that one son, Shamash-shum-ukin, was to be king of Babylonia, with Ashurbanipal holding the senior kingship, that of Assyria.

Ashurbanipal had been carefully trained for the role he was to play. Installed in a special 'Palace of the Succession', the formal residence of the Crown Prince, he received an education in the scribal arts, in mathematics ('I can solve the most complicated divisions and multiplications', he claimed), and in the practical accomplishments of riding, driving a chariot, shooting with the bow, and hurling the javelin. He was also trained in royal administration and protocol. According to his own account, he achieved a high standard in his literary education, including not only Akkadian, the language of which Assyrian and Babylonian were dialects, but also the older language Sumerian, which had much the same status as Latin in education up to recent times. He even read archaic texts. As he put it: 'I have read complicated texts of which the Sumerian version is obscure and the Akkadian version is difficult to get clear. I research into cuneiform writing on stones from before the Flood.'

The shooting and riding skills he had to acquire were necessary to him not only for warfare, but also for hunting, which was a ceremonial requirement for the Assyrian king whatever his personal tastes, and we have bas-reliefs from Ashurbanipal's palace showing him not only shooting lions from his chariot but also engaging one on foot. This was no longer, as at an earlier stage in Assyrian history, hunting in the wild; rather, the unfortunate lions were caught by trappers and then released from cages in a special park so that the king could display his prowess in shooting them down.

The succession came into operation smoothly, and

Left: Figurine from Larsa showing Hammurabi praying. *Right:*
The laws of Hammurabi inscribed in cuneiform on a seven-
foot-high stone stele. At the head of the stele a relief shows the
law-giver in converse with the sun-god Shamash.

The temple of Queen Hatshepsut at Deir el-Bahri (*above*). *Below left:* A relief within the temple depicts the queen drinking from the udder of the cow-goddess Hathor. *Below right:* A black marble head of the queen, probably deliberately defaced by her successor.

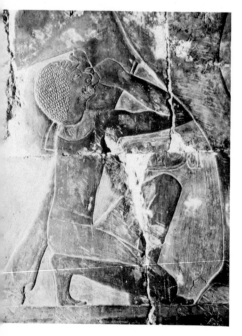

Ashurbanipal took up the tasks facing him. The first concerned Egypt. Shortly before his death, Esarhaddon had initiated a major extension of the empire by invading Egypt, a feat only made possible by the assistance of friendly Arab tribes who helped him across the Sinai desert. His initial success in taking Egypt, capturing the capital Memphis, and receiving the submission of the princes of Lower Egypt (the Delta) had been reversed as soon as the main Assyrian army withdrew. Ashurbanipal acted to continue his father's policy in Egypt, and in 667 B.C. sent a strong Assyrian army, which again took Memphis. The leading vassal princes, after being arrested, were released and treated with clemency, the chief among them, Neco of Sais, being taken to Ashurbanipal at Nineveh, treated with conspicuous honour, and then reinstalled as paramount Egyptian prince with Assyrian military backing.

But there was an independent native Egyptian king, Tarqa, ruling from Thebes in the south. In 664 B.C. he moved north and besieged the Assyrians in Memphis. When an express messenger reached Nineveh with a dispatch, Ashurbanipal immediately sent a powerful army, which in 663 B.C. repelled Tarqa, and then followed him up to capture and loot Thebes, an event mentioned in Nahum 3:8–10 (where No-Amon is Thebes).

This period also saw the maximum extension of Assyrian influence in the north-west, in Asia Minor. Halfway along the southern coast of Asia Minor was the kingdom of Lydia, with a ruler named Gyges. In the hinterland, Cimmerian tribes were on the move and threatening Lydia. Ashurbanipal tells us that he received an embassy from Gyges, who said that the gods had instructed him in a dream to ask Ashurbanipal for military assistance against the Cimmerians. This was evidently given, since Gyges defeated the Cimmerians and sent some of his spoil to Ashurbanipal in Nineveh.

Events after Esarhaddon's first attack on Egypt had shown that the lines of communication were too long, and across the Sinai desert too hazardous, for Assyria to hold Egypt permanently solely by campaigns by its main army. The only practicable course was to use an acceptable Egyptian prince as viceroy, backed by Assyrian garrisons at key points. This was the role Neco filled, and he loyally served Assyrian interests. In pursuance of this policy, when Neco died in 663 B.C., Ashurbanipal appointed his son Psammetichus, who already held a senior position in the Assyrian administration, as viceroy in his place. Ashurbanipal had, however, misjudged the situation. The proud Egyptian was not content to remain an Assyrian underling, however exalted, and he soon began to assert his independence. Shipping links between north and south of the Mediterranean fostered common interests between Psammetichus and Gyges of Lydia, and the latter, with the Cimmerian threat removed, now also sought independence from Assyria. In Egypt, Ashurbanipal had to accept the inevitable, and by 651 B.C. Psammetichus was independent ruler of his country, free from Assyrian garrisons. Gyges was not so fortunate: Ashurbanipal gave the signal to the Cimmerians that they were free to attack him without Assyrian intervention, and the kingdom of Gyges was overrun.

The fact was that Assyrian military and economic resources, great as they were, were not sufficient to hold at the same time the whole region from Egypt and Asia Minor to Iran, and Ashurbanipal's relinquishment of Egypt and Lydia had involved a choice of priorities. Provided Egypt were prevented from interfering militarily in Palestine, it in no way threatened Assyrian imperial interests. The major problems of the empire hinged on Babylonia, with which Assyria was inextricably interlinked by history, culture, language and trade. Ashurbanipal's brother, king in Babylonia, faced two main problems there: the Aramaean and Chaldaean populations of Babylonia itself, and the ancient kingdom of Elam to the east in south-west Iran. The two problems were linked. In Babylonia there was a basic division, extending even to language, between the Akkadian-speaking citizens of the great cities with their culture and traditions going back to the third millennium, and the Aramaic-speaking Aramaeans and Chaldaeans of the countryside and marshlands, who had entered Babylonia as nomads a bare half millennium earlier. Like many peoples of nomadic origin, these Aramaeans and Chaldaeans disregarded national boundaries, and when under pressure in Babylonia were accustomed to take refuge in Elam. This in turn affected Elam, which at the same time was experiencing pressure from Iranian migrations occurring to the north of the kingdom. Elam was already facing internal difficulties when Ashurbanipal came to the throne, and at the beginning of his reign he attempted to assist its stability by economic aid. He tells us: 'When there was famine in Elam and a food shortage developed, I had corn sent. People who had fled before the famine and taken up residence in Assyria until the rains came and a harvest followed, these people I sent back.'

Despite Ashurbanipal's initial policy of friendship, the links of Elam with tribal leaders in Babylonia resulted in an Elamite attack on Babylon in 665 B.C., at a time when Ashurbanipal was apparently fully occupied with Egypt; nevertheless, Ashurbanipal possessed the resources at that time to send an army to Babylonia adequate to repulse the Elamites. Shortly after this, the Elamite king died, whereupon a usurping member of the royal family seized the throne, and attempted to murder all possible royal rivals. Over sixty members of the Elamite royal family fled for protection to Ashurbanipal, thereby involving him still more closely in internal Elamite affairs. In this incident Ashurbanipal showed his recognition of certain principles of international law. The new Elamite king applied for the extradition of the fugitives, and Ashurbanipal felt it necessary to offer a reason for his refusal to comply: 'I did not order the extradition, because of the insolent messages which he kept sending me.'

Ashurbanipal held by inheritance substantial parts of Iran further north, and made intermittent campaigns to maintain his position there. But these regions were all either minor kingdoms or tribal areas, lacking the traditional international status of the ancient kingdom of Elam, and Ashurbanipal's activities further north in Iran implied no intention of annexing Elam. The new king of Elam now engaged in a period of expansion within Iran, by which he increased his resources and power, and in 653 B.C. mobilised his army for an attack against Ashurbanipal. Learning of this, Ashurbanipal made a pre-emptive attack, and the Elamite king was defeated and killed. Ashurbanipal now showed an unpleasant side of his character, a vindictiveness which was to grow on him. He slashed the dead king's face and spat on it, and hung his head on a tree in the garden where he celebrated his victory in a banquet with his wife, a scene shown on a bas-relief.

Intrigues had continued between the Elamites and tribal factions in Babylonia. This caused problems for Ashurbanipal's brother, Shamash-shum-ukin, king of Babylonia. Until at least 654 B.C. the two brothers remained on good terms, but the need for Ashurbanipal to intervene directly against Elam produced stresses by underlining the inferior status of Shamash-shum-ukin. The problem was complicated by the fact that there were several members of the Elamite royal family who were making a bid for the throne, of whom some were seeking Ashurbanipal's support, with the likelihood that others sought that of Shamash-shum-ukin. Eventually Shamash-shum-ukin became caught up in intrigue with an Elamite faction; this escalated to civil war when in 652 B.C., backed by an Elamite army, he attacked the main Assyrian garrison in Babylonia. The war culminated in Ashurbanipal's forces besieging Babylon, held by Shamash-shum-ukin. The city surrendered to Ashurbanipal in 648 B.C. after famine had become so severe that the inhabitants turned to cannibalism. Shamash-shum-ukin died, perhaps by suicide, and Ashurbanipal, with proper fraternal feeling, gave his brother respectable burial. But the vindictiveness shown earlier became apparent again in his treatment of subsidiary rebel leaders, who were hunted down and their bodies carved up and fed to dogs, pigs, wolves and vultures.

For some years further, Ashurbanipal continued his attempts at producing stability in Elam, intervening several times in the succession. But the situation steadily deteriorated, partly from the inability of any member of the extensive Elamite royal family to obtain general acceptance, and partly from the pressure of Persian tribes on the country's northern borders. The problem from the point of view of Ashurbanipal was that an unstable Elam had already brought catastrophe in Babylonia and might in time infect Assyria. Eventually Ashurbanipal seems to have decided that statesmanship had had a fair trial and failed, and that the solution now lay in military terrorism. During the first half of the 640s he sent his army into Elam twice to ravage the country. They marched through the whole land, devastating and looting its major cities including its capital Susa, desecrating temples, and even violating royal tombs. The population was deported in large numbers and many districts of Elam were left without occupants, like a wilderness. Ashurbanipal describes the end he achieved: 'I left the fields empty of the sound of mankind and the tread of cattle and sheep; in them I made wild asses couch, and gazelles, and all manner of wild beasts.'

Ashurbanipal had solved the immediate problem of Elam, but in doing so he had left the land wide open for migrating Persian tribes, who two centuries later were to inherit what had been the Assyrian and afterwards the Babylonian empire.

Despite his problems in Egypt and Elam, Ashurbanipal was able to maintain a substantial measure of security and good order over the greatest empire the world had yet known, extending to about a thousand miles by eight hundred even without Egypt and Elam. After his Elamite campaigns he achieved some further extensions of control, notably over the Bedouin Arabs of the Syrian and north Arabian deserts. His ancestors had already come into contact with these people, whose importance to Assyria lay in their control of the trade routes from southern Arabia. Ashurbanipal brought them more effectively under his control, by sending troops into the desert to seize oases, until the Arabs were forced to make submission. He appointed a king of the Arabs, and when this vassal gave trouble he caught him and tied him like a dog to guard a city gate.

Not all Ashurbanipal's energies were directed to running the empire. He was also a builder and restorer of temples and palaces. We are fortunate in the survival of a splendid series of bas-reliefs from one palace of his at Nineveh, showing vivid scenes of warfare and hunting from the life of Ashurbanipal.

The most important of all Ashurbanipal's achievements in the long term was, however, his creation of a library of cuneiform texts at Nineveh. Earlier Assyrian kings had made collections of texts, but this was on a much bigger scale. There were about five thousand tablets altogether, comprising principally texts in the area of religion and literature, both terms to be understood in their widest sense. The main categories were: lists of omens; sign lists and synonym lists for scribal education; rituals and incantations relating to magic; myths and epics; and wisdom literature, that is, works of the same kind as the biblical Job and Ecclesiastes. This library was excavated last century and brought to the British Museum, where it constitutes the most significant single source for our knowledge of ancient Mesopotamian culture.

Little is known of the final years of Ashurbanipal's reign, though it seems that except for minor disturbances he continued to hold the empire in firm control until his death in 627 B.C. Then, with the master hand gone, the tensions which had built up within the empire brought its final collapse with astonishing speed, within less than two decades.

Nebuchadnezzar

(c. 630–562 B.C.)

Nebuchadnezzar (more correctly, Nebuchadrezzar) was the most celebrated king of the Neo-Babylonian (or Chaldaean) dynasty, famous for his military power and the splendour of his capital Babylon. His name meant 'O Nabu, protect my succession!' He is known from cuneiform inscriptions and from classical and Jewish sources. He was the oldest son of Nabopolassar, earlier an official in Assyrian service, who in 626 B.C. had seized the throne of Babylon, and allied himself with the Medes of north-west Iran and other peoples in the north to overthrow Assyria. The Assyrian capital Nineveh was taken in 612 B.C., after which the Assyrian army moved westwards to establish new bases.

Nebuchadnezzar, born not earlier than 630 B.C., was trained for succession to the throne of Babylon, and had officiated (along with a younger brother next in line) as his father's representative in certain religious rites soon after 612 B.C. The family was not royal in origin. Nebuchadnezzar himself spoke of the third-millennium king Naram-Sin as 'my ancient ancestor', but the fact that he had to search so far back for a putative royal ancestor tells its own story, and his father Nabopolassar quite frankly spoke of himself as having been 'a nobody' in his youth.

Nebuchadnezzar made his first appearance as an army commander alongside his father in 607 B.C., and two years later had been promoted to the supreme command. After the fall of Nineveh, Egypt had taken control of Palestine and Syria, and in 609 B.C. the Egyptian king Neco, in order to guard these territories from the Babylonians, had led an army to join forces with the Assyrians at their base at Carchemish on the Euphrates (2 Kings 23:29). By 605 B.C. Nabopolassar was in a position to attack, and it was now that, probably because of illness, he stayed at home and handed over the main Babylonian army to Nebuchadnezzar. Carchemish lies on the west bank of the Euphrates, and the expected route of approach by an army from Babylonia would be up the west bank. However, Nebuchadnezzar gained the element of surprise by advancing up the east bank and crossing the Euphrates near Carchemish, to make a direct attack on the city. There was ferocious fighting, with the Egyptians finally being defeated and fleeing in disorder. Following up, Nebuchadnezzar inflicted a further slaughter on survivors in the province of Hamath, between Aleppo and Damascus. The people of Judah, who knew that they were destined for vassaldom to either Egypt or Babylonia, followed events keenly, and the prophet Jeremiah gave an oracle on the fate of 'the army of Pharaoh Neco, king of Egypt, which was by the river Euphrates at Carchemish and which Nebuchadnezzar king of Babylon defeated':

> Their warriors are beaten down, and have fled in haste; They look not back – terror on every side! says the Lord. The swift cannot flee away, nor the warrior escape.
>
> (Jeremiah 46:2, 5–6)

Nabopolassar died in August 605 B.C. and Nebuchadnezzar returned to Babylon to ascend the throne three weeks later.

The international situation largely dictated the general course of Nebuchadnezzar's activities during much of his reign. The Assyrian empire had held territories, either as provinces or vassal kingdoms, with all that this implied for the control of resources by way of trade or booty, both beyond the Zagros in Iran and up beyond north Syria in Anatolia and Asia Minor. The downfall of that empire had come about through common action by Nebuchadnezzar's father in a coalition with various peoples of which the most powerful and best organised were the Medes in Iran. After the Assyrian collapse, there was a *de facto* partition of the empire, with the Medes taking not only everything east of the Zagros but also a wide band of the northern areas as far west as Asia Minor. The share of the Assyrian empire which fell to Nabopolassar and to Nebuchadnezzar after him was the whole of Mesopotamia, some parts of the north-west as far as Cilicia in south-east Asia Minor, Syria and Palestine, and the accessible fringes of the Syrian and north Arabian deserts. But Egypt, which had close ties of trade with the Philistine and Phoenician coasts, was in defence of this seeking to reassert over Palestine and Syria the control which it had exercised on many earlier occasions. These factors resulted in Nebuchadnezzar's having to devote his main military operations during his first decade and frequently afterwards to Syria and Palestine.

Immediately after his enthronement he returned to Syria to make an extended demonstration of his power; the fact that he could safely leave Babylonia so soon showed the firm basis on which his kingship stood. In the following year, 604 B.C., he again spent about six months marching about in Syria and Palestine, receiving submission and tribute from subject kings, including the king of Judah, who had now reversed his allegiance, since he originally owed his position to the king of Egypt. However, Egypt remained politically active in the region, and in December 604 B.C. the Philistine city of Askelon rebelled, only to be reduced to rubble by Nebuchadnezzar. Nebuchadnezzar clearly took the threat of Egyptian interference seriously, for he undertook further campaigns in Syria and Palestine in each of the following three years, and at the end of 601 B.C. attempted to invade Egypt. This was not a success; there were heavy casualties on both sides and Nebuchadnezzar was forced to withdraw. The fact that he now spent well over a year mustering a large force of chariotry is indicative of the scale of his losses. For the time being the Egyptian Pharaoh was actually able to advance into south Palestine, according to Jeremiah 47:1, which refers to his attacking Gaza; and this had an unsettling effect on some other vassal states, notably Judah, which withdrew allegiance from Nebuchadnezzar.

Nebuchadnezzar brought in his army to put Jerusalem under

siege at the end of 598 B.C. The rebel Judaean king died as the siege began, and after three months his son Jehoiachin surrendered to Nebuchadnezzar, and was deported along with other captives. A cuneiform chronicle speaks of Nebuchadnezzar taking away heavy tribute, which the Bible identifies as the treasure of the royal palace and of the Temple, including gold and silver vessels of Solomon (2 Kings 24:13). Nebuchadnezzar treated Jehoiachin without harshness: we have cuneiform records dating from about 592 B.C. showing that he housed him and other captives in a building near the centre of Babylon, supplied deliveries of food, and still accorded him the official title 'king'.

Despite the inherent stability of Babylonia under Nebuchadnezzar, his repeated long absences produced a situation in which the inevitable small discontents could build up to major opposition. In 594 B.C. we hear of a rebellion in Babylonia, and although this was put down within a month, it must have had repercussions throughout the empire, for Jeremiah 28:2–3 reports a false prophet in Judah as foretelling at this date that Nebuchadnezzar would be overthrown within two years. It may be observed that Jeremiah himself had already expressed a quite different view, prophesying continuing success for Nebuchadnezzar, whose dynasty he said would last for three generations (Jeremiah 27:1–7).

After putting down the rebellion, Nebuchadnezzar continued with his campaigns in Syria and Palestine. But Egyptian diplomacy was still destabilising the area, and in 588 B.C. the new vassal king of Judah, who had been appointed by Nebuchadnezzar, withdrew allegiance from him and sought military aid from Egypt (Ezekiel 17:15). Nebuchadnezzar responded by investing Jerusalem. The siege was lifted temporarily when an Egyptian force approached (Jeremiah 37:5), but reinstated when the Egyptians withdrew without giving battle. Such was the reputation of the Babylonian army under Nebuchadnezzar that Jeremiah warned (37:10) that resistance was useless and that the Babylonian wounded could by themselves alone take the city. Famine compelled surrender after a year and a half, in 586 B.C. The city was burnt down and the more important sections of the population were deported, including the king, who had been blinded. Nebuchadnezzar clearly had an efficient intelligence service, for he now sent orders for the protection of Jeremiah, who had throughout prophesied in favour of submission to Nebuchadnezzar (Jeremiah 39:11–12). There was a further deportation in 582 B.C.

This was not the end of Nebuchadnezzar's problems in

Palestine resulting from Egyptian attempts to reassert influence there. Shortly after the final fall of Jerusalem he found it necessary to begin a siege of the maritime Phoenician city of Tyre, which because of its ability to supply itself by sea was able to hold out for thirteen years. Shortly afterwards, Nebuchadnezzar again attempted the invasion of Egypt, alluded to in Ezekiel 29:20, but no details are known. Classical sources say that he actually conquered Egypt and even Libya, but this is certainly unhistorical.

Nebuchadnezzar retained good relations with the Medes, and indeed his wife, who is named in classical sources as Amuhea, was a Median princess. Apart from one possible obscure minor incident, there were no problems during Nebuchadnezzar's reign on his eastern and northern borders, which extended to Cilicia in south-east Asia Minor. The interests of Nebuchadnezzar in the latter area, along with his good international reputation, led to his representative Nabonidus (later a successor) being found acceptable to the parties concerned for the settlement of a border dispute in Asia Minor between the Medes and their Lydian neighbours further west. Nebuchadnezzar died a natural death in October 562 B.C., being succeeded by his son Amel-Marduk, the Evil-Merodach of the Bible.

In the reports of Nebuchadnezzar's campaigns in the west, both in the cuneiform chronicles and in the Bible, a recurrent theme is that considerable booty or tribute was collected and sent to Babylon. This was directly related to Nebuchadnezzar's plans for his capital, Babylon. His father had begun restoring the damaged ziggurat (temple-tower) of Babylon soon after his overthrow of Assyria, as a work of piety in honour of Marduk. Nebuchadnezzar, soon after his accession, continued this piety with an ambitious building programme, particularly splendidly conceived at Babylon but by no means limited to that city. In all, he built or restored temples at at least eleven cities, in addition to not less than fourteen temples in Babylon itself. His building projects also included defence works, canals and palaces, all on a sumptuous scale. His most spectacular results were achieved at Babylon, which he made into one of the wonders of the world, leading the Greek traveller and historian Herodotus, just over a century later, to say that its beauty and magnificence exceeded anything he had known.

In the time of Nebuchadnezzar Babylon lay on both sides of the Euphrates. It had long possessed fortifications, but Nebuchadnezzar added considerably to their strength. In the form he finally achieved, there was a powerful double system of defence. The inner ramparts, about five miles long and surrounding Babylon on both sides of the river, consisted of two walls of mud brick, the inner 21 feet thick with towers 60 feet apart, then at a distance of 23 feet the outer wall, 12 feet thick, also with towers. Outside them, at a distance of about 65 feet, lay a moat lined with burnt brick and bitumen and fed with water from the Euphrates. Further out on the eastern side of the city were the outer ramparts, again of two walls, the inner of mud brick 23 feet thick and the outer of burnt brick up to 25 feet thick. This system ran south-eastwards from the Euphrates a mile and a half north of the city, returning to the river about 250 yards south of the inner ramparts. Where the inner ramparts approached the Euphrates at the north, in the eastern half of Babylon, Nebuchadnezzar built two powerful citadels. Alongside them was the Ishtar Gate, a structure with twin towers, splendidly decorated with a façade of 575 dragons and bulls in alternate brown and white enamel on a blue background. Through the Ishtar Gate passed a road used for ceremonial purposes, which we know as the Processional Way. This road, paved with stone, ran between walls of baked brick decorated with enamelled lions to the great temple of Esagila, sacred to the city-god Marduk, standing in an enclosure of about 470 yards by 240 yards, that is, about 23 acres. This temple was dominated by a great ziggurat, a tower in seven stages of different colours, with three broad staircases, reaching a height of almost three hundred feet. In addition to this complex there were more than fifty other temples or chapels within the city. From Esagila the Processional Way turned to cross the Euphrates by a stone bridge, supported on piers, to the western part of the city. Nebuchadnezzar also built himself a fortified palace, somewhat away from the city, near the northern end of the outer defence system.

One of the features of Nebuchadnezzar's Babylon famous in classical authors was that called the 'Hanging Gardens'. These were described as high stone terraces planted with trees, which Nebuchadnezzar built to please his Median wife, who was pining for the mountains of her native land. The principal excavator of Babylon considered that some curious chambers he found were the sub-structure of these terraces.

The crucial part Nebuchadnezzar played in the destruction of the kingdom of Judah ensured his survival in Jewish tradition. His activities feature near the end of the Books of Kings and Chronicles, and he is alluded to frequently by his contemporaries the prophets Jeremiah and Ezekiel. Jeremiah clearly regarded him favourably, and the same attitude is reflected in some apocryphal Jewish works, such as the Book of Baruch, of the second or first century B.C., which speaks of Jews paying for the life of Nebuchadnezzar as their protector.

Nebuchadnezzar was particularly prominent in the Book of Daniel, where he figures in a number of legends as a king who, initially led astray by paganism, finally accepted the truth of the Jewish religion. One of these legends can be linked to an historical situation. In it, Nebuchadnezzar is represented as an arrogant and wicked king whom God punished by depriving him of his reason, so that he left the abodes of men and for seven years lived in the wilds like an animal. Finally his reason returned and he acknowledged that all power came from God. It seems likely that, as with many another famous person, anecdotes originally told of another person have been fixed on him, and that the foundation of this legend lies in the activities of Nebuchadnezzar's principal successor, Nabonidus. We know that Nabonidus left Babylon for nearly a decade, during which time he resided at the oasis of Tema in the north Arabian desert, to the intense disapproval of the religious establishment in Babylon, where some rites could not take place without the participation of the king. The withdrawal of Nabonidus to the desert had become Nebuchadnezzar's living in the wild, and the subsequent rejection of Nabonidus by the polytheists of Babylon opened the way to the claim that he – and Nebuchadnezzar by transference – had been converted from polytheism to Judaic monotheism.

The texts of Nebuchadnezzar himself, almost all building inscriptions, give no suggestion of any deviation from standard Babylonian polytheism. They are full of pieties about Babylonian deities, and although this has sometimes been interpreted as showing a particularly strong religious feeling in Nebuchadnezzar, they are in fact largely the standard phrases of the Babylonian religion.

Seleucus I

(c. 356–281 B.C.)

Seleucus I, known as Nicator ('Conqueror'), was the most important successor of Alexander the Great and the founder of a dynasty which ruled much of the Near and Middle East for 240 years and affected its history for much longer.

He was born between 358 and 354 B.C., his father Antiochus being a Macedonian of good birth who had distinguished himself in the service of Philip of Macedon. Seleucus, of about the same age as Philip's heir Alexander the Great, accompanied him from the beginning of his invasion of Asia in 334 B.C. as one of the 'Companions', an elite body of about a hundred officers. By the time the Macedonian army reached India, Seleucus had acquitted himself in such a distinguished manner that he was one of the senior generals. He was evidently in the immediate entourage of Alexander, since there is a story that at the crossing of one Indian river he was one of four officers in the boat with Alexander, the other three being Macedonian generals of the highest eminence who were afterwards central figures in the struggle for succession to Alexander.

The high esteem in which Seleucus was held by Alexander is again reflected in events at Susa, an ancient capital in south-west Iran, where Alexander temporarily established his court after returning from India. Alexander, with a vision of a fusion of the races of his empire, in 324 B.C. arranged a great marriage festival in which he and eighty of his senior officers took brides from the Iranian aristocracy. The lineage of the lady bestowed upon Seleucus made her equal in Iranian eyes to Alexander's own principal wife. The bride of Seleucus was Apama, the daughter of one of two great lords in eastern Iran who had powerfully opposed Alexander's advance; Alexander had already made Roxane, the daughter of the other great lord, his chief queen. The union of Seleucus with Apama had a happy outcome; Seleucus was the only one of Alexander's generals to make a permanent marriage with his Iranian wife, she was the mother of his heir, and he did her the honour of naming three cities after her. By this marriage the subsequent Seleucid dynasty inherited noble Iranian as well as Macedonian ancestry, with all that meant for legitimacy in the eyes of Iranian subjects.

Alexander died in Babylon in 323 B.C., leaving no heir apparent. This led to a power struggle between Alexander's generals. One after the other they were removed, by natural death, battle or intrigue, until the final survivor, who briefly reunited most of Alexander's domains under his rule, was Seleucus. The details of the power struggle are complex and at some points uncertain, but the attainment of supremacy by Seleucus cannot be understood without a summary of its main features.

Initially there was a compromise. Alexander had a half-brother, and his wife was pregnant at his death. The generals agreed that if the posthumous child were a boy (which proved to be the case), he and the half-brother were to be nominal joint-kings, with imperial authority wielded (with checks) by Perdiccas, the senior Macedonian nobleman in Babylon and commander-in-chief of the army. Other generals were given satrapies (provinces), the most significant appointments being Ptolemy in Egypt, the very senior general Antigonus in Phrygia in Asia Minor, and Lysimachus in Thrace. The veteran Antipater, formerly in the service of Alexander's father, commanded the homelands of Macedonia and Greece. Seleucus was less self-seeking than some and received no province at this time, but was given a prestigious military post which made Seleucus in effect second in military command to Perdiccas.

In 321 B.C. the uneasy settlement gave way to war between Perdiccas and other Macedonian leaders including Ptolemy and Antipater. Whilst allies of Perdiccas acted in Asia Minor, he moved against Ptolemy in Egypt, Seleucus accompanying him. But after Perdiccas had failed in several attempts to break through Ptolemy's defences, there was a mutiny in his forces. Perdiccas was assassinated; one classical source suggests that Seleucus was directly involved.

Antipater was now elected regent in place of Perdiccas. But the appointment was unpopular with part of the Macedonian army, and Seleucus and Antigonus had to intervene in person to save Antipater from mob attack; once again Seleucus was seen as one of the most influential of the generals. In a subsequent redistribution of territories, this prominence of Seleucus was recognised by his receiving the important province of Babylonia, the wealthiest of Alexander's territories.

In 319 B.C. Antipater died. His designated successor, a veteran, was no match for the younger and more ambitious generals, several of whom at once took measures to increase their power at the expense of the central authority. Ptolemy occupied Syria, and Antigonus extended his control over neighbouring satrapies. Eumenes, a distinguished Greek who loyally supported the joint kings, moved eastwards to seek support for the royal party against Antigonus. Seleucus attempted to avoid involvement, but finally made alliance with Antigonus. Antigonus, with assistance from Seleucus, defeated Eumenes in 316 B.C. in Iran, but his autocratic policy there, where he liquidated certain powerful satraps and replaced them with his own nominees, created the suspicion that his ambitions were directed to Alexander's kingship. It was consistent with this that on his return to Babylon he attempted to treat Seleucus, although appointed by the council of Macedonian generals, as directly responsible to himself. Seleucus, mindful of the fate of the satraps in Iran, feared imminent arrest, and so fled to take refuge with Ptolemy in Egypt, whom he warned of the suspected intentions of Antigonus.

The warning of Seleucus was heeded. Already Antigonus held the greater part of Alexander's territories, and the principal other generals of Alexander still alive – Cassander the son of Antipater, and Lysimachus – decided upon action. War broke out in 315 B.C. Seleucus commanded a fleet of a hundred ships which patrolled the coasts from Palestine to Asia Minor as a demonstration of force to undermine the morale of the troops of Antigonus. Subsequently he commanded part of Ptolemy's army in an advance through Palestine against the forces of Antigonus in Syria. This opened routes to the east, and although Antigonus still controlled garrisons throughout most of the eastern territories, Seleucus now set out to regain his satrapy in Babylonia. This was a bold and self-confident move, since although he had the promise of Ptolemy's support, his initial force was only about a thousand men. But his reputation was such that further Macedonian settlers joined him on the way. Moreover, his generous and tolerant conduct during his earlier years as satrap of Babylonia had won him influential friends and the goodwill of the population, so that he received local support against the garrison left by Antigonus, and was able to re-establish himself. Although Seleucus did not formally adopt the title 'king' until later, from the point of view of his oriental subjects he was king from this time, and subsequently the year 312 B.C. was taken as the beginning of the Seleucid era, which was still used for calendar purposes in some parts of the Near East down to modern times.

Seleucus still had to deal with Iran, where Antigonus had left his own satraps. The most prominent of these moved against Seleucus, but the superior generalship of Seleucus – almost the greatest of Alexander's generals, according to the judgement of one classical author – won the encounter, although the attacking army was five times the size of his. The personal reputation of Seleucus now once again had its effect, leading much of the defeated army to desert to him. Within Iran, many of the Macedonian garrisons were favourably disposed to Seleucus, and he quickly received the submission of the provinces of south-west Iran, and with an augmented army was able to overcome the resistance of Media further north.

Detailed information about Seleucus in the following years is lacking, but it is clear that between 311 and 302 B.C. he made himself master of all Iran, except the north-west, as far as the frontiers of India. But although he might have claimed part of India as a legacy from Alexander's conquests, he renounced this, and also gave up part of Afghanistan in the interests of friendly relations with India. Not only did this ensure Seleucus a steady supply of elephants for war, but it also served to encourage trade more generally.

Meanwhile, the last of Alexander's potential blood heirs had been murdered, and by 305 B.C. all the competing dynasts, including Seleucus, had formally adopted the title 'king'; Seleucus now wore the diadem which the old Persian kings had used as the symbol of royalty.

In the west an uneasy balance of power between Antigonus, Cassander, Lysimachus and Ptolemy broke down when a campaign by Antigonus's son Demetrius in 303 B.C. left the whole region from Greece to north Syria in the hands of Antigonus. This reactivated the alliance between the other dynasts. Seleucus returned from India with a considerable army including recently acquired war elephants, and in early 301 B.C. advanced into central Asia Minor, where he joined forces with Lysimachus. Antigonus was defeated and died in battle. Except for Egypt and the provinces from Babylonia eastwards, most of Alexander's empire had been in the hands of Antigonus, and the victors now dismembered it. Seleucus annexed Syria and the southern part of Asia Minor, whilst Ptolemy took Palestine. It was typical of Seleucus that although he also considered he had a claim to Palestine and registered a protest, he took no further steps in the matter, recognising his indebtedness to Ptolem for earlier friendship.

Seleucus had already built a major imperial city at Seleucia on the Tigris, a foundation which replaced the old capital Babylon and drew off its population. But he now needed a capital for his western territories, and for this he founded Antioch on the Orontes. Two major road systems connected the two capitals. Subsequently Seleucus appointed his son Antiochus as joint king in charge of the eastern provinces, governing from Seleucia, whilst he himself ruled from Antioch.

The two new capitals bring out the fact that the activities of Seleucus were by no means limited to successful warfare and diplomacy. He was, indeed, a creator on a large scale and founded scores of cities. These included sixteen Antiochs named after his father, five Laodiceas after his mother, nine named Seleucia after himself, as well as three cities named for his first wife and one for his second. Many of these were, of course, on the sites of former towns. Their common feature was that they were all settlements of

Graeco-Macedonian colonists, with the status of free Greek cities with their own laws and administrations, and generally with a royal cult in honour of Seleucus. These cities, by being not only links in the chain of Seleucid military control but also industrial and commercial centres and foci of Hellenistic culture, played an important role in integrating the whole of Asia as far as the Indus.

The creative impulses of Seleucus were not limited to city-building. He promoted agriculture, both by irrigation works and by attempting to introduce foreign plants from India. There is also mention of an ambitious plan of his linking the land-locked Caspian to the main seaways by cutting a canal from it to the Sea of Azov, north of the Black Sea.

The years after 301 B.C. were a period in which Seleucus was consolidating and developing his territories from southern Asia Minor and Syria eastwards. There was a thriving trade across the whole area, with links with India and Arabia. In many places temples played an important economic as well as religious role in society, and throughout his empire Seleucus showed tolerance to the temples, giving them special privileges and protection. Mints were established in a number of cities to provide an acceptable coinage to assist trade, one of the most important being at Seleucia on the Tigris.

The years from the turn of the century saw a succession of changing alliances between the remaining dynasts, during which the standing of Seleucus steadily increased. Incidents in the course of this show something of the character of Seleucus. Demetrius, son of Antigonus, had made himself king of Macedonia but had been driven out into Asia Minor, from where in 285 B.C. he made a raid into Syria and attacked the camp of Seleucus. Seleucus, though now an old man, again showed his coolness. Removing his helmet, he rode up to the enemy lines and invited the soldiers to surrender. Such was the prestige of the veteran general of Alexander that most of Demetrius's forces went over to him. Demetrius was captured, and by the usual graciousness of Seleucus was held as an honoured guest rather than as a prisoner. Lysimachus, the last of Alexander's generals other than Ptolemy and Seleucus, who had taken the kingship of Macedonia after the expulsion of Demetrius and saw his survival as a threat to his position, offered Seleucus a considerable bribe to put his prisoner to death. Seleucus rejected the proposal with indignation.

Events now conspired to give Seleucus an even greater share of the legacy of Alexander. Lysimachus executed his heir, who had already won distinction as an army commander, on false suspicions of treason. The victim had been popular, and in consequence of this unjust act there was widespread disaffection in the territories of Lysimachus, with calls for Seleucus to act against the tyrant. Seleucus attacked the forces of Lysimachus in Asia Minor; Lysimachus was defeated and killed. This was in 282 B.C.; Ptolemy had died a natural death the previous year. Seleucus was now the only survivor of Alexander's generals, and all Alexander's former empire, except Egypt and Palestine, now belonged to him.

The death of Seleucus came as a result of his own generosity. In 281 B.C. he crossed the Hellespont into Europe. With him was Ceraunos, the disinherited son of Ptolemy of Egypt, to whom he had given sanctuary. This man was unscrupulous and unstable, and had a grudge against Seleucus for not setting him on the throne of Egypt. When Seleucus turned aside from the main army to examine an ancient monument, Ceraunos murdered him and made his escape.

In person, Seleucus was a kindly, modest man; he must have been of massive build, for there is a story that when a wild bull intended for sacrifice broke loose he restrained it with his bare hands. He was the noblest of the successors of Alexander. He showed generosity to defeated opponents, and gratitude to benefactors; he honoured his Persian wife when other generals divorced theirs, and he trusted his eldest son and made him joint king when the heirs of two of his contemporaries suffered respectively disinheritance and death. He did later make a diplomatic second marriage with a granddaughter of Antigonus, but he subsequently divorced the lady without dishonouring her, making her the wife of his son and heir. The ancient historian Arrian described Seleucus as 'the greatest king of those who succeeded Alexander and of the most royal mind, and ruler over more territory than anyone except Alexander'.

Antiochus III

(*Ruled* 223–187 B.C.)

Antiochus III, a major king of the Seleucid dynasty which ruled much of western Asia for nearly two and a half centuries, was one of the more enigmatic rulers of the ancient world. Alongside exploits which earned him from his contemporaries the title 'the great king', there were disasters which led to a saying 'There *was* a king – Antiochus the Great'. Whilst he possessed considerable energy and personal courage which for a time gave his empire the greatest territorial extent since its founder, Seleucus I, he sometimes showed poor judgement, both military and political. Above all, it was Antiochus whose policies drew the Romans into Asia Minor (Asiatic Turkey), from where they ultimately spread their influence eastwards and southwards to absorb and supersede the Seleucid empire.

Antiochus came to the throne in his late teens, when his predecessor, his elder brother, campaigning in Asia Minor, was assassinated. Circumstances were not propitious for a successful reign. Though the Seleucid rulers had always claimed the whole region from Asia Minor to the borders of India together with Palestine to the borders of Egypt, their hold on Asia Minor had recently been challenged, parts of Iran were under local rulers who exercised independence and were extending their powers, and Palestine had never been effectively held. Even the main Mediterranean port near the western capital of Antioch was in Egyptian hands. But on the favourable side, there was widespread allegiance to the Seleucids as a dynasty. There were colonies of Graeco-Macedonian settlers across the whole region conquered by Alexander the Great, planted either by Alexander himself, by Seleucus I, or by later Seleucids; these people formed the nucleus of the armies of the period, and for them the Seleucids were the legitimate successors of Alexander. Many non-Hellenistic oriental populations also accepted the legitimacy of the Seleucid dynasty, though on a different basis; a policy of tolerance and patronage of local temples had resulted in the assimilation of the Seleucid rulers into the ancient native royal cults.

At the time of his predecessor's death, Antiochus was acting as viceroy at the great wealthy city of Seleucia on the Tigris, the subsidiary capital from which the east was governed. The circumstances of his accession brought an urgent need for major decisions, but Antiochus, under the sway of a powerful vizier, was not yet his own master. The immediate problem was Asia Minor, disturbed by earlier challenges and now by the assassination of the king. Fortunately for Antiochus, the governor Achaeus, a cousin of his, took control, and although he later aimed at the kingship for himself, at this time he threw his weight behind Antiochus as legitimate successor.

Asia Minor was not the only problem. Egypt was always in competition with the Seleucids for control not only of Palestine but also of the trade routes around the coasts of the eastern

Mediterranean, and there were fears that Egypt – which already held Cilicia on the south coast of Asia Minor – might attempt to benefit by the situation. Antiochus therefore moved to the senior capital, Antioch in Syria. But this left problems in the eastern territories, Babylonia and Iran. Much of eastern Iran was not effectively under Seleucid control, whilst in western Iran, amongst representatives of Seleucid authority, there were two powerful satraps in Media (with its capital at Ecbatana, modern Hamadan) and Persia (south-west Iran). After the departure of Antiochus, these two governors revolted. Antiochus, under pressure from his vizier and against his better judgement, remained in Syria, until Molon, the governor of Media, took Seleucia and entered the vital province of Babylonia, to which it was the key (221 B.C.). In this serious position, the vizier was overruled, and in 220 B.C. Antiochus led an army against Molon, who committed suicide when his troops, from the reverence in which they held the young Antiochus as the legitimate Seleucid ruler, began to desert. Antiochus, now in a position to assert himself against his tyrannous vizier, stopped the savage reprisals which the latter was beginning to inflict upon the rebels, and shortly afterwards was a party to the disposal of the vizier by assassination. Antiochus reorganised western Iranian satrapies under royal governors and with his new prestige was able to bring north-west Iran under Seleucid suzerainty for the first time.

Antiochus returned to Syria in late 220 B.C. The situation in the west was now very complex. Alongside the Ptolemies in Egypt and the Seleucids as heirs of parts of the domains of Alexander the Great, there was a dynasty ruling Macedonia and Greece. There had already been clashes between Macedonia and the rising power of Rome, and some of the Greek city-states were looking to Rome, which shared their anti-monarchical ideals, for assistance in their struggle for freedom from the king of Macedonia. On the south side of the Mediterranean was Carthage, in conflict with Rome for control of the sea-routes. At the eastern corner of north Africa was Egypt, which controlled the coast of Palestine and even the port originally founded for the Seleucid capital Antioch. In Asia Minor, part of the south coast was under Egypt, some areas were independent, and the remainder was controlled by Achaeus.

During the absence of Antiochus in the east, Achaeus had begun to act as an independent king, but was prevented from direct hostilities against Antiochus by a mutiny of his troops when they suspected that he intended them to fight against the legitimate Seleucid ruler. Thus, although Antiochus did not hold Asia Minor, he was secure against attack from that direction, and could now turn his attention to Palestine, which his dynasty had always claimed but never firmly held. He began well enough in 219 B.C. by retaking Antioch's port, Seleucia in Pieria, which had been in Egyptian hands for over twenty years. Then he moved southwards into Palestine. Here initial military successes were frustrated by political immaturity. The Egyptians hoodwinked Antiochus by stretching out negotiations to make him suppose that Egypt would surrender Palestine rather than fight; meanwhile the Egyptians were organising a powerful army. In consequence, when negotiations were broken off and Antiochus invaded Palestine in 217 B.C., his army was stopped by a major Egyptian force south of Gaza. The ensuing battle highlights both the strength and the weakness of the military skills of Antiochus, who in a static battle between large armies more than once showed a curious combination of inspiring leadership and personal valour in his immediate sector with defective generalship in control of the total battle plan. On this occasion Antiochus put to flight the forces opposite to him and led his cavalry in furious pursuit, but was unaware that his main army was in headlong retreat. An ancient author credits Antiochus with the comforting view that he himself had won the battle, but that he had suffered disaster owing to the cowardice of others.

Antiochus needed a success, both politically to compensate for his setback against Egypt, and on economic grounds to gain control of eastern Mediterranean trade routes, and in 216 B.C. he invaded Asia Minor. Coming to an understanding with the main independent ruler, the king of Pergamum in the west, he campaigned against Achaeus, who was captured by treachery in 214 B.C. and executed with disgraceful savagery. Antiochus accepted a *de facto* partition of spheres of influence in Asia Minor between himself and Pergamum.

Now began the expansion of empire which earned Antiochus the title 'the Great'. Superficially, he re-enacted the exploits of Alexander the Great, in reconquering the whole of Iran and Afghanistan as far as India. The reality was less sensational, but none the less a major achievement. Whatever his military abilities, Antiochus seems to have seen the economic realities. He was not so much concerned with conquest for its own sake as with ensuring supremacy over the trade routes from Bactria and India which brought merchandise and wealth to the great eastern capital, Seleucia on the Tigris. We hear first of his attacking Armenia, on the north-eastern borders of Asia Minor; instead of appointing a satrap to give himself the glory of acknowledged conquest, he took the statesmanlike step, when the king had made submission, of confirming him in his dominions as a tributary, bound by a marriage alliance.

Antiochus then moved into Iran. At his first destination, Ecbatana, capital of Media, there was an incident which sheds light on one of the unstated objectives of the eastern operations of Antiochus. His inability to secure Palestine from Egypt, and his partial loss of Asia Minor, had had adverse consequences for Seleucid revenues owing to the loss of trade routes in the Mediterranean area. In parts of the east, temples had long played an important economic role, providing a kind of rudimentary banking system, and some of them had enormous wealth in the form of precious metals. Antiochus now initiated the policy, followed by later Seleucids, of confiscating temple wealth, and it was at Ecbatana that he is first recorded as stripping a temple of its precious metals.

East of Media, beyond the great desert of central Iran, were two major areas, Parthia and Bactria, which had earlier been conquered by Alexander but whose rulers now claimed independence and were extending their powers. The Parthian ruler did not expect Antiochus to venture east of the desert. However, advancing by the trade route north of it, Antiochus brought the Parthian army to battle, in a mobile engagement in difficult terrain which allowed him to use his specialist units and which reflected considerably more credit on his tactical and logistic skills than did the earlier battle with Egypt.

The furthest north-east of Alexander's conquests had been Bactria (today, approximately, the U.S.S.R. north-west of Afghanistan). At this considerable distance from his base – some eleven hundred miles as the crow flies – Antiochus defeated the Greek ruler of Bactria, here again showing skilful generalship and great personal courage in the type of mobile cavalry engagement in which he excelled. Both in Parthia and Bactria conquest was clearly secondary to Seleucid economic interests: the rulers of both regions were allowed to remain as kings subject to acceptance of the suzerainty of Antiochus and the payment of heavy tribute.

Antiochus completed his oriental expedition by visiting north-west India, where he entered into an alliance with the Indian king. The immediate result of this was the obtaining of elephants for military use and tribute; the long-term result was to ensure that trade from India would pass through the Seleucid empire rather than by more southerly routes into Egyptian-controlled territory.

The enhanced prestige gained by Antiochus in his eastern expedition did much to consolidate his position in the west. In

198 B.C. he was in a position to avenge his earlier defeat by Egypt, and now for the first time brought Palestine firmly under Seleucid control. By his defeat of Egypt he also regained areas of south Asia Minor, where he began a vigorous policy of settlement of military colonists, who included Jewish families from Babylonia. Mention by the Jewish historian Josephus of this and other real or supposed instances of Antiochus's benevolent treatment of the Jews has contributed to the generally favourable assessment of this king. Circumstances now seemed favourable for making good the Seleucid claim to the whole of Asia Minor, and beyond that to Thrace, the region on the European side of the Bosphorus. In 197 B.C. Antiochus undertook an expedition through Asia Minor, quickly overcoming most of the opposition, and in 196 B.C. he invaded Thrace.

Meanwhile, there were some Greek cities on the west coast of Asia Minor which had resisted Antiochus and appealed for assistance to Rome, now beginning to be recognised as a major power by reason of its recent victories over Macedonia and Carthage. The Egyptians also sent an embassy to seek Roman support against further aggression. In consequence, the Romans warned Antiochus against further interference with either Egypt or the Greek cities.

Antiochus, however, was over-confident from the knowledge that he had now raised the Seleucid empire to its greatest extent, and he did not yet adequately appreciate the potential might of Rome. Denying that Rome had any standing in Asiatic matters, he began to prepare for further advances in Europe: he clearly saw himself as the new Alexander. He flaunted his defiance by giving a magnificent reception to Hannibal of Carthage, who had fled to Antiochus after his defeat by the Romans.

In 192 B.C. Antiochus, promised support from within Greece, invaded that country, though with what Hannibal warned him were inadequate preparations and an inadequate force. In any case, Hannibal, the most brilliant military strategist of his time, had advised Antiochus to attack the Romans in Italy rather than get into a war in Greece, but had been overruled.

As promised, Antiochus received widespread acclamation in Greece, although some cities stood out against him. In early 191 B.C. the Romans declared war. Greek support at once crumbled, and when Antiochus gave battle at Thermopylae, with all the disadvantages of which Hannibal had warned, he was disastrously defeated.

Antiochus retreated into Asia Minor. The Romans offered him peace terms, requiring withdrawal east of the Taurus and payment of war indemnity. Antiochus, still misjudging Roman strength compared with his own huge empire, declined. He proposed to re-establish himself by means of the considerable army he now proceeded to muster. All parts of the empire contributed. There were elephants, scythed chariots, archers mounted on camels, and specialist ethnic units armed with their traditional weapons, as well as the usual nucleus of cavalry and infantry. But when battle was joined at Magnesia in western Asia Minor in 190 B.C., the very size and diversity of the army of Antiochus made it a very inefficient fighting machine which the disciplined and well-trained Romans were easily able to throw into confusion. Antiochus, now over fifty, showed the same personal courage as a cavalry officer as when fighting against the Egyptians nearly thirty years before, but he also showed the same lack of organisational skill in manoeuvring a large army in a static battle. According to the classical author Appian, Antiochus made a disastrous disposition of his troops, with his best soldiers, the Macedonian phalanx, 'crowded together unskilfully in a narrow space'. He was again defeated.

The Romans again offered the former peace terms, with some additional penalties. This time Antiochus had no choice but to accept. The next two years were spent in finalising the details of the peace treaty.

With the loss of Asia Minor and with heavy annual payments to make to Rome, Antiochus now faced severe economic difficulties, but he still held the east, though even there allegiance began to be withdrawn in some areas as a result of the Great King's diminished status. It was probably with the dream of re-enacting the military and economic successes of his earlier glorious eastern expedition that in 188 B.C. Antiochus left his son as joint king in Antioch and set off to the east. But although there were still wealthy temples as sources of revenue, his earlier successes were not to be repeated. In the following year, in the course of attempting to confiscate the treasures of a temple in Elam, Antiochus lost his life at the hands of outraged tribesmen.

David

(*c.* 1010–970 B.C.)

When the Philistines threatened to overrun Canaan (Palestine), moving up from their city-states on the coastal plain, the Hebrews in the hill country determined to elect a king to unite their tribes. The decision was far from unanimous. The Hebrews were surrounded by petty kingdoms, but for two hundred years had remained faithful to their theocracy, acknowledging no supreme authority but their god Yahweh. It was with some reluctance that the prophet Samuel anointed the first king, Saul, from the northern tribe of Benjamin. Though divinely chosen, and a heroic figure – 'from his shoulders and upward higher than any of the people' – and initially successful in battle, Saul soon incurred Yahweh's displeasure; Samuel told him bluntly that the succession would not follow his line. Saul became unbalanced, probably manic-depressive, and for the rest of his reign was subject to moods of black despair.

It was to lighten such a mood that the boy musician David, great-grandson of the biblical Ruth, was first introduced to Saul's court. David at this time is described as fair-complexioned, 'of a beautiful countenance, and goodly to look at'. His skill with the lyre had the desired effect: Saul recovered his spirits, and made the youth his personal attendant.

Unknown to Saul, Yahweh had already named David as next in line to the throne; indeed, the anointing was carried out by Samuel with such secrecy in David's southern home town of Bethlehem-judah, that David himself was almost certainly unaware at the time of its significance. He had been out tending his father's sheep when Samuel appeared, this being his allotted task as the youngest of seven or eight sons; but it would be a mistake to think of David as a simple shepherd. We know that he had stockmen under him, and his father Jesse was evidently a man of substance. David's description of himself at court as 'a poor man, and lightly esteemed' is evidence only of the diplomacy that was but one facet of an extremely complex, not to say devious character.

An alternative account sets the meeting of David and Saul in the vale of Elah, south of Bethlehem: site of the youth's famous destruction of the Philistine giant Goliath of Gath, who challenged Saul's Israelites to send down a champion to meet him in single combat. Some authorities have cast doubts on David's part in the affray, but there is nothing intrinsically improbable in the story. The sling was often used as the shepherd's sheepdog, handled with hair's-breadth accuracy to lob a stone before or beside a stray to turn it, and David claimed to have killed both bear and lion in defence of his father's flocks. Goliath fell, stunned or dead, and David cut off his head with the giant's own sword. Again we are told Saul took David into his court, not only as court musician but also as war lord: a career David followed ruthlessly. The resultant popular jingle:

> Saul has slain his thousands,
> And David his tens of thousands

was not only an affront to the king. Saul's authority depended mainly on his personal courage and leadership. It was this challenge that determined him to be rid of the popular hero. Having promised his elder daughter to the slayer of Goliath, he gave her to another. In her place he offered the younger Michal, asking not the customary bride-price (which for a king's daughter could have been enormous) but the foreskins of a hundred Philistines. That is to say, he sent David on a suicide mission. When David returned with twice the required number of gruesome trophies Saul had no choice but to keep his promise. David was now the king's son-in-law. Michal loved him. He formed an attachment with Saul's son Jonathan so close that they became virtually blood brothers.

There can be no doubt that Saul too, in his saner moods, was deeply attached to David. But on more than one occasion he turned violently against him, even hurling a lethal javelin at him without warning. With the help of Jonathan and the faithful Michal, David escaped from the very real danger to his life, eventually making his way up to the priests of Nob, a town just north of Jerusalem, on the pretext that he was on a secret mission from the king. The ferocity of Saul's pursuit may be judged from the fact that he ordered the slaughter of no less than eighty-five of the priests for the crime of harbouring the fugitive, together with their women, children and livestock, despite their protestation of innocence.

There followed many fanatical attempts by Saul to hunt down and kill David, who each time evaded him. Driven into the role of outlaw, David became in fact a bandit chief, attracting to himself in his caves and strongholds some 600 malcontents, whom he welded into a formidable fighting force. Few if any were Hebrews; many were in all probability from the Philistines themselves. To provide for his little army, David resorted to extortion, offering 'protection' to local landowners at a price; though the protection may have been real enough.

Popular sympathy was with David, and when Saul mounted yet another expedition in the wilderness of Ziph, there was no lack of spies to warn his quarry. Informed of the position of Saul's camp, David slipped through the sentries under cover of darkness accompanied by only one man and reached the sleeping king's tent undetected. Urged to kill Saul, David refused: 'The Lord forbid that I should stretch forth mine hand against the Lord's anointed.' Instead he took Saul's spear and water pitcher, and safely out of range shouted out what he had done. Saul was overcome with remorse and swore to do him no more harm. However, David retreated to Philistine Gath, out of Saul's reach, and offered the services of his band as mercenaries.

It was a daring move, considering David's record; but Achish king of Gath welcomed him, well aware of the enmity between Saul and David. The Philistines, not themselves numerous, were accustomed to fighting with 'native' forces, perhaps not unlike the British in India, and certainly numbered Hebrews among them. David was given the town of Ziklag, well south of Gath, probably to protect a Philistine flank. From Ziklag David carried out long-range raids far into the desert, down towards Egypt, against the nomad Bedouin who had long preyed on Judah; representing to Achish that he was fighting the Judahites themselves. As he ensured that none of the nomads encountered was left alive to tell the tale, the deception was successful; so successful that when Achish mustered his fighting men for a mass attack on Israel, he planned to take David with him. David could scarcely refuse, and was saved from an awkward dilemma only when others of the Philistines, less happy with the plan, insisted that he should be sent back.

During his reign Saul had successfully held the Philistines back from the highlands; but this final battle was disastrous. Routed at Mount Gilboa, with his sons slain and himself wounded by an arrow, Saul fell on his sword rather than be taken alive, perhaps mindful of the fate of Samson. David's lament for the deaths of Saul and Jonathan, beautifully composed as might be expected from the author of at least some of the psalms attributed to him, was politic in proclaiming his sympathy with the northern tribes' loss, but undoubtedly expressed his genuine feelings. When a messenger brought him the dead king's crown, claiming (untruthfully) that he had slain Saul, David had him put to death for the crime of killing the Lord's anointed.

It was now, with Saul dead and the northern territory at least partially occupied by the enemy, that David was popularly proclaimed king of Judah, though still as suzerain under the Philistines. Similarly a surviving son of Saul, Ish-bosheth, was crowned king of Israel, the name now limited to the northern tribes. Intermittent civil war followed between Israel and Judah; when the northern warlord Abner moved to make David king over both, David refused, content to play a waiting game. When Ish-bosheth was murdered by two brigands, who expected to gain David's favour, he had them brutally executed. But Abner too had been assassinated, and with Israel virtually leaderless, a deputation approached David and he felt confident enough to accept the double crown.

It will be seen that the division between the two halves of the old federation of Hebrew tribes had become absolute, and so long as it remained so, the Philistines could regard David as their man. But with the tribes reunited, he posed a considerable threat; this became more alarming when David took the Jebusite city of Jerusalem, which stood on a commanding height between the two and had hitherto belonged to neither. To consolidate his position, David had the Ark of the Lord fetched up from Gibeah, where it had lain neglected since its appalling loss to the Philistines at the battle of Aphek. The Ark represented the central shrine of all Israel, and its presence confirmed Jerusalem as the new capital.

There is no suggestion that the Jebusites were put to the sword, and every reason to believe that they were absorbed into David's kingdom. Nor were the Hebrew tribal levies introduced into Jerusalem, which remained the personal city of David, with the king's mercenary 'household troops' as the nucleus of his army and his court.

His position secure, David turned his attention to the Hebrews' traditional enemies: the Philistines; the remaining Canaanite city-states which, like Jerusalem, had never been conquered; the desert Bedouin, and the neighbouring kingdoms east of Jordan. We are given few details of the campaigns, but their success was nothing short of spectacular. The Philistines were driven back to their coast, never again to pose a major threat, and within a few short years of Saul's death the Hebrews had risen from near-subjugation to the command of an empire extending well beyond Palestine, taking in southern Syria. They also exercised control over the surrounding states, as well as the all-important coastal 'King's Highway', which was the main international road from

Mesopotamia to Egypt.

An incident which throws light on the relationship between the Hebrew monarchy and priesthood is the well-known adultery of David with Bath-sheba, the beautiful wife of one of David's 'thirty heroes' or inner circle, then absent at a battle against the Ammonites. David conceived a violent passion for the woman when from the rooftop of his palace he observed her bathing, and promptly sent for her. In due course, when she sent word that she had conceived, he called her husband Uriah back on the pretext of wanting a report on the war; actually to father the child on him. Soldiers customarily took an oath to abstain from intercourse while on active service, and despite David's making him drunk, Uriah was faithful to it. In desperation David sent him back to the battle bearing a sealed order to the local commander to have him put 'in the forefront of the battle' and abandoned. Inevitably Uriah was killed, and David took Bath-sheba to wife.

It must be said that another king of those times would scarcely have felt the necessity to excuse himself in taking the wife of a subject. But when the prophet Nathan denounced David to his face, David accepted the rebuke; he fasted and prayed for forgiveness. Punished by the death of his son by the union, he accepted the calamity as just. Later, evidently in token of divine forgiveness, Bath-sheba bore him a second son: Solomon.

The loyalty David expected from, and gave to, his own was at once his greatest strength and perhaps his greatest weakness. When his beloved eldest son Absalom murdered his brother in revenge for his rape of their sister Tamar, David took no action, unaware that Absalom was plotting to gain the throne for himself. The conspiracy took the king by surprise, and he was forced to flee from Jerusalem. However, he took his faithful mercenaries with him, together with the Ark, and from east of Jordan launched a counter-insurrection in the course of which Absalom was slain. David mourned him bitterly, with that generosity of spirit so much at odds with a nature that was well capable of being as violent and merciless as the times in which he lived.

On his deathbed, represented as prematurely aged, King David's last public act was to name Solomon as his successor, despite the claims and threatened revolt of an older son, apparently honouring a promise to Bath-sheba of which we have no record.

It was Nathan who promised David in the name of the Lord that his 'house' or dynasty would be established forever: a promise obscured by the destruction of Israel, leaving only Judah – the Judahites, or Jews – who in turn were to be conquered and scattered over the known world, partially returning only as subjects of foreign rulers up to our own time; but a promise that Christians believe was wholly fulfilled in the person of David's descendant, Jesus Christ, the Messiah.

Solomon

(Ruled c. 970–*c.* 930 B.C.*)*

King of the united realm of ancient Israel for some forty years from about 970 B.C., Solomon was one of the younger sons of King David. The child of Bath-sheba, whose first husband Uriah had been sent by David to die in the heat of battle, Solomon was born in the purple and lacked the experience of struggle which had shaped his father's character and policies. Modern scholars have called Solomon ostentatious and tyrannical, yet legend honoured him for wealth and wisdom, attributing to him books with which he probably had little to do.

In David's old age it seems that there was no rule of succession but, according to the first Book of Kings in the Bible, Adonijah, an elder son, gained the support of the priest Abiathar, who had been with David from early years, and Joab the army commander. Adonijah made a great feast and invited his royal brothers and men of their tribe of Judah, but Solomon was not invited; nor was Nathan the prophet or Zadok the priest. Nathan told Bath-sheba what was going on; she went to the old King David, claiming that he had sworn that her son Solomon should reign after him. David, backed by Nathan, confirmed this. Solomon was anointed by Nathan and Zadok and proclaimed king publicly with the support of Benaiah, captain of the foreign bodyguard.

Adonijah was taken by surprise. His guests dispersed hurriedly, while he himself did obeisance to Solomon on promise of safe conduct. But soon, on a charge of coveting the dead David's last concubine, Adonijah was murdered by Benaiah. Joab had long been a faithful servant of David, but although he took sanctuary at the altar Solomon ordered Benaiah to kill him there. Abiathar was banished to his home town and Zadok became chief priest in his place. By this palace coup young Solomon became king of all Israel and crushed his rivals.

Saul, the first king, had united the Hebrew tribes, but he died whilst fighting the Philistines at Mount Gilboa. David served and then rivalled Saul. Succeeding him, by strategic battles and judicious policies he enlarged the country, secured its frontiers, made Jerusalem the capital, and made alliances with neighbouring states. Solomon only added to this realm the site of Gezer, given by the Egyptian pharaoh as dowry for a princess whom Solomon married. Copying other oriental despots he contracted many marriages, traditionally 700 wives and 300 concubines. Some were foreign women, married for political alliances, but this involved introducing their religion into Israel and Jerusalem itself, and later scribes condemned Solomon because 'his wives turned away his heart after other gods'.

One of Solomon's chief claims to fame was his building programme, building fortresses at the frontiers and key places. Then he set out to make Jerusalem comparable to great foreign cities. David had bought a threshing-floor, perhaps an ancient place of sacrifice of the original inhabitants of Jerusalem. The bare stone of this rock is said to be the same which still today forms the floor of the great Islamic shrine in Jerusalem, the Dome of the Rock or Mosque of Omar.

Solomon extended Jerusalem northwards to enclose this site, and here he built the first permanent temple of the Hebrew people. It was not large, about 100 feet long and 50 feet high, and massive rather than elegant. The outside was of stone; the inside was covered with cedar and cypress wood, and decorated with figures of angelic beings or cherubim, palm trees and flowers. There were two main chambers, a larger one with lattice windows and an inner sanctuary, the Holy of Holies, which was either in complete darkness or lit by a lamp. Here was the Ark, held to contain the tablets of the Law which Moses had brought, protected by two winged cherubim. Outside the temple there were open courtyards with altars of sacrifice.

Other buildings were the king's own house nearest the temple, and attached to it was the palace of pharaoh's daughter. Then came a hall of pillars, a hall of justice, and 'the house of the forest of Lebanon'. The last is the only one described in detail; it was a great hall with rows of pillars of cedar from Lebanon and a ceiling of cedar wood. The other buildings were probably much the same, and were simple though undoubtedly expensive.

The financial and construction arrangements for this building work were very heavy, yet the kingdom of Israel was small and poor compared with the great empires nearby. Solomon's ally, King Hiram of Tyre, supplied some of the timber, provided skilled workmen, and controlled the transport, sending material by sea, though even then there was long haulage from the coast up to

Jerusalem in the mountains. Not only wood was used in building, and stone which could be quarried locally, but bronze and gold and ornamental stones, much of which would be imported. In addition there was all the cost of maintaining Solomon's court, his wives and his fortresses. He had 1,400 chariots, purchased from Egypt, and both maintenance and the displays which Solomon loved required constant expenditure.

Solomon has been called the first commercial king of Israel, perhaps the first great Israelite merchant. He exacted tolls from travellers passing down the international highways, by the pass of Megiddo and the coastal plains which connected the empires of Mesopotamia and Egypt. The coastline of Palestine has no natural port, so Solomon made a port at Ezion-geber on the gulf of Akabah in the far south, and from here he traded down the Red Sea south and east. The Book of Kings mentions his navy bringing ivory, apes and peacocks which could have come from India.

On his own people Solomon bore heavily. Taxation in money and goods, and also unpaid labour, were oppressive. He raised levies out of all Israel, sending men to work for a month in the forest or quarries and back home for two months, making four months in the year away from their homes and fields under what were sometimes like slave conditions. It has been estimated that the building operations required 200,000 men, and it is said that there were 3,000 overseers. Some mercenaries, or slaves, may also have been sent from Israel into Egypt to pay for the chariots and horses. Solomon's kingdom was divided into twelve districts, both to provide workmen and to supply the needs of the royal household.

It is not surprising that there were revolts from the tribes, which before the time of the monarchy had been used to independence and still resented central government, especially if it was tyrannical. The records put it that 'the Lord raised up adversaries to Solomon' and several are named. One of the most significant rebels was Jeroboam of the northern tribe of Ephraim. Solomon had given him charge of a district, but a prophet named Ahijah met Jeroboam and told him that the Lord would take ten tribes from Solomon and give them to him, tearing his cloak into twelve pieces and giving Jeroboam ten as a symbol, because of the foreign gods that Solomon had introduced into Israel. Solomon found out and sought to kill Jeroboam, who fled to Egypt till Solomon's death.

When Solomon died his son Rehoboam went to the ancient town of Shechem to meet the tribes and be crowned. Jeroboam returned and led a demand that the 'grievous service' and 'heavy yoke' imposed by Solomon should be lifted. The old counsellors advised Rehoboam to negotiate, but young men who had grown up with him urged Rehoboam to threaten even heavier burdens and he replied, 'my father chastised you with whips, but I will chastise you with scorpions'.

Thereupon Jeroboam led the ten northern tribes to rebel. They established the rival capital at Shechem, founding the northern state of Israel with a sanctuary at Beth-el, 'the house of God', to prevent people going up to Jerusalem. Rehoboam was left with the small and weak kingdom of the south, with only the tribes of Judah and Benjamin, centred on Jerusalem. So Solomon's kingdom and its luxury crumbled, as a result of his vanity and oppressiveness, and the feeling of the northern peoples of Galilee was later expressed in the saying of Jesus that 'Solomon in all his glory was not arrayed like one of these' – wild lilies of the field.

Yet the wisdom of Solomon was legendary in later ages, exceeding 'all the wisdom of Egypt', and 'all peoples' were said to have come to hear him. He is said to have spoken of trees and flowers, of animals, birds and fishes, which later legend took to mean that he understood their language. This notion entered into both Jewish and Islamic mythology, of which Kipling's oriental tale of *The Butterfly that Stamped* is a modern rendering.

Solomon is said to have spoken 3,000 proverbs and composed 1,005 songs. The Bible Book of Proverbs was traditionally attributed to him (1,1; 10,1), though there are many sayings here assigned to other men and scholars consider that the book was compiled centuries after Solomon. The Canticles or Song of Songs is also ascribed to Solomon (1,1), though it seems to be a collection of ancient love lyrics. Ecclesiastes or The Preacher, 'the son of David, king in Jerusalem', is a late composition in the Bible whose pessimism seems far removed from the spirit of Solomon. In the Apocrypha, books of late date and not included in the Bible, there is a so-called Wisdom of Solomon, which dates perhaps from the second or first centuries B.C. The even later so-called Odes of Solomon are short psalms, written in Syriac or Greek, which may be late Jewish or early Christian works.

Solomon is said to have had a dream in which God gave him an understanding heart. He may have had a quick wit, as illustrated in the story of the judgement of Solomon between two women who disputed over a baby. Solomon ordered it to be cut in half, and the true mother was revealed when she cried out that the child should be given to the other woman rather than be killed. Solomon is said to have recognised that God could not be confined to live in the temple that he had built, but the prayer attributed to him at the

Sculpture of Akhenaton revealing his adherence to one of the royal titles he assumed on coming to the throne – 'He who Lives in Truth'. It is not stylised, and bears all the signs of being true to life. *Below:* A carving depicting Akhenaton and his wife, Nefertiti.

The mummy of the great 19th-dynasty pharaoh Ramesses II, discovered in the late nineteenth century. Radiological examination confirmed his advanced age at death. By contrast with his mortal remains the colossal head of the king at Abu Simbel suggests unending endurance.

dedication of the temple breathes the feelings of prophets and priests of a later age.

The Queen of Sheba, perhaps from Saba in southern Arabia, is said to have come to test Solomon with hard questions and to have admitted that 'the half was not told me' before she returned home. In Islamic legend the Queen of Sheba was named Bilqis and she became one of Solomon's queens. In our time the emperors of Ethiopia claimed to descend from Solomon and the Queen of Sheba, as do also the Falasha Jews of Ethiopia.

The wisdom ascribed to Solomon was not illustrated in the facts of his life. As a king he was much inferior to his father David, in character and policy, and in religion he was far below the high standard of the Hebrew prophets who came after him. He was selfish and extravagant, his foreign wives made him unfaithful to the religion of his people, and his oppressive treatment of his own tribes led to the inevitable revolt. The united kingdom which had been built up by Saul and David was fatally undermined. United it might have long resisted outside pressures; when it was divided into Israel and Judah these two small kingdoms fell one after the other to the invading armies of Mesopotamia. Yet people forgave and forgot, and looked back through the rosy mists of history to the luxury and vaunted wisdom of Solomon, when their land seemed to be united, rich and powerful.

Herod I

(73–4 B.C.)

Herod I (King of Judaea 37–4 B.C.), known as the Great, was the most important Jewish ruler after Old Testament times.

In the second century B.C., Jewish nationalists achieved independence under the priestly Hasmonean family, their rulers eventually taking the title of king as well as high priest. In 67 B.C. a struggle for the royal office developed between two sons of the previous ruler.

During the Hasmonean expansion, the Idumeans (Edomites) to the south had been incorporated into the Jewish community by forcible circumcision, and a rich Idumean named Antipater had been appointed governor. His son, bearing the same name, inherited his prominence and wealth, and now intervened to support the legitimate heir, Hyrcanus II, against his younger brother Aristobulus. The second Antipater had four sons, of whom the second was Herod, born in 73 B.C. By Israelite law (Deuteronomy 23:8), Herod and his brothers, as Idumean converts of the third generation, were full Jews.

In 64–63 B.C. Rome, expanding in the east, annexed Syria and Palestine. Both Hasmonean claimants now sought the support of Pompey, Rome's representative in the east. Pompey decided in favour of Hyrcanus, leaving him as high priest and thus head of the Jewish community, although without the title of king. Pompey used Antipater to set up a native administrative network.

Civil war between Pompey and Julius Caesar threatened the position of Antipater and Hyrcanus. But Antipater gave help to Caesar in taking Egypt after Pompey's defeat in 48 B.C., and was rewarded by Roman citizenship and the post of procurator (governor) of Judaea. His oldest son, Phasael, was put in charge of Jerusalem, and Herod, now twenty-five or twenty-six, became *strategos* (commanding officer) of Galilee. Hyrcanus was confirmed as high priest and given the title of ethnarch (ruler of the nation).

Herod, finding that Galilee was infested with bandits, took vigorous measures, putting the ringleaders to death. In Galilee he received general approval. But Antipater and his sons had enemies within Jerusalem. The aristocracy there despised them for their Idumean strain, and were jealous of the wealth and influence of Antipater. Now was their chance to attack Herod, for inflicting the death penalty without authority from the Sanhedrin, the supreme religious court, and they persuaded Hyrcanus to summon Herod for trial.

Herod complied, but in defiant manner, arriving with a bodyguard. So formidable was he that only one member of the Sanhedrin dared to speak against him, and the case was dropped. But Herod felt insulted, and it was only with difficulty that his father and brother were able to dissuade him from an attack to dethrone Hyrcanus.

After the murder of Julius Caesar in 44 B.C., an anti-Caesar general, Cassius, commanded the Roman forces in Syria for two years. Needing money for his troops, he imposed heavy taxation, to be collected through Antipater. Antipater shared out the task between his sons and other officials. Herod again showed his energy, efficiency, and pro-Roman attitude, by being the first to deliver his quota. But others resented Roman taxation, and one leading Jew, close to Hyrcanus, instigated the murder of Antipater, possibly with the connivance of Hyrcanus.

Although Hyrcanus had sometimes sided with enemies of Antipater and his sons, he owed much to their support. This became explicit when Antigonus, the son of his brother and rival Aristobulus, invaded Galilee. Herod defeated him, but Antigonus had a dangerously strong following in Judaea, and his attack emphasised the need for Hyrcanus and the sons of Antipater to stand together. A marriage alliance was therefore arranged, by which Herod (although already married, with a son) became betrothed to Mariamme, granddaughter of Hyrcanus.

In 42 B.C. the eastern part of the Roman empire fell to Mark Antony, and Cassius was killed. Herod and his brother had collaborated with Cassius, and Jewish delegations went to Antony to denounce them. But Antony, who had long before been on terms of friendship with Antipater, decided in favour of Phasael and Herod, and gave both brothers the title tetrarch (ruler of a district). Some suppose that the new arrangement vested all political authority in Herod and his brother, with Hyrcanus limited to religious affairs; but since Hyrcanus retained the title of ethnarch, it is more likely that Phasael and Herod were regarded as subordinate princes under him.

Two years later, the Parthians from Iran invaded Palestine. Antigonus allied himself with the invaders and seized Jerusalem. The Parthians, under pretext of negotiating, summoned Hyrcanus, Phasael and Herod to a meeting. Against the advice of the more suspicious Herod, the other two complied and were arrested. Herod, after taking his family to safety, went off to seek assistance. Meanwhile Antigonus had lopped the ears of Hyrcanus to disqualify him for the high priesthood, and had had him deported and Phasael killed.

Herod set off for Rome, where he met Antony, and through him Julius Caesar's heir Octavian, later to become the emperor Augustus. With such diplomatic skill did Herod present his case that the two Roman leaders argued before the senate that it was to Rome's advantage that Herod should become king of Judaea. The senate voted in agreement.

Meanwhile the Romans had expelled the Parthians, but Antigonus still held Jerusalem. Herod returned to Palestine, but his final conquest of his kingdom was delayed whilst the Romans dealt with problems in Asia Minor. Antony had come there to take charge, and Herod, always careful to remain on good terms with his current patron, went there to pay his respects and give military assistance. It was not until the winter of 38–37 B.C. that he was able to begin the siege of Jerusalem, with Roman assistance. During the siege, he left to complete his nuptials with Mariamme, to whom he had been betrothed for five years. Herod was not deserting the martial arts for love; rather, he knew it would assist his acceptance in Jerusalem to enter as the newly wed husband of a Hasmonean princess.

Herod's forces duly captured Jerusalem, but the Roman soldiers got out of hand and began looting. Herod, with his father's considerable wealth behind him, was able to buy the looters off and save the city, thereby winning support from many Jerusalem property-owners. Antigonus was taken prisoner, sent to Antony and executed. Herod, well aware that the old aristocracy of Jerusalem remained opposed to him, took this opportunity to purge the aristocracy-dominated Sanhedrin, killing forty-five of its members. But not all Jewish religious leaders opposed Herod. We hear of his being on good terms with some Pharisees, and with the sect called Essenes.

With the death of Antigonus, the only remaining Hasmoneans were closely related to Herod by marriage. This appeared to promise an end to dynastic conflict, but it worked out otherwise. Josephus commented that 'fortune was avenged on Herod for his great successes in public matters by raising him up domestic troubles'. The first crisis concerned the high priesthood. This office was hereditary and the proper successor was the younger brother of Herod's bride Mariamme, another Aristobulus, but Aristobulus was under age, a fact which Herod used to pass him over and appoint a priest of obscure origin. The real objection to Aristobulus went deeper. The high priesthood was the most influential office in the Jewish religious community, more ancient than the kingship and held by many Jews in equal or greater honour. A Hasmonean high priest would be a focus of any opposition to Herod.

But Herod had reckoned without the women of his household. Alexandra, his new mother-in-law, had powerful connexions. She complained to Cleopatra, Queen of Egypt, with whom Antony was besotted, and brought pressure to bear. Mariamme added her persuasion. Herod had to eject his former nominee and install Aristobulus. Popular acclamation followed, confirming Herod's fears. He removed the danger of a Hasmonean high priest by secretly having the young man drowned.

Herod's guilt did not remain hidden. His mother-in-law informed Cleopatra, who induced Antony to summon him to interview. In the event Herod convinced Antony that he, as a client king, should not have his authority questioned in his own land. But the affair increased the tensions in Herod's family.

Eventually war broke out between the two Roman leaders,

Antony and Octavian, and Antony was defeated in 31 B.C. Herod's past allegiance to Antony put him under a cloud, but, ever bold and decisive, he went to make submission to Octavian. He made no secret of his former attachment to Antony, and theatrically surrendered his diadem. Octavian, recognising the value in an outlying part of the empire of an honest ruler steadfastly loyal to Rome in the face of all local pressures, confirmed the kingdom to Herod. Shortly afterwards, Octavian passed through Palestine to Egypt, and was so impressed by Herod's efficiency over commissariat arrangements that he added the whole Palestinian coastline and Samaria to Herod's kingdom, and subsequently gave him regions east of the Jordan.

Herod carefully cultivated friendship with Octavian (from 27 B.C. known as the emperor Augustus) and with his powerful counsellor Marcus Agrippa. This was not mere sycophancy. Doubtless he recognised the advantages of links with the great, but he also had a strong sense of the duty of co-operating with the forces of stability, which each Roman leader in turn represented.

The other side of Herod's concern for stability was his ruthlessness against anyone he saw as a threat to his own rule. The captured former ethnarch Hyrcanus, now a septuagenarian, had been allowed to return to Palestine. Before Herod went to see Octavian, he had the old man murdered. This was a calculated act rather than vindictiveness. Octavian had to ensure efficient government for parts of the empire under native rule. With Herod under a cloud, if Octavian learned of a former ethnarch still living and generally acceptable to the Jews, he might well reinstall him in Herod's place. The removal of Hyrcanus, the last adult male Hasmonean, meant that Octavian could not dethrone Herod without leaving a dangerous vacuum.

However advantageous in political terms, the murder of Hyrcanus brought further tragedy to Herod's family. Josephus reports that after the murder of her brother and grandfather, Mariamme, by whom Herod had three sons and two daughters, developed bitter hatred against her husband, with no attempt to conceal it. Alexandra had already publicly shown her dislike of Herod. Now that his wife was estranged, she and her mother, as Hasmonean princesses, were from Herod's point of view dangers to be removed. Herod had Mariamme tried on a trumped-up charge of adultery and attempted murder. She was condemned and executed (29 B.C.). Josephus reports that Herod was afterwards distracted at her loss, but his account suggests mental illness rather than remorse. His supposed grief did not prevent him from shortly afterwards executing Mariamme's mother on his first cousin's convenient evidence that she had attempted to involve him in a plot.

Although his private life was now in ruins, Herod's public affairs were entering a most illustrious period. Augustus needed him. Palestine was vital as the link between Syria, the most important of Augustus's fifteen provinces, and Egypt, regarded as his personal domain. Furthermore, it led to the kingdom of Petra, which controlled the rich spice routes from South Arabia, and it had a vulnerable border.

A native king of Palestine could not survive if he failed to defend the interests of Rome. But he must also serve Palestinian interests, or there might be risings to alarm Rome. Palestine had a population which culturally and ethnically was mixed. There were non-Jewish populations in such areas as Samaria and old Philistine cities such as Gaza. Moreover, the Jews themselves were culturally mixed. Despite three centuries of Hellenism, there were still fanatical nationalists to be found in Judaea, alert for any suspicion or offence against Mosaic law in its narrowest interpretation. But there were many Palestinian Jews who, like almost all in the Diaspora, were content to accept Graeco-Roman culture provided monotheism and Sabbath observance were not compromised. Herod acted sternly against any group whose nationalism might threaten conflict with Rome, but where no such problem arose, he showed himself a good Jew.

The most conspicuous mark of Herod's piety was his rebuilding of the Temple of Solomon: substantial parts remain today. An ancient temple always stood in a sacred enclosure, and Herod enlarged that of the Jerusalem temple to 35 acres, three-quarters the size of Buckingham Palace Gardens. It was surrounded by a continuous wall, with a fortified palace, the Antonia, at its north-west corner. The temple itself was a magnificent structure with colonnades and porticoes, occupying about three and a half acres, inside a wall 60 feet high.

Herod changed the face of many other parts of Palestine. In Samaria, he laid out a splendid new city, named Sebaste after the Greek form of the name Augustus. On the coast he built a major port, Caesarea, with all the amenities of a Graeco-Roman city, such as amphitheatres, market places, temples and colossi, and equipped it with a great artificial harbour with sea walls and breakwaters. He built or restored a series of fortresses in the wilderness, the most famous of them being Masada, and the most impressive being one near Jericho, associated with a fine new city.

His display was not limited to his own land. He made large endowments elsewhere. Some beneficiaries were cities which had helped him in times of trouble. Others were places where Jews of the Diaspora were to be found: Herod was not neglectful of their interests, and conspicuous generosity by the Jewish king brought much advantage to Jews in those cities. Thus we find him endowing gymnasiums at Damascus, temples and market places at Beirut and Tyre, theatres at Sidon and Damascus.

Herod continued to receive imperial favour. He could be relied upon to maintain order, and border disturbances led to his receiving further additions of territory, until his kingdom rivalled that of Solomon. In 15 B.C. the powerful Agrippa publicly showed his close friendship with Herod in a tour of Palestine. The following year Herod joined Agrippa on a tour through western Asia Minor, assisting in settling disputes between the cities and the government and greatly augmenting his international reputation. The Jews there now approached Herod to secure them redress for infringement of their religious traditions. At Herod's persuasion, Agrippa held an investigation, and confirmed all their ancient rights. When Herod returned to Jerusalem and announced what he had achieved for the Jews of Asia Minor, he received general acclamation, heightened by his granting a 25 per cent remission of taxes.

Herod's final decade was clouded by a breakdown of health and by family problems. He was ageing, and needed to plan for the succession. He had three adult sons: Antipater, by his first wife, a commoner, and Alexander and Aristobulus by the royal Mariamme. With a Roman education and Hasmonean blood, Alexander was the obvious successor. But Herod had misgivings and in 13 B.C. named Antipater heir. Family in-fighting now brought disaster. Josephus recounts Herod's growing estrangement from his Hasmonean sons: the young men, understandably bitter about their murdered mother, were indiscreet in speaking about their father, and Antipater and other non-Hasmonean members of Herod's family told tales to benefit by this. The final outcome, after several reconciliations, was that Herod had the two young men arrested, tried, and against the verdict of the senior Roman judge, taken to Sebaste and strangled.

Antipater now considered his succession assured, and to advance his prospects went to Rome. During his absence, circumstances arose implicating him in a plot. He was called home by Herod, arrested, tried, found guilty and imprisoned.

After the murder of the Hasmonean queen Mariamme, Herod had married a further eight times. Four of these ladies had borne him sons, though they had been too young to become involved in the succession struggle. Now, in 5 B.C., Herod named as his heir

Antipas, the second son of his fourth wife, a Samaritan lady, passing over his older full brother Archaelaus because he had associated with Antipater.

Herod, though now seriously ill, remained firmly in control to the end. His final act was a new arrangement for the succession. He had Antipater executed, and, relenting towards Archaelaus, appointed him king of Judaea, and Antipas and another son, Philip, tetrarchs. Five days later he died, from what has been diagnosed, from the symptoms described by Josephus, as gangrenous complications from arterio-sclerosis.

It was shortly before Herod's death that the most important event of his reign occurred – the birth of Jesus. There is no evidence outside St Matthew's Gospel for the story of Herod's massacre of all newborn babies.

Herod combined great ability with an obsessive suspicion of potential rivals which led him into foul acts of murder. He was a brilliant administrator, a quality evident in the way he saved his country in a severe famine in 25 B.C., when he stripped his palace of gold and silver, and used it to buy corn from Egypt, distributing it through government depots. To win the trust and friendship of men like Pompey, Antony, Augustus and Agrippa, he must have had not only considerable charm and diplomatic ability but also reliability and probity. He could use stern measures to achieve his ends, but those ends included peace, security, major projects of city development, and prosperous agriculture, which Palestine desperately needed after a century and a half of unsettlement.

Persia

Cyrus the Great

(*Ruled* 553–530 B.C.)

In 330 B.C. flames swept through Persepolis after its capture by Alexander the Great, signalling an end to the greatest empire the world had yet seen, the empire of the Persians founded some two centuries earlier by Cyrus the Great. Yet there was little to suggest a couple of hundred years before the birth of Cyrus that the Iranians would control a vast empire.

From the late Assyrian records it is clear that in the ninth and

eighth centuries B.C. both the Medes and the Persians, closely
related groups of Iranian-speaking people who had infiltrated on
to the plateau from further north, were nothing more than loose
confederations of tribes. Nevertheless, by the seventh century B.C.
the Medes had control of a wide area around their capital at
Ecbatana (modern Hamadan) while the subject Persians were
settled in the modern province of Fars. Together with the
Babylonians, the Medes were responsible for the overthrow of the
Assyrian Empire, and in the political vacuum that followed they
were able to extend their sphere of influence across Turkey as far
as the Halys river, where the frontier between them and the
Lydians was established.

According to Herodotus, Cyrus was the offspring of a union
between a Persian noble called Cambyses and Mandane, a
daughter of the Median king Astyages. After the marriage
between Cambyses and Mandane, Astyages had a dream in
which a vine grew out of his daughter's womb and spread until it
overshadowed the whole of Asia. This dream was interpreted to
mean that his daughter's son would usurp the throne.
Consequently, when the child was born Astyages instructed one of
his nobles, Harpagus, to dispose of it. Reluctant to carry out this
wicked deed himself, Harpagus passed on the child and
instructions to kill it to a herdsman called Mithradates. At that
time, though, the herdsman's wife gave birth to a stillborn son and
this they substituted for the infant prince. Cyrus was then brought
up by the herdsman and his wife until he was ten years old. At this
point his true identity was recognised, but his life was spared and
he was sent to his father's palace in Persia. However this may be, it
is clear from the cuneiform record that Cyrus belonged to the
ruling house of Persia and that he was known as 'King of Anshan'.
All sources are agreed that by 553 B.C. Cyrus had overthrown
Astyages and established himself as undisputed king of the Medes
and the Persians.

About Cyrus's appearance we can say little except that
Plutarch describes him as griffin-nosed. No contemporary
representations of him exist, and even if they did they would
probably be uninformative as portraits in ancient western Asia
tended to be very stylised. But the classical authors – who together
with the Babylonian Chronicle are our main source for the life and
times of Cyrus – are unanimous in speaking of his comely
qualities. Thus Herodotus describes him as 'the manliest and the
best loved of his peers', while Xenophon goes even further and
says that 'Cyrus was most handsome in person, most generous of
heart, most devoted to learning, and most ambitious'. But these

accounts cannot really be taken at their face value, for Cyrus became to his contemporaries and successors a heroic figure, and in consequence eulogy was heaped upon him. Much of it might have been deserved, but doubtless there was more than a little exaggeration.

For the first few years after his defeat of Astyages Cyrus was probably occupied in consolidating his position at home. But it was not long before Croesus, the fabulously wealthy king of Lydia, saw an opportunity to take advantage of the turn of events in Iran, and according to Herodotus he crossed the Halys, long recognised as the border between the Lydians and the Medes. Cyrus advanced to meet him, and after an indecisive encounter Croesus retired to Sardis, not thinking that Cyrus would dare to follow him. He had clearly underestimated the determination of the Persian king, though, for Cyrus pressed westwards with all speed and was within striking distance of Sardis before the Lydians realised what was happening. In a second battle outside the city, legend has it that Cyrus resorted to a clever ruse to gain the advantage. Knowing the unsettling effect that camels have on horses, he sent a contingent of these beasts ahead of his main force and caused chaos amongst the Lydian cavalry. The Lydians were obliged to retreat within the city, but in due course this was taken by Cyrus. This capture of Sardis – probably in 547 or 546 B.C. – and the defeat of Croesus must rank as one of the great victories of antiquity. Afterwards Cyrus himself returned eastwards, entrusting the Mede Harpagus with the task of reducing the various Greek cities in Asia Minor; in this way even Lycia and Caria were brought within the empire.

It was probably now on his return to Iran that Cyrus embarked on his ambitious building programme at Pasargadae in Fars, which he made his capital. We know quite a lot about this site thanks to a series of excavations, the most recent being the brilliant investigations of Professor David Stronach between 1961 and 1963. Scattered about in a large park were at least two grand pavilions, both with the colonnades that are so distinctive of later Achaemenid architecture. Now just a solitary column is still standing, which, complete with stork's nest on top, imparts to the visitor a sense of melancholy grandeur. Access to the enclosure was via a gatehouse where a relief is still preserved showing a winged figure wearing an elaborate crown; it used to be thought this figure represented Cyrus, but this view is not now generally accepted. Very probably the buildings at Pasargadae were reproductions in stone of traditional wooden forms. Indeed, it has been written that Pasargadae still retains the character of the settlement of a nomad chief. To make the transition from wood to stone Cyrus needed skilled workmen, and for this reason he imported stonemasons from the newly conquered territories of Ionia and Lydia.

The next years seem to have been spent campaigning in the east, partly to reassert authority over the various east Iranian tribes that had formerly been subject to Astyages, and partly to make fresh conquests. He certainly reached the River Jaxartes (Syr Darya) and may even have got to the Indus. By 539 B.C. Cyrus was ready to turn his attention to Babylon and its wayward king Nabonidus. A conflict had been brewing here for some time. Once – when Cyrus was rebelling against Astyages – he and Nabonidus had been allies, but it was inevitable that sooner or later these two great powers would clash. Relations seriously deteriorated when Nabonidus entered into an alliance with Croesus against the Persians, but what really gave Cyrus his opportunity was the growing unpopularity of Nabonidus in Babylon. He had spent much of his reign away in Arabia and – so it is said – he had grossly neglected his religious duties, including attending the New Year festival in Babylon. There is even a suggestion that he intended to make Sin the chief god of the Babylonian pantheon instead of Marduk. The upshot of all this was that the priests of Marduk, at least, were deeply resentful of Nabonidus and may even have encouraged Cyrus to depose him.

Herodotus has a dramatic account of how the city was captured. He says that first it was unsuccessfully besieged, but that Cyrus then managed to force an entrance by diverting the course of the Euphrates. Consequently, the water-level dropped so low that his men were able to wade along the river-bed and so into the city. More probably, though, the occupation was achieved without force: the Babylonian Chronicle records that Cyrus's capture of the city was entirely peaceable. Whatever may be the truth of this, after the capture of Babylon those parts of the Babylonian Empire that had not already defected to him fell into his hands, and Cyrus was now master of an empire stretching from eastern Iran to the Mediterranean, and from the Black Sea to the borders of Arabia. Now he was truly 'ruler of all the world'.

Fortunately a clay barrel inscribed in Babylonian cuneiform recording the capture of Babylon has survived, and is now in the British Museum. It is known as the 'Cyrus cylinder', and provides us with a remarkable insight into Cyrus's conduct on this occasion. It is clear that he bent over backwards to justify his capture of this, the most prestigious city in the ancient Near East, and he went to some lengths to ingratiate himself with the local population. He claims to have been the agent of Marduk, the god who had been so shamefully wronged by Nabonidus. Images were apparently restored to temples, and many deported peoples were repatriated. Among these were the Jews whom, as we know from the Book of Ezra, 'Nebuchadnezzar the king of Babylon had carried away into Babylon', and in addition he ordered that the temple in Jerusalem should be rebuilt. It was as a result of these latter actions, no doubt, that references to Cyrus in the Old Testament are so sympathetic – for example, he is described in Isaiah as the Lord's anointed.

In matters of religion Cyrus does seem to have been remarkably tolerant. About his own beliefs we can say little: he may have been an early follower of the prophet Zoroaster, or he may have supported the 'daivas', the old Iranian gods of war and strife rejected by Zoroaster. The evidence is inconclusive. In any event, he does not seem to have forced his own views on any of his subject peoples, but of course this religious tolerance may well have been dictated by political expediency. For it seems to have been a hallmark of Cyrus's rule to observe local customs wherever he went, to preserve local institutions if possible and in general to avoid creating disruption.

There is no doubt that he was a brilliant military commander, but clearly he was also remarkably astute. Although supremely confident in his ability to emerge victorious from military campaigns, he obviously realised that the easiest way to keep a hold on such a large empire was to rule by consent rather than by force. This was particularly important during the reign of Cyrus, for the elaborate administrative system that was to prove so effective in the later years of the Achaemenid empire had not yet been set up. It may well have been these sorts of consideration, then, that determined Cyrus's apparently tolerant outlook. If this sounds rather cynical, there was another side to Cyrus's character that we have not yet touched on. He is often regarded as a magnanimous person, and there is some evidence to support this view. We have the stories in Herodotus, for example, of how he treated the deposed Astyages with great consideration until his death, and how at the last moment he felt sorry for Croesus and ordered that the flames of the pyre on which he had been set should be put out. It was partly because of acts of kindness such as these, no doubt, that the memory of Cyrus was universally revered in the ancient world.

Cyrus was eventually killed in 530 B.C. campaigning on his north-eastern frontier against the Massagetae, a people probably living to the east of the Aral Sea. He appears to have crossed the

River Jaxartes, and in the ensuing battle lost his life. His body was taken back to Pasargadae and placed in the imposing stone tomb, set on a stepped platform and with a gabled roof, that is still such an impressive landmark at the site. Claudius James Rich, the famous traveller and orientalist, who visited the tomb in 1821, wrote of it: 'The very venerable appearance of this ruin instantly awed me. I found that I had no right conception of it. I sat for nearly an hour on the steps, contemplating it until the moon rose on it; and I began to think that this in reality must be the tomb of the best, the most illustrious, and the most interesting of Oriental Sovereigns'.

Cambyses

(*Ruled* 530–522 B.C.)

Few historical figures have received such a bad press as Cambyses, king of Persia from 530 to 522 B.C. This is largely due to Herodotus, who depicts him as a vicious tyrant, even a madman. Yet where we have a chance to check Herodotus's story, it emerges that he was very biased. This is not to say that as a character Cambyses should be fully rehabilitated. But it is clear that the old view of him as 'a wild despot, committing many atrocities in his drunkenness' (*Encyclopedia Britannica*, 1929) is no longer acceptable.

Cambyses (old Persian *Kambūjia*) was the elder son of Cyrus by his wife Kassandane, and from an early age was groomed to succeed to the throne. Thus after his capture of Babylon in 539 B.C., Cyrus associated Cambyses with himself in the famous cylinder, and in 538 B.C. Cambyses was made the king of Babylon. Although this arrangement seems to have been short-lived, it was repeated in 530 B.C., probably just before Cyrus marched off to his north-east frontier to fight against the Massagetae. According to Herodotus Cambyses accompanied his father on this campaign, but before crossing the Jaxartes to engage the Massagetae Cyrus sent him back to Persia, having put Croesus under his protection, with instructions to treat him decently should the expedition end in disaster.

In the event, of course, Cyrus was killed. The succession seems to have been smooth enough, but inevitably Cambyses must have spent the next few years consolidating his position. By 526 B.C. he was ready to embark on an enterprise that may even have been planned during the lifetime of his father, the invasion of Egypt. Herodotus lists various reasons for this invasion, the main one being that Cambyses sent to the Egyptian pharaoh Amosis II requesting the services of the best oculist in Egypt. The oculist who was selected was resentful at being sent abroad, and in revenge suggested to Cambyses that he should ask for the hand of Amosis's daughter, knowing that this would cause the pharaoh great distress. This he did, but Amosis sent another girl pretending that it was his daughter. When Cyrus discovered the deceit he was so furious, so the story goes, that he determined to invade Egypt. It is much more probable that the plan had been a long time in germination, and was seen as a logical extension of the conquests of Cyrus. Some pretext may have been drummed up to justify this aggression, but about this we cannot be sure. Herodotus's story that Cambyses was aided in the enterprise by the defection of one of Amosis's Greek mercenaries has much more of a ring of truth about it. This was a man called Phanes from Halicarnassus. He made his way to the Persian court, and suggested that the best way of securing safe conduct through the northern part of the Sinai desert would be by concluding an alliance with the appropriate Arab king. This was done, and the water supplies essential to the Persian army during this crossing of the desert were organised by the Arab king.

Before the invasion actually began Amosis II died and was succeeded by his son Psammetichus III. Near Pelousion on the Delta the Egyptian army was routed and fled in disorder to Memphis. After a siege of some duration the pharaoh surrendered. His life was spared and indeed he might have recovered something of his former glory had he not tried to raise a revolt against his new masters. It was this that signalled his end. Cambyses's next target was Sais in the western Delta, after which he proceeded to Thebes. The whole of Upper and Lower Egypt was now in Cambyses's hands, and in 525 B.C. he became the first king of the 27th Dynasty.

Libya and Cyprus capitulated without a struggle, but offensives against Ethiopia and the people of the Oasis of Amun were less successful. Herodotus tells us that the Ethiopian campaign was a complete disaster, but this cannot be corroborated. According to Herodotus, the army set off without proper preparation and with inadequate provisions. When the food gave out the soldiers were forced to eat the pack-animals, and eventually they were reduced to cannibalism. It was only at this point that Cambyses abandoned the campaign and returned to Thebes. However this may be, the southern limit of Egypt remained at the First Cataract after Cambyses as it had been before him. The force of 50,000 men sent across the desert to the Oasis of Amun (Siwa) was, according to Herodotus, overwhelmed by a sandstorm before it reached there and completely disappeared. The story about the disappearance of this army may or may not be true, but it has not failed to attract popular interest and imagination ever since. For example, generations of pre- and post-war English schoolboys will remember that in one of his adventures the lost army was found by the redoubtable Biggles. From time to time there have been reports in the press about the discovery of this army, most recently in 1977 when it was reported that an Egyptian archaeological expedition had found in the western desert thousands of bones, swords and spears which it was assumed represented the vanished army of Cambyses. However, none of these reports has been confirmed.

It is concerning Cambyses's behaviour in Egypt that Herodotus becomes really scathing about him. In particular, he alleges that shortly after his return to Memphis following the unsuccessful Ethiopian campaign a sacred Apis bull appeared among the Egyptians. This was a bull with distinctive markings thought to represent the god Apis who became manifest among the Egyptians from time to time, and whenever he did so the people celebrated. Cambyses was annoyed to find the people celebrating, and thought it to be connected with his recent setbacks. When he discovered the festival was about the Apis bull, he ordered it to be brought before him and pierced it in the thigh with his dagger. The festival was thus broken up, and Apis subsequently died from its wound. However, this story seems to be a complete fabrication. The Egyptian evidence shows that a sacred Apis bull was buried in the Serapeum at Memphis in 525 B.C. in a sarcophagus dedicated by Cambyses himself. Further, another sacred bull is known to have replaced this one, and he survived into the reign of Darius. As he got this story so wrong, it is probable that Herodotus's other stories about Egypt should be treated with scepticism. These are that when Cambyses reached Sais the body of the late pharaoh Amosis was removed from its tomb and wickedly desecrated, being first mutilated and then burnt, a practice contrary to the beliefs of both Egyptians and Persians. Herodotus also claims that Cambyses broke open ancient tombs and examined the bodies, and made unauthorised entry into temples.

In fact, Cambyses seems to have been careful to follow Egyptian customs and religious practices. Thus, on the sarcophagus for the dead Apis bull he is depicted wearing pharaonic dress and kneeling before the bull in the standard Egyptian posture. Also, we have the testimony of one Udjeharresne, who had been a naval commander under Psammetichus and was made Cambyses's chief physician and director of the palace. He records that Cambyses restored the Temple of Neth at Sais to its former glory, and caused it to be provided with revenues. Of course, Udjeharresne was probably a collaborator and his testimony should be treated accordingly, but it does represent the alternative to Herodotus's biased statements. Very probably Herodotus's hostility towards Cambyses is to be explained by the fact that his main informants were the Egyptian priests. They had good reason to dislike Cambyses, for it seems from the later Demotic Chronicle that he reduced temple revenues and forced the priests to provide sacrificial animals themselves. Also, Herodotus's visit to Egypt – shortly after 450 B.C. – was fairly soon after the revolt of Inaros had been put down, probably with some harshness, and anti-Persian feelings were no doubt running high.

If, then, Herodotus's account of Cambyses's dealings with the Egyptians are so unreliable, what are we to make of Cambyses's supposed relations with his fellow Persians whom, we are told, he treated 'with the savagery of a lunatic'? As examples of this behaviour Herodotus related a number of stories. There is the killing of his sister whom he had married and was expecting his child; in a fit of temper Cambyses kicked her, she had a miscarriage and died. Then there is the story about the son of his trusted servant Prexaspes, whom he shot through the heart with an arrow to prove that he was neither mad nor drunk. Again, it is alleged that on some trifling charge he arrested twelve Persians of the highest rank and buried them alive, head downwards. These stories cannot be dismissed lightly, and indeed it is possible that Cambyses may have been something of a tyrant – he was after all an absolute monarch – but neither, in view of Herodotus's known bias, can they be taken at their face value.

Yet the real scandal of Cambyses's reign concerns his alleged treatment of his brother Bardiya. Stripped of its embellishments, Herodotus's story is that Bardiya (Greek Smerdis) accompanied Cambyses to Egypt, but was sent back home because the king was jealous of him. Then Cambyses had a dream in which he saw Bardiya sitting on the throne, and believing this to mean that he intended to usurp it he gave instructions that Bardiya should be secretly murdered. Some time later there was a revolt in Persia, at the head of which were two Magi, members of the Median priestly caste, one of whom pretended to be the murdered Bardiya. The news reached Cambyses while he was in Syria, and he determined to march to Susa with all possible speed. As he was mounting his horse, though, the chape fell off the end of his scabbard and the exposed point of the sword pierced his thigh and he subsequently died from the wound. This would have been in 522 B.C. After a lapse of some months the impostor was killed by a group of seven conspirators, one of whom was Darius, who then seized the throne. So runs the account of Herodotus, and on the whole it agrees with the version of these events recorded by Darius in his Bisitun inscription. The only significant difference is that according to Darius Bardiya was murdered *before* Cambyses set off for Egypt. Darius also names the impostor as Gaumata.

It is perhaps not surprising that the two accounts should be so similar, because of course it is possible that Herodotus's source was Darius's inscription or one of the copies of it that were probably distributed around the empire. In any event, some scholars have chosen to regard this version of events as unlikely, thinking it much more probable that the person whom Darius killed was the *real* Bardiya and not an impostor. This is an attractive theory, but it cannot be substantiated. In the absence of proof to the contrary, it is much safer to stick to the traditional view of events.

This would mean, of course, that Cambyses did indeed kill his own brother, a deed for which Herodotus indicts him severely. Also, the fact that there was an uprising while he was away may be taken as a sign that Cambyses was not very popular. Very probably his behaviour towards his fellow Persians did tend to be arrogant and dictatorial. However the worst excesses of his behaviour are not proven, and Herodotus as we have seen was certainly biased. On the positive side Cambyses added Egypt and Cyprus to the Persian Empire, no mean achievement when we consider that he was only on the throne for seven years. In addition he held all the territory acquired by his father. In short, Cyrus and Cambyses may be considered as the empire-builders; it was left to Darius to consolidate their gains.

Darius the Great

(*Ruled* 522–486 B.C.)

For hundreds of years travellers passing along the great Khorasan road, one of the great arterial routes linking east and west, have gazed in awe at the rock-carving on a cliff high above the road at Bisitun near Kermanshah in western Iran. It is a legacy of Darius, perhaps the greatest of the Achaemenid kings, who ruled from 522 to 486 B.C. The relief shows him with his foot on the prostrate Gaumata, behind whom are standing nine rebel leaders roped together at the neck and with their arms bound behind their backs. We have already described in the chapter on Cambyses how after his death a priest seized the throne, claiming to be Bardiya the brother of Cambyses, but in all probability an impostor named Gaumata. This impostor was removed by a band of seven conspirators, one of whom was Darius.

Herodotus has an amusing account of how the conspirators decided which of them should be king. They agreed that before dawn they would take their horses to the outskirts of the city, and whosoever's horse should be the first to neigh after the sun rose should be king. Now Darius had a cunning groom called Oebares, who devised a clever plan to make sure that his master was successful. In the middle of the night he took a mare to the selected spot and allowed Darius's horse to mount her. Early next morning when Darius's horse reached the place where the mare had been tethered he started forward and neighed. Another version records that Oebares rubbed the mare's genitals with his hand and when the sun rose drew his hand across the nostrils of Darius's horse, causing it to snort and neigh.

Darius was the son of a Persian noble called Hystaspes (Old Persian Wishtaspa), and in the Bisitun inscription and elsewhere he claims to be of royal descent. However it seems clear that his claim to the throne was far from being universally accepted, for in his first year there were a number of rebellions. There were uprisings in Elam, Babylonia, Armenia, Parthia and even Persia and Media, but these Darius suppressed in a forceful fashion. He himself boasts in the Bisitun inscription that he fought nineteen battles and took captive nine kings (those shown on the relief) in just one year. While the time taken to deal with these rebels might be disputed, there can be no doubt that he stamped his authority on the empire with conviction.

In the first half of his reign Darius and his generals were campaigning in many different parts of the empire, but two campaigns in particular stand out. His expedition to India resulted in the annexation of Sind and possibly the Punjab; the wealthy province of India was an important addition to the empire, for it became the most heavily taxed province, paying annually 360 talents of gold-dust. Less successful was Darius's expedition against the Scythians, a nomadic people living on the steppes to the north of the Black Sea. The reasons for this campaign are obscure, but perhaps Herodotus is not far from the mark when he implies that Darius, with immense revenues and huge resources of manpower at his disposal, was simply looking for fresh fields to conquer. In any event, Darius crossed the Bosphorus, marched through Thrace and went round the Black Sea as far as the mouth of the Danube, where he met the Ionians who had been sent ahead by boat with instructions to bridge the river. The army was therefore able to cross over, but they failed to engage the Scythians. As Darius and his army advanced so the Scythians withdrew, seeking at all costs to avoid a pitched battle. Try as he would Darius could not get to grips with them, and in the end he had no alternative but to withdraw.

But it is not for his military exploits that Darius is given the epithet 'Great'. He deserves this for his great organising ability and his considerable administrative achievements. Herodotus calls him a 'tradesman', and while some scholars have seen this as a term of disparagement it is more probably a genuine tribute to his good book-keeping. Under Darius the empire was formally divided into provinces (satrapies), and provincial governors (satraps) were appointed. Herodotus lists twenty of these provinces, but there may have been more. During the reigns of Cyrus and Cambyses there had been no fixed tribute, with much of the revenue coming from gifts. Now, however, each of the provinces was assessed for tax purposes and obliged to provide a fixed annual tribute. For the purposes of this assessment it was often necessary to know more about the area in question, and this led to some interesting geographical research. Thus Scylax of Caryanda was entrusted with the task of exploring India. He started from Gandhara, sailed down the Kabul River as far as its confluence with the Indus, and then sailed right down the Indus and into the Arabian Sea, carefully recording everything he saw in a book which sadly has not survived. From there his route took him along the southern coast of Iran, right round the Arabian peninsula and up the Red Sea to Suez. Darius also sent Scylax to investigate the Black Sea and the Caspian Sea.

Among Darius's many other achievements he was the first Persian king to mint coins, the Old Persian cuneiform script was introduced during his reign for monumental purposes, and communications were much improved. It is now for the first time that we hear of the Royal Road, a major highway linking Sardis and Susa with posting stations at regular intervals all along its length. Darius also built a canal connecting the Red Sea with the Nile, a forerunner of the modern Suez canal. The project had been started one hundred years earlier by the pharaoh Necho II but soon abandoned. Under Darius 52 miles (84 km) were dug out in ten years, a formidable undertaking. In 497 B.C. Darius travelled to Egypt for the inauguration of the canal, and the event is commemorated by a stela inscribed in Old Persian, Elamite, Akkadian and Egyptian hieroglyphs.

Also in Egypt qanats or underground water channels were probably introduced under Darius. He also ordered that the laws should be codified, and temples, at least in Sais, were restored. This is hardly the behaviour of a tyrant, a label which has often been applied to Darius. As far as the Greek authors were concerned, of course, Darius like other Persian kings *was* a tyrant, but it must be remembered they were far from being impartial commentators. Certainly, like many other oriental sovereigns Darius was an absolute monarch, but there is no evidence that he behaved in the unreasonable way usually associated with tyrants. Admittedly some of the provinces were extremely heavily taxed, and a number of people were deported during his reign – for example, inhabitants of Miletus were resettled near the head of the Persian Gulf and a number of Thracian tribes were transferred to Asia – but in these respects he was merely doing the sort of thing that had been going on for centuries, notably under the Assyrians.

Any discussion about the life and times of Darius would be incomplete without a brief description of Persepolis, which is still one of the most impressive archaeological sites in the world. Building here started in Darius's reign and continued under his successors. Curiously none of the Greek authors refers to Persepolis, perhaps because it was neither an administrative centre nor a capital. In fact the main purpose of the site seems to have been ceremonial, and festivals such as that on the occasion of the New Year were probably celebrated here regularly. The site is located in the heart of Fars province, about 27 miles (43 km) south-west of Pasargadae. Built on a huge terrace are a number of monumental buildings, all characterised by the widespread use of columns. There are palaces, a building known as the Harem, a vast building called the Treasury which incorporated store-rooms and military quarters, the Hall of the Hundred Columns founded by Xerxes and, most spectacular, the Apadana or Audience Hall of Darius. Here the façades and stairways were covered with reliefs showing tribute-bearers from all corners of the empire. There are Bactrians bringing a camel and vessels of precious metal, Lydians with horses and gold bracelets, and so on. In spite of the ravages of time and Alexander the Great, by extraordinarily good fortune many of these reliefs are still in their original positions at Persepolis and provide a dramatic illustration of the power and splendour of the ancient Persian empire.

But for all his considerable achievements, in 492 B.C. Darius embarked upon an enterprise that in the end was to contribute substantially to the downfall of the Achaemenid empire. This was the war with Greece, which although a small and disunited country was capable of spirited resistance and resoundingly demonstrated that the Persians were far from being invincible. Although the war petered out in 479 B.C., the animosity it engendered was not forgotten and ultimately resulted in Alexander the Great marching through the Achaemenid empire and destroying Persepolis. It was perhaps foolish of Darius ever to have got involved in this war, for even if the Persians had succeeded in conquering Greece it is doubtful whether they could ever have held a country largely surrounded by sea so far from the heart of their own empire. What, then, was the background to this conflict?

In the last years of his life Darius was very much occupied with the Ionian revolt and its aftermath. In an attempt to throw off the Persian yoke, the Ionians in Asia Minor sought and obtained assistance from Athens and Eretria and proceeded to sack Sardis. The revolt was fairly easily suppressed, but this interference in Asian affairs by Greek mainland states must have convinced Darius that there would be no lasting peace in Asia Minor while Greek intervention remained possible. Consequently he put Mardonius, son of Gobryas, in charge of a large army and fleet; this army crossed the Hellespont and advanced through Europe, with Eretria and Athens as its main objectives. Macedonia was subjugated, but the fleet was severely damaged in a gale off the Athos peninsula and the army was mauled in a night-time attack by the Brygi, a Thracian tribe. As a result of these setbacks Mardonius was forced to retreat, but, undeterred, Darius determined to send a still larger force in 490 B.C. This was under the command of Artaphernes, his nephew, and a Mede called Datis. After capturing Eretria with little difficulty, the troops sailed for Attica. Crossing the Gulf of Euboea, they landed on the coast near the plain of Marathon. Here they were opposed by the Athenians under the command of Miltiades. In response to an appeal for help the Spartans arrived too late to participate in the fighting, but the Athenians were joined by some troops from Plataea. In the ensuing battle the Athenians were victorious, chiefly it is claimed through the superior military tactics of Miltiades. He deployed his force so that it was weak in the centre and strong on the wings. When battle was joined the Persians forged ahead in the middle but lost ground on the wings. Consequently the Athenians were able to execute a pincer movement. But it would be wrong to think of this as a great military encounter. The number of casualties given by Herodotus – 192 Athenians, which is probably an understatement, and 6,400 Persians, which is probably an overstatement – are relatively small, and, far from being routed, most of the Persian force was apparently able to get back on board ship. Nevertheless, Athens was saved for the time being.

Next, the Persian fleet sailed round the peninsula to Athens, hoping to find the city unprepared, but the Athenian army had hurried back from Marathon and was there before them. First to arrive, though, had been the athlete Pheidippides, whose epic run is still commemorated in the modern marathon race. Datis had little alternative but to withdraw. When news of the defeat at Marathon reached Darius he at once began to make preparations for a third invasion. Shortly afterwards there was also a rebellion in Egypt. But before he could tackle either of these matters he died, in 486 B.C. He was buried in a rock-cut tomb, still visible today, at Naqsh-i Rustam near Persepolis.

Xerxes

(*Ruled* 486–465 B.C.)

'If we crush the Athenians and their neighbours in the Peloponnese, we shall so extend the empire of Persia that its boundaries will be God's own sky, so that the sun will not look down upon any land beyond the boundaries of what is ours' – so, according to Herodotus (Penguin translation), spoke Xerxes, king of Persia from 486 to 465 B.C.

But there was much more behind the Persian invasion of Greece than this. Indeed, there is some indication that at the beginning of his reign Xerxes was not enthusiastic about attacking Greece, and it was not until his sixth year that he in fact did so. What ultimately persuaded him to follow this course of action is not at all clear, but there may have been a genuine fear that if he did not take the initiative then the Greeks themselves would invade the Asiatic mainland. After all, in the reign of his father Darius the Greek states had come to the assistance of the Ionians, and it had been the Athenians acting in conjunction with the Ionians who had sacked Sardis. It was this that prompted Darius to launch his ill-fated expedition to Greece that ended in ignominy at Marathon in 490 B.C. A contributory factor in Xerxes's decision, then, must have been a desire to complete his father's unfinished business. Not to have done so would surely have resulted in considerable loss of face.

Xerxes was not the automatic heir to the throne, as Darius had older sons from his marriage to the daughter of Gobryas. But Xerxes was an offspring of Darius's marriage to Atossa, the daughter of Cyrus and sister of Cambyses. He was therefore a direct descendant of the founder of the empire and this, coupled with the fact that he was born after Darius had become king, seems to have secured his right to the throne and he was recognised as heir presumptive a few years before Darius's death.

He was in his early thirties when he succeeded his father. Before he could turn his attention to Greece, however, he had to deal with a rebellion in Egypt that had broken out in 486 B.C., probably inspired by the Persian reversal at Marathon. This uprising was finally put down in Xerxes's second year, according to Herodotus with a good deal of severity. He says that Xerxes 'reduced the country to a condition of worse servitude that it had ever been in the previous reign'. For Egypt he did practically nothing: there are no records of building works during his reign, and there is some evidence that he confiscated temple property. Worse, Xerxes ignored Egyptian protocol and went to Egypt as the king of Persia. His brother Achaemenes was installed as governor, and thenceforth Egypt was merely another Persian province. There was trouble too in Babylonia which was harshly suppressed. The city of Babylon was partially destroyed and the famous gold statue of Marduk was removed from Esagila, the temple built by Nebuchadnezzar, and melted down. No longer did the Persian king pay homage to Marduk, and no longer did he describe himself foremost as king of Babylon.

The force that Xerxes assembled for his invasion of Greece was huge, though it is scarcely likely to have amounted to the 1,800,000 fighting men that Herodotus says were taken across to Europe. This army was supported by an enormous fleet, probably having more than 1,000 triremes at its disposal. Both army and fleet were composed of men drawn from all the nations of the empire, including Persians, Medes, Lydians, Assyrians, Phoenicians, Indians, and so on. Further, as both army and fleet got nearer to their objective, their numbers were swelled by peoples anxious to show their allegiance to the Persian king. First, however, the Hellespont had to be crossed, and this was achieved by building two bridges of boats. Other preparations included cutting a canal through the Athos peninsula to avoid the disaster that had overtaken Darius's fleet in 492 B.C. By the early summer of 480 B.C. all was ready, and Xerxes crossed over into Europe.

The army marched through Thrace, Macedonia and Thessaly without check, and it was not until they came to the pass at Thermopylae that they encountered serious resistance. Here the Greek allies made a stand in an effort to keep the invaders out of central Greece. The Greek forces occupying the pass at Thermopylae were relatively small, but their position was a strong one. The pass was narrow, and the superior numbers on the Persian side were of little advantage. After waiting a few days the Persian army attacked, but they were not able to force their way through. For two days there was a stalemate, but on the evening of the second day a certain Ephialtes told the Persians about a mountain track leading over the hills to Thermopylae. A detachment of Persian troops followed this track during the night, brushing aside the Phocians who had been detailed to guard it, and at dawn were in a position to attack the Greeks from behind. Most of the confederate troops, seeing the hopelessness of their position, withdrew, leaving behind Leonidas and his 300 Spartans together with the Boeotians to make a last stand, presumably in order to cover the retreat of the remainder of the army. All were annihilated, and the way was now open for Xerxes to advance on Athens.

Meanwhile there had been some naval engagements, and although these were inconclusive the Greek fleet, seeing the turn of events at Thermopylae, withdrew to Salamis to cover the expected battle at the Isthmus of Corinth for control of the Peloponnese. The Athenians too withdrew to Salamis, leaving an almost deserted Athens for Xerxes to occupy. But his success was short-lived. The two fleets clashed in the straits of Salamis, and the Greeks under Themistocles won a convincing victory. On the Persian side there was great loss of life, largely because, it is claimed, most of the Persians were unable to swim and any that were shipwrecked were drowned. Demoralised, the Persian fleet withdrew to the Hellespont. Xerxes was now in a dilemma. He could not advance into the Peloponnese without naval support, and yet he was reluctant to abandon his campaign. So he compromised, leaving Mardonius behind in northern Greece with a selection of picked troops and himself returning to Asia with the remainder.

After wintering in Macedonia and Thessaly, in 479 B.C.

Mardonius again advanced into Attica and proceeded to Athens which, as before, was deserted. In the words of Herodotus he 'burnt Athens and reduced to complete ruin anything that remained standing'. For this act the Persians have been much indicted, but in fairness to them it must be pointed out that it was a standard practice of ancient armies to destroy captured cities. The Athenians had participated in the sack of Sardis in 499 B.C., and Alexander the Great was to burn Persepolis in 330 B.C. In any event, largely as a result of Athenian pressure the Spartans and their allies were eventually persuaded to carry the war to the enemy and they advanced northwards from their position on the Isthmus of Corinth. The two armies came together on the plain of Plataea near Thebes, the Persians under Mardonius and the Greeks commanded by Pausanias of Sparta. In the ensuing mêlée, the Persians were routed and Mardonius himself was killed. Those Persian troops under Artabazos which had not been committed to the battle, returned with all haste to Asia, crossing over via the Bosphorus.

Shortly after Plataea, on the afternoon of the same day if popular tradition is to be believed, the Persians were overtaken by another disaster at Mykale on the coast of Asia Minor. The remnants of the Persian fleet, having seen Xerxes safely across the Hellespont, had proceeded to sail round the coast of Asia Minor. Near Samos they were intercepted by a Greek fleet under Leotychidas of Sparta, and forced to beach their boats. In the following land battle the Persians were again beaten, and Xerxes's attempt to force the Greeks into submission was now at an end. Never again would a Persian army cross over into Europe.

The repulse of Xerxes's invasion has often been heralded as one of the great turning-points in the history of Europe, even in the history of civilisation. Such views are fuelled by the Greek authors, who sometimes refer to the Persians as 'barbarians' and polarise the conflict as one between slavery and freedom. Many commentators have been happy enough to go along with these views, but they are not really borne out by the available evidence. For one thing, there are many indications that the Persians were prepared to assimilate all that was best in the lands they conquered, and had they succeeded in overwhelming Greece, so far from stamping out democracy they might well have introduced an element of it into their own system. Indeed, after the Ionian revolt had been suppressed in the reign of Darius, Mardonius promoted democratic rule in the mainland Ionian cities. In fact, each side had much to give to the other, and it is perhaps a pity that west and east were to go their separate ways until the reign of Alexander the Great.

To return to Xerxes, there is no doubt that his conduct of the war left much to be desired. The invasion of Greece was a rash undertaking in the beginning, and subsequently Xerxes made a series of tactical blunders. For example, it was a mistake to commit his fleet to battle at Salamis when to do so was apparently unnecessary. If Herodotus is to be believed, the Greeks were divided about the desirability of making a stand at Salamis, but the Persians forced the issue. After the battle Xerxes was in a precarious position, as theoretically the Greeks could have sailed to the Hellespont and cut off his retreat to Asia. His handling of the war, then, was poor, and resulted in considerable losses for the empire including, for the time being, Cyprus. Further, the way that he put down uprisings in Egypt and Babylonia was guaranteed to incite further unrest. But for all this, there is no reason to suppose that he was the sort of megalomaniac depicted in Greek sources. This hostility is reflected in a number of stories in Herodotus, such as Xerxes ordering that the Hellespont be given 300 lashes after the bridges had been swept away by a storm. Again, on his march through Greece Xerxes is supposed to have buried alive nine native boys and nine girls as a sacrifice to a local god. Herodotus goes on to claim that burying people alive was a Persian custom. This is hard to credit, and raises doubts about Herodotus's reliability as a story-teller.

In religious matters, Xerxes seems like his predecessors to have been remarkably tolerant. For instance, Herodotus tells us that after his capture of Athens he ordered the Athenian exiles who were serving with the Persian forces to go up into the Acropolis and offer sacrifices there. About Xerxes's personal beliefs, as with the other Achaemenid monarchs, we are on difficult ground. Some scholars have assumed that they were Zoroastrians, and in the case of Xerxes this view is reinforced by the fact that in inscriptions from Persepolis he claims that with the help of Ahuramazda he destroyed a sanctuary of the daivas, the ancient gods of war and strife that are known to have been rejected by Zoroaster. However, there are some difficulties in accepting the Achaemenid kings as orthodox Zoroastrians. For example, there is no mention of Zoroaster in the classical authors who commented so fully on Achaemenid history, and the Achaemenids buried their dead rather than exposing corpses to the elements to avoid pollution of the earth. It is perhaps safest to assume that they believed in a dualistic system, with opposing forces of good and evil, which may be parallel to the tradition preserved in the Avesta, the Zoroastrian holy book, but did not necessarily derive from the teachings of Zoroaster.

The latter part of Xerxes's life seems to have been spent mostly in Iran. We know little about his activities during this time, but he was clearly much occupied with building projects at Persepolis, where he made a substantial contribution. Many of the structures now standing were completed or built during his reign.

During this period he was also occupied, apparently, with harem intrigues and domestic difficulties of a sort that it is difficult to imagine Cyrus or Darius getting involved with. A reflection of these is probably to be found in the Book of Esther, which though largely fictional clearly contains elements of truth. The book describes how Esther, a Jewess, became the wife of King Ahasuerus, usually identified as Xerxes. From her cousin Mordecai she learns of a plot to kill the king, and the conspirators are arrested and found guilty. Esther and Mordecai are thus assured of the king's favour, and are able to prevent a massacre of the Jews that is being planned by the king's favourite, Haman. Whatever may be the truth of all this, in 465 B.C. Xerxes was assassinated, killed in his palace by the general Artabanos acting in concert with the eunuch of the bedchamber. So passed away a monarch who had the ambition of his predecessors but lacked their ability. The seeds of decline in the mighty edifice constructed by Cyrus were already apparent.

Greece

Cleisthenes

(*fl.* 525 B.C.)

In the late seventh and early sixth centuries B.C. the Greek city of Sicyon, on the southern shore of the Gulf of Corinth, a fertile and prosperous area, was ruled over by a dynasty of autocrats ('tyrants', in the Greek terminology), the descendants of Orthagoras. In the first part of the sixth century the dynast was called Cleisthenes. As part of his dynastic policies, he wanted to marry off his daughter, Agariste, to a well-connected young man, and therefore announced a gathering to which all suitable candidates were invited. They came from various parts of Greece (it is interesting to notice that in such a dynastic marriage the fixed boundaries of Greek city-state patriotism were easily broken). Some came from Athens, including Hippocleides, son of Teisander. As part of the tests imposed on them the suitors were required to entertain their fellow guests at a dinner party. Hippocleides performed a dance, which he ended by standing on his head on one of the low tables by the side of the dining couch, moving his legs in time to the music, a performance that was, to say the least, undignified. 'O Hippocleides,' said Cleisthenes, 'you have danced away your marriage.' To which Hippocleides replied, 'Hippocleides doesn't care', a saying which became the earliest catch-phrase in the history of European entertainment.

Instead, Agariste was married to another Athenian, Megacles, a member of the Alcmeonid family, which had disgraced itself by its responsibility for the sacrilegious slaughter of Cylon's followers at the altar of Athena on the Acropolis (for this, see the life of Solon). The family connexions are interesting, and important. The Alcmeonids formed a powerful group, but are frequently put in the shade by other combinations of families. Hippocleides belongs to the family of the Philaids, which had at an early date intermarried with the dynasts of Corinth, the family of Cypselos, who controlled the part of Greece adjacent to Sicyon; one wonders whether Hippocleides's performance on the table was intended to sabotage an alliance which he did not particularly welcome. Megacles, on the other hand, was probably anxious for dynastic connexions to strengthen the position of his own family at Athens, which was certainly under a cloud since the time of Cylon's conspiracy.

The third important family group at Athens at this time was that of Peisistratos (who claimed descent from a Homeric hero, Nestor, King of Pylos). He had estates in the area of Marathon; rural aristocrats found it was more difficult to dominate the faction politics at Athens. He had been a friend and associate of Solon, and was responsible for a successful war against Athens's neighbour Megara which gave Athens control of Salamis. His various attempts to win power at Athens, relying on prestige and marriage alliances, came to nothing, and finally, about the middle of the sixth century, he seized power with foreign military support, provided by friends in Thessaly, by which he set himself up as a tyrant. Athens flourished as a result; the Acropolis, in particular, was embellished with splendid sculpture. Peisistratos's rule was mild; there was no slaughter of his opponents, or confiscation of land, and he chose instead to develop the work of Solon, strengthening the Athenian economy and protecting the ordinary Athenians from the greed and oppressiveness of the powerful aristocratic families. They, of course, found their greed – and their political ambition – restricted, but there were other ways of making wealth, particularly by exploiting the resources of the northern Aegean.

In this period, the fortunes of Megacles and his family varied. His oldest child was a daughter, who featured in a brief political (and so marriage) alliance with Peisistratos, in perhaps 557 B.C. Megacles's first son was named after his maternal grandfather, Cleisthenes, and it is he who emerges as head of the family, in the political sense, after his father's death (the date of which is uncertain, but probably falls in the time while Peisistratos was tyrant). Whether the family had remained in Athens all this time is uncertain. The breach between Megacles and Peisistratos may well have been so severe that some, at least, of the Alcmeonids went into exile when Peisistratos firmly established himself as tyrant; certainly they later boasted of their stalwart hatred of the tyranny. Despite this, an inscription found in the Athenian agora records that in a year equivalent to 525/4 B.C., three years after Peisistratos's death, Cleisthenes, the son of Megacles, was not only in Athens, but was elected archon for that year. By this time Peisistratos's son Hippias was ruling; he may have attempted a reconciliation with the rival aristocratic families, but it came to nothing. His rule was challenged, he became harsher and more autocratic, and Cleisthenes found it prudent to leave Athens, to continue his opposition to the tyrant from outside.

The murder of Hippias's brother, as the result of a personal quarrel aimed at Hippias himself, increased the tyrant's harshness, and a group of exiles, including Alcmeonids, seized a frontier stronghold, Leipsydrion, with the intention of overthrowing him by force. The attempt failed, with loss of life, and the disaster was bewailed in a song which was remembered – and sung – at aristocratic drinking parties for a long, long time to come.

Despite this exile, Cleisthenes still had access to considerable wealth, and with this he undertook the necessary guarantees for the reconstruction of the Temple of Apollo at Delphi which had been ruined in one of the rock-falls that regularly occur there. The contract specified that the temple was to be rebuilt in local lime-stone, but Cleisthenes, at his own expense, paid for part at least of the work to be done in high-quality island marble, with all the extra transport costs involved in shipping it from Paros, in the Aegean, and up from the coast to the sanctuary. He thus gained the support of the priests who manipulated the Delphic oracle, and they began to put pressure on the Spartans (who had a close connexion with Delphi), telling them to overthrow the tyrants at Athens. This, at least, is the version told by Herodotus, who probably got his information from the Alcmeonid family in the fifth century. It is equally likely that the Spartans did not need to be pressurised by Delphi. In the earlier part of the sixth century they had been the allies of Croesus of Lydia, and though they did not intervene when he was overthrown by Cyrus the Great of Persia, it is clear that they were hostile to the Persian Empire. That empire tended to rule through local autocrats, and the Greek tyrants therefore instinctively turned to Persia for support. One of the two Spartan kings of this period, Cleomenes, appears as the instigator of a Spartan policy aimed at strengthening Greek opposition to Persia, and the removal of potentially pro-Persian tyrants was part of this policy (in addition, such autocratic administrations were contrary to Sparta's aristocratic system).

For whatever reason, Cleomenes decided to intervene at Athens. He arrived with a small army, but one which was more than sufficient to deal with the only troops Hippias had available, mercenaries recruited from other parts of Greece – the Athenian citizen soldiers had been deprived of their arms and armour, at least since the murder of Hippias's brother. Hippias fled to the Persian Empire; his supporters were overthrown. The sequel was a struggle for power, in which it is interesting to note that, despite the stories about the Delphic oracle, Cleomenes the Spartan did not support Cleisthenes. The victor was another aristocrat called Isagoras, and he set about creating a system at Athens which restricted full rights of citizenship to the relatively well off – many poorer Athenians, who had had their rights guaranteed under the tyranny, were deprived of their citizenship. Cleisthenes, beaten in the power struggle, took these people into alliance, and in a coup secured the downfall of Isagoras. This was not what the Spartans expected, or wanted, and Cleomenes, with a small force, again intervened, seizing the Acropolis. But by now the Athenian citizen soldiers had been rearmed, they rallied round Cleisthenes, and besieged the Spartans in the Acropolis. Cleomenes was forced to give way ignominiously.

This was, for Athens, a historic moment. Herodotus records (or, more likely, invents) a debate at Sparta on the action they should take. The Spartans considered the restoration of Hippias, but were argued down by the Corinthians, who spoke about their own evil experiences under their tyrants. Isagoras, on the other hand, could not command the support of the Athenian people, and the Spartans therefore were forced to acquiesce in the setting up of a form of government which necessarily had broad-based support, rather than one which depended on the narrow factional interests of the more powerful aristocratic families. It was Cleisthenes's task to bring about a reformation of the Athenian system which guaranteed not only the rights of all citizens, but put the real basis of the constitution in their hands, reducing the danger of aristocratic, factional domination.

His reforms are described by Herodotus, and in a treatise on the Athenian constitution which was rediscovered in the last century on a papyrus document, found in Egypt and now in the British Museum. The reforms are ingenious, but complicated. The city state of Athens had been formed, gradually, in the early years of the first millennium B.C. by the coalition of different groups of peoples living in the region known as Attica. The unifying element seems to have been that they all spoke the same dialect of the Greek language, which is related to that of the eastern Greeks, in the islands of the central Aegean and on the coast of Asia Minor, and which differed from the dialects of their neighbours to the west, south and north. With this, of course, went other elements which they shared in common, particularly in religion. They believed this unity went back at least into the Bronze Age, and that the state was originally unified by a founding hero, Theseus. By ancestry, all true Athenians belonged to a 'tribe' and this arrangement is found, in fact, in all Greek cities. The traditional Athenian tribes differ in name from those of their Dorian neighbours, but are shared, along with their dialect, with the Ionic neighbours to the east.

Despite this belief in a common origin and ultimate unity, politically Athens had been divided; it is these divisions which had been forcibly suppressed by Peisistratos, but which had immediately re-emerged on the overthrow of the tyrant. Essentially the divisions were geographical, and consisted firstly of the central plain, round the Acropolis (that is, the area now occupied by the urban sprawl of modern Athens) together with the adjacent plain of Eleusis. To the east of this are the mountains of Hymettus and Pentelicus, separated by an easy but distinct pass; beyond these mountains are more plains, divided from each other by lesser ranges of hills, some of them being fair-sized areas, and including substantial populations. Behind Pentelicus there are still further inhabited areas, especially the plain of Marathon where Peisistratos had his estates. The aristocratic leaders of Athens held estates in these different regions, whose inhabitants formed their supporters. It was the relatively well-to-do plainsmen of the area around Athens who were the most powerful, and who were attempting to exclude the inhabitants of other regions, in particular, from

citizenship. Cleisthenes and the Alcmeonids are associated with
the area beyond Hymettus, though they may well have held other
estates elsewhere. Here were their burial grounds, whose memo-
rials and statues had been savaged in the upheavals at the end of
the tyranny (the splendid statue of Phrasicleia, found recently at
Merenda in eastern Attica, the ancient Myrhinous, and now on
display in the National Museum of Athens, may come from an
Alcmeonid memorial destroyed at this time).

Cleisthenes used these regional divisions of Attica as the basis of
his new system, but at the same time ended their separation. Each
of the three main regions of Attica, which he termed the city, the
coast and the 'inland' (not quite coinciding with the earlier,
traditional division and neighbours) was divided into ten. These
divisions comprised existing villages, grouped together as necessary, while the city of Athens itself was divided into similarly sized
units. One division was then taken from each group of ten;
together these formed a tribe (so each division was called a 'third
part', a trittys, a 'thirding'). There were thus ten new tribes
formed, each cutting across the regional divisions of Attica, but
each having, in its trittys, a local unity within the region. These
new tribes now formed the basis of the Athenian political system.
Each tribe contributed fifty members to a council, which had
important administrative responsibilities, checking the magistrates and, above all, being responsible for the presentation of
business to the citizen assembly. Election to this was random, by
lot, and only one re-election was permitted, and that only after an
interval of ten years. It was thus impossible for the aristocrats to
control the council, and this must have weakened their domination over the citizens' assembly.

The tribes were given names, chosen by the Delphic oracle,
based on those of traditional Athenian heroes, and a monument
commemorating them was set up in the central meeting place of
the city, the Agora. All citizens had their names registered on the
lists kept in the village or village group. Newborn sons had to be
presented to the village officials for registration, and once this had
been done, and the child thus acknowledged by his fellow villa-
gers, his right to citizenship was secure; there was no longer any
question that an aristocratic faction could exclude people from
citizenship. It is doubtful whether any real outsiders acquired
citizenship as a result of Cleisthenes's reforms – citizens had to
possess land, and as land could not be acquired by non-citizens it
was not really possible to buy one's way into citizenship; those
who had been excluded by Isagoras and his friends were merely
poor, not immigrant foreigners (though Cleisthenes was misrep-

resented as having admitted such people to citizenship by his opponents).

By this means Cleisthenes established on a lasting basis the Athenian democratic system. Yet it is more than a reform for political purposes, and therein lies its strength, and its cleverness. The origin of it is almost certainly a series of reforms which had been carried out at Sicyon by Orthagoras, Cleisthenes's ancestor. He too had taken a traditional tribal system and reorganised it, though the details of what he did have been hopelessly distorted in attempts to ridicule them by the more aristocratic governments which at Sicyon succeeded to the tyrants. There, also, the purpose seems to have been more than political. Under the traditional systems the armies of the Greek city states had been organised in tribal groups. At Athens, the traditional Ionic tribes were linked to the aristocratic system, and their members in some way distributed so as to act as supporters to the factions.

Cleisthenes continued the tribal organisation of the Athenian army, but on the basis of the new ten tribes. Each tribe was called on to contribute 1,000 infantrymen to the Athenian army. The most developed infantry army in Greece, that of Sparta, was organised in regiments of 1,000, and the tactics employed seem to have resulted in this being the optimum unit. It is not unlikely, therefore, that Cleisthenes decided to organise Athens with ten tribes because he knew that the total population was of a size to give him 10,000 infantry of military age. Because of the way the new tribes were based on village divisions, it was now possible for each subdivision of the tribal regiment, that of the trittys, to train together. Citizenship and membership of the village were hereditary, and this ensured that the villages' military contribution to the city, within reason, remained constant. The new system meant that the loyalties of the regiment were to the tribe and thus to the city as a whole; as in the political aspect, the factional element was now played down. By the standard of the ancient Greek city states this was a substantial army, twice the size of the Spartan, even though, as it consisted of working farmers rather than landowners whose fields were worked for them by helots, as at Sparta, it did not quite have the same fighting skill, man for man.

After these reforms, Cleisthenes disappears from the record of Athenian history. There is nothing surprising in this. When the reforms were carried through he must have been approaching his seventies, and the assumption is that he died shortly afterwards. It is impossible to exaggerate the contribution he made to the well-being of Athens in these last years of his life. Some twenty or so years later, in 480 B.C., the tyrant Hippias at last returned, as an

old man. He had been brought back to his own region of
Marathon by a Persian fleet and army. From here his father had
marched on Athens, with his own alien army, when he finally
succeeded in establishing himself as tyrant; doubtless, Hippias
hoped to do the same.

Before the Persian forces could be organised for the march, the
Athenian citizen army, in its Cleisthenic tribal regiments, came
out to occupy the foothills over the plain of Marathon. Its commander, Callimachus, still held the old aristocratic office of military command, the 'War Leader' or 'Polemarch', but each tribal
regiment had its own general, one of them the Philaid Miltiades,
descended probably from the brother of Hippocleides who had
danced away his marriage to Agariste. At the battle of Marathon,
Cleisthenes's new citizen army won its proudest victory. The
Athenian democracy had shown that the Persians, for all their
resources, could be beaten, and there could be no turning back for
the city.

Themistocles

(*c.* 525–449 B.C.)

When the historian Thucydides wrote his account of the great war
which Athens and Sparta fought between 431 and 404 B.C., he
prefaced his narrative with an outline of earlier Greek history,
tracing the development of the rivalry between the two great city
states, from the end of the Persian war in 479. This was the time
when Athens became an imperial power, dominating the Aegean
with her navy, and contending for the leadership of all the Greek
states.

Three men stand out as responsible for Athenian success:
Themistocles, who established the Athenian navy and gave
Athens the basis for supremacy; Thucydides's own kinsman,
Cimon, who led that navy successfully, in the Aegean and further
afield, keeping the defeated Persian Empire at bay and winning
Greek cities over to the Athenian alliance; and Pericles, under
whose domination of Athenian affairs that alliance was converted
into an empire. Themistocles and Pericles belonged to families
and a political grouping which were, in many senses, the
opponents of Cimon (and so of those to whom Thucydides is
naturally sympathetic). Even so, he cannot conceal his admira-

tion of these two, and their contribution to the future of Athens.

Themistocles was born about 525 B.C. His father was Neocles, his mother almost certainly not a Greek but a Carian or Thracian called Abrotonon (the Athenians had established interest in Thrace, the mainland regions of the north Aegean coast, the Dardanelles and the sea of Marmara, and several important Athenians intermarried with Thracian families). Plutarch says that Themistocles's family was too obscure to give him any distinction when he began his political career, but this is almost certainly false. His early political career, particularly the fact that he was elected to the archonship in 493, demonstrates that his family connexions were already with the leading, dominant groups in Athenian public life. Plutarch, in fact, contradicts himself and tells us he had connexions with the family of the Lycomidai. At the same time, it is likely that Themistocles took advantage of the new basis given to Athenian politics by the reforms of Cleisthenes, and the continued division of Athenian political life between supporters of the new order and those of the descendants of Peisistratos, to enhance his own political position; families formed groups, and Themistocles cannot have acted alone. Whether his holding of the archonship was anything more than a formality is uncertain. He is credited with the creation in his archonship of a new town at Athens's harbour, Piraeus; that he was responsible for the new town is certain, but it is unlikely to have happened as early as 493.

The first great military crisis for Athens came in 490, when a Persian expeditionary force landed at Marathon. Its purpose was to restore to power Peisistratos's son Hippias; the resistance was led by Miltiades. Themistocles may well have fought at the battle, but his name is not associated in any way with this campaign; clearly, he was not yet prominent.

His opportunity came after Athens's victory. The city was still divided between those who supported Hippias (and so the Persian supremacy) and those who wished to keep Athens independent. It is at this time that the process of ostracism, a device for getting rid of unpopular politicians, is first used in Athenian political life. Athenian citizens were summoned to gather in the central meeting place, the Agora. As they passed in through one of the entrances they cast a vote, in the form of a broken piece of pottery (an *ostrakon*) on which was scratched the name of any politician whose removal was desired. If sufficient votes were cast against him, the politician had to leave Athens for ten years, crippling him politically but not going to the extremes of exile, banishment for life and confiscation of property. The introduction of the process is attributed to Cleisthenes; but it is noticeable that it first came into effect long after Cleisthenes's reforms, and it may have been the work of others – possibly of Themistocles himself. The process was, in fact, highly organised. Collections of potsherds have been found by the American excavators of the agora, dumped in a well, inscribed in the same handwriting, with the same name, for distribution to the voters. Ironically, the name they bear is that of Themistocles.

Once the device of ostracism had been tried, it was used relentlessly; each year from 487 onwards someone suffered, first the relatives of the tyrants, then Megacles the Alcmeonid, suspected of wanting to secure the return of Hippias and signalling treacherously to the Persians during the battle of Marathon.

Another reform introduced in 487 seems to be aimed against the established order; selection by lot was now used to appoint the archons, instead of direct election, and they consequently cease to be people of importance. Again, it is suspected that this new law was the work of Themistocles. Whether this is so or not, he was by this time clearly associated with a group of progressive politicians, who may have included Aristeides, known as 'the Just'.

At this time Athens was given a breathing-space before the anticipated renewal of the Persian onslaught by the death of the Persian king, Darius, and the subsequent rebellion of Egypt, Persia's most valuable, but most turbulent possession. It was not until the later 480s that Darius's successor, his son Xerxes, was firmly in control and ready to invade Greece. Athens had at first used the lull to celebrate what appeared to be a decisive victory at Marathon. A great new temple was begun on the Acropolis, as a thank-offering to the protecting deity, the goddess Athena, and a splendid new ceremonial gateway planned at the entrance, previously marked by a centuries-old fortification. All this again may be the work of the progressive group, who also secured the eclipse of Miltiades, the victor of Marathon, following his failure to take the strategic island of Naxos. He was fined a huge sum, but died in prison before it could be paid; the fine was inherited, and paid, by his son Cimon. It was over a decade before Cimon gained his vengeance.

Themistocles's progressive policies went with a greater realisation that the Persians were still the main threat, and his aims were directed to strengthening resistance. His chance came in 484–3. Athens possessed at Laurion the richest source of silver in southern Greece, exploited by private Athenians, but with the state taking a share, since the mineral rights belonged to the whole people, rather than any individual landowner. In that year a particularly rich vein of silver was found, and the profits that went to the city were correspondingly large. Two proposals were made for spending it. One, that it should be divided equally among all Athenian citizens, would have appealed to individual hopes of gain. The other, put forward by Themistocles, was that the money should be used to build a new and enlarged fleet of warships to resist the Persians. Whether the first proposal was made by Themistocles's enemies (or the friends of Persia) to prevent the construction of a fleet is not clear; but Themistocles's policy, and the safety of Athens, prevailed over individual greed, and the fleet was built.

His ideas are clear. Almost twenty years earlier the Greek cities on the east side of the Aegean, including Miletus, which were already under Persian domination, rebelled; their resistance was heroic, and successful for several years. These cities were situated either on the offshore islands (such as Samos and Chios) or, if on the mainland, were immediately adjacent to the sea and heavily fortified. Though the Persians could attempt to put their cities under siege, so long as the east Greeks had control of the sea they could bring in supplies and attack the Persians in the rear, so that no successful siege was possible. In the end this strategy failed, but it was only because part of the Greek fleet deserted, giving the Persians that naval superiority they could not win by their own actions. The remains of the allied fleet were defeated in 494, Miletus fell, and the rebellion was at an end. Themistocles, however, had seen the strategic lesson. His policy for the Greek resistance was to build up, at Athens itself and in alliance with other Greek cities, a fleet large enough to control the Aegean, and so to hamper the Persian army and its supplies that it could not bring its full forces into action in southern Greece.

Ideally, like an east Greek city, Athens should have been situated on the sea, so that its fortifications could be defended and supplied. Unfortunately it was not – it is some four miles inland – and this failing may explain Themistocles's desire to develop instead the harbour town of Piraeus. When the Persians finally arrived in 480 it was too late to do this, so (apart from a token resistance on the Acropolis) Athens had to be evacuated, its inhabitants taken either to the nearby island of Salamis or to the towns on the opposite side of the gulf, such as Troizen. A few years ago an inscription was found at Troizen relating to these events, the so-called 'Themistocles decree'. Though it belongs in fact to a much later date (perhaps the second century B.C.), its text must derive from decisions actually made in Athens in 480, when the Persians were in northern Greece, and before they had reached

Athens. In every sense, the far-sightedness and organisational skills of Themistocles are clear.

Themistocles's policies were completely vindicated. Leadership of the Greek alliance was conceded voluntarily to the Spartans, whose infantry soldiers had long been the best in Greece. Even these could not prevent the Persian breakthrough at Thermopylae, but in the naval battle fought at the same time off Cape Artemision the Greek fleet was victorious, and many Persian ships were destroyed (admittedly, by bad handling and lack of appreciation of climatic conditions by the completely unnautical Persian king, so that his fleet was caught off a mountainous lee shore in a gale). The Persians marched south and occupied Athens; but the Greek fleet held firm at Salamis. The Persian fleet was lured to attack in waters entirely favourable to the Greeks, perhaps another instance of Xerxes's nautical incompetence (but it was afterwards said he had been trapped by a false message sent to him by Themistocles himself). The Athenian fleet played a major part in the Greek victory. Cimon put aside his personal animosities, serving in one of the ships, and Aristeides was summoned back from ostracism.

The Persians still held Athens, and during the winter Xerxes sent his vassal, Alexander, King of Macedon, to offer favourable terms to the Athenians in order to split the anti-Persian alliance. The Athenians withstood, though in the end they had to threaten that they would abandon Greece en bloc and migrate to Italy, before the Spartans would march against the Persian forces. Again, this was Themistocles's work. The culmination of this endeavour came with a double victory of the Greeks: by land, at Plataea and over the remnants of the Persian navy at Mykale opposite Miletus, when the allied – largely Athenian – fleet provoked the second rebellion of the east Greeks against the Persians, the starting-off point for the Athenian alliance and empire.

At this moment, however, the Greek alliance was still dominated by the Spartans. Their policies inevitably were directed towards their infantry army: naval affairs placed too great a strain on their complex social organisation, and for these they preferred to rely on the Athenians and other allies. The Spartans would not support (or perhaps could not understand) the idea of the defended city supplied by sea, so, when the Persians withdrew and Greece was once more free, the Spartans kept to their defensive system, sheltering behind the fortified Isthmus of Corinth, and insisted that Athens, outside that defence, should not rebuild her walls in case the city became a Persian base (were the Spartans still afraid that Athens might after all go over to the Persian side?

Or was this an attempt to keep Athens weak and subservient?).
Themistocles told the Athenians to send him to Sparta, where he
procrastinated while, at his bidding, the Athenians made haste to
rebuild their walls, using the broken gravestones and other debris
from the Persian sack of the city, which, Thucydides says, could
still be seen in his day (and, indeed, parts of this wall, with its
mud-brick superstructure, still survive at the present day).
Rumours of the rebuilding reached Sparta, putting Themistocles,
as he knew, at grave risk; but his reputation amongst the Spartans
was high, and soon news reached him that the wall was complete.
The Spartans were faced with a *fait accompli*, and could do nothing
but let Themistocles return.

This was his last great triumph, and thereafter his fortunes
changed. We do not know the exact reason for this, but his support
may have dwindled as fear of Persia was removed. True, he seems
now to have achieved his long-cherished development of Piraeus,
but it was Aristeides who organised the east Greek cities liberated
from Persia into the Athenian-dominated Delian league, after
they had rejected Spartan leadership; and it was Cimon who now
led the allied fleet to victory after victory over the Persians,
culminating at the battle of Eurymedon (probably in 468) when
the Persian fleet was driven altogether from the seas. By that time
Themistocles was gone from Athens. After earlier unsuccessful
attempts to secure his ostracism (the evidence is the dumped
inscribed potsherds found in modern archaeological excavations),
his enemies at last succeeded in having him driven out.

In 472 his young supporter, Pericles, paid for the production of
Aeschylus's drama *The Persians*. This play, which of course survives, tells of the arrogant pride of Xerxes and his failure at
Salamis, a rare example of a Greek tragedy that is concerned with
contemporary events rather than myth and legend. Clearly it was
intended to remind the Athenians of their debt to Themistocles. It
did not succeed, and he left Athens to live at Argos. Here (though
the details are obscure) he seems to have been involved in plotting
against the Spartans. Representations were made at Athens; he
was impeached for treason and, says Plutarch, the Spartans
joined in the indictment. Themistocles got word of this and,
anticipating arrest, fled from Argos to the remote, backward
north-western regions of Greece, where he was received, in the
old-fashioned, honourable way, as a suppliant by Admetos, king
of the Molossi. Even here he was not safe: he crossed the Pindus
mountains to Macedon, and took ship to Ionia, narrowly avoiding
accidental capture by an Athenian fleet operating in the Aegean.
When he arrived he threw himself on the mercy of the new Persian

king, Artaxerxes, who had just succeeded: the final irony of Themistocles's extraordinary career. He was well received, despite the previous harm he had inflicted on the Persians (rather, perhaps, than for his dubious services of which it was said, he reminded the Persians, such as the message to Xerxes before Salamis). He was given the Greek cities of Lampsacus, Magnesia and Myus that were still part of the Persian empire. It was at Magnesia that he died (later, he was commemorated on that city's coins).

The people of Magnesia, says Plutarch, have a magnificent tomb of Themistocles in their agora (a signal honour: normally the Greeks bury their dead outside the city limits). Yet there is another tradition – surely a true one – that his body was brought back to Athens and buried, overlooking the waters where his fleet won its victory, on the promontory of Piraeus, the Akte Themistocleous which bears his name to the present day.

Pericles

(*c.* 495–429 B.C.)

Pericles dominated Athens from the mid-fifth century B.C. until his death in 429. Athens, during that time, says Thucydides, was only nominally a democracy; in fact, it was ruled by the leading citizen – Pericles. He belonged to an aristocratic family. His father was Xanthippos; his mother Agariste was a member of the Alcmeonid family, and a niece of Cleisthenes the reformer. He was born, the second son, probably in 495 B.C.. He grew up, therefore, during the Persian crisis, and must have seen from inside the shifts of political fortune, the changing family alliances which accompanied that hectic period of Athenian history. In particular, the fortunes of the Alcmeonids varied: dominant in Athens during the time of Cleisthenes, they were accused, rightly or wrongly, of trying to maintain their position through collaboration with Persia. As Pericles emerged into political life as a young man, his own attitudes became clear. As Cleisthenes had done before him, he was to use his aristocratic talent – and status – to win the popular support which would be the deciding factor in politics under the new constitution. It was his control, and dominance, of the popular assembly which was to give him the basis for his new autocratic rule; hence Thucydides's paradoxical summing up.

His first alliance was with Themistocles, even at the time when Themistocles's fortunes were in decline. After Themistocles's departure from Athens, political life would seem to have been dominated by Cimon, whose policy was to collaborate with Sparta in Greece, and to prosecute vigorously overseas the war against Persia. This was successful, but meant that at home Athens was failing to secure the prominence and domination her overseas efforts were winning for her. Fear of Sparta was the key to this; by land, the Spartan army was invincible, and the Athenians were afraid to provoke her. Cimon symbolised this attitude; and though the associates of Themistocles, the young Pericles and the lesser known Ephialtes, continued their opposition to him, it had small hope of success. Their fortunes changed when a disastrous earthquake destroyed Sparta, probably in 464. Her population and her army suffered severe loss of life, and she no longer presented a military threat to Athens, especially as her subservient rural population, the helots, rebelled.

The Spartan leaders turned to Athens, and Cimon, for help, probably under the terms of the alliance between them, and Cimon complied; 4,000 Athenian infantry marched to Sparta's aid. The policy was unpopular; freed from fear of Sparta, the Athenians turned against Cimon, and ostracised him. Pericles and Ephialtes seized their opportunity, and in 461 Ephialtes carried through the assembly a series of reforms which, effectively, gave complete control of the city to the popular vote. The old aristocratic council (called the Areopagus, the name of the hill by the Acropolis on which it met) lost all its powers except for religious matters. The aristocrats took swift vengeance on Ephialtes, and he was murdered; it was Pericles who was to reap the benefit.

How far he dominated Athens in these early years is unclear. Inscriptions have been found in Athens which record various decrees passed by the assembly during the period of Pericles's supremacy, several of them dealing with important matters. They record the names of the individual Athenians who made the proposals, but Pericles's name does not appear among them. In all likelihood this is the result of the Athenian system and the proposers may be members of the council, appointed by lot; but this is not necessarily so. Probably the convention was to act through nominees and supporters, rather than directly. Even if Pericles's name is not recorded, we are told his influence was in part due to the skills with which he addressed the assembly, and his prestige was guaranteed by his repeated re-election to the military command, even though his military skills seem to have been deficient.

After 461 Athenian policy was to challenge the supremacy of Sparta in Greece, and to continue the maintenance of her own anti-Persian alliance. Both aspects suffered setbacks. The Spartan army recovered from the losses inflicted by the earthquake: the helots were put down, and an army sent to central Greece to reassert Spartan influence. That army fought the Athenians at the battle of Tanagra, where the Athenians and their allies suffered heavily, and though not a great Spartan victory it announced to Greece that once more the Spartans were the dominant force in Greece. Shortly after the Athenians sent help to Egypt, which had rebelled against the Persians, but their fleet was trapped and many ships lost: for a moment Greek (and that means Athenian) naval supremacy was shaken. At some point in this crisis Cimon returned from ostracism, and was sent, as a commander with the Athenian fleet, to retrieve the situation in the east Mediterranean. He died before the victory the fleet won off Salamis in Cyprus. Athenian naval supremacy was restored, but it was Pericles who profited. Probably the Athenians now made a deal with the Persian king which guaranteed them a free hand in the Aegean. A Spartan army attacking Athens was recalled, because Pericles had bribed its commander (in his accounts for that year Pericles put down the cost to 'miscellaneous necessary expenses' – this remained a famous joke for years to come). Even so, faced with a rebellion by some of her allies, Athens was forced to come to terms with Sparta, and signed a treaty which was supposed to last for thirty years, effectively dividing the Greek world into two spheres of interest, Spartan and Athenian.

By this time, Athens was exploiting her alliance for her own benefit. The allies became subjects, paying tribute which was supposed to go to the cost of fighting the Persians – except that there was now peace with Persia. Pericles's opponents protested: Athens, a relative of Cimon said, was using the money to deck herself out with splendid new temples, as a harlot bedecks herself with jewels. The criticism was rejected, the critic ostracised: and the temple building went on. The policy was undoubtedly Pericles's own; Thucydides attributes to him, in a speech, the proud boast that Athens was now the 'School of Greece', showing the way forward in artistic endeavour and achievement. The words are, perhaps, Thucydides's, but the ideas must have been those of Pericles himself. It is a proud boast, but a justified one, for the fifth century B.C. marks the height of Athenian literary achievement, the great surge of sculpture, the construction of the most famous temples: and though this began before the supremacy of Pericles, and certainly continued after his death, it is this which marks out the age of Pericles as supreme in the annals of Greek intellectual and artistic life, and a lasting influence on succeeding civilisations.

Politically, this world was still on edge. The thirty years' peace was a breathing-space, not a solution. Pericles used it, as best he could, to strengthen Athens's position. Subject states which rebelled against her were put down with increasing ruthlessness. Athens interfered in the internal affairs of subject cities, governments controlled by the well-to-do, which might favour Sparta or Persia, being put down and replaced by democracies modelled on the Athenian system. Increasingly Athens treated the east Greek cities as though they were dependent colonies (the colonisation being an extension of the traditional Athenian reputation as the organiser of the east Greek settlements in the remote 'Dark Age' around 1000 B.C., almost certainly a fiction). The great festival of Athena, Athen's patron deity, held every four years, was the occasion when they had to render the visible signs of dependence; each city had to send a cow to be sacrificed in honour of Athena, and a suit of infantry armour, to be deposited in the sacred armoury on the Acropolis. All this time the temples were building: the Parthenon on the Acropolis, other temples in those shrines of Athens whose gods were particularly responsible for victory over the Persians: Hephaistos the armourer by the Athenian agora; Poseidon the god of the sea, at Cape Sounion, the Land's End of Athens; Ares the god of war, in the village of Acharnai north of Athens, where the Athenian youth continued to take the oath of Plataea, sworn before the great victory over Xerxes' army; and Nemesis at Rhamnous, symbolising how, appropriately, the Persians had met their fate.

More prosaically, under Pericles Athens accumulated considerable financial reserves. There was, of course, heavy expenditure on the architectural programme and the embellishment of buildings. The Parthenon contained Pheidias's statue of Athena, ivory and gold plates over a wooden core; but the moulds for the gold plates were kept, so that the gold itself could, if necessary, be removed and melted down. Pericles sensed that the balance between Athens and Sparta was unstable, and that war, inevitably, would come. He prepared the strategy, an extension of Themistocles's use of that employed in the rebellion of the east Greeks against the Persians. Athens would use her command of the sea to bring in all necessary supplies. The population would withdraw behind the fortifications, which were impregnable to Spartan attack. Since the 450s the walls of Athens had been extended to join those of the Piraeus, achieving, in a different way, Themistocles's intention when he had proposed moving the city to Piraeus. It is surprising that Pericles had not been prepared to sit out a siege earlier, when he bribed off the Spartan army, but it must have been difficult to persuade the Athenians, most of whom lived in the rural villages, to abandon their homes and their fields. Nevertheless, this is what Pericles proposed – and the Athenians accepted – when the prospect of war loomed again in the mid 430s.

The preparations for the inevitable were methodical. An alliance was made with Kerkyra (Corfu), the only independent state outside the Greek settlements in the west with a substantial fleet. Colonies of Corinth (Sparta's staunchest ally) which were now subject to Athens were forced to break their ties with their mother city. Finally, Athens was put on a war footing as the treasures of the rural temples were moved into safe-keeping on the Acropolis. Sparta, with her conservative superstition, was reluctant to be the first to break the terms of the thirty-year truce, which both sides had sworn by oaths on the gods to observe. She feared – and her allies, like Corinth, feared even more strongly – that if action was not taken, Periclean Athens would be invincible. The Spartans, rightly, considered that in Pericles's own person resided the greatest strength of the Athenians, and they tried to undermine him. They sent envoys to Athens, calling on them to purify the city from the 'Curse of the Alcmeonids', by implication, by expelling Pericles, whose mother, as we have seen, was a member of that family. It is doubtful whether the Spartans hoped to succeed in this; but they might weaken Pericles's popularity, and perhaps give themselves a proper religious pretext for breaking the peace.

When war came Athens carried out the evacuation of the countryside. She lost the revenue from the land, and possibly the silver mines, but this was compensated for by the tributes and the income from her empire. The Spartans were helpless; they invaded but could not attack the walls, and had to content themselves with destroying the crops, and cutting down the olive trees. It looked as though Pericles's strategy for the war would be successful, when the unexpected, the uncalculated intervened. Crowded into the restricted space protected by the walls, with inadequate water supplies and non-existent sanitation, the Athenians were all unwittingly vulnerable to epidemic. The infection of plague was brought by sea, and spread like wildfire through the population. Thucydides, who experienced it, gives a vivid description; all Athenians, rich and poor, were vulnerable, and Pericles himself caught the disease. The Athenians were demoralised, and turned against Pericles. He was not reappointed general, for the first time in his long political career. Then they repented, but to no purpose. Weakened by the disease, Pericles died in 429, two years after the war had broken out.

It is difficult to assess Pericles as a person. His qualities as a statesman and politician, his patriotism for his city, show clearly in Thucydides, but that austere historian was not concerned with personalities. Like all politicians in the Athenian democracy, Pericles was subject to attack in his own lifetime. His prominence and prestige made him immune to legal prosecution, except in the crisis of the plague, though he himself as an up-and-coming politician had not hesitated to use legal attacks on his rivals to improve his own position; this was normal Athenian practice. During his supremacy, however, his enemies had to be content with attacking his friends and associates, with some success. The philosopher Anaxagoras was charged with impiety and forced to leave Athens, the sculptor Pheidias with embezzlement. The other form of attack was public mockery in the comedies performed at the religious dramatic festivals. None of the comedies in which Pericles was ridiculed has survived (the plays of Aristophanes, which continue the tradition with later politicians, were written after Pericles's death). We have quotations from some earlier comedies which show what Pericles experienced, and these include jokes about his personal appearance; he had a tall, domed forehead (like a 'squill', or onion) which in public he tried to conceal by wearing a military helmet. 'Here comes our squill-headed Zeus', says Cratinus, 'carrying on his head....' not the helmet one would expect but the 'odeion', the music hall built next to the Theatre of Dionysus by Pericles himself.

More personal information is given, of course, by Plutarch, but much of this is unreliable. The comic poets were not restricted by any law of libel, and innuendoes and downright lies, often of a sexual nature, were all part of their stock-in-trade. The problem is that Plutarch, living in a very different Greek world centuries after Pericles's time, is not able to distinguish this, and treats it all with too naïve a belief. For us, it is next to impossible to unravel truth from libel. It is clear that Pericles enjoyed intellectual company. His circle, as we have seen, included the Ionian philosopher Anaxagoras. Plutarch regards this relationship as similar to that which later politicians had with the sophists, teachers of wisdom and rhetoric, and explains that from Anaxagoras Pericles learned a style of speaking, 'tinged with natural philosophy'. This, again, may be an anachronism: it was the thought, not the rhetorical skill, that attracted Pericles. His relationship with Aspasia is treated elsewhere; but, here again, the attraction of this non-Athenian woman may well have been her greater intellectual attainment, compared with that of Athenian aristocratic women, trained instead to fulfil their duties of dynastic marriage. Pericles seems to have been interested in the arts, and in Plutarch appears not only as the patron of Pheidias, but as the chief instigator of the artistic and architectural programme which brought such glory to Athens. That he was aware of the significance of his achievement there was no doubt: Thucydides is witness to this. Earlier politicians had sought prestige by sponsoring building programmes and supporting them financially from their own resources. Cleisthenes, exiled by the sons of Peisistratos, bought the support of the Delphic oracle by paying for the reconstruction of the temple of Apollo. Despite his family connexions, Pericles as a younger son may not have had wealth at this level; at any rate, he was charged, in effect, with paying for the building programme out of state funds (which was true) to further his own prestige. In a sense, his reputation outstrips the evidence (how much more we would know about him if he had lived only thirty years later): the reputation, nevertheless, is secure even if the evidence is, perhaps, distorted.

Much of the achievement of Athens was the result of factors over which Pericles had no control – the existence of the fleet, created originally by Themistocles; the system of the Athenian alliance, worked out by Aristeides. Athens depended, too, on her wealth, both from tribute and trade, and none of this was created by Pericles. His military skills were limited, despite his continuous holding of the generalship – the victories, on the whole, were won by other men, such as Myronides.

Even so, Pericles's own achievement is clear. He held the Athenian democracy on course when it was at its height, successful in politics, in war, in the arts. By interposing his own personality between the realities of political existence, and the unstable nature of the Athenian democratic system, Pericles was able to direct the city when it reached its peak. The failures, the uncertainties, the acts of crass political stupidity after his death, which led to the final defeat of Athens by the Spartans in 404, give his true measure.

Philip II of Macedon

(*c*. 382–336 B.C.)

The kingdom of Macedon formed the northern frontier of the Greek world. Beyond were the barbarians; Illyrians to the north-west, Dardanians to the north, Thracians to the north-east. It was dangerous country, involved incessantly with the risk of plundering invasions. To the sophisticated Greeks of the city states it was primitive, and backward. The monarchy itself, in its application and as an institution, was comparable only with the long-superseded forms described in the poems of Homer. The people were uncouth, and, possibly, not even Greek. Their language (for which very little real evidence survives) seems to be a dialect form of Greek, but this is a point still debated by the experts, and a problem not untouched by modern politics. They had a hard life, and were, perhaps, pastoralists rather than farmers.

In a speech of rebuke when his Macedonians had crossed him, Alexander the Great reminded them that his father, Philip, 'had found you vagabonds and helpless, most of you clothed in sheepskins, pasturing a few sheep on the mountains, and fighting for them, without much success, against the tribes on your borders'. The picture may be exaggerated (and the words more likely those of the historian, Arrian, imagining what Alexander said) but the impression is clear.

The Macedonian royal family were called the Argeadai; and from this grew up the fiction that they were immigrants from Argos, related to the Argive royal family. This seems impossible. It was propounded, almost certainly, by the first Macedonian king to get involved in southern Greek affairs, Alexander I, nicknamed the Philhellene. By the time he became king in 498 B.C. the Persians had extended their empire into Europe, and converted Thrace into a province. Alexander was seeking the support of the Greeks, and in pursuit of this wished to compete in the Olympic Games, which were restricted to those of Greek birth. It was argued that the Macedonians were not Greek; hence the invention of the story that the royal family was of respectable Argive descent.

In the fourth century B.C. Macedon was particularly unstable.

The succession to the monarchy was disputed; there were assassinations and usurpers. To the west, the Illyrian tribes, usually divided amongst themselves, were united by a particularly vigorous leader, Bardylis, and thus the external threat to Macedon grew more severe, even though the Illyrians were more interested in plunder than permanent occupation. Philip II was born in this period of chaos, in 382 or 381. His father was Amyntas III, whose career included a series of expulsions from his kingdom at the hands of the Illyrians, and who, on his death in 370/69, left a kingdom impoverished and weakened as a result. A period of dispute succeeded, with Macedon coming briefly under the domination of the leading power in Greece, the Boeotian League, whose authority in Greece had been extended through the activity above all of two men, Epameinondas and Pelopidas. Pelopidas had the responsibility of dealing with the north; to achieve settled conditions there he took hostages back to his own city, Thebes, in Boeotia, including the young prince, Philip. Amyntas had been succeeded by his eldest son Alexander; he was assassinated in 368 or 7, and after a struggle the next oldest son, Perdiccas, became king. He died in battle, his army overwhelmed by Bardylis and the Illyrians in 359. At this point, the fortunes of the Macedonian state had never looked bleaker.

Philip had spent three years at Thebes. He was an intelligent young man, and learned quickly. In particular he had appreciated the military innovations developed by the Boeotians, which, with devastating effect, had put an end at last to the hitherto invincible Spartan armies at the battle of Leuctra in 371. These developments included the special selection and training of an élite corps, the 'Sacred Band', which could be used to deliver a knock-out blow against a thinner but longer enemy line by being massed in greater depth, while the risk of encirclement was avoided, in part at least, by the intelligent use of cavalry protection. Philip saw how these new tactics could be adopted to save Macedon, and he introduced them there.

When Perdiccas died, it appears that Philip was in charge of another contingent of the Macedonian army, now the only part left. He was the obvious successor. Perdiccas had left an infant son, but this crisis was no time for an infant to become king; Macedonian kings had to be able to lead the army in battle and primogeniture was not the best criterion for that. Philip took the remnants of the Macedonian army and spent the first few months of his reign training them in the Theban tactics. Before countering Bardylis he had to deal with another pretender to the throne, supported by Athens, and defeated him without much ado. By 358 he was ready. In the ensuing battle the new Macedonian army, arranged in its massed phalanx formation, and armed with the long lance, the sarissa, confronted an enemy for the first time. After fierce fighting they broke open the Illyrian ranks, and, under Philip's command, the incomparable Macedonian cavalry swept in to deliver the decisive blow. Philip had not only learned the Theban lesson, but had improved on it. The Illyrians were utterly defeated, and Macedon was saved.

Philip's next moves were to strengthen and extend his kingdom. Apart from defending Macedon from the tribes of the north, he had to consider his relations with the Greek states. Thessaly, to the south, had formed part of the Boeotian involvement in northern Greece, and had had territorial and other ambitions of its own. To attach it to the Macedonian kingdom would give security on the southern frontier, and make available to Philip the excellent Thessalian cavalry. Philip made tentative moves, but without complete success; it was several years before Thessaly fell fairly into his grasp.

Meanwhile, an opportunity arose to acquire a valuable and strategic city to the east of Macedonia. Amphipolis had been settled, in the fifth century, by the Athenians, to control the valley of the river Strymon and the rich resources of that area, timber and silver in particular. It had been a restless colony, and effectively rebelled from Athens during the wars with Sparta. Athens had always wanted to regain control, but had not succeeded; Amphipolis remained independent. On his succession Philip sought to gain Athenian support, in the time of emergency, by promising to return Amphipolis to them. He called on the people of Amphipolis to let him install a garrison; they refused, and he took the place by storm. It was his prize, and, whatever undertaking he had given to Athens, he held on to it. The Athenians were outraged, and, though many leading Athenians continued to be favourably disposed to Philip, in general the enmity of the city grew. Philip must have realised it, and discounted it. He emerges as a political realist, clever and quick to take whatever was advantageous to himself and his kingdom.

The Greeks of the cities, whose enemy he became, constantly underrated him, believing him to be unsophisticated and lacking in cleverness, 'Philip the barbarian'. They were completely mistaken; as Philip's acquisitions grew, he demonstrated over and over again the astuteness of his political acumen, as well as outstanding military skills, in planning battles and winning the unswerving support and loyalty of his troops.

After this, Philip's attention was switched to the Greek cities on the coast of Macedon itself; Methone, an ally of Athens, was put under siege. The city resisted strongly, but finally capitulated. Philip, however, had suffered in the siege, losing his right eye when it was struck by an arrow. He survived the wound, but it was to have an interesting, and unexpected, sequel.

In the late 350s Philip steadily increased the area under his domination. His policies in this respect were clever, and effective, as his Athenian opponents were to observe. He had several fronts on which he could operate: eastwards and north-eastwards against the various Thracian tribes; northwards and north-westwards, particularly against the Illyrians, whose unity had disintegrated after the death of Bardylis; southwards and south-westwards against the equally fragmented Greeks. Whenever he ran up against excessive opposition on one front, he could disengage and try elsewhere. In the meantime, he sought friends and collaborators who might swing affairs in his interest. From the Greek point of view a major crisis was the quarrel with Olynthus, a Greek city in territory adjacent to Macedonia. Earlier in the century this city had been powerful enough to defeat the Macedonians, and it had an obvious interest in keeping Macedon weak. The Olynthians offered refuge to Philip's half-brothers, with the intention of promoting civil war in Macedon, so that Philip was bound to attack. In defence, Olynthus made an alliance with Athens, where the orator Demosthenes, suspicious of the growing power of Philip, urged full intervention and help. But Athens was financially enfeebled; support was not wholehearted, and in the end was sent too little and too late. Olynthus fell in 348 and was totally destroyed, its population put to death or dispersed.

This ruthless end must have sent a shiver through the other Greek cities, but Olynthus and Macedon were remote, and other Greek cities in that area had been sacked before. Philip was doing no more than had been achieved, from time to time, by the various kings of the barbarous northern tribes, and no doubt his kingdom would disintegrate as had these others. These northern kings were to be exploited rather than feared by the southern Greek cities. Athens, in particular, had done this before, and saw no reason to regard Philip in any other way. Philip was successful; Athens, therefore, must come to terms with him and use him. However much Demosthenes might try to urge the Athenians to oppose Philip, the sensible course – it seemed to the majority – was to placate and win him over. An embassy was sent to negotiate.

Philip was anxious for peace with Athens, since not only would it help his own advancement, but he had a high and genuine respect for that city and its past achievements, as well as its intellectual and artistic attainments. So he set out to charm the embassy, and, where charm was not enough, to bribe. The Athenian envoys were pleasantly surprised to find that Philip was not the uncouth ogre many of them expected, and only Demosthenes, who was one of them, was not so impressed. When his fellow envoys praised Philip for his handsomeness and his qualities as a drinking partner, he grumbled that these were, respectively, the attributes of a woman and a sponge. Yet he did not prevail. Opinion in Athens saw Philip as a friend, while Isocrates, the speech-maker and pamphleteer, who years before had preached for a Greek crusade against the Persian Empire, saw even more; here was the leader who could unite the Greeks, and lead them against the traditional enemy.

Philip was not so pleased with this. As his kingdom extended further to the east, he came closer to Persia, and he could not yet afford to provoke the Persian king. During the fourth century, under the long and feeble rule of Artaxerxes II, Persia had been weak and had lost territory. His successor Artaxerxes III was more vigorous, and was effectively restoring the empire to its former limits. In 344 he asked the Greeks (but not Philip) for help and, in particular, mercenary soldiers, for an invasion of Egypt, which had been independent of Persian rule for more than half a century. It is likely that he was even then suspicious of Philip's intentions. In 340 Philip intervened at Byzantium, on the threshold of the Persian Empire, a city which dominated the sea route through the Bosphorus, by which Athens imported the corn from southern Russia, vital for the feeding of her population. Athens at last resisted and Philip was checked.

By now Athenian opposition was roused, and Demosthenes was in the ascendancy. It is not unlikely that Persian subsidies were now coming into Greece. Philip's intervention in a dispute within the Amphictyonic Council which controlled Delphi and the oracle of Apollo led to his appointment as its champion, opposed by the two most powerful cities, Athens and Thebes, long since enemies but at last driven to co-operate by the greater threat.

The opposing armies met, in 338, at Chaironeia, in northern Boeotia. Philip's generalship, as always, was brilliant. He used his phalanx defensively, as a holding force facing the Athenians, not pressing forward but, in a controlled, disciplined way, giving ground slowly. The Athenians, urged on by Demosthenes, took this as a sign of defeat: 'On to Macedon.' A gap, as Philip intended, opened between the Theban and Athenian armies, and into this charged the Macedonian cavalry, led by Philip's eighteen-year-old son Alexander. The Theban sacred band fought to the death, but the Macedonian victory was complete. In the aftermath the darker side of Philip's character emerged. As Demosthenes had noted, he was a hard drinker; and in celebration of his victory he became roaring drunk, rampaging round the battlefield, trampling on the corpses, chanting in mockery the name of his opponent 'Demosthenes, son of Demosthenes, of Paiania'. The barbarian under the skin?

Yet his settlement after the victory was a masterpiece of diplomacy. All the Greek cities, except the proud Spartans – who could be ignored – accepted it. No Greek cities were plundered. Instead they were to be members of a league, each one enjoying its own laws. They were to observe peace with each other, and to police the seas to prevent the piracy which had become endemic in the troubled years of the 340s. They were to be allies of Philip, and their forces, united under Philip as leader, were to join with the Macedonians, at last, in the great crusade against the Persians. A Macedonian force was sent to Asia to prepare the ground for Philip's – and the Greeks' – invasion.

Philip's private life had been turbulent (for some account of this, see the life of Olympias). He had had a succession of wives; polygamy was part of the tradition of the Macedonian monarchy. Olympias quarrelled with him, and had been banished from the court, when in 337 Philip was married for the last time, to a Macedonian noblewoman, Cleopatra. He was in love with her. Her uncle, at a drinking party, invited the Macedonians to pray for a legitimate heir to the throne. A brawl ensued, in which Philip distinguished himself by falling flat on his face, blind drunk. He had offended not only Olympias, but their son Alexander; and there were other frictions irritating the Macedonians.

Alexander was recalled in 336, and, as part of the reconciliation, Philip's daughter, another Cleopatra, was to be married to the King of the Molossi. The celebrations were held at the Macedonian capital, Aegae. As Philip entered the theatre there, in the midst of the celebrations, he was assassinated by a Macedonian noble, probably because of a personal grudge.

Whatever their differences may have been, Alexander gave his father an appropriate burial. A vaulted tomb was hurriedly constructed, and by it, he was cremated on a funerary pyre. His ashes (the bones remaining, according to the Greek practice) were placed in a gold casket in the tomb, along with his breastplate, his great shield, decorated with gold and silver and ivory, and a couch on which he could recline at the everlasting feast that the dead enjoy, his drinking vessels placed there with him. In the antechamber in front was another gold casket, containing richly embroidered material, and the ashes of a young woman, almost certainly his last wife, Cleopatra. Later the tomb was covered, for its protection, by a huge mound, and there Philip remained until in 1978 Manolis Andronikos, Professor of Classical Archaeology at Salonika University, having laboriously had the mound dug away, removed a block from the vault, and revealed the contents of the tomb. Philip's casket is now on display in the Salonika Museum. The cremated remains have been studied, and though some scholars have doubted the identification, the discovery that they belonged to a man, aged between forty and fifty, who had been blinded in his right eye by an arrow, which had left the marks of its penetration on the bone, indicated beyond dispute that this was indeed Philip, the greatest of the Macedonian kings.

Alexander the Great

(356–323 B.C.)

On the death of his father, Philip II, Alexander inherited not only the kingdom of Macedon, but his commitment to carry on a war of vengeance against the Persian Empire. In this he was completely successful. With a fine sense of the historic significance that would be attached to the campaign, Alexander took with him his own historian, Callisthenes. The war, however, became more than a crusade of vengeance. The Persian Empire, weakened after many years of ineffective rule which the last vigorous king, Artaxerxes III, had been unable to counteract before his death, fell into Alexander's hands complete; from being the king of a small Balkan state, he became the Great King, the King of Kings, the King of the Lands – all the grandiloquent titles that the mighty, god-like rulers of the Near East had had bestowed on themselves for centuries.

Many of Alexander's Macedonians could not accept the transformation in the monarchy that thus ensued. They plotted or rebelled against this new Alexander, and were ruthlessly put to death, Callisthenes himself perishing in the process. It was not a time for the disinterested writing of history, so despite the magnitude of Alexander's achievements, we have no contemporary record. After his early death he became a legend, and stories of his great doings, more akin to myth than history, began to circulate;

the beginnings, in fact, of the *Alexander Romance*, a fairy tale, exaggerated and distorted, which was added to, and altered, for centuries to come; even now, Alexander is part of the folklore in the areas he conquered.

It was virtually fifty years after Alexander's death that, at last, factual, authoritative accounts could be written (perhaps to counteract those embellished romances). Alexander's commanders, in old age and approaching death themselves, thought the time had come to put down in writing the true account. Sober histories were compiled by Aristobulus, one of Alexander's engineers, and by another general, Ptolemy, son of Lagos (who, after Alexander's death, established himself as king of Egypt). These accounts have not survived, but they form the basis of the best later versions which have come down to us, that written by the Roman senator Arrian, for example, who refers to both of them, and places great reliance on Ptolemy, for, as he puts it, kings cannot tell lies.

At times it is difficult to separate the reality of Alexander from the myth. His achievements speak for themselves; his character and his personality are less easy to interpret. He was born in July 356 B.C., and was destined by Philip to be his heir. Of his training as a military leader we know nothing; but we have seen him already, at the age of eighteen, given the crucial command of the Macedonian cavalry. His education was entrusted to Aristotle, not simply through his reputation as a philosopher (which, in fact, he was still in the process of achieving) but because he was known to the court; his father had been the personal physician of Philip's father, Amyntas.

Aristotle brought to Alexander's schooling a combination of Macedonian origin and Athenian sophistication (he had moved to Athens at the age of seventeen in 368); respect of Athens's achievement was to be a cornerstone of Philip's and Alexander's careers alike. Nevertheless, Alexander's position as heir to the throne was never certain; uncertainty flourished in the Macedonian royal family. His mother, Olympias, was not a Macedonian, and her fall from favour weakened Alexander. Philip was still in his forties when she was banished, and the hope that the new queen would present the king with a legitimate (and completely Macedonian) heir represented to Alexander a significant threat.

When his father was assassinated, however, Alexander was the obvious successor. There was no other effective son of Philip, no one who had, like Alexander, successfully demonstrated his ability to command. In the shadows there was a cousin, Amyntas, the son of Perdiccas, the infant who could not have ruled effectively at the moment of crisis in 359. He was certainly still alive, and might have become a focus of opposition, but if so, he soon disappears. Alexander acted swiftly to confirm his authority as king in Macedon, as son and heir to his father (all quarrels forgotten in the lavish funeral that Alexander properly and piously carried out); and then, to confirm the position of Macedon, a military campaign against the Balkan tribes who had hoped to secede, followed by an equally ruthless campaign against the rebel Greek cities.

There had been rumours that Alexander had perished in the Balkan campaign; his appearance at Thebes put the lie to that story. Thebes resisted strongly, but was taken by storm. Alexander then gave a terrible – and deliberate – lesson to the Greek cities. Thebes, like Olynthus a decade previously, was completely destroyed (as a gesture to the power of Greek literature only the house of the early fifth-century poet Pindar was spared). Subsequently, Alexander gave out that he was remorseful, that he had been carried away by his anger; and such stories have been used to demonstrate the emotional, quicksilver nature of Alexander's character. It is more likely that, his object lesson achieved, Alexander wished to modify the reputation for barbaric harshness such actions might otherwise gain him. Athens waited in fear and trembling, but was spared.

Alexander could not afford to delay the campaign against Persia. It was needed as a rallying cry for the Greeks, to hide the fact that under the alliance and leadership of Alexander they were effectively his subjects. There was a danger that the Persian king, Darius III, would try to strengthen the opposition in Greece, at least by means of subsidy. Alexander's own resources were low. He had insufficient funds to support his army – the cost of Philip's funeral, and the gold and silver buried with him, must have made a difference – and it would have to support itself with the rewards of victory. In 334 he set out. His army was not large: about 40,000 men, 16,000 or so Macedonian, 12,500 Greek 'allies', plus various light-armed and specialised troops. Though the Greek cities – above all Athens – provided him with a fleet, its loyalty was uncertain, and the Persian fleet (commanded by a Greek) could easily establish domination in the Aegean, and cut Alexander's line of communication. In effect, Alexander had to act as though he were isolated from Macedon, which was left in the loyal charge of Antipater, one of Philip's generals.

Swiftly, Alexander won the successes he needed, and these demonstrate the qualities of his generalship. The first Persian army was met at the River Granicos, in north-west Asia Minor. The accounts are distorted. Alexander had to attack the Persians across a river which, in actuality, did not present the substantial barrier of the later, literary descriptions. From here he advanced down the west coast, liberating the Greek cities, which welcomed him. Only Halicarnassus, with a Persian governor, resisted, giving Alexander an ideal opportunity to try out his siegecraft, and the new siege engines which had been made for him. The walls of Halicarnassus had been built some twenty-five years earlier by the dynast Mausolus to the latest design; they were already outdated, and were swiftly breached. The Persian governor was expelled, and Alexander restored the city to Mausolus's sister, Ada, whom he recognised, diplomatically, as his mother (thus ensuring the legitimacy of his own rule there).

Alexander then split his army, sending the main force along the Persian royal road, while he himself took a contingent through the difficult mountain country of southern Asia Minor. Persian resistance behind him was stiffening; he had to advance swiftly to cut off the Persian bases in the Phoenician cities. The policy was not a new one – the Spartan king Agesilaus had planned such a raid sixty years previously, but had been prevented from carrying it out by Persian subsidies to the free Greek cities. Alexander had a stronger grip on Greece, and moved more swiftly; he soon emerged into Syria.

Now Darius himself had to bring out the full Persian army against Alexander; ironically the two armies passed each other before learning of the other's presence, and had to turn, Alexander facing north and Darius south, by the river Issus. Darius's army must have outnumbered Alexander's (by how much is quite uncertain – figures given by the historians are prone to exaggeration) and he anticipated victory, so he had brought with him his harem to watch his achievement. The battle was in fact hard fought – this was, in many senses, the most critical of Alexander's engagements – and particularly stiff resistance was offered to him by the Greek mercenary soldiers fighting on behalf of the Persian king. Alexander engaged, or rather attempted to engage, in hand-to-hand combat with Darius himself, Alexander on horseback, Darius fighting from his chariot, but Darius turned and fled. Alexander was in victorious possession of the field – and of Darius's harem.

Various stories grew out of this. Alexander's courtesy towards the Persian women is used to illustrate his gentlemanly nature (though this was obviously good policy also). More important is the story that Darius sent a message to Alexander offering, in the fairy-tale manner, half his kingdom, and his daughter's hand in marriage, if Alexander would release the harem. Alexander is said to have consulted his staff. 'If I were Alexander', advised his general, Parmenio, 'I would accept'. 'So I would', replied Alexander 'if I were Parmenio'. That this belongs to romance is obvious; historically it is more likely that Alexander knew, from the moment he set out from Macedon, that his aim was to make himself ruler of the whole Persian Empire.

Darius withdrew to Mesopotamia. Alexander did not pursue him, but consolidated his gains methodically. Darius could wait. More important was to secure the Phoenician cities and Egypt. Of the Phoenician cities Sidon was ruled by a dynasty already well disposed to the Greeks. Tyre, an island stronghold, resisted strenuously, putting Alexander's siege train to a much more severe test than Halicarnassus. The siege lasted seven months. Egypt, on the other hand, welcomed Alexander as a liberator. The Egyptians had thrown off their allegiance to the Persians at the end of the fifth century, and only recently had they been resubjugated by Artaxerxes III. They were, moreover, accustomed to welcome into their armies Greek mercenary commanders and their troops. No doubt they regarded Alexander as another example. Instead Alexander came as king, as pharaoh, making a much publicised visit to the oasis sanctuary of Amon, in the western desert, where the god recognised him as his son.

His arrangements for Egypt included the appointment of two Egyptian governors, but there was a military garrison, and the most effective power seems to have been wielded in Alexander's name by Cleomenes, a Greek from Naucratis, in Egypt. One of Cleomenes's tasks was to supervise the construction of a new city, in the Delta, to be the essential link between the Egyptian world of the Nile, and the Graeco-Macedonian world of the Mediterranean. This was to be Alexandria – *by*, not *in* Egypt, and the greatest of Alexander's city foundations.

After Egypt, Darius again. Alexander turned east, and defeated the Persian king in the last battle of the organised Persian empire, Gaugamela. Darius fled towards the Caspian, and was assassinated by a potential – but futile – rival. The rest of Alexander's campaigning was in the nature of a demonstration in force, to remind the turbulent local rulers in the remote eastern provinces of the former Persian empire that the defeat of Darius did not mean the restoration of their independence. This took him to Bactria (Afghanistan) where he soon secured the allegiance of the local king, and married his daughter Roxane. Thence he crossed the Hindu Kush into the Indian sub-continent to the Indus valley and his last set-piece battle, against an Indian prince, Porus. Here Alexander had reached the limits of the Persian Empire, and it was time for him to return and consolidate his kingdom.

Again the *Romance* seems to get between us and historical reality. Alexander knew – or thought he knew – that in the Indus valley he was nearing the edge of the earth. One more campaign, to the Ganges, and the world would be his. But here, we are told, at last his Macedonian troops let him down. Weary of fighting, far from home, they had had enough, and refused to go further. Alexander raged and sulked, but to no avail; he was forced to give the order to withdraw. Fact, or an invention? Was Alexander merely trying to hide the victory of commonsense over illusion? It is impossible to tell. The horrors of the withdrawal were real enough, though, by the direct route across the Persian desert, along the coast to Mesopotamia. The severity of the return journey seems to betoken a certain urgency, the need to get back to the heart of his new kingdom to put it in order. The campaign had lasted long enough, and had reached its proper boundaries, at least for the time being. A great feast of reconciliation was held with the army; Alexander with his immediate followers in a banqueting tent, the army in the courtyard round him.

Alexander made his capital at Babylon. He had burned the Persian palace at Persepolis (a propaganda achievement, to show he remembered that the real pretext of his invasion was to avenge the Greeks). It was unlikely that he intended to return to Macedon, or that he could afford to. He had established himself as the ruler, by force and success of his armies, of the Persian Empire; Babylon was central, and a convenient place from which to rule. His new subjects expected traditional signs of authority from their rulers, and Alexander could not go against them without losing credibility. He had to be remote and godlike. Subjects could approach him only after abasing themselves to the ground. Such adoption of the customs, and of the paraphernalia – and dress – of Persian kingship offended the Macedonians. The Macedonian nobles, in particular, considered themselves his equals – many of them were the descendants of the kings who formerly ruled the independent, neighbouring peoples whom Philip had incorporated into the Macedonian state. Some protested and were put to death, others were banished from court. In many ways, Alexander seemed to be surrounding himself with less assertive, and less capable men. The Macedonians expected that they would be allowed to exploit the fruits of victory. Alexander realised that he could not afford to alienate his new subjects, or, more particularly, their own noble families. Some form of reconciliation had to be achieved. He, himself, had married Roxane, daughter of the king of Bactria. His Macedonians had to follow suit, generals, commanders and ordinary soldiers alike. The new élite of the new order would not come from Macedon alone.

The more restrained of the ancient narrators concentrate on Alexander's military career. His prowess in military matters, his personal courage, his powers of leadership, his ability to adapt established tactics to meet the unexpected challenge of new terrains and (in the case of Porus and his elephants) strange new weapons, all come over clearly, though it must never be forgotten that his conquests, which earned him the title of 'the Great', were based on the Macedonian army, trained and organised and brought to perfection by his father, Philip. It is more difficult to assess the personality, statesmanship and political skills of Alexander. Unlike his father, he was hesitant of marrying, and less cavalier (if what we are told is the truth) in his treatment of women. This may all be part of the romance; it may rather be the consequences of Philip's behaviour towards Olympias. This had obvious disadvantages. In the struggle to maintain his claim to the throne, Alexander had acted ruthlessly towards other, male members of the Argead family. Amyntas, son of Perdiccas, disappeared. All other possible rivals were hunted down and put to death. For much of the time during his campaign Alexander had no heir, or prospect of an heir. Even so, this did not obstruct him from reckless acts of daring, exposing himself to the threat of immediate death. He was, in fact, severely wounded on one occasion. At these times, if he had died the whole enterprise would have collapsed.

No clear indications survive of an administrative reorganisation of the empire. Perhaps it is unthinkable. The Macedonian state had barely, if at all, emerged from a primitive (and, in essence, prehistoric) system. The sophistication that Aristotle had brought was Greek; and for Aristotle, the ideal state had a mere six thousand citizens. Such an ideal is that of the archaic, small, self-contained Greek city, which was already a political anachronism in the fifth century B.C., and it could not serve as a model for Alexander's new empire. He founded cities of the Greek type, and the Greek city system was given a privileged level of at least local independence in his empire. They could not, in practice, be independent in the Greek sense, and the remoter Alexandrias which he founded were completely surrounded by an ocean of Alexander's oriental subjects. Politically, Alexander could do no better than adapt himself, and his Macedonians, to the system he found.

Aristotle proclaimed the doctrine of Greek supremacy. Alexander's Macedonians had established their own supremacy, at least as soldiers. Yet Alexander had to depend on his orientals. There were not enough Macedonians to go round, and it was a sensible move to train, and equip, the best oriental troops in the Macedonian manner, even though that gave offence to the Macedonians. It is wrong to regard this as more than expediency. Sir W. W. Tarn, who wrote in the 1920s a substantial and brilliant study of Alexander, and who was, it is fair to say, imbued with the spirit of reconciliation that lay behind the League of Nations, saw in Alexander the protagonist of 'the brotherhood of man'. The real Alexander was more pragmatic, and hard-headed (though more recent studies are equally wrong to be too influenced by the harsher realities of modern politics).

Alexander may have proclaimed, certainly encouraged in the right places, belief in his divinity. The Greeks could treat it with contempt, if it suited them, or with the flattery of acceptance. They could not avoid the realities of Alexander's political might, which could – and did – interfere in their independence and autonomy, whatever treaties they might have with him. Alexander was feared, not loved.

His end came suddenly. Hard drinking was a Macedonian fact of life. Religious and other celebrations included prolonged drinking parties. The story of Alexander's progress is marred by the accounts of drinking bouts in which, frenzied and out of control, he put his associates to the sword, or, at best, was restrained by his fellow drinkers. It was, in all probability, as the result of such excess in the non-Macedonian climate of the Babylonian summer of 323 that Alexander caught a high fever. Soon it was obvious to all that he was dying, and his Macedonians paid their last respects. He was not universally mourned, certainly not by some of the leading Macedonians, and there were stories – untrue – that he was poisoned.

He left no obvious heir. He had not expected to die, and the crisis should not have happened. Roxane was pregnant, and produced a posthumous son, but that was not sufficient to keep the Empire together. Alexander indicated (or is said to have indicated) at the end that his ring, the symbol of his authority, was to be taken by his general, Perdiccas. It was not enough. Alexander had changed the course of history, and the Macedonian supremacy was not to be turned aside. It was his victories that had earned him the title of the Great: his short-sightedness foredoomed his empire to disintegration.

Attalos I of Pergamon

(*Ruled c.* 236–197 B.C.)

Pergamon is situated in north-west Asia Minor, in the area
settled during the migration period at the beginning of the first
millennium B.C. by Aeolian Greeks. Few of these settlements
developed into sizeable cities, and in the fourth century B.C. the
area was ruled, more often than not, by petty dynasts, established
in strongholds where they maintained their residences and
sufficient troops to keep the area under their control.

Pergamon is such a stronghold, a steep-sided hill some twenty
miles inland, dominating the northern side of the valley of the
River Kaikos. After the wars of the successors of Alexander the
Great, and as a result of the decisive battle of Ipsus in 301 B.C., it
formed part of the kingdom of Lysimachus; this included the
regions of Thrace and western Asia Minor. Under his rule the
hilltop of Pergamon was developed as a citadel, and a safe place to
deposit part of his treasury. There may have been some
population on the lower slopes of the hill, and a small sanctuary of
Asclepios on the flat ground to the west; but there was no Greek
city here. The man in charge was Philetairus, son of Attalos, who
came from Paphlagonia, a district of Asia Minor further to the
east.

The amount of money deposited in the citadel under
Philetairus's control amounted to 9,000 talents, a colossal sum (at
the height of their power and prosperity in the fifth century B.C.
the Athenians had financial reserves worth only two-thirds of that
amount). Philetairus was therefore in a position of considerable
trust. Late in life Lysimachus married Arsinoe, daughter of
Ptolemy I of Egypt. She set her husband against his son,
Agathocles, hoping to shift the succession to her own family. Her
ambitions offended many of Lysimachus's supporters, including
Philetairus; when Lysimachus had his son murdered there was
outright rebellion, and Philetairus changed his allegiance to
Seleucus. The Seleucids were more remote than Lysimachus, and,
in the manner of the region, Philetairus began to build up his
authority as a local dynast, though taking care always to maintain
the signs of allegiance to the king (much as earlier dynasts had
done when this area was part of the Persian Empire). He

strengthened the citadel, and began its embellishment as a capital.

Enough remains of this 'Philetairus' period have been discovered by the modern excavators of Pergamon for it to be recognisable as its first major phase. It began to attract a population to the slopes below the fortifications, and so became a town. Philetairus attracted artists, and made endowments to Greek cities in Asia Minor and sanctuaries in the mainland, building up his reputation as a Philhellene, the protector of the Greek ideal.

He died in 263, and Pergamon passed to his nephew and adopted son Eumenes. Eumenes began to pursue a more independent policy, and soon came into conflict with his king, whom he defeated at Sardis. He now began to strike coins in his own right, putting on them the head of Philetairus. He extended the territory under his control inland up the Kaikos valley, and westwards to the sea, where he acquired a harbour; nevertheless, he still remained only a dynast, refusing to take the title of king.

During the last years of his life (he died in 241) Asia Minor became a major theatre of war in the third of a series of conflicts between the Seleucids and the Ptolemies. To strengthen his position the Seleucid king, Seleucus II, appointed his brother Antiochus Hierax as co-regent in Asia Minor. Inevitably the brothers fell out, and the lesser rulers of Asia Minor, the kings of Pontus (in the north) and Cappadocia (in the east) were forced to take sides. They chose to support Antiochus. Eventually the brothers made peace, in 236, but only after Hierax had inflicted a crushing defeat on his brother. In the meantime Eumenes was succeeded, as dynast of Pergamon, by Attalos, his adopted son (a grandson of his uncle, another Attalos).

No clear account of the history of this period survives, and much is obscure. It is known, however, that unlike the kings of Pontus and Cappadocia Attalos became the enemy of Hierax. The cause of the war between them is uncertain. Earlier in the century Celtic tribes had migrated from central Europe through the Balkan peninsula. Some had made their way to Macedon and Greece, where they were defeated and expelled; others had gone further to the east, through Thrace and across the straits into Asia Minor. Here they had settled in the district of Phrygia, where they established a permanent state, being usually referred to by the Greek version of their name, the Galatoi, or Galatians (it was, of course, to their descendants that St Paul wrote his epistle: their chief town was Ankyra, the modern Ankara). They were fierce, vigorous and terrifying warriors, unreliable and mainly interested in plunder, though they were recruited as mercenary soldiers, and as allies by Hierax who used them to attack Attalos.

In the ensuing war Attalos was victorious in several battles. Hierax withdrew to the east, to attack his brother once more; the Galatians succumbed to Attalos. All the Seleucid lands in Asia Minor as far as the Taurus mountains were now under his control, and he had emerged (despite his own use of Galatian mercenaries at times) as champion of Hellenism against the barbarians. His power and position were no longer those of a dynast; the time had come to take the title of king, as Attalos Soter, Attalos the Saviour.

The victories – one of them was under the walls of Pergamon itself – had been considerable. Quite apart from his claim to be the champion of Hellenism, Attalos had in fact saved many of the Greek cities from plunder, if not destruction. His reputation was a useful adjunct to his authority; and he advertised this by commissioning works of art, some of which were set up at Pergamon, others in influential cities, such as Athens. These included sculptures, the originals of which are lost, but of which Roman copies survive, including the Dying Gaul (once popularly misnamed the Dying Gladiator) and the related group, the Gaul killing himself after putting his wife to death.

Pergamon and its rulers, for all their philhellenic sympathies, were not Greeks; the population came only as its importance as a city developed, and though many were doubtless Greek (and all of them Greek-speaking) it is not really a Greek town, though Attalos's successors were to invent a fictitious early Greek foundation, and an appropriately Greek foundation myth.

By 226 Attalos was ruling a substantial kingdom, and Pergamon was being embellished in a manner suitable for a Hellenistic capital. His fortunes now go into reverse. A relative of the Seleucid kings, Achaeus, accompanied an expedition to north-west Asia Minor of Seleucus III in 223. On this expedition, Seleucus was assassinated, and Achaeus remained as governor of the area on behalf of Seleucus's successor, Antiochus III. He acted vigorously, and gained control of most of this region, including towns quite close to Pergamon itself. Attalos's kingdom was reduced, until little was left except Pergamon itself and its adjacent territory. Achaeus was then tempted by the hope of superseding Antiochus; and though an invasion of Syria proved abortive this at least gave Attalos a breathing-space. With an army augmented (despite his reputation) by Gauls (from Thrace, rather than Galatia) he recovered the allegiance of the Greek cities, and re-established friendly relations with cities in the Hellespont region, Lampsakos, Ilion, and Alexandria Troas.

(These places, it would seem, had been friendly to him since the time of his war with Hierax.) Attalos was well on the way to recovering his power, and by 216 had made an alliance with Antiochus for a joint campaign against Achaeus. Achaeus was trapped at Sardis by Antiochus, captured and beheaded.

During the third century B.C. control of the Aegean, relying on sea power, had been disputed between the kingdoms of Macedon and Ptolemaic Egypt. In the first half of the century Macedon had emerged victorious, but her naval power then went into decline. Egypt tried to take advantage of this, but without lasting success, and the emergence of new naval powers was inevitable. One of these was the island of Rhodes, the other, Pergamon. Rhodes had intervened in 220 when Byzantium attempted to impose a toll on traffic passing through the Bosphorus, and now assumed the major role in policing the seas. Nevertheless, Macedonian interest in the Aegean was still active.

In 227 the Macedonian king had made an expedition into Caria, the mainland opposite Rhodes and adjacent to regions within the Pergamene interest. (It is not unlikely that this was done with the support of Rhodes, worried by the growth of Pergamon.) Pergamene suspicion of Macedon was consequently aroused. One offshoot of this was rivalry between Macedonian kings and Pergamon in supporting the sanctuary of Apollo on Delos (where festivals for the Macedonian kings had long been established). There were many Macedonian monuments in Delos and Attalos built a colonnade which seems deliberately to have obscured one of them.

This enmity towards Macedon was shared by states on the mainland of Greece, particularly the federal league of Aetolia, which controlled Delphi, after successfully defending it against the Gauls. There was sympathy of interest, and anti-Gallic patriotism, between the Aetolians and Pergamon. Philetairus had made gifts to Delphi, and Attalos built a portico there to celebrate his victory over the Galatians, as well as making other gestures of friendship towards the Aetolians.

In 215 the fortunes of the Hellenistic east and the future of Pergamon were profoundly affected by an unexpected turn of events. During the third century the western Mediterranean had been largely neglected by the Hellenistic states. The dominant powers there were Carthage and Rome. A first war had seen the Romans drive the Carthagians from Sicily, when the Greek cities, like those in Italy, now came under Roman protection. In 218 the war was resumed: Hannibal crossed the Alps, and inflicted a series of stunning defeats on the Romans. The young king of

Above: Assyrian bas-relief showing one of the campaigns of Tiglath-Pileser III. A captured city is being evacuated, and Assyrian scribes are taking note of the spoils. *Below:* Ashurbanipal spearing a lion.

Above: The tomb of Cyrus the Great at Pasargadae. *Below:* A relief from Persepolis showing the enthroned Darius the Great receiving tribute.

Macedon, Philip V, saw his opportunity. An alliance with Hannibal might give him the Greek cities of the west, and this would in turn strengthen him in his ambitions in the Aegean. He sent envoys to Hannibal; they were captured by the Romans, and Roman intervention in Greece was inevitable. Preoccupied with the critical situation in Italy, they needed friends in Greece itself to counterbalance Philip. The Aetolian League was an obvious choice; Attalos of Pergamon another.

This was a fateful development, and Roman success led ultimately to the downfall of the Hellenistic kingdoms. Philip was defeated at Cynoscephalae in 197; then it was the turn of Antiochus III. Ptolemaic Egypt survived, with Roman support, until the death of Cleopatra VII. In contrast, Pergamon did well out of the Roman alliance, and, in a sense, this was Attalos's greatest contribution to his kingdom. He acquired a foothold in mainland Greece – the Aetolians 'sold' him the island of Aegina for thirty talents. His troops operated in Greece, expelling Macedonian garrisons from strategic strongholds, and constructed, in great haste, a substantial fleet, which collaborated with a smaller Roman fleet in the Aegean. The Romans came to trust and respect him; certainly, during this first war, Attalos emerged as the staunchest of Rome's supporters in the Hellenistic east.

After the war Philip built a fleet, and began demonstrations of naval strength in the Aegean. This, obviously, caused alarm to Attalos, but also at Rhodes, which had not been involved in the earlier fighting. In 201 a combined fleet of Rhodes and Attalos severely mauled Philip's at Chios, but afterwards allowed Philip a breathing-space by separating. Philip invaded Asia Minor, attacking Rhodian possessions on the mainland rather than Pergamene territory at first, but then, suddenly, advancing to Pergamon itself. The citadel was impregnable, but sanctuaries and everything else outside the protection of the walls were devastated. Though this came to nothing (Philip was short of supplies, and had to withdraw) the threat to Attalos had been considerable.

Not surprisingly he turned to Rome for help. The Romans hesitated. They had fought a long wearisome war against Hannibal, in which they had suffered severe loss of life. Italy – or parts of it – had been devastated, and the ordinary pattern of life severely disrupted. The Romans were obviously reluctant to become embroiled in further fighting, in a remote country and for reasons that did not seem to affect them directly. It is likely that Rome had imposed on Philip an obligation to be at peace with her allies, the Aetolians and Attalos, but it is not certain whether this meant Rome would fight on their behalf. Clearly, in 201 the Romans were reluctant to do so. Here again, this is a turning-point in history. Rome might have withdrawn her interests in Aegean affairs. It was the envoys of Attalos and Rhodes who made clear to the Roman Senate their obligation to defend them against Philip, and since Philip had irrevocably offended the Romans by his stab-in-the-back alliance with Hannibal, in the end the Senate agreed to intervene. Rome joined with Attalos as the champion of Greek freedom, and envoys were sent to Philip forbidding him to make war on the Greeks.

Even so, the Greeks made their alliance with Attalos, or Rhodes, rather than with Rome; presumably this was Rome's wish (it would be a nuisance to be bound to intervene in petty inter-Greek quarrels). Athens was already on good terms with Attalos. Nevertheless, it took a Roman army, stiffened with a Pergamene contingent, to win the decisive battle at Cynoscephalae. The Roman commander, Flamininus, made peace, and the terms were announced by him in a speech he delivered (in Greek) at the Isthmian Games the following year, in 196. Philip's power was broken. The Greek cities were to be free. Pergamon progressed to its greatest prosperity.

By that time, Attalos was dead. Pergamon, which he inherited as a petty state, had become a major force in international politics, a kingdom in its own right. His successors were to extend its territorial possessions still further, but the basis on which they built was essentially Attalos's work. In a sense, there is a paradox about him, for by basing his policy of championing Greek freedom, as the protector of the Greeks, on co-operation with the Romans he can be depicted as a traitor to Hellenism. This is hardly fair. The real traitor was Philip. Whatever reservations there might have been at Rome, or whatever subsequent changes of policy, there can be little doubt of Flamininus's sincerity at the Isthmian Games, since at that time leaving the Greeks to enjoy their freedom was sensible policy from Rome's point of view. What happened later was not Attalos's fault. There seems little doubt that he could accept Rome as a disinterested protector, though this is not the same attitude as that of his grandson, Attalos III, who on his death bequeathed his kingdom to Rome.

It is impossible to judge the personality of Attalos. His behaviour as dynast and king is attested by inscriptions. It is invariably, from the Greek point of view, 'correct'. He respects the city system of administration in Pergamon itself, but this is a politeness. He himself controlled the realities of power. He was interested in the well-being of his people and his city, and Pergamon developed considerably as an artistic centre, producing works of art modelled on Athenian classicism, as well as the more extreme, almost baroque works such as the great monument to the victory over the Gauls. Pergamene architects, confronted with the engineering problems of building on the steep slopes of the citadel, developed a distinctive style of buildings supported on great terraced platforms, and made some use of the vault and the arch, techniques they had taken over from Macedon. Attalos's gifts of buildings, for example at Delphi, are immediately recognisable from their style.

His wife was Apollonis of Cyzicus. Much younger than her husband, she lived for a long time after his death. She seems to have been a pious woman, and was responsible for a substantial reconstruction of the Sanctuary of Demeter at Pergamon. Attalos appears as an honourable, reasonable man, a contrast to the greater violence of the successors of Alexander, as his wife is in direct contrast to the more virulent queens, such as Olympias.

Carthage

Hannibal

(c. 246–182 B.C.)

Hannibal, the Carthaginian whom Rome regarded as the city's greatest and most dangerous enemy, was born about 246 B.C. during the First Punic War between his native city and the Romans. That war, fought for the mastery of the western Mediterranean, had seen Carthage lose naval supremacy and compelled to give up her colonies in Sicily and pay a heavy indemnity to Rome. This defeat determined the shape of Hannibal's life; Roman historians told the story of how, when the boy was nine, his father had made him swear that he would never be a friend of the Roman people. More important however was the reappraisal which the failure of the first war forced on the Carthaginians: they concluded that they could not defeat Rome by seapower, and that any victory depended on their ability to destroy Roman power in Italy itself. That was to be Hannibal's lifelong policy.

He was the son of Hamilcar Barca, a leading member of one of the great families of Carthage. Hamilcar was principally responsible for the new direction of Carthaginian policy, and the decision to repair the loss of Sicily by building a new empire in Spain. Spain offered mineral wealth to enrich both the state and the Barca family (Hannibal was to draw three hundred talents from one mine). When, at the instigation of their ally, Massilia (Marseilles), a city which had commercial interests in Spain, the Romans demanded to know Hamilcar's intentions there, he replied that he was trying to obtain the money with which Carthage could pay off her indemnity to Rome.

Hamilcar was killed in battle in 229, and was succeeded as Carthaginian commander in Spain by his son-in-law Hasdrubal, who continued his policy by diplomatic means and also strengthened the links already formed with some native tribes by marrying an Iberian princess as his second wife. (Hannibal was to make a similar marriage.) Hasdrubal founded a new city as the Carthaginian capital in Spain, the modern Cartagena, which the Romans called Carthago Nova. By the time the young Hannibal was grown up, Carthaginian power in Spain had reached a point when the damage of the first war had been repaired and they were ready to resume the struggle with Rome. Meanwhile, an agreement had been reached which implicitly recognised Spain south of the Ebro as the Carthaginian sphere of influence.

Hasdrubal was murdered by a Celt in 221. Hannibal, then twenty-five, was chosen by the army as his successor. He had spent most of his life in Spain and immediately resumed the more aggressive military policy favoured by his father. Within two years he had brought a large part of central Spain south of the Douro under his control. Then in the winter of 220–19 occurred the incident which provoked a new war with Rome.

Saguntum was a town on the Mediterranean coast to the south of the Ebro. At some date it had become a 'friend' of the Roman people, but there was in the city a pro-Carthaginian party also; and in 221 the Romans had to intervene to maintain the supremacy of the party favourable to them. It was clear that the development of Carthaginian power in southern Spain threatened the independence of Saguntum, and the Romans accordingly sent Hannibal a message warning him that they considered the town to be under their protection. He replied that he considered the Roman intervention there a breach of the Ebro Treaty. The Saguntines had meanwhile become involved in hostilities with a pro-Carthaginian tribe, the Torpolatae, and Hannibal indicated that he intended to fulfil his obligations to them. So, early in 219, he besieged Saguntum, and, though the Romans made no move to help their allies during the eight-month siege, this was the ostensible cause of war.

Hannibal acted swiftly, even before a formal declaration of war had been made, and crossed the Ebro in the spring of 218. The war-plan was the result of long meditation in the Barcid family. It was based on the judgement that Rome could only be defeated by the destruction of her armies in Italy. Accordingly Hannibal must invade the peninsula, and since it was likely that the resources of Carthage could not maintain a large army and a large fleet on a war footing, he must do so by land. Moreover, speed was essential. Italy must be invaded before the Romans could attack Carthage itself.

Hannibal's march was rapid, though one of the Roman consuls, Publius Cornelius Scipio (the elder) only just failed to intercept him. By late September he was in the Alps. His crossing of the mountains was to be regarded with awed admiration, though they had been crossed by Gallic tribes on several occasions; nevertheless, Hannibal's was the first crossing by the army of a civilised power. It cost him almost half his infantry, many horses and most of his elephants. When he descended into north Italy (Cisalpine Gaul) he had perhaps 20,000 infantry and 6,000 cavalry. However, most of the Gallic tribes there welcomed him and he was quickly able to recruit some 15,000 fresh troops.

Then, though Scipio wished to avoid battle, Hannibal lured the other consul Sempronius into attempting an attack across the River Trebia. Hannibal's cavalry broke the Roman flanks and attacked their rear. Only the centre managed to break through and regain their base at Placentia. Hannibal's military genius was displayed in this battle, for he had compelled the Romans to fight on ground and at a time of his choosing, and they had lost two-thirds of their army.

The sequel revealed his political strategy. He released his Italian prisoners without any ransom, proclaiming that he intended to liberate the Italian cities which had been reduced to satellite status by the Romans. The success of his Italian campaign and therefore of the war depended on his ability to break Rome's Italian confederacy, which provided about half the strength of the Roman army.

The following year, after wintering at Bologna, he crossed the Apennines. He caught a chill in the Arno marshes and lost the sight of one eye, but still out-manoeuvred the new Roman commander Flaminius, trapping him on the north shore of Lake Trasimene. The Romans had neglected their intelligence and reconnaissance, and were caught between the foothills and the lake. Their army of 25,000 men was almost completely destroyed; again Hannibal treated the Italian allies with clemency and sent them home. 'I am not come to fight against Italians, but on behalf of Italians against Rome'; but there was still no sign of a general Italian revolt.

The Romans appointed the experienced general Quintus Fabius Maximus dictator. He adopted those tactics of delaying Hannibal and avoiding battle which were to bring him the name 'Cunctator' ('the delayer'). Maximus had determined that he would only fight a battle if he had managed to force Hannibal on unfavourable ground. Only once however did he seem close to success; even then Hannibal outwitted him and managed to make his escape across the River Volturnus.

All Italy was now the battlefield. In the autumn of 217 Hannibal had devastated Campania. Then he returned to winter in fertile Apulia. The Romans became impatient with Fabius Maximus's tactics. They probably feared that Hannibal's freedom to range Italy with impunity would lead some of the Italian cities to conclude that they could no longer depend on Rome and would be wiser to throw in their lot with the Carthaginian. Therefore the consuls for 216, one of whom, C. Terentius Varro, had been elected in the face of aristocratic opposition, were given permission to seek a decisive battle. Hannibal awaited them at Cannae, north of Taranto, on the maritime plain, in country that would allow him to exploit his superiority in cavalry.

Cannae was to be Hannibal's tactical masterpiece, and the greatest military disaster experienced by the Roman Republic. He drew up his army in a convex crescent formation, with the Spanish and Gallic infantry in the centre, his Africans on either side of them, and the cavalry on the wings. The Romans were drawn up in conventional parallel formation. First, the Carthaginian cavalry swept the inferior Roman horse from the field. Then Hannibal allowed his centre to receive the brunt of the legions' attack, gradually giving way, till he suddenly launched the African infantry on either side of the now concave crescent. The horns closed on the legions. Their annihilation was completed when Hannibal's cavalry returned to the field to take them in the rear. In the words of Major-General Sir John Fuller: 'The Roman army was swallowed up as by an earthquake.' A force of 70,000 men ceased to exist.

Cannae brought Hannibal to the peak of his success. Capua, the second city in Italy, defected to him. He was joined also by the

Samnites, the Lucanians, the Bruttians, and some Apulian cities. Nevertheless, most of the Italian confederacy remained loyal to Rome; perhaps the fact that Hannibal's army contained so many Gauls, against whom Rome had long defended Italy, influenced this decision. Perhaps the Italians merely considered that Rome was likely to win in the end. Whatever their reason, the failure to attract more defections marked the failure of Hannibal's Italian policy.

Rome expected an attack after Cannae, and Maharbal, Hannibal's cavalry commander, is said to have urged it. When Hannibal refused to take his advice, Maharbal told him he knew how to win a victory, but not how to use one. Many historians have echoed that judgement. Yet Hannibal's difficulties were considerable. He was short of manpower and of siege-engines. He was unfortunate to live in an era when defensive fortifications had the advantage over the besieger. Most cities which fell in the war had to be starved out. Hannibal had hardly the resources to do this; when the Romans besieged Capua in 211, they devoted six legions to the siege. It is doubtful too if Hannibal could have supplied his army at a siege of Rome. His failure to take several smaller cities in the course of the war suggests that his judgement after Cannae was sound.

The Romans resumed the strategy advocated by Fabius Maximus. The war in Italy turned into a war of attrition. Hannibal, compelled to live off the country, unable to demand as much from his new allies as Rome could from hers, found himself penned in. His problem was one of manpower, and Roman successes in Spain made it impossible for him to receive the reinforcements he had expected. He turned to diplomacy, attempting to encircle Rome by making an alliance with Philip V of Macedon. But the decline of Carthaginian seapower rendered this alliance ineffective.

A coup by anti-Roman elements in the Greek city of Syracuse in 214 offered hopes of recovering Carthaginian influence in Sicily. For three years the situation there remained in balance. A victory for the Carthaginians might have transformed Hannibal's position, but in 211 Syracuse fell to the Romans.

Hannibal was already confined more or less to the south of Italy. Whenever he advanced beyond the area he held he found it difficult to feed his troops. He had, only a few years after Cannae, lost the initiative, and in 212 the Romans undertook the siege of Capua. That city fell in 211 also, the Romans having refused to be diverted to a desperate march Hannibal made right up to the walls of Rome itself: the senate knew that he was not strong enough to take the city.

Meanwhile the Romans, under the younger Publius Scipio Africanus, were destroying the Carthaginian empire in Spain. New Carthage fell in 210, Hasdrubal (Hannibal's brother) was defeated in 208 (the same year as a naval victory left Hannibal finally isolated in south Italy) and Mago in 206. By 205 the Romans had cleared the Carthaginians out of Spain. The Barcid strategy was in ruins.

The initiative had now quite passed to Scipio. Ignoring Hannibal and those who now wished to attack his weakened forces, he launched an attack on Africa itself. The Carthaginians sued for peace, and recalled Hannibal in 203. He landed at Leptis Minor with perhaps 15,000 men, of whom rather more than half were veterans of his long Italian campaign. Livy says he left the land of his enemies with as much grief as most men feel on going into exile. His return encouraged the Carthaginians to break the truce that had been agreed and try the chance of battle in the hope at least of getting better terms of peace. In the early autumn of 202 Hannibal confronted Scipio at Zama in the upper part of the Medjerba valley. Before the battle he met Scipio to propose new terms, possibly in the hope that his reputation would encourage the Romans to accept them. But the terms he proposed were more favourable to Carthage than those agreed before the truce had been broken; they were therefore rejected.

For the first time in his career Hannibal met a general of comparable skill, and one who was superior in cavalry – the weapon which Hannibal had used so well in his great victories. This meant that he could not use the enveloping tactics which he favoured, but was compelled to fight on the defensive, unless his elephants managed to break the Roman front. Hope placed in the elephants was hope misplaced, and after the Roman cavalry had scattered the Carthaginian horse, the battle turned into an infantry struggle. Hannibal's Italian veterans, placed in the third line, at least held their own, and it was not until Scipio's cavalry returned to take them in the rear that they broke. Hannibal at once advised the Carthaginians to sue for peace.

Carthage was humbled. After a few months Hannibal retired into private life, but the incompetence and corruption of the aristocratic government (which had even tried to pay the Roman indemnity in debased silver) caused an outcry and a demand that Hannibal be recalled. He was therefore elected *sufet* and proceeded with major reforms, proposing a law that judges should be chosen every year and that none should serve more than two years. These reforms would have established a democratic government on the model of the old Greek city-states; the discredited opposition politicians therefore wrote to the Roman senate accusing Hannibal of being in communication with King Antiochus of Syria and of planning a new war against Rome.

Hannibal was forced into exile, and indeed fled to the court of King Antiochus, thereby suggesting that there might be some truth in the accusations. On several occasions over the next years he advanced his view of how a successful war might be waged against Rome; he saw that the Hellenistic states of the eastern Mediterranean were bound to come into conflict with Roman imperialism, and advised that they should take the initiative. His proposals were disregarded, and when a brief war did break out between Antiochus and Rome, Hannibal played only a minor part. After that he was in continual flight from Roman vengeance. In 182 he arrived, a frustrated exile, at the court of King Prusias of Bithynia. The Romans demanded that the king hand over their enemy; to avoid disgrace Hannibal took poison and killed himself.

His career was a failure, but of the most glittering kind. No enemy of Rome ever impressed himself so indelibly on the Roman imagination. His qualities as a general were outstanding. It was a remarkable feat to have held the loyalty and maintained the discipline of a largely mercenary army over the sixteen years of his Italian campaign. He was tactically brilliant, and was only defeated when Scipio had learned from him how to use cavalry and had the advantages of a better trained army and greater resources. His genius for almost two decades neutralised Rome's inherent superiority, and even the Romans felt bound to praise him. Livy wrote: 'He waged war, far from home, in enemy territory ... at the head of an army not of his own country, but a mixed force ... differing in laws, customs and language, and having nothing in common in their behaviour, dress, arms and religion; yet he bound them as with a chain so that there was never any division among them of mutiny against their leader, though money and supplies were often lacking.'

Scipio

(236–183 B.C.)

Publius Cornelius Scipio Africanus was the greatest soldier of Republican Rome; his outstanding achievement was the defeat of Hannibal, Rome's most dangerous enemy. This victory not only brought the second war with Carthage to an end, but ensured Rome's supremacy in the western Mediterranean.

Scipio was born in 236 B.C. into a great patrician family; the three preceding generations had all supplied consuls. His father, also Publius, was consul in 218, the year of Hannibal's invasion. Failing to stop him in Gaul, he was forced to withdraw to Italy, where he tried to halt Hannibal's advance at the River Po. In one action fought there the young Scipio was reported as having saved his father's life.

In 216 Scipio served as a military tribune (a junior staff officer) at Cannae. He survived the disaster, escaping to Canusium where he thwarted the attempted desertion of 4,000 troops. In 213 he stood for election as curule aedile. To the objection that he was under age, he replied: 'If the Roman people desire to make me aedile, I am old enough.' In 211 his father and uncle were both killed in Spain, as the Carthaginians drove the Romans north of the Ebro; at the age of twenty-five Scipio found himself head of his family.

It was necessary to send reinforcements to Spain. Apparently no experienced general was willing to take up so dangerous a post. Scipio therefore offered his services and was elected general, even though he was technically ineligible since he was not a magistrate. This grant by the popular assembly of a military command to a man who had been neither praetor nor consul created a dangerous constitutional precedent.

Scipio's Spanish policy was ambitious from the start. It might be described as a mirror-image of Hannibal's. Just as Hannibal had boldly struck at the enemy's heartland, Scipio intended to conquer the economically vital Spanish colonies, and so hobble Carthage's war effort. In doing so, he would also avenge his father, and make it impossible for Hannibal to receive reinforcements in Italy.

In 210 this policy seemed over-ambitious; yet it was

successfully achieved in four years. In 209 Scipio launched a combined naval and military attack on the chief enemy city, New Carthage (Cartagena), from his headquarters at Tarragona. He covered the 300 miles in a week, outstripping the nearest of three Carthaginian armies. The defenders were surprised in a fortress considered impregnable. Scipio led his men through the shallows of the lagoon to scale the weakest part of the wall. This victory allowed him to establish himself on his enemy's eastern flank and rear. The attack through the lagoon had been made possible by a sudden drop in the water-level, attributed by the soldiers to the direct intervention of Neptune, evidence that their general was a favourite of the gods.

In 208 Scipio defeated Hasdrubal Barca, Hannibal's brother, at Baecula in Andalusia, and in 206 overcame the two other Carthaginian armies in Spain, commanded by Mago and Hasdrubal Gisgo, at Ilipa. In both these battles he employed tactics which were new for a Roman army, attacking in horn formation, with a weak centre and the strongest legions placed on the wings. By these victories he ended the Carthaginian empire in Spain.

In 205 he was back in Rome, having been elected consul for that year. Hannibal was now contained in the south of Italy, and many in the Senate urged a direct attack. Scipio proposed an alternative strategy. He was in favour of keeping Hannibal penned in Italy while he struck directly at Carthage itself; again he showed how he had learned from Rome's master enemy. Though the senate was dubious, he was permitted to go with two legions to Sicily, where he passed the autumn and winter training his recruits, who were mostly volunteers. He also raided the mainland and snatched Locri from Hannibal. More important, he concluded an alliance with Masinissa, King of Numidia, who could supply him with first-class cavalry, an arm in which the Romans were notoriously deficient. In the spring of 204 he landed in North Africa. His army has been variously estimated at between 25,000 and 35,000 men.

He first besieged Utica, which thereafter could serve as a base. Early in 203 he burned the camps of Hasdrubal Gisgo and his Numidian ally Syphax; the morality of this was dubious, for it took place during negotiations for a cease-fire. Scipio then pursued Hasdrubal and Syphax into the Bagradas plain (modern Suq al Khamis, on the Majardah in Tunisia) where he defeated them by the un-Roman tactics of outflanking them with his cavalry.

Carthage now sued for peace and recalled Hannibal from Italy, complete justification of Scipio's strategy. On the arrival of their great general the Carthaginians decided to resume the war. In 202 Scipio first ravaged the rich valley of the Bagradas, the chief source of Carthage's corn supply, and by this manoeuvre drew Hannibal from the city; it enabled him also to link up with Masinissa and thus ensure that he would have a decisive superiority in cavalry. The two armies met at Zama.

According to Livy Hannibal and Scipio met on the eve of the battle at the Carthaginian's request. Presumably he offered peace terms which Scipio rejected.

Scipio adapted the usual disposition of the legions in order to cope with the danger posed by the Carthaginian elephants and to enable him to exploit his superiority in cavalry. He drew up the maniples in columns leaving gaps or lanes between them, down which the elephants might pass assailed by the velites (lightly-armed slingers). The lines were spaced more widely apart than usual, to give the velites room to retire between them. The cavalry were disposed on either wing, Masinissa's Numidians on the right, Laelius's Italian horse on the left. Their strength made it impossible for Hannibal to employ the enveloping tactics which he usually favoured and which had previously proved so successful.

Scipio's tactics rendered the elephants nugatory. Indeed, many of them apparently charged back into the Carthaginian ranks, causing especial confusion among the cavalry which Masinissa and Laelius were able to exploit. The infantry struggle in the centre was a dour affair, however, and the victory was only achieved first by Scipio's own coolness, when he re-formed his well-trained troops in the midst of the battle, and second by the return of the cavalry to attack the Carthaginian rear.

Scipio did not attack Carthage, since he had not the equipment to besiege so great a city. Anyway he favoured a moderate peace, rather than a punitive one. His leniency was later to be criticised. At the time, however, Roman relief at the end of the long war was overwhelming; Scipio was named Africanus.

In 199 he was censor and became *princeps senatus* (the titular head of the senate). The next decade was dominated by Greek affairs. Scipio was a vigorous philhellene, but he argued during his second consulship (194) against the evacuation of Greece after the defeat of Philip V of Macedonia, since he feared that the power vacuum would be filled by Antiochus III, King of Syria. His fear was justified, Antiochus advanced into Greece and had to be expelled. Scipio's brother Lucius was given command against him, and carried the war into Asia, with the more distinguished elder brother serving under him. His acceptance of the subordinate role may have been because of ill-health; at any rate he was too ill to take part in Lucius's victory at Magnesia.

Meanwhile however the liberal and magnanimous policy of the Scipios had come under attack in Rome, their chief accuser being the elder Cato. Lucius's command was not renewed, and the generous peace terms offered to Antiochus were not confirmed by the senate. In 187 Lucius was accused of financial irregularities; Publius may also have been arraigned. He was not convicted, but nevertheless withdrew from Rome, his influence much reduced. He settled on a farm at Liternum in Campania, living simply and cultivating the fields himself; the Stoic philosopher of the first century A.D., Seneca, would contrast the simplicity of Scipio's life with the luxury of his own day. Scipio died there in 184 or 183, virtually an exile. He reputedly expressed his disillusion by requesting that he be buried in Liternum rather than in the family tomb on the Appian Way.

Scipio was not only one of the greatest, but one of the most attractive figures of the Republic. His sympathies were wide and generous; his troops were devoted to him, and he also won the friendship of foreigners like Philip of Macedon and the native princes of Spain and Africa. He was sympathetic to Greek culture and saw Rome as its protector, a civilised view that aroused the hostility of the boorish Cato. He would seem to have been a man of genuine religious feeling; he used to visit Jupiter's temple on the Capitol by night in order to commune with the god. Later his portrait bust was placed there, for it was rumoured that he was in fact the son of the god who had appeared in his mother's bed in the form of a snake. Though his biographer Polybius (a rationalist) discounted this element in his character, it seems likely that Scipio had a streak of mysticism in his character unusual for a Roman. Certainly, like many great commanders, he believed in his star and that he was a favourite of fortune.

Nothing is known of his marriage to Aemilia, daughter of the consul Aemilius Paulus who was killed at Cannae. He had two sons, Publius, whose poor health made a public career impossible, but who adopted the second member of the family to gain enduring fame, Scipio Aemilianus; and Lucius, praetor in 174. More famous than the sons was his daughter Cornelia, the mother of Tiberius and Gaius Gracchus.

Scipio was one of the greatest soldiers of the ancient world, a great trainer of men, a great leader, capable of learning from the tactical innovations of Hannibal, and greatly superior to him in strategical ability. It was in the originality and vision of his strategy that his genius shone; and it was his boldness and willingness to take well-judged risks that enabled him to defeat Hannibal.

Scipio was hailed as a king by Spanish tribes and he may have been the first Roman general to be acclaimed as imperator by his troops, but he never tried to break out of the conventional pattern of Roman politics. He saw himself as a servant of the Republic who never aspired, as Sulla, Marius, Caesar and Pompey later did, to become its master. His foreign policy was generous – he saw no reason to humiliate a defeated enemy – but his career ensured that Rome would be a Mediterranean, not merely an Italian, power.

To later ages he became the pattern of Republican virtue and the humanists of the early Renaissance idealised him as one who had served the divine purpose. Petrarch made him the hero of his epic, Africa. He thus stood between Aeneas, Augustus and Constantine in the line of those who had made the Roman Empire, and hence Roman Christendom, possible.

Marius

(*c.* 157–86 B.C.)

Gaius Marius was born about 157 B.C. in Arpinum, a hill-town some sixty miles south-east of Rome. He was to be the first *novus homo*, a man from outside the traditional governing classes, to achieve political power in Rome. (His fellow-townsman Cicero was the second. Both in fact came from middle-class equites or equestrian orders.)

This was the first important fact of his career; he showed that it was possible to break into the magic circle. But his career was important for two other reasons; the first of which preserved Rome, the second of which undermined the Republic. He converted the old citizen army into a full-time professional force, modernising its organisation and training in the process; he broke through the traditional pattern of political power, destroyed the authority of the senate, and inaugurated the era of the Dynasts, dependent on the possession of military force.

Marius was a grown man, already with military experience, by the time the brothers Gracchi first challenged the authority of the senate in the name of the people. Their failure and death did nothing to repair the cleavage that had opened in Roman society.

Marius was eventually to inherit the leadership of their party, known as the *Populares*; but, because he was an outsider, his political importance grew very slowly.

He began indeed as a client of a great noble family, the Caecilii Metelli. He had acquired a military reputation on the staff of Scipio Aemilianus in Spain long before the Metelli backed his candidature as a tribune of the plebs in 119. That was his first elected office, and he was almost forty. As tribune he sponsored a law, the effect of which was to reduce aristocratic influence on elections, but he also vetoed a popular corn bill, which would have distressed his noble patrons. His political career advanced slowly and uncertainly. He failed to be elected aedile in 117, and only just managed to be elected praetor for 115, coming at the bottom of the list of successful candidates; he was accused of bribery and barely acquitted. However, this election laid the foundation of his fortunes, for he secured a governorship in Spain, where he was able to make successful investments in silver mines. This secured him a degree of political independence, for without wealth, or at least access to wealth, a man was doomed to remain a client in Roman politics. In 111 he improved his position further by marrying into a great patrician family; his wife was Julia, the aunt of Julius Caesar. By his middle forties he was becoming a man to be reckoned with.

The Numidian War against King Jugurtha provided him with further opportunity. Though his links with the Metelli may have been weakened by some of his actions as tribune, he contrived to get himself appointed as legate on the staff of Metellus Numidicus. The war against this client kingdom, undertaken originally to protect the commercial interests of the Roman Equites, had so far been unsuccessful, and the Roman conduct of the war was disfigured by accusations of senatorial corruption and inefficiency. Though the strategy with which the initiative was wrested from Jugurtha may well have been devised by Metellus, it was Marius who benefited.

First, he agitated for permission to return to Rome and stand for the consulship. When Metellus denied him this, he stirred up agitation in the army and among the equites, claiming that Metellus was unnecessarily prolonging the war, either through incompetence or because of his ambition. At last he got his way, returned to Rome and was elected consul for 107. At the age of fifty he had achieved, by means of popular support, what no *novus homo* had managed before. Then, in an unprecedented step, the Popular Assembly overruled the senate's decision that Metellus should have his African command prolonged, and appointed

Marius to succeed him. This disregard of the senate's long-established right to allocate the provincial commands was fraught with danger for the Republic; it anticipated the developments of the next century by which generals like Caesar and Pompey were to obtain extraordinary commands that led to the overthrow of civil authority and the ruin of the Republican state.

Moreover, Marius's next action looked in that direction also. To make sure of victory in Africa he determined to raise more troops; to obtain these he disregarded the rule that the army should be drawn from the propertied classes, and called for volunteers. This innovation prepared the way for military dictatorship, since such soldiers attached themselves to the general, from whom they might expect rewards, rather than to the state. At the same time Marius created for himself an extensive *clientela*, that indispensable power-base for a Roman politician, which his lack of family connexions had hitherto denied him.

He pursued the Jugurthan war successfully. Jugurtha, who had previously derided Rome as 'a city up for sale and destined to perish, if it finds a buyer', now found himself faced by an implacable adversary whose career could only be advanced by victory. With the aid of his enterprising staff officer, L. Cornelius Sulla, Marius first reduced the strongholds of the Numidian king, then defeated him in battle, and captured him by a ruse. Marius was granted a triumph (104) in which the Numidian king featured before being put to death in the Mamertine prison at the Capitoline end of the Sacred Way.

The Numidian war had ended none too soon. Rome now faced a real danger in the north. Two barbarian tribes, the Teutones and the Cimbri, who had been on the move from their northern forests for some ten years, now threatened an invasion of Italy. In 105 a Roman army was heavily, and, it was thought, disgracefully, defeated at Arausio (modern Orange). It was Rome's heaviest defeat since Cannae; losses were put at 80,000 men; the consul of 105, P. Rutilius Rufus, decreed that no man under the age of thirty-five should leave the country.

In this crisis, Marius, as the people's hero, was elected to his second consulship in defiance of the law that an interval of ten years should pass between consulships. He set off for the north to train a new army, and was in fact to be elected consul every year till 100. He was thus one of the two chief magistrates for five successive years, and he held the office by the will of the people. It was unprecedented, and unnecessary: the senate could legally have confirmed him in a proconsular *imperium*.

If Marius's role in this boded ill for the Republic, and was indeed destructive of its institutions, his work in the reorganisation of the army made it possible for the Empire to spread over the Mediterranean world, and for the military commanders eventually to overthrow the Republic. He was fortunate to be given time to effect his reforms by the lack of direction and purpose shown by the barbarians, but the reforms themselves were of permanent importance.

In the first place he transformed the old citizen-militia into a professional force. The army became a career. Fewer men of property were to be found in its ranks; instead soldiers looked to their army service as a means of acquiring property. The dangerous effects of this have been noted. Since the senate failed to establish any system of pensions or to take responsibility for the soldiers' retirement, they naturally looked to their general for reward, to provide allotments for them by passing a *lex agraria*.

But there were advantages too. The new army Marius created was much more efficient than the one it replaced. He made tactical changes of importance. The legions had been accustomed to fight in three lines, differing in age and equipment (*hastati*, *principes* and *triarii*). Marius abolished these distinctions. Henceforth all the infantry were armed alike. He made the cohort, a battalion of 600 men, the standard tactical unit. Each legion was divided into ten cohorts, each of which was subdivided into six centuries. He introduced the eagle as the standard of each legion, and encouraged regimental loyalty. He standardised equipment too; each legionary was now armed with a javelin (pilum) and sword. He trained his men thoroughly in arms-drill developed on the model of the gladiatorial schools. Finally, he took measures to encourage mobility and self-reliance. The men now carried their own entrenching-tools and the necessary equipment to fortify their night's camp; known as Marius's mules, they no longer had to depend on slow-moving baggage-trains. By these reforms – many, of course, developments of what was already happening – Marius made the Roman army the most efficient in the ancient world; he forged the force with which Sulla and Pompey would conquer Asia, and Caesar bring Gaul within the Empire. His military reforms constitute his lasting and positive contribution to the spread of Roman power; they were so effective that it was to be some four hundred years before the Romans found it necessary to revise them.

During the years of training Marius also employed his army in digging a channel at the mouth of the Rhone to improve navigation; this secured his supply-line, encouraged commercial development and foreshadowed the way the imperial armies would be used. At last in 102 the barbarians desisted from their ramblings and planned a three-pronged attack on Italy. Marius first defeated the Teutones at Aquae Sextiae (Aix-en-Provence), then the following year pursued the Cimbri, who had crossed the Alps by the Brenner Pass, and routed them at Vercellae (near Turin). By these two victories he saved Italy. Terrors aroused by the memory of the Gallic sack of Rome in 390 receded; they would not be renewed for five hundred years. Marius was regarded as the saviour of Rome, his glory was assured, and he was granted a second triumph in 100.

It would have been happy for his reputation if he had died then. He soon showed himself as inept a politician as he had been resolute and skilful in war. Indeed it was at once clear that beyond rewarding his soldiers and confirming his own *dignitas*, he had no clear political aims; and he had already broken the law and alienated a section of the people by granting Roman citizenship to two cohorts of Italians who had fought against the Cimbri. Now he became the tool of radical politicians, C. Servilius Glaucia and L. Appuleius Saturninus, who sought to bribe the people with promises of cheap bread and free land in an attempt to break the power of the senate. Marius, finally alarmed by the violence of his associates, turned on them and became the agent of their defeat. But his early association with them had lost him the respect of the senate; his abandonment of them cost him the support of the people. In 98 he retired to exile in Asia and ten years' obscurity.

Those years saw the terrible Social War between Rome and its erstwhile Italian allies. They saw the opening of the long war against Mithridates in Asia. Both reawakened Marius's ambitions and seemed to promise new opportunities to revive his moribund glory. He returned to Rome and sought the command against Mithridates which the senate had already given to his old lieutenant Sulla. A resolution to this effect was passed in the popular assembly. Sulla however was made of sterner stuff than Metellus Numidicus. He refused to give up his legal right to the command. Instead he marched on Rome. This was itself illegal, but it was effective. Marius, who had no troops of his own, fled. In his absence, untried and unheard, he was declared an outlaw. His adherent, P. Sulpicius Rufus, though a tribune, was seized and put to death. Marius's own life was in danger. Found hiding in the marshes, he was imprisoned in a hut. A slave was sent to kill him. The old man's eyes flashed in the darkness (or so we are told). 'Slave', he cried in a voice of grim authority, 'do you dare kill Gaius Marius?' The terrified slave fled, and the old man was able to escape by a tortuous route to Africa, where many of his veterans were settled. Meanwhile Sulla, having made such constitutional arrangements as he thought would safeguard his position, departed for the east.

He had miscalculated. One of the consuls, L. Cornelius Cinna, immediately broke the oath of loyalty Sulla had compelled him to swear. He was opposed by his fellow-consul, Octavius, and withdrew from Rome to collect troops; Sulla had shown men the way to impress their will on the city. The news was brought to Marius, who returned to Italy and at once recruited an army from his veterans. He joined with Cinna. Together they marched on the city and easily overcame such resistance as Octavius and his associates could offer. Then Rome tasted for the first time the true meaning of military despotism. Marius and Cinna set themselves to secure their position by liquidating their political opponents. Marius rewarded his troops and slaves by letting them loot and murder; it was his revenge on the city which had so insulted his *dignitas*. The bloodbath lasted the best part of a week before Cinna called a halt. Then Marius and Cinna were elected consuls; Sulla was formally outlawed and his laws repealed. The old man, however – he was at least seventy – had hardly entered on this, his seventh consulship, when he died.

So ended a career of enormous and in many ways dire significance. He had saved the Republic; he had forged the instrument that would expand and protect the Empire. He had shown the fragility of the state's institutions; he had prepared their destruction. His character, owing to the paucity of sources, and their partisan character, remains a mystery. He displayed prudence, balance, and resolution for most of his life; in his sixth consulship he vacillated, and was revealed to have no policy and no understanding of the complicated political situation; thereafter he slid first into torpor, then into megalomania.

Any interpretation of such a contradictory history can only be tentative. Nevertheless it is reasonable to suppose that the contrast between his unprecedented glory and success (106–101) and the failure of that sixth consulship, which ended in the loss of respect and his ignominious withdrawal from public life, unbalanced him; that he spent the years of exile brooding on the ingratitude of the senatorial class and on the insults inflicted on his dignity; and that he was indeed hardly sane when he seized power again in 87. His end was terrible, the implications of his career disastrous for the Republic, and yet his positive achievements were such as to have deserved to have been better requited.

Sulla

(138–78 B.C.)

Lucius Cornelius Sulla, born in 138 B.C. to a minor branch of the Cornelian gens, was one of the most remarkable figures in Roman history. His career illustrated the demoralisation of the Republic and contributed to its sharper deterioration: the measures he took in his last years of power which were intended to preserve Republican institutions by reforming them did not last; they were altogether ineffectual compared to the example of Sulla's own career.

He distinguished himself first in the war against Jugurtha (107–6). Much of the credit for Jugurtha's defeat belonged to Sulla, though it was appropriated by the commander-in-chief Marius. Yet Sulla's use of cavalry and diplomatic skill had hastened the end of the war, and it was Sulla who had captured Jugurtha. He showed in this war the peculiar ability to win the respect, affection and confidence of the soldiers under his command, on which ability his career was founded. He managed to maintain his own control over the troops while still granting them unusual licence. Sallust considered that 'Roman soldiers in Sulla's time began to drink, to make love, to have a taste for works of art, to rob temples ...'

From 104 to 101 Sulla again served under Marius in the war against the German tribes, the Cimbri and the Teutones, who threatened an invasion of Italy. He played a leading part in their final defeat near Verona and pursued them into Sicily. By this time a rift appears to have opened between Marius and Sulla, principally because the old general seems to have been jealous of his younger colleague's aristocratic connexions and popularity with the army.

Sulla returned to Rome, living quietly for some years and taking no part in politics. His temperament was sociable; he was a man of genuine culture, fully capable of enjoying leisure. In 97 however he was elected praetor; he sought popularity by exhibiting a hundred African lions, sent him by King Bocchus, whom Sulla had earlier persuaded to betray Jugurtha, and whose treachery had been rewarded by the Romans.

The year after his praetorship Sulla was dispatched to the east to confront Mithridates, King of Pontus, whose own imperial ambitions were beginning to alarm the Romans. His immediate purpose was to restore the Roman client-king of Cappadocia, Ariobarazanes, whom Mithridates had deposed. He succeeded in this task and also became the first Roman to establish diplomatic contact with the Parthian empire.

Resolution of the conflict for empire with Mithridates which was looming in the east was made less urgent for the Romans by a new danger which arose in Italy itself in 91. This was the outbreak of the Social or Italian War. (The designation 'social' derives from the fact that the war was fought against Rome's allies [*socii*]; the term is slightly misleading because the Latin cities did not join in, but remained loyal to Rome.) In this war Sulla commanded the legions against the Samnites, the southern group of the allies. It was a war of peculiar bitterness, for the Italian grievances ran deep. They had been loyal to Rome in the long wars with Carthage; they had contributed to the spread of empire, but they had been denied any share in its rewards, and were not treated as equals by the Romans. After initial checks, Sulla was able to move over to the offensive in 89. He defeated an Italian army which was trying to relieve Pompeii, advanced into the mountains and captured Bovianum Vetus, the Italian headquarters. Leaving his lieutenants to crush the final Italian resistance (which had now reached so desperate a pitch that they were negotiating an alliance with Mithridates) he returned to Rome to stand for the consulship of 88.

He played a great part in the military victory. What part he played in the intelligent and generous settlement that converted the discontented Italians into Roman citizens is uncertain. It is probable that it was not great, for the tribune P. Sulpicius Rufus, who in 88 proposed that the newly enfranchised Italians should be distributed over the thirty-five tribes, was an enemy of his. He also proposed that the province of Asia, and hence the command in the war against Mithridates that was imminent, should be transferred from Sulla to Marius. Sulla tried to block all Sulpicius's legislation by proclaiming a suspension of public business (*iustitium*), which in turn Sulpicius declared illegal. There was rioting in the city. Sulla withdrew to Campania where his legions were mustering for the war against Mithridates and Sulpicius passed all his measures.

Sulla reacted violently. He marched on Rome at the head of six legions, thus becoming the first Roman to enter the city at the head of a Roman army. He took the city after a few hours' street-fighting. Marius, the leader or at least the figurehead of the

popular party, and Sulpicius were declared outlaws, without trial.
Sulpicius, a tribune in office, was found and killed. His laws were
abrogated. Sulla hastily passed measures to curtail the power of
the tribunes and increase that of the senate. He made the new
consuls swear they would not interfere with his arrangements, and
then set off for the east. This first violent military intervention in
Roman politics represented a hideous precedent of brutal
illegality. It would be even more bloodily revenged in Sulla's
absence.

Mithridates, king of Pontus, was no ordinary man, but rather
the most formidable enemy Rome had met since Hannibal. In a
few years he had extended his kingdom round the Black Sea to
Colchis (modern Georgia) and the Caucasus. This enabled him to
build up and supply a large army and navy. He had then taken
advantage of Rome's involvement in the Social War to seize
Bithynia and Cappadocia (90). In 88 he defeated Nicomedes, the
former king of Bithynia, who had obtained modest Roman
support, and then overran the Roman province of Asia, where he
posed as the champion of Greek interests, promising freedom and
remission of taxes to the Greek cities. He massacred tens of
thousands of Roman and Italian businessmen resident in these
cities – as many as 80,000 according to some authorities. He then
crossed over into Greece where he established a puppet
government in Athens, though the Roman governor of Macedonia
managed to check his progress into northern Greece.
Nevertheless, when Sulla landed in Epirus with five legions in 87,
he was faced with the prospect not only of the loss of Rome's
influence and possessions in Greece and Asia but also with the
likelihood that Rome would be replaced by an energetic,
acquisitive and hostile power. The task facing Sulla was therefore
of the utmost importance.

His war against Mithridates lasted four years. They were years
of turmoil back in Rome where his enemies took advantage of his
absence to resume power, annul his legislation, dismiss him from
his command and declare him an outlaw. But Sulla's army was
loyal to Sulla, not to the Republic; he could afford to ignore his
dismissal and prosecute his war.

Nevertheless his military position was dangerous too.
Mithridates commanded the sea, and so Sulla's freedom of
operation was restricted. One of his first actions was to dispatch
his lieutenant Lucullus to collect a fleet. Meanwhile he ensured
that he would be able to finance his campaign, and reward his
soldiers, by plundering the treasuries of Delphi and Olympia. In
86 he stormed Athens successfully, allowing his legions to sack the

city and himself appropriating a library which contained the works of Aristotle. Then he defeated an army which outnumbered his by three to one at Chaironeia, the scene more than two hundred years earlier of Philip of Macedon's great victory. Another Pontic army was however sent to Greece. Sulla brought it to battle at Orchomenus, and defeated it. The invasion of Greece was ended; Sulla could now turn to the attack.

He was now faced with a new danger, a new complication. A Roman general, Flaccus, had been sent to replace him. Aware that he could not hope to do this after Chaironeia, he attempted to outflank Sulla by himself marching into Asia. Flaccus was however murdered by his lieutenant Fimbria, who appears to have offered to co-operate with Sulla's man Lucullus and those Greek cities now disillusioned with Mithridates's rule. Lucullus declined the offer, and Sulla himself crossed over into Asia. He was now irresistible and Mithridates sued for peace. He met Sulla in 65 at Dardanus near Troy. He was compelled to surrender a large part of his fleet (70 ships), evacuate such conquered territory as he still held in Asia, and pay an indemnity of 2,000 talents; but Sulla permitted him to retain his own kingdom and granted him the title of 'friend and ally of the Roman people'.

Sulla's achievement in this war was great and of lasting importance. He had not completed Rome's conquest of the east; that would be the work of his lieutenants Lucullus and Pompey. Nor had he made any definitive settlement. But he had done more than check the progress of Rome's only rival for domination in Greece and Asia; he had ensured that these provinces would form part of the Roman Empire. His settlement was harsh for those cities which had welcomed Mithridates. They lost their autonomous status and became subject to Roman tax-collectors. Sulla imposed an enormous indemnity on the province of 20,000 talents, calculated as the cost of the war and five years' lost taxation; and he compelled the unfortunate provincials to pay for the expense of his army of occupation through the winter of 85–4. One result of this was to leave much of Asia heavily in debt to Roman business interests.

Sulla landed at Brundisium in 83 with perhaps 40,000 men. He had been declared a public enemy; his friends had been persecuted, some of them killed, his own property confiscated. Marius was dead, but the popular party, Sulla's enemies, remained in control of Rome, and could count (it was believed) on the support of most of the Italian cities. It was clear that Sulla would have to be prepared to fight for his political future and, very possibly, for his life. He was however soon joined by others who had reason to fear the Populares, or to believe that Sulla would win. These included men of future note: M. Licinius Crassus, whose father had been killed in Marius's terror, Metellus Pius, and the young Gnaeus Pompey, to whom Sulla was later to give the surname 'Magnus' (the Great).

With these reinforcements Sulla advanced into Campania, where he defeated the consul C. Norbanus near Capua. He then negotiated with the other consul L. Scipio and managed to persuade most of Scipio's army to join him. He conciliated the Italians by promising to respect the rights of those newly granted citizenship; only the Samnites, who had been in direct opposition to Sulla in the Social War, remained obdurate.

The consuls for 82 were Carbo and the younger Marius. Sulla forced Marius into Praeneste (Palestrina), but was unable to take the town. Leaving an investing force, he marched north against Carbo, who, dismayed by the successes of Sulla's lieutenants and three failures to relieve Marius, gave up the struggle and fled to Africa. The siege of Praeneste continued into the autumn. Then the Samnites and the remnants of 'Marian armies' made a desperate attack on Rome itself. Sulla only managed to intercept them outside the city. On 1 November a hard battle was fought by the Colline Gate. Sulla, commanding the left wing, was almost overwhelmed, but Crassus on the right won the battle for him. The captured and wounded Samnites were put to death on Sulla's order. Soon Praeneste fell and young Marius killed himself. Though a few pockets of resistance remained in Italy, Spain and Africa, Sulla was effectively master of the Roman world.

He embarked on a course of deliberate terror. Revenge was doubtless one motive. His friends and adherents had suffered in the years of the Populares' ascendancy. He was determined also to liquidate all possible opposition. He needed money and land, which confiscations could provide, for his veterans. As H. H. Scullard puts it, 'the vicious nexus between an army and its commander, which Marius's career had first demonstrated, now began to get its stranglehold on Roman life'. What differentiated Sulla's terror from the one that had preceded it was its deliberation: proscription lists of his victims, by which they were outlawed with a price on their head, were posted. The first contained the names of 40 senators and 1,600 equites. It has been claimed that as many as 9,000 were eventually proscribed. The punishment extended to their children and grandchildren, who were debarred from holding public office by a general who thought to control the future as he dominated the present.

In the constitutional vacuum created by the deaths of the

consuls, Sulla was named 'dictator', an old office which had not been filled since the second war with Carthage. The senate heaped honours on him. He was granted a triumph which he celebrated in 81. An equestrian statue to Cornelius Sulla Imperator Felix was set up in the Forum. He was granted an escort of twenty-four lictors and his authority was unimpeded by any veto or right of appeal. No one in the history of Republican Rome had possessed such power; unlike previous dictators, no limit was set to his term of office.

Sulla had come to power by the sword and in defiance of legality. To confirm his power he resorted to measures which were both illegal and cruel. His position was full of ironies, for he had shown the fragility of the Republican institutions which he now set himself to reform. He seems to have judged that only by strengthening the senate and reducing the power of the popular assembly and the tribunes could authority and stability be restored.

First he raised the membership of the senate from the 150 to which it had fallen to about 600. In doing so he rewarded his supporters and placated the equestrian order which supplied some 300 of the new senators. He arranged that in future the senate should be automatically recruited from the magistrates: anyone elected quaestor became a senator at the end of his year of office. He increased the number of quaestors from twelve to twenty, but at the same time revised the Lex Villa of 180 in an attempt to prevent young men from getting political power too early: the *cursus honorum* was to be enforced more strictly; no one was eligible for election as quaestor before he was thirty, for praetor before thirty-nine or for consul before forty-two. In an attempt to prevent the acquisition of personal power he decreed that no one man was to hold the same office twice within ten years. This was no doubt well-intentioned, but it missed the real defect of the system: for it was not in Rome but in the provinces that the Republic would be overthrown. The real danger to the state came from a dissatisfied proconsul backed by a loyal army. Sulla himself had set the example that Pompey and Caesar would follow.

Having effected his reforms, which also included a new treason law and the creation of new standing courts controlled by the senate to deal with major crime, and having demobilised twenty-three legions and settled 120,000 veterans in colonies throughout Italy, Sulla abruptly retired into private life in 79. His retirement puzzled contemporaries: Julius Caesar said it showed that Sulla 'did not know his political alphabet'. One modern historian,

Jerome Carcopino, has suggested that his retirement was forced on him by associates who were unwilling to support his hope of becoming a monarch. Yet it is possible that, as a conservative, he felt he had done his work in restoring the balance of the state (short-lived though it was to prove) and wished to enjoy his last years.

At any rate he withdrew to his country estate in Campania with his new wife Valeria. There he wrote his memoirs, which have unfortunately been lost, but which formed the basis for Plutarch's biography. He hunted, fished and lived the life of a country gentleman of sporting and literary tastes. (His enemies, after the usual fashion of Roman scandal, imputed other less reputable pleasures to him.) He died the following year, 78. He was granted a magnificent funeral; no friend, his epitaph observed, excelled him in kindness, no enemy in harsh reprisal.

Sulla was an odd mixture of cynicism and superstition, public sobriety and private self-indulgence. He brought an unprecedented ruthlessness to Roman life; and, though it may be conceded that his political intentions were good, his methods contributed more than those of any other man to the debasement of the Republic he avowedly restored.

Cicero

(106–43 B.C.)

Marcus Tullius Cicero, intellectual and supreme orator, was a rarity among Roman politicians, being a self-made man, and an outsider. He was born in 106 B.C. in the municipality of Arpinum (also the birth-place of Marius), seventy miles south-east of Rome. His father, also Marcus Tullius Cicero, was of equestrian rank; Cicero would inherit a villa and substantial farms from him, but he could do little to advance his son's political career.

That was made by his genius as an advocate. After serving in the army during the Social War (89 B.C.), the young Cicero studied rhetoric and philosophy in Rome, Athens and Rhodes. He distinguished himself as a pleader in the courts, even taking the risk of defending enemies of the dictator Sulla. Legal services were given free, for there was no class of professional lawyers; but they were not unrewarded: he could accept 'presents' and legacies, and towards the end of his life claimed that he had received twenty million sesterces in legacies from grateful clients. The first purpose of his advocacy however was to force himself on the attention of the public; lacking family connexions, it was the only means by which he could make himself a political career.

In 75 he stepped on the first rung of the ladder when he was elected one of the quaestors for the following year. These junior magistrates were principally responsible for managing the state's financial affairs: Cicero served his quaestorship in the rich province of Sicily. Becoming a quaestor was important for another reason. As a result of Sulla's reforms it provided automatic entry to the senate, where Cicero's peculiar abilities could shine. In 69 he became curule aedile, responsible for the public games and the maintenance of the city; in 66 praetor, an office with largely legal responsibilities; and in 64 he was elected consul for the following year.

It was a remarkable advance and, if it was made possible by merit, it also showed that Cicero possessed considerable political acumen. He had declined to take up the governorship of a province after his year as praetor, preferring to remain in Rome to plan his campaign for the consulship. Two years had to elapse before he was eligible to stand, and the magnitude of the enterprise is made clear when it is realised that at any time there might be up to a hundred Roman politicians qualified for the position, and that almost all of his possible rivals would have more distinguished family connexions. Nevertheless he was elected consul for 63. At the age of 43 he had attained the highest position open to a Roman citizen.

It was to be a momentous year. The crisis of the Republic, first fomented sixty years earlier by the Gracchi, then bursting into flames in the civil war between Marius and Sulla, then smouldering since Sulla's death, was approaching a new intensity. Essentially it was caused by the social strains engendered by the expansion of empire and by the failure to adapt the Republic's institutions to the demands made by empire. No means had been found to attach the loyalty of the armies to the Republic rather than to their commanders, or to control the influence exerted by a few rich men over political life. The conservative senatorial grouping to which Cicero was gravitating had neither programme nor philosophy that went beyond a desire to keep things ticking over and restrict office to safe and respectable men. Their opponents, however, known as the Populares, threatened all stability by their lack of respect for property and their willingness to bribe the poor and dispossessed with extravagant promises of land reform, remission of debts and the lavish distribution of public bounty. All Cicero's instincts inclined him to the conservative party; he set out to make himself indispensable to them.

His consulship gave him that opportunity. The aristocrat Caesar and the millionaire Crassus, both fearful of the power of the great dynast Pompey, noisily espoused the popular cause. They put up a tribune, Rullus, to initiate a bill proposing vast measures of confiscation and resettlement as part of a plan to redistribute land among the urban poor. That promise secured the bill popular support. Properly drafted, the bill might have seemed more reasonable; but it also proposed a commission of ten to administer its provisions, and these included the incorporation of Egypt (a Roman dependency, but not a province) in the Roman domain. It was clear to Cicero that the true purpose of the bill rested here; Caesar and Crassus would have the fabulous wealth of Egypt at their disposal. The bill had a secondary purpose: it was intended to stir up popular animosity against the conservative politicians who would oppose it. Cicero did not flinch from the challenge. The bill offended his idea of justice and of political virtue equally. He spoke three times against it and secured its defeat. It was a momentous victory, for it ensured that his own political future must rest with the conservative classes, known as *Optimates*.

He was then faced with a more immediate danger. Among his defeated rivals in the election had been a dissolute and near-bankrupt nobleman, L. Sergius Catilina (Catiline). He had run Cicero close in the election, in which Cicero had set himself to destroy Catiline's reputation. When Catiline failed again in the elections in June 63, he tried in desperation to overthrow the state. He planned a *coup d'état*, and was even ready to ally himself with a Gallic tribe, the Allobroges, to secure troops. Cicero, even before full proof of the conspiracy was forthcoming, persuaded the senate to pass an emergency decree empowering him 'to see to it that the Republic incurs no injury'. He then provoked four of Catiline's followers to more drastic and open action, putting their names to a document of agreement with the Gauls. He was then able to denounce them to the senate, and prove that his suspicions of Catiline had been fully justified. He demanded the death penalty. Most senators agreed, though Caesar, whose relations with Catiline made his own position dangerous, called for life imprisonment. Cato supported Cicero, and the senate voted in his favour; Cicero therefore had the four strangled in the Mamertime prison. It was an extraordinary blunder on the part of a lawyer and constitutionalist, for they were Roman citizens and there had been no trial.

Catiline himself fled the city, and tried to raise an army. It was easily dispersed by the force of three legions sent after him, and Catiline was killed in the skirmish. Cicero had reached the peak of his fame. He had saved the state. The senate granted him the title 'Father of his Country', and Cicero had medals struck to commemorate his achievement. Nevertheless his rash and illegal execution of the conspirators would return to plague him.

His consulship represented not only the summit of his career, but his only taste of real power. In 60 the First Triumvirate came into being: it was formed by a compact between Pompey, Caesar and Crassus as a result of which they carved up power in the state. Caesar became consul in 59. Five years later Cicero summed up the significance of what had happened: since then there had been 'no genuine consuls, but mere hucksters of provinces, mere agents and slaves of sedition'. He himself was offered a chance to join in the domination of the Free State, for Caesar invited him to become his lieutenant in Gaul. Cicero declined.

He was soon in danger from the new régime. The demogogue, agitator and gang-leader Clodius was encouraged by Caesar and Crassus to prevent any restoration of stability in political life. Now a tribune of the people, Clodius was an old enemy of Cicero's. He proposed a law making death or exile the penalty for anyone who should condemn or had already condemned a Roman citizen to death without trial and without the right to appeal against the sentence to the vote of the people. The measure was clearly aimed at Cicero; only the self-satisfaction with which he viewed his defence of the Republic against Catiline had prevented him from foreseeing the danger. Consequently he had failed to build up a party among those who owed him gratitude strong enough to defend him now; and he had antagonised each member of the Triumvirate on either personal or political grounds. His appeals for protection now failed. In March 58 he fled to Greece. Clodius at once had his town house destroyed.

From Greece he repaired relations with Pompey, himself now the victim of Clodius's intemperate attacks. Pompey got Caesar to agree to Cicero's return provided he promised to make no further trouble for the Triumvirate. But when a bill authorising Cicero's return was proposed, Clodius set his gang to break up the meeting. It was not till another tribune, Milo, a client of Pompey's, organised a rival gang that, after another riot, a law was passed in August 57 recalling Cicero from exile.

He returned, but on a leash. Cicero had his own programme for the revitalisation of the Republic. He called it the *concordia ordinum* – the agreement of the classes. He invited the *boni* (all men of good will and good standing) to come together and work in harmony. Presumably he envisaged this as the preliminary to some structural reform, for he could hardly have imagined that a change of heart could by itself rescue the Republic. But now he found that the ascendancy of the Triumvirate (reaffirmed at Luca in April 56) had cost him his freedom of action. In the autumn of 54 he wrote to his brother Quintus (who was serving on Caesar's staff in Gaul): 'You must see that the Republic, the senate, the law courts are mere ciphers, and that none of us has any constitutional position at all.' So, immediately after his return from exile in 57, Cicero had found himself compelled to repay his debt to Pompey by proposing that Pompey be given proconsular authority to reorganise Rome's corn supply. It was an indication of the state's decadence that Cicero, the champion of constitutional government, should be reduced to urging one of those extraordinary commands which were a mark of that government's failure. His search for the *concordia ordinum* now seemed to depend on the desperate remedy of first detaching Pompey from Caesar and Crassus.

The 50s were a miserable decade for Cicero as Rome plunged into chaos and stumbled to civil war. Nevertheless he still found the fascination of the city such that it was only with extreme reluctance that he allowed himself to be sent to Cilicia as proconsul in 51. Twenty years before, Cicero had prosecuted Verres for his misgovernment of Sicily; he governed his own province with admirable honesty and self-restraint. The members of his staff complained that they were not permitted to grow rich at the expense of the provincials.

When civil war broke out between Pompey and Caesar in 49, Cicero could hardly fail to be on Pompey's side, supported as he was by the majority of respectable and conservative senators. But he did so despairingly: 'The sun seems to me to have disappeared from the world ... the worst has come to the worst.' He regarded the Republic as 'completely abolished'; he joined Pompey 'because I cannot endure the sight of what is happening or of what is certain to happen'.

Nevertheless, he did not follow Pompey to Greece, but languished in Brundisium from July 48 to September 47. His fate was in the victorious Caesar's hands. In fact Caesar both liked and respected Cicero; he hoped that Cicero would lend respectability to his régime. He pardoned him, but could not promise him the freedom of speech without which Cicero could not contemplate a return to public life. Cicero's feelings about Caesar were now ambivalent. On the one hand he declared himself 'astonished by Caesar's sobriety, fairness and wisdom'. On the other hand, Caesar's supremacy meant the end of the old political life in which Cicero had delighted: 'The men, the forum and the senate house are all utterly repulsive to me', Cicero now wrote. From the time of his return from Brundisium to Caesar's murder in March 44, Cicero retired into private life.

In these years he wrote works on philosophy and literature which were to establish his enduring reputation in post-Roman Europe. Some of these, *On the Nature of the Gods*, *On Divination*, *On Fate*, *On Old Age*, were rather popularisations of Greek philosophy than works of original thought; others, *The Republic*, *The Laws* (both largely lost) and *On Duty* represented his mature reflections on his long political career, and constituted an analysis of Rome's broken commonwealth. They could not influence the struggle for power in the dying Republic, but they stimulated and enlightened future generations. Cicero may not have been a strikingly original thinker, but very few men gifted with his power of expression have spoken from a comparable experience on practical politics.

Caesar's murder brought him back into public life. He had not been privy to the conspiracy, but he could not help approving what had been done. He deplored however the lack of foresight shown by the liberators, their failure to eliminate Caesar's lieutenant Antony, to seize the treasury and take control of the state. He regarded Antony as possessed of all Caesar's vices and none of his virtues. Between September 44 and April 43 he denounced Antony before the senate and the people in speeches of such masterly invective that they were compared to those classics of ancient oratory, the speeches in which Demosthenes had defended the liberties of Athens against Philip of Macedon. If Cicero's life had sometimes displayed timidity, his courage in old age was unmistakable. He remained, though, the devious politician. Desperately seeking to check Antony, he had favoured Caesar's nephew, the young Octavian. This was a measure of the fragility of the Republic: to defeat the adventurer he had to turn to another adventurer. It was a measure of his cynicism too: 'The young man', he said, 'should be praised, decorated and disposed of.'

In fact it was Cicero himself who was outwitted. He had thought to use Octavian against Antony; Octavian used him to force the reunion of the Caesarean party on Antony. When this was achieved, Cicero found himself on the proscription list. His attacks on Antony had made this inevitable. Octavian did nothing to save him; he knew how Cicero had planned to use him. Antony's soldiers caught the old man as he was being carried in a litter to a ship which might have taken him at least to a temporary refuge. A centurion killed him with one blow.

The forces that destroyed Cicero's career were the same as those which destroyed the Republic. He was the victim far more of circumstance than of the failure of his judgement or the faults of his own character. Vain, self-admiring, over-susceptible to flattery, sometimes irresolute, Cicero was nevertheless a good and, within the limits of Roman politics, honourable man. He was devoted to liberty, but he did not realise the sacrifices that might have to be made to preserve it.

Cicero was married twice, first to Terentia in 77 B.C. They had two children, a son, Marcus, born in 65, and a much-loved daughter, Tullia, born in 76. Cicero divorced Terentia in 46, and the same year married Pubililia. This second marriage, to a girl young enough to be his granddaughter, was probably undertaken for financial reasons, but lasted only a few months.

Julius Caesar

(100–44 B.C.)

Gaius Julius Caesar was born in 100 B.C. to a great patrician family; the Julians claimed descent from the goddess Venus and from the old royal house of Alba Longa. Yet his immediate political connexions placed him in the Popular camp. His aunt had been married to Gaius Marius, and his own first wife was Cornelia, daughter of the Popular leader L. Cornelius Cinna, who had been Marius's colleague in his last consulship. Caesar indeed nearly lost his life in the proscription that followed Sulla's victory over the Populares; 'in that young man there are many Mariuses', the dictator said, sparing him reluctantly.

Caesar's career started ominously and slowly; for twenty years he struggled up the foothills of Roman politics. He showed courage at the siege of Mytilene in 80, when he was decorated with the *corona civica* (civil crown), and energy and resourcefulness in 75, when he commandeered a fleet to pursue a band of pirates who had previously captured him and held him to ransom. In 63 he displayed moral courage and confirmed his standing with the Populares when, almost alone in the senate, he opposed the death

Above left: Homer, the great epic poet of antiquity, to whom the *Iliad* and the *Odyssey* are attributed. An imaginary portrait. The two greatest Greek historians: (*above right*) Herodotus, frequently described as 'the Father of History'; and (*left*) Thucydides, author of the *History of the Peloponnesian War*. Like the portrait of Homer, these are probably imaginary versions by sculptors of a later age.

Bust of Pericles in the British Museum. The Age of Pericles was supreme in the annals of Greek intellectual and artistic life. Among the works undertaken under his auspices was the building of the Parthenon on the Acropolis.

penalty demanded by Cicero for the Catilinarian conspirators. Before then in 65 he had, as aedile, courted the favour of the people by holding games of unprecedented splendour and extravagance; they left him heavily in debt, but that was of little importance compared to the political credit he had won.

Through the family influence he became *pontifex maximus*, virtually head of the state religion, a position that enhanced his *dignitas* and, to some extent at least, ensured that his numerous political enemies must treat him with circumspection. In 62 he became praetor, and that year divorced his second wife who had become embroiled in a scandal: 'Caesar's wife must be above suspicion.'

The following year he got his first overseas command, proconsul in the province of Further Spain, where he campaigned successfully against the Lusitanians. He was awarded a triumph, but did not celebrate it: he had decided to stand for election as consul in 59, and this required him to fight the 60 elections. He could not campaign as a military commander; he could not receive the triumph as a civilian. With that sense of political realism which was to be his peculiar quality till the year of his murder, he chose to forgo the glory of a triumph.

Aware of the hostility and distrust which surrounded him, he sought allies. He found them in the millionaire Crassus and the great general Pompey. Both had reason to be discontented with the oligarchy which controlled Rome. Crassus had already financed Caesar, and saw him as the means of re-establishing the political influence he had himself been losing since his consulship in 70. Pompey's grievances were more specific: the senate had insulted him by refusing to accept his settlement of affairs in Asia without investigation and scrutiny, and by declining to provide land which could satisfy Pompey's veterans. Both men were seeking a means of redressing their private grievances; both saw Caesar as the instrument which could provide it. They disliked and distrusted each other, but this very coolness offered Caesar his opportunity. He could act as the middleman who would reconcile the resentful dynasts; together the three could dominate the state. This compact, later known as the First Triumvirate, ensured Caesar's first consulship of 59.

As consul he first brought in an agrarian bill to satisfy the land-hunger of Pompey's old soldiers. The senate rejected it. Caesar promptly brought it before the popular assembly, where it was carried despite the obstruction attempted by his fellow-consul, M. Calpurnius Bibulus. Then Caesar had his henchman, the tribune P. Vatinius, carry a bill confirming everything

Pompey had done in Asia. These measures satisfied Pompey; the alliance between him and Caesar was sealed by the marriage of Caesar's daughter Julia to Pompey. Meanwhile Caesar repaid his debt to Crassus by a measure which remitted one-third of their contract to Crassus's clients, the tax-collectors of Asia.

This consulship was the watershed of Caesar's career. It established him as one of the great men of Rome. It also won him the undying hatred of the Optimates. Despite good legislation like the *Lex Julia de Repetundis*, which defined and controlled the power of provincial governors, they read in all his actions a revival of the old Popular programme; they feared confiscations and domination. Moreover, the refusal of Caesar's colleague to co-operate in any of this legislation meant that the legality of Caesar's measures could be challenged. Bibulus had tried to prevent the passage of any public business first by declaring the omens unfavourable, then by nominating all the remaining days of the year as public holidays. Caesar paid no attention and pressed ahead with his legislation.

The consulship was the means of providing for his own future also. Anticipating his election, his Optimate enemies had tried to shackle him by passing a measure in 60 which decreed that the proconsular province for 58 should not be the usual overseas command but the 'woods and forests of Italy'. This would deny Caesar any power-base. He therefore again had Vatinius inter-vene and carry in the assembly a bill granting him Cisalpine Gaul and Illyricum for five years, with command of three legions and the right to appoint his own officers and to found colonies – two provisions which gave him enormous opportunity for patronage and to build up that essential requirement for success in Roman politics, an extensive and grateful clientage. Then, when the proconsul for Transalpine Gaul died unexpectedly, Pompey proposed in the senate that this province too should be added to Caesar's command. Unnerved by the solidarity displayed by the dynasts, the senate yielded. Caesar's future was secured. Moreover, being in office he was immune from prosecution for any alleged irregularities of his consulship for at least five years.

Gaul made Caesar great; his command there also, in Cicero's words, 'led to the murder of the ancestral constitution'. Cicero had been aware of the danger. He had opposed the addition of Transalpine Gaul on the grounds that 'the senate was placing the tyrant in the citadel'. As for Caesar himself, the historian Sallust summed up what the Gallic command offered him: 'Caesar passionately desired a great command, a great army, and an unprecedented war which would give his ability the chance to display itself.'

Three features of the command made it ideal.

First, it made him a patron on a huge scale. In the peaceful provinces of Cisalpine Gaul and Illyricum, he was able to establish colonial settlements and win the gratitude of the civilised provincials by treating all townships on the north side of the Po as colonies of Roman citizens. It was from this region that he drew his reinforcements for the Gallic Wars, and created the devoted army that stood by him in the subsequent civil war.

Second, the province was close enough to Rome for Caesar to be able to remain alert to political developments in the city. He usually spent his winters in Cisalpine Gaul near the Roman frontier. There he was in constant touch with his agents in the city. In the words of his biographer Gelzer: 'He never lost himself in activity on the periphery of empire; what mattered was always its effect on Rome.'

Third, the addition of Transalpine Gaul, then a mere strip of territory on the Mediterranean coast, gave him the chance of winning military glory equal to Pompey's and of adding to the Roman Empire.

His achievement in Gaul was extraordinary. In two years he overran the greater part of the country up to the Rhine. He employed the strategy of favouring, and promoting the interest of, certain tribes which were then willing to act as allies or clients of the Roman people. Even so, the speed with which the northern barbarians, who only fifty years back had threatened Rome's frontiers, were conquered, dazzled the city; fifteen days of thanksgiving for Caesar's achievements were ordained. The rejoicing was premature, for the first conquest was superficial. Sporadic risings broke out, aided by the Germans and the Celtic tribes of south-east Britain. Caesar's response was brutal. In 55 two tribes, the Usipetes and Tencteri, were wiped out, even the women and children being killed. Back in Rome, Caesar's enemy Cato proclaimed himself appalled by this genocide: Caesar should be handed over to the Germans as a war criminal. Yet the people were less impressed by the cruelty than by Caesar's first expedition that same year to the fabled island of Britain.

The greatest rising against the Romans came in 52, when Vercingetorix raised all central Gaul in the last effort to preserve liberty. Caesar forced him into the hill-town of Alesia, threw up lines of investment, fought off a relieving army and compelled surrender. Gaul was finally secured as a Roman province; the Rhine was established as the frontier of empire. Vercingetorix himself was hustled off to Rome where he was preserved to make a show at Caesar's triumph six years later before execution in the Mamertine prison.

Caesar's methods in Gaul had been cruel: 'No man ever made war so horrible as Caesar in Gaul', wrote Field-Marshal Lord Montgomery. But his achievement was immense and enduring. Mediterranean civilisation was carried into northern Europe. His conquest of Gaul eventually made medieval Christendom possible; it made France; it made modern Europe. It was the most important single action between the defeat of Carthage and Constantine's adoption of Christianity as the official religion of the Roman Empire.

Meanwhile the constitutional crisis of the last years of the Republic grew more intense. The compact between the three dynasts was fragile, and the mob-leaders, Clodius and Milo, sponsored by Crassus and Pompey respectively, came near to breaking it by involving their principals in their dissensions. Pompey was being wooed by Cicero, who, having been exiled in 58, returned to Rome and active politics in 57, and demanded that Pompey be given proconsular authority to reorganise the corn supply. It was symptomatic of the state's decadence that Cicero, the constitutionalist, should find himself proposing one of those extraordinary commands which were undermining the constitution; but the wooing of Pompey held danger for Caesar. He was alarmed too by the threats of the Optimate senator, L. Domitius Ahenobarbus, who was a candidate for election as consul for 55, and who had declared his intention of recalling Caesar from Gaul.

Caesar's response was swift. He called Crassus to Ravenna; then the two moved to Luca to meet Pompey, who arrived there with an entourage of one hundred and twenty senators. There, by means of Caesar's diplomatic skills, the compact was renewed, the Triumvirate reaffirmed. Plutarch described what happened at Luca as 'a conspiracy to share the sovereignty and destroy the constitution'. It was agreed that Pompey and Crassus should be consuls in 55. To ensure their success the elections would be postponed till the autumn when, the campaigning season over, Caesar would send his legions on leave to cast their votes as instructed. The elected consuls would then prolong Caesar's Gallic command for another five years and pass another bill allowing him to stand for his own second consulship in 49 in his absence, thus avoiding any period when he would be out of office and liable to prosecution for the alleged misdeeds of his first term of office. After their consulships Pompey would take Spain (as well as the corn supply commission) and Crassus Syria. It seemed that the three had satisfactorily arranged the affairs of Rome.

Events destroyed the compact. First Julia, Pompey's wife and Caesar's daughter, died; one link of sympathy was broken. Then Crassus, moving from Syria against the Parthian Empire, was surprised, defeated and himself killed at Carrhae. The triumvirate destroyed, Caesar and Pompey were left gazing across a widening gulf of distrust; and Pompey was in Rome, since his corn commission allowed him exemption from the rule that proconsuls must reside in their province, and, being in the city, was open to persuasion that he alone could save the Republic.

Disorder grew. It was impossible to hold elections in 53. When the gang leader Clodius was murdered, his followers burned down the Senate House. For the moment Pompey held to his agreement with Caesar; he arranged that all ten tribunes should sponsor that bill promised at Luca which would permit him to stand for the consulship in his absence. But then the senate proposed that Pompey should be made consul without a colleague. It was clear to Caesar that they were trying to drive a wedge between them. He responded by publishing his memoirs of the Gallic War, a propaganda device that was simultaneously witness to what he had achieved for the Roman people, a defence of the necessity of his actions and a warning to his enemies.

M. Marcellus, however, consul in 51, seized on the memoirs as evidence that the Gallic War was over, and that Caesar should be recalled. He argued also that the Law of the Ten Tribunes was invalid, and proposed that the senate debate the question of Caesar's successor on 1 March 50. Caesar's agent, the tribune, G. Scribonius Curio, vetoed the proposal.

Fear dominated both sides. Caesar's Optimate enemies were convinced that his second consulship meant ruin for the free state. He was equally sure he was fighting for his life. He attempted conciliation: Curio proposed that Caesar and Pompey should both give up their commands. The longing for peace, and the fearful memories of the civil war between Marius and Sulla, persuaded the senate to pass the bill by 370 votes to 22. But a tribune was found to veto this in its turn; the Optimates could not believe in Caesar's sincerity. Instead, Marcellus asked Pompey to assume command of all forces in Italy and save the Republic. Still Caesar proposed compromise. Mark Antony, tribune in 49, was sent to Rome to renew Caesar's offer to carry out Curio's proposal. The offer was rejected. Instead, the senate decreed that Caesar must disarm within two months or be deemed a public enemy. When Antony interposed the tribunician veto, the defenders of legality disregarded it. Antony and a fellow-tribune fled the city. On the seventh of January Pompey was named dictator. A few days later Caesar crossed the Rubicon, the narrow stream that divided Cisalpine Gaul from Italy, and so launched civil war on the Republic.

He had not desired the war; nor had Pompey. Caesar believed that his political career, possibly his life, were at stake. Looking at the bodies of his enemies on the field of Pharsalus, he excused himself with the words *'hoc voluerunt'* ('they wanted it'). Yet he himself was fighting for no principle, only for his own *dignitas* and safety.

The first stage of the war was rapid. Caesar's speed surprised his enemies and drove them from Italy. Master of the peninsula, he pursued a policy the exact opposite of that which he had followed in Gaul: clemency, not terror, was now the watchword. He attempted to win Cicero to his side; in vain. Nevertheless his moderation did conciliate some who had feared him.

From Italy he first destroyed the Pompeian legions in Spain in the summer of 49, then crossed over to Greece. Pompey had built up a force of some 36,000 legionaries, and took up a strong position at Dyrrhachium, where he could be supplied by sea. Caesar found it impossible to break these lines, and withdrew to Thessaly. Pompey followed and the armies met at Pharsalus. Caesar's victory was complete. Pompey fled to Egypt, where he was murdered three days before Caesar arrived in pursuit.

Caesar delayed some months in Egypt, having an affair with the young queen Cleopatra and consolidating Roman power in the country that served as the granary of the Mediterranean. Though there were still Pompeian armies in Africa and Sicily, Caesar had established himself as master of the Roman world. In the spring of 46 he defeated Cato and an Optimate army at Thapsus. The same year he was named as dictator for ten years and entered on his third consulship. A fourth followed in 45, when he defeated the last army of his enemies, commanded by his old lieutenant T. Labienus, at Munda in Spain. Extravagant decrees were passed in his honour; he was named dictator for life and consul again for 44. The question remained: what would he do with his power? Would he restore the Republic or would he supplant it?

No answer to the question is possible. His intentions mystify us as they mystified his contemporaries. Perhaps he had no solution himself. He began preparing for a Parthian war which would avenge Crassus's defeat. It looked as if he was ready to shelve the constitutional dilemma and seek further glory. There were many in Rome however who feared that he was dissatisfied with the position of perpetual dictator and wished to revive the obnoxious title of king. Neither his remark 'I am not king, but Caesar', nor his refusal of a kingly crown offered him by Mark Antony during the Festival of the Lupercal in February 44, convinced the doubters. A conspiracy was formed. Caesar disregarded warnings and doubtful omens alike. Attending a meeting of the senate in the Theatre of Pompey on the ides of March 44, he was surrounded by the conspirators and stabbed to death. They ran through the streets proclaiming liberty. Many of them were men to whom Caesar had shown friendship and mercy; one of their chiefs was Marcus Brutus, the son of his lifelong friend and mistress Servilia. The conspiracy involved at least sixty men, but support for it went wider still. As Cicero said in the senate: 'Is there anyone, except Antony and those who were glad to have Caesar reign over us, who did not wish for his death or who disapproved of what was done?'

Caesar had achieved two things of lasting importance. First, his conquest of Gaul had extended the Roman Empire to northern Europe. Second, he had destroyed the old Republic. He had failed to establish anything durable: Rome would experience another, more terrible, civil war before a settlement came in sight. But what Caesar had destroyed was never repaired. The old oligarchic constitution lay in ruins. He himself had said that 'the Republic was a mere name, without form or substance'. His career had revealed that to be true; the self-styled liberators could not restore that substance.

Julius Caesar and Shakespeare

Julius Caesar and Alexander the Great are the two men of action from antiquity who have most affected European imagination. Of the two Julius Caesar naturally stood out more in Shakespeare's mind, for he knew no Greek and more Latin than he has been given credit for. Elizabethan grammar-school education was based on Latin, and there is more about this in his work than with any other dramatist of his time, confirming the early tradition that before taking to playing he was an usher in a country school.

The earliest plays are school plays, reflecting what was taught in school – Plautus, Ovid, Seneca, Cicero, Caesar's *Commentaries*.

In each of the very first plays, the three parts of *Henry VI*, we find
these tell-tale pointers. In *3 Henry VI*,

> Kent, in the *Commentaries* Caesar writ,
> Is termed the civil'st place.

In *1 Henry VI* we find

> – like that proud insulting ship
> Which Caesar and his fortune bare at once.

This refers to the young Caesar's insistence on crossing the
Adriatic in the teeth of a storm. In *2 Henry VI* we find 'Brutus's
bastard hand/Stabbed Julius Caesar': which shows that Shakes-
peare knew the story from antiquity that Brutus may have been
Caesar's son, for he had been the lover of Brutus's mother.
(Hence, by the way, the redoubled poignancy of Caesar's last cry,
'*Et tu, Brute!*')

Julius Caesar's astonishing – and dramatic – personality
occupied Shakespeare's mind more than any other. There are
references to him in some eighteen of the plays (half the total),
apart from the play wholly devoted to him and references back in
Antony and Cleopatra. Four times Caesar's 'thrasonical brag', *Veni,
vidi, vici*, is referred to or quoted. Plutarch gives us a further
reason, which we may not realise, why the words made such an
impression in the Roman world: 'These three words, ending all
with like sound and letters in the Latin, have a certain short grace,
more pleasant to the ear than can be well expressed in any other
tongue.' In addition to the implicit boastfulness, Caesar was
conscious of style; a highly educated man besides everything else,
he was an excellent writer, an admirer of Cicero for his style, and
author of a lost book on grammar.

The ancients thought of Caesar as possessed of a daemon, for
which the Latin word was genius. Shakespeare knew of this
(genius speaks to genius, not to fools): in *Macbeth* we find:

> My Genius is rebuked, as it is said,
> Mark Antony's was by Caesar [Octavius].

The characteristic of genius is to be obsessed in nature – virtually
from birth, with which the word is cognate – and Caesar was
obsessed by the desire for power, to rule and to govern. And why
not? He has usually been condemned for his ambition; but why? –
he was far more able to rule and govern than anybody else, and
knew it.

This well-justified assumption of superiority often arouses the
envy of the second-rate, the Cassiuses of this world who have

pretensions of their own, and talents which cannot, however, rival the gifts of a man of genius. It does not arouse so much envy among the third-rate, for they know their place. As for the people at large, Caesar well knew what to think of them (as did William Shakespeare): Plutarch tells us that, in depriving the tribunes of the people, Flavius and Marullus, Caesar 'spake also against the people and called them Bruti and Cumani, to wit beasts and fools'. This did not prevent him, an aristocrat, from always culti-vating popularity.

Julius Caesar had precisely this quality – as Elizabeth I and Burghley had, without his challenging and intolerable gifts, his consuming self-confidence, what people who do not understand it are apt to call 'arrogance'. (The word should be properly applied only when it is unjustified; with Caesar it was only too well justified, and this again was maddening to the inferior with *their* pretensions.) Brutus, who had more justice of mind, recognised that Caesar was not motivated by partiality, and this is credited to him in the play:

> To speak truth of Caesar,
> I have not known when his affections swayed
> More than his reason.

Here is a prime qualification for a ruler; Caesar had it, when others had not – except Brutus, but he had other disqualifications for rule.

Then why was Caesar brought low, after such an unparalleled career of success, good luck and achievement? – unparalleled by anybody but Alexander the Great, the only person who gave Caesar cause for envy. The answer is probably that the time was not yet ready for the only solution to the Roman Republic's troubles – the imperial government inaugurated by his great-nephew Augustus, but only after a second civil war unleashed by Caesar's assassination.

What looks obvious is that the Republic could not administer the empire Rome had won. Republican government was evidently tottering to its fall, as witnessed not only by shocking exploitation of the provinces but also by corruption, inefficiency, and popular disorder at home. The incompetence of the Republic, increasingly breaking down, obviates the necessity of arguments pro or con in accordance with our own prejudices. The leading Roman historian in Britain in our time, A. H. M. Jones, with his Leftist sympathies, was pro-Republic, anti-Julius Caesar; the Prussian Mommsen was, of course, pro-Caesar. History has its inevitabilities, at least its unavoidable dilemmas – as Caesar's had.

The extraordinary personality of Julius Caesar has thus been subject always to controversy. Ordinary folk are apt to think 'controversial' what they are too simple to understand; and many historians have found Julius Caesar 'enigmatic'. But Julius Caesar – with his genius, his lust for power, his exceptional gifts – is understandable. To understand Shakespeare's presentation of him we have to see him in the perspective of Shakespeare's own time, what that age made of him, what the tradition was as well as what the classical authorities they read, especially Plutarch, wrote about him. This approach is far more illuminating, and rewarding, than the purely literary treatment of the play unhistorically *in vacuo*.

Shakespeare's attitude to Caesar in the play was rather an ambivalent one, but this was in accordance with tradition. In antiquity Caesar was criticised as much as he was praised – chiefly by Republican sympathisers among intellectuals, who rarely understand the conditions under which men of action operate. Even Plutarch, who was sympathetic to the man and appreciated his greatness, noted his physical failings, his proneness to headaches and to the 'falling sickness', presumably epileptic attacks – without giving him credit for his superhuman efforts in spite of them. No doubt these physical symptoms came from the intense strain under which Caesar lived and to which his will subjected his body. Will-power consumed him, the will to power and to govern well when he got there.

To the medieval mind, not much given to rational criticism, Caesar, like Virgil, was a legendary figure, with something magical about him (he certainly had charisma). To churchmen he was anathema. The great exception to medieval moral disapprobation was Dante: genius spoke to genius. He placed Brutus and Cassius in the lowest reach of Inferno, as traitors to their benefactor, who had pardoned their hostility in fighting for Pompey and treated them with characteristic clemency.

The Renaissance – naturally, with its liberation from medieval values – had a higher and a better appreciation of Caesar. The English attitude was, however, somewhat mixed; again characteristically, for Tudor England was not Renaissance Italy, and medieval tradition – as one sees in its drama no less than its architecture – was stronger than the new classical impulse. Not the least remarkable thing about Shakespeare's play is how comparatively classical it is: it has a classicism of its own, in keeping with the subject, artistic decorum, a self-consciousness as to style witnessed in the contrasting rhetoric of Brutus, stoical and laconic, with its prosaic appeal to reason, as against the Alexandrian rhetoric of Mark Antony, with its oratorical tricks, its repetitiveness and appeal to emotion.

Julius Caesar was something quite new in Shakespeare's work, a marked contrast with the rambling chronicle plays. The play is much more carefully worked; he evidently took trouble over it, gave it more thought – and produced something quite new, of significance for future development, which would influence other people's work as well as his own.

Our best critic in the proper terms of theatre, Granville-Barker, tells us: '*Julius Caesar* is the gateway through which Shakespeare passed to the writing of his five great tragedies.' He adds that 'Plutarch was a godsend to Shakespeare' – in Sir Thomas North's beautifully Englished translation of course. He read up the relevant accounts in the three Lives, of Caesar, Brutus, and Antony; no reason why he should not have looked at that of Cicero too – though there is no reason why we should waste time ferreting about for more and more remote 'sources'. Shakespeare *was* a reading man,* also a practical man of the theatre, who would not waste *his* time on what was not relevant to writing his play. He would already have read the best-selling *Mirror for Magistrates* and Sir Thomas Elyot's magistral *Book of the Governor* with its sympathetic account of Caesar. Still, Plutarch's three Lives 'contain the main incidents of his plot, and treat Caesar, the conspirators, and Antony in much the same way'.

What is revealing of Shakespeare's way of writing is that, partly in consequence, the play has a threefold structure. The first centres on Brutus and his persuasion by Cassius to head the conspiracy; the second on Caesar himself and the assassination; the third, Brutus and Cassius again, and their nemesis, with Antony and Octavius to round off as victors, Octavius the heir of Caesar's spirit. Granville-Barker notes that the populace give unity to the first three acts; they have a collective character and are given the derisory depiction Shakespeare reserves for the mob.

His was always a responsible governing-class point of view (unlike Marlowe, for instance). To Tudor England nothing was worse than civil war, the danger of disruption of the social order and consequent anarchy – and such was the consequence of Caesar's assassination.

To Shakespeare the mob was always good for a laugh, as well as

* *cf.* my *Shakespeare's Globe* (American title, *What Shakespeare Read and Thought*).

serious warning. Casca reports that upon Caesar's reluctant refusal of the title of king, 'the rabblement hooted and clapped their chopped hands, and threw up their sweaty nightcaps, and uttered such a deal of stinking breath that it had almost choked Caesar, for he swounded and fell down at it. And for my own part, I durst not laugh for fear of opening my lips and receiving the bad air.'

The superior, gentlemanly Shakespeare repeats this reflection elsewhere. We now know that, in addition to his being the favourite dramatist at court, his audiences at the Globe would be mainly middle and upper class, those who could afford to pay, the groundlings being very much a minority.*

He downgrades Caesar's character, in accordance with tradition, as against Plutarch's more favourable view. This may be, as is usually thought, partly in order to keep dramatic balance, while on the other side he upgrades Brutus, partly to even things up. Cassius is allowed to claim that Caesar called on him to rescue him when swimming in the Tiber, and that Caesar lacked courage in danger. Nothing could be further from the truth: his courage was notorious, to the point of foolhardiness. He was a gambler, and always took risks, trusting in his stars even to the last – his over-confidence may be regarded as a fault. Historically, his prowess in swimming saved him from danger of capture at Alexandria – and Sir Thomas Elyot gets this right.

Again, historically, Caesar's decisive crossing of the Rubicon to invade Italy, contrary to the law and the senate's proscription, was a necessary decision for his self-preservation, or his enemies would have got him. It is like Bolingbroke's taking Richard II's throne: apart from his being called to undertake it by Parliament and Church – on account of Richard's incapacity as a ruler – Bolingbroke *had* to take the throne or, at the next turn in the wheel of Fortune, Richard would have had him by the neck. Certain steps in high politics are forced by necessity upon the actors – mere intellectuals with no political sense often cannot see this. Shakespeare did.

We may think that he makes too much of Caesar's brags, his boastfulness – a weakness, for it offends other people's self-esteem, and in Caesar's case aroused widespread envy. He was open and fearless in his self-confidence and too-great trust in his stars – unlike the great Lord Burghley, at the time of the play, who disguised his pre-eminence under a show of bogus humility. That was not Caesar's way – utterly contrary to his temperament

* *cf.* Ann Jennalee Cook, *The Privileged Playgoers of Shakespeare's London*, which puts out of court A. Harbage's *Shakespeare's Audience.*

(after all, he was more of an Italian than a Roman Republican, like Cato or Brutus).

In the play, when Artemidorus tries to inform Caesar of the conspiracy against him –

> O Caesar, read mine first; for mine's a suit
> That touches Caesar nearer –

Caesar replies too grandly,

> What touches us ourself shall be last served.

(Note here the contemporary Elizabethan touch, the word 'ourself' – the royal 'We'.) Again, Shakespeare turns Plutarch's point against Caesar; Plutarch makes it clear that the dictator tried several times to read Artemidorus's document, but simply could not for the press of suitors. We may legitimately infer, from the marked emphasis Shakespeare lays upon Caesar's boastfulness, that this was a feature that the dramatist personally disliked. After all, it was very unlike himself, and hubris calls for nemesis.

It is significant that Caesar is given none of the charming, redeeming touches that Brutus gets; even Caesar's greatness is merely reported indirectly, unfavourably by Cassius – bestriding the world like a Colossus. No indication either that, in historic fact, Caesar had treated Cassius magnanimously, pardoned his taking part with Pompey, and promised him promotion.

Brutus is treated far more favourably, his considerateness for his little slave-boy highlighted, and his love for Portia brought out with inner feeling –

> As dear to me as are the ruddy drops
> That visit my sad heart.

Why is it that, in a play on Julius Caesar, Brutus is treated much more favourably?

I think the answer points directly to the nature of Shakespeare's own genius. In this play he was developing his interest in the mixture of motives, the inconsistencies and dubieties of human character, that led to the great tragedies. *Hamlet* followed immediately upon the heels of *Julius Caesar*, still in mind as we can tell from the reminder in the first scene upon the battlements of Elsinore:

> In the most high and palmy state of Rome,
> A little ere the mightiest Julius fell,
> The graves stood tenantless, and the sheeted dead
> Did squeak and gibber in the Roman streets . . .

Apart from the high drama of the assassination, there was no inner conflict in the mightiest Julius to inspire the dramatist's interest: in a sense, Caesar was too obvious, like the Colossus itself. Whereas Brutus, with his conflicting motives, his inner dilemma, the necessity to persuade himself that the criminal deed was in the public interest, apart from private respects – all this makes for a character in depth. His relations with Cassius are given a further dimension in the quarrel before Philippi, the most humanly affecting scene in the play.

Brutus's faults are not overlooked, but they come from Plutarch. His bad judgement is shown up in letting Mark Antony go free after Caesar's death and even allowing him to speak to the mob and turn them against the conspirators. Again, his military judgement was at fault before Philippi, the more human and less exalted Cassius in the right. The historic crime of Brutus – that he murdered his benefactor and unleashed civil war – is overlooked, if not forgiven him, for at Philippi he got his come-uppance and Caesar's spirit his revenge.

Then, *pour comble de tout*, Brutus receives the noblest tribute of all, from Antony:

> This was the noblest Roman of them all.

It is really very curious, for the last word on Brutus, historically, was said by himself at Philippi, in quoting from a lost Greek tragedy:

> Poor Virtue, I find you now a fable, yet I practised you as if you were real.

That is, the doctrinaire intellectual died disillusioned. Shakespeare would not have known that, for it is not in Plutarch.

Nor is the circumstance of Cicero speaking in Greek at the offer of the crown to Caesar. A classical scholar tells us that 'it is deliberately invented and inserted in the play by Shakespeare himself. He must have had a reason for this.'* What was it? 'The delineation of Cicero is slightly satirical. And this must be intentional, because (apart from his jibe about the Greek) the record has been altered.' The real reason for the conspirators not recruiting Cicero is given by Plutarch: his timidity. Shakespeare changes this to –

> he will never follow anything
> That other men begin.

Had he somebody particular in mind?

* J. A. K. Thomson, *Shakespeare and the Classics*, 206ff.

Our classical scholar, Professor J. A. K. Thomson, thinks it 'much more likely that what we have is a sketch from his hand of a typical scholar'.

With *Julius Caesar* Shakespeare produced something entirely new, quite different from the dead academic plays on the subject, such as the *Caesar Interfectus*, or *Octavia*, or *Caesar's Revenge* from Oxford. 'In Shakespeare's own time,' Professor Thomson thinks, 'it called for real courage to defy the majority vote of the critics and the universities.'

Augustus

(63 B.C.–14 A.D.)

Augustus put an end to the disorder of the late Republic, ensured the territorial integrity of Rome's conquests, and established the pattern of empire. He curtailed the freedom of traditional institutions and prepared the way for despotism, though he was not a despot himself and indeed respected the customary forms of the constitution.

He was born Gaius Octavius Thurinus in the old Volscian town of Velletri in 63 B.C. His father's family was undistinguished, though of equestrian rank. They owed their elevation to the marriage of his maternal grandfather to Julia, the sister of Julius Caesar. He, having no legitimate son, adopted the boy as his heir. (On adoption he became Gaius Julius Caesar Octavianus; it is convenient to refer to him as Octavian till 27 B.C. when the senate granted him the honorific name Augustus.)

He was eighteen at the time of Caesar's murder. His stepfather L. Marius Philippus advised him to decline the dangerous inheritance. But the boy hurried to Rome where he found Mark Antony, the consul and natural leader of Caesar's followers, hostile and suspicious. Antony refused to hand over Caesar's treasure to Octavian, who therefore began to pay his uncle's legacies from his own resources and from money advanced by the Spanish banker Balbus.

The state of Rome was confused throughout 44. Caesar's murderers (the Liberators) had neglected to prepare a coup, and the Caesareans remained in control of the armies, legally at least during Antony's consulship, and had the chance to ensure their continuing predominance by their power to dispose of provincial governorships. Brutus and Cassius, the chief Liberators, withdrew to the east to prepare civil war. Sextus Pompeius, the unreconciled son of the great Pompey, held the strategically important island of Sicily. In Rome itself Cicero, hating and fearing Antony, sought to restore the old form of the Republic.

Octavian manoeuvred skilfully between these parties. His methods were devious and empirical; yet his strategic aim was constant: he must compel Antony to accept him as an equal partner in Caesar's political legacy. To achieve this he was ready to combine with anyone, even Caesar's murderers. Yet he had to be cautious: he depended on his position as Caesar's heir and on the loyalty of Caesar's legions.

In January 43 Antony was no longer consul. Cicero called on the senate to declare him a public enemy, and to accept Octavian and his legions. The boy was made a senator, granted the *imperium* of a pro-praetor, and joined with the new consuls, Hirtius and Pansa, in the command of the army against Antony.

The campaign of Mutina saw Antony driven over the Alps, both consuls killed and Octavian general of the only army in Italy. He promptly opened negotiations with Antony and at the same time demanded the vacant consulship from the senate. When this was refused he marched on Rome and seized power. On 19 August 43 he had himself elected consul. He was still nineteen, ineligible for even the most junior office.

He now came to terms with Antony. They associated M. Aemilianus Lepidus, governor of Spain and Caesar's master of the horse, with them in what is known as the Second Triumvirate. The three imposed their rule on the Republic. They instituted proscriptions: to avenge themselves on their enemies; to ensure no seditious elements remained in Italy when they turned against Brutus and Cassius; to finance that campaign. Cicero was the most distinguished victim. Octavian has been reproached with cruel ingratitude. But Cicero had been equally ready to dispose of him: 'The boy', he had said, 'must be praised, decorated and got rid of.'

The Triumvirate was formally instituted for five years, later prolonged for five more. Elections were held for the traditional offices, but the triumvirs prepared lists of approved candidates years in advance. It was an uneasy partnership, but it endured till its enemies had been overcome. The Liberators were defeated at Philippi in 42, but Sextus Pompeius remained as a focus for disaffection till 36.

After Philippi the triumvirs divided responsibility in the

Empire. Antony took the east and the chance of glory in a war against the Parthian empire. Octavian undertook the huge task of managing the demobilisation and resettlement of the army raised for the civil war. He marked down nineteen Italian municipalities, confiscated one-third of their estates, and settled 100,000 veterans; a feat of supreme administrative competence.

It aroused inevitable resentment, fanned by Antony's wife, Fulvia, and brother, Lucius, who claimed Octavian had favoured his own veterans at the expense of Antony's. A new war broke out in Italy. This War of Perusia (Perugia) ended in complete victory for Octavian, but shook the Triumvirate. Common interest and the general fear of civil war yet held them together. Antony married Octavian's sister Octavia, and they combined against Sextus Pompeius.

Nevertheless Antony's eastern interests, which led eventually to his rejection of Octavia in favour of the Egyptian queen Cleopatra, drove them apart. When, after the defeat of Sextus Pompeius, their disregarded partner Lepidus tried to assert himself at Octavian's expense and was easily disposed of, they were left joint masters of the Roman world. No common enemy now held them together; their rivalry was soon open.

Octavian took steps to ensure the loyalty of Italy. In the autumn of 32 he summoned senators, soldiers, municipalities and civilians to swear an oath of loyalty to him, and to accept him as Rome's leader against Antony and Cleopatra. He set himself to blacken Antony's reputation, seizing and publishing the will Antony had deposited with the Vestal Virgins: its terms led Romans to believe that he was preparing to transfer the capital of the Empire to Egypt.

War was declared against Cleopatra, for Octavian wished to mass resentment against the foreigner. But it was really the last civil war of the dying Republic. The victor would be its master, in a position to reform its political structure. The total defeat of Antony's fleet at Actium in 31 ensured that that master was Octavian.

Two problems faced him: the army and the constitution. They were connected, for it was the existence of large armies attached to their generals rather than to the state which had wrecked the republic. They could however be tackled separately.

After Actium Octavian commanded seventy legions. Antony's had crossed over to him, and these seventy legions, perhaps 350,000 men, represented the military force of the whole Empire. In the next three years, forty-two legions were disbanded. The demobilised men were settled on lands brought from Italian or provincial municipalities. Octavian kept twenty-eight legions, a force of about 150,000, and these were stationed in frontier provinces. They were joined there by an equal number of *auxilia*, provincial troops officered by Romans. He attached this army to himself by extracting a personal oath of loyalty and by appointing commanders connected to him by blood, friendship or obligation.

This done, he could turn his attention to the constitution. In 27, as he was to claim in the *Res Gestae*, his own record of his achievements, Octavian 'transferred the state from my own power to the control of the Roman people. For this service of mine I received the title of Augustus by decree of the senate ... henceforth, though I excelled all in authority, I had no more power than those who were my colleagues in any magistracy.' The imperial historian Velleius Patroclus said, 'the old forms of the Republic were restored'. Even Tacitus, ever suspicious of the Empire, recognised that January 27 marked the end of civil strife and the establishment of civil order.

Competition for the traditional offices was resumed, though Augustus was himself elected consul every year till 23. The senate also resumed its old powers, and even added to them, becoming a court of law. Augustus was granted the Republican title *princeps senatus* (chief of the senate). Consequently he is often referred to as the princeps and the order he instituted as the principate; the word *imperator* (emperor) retained a purely military significance.

Nevertheless the restoration of the old order was more apparent than real. Government of the provinces was divided between the senate and the princeps. The senate appointed governors for, and controlled the taxation and administration of, the heartland of the Empire; Augustus remained proconsul of all provinces where there was a military establishment. Political realism could hardly be expressed more effectively.

An aristocratic conspiracy in 23, revealing enduring resentment, produced a further refinement. Augustus ceased to monopolise a consulship. This created a problem, for his legal authority in Rome had depended on that office. However he had the senate vote him a superior *imperium*, overriding that of any other magistrate, and he was now invested with the full power of a tribune, which rendered his person inviolable and permitted him to initiate and veto legislation.

The next twenty years saw the flowering of the Augustan peace before uncertainty about the succession darkened the end of his principate. With his lieutenant and son-in-law Marcus Agrippa as commissioner of public works he set himself to beautifying and enriching the city; it was his boast that he 'had found Rome of brick and left it of marble'. Among many buildings they constructed the Temple of Apollo on the Palatine, the Theatre of Marcellus and the first version of the Pantheon. (The frieze above the present building reconstructed by Hadrian still bears Agrippa's name.) The Ara Pacis (Altar of Peace), unveiled in 13 B.C., represents what Augustus had achieved for Rome.

With his friend Maecenas, Augustus was a patron of the arts. Maecenas brought Virgil and Horace into the imperial circle. Augustus himself suggested the theme of the *Aeneid* to Virgil. The poem celebrates him in turn: '*Augustus Caesar, divi genus, aurea condet / Saecula qui rursus Latio regnata arva / Saturno quondam . . .*' ('Caesar Augustus, son of a god, who shall establish the age of gold in Latium over fields that once were Saturn's realm . . .'). When in 17 Augustus held the Ludi Saeculares, games instituted in the year of the Republic's foundation and repeated every century, in order to demonstrate how health had been restored to the state, Horace wrote the celebratory ode.

Yet the Roman peace was internal only. Roman expansion continued in the north and in Africa, though Augustus abandoned the dream of a Parthian war. By the end of the reign the frontier had been pushed south to the Sahara, north to the line of the Upper Danube and Rhine. Only a disaster in 9 A.D., when Quintilius Varus lost three legions in the forests of Germany, persuaded Augustus not to advance to the Elbe. He advised his successor to eschew further conquests, but he himself had annexed more territory than any general of the Republic.

The question of the succession loomed early. When he fell ill in 23 B.C. he gave his ring to Agrippa, whom he had married to his daughter Julia. Afterwards Agrippa was associated in government till his death in 12. Augustus had the dynastic ambitions proper to a family man, but neither of his first two brief marriages nor his third to Livia (whom he married in 39 B.C. and who survived him) produced a son. Julia was his only child. After Agrippa's death, her father quickly married her to Tiberius, Livia's son by her first marriage, who was compelled to divorce Agrippa's daughter Vipsania. Meanwhile Augustus adopted his grandsons Gaius and Lucius, the children of Julia and Agrippa. These were intended to succeed him, with Tiberius acting as regent if necessary. The boys were given the title *principes iuventutis* (Princes of Youth). When they grew up, Tiberius, disgruntled, withdrew to Rhodes, against Augustus's will. The boys however both died by 4 A.D., by which time Julia had been involved in an unsavoury and politically dangerous scandal and had herself been exiled to the island of Pandateria. Augustus, whether reluctantly or not, had to fall back on Tiberius, who played an increasingly important part in the government of the Empire during Augustus's last years.

Augustus died in A.D. 14. He had always lived simply and without ceremony; his health, poor in youth, had improved with age. His funeral was of unprecedented splendour, and a few days later the senate decreed his divinity, an ex-praetor Numerius Atticus obligingly swearing that he had seen him ascending to the heavens.

Augustus had effected a revolution and made it seem natural. The constitution he had constructed from the rubble of the Republic and civil war appeased the nobility, and permitted the cities of the Empire to prosper in security, the majesty of Roman peace, Roman law and Roman civilisation to spread over the Mediterranean world. Viewed in his time, he had saved the Empire from disintegration and rescued it from civil strife; viewed historically, no man did more to make the passage from the ancient world to European civilisation possible.

Tiberius

(42 B.C.–A.D. 37)

In 42 B.C., the assassinated Julius Caesar's great-nephew and official heir, Octavian, in association with Caesar's fellow consul and loyal general, Mark Antony, defeated the forces of Brutus and Cassius in two engagements at Philippi in Macedonia. Subsequently, Octavian and Mark Antony, who had been past rivals, fell out again, largely due to the latter's infatuation with the Egyptian queen Cleopatra and his scheme to appropriate the Eastern Empire.

Civil war ensued. Antony and Cleopatra were defeated by Octavian at Actium in 31 B.C., and fled to Egypt, where Antony killed himself. Octavian was left as sole ruler of the entire Roman army, and therefore of the whole vast empire.

He took the name Augustus ('Exalted') as befitting the first Roman emperor, and set about instituting widespread financial and organisational reforms in almost every sphere of administration. With a strong regular army, and the shrewd device of keeping his subjects happy with sumptuous entertainments and gifts of money, Augustus ruled easily enough and, in general, enjoyed the support of the ruling class. But his health was not good. Sooner or later he would have to nominate a successor. In ancient Rome, this was where the rivalries and plottings invariably intensified. The simple system of the eldest son automatically stepping up did not exist, and prospective heirs were inclined to die prematurely, by chance or design. By such a process of elimination Augustus's successor, when he died of a chill in A.D. 14, was his stepson Tiberius Claudius Nero, an aristocratic soldier of long service and much distinction, whom he had been grooming for the highest office.

Tiberius had been drawn into the royal family in the first place when Augustus had married the young man's mother, Livia. Tiberius had been ordered to divorce his own wife, Vipsania, who was pregnant at the time and whom he happened to love, in order to marry Augustus's widowed daughter, Julia, whose reputation for immorality was widespread. Their unhappy marriage, which produced one son, Drusus (born c. 15 B.C.), lasted only a few years before Augustus annulled it without even troubling to ask Tiberius if that was his wish. Being moved about like some matrimonial pawn had embittered a man whose nature was proud and reserved, and he spent some years brooding in exile in Rhodes. All the same, he remained destined to succeed his stepfather, and virtually ruled beside him during the old emperor's last years.

Having been born in 42 B.C., that same year of the vengeful victories at Philippi, Tiberius was already fifty-six years old when he became Rome's second emperor in A.D. 14. There appeared to be no opposition to his succession, except from himself. He did not leap eagerly into office, but demurred. This was not from delicacy of feeling for his predecessor, who had, after all, made him give up a beloved wife for one he was to detest, and had alienated him through long absence abroad (he had campaigned in Germany alone nine times, and in many other parts) from the aristocratic Claudian family of which he should now have been head. Tiberius's objection was that he had served the state enough already, that he was unworthy of the honourable and onerous task of ruling in the aftermath of so great a personality as Augustus (now declared a god, with a temple dedicated to him), and that, in any case, so responsible an office ought no longer to be entrusted to one man.

No one of consequence was taken in by this. Tiberius's reputation as a hypocrite, with the almost oriental habit of saying one thing while meaning something quite different, was well known. The historian Dio Cassius expressed it perceptively:

His was a most peculiar nature. He never revealed in his conversation that which he really wanted, while what he *said* he wanted he usually did not want at all. On the contrary, he conveyed the exact opposite of his intention; he made out that he had no interest in what he really longed for, but would much prefer that which he was known to detest. He would behave angrily about things which did not anger him, but put on a show of affability when he was actually furious. He would express pity for those whom he ordered to be severely punished, while never forgiving ones whom he had pardoned. Sometimes he would treat his bitterest enemy as his closest friend, yet behave towards a dear friend as if he were an utter stranger. The fact is, he thought it bad tactics to reveal his true thoughts, which he said often led to downfall, whereas there was far more likelihood of success by dissembling.

An even more disconcerting trait was to leave his hearers uncertain whether he was pretending or being truthful. He achieved this – not necessarily deliberately – from a habit of speaking hesitantly, in obscurities and double meanings. He was very well educated, deeply fond of the Greek language, literature and culture, but even what he said in Latin often emerged as 'all Greek' so far as his hearers were concerned. Life had taught him extreme caution. He weighed every thought and every word, causing uncomfortable silences while people waited for him to speak. Like lawyers and public servants still, when he did at length utter he qualified everything, so that he could claim to have been misunderstood if he might subsequently regret having committed himself.

It was due to genuine caution, rather than intention to deceive. Tiberius was not an open man. He had lived long, seen sufficient and become cynical enough for evasiveness to have become his natural way. But woe betide those who 'read' him wrongly, failing to grasp what he thought or felt but would not say outright. He would produce some witheringly sarcastic retort – his manner was acidulous at the best of times – or erupt in a fury that was all the more petrifying coming from one habitually cold, grim and hesitant. Yet he could be apologetic, too; for although he gave people every cause to misunderstand him, and made nothing easy for them, he hated being misinterpreted in a way that would leave anyone thinking badly of him, and he hastened to set them right, sometimes mystifying them further in the process. At the same time, he professed not to care whether he was liked or hated and made no effort to become popular, for instance by showing contemptuous indifference to the Games by which Romans, high and low, set such store.

The physical appearance which might be expected of such a man is perhaps lean, puny of stature, with shifty eyes in a pallid face. In fact, Tiberius was big and burly, with a jutting chest and wide shoulders, proportionately built in all respects. According to Suetonius, his left hand was so powerful that he could thrust his extended finger 'through a green and sound apple, or the skull of a boy or grown youth', a party trick which, in the light of his later life, may have become uneasily familiar to his guests.

He wore his hair long down the back of his neck, as a reminder of aristocratic Claudian origins. He was good-looking, though given to pimples and perhaps acne, and his exceptionally big eyes were remarkable for the power of seeing in the dark immediately after waking, which must have been a comfort in case of possible assassination attempts. He drank rather too much, but was otherwise healthy, needing neither physicians to tend his body nor astrologers to protect him from the fates.

After his show of reluctance he allowed himself to be enthroned. He declared that the state would continue to be run as Augustus had run it. He refused to accept personal glorification and honours, to have statues and busts of himself put up, or months renamed after him and his mother. He would not even be called 'Emperor' or 'Father of His Country', and anyone addressing him in flattering terms was sharply warned not to 'insult' him thus again.

His rule was, on the whole, as passive as he had said it would be, consisting to a large degree of economy campaigns. He reduced public entertainments and the pay of actors and gladiators. Wastrels faced exile. The sale of luxury foodstuffs was curtailed and banquets ordered to be less lavish. The giving of New Year gifts was discouraged. Immoral behaviour by married women was punished.

Along with this imposition of austerity, which did not suit the pleasure-loving Romans at all, went restrictive measures of a harsher kind. Magistrates were required to apply the law to the letter. Astrologers were banned. Jews, Egyptians and others were made to destroy the trappings of their alien faiths and were exiled or enslaved. The police were strengthened and Rome's garrison was increased, ready to act against any riots, while the old rights of sanctuary in holy places were abolished.

Things continued to run well enough, especially in the provinces which Tiberius never troubled to visit – he scarcely ever left

Rome – and his economies ensured that the treasury was in good shape. Personally, though, he was becoming an increasingly unpopular figure: unamenable, a kill-joy, and a negative ruler, who expected the senate to oversee things, while it in turn looked to him in vain for firm leadership such as Augustus had given. A disturbing element for those nearest the seat of power was the proliferation of trials for alleged treason. The prescribed punishment for anything from a plot to a direct insult had been exile, and to a large extent remained so; but gradually the death penalty began to creep in, and with it the informant and the blackmailer.

One of the influences behind the treason trials was Tiberius's principal adviser, Lucius Aelius Sejanus, an outwardly extrovert man of high connexions who had held prefectural office from Augustus's time. Serving an aloof and retiring emperor, such a man was able to advance his own influence, to a point where Tiberius had come to rely on and confide in him. Drusus, Tiberius's son, distrusted this growing intimacy; but since he was away on foreign service with the army he could do nothing to try to influence his father. He was never to get the chance, for he died in A.D. 23, four years after Tiberius's adoptive son, the popular commander Germanicus, the obvious alternative successor to the throne.

Tiberius was now isolated, and proceeded to make himself literally so. With the few close friends he really trusted he made the short voyage to the island of Capreae (Capri), whose unscaleable cliffs and easily guarded landing-places gave him the feeling of security which the scheming Sejanus had persuaded him he badly needed. The danger cited was Germanicus's widow Agrippina, who Sejanus alleged had designs on the throne for one or another of her three young sons.

This and other fears kept Tiberius virtually his own prisoner on Capreae for the rest of his reign, eleven years of it. He never entered Rome again, but carried on the governance of the mighty empire by correspondence with his senate, much of whose time had to be devoted to debating the precise meaning behind his convoluted prose. Agrippina and her sons were denounced by Sejanus and imprisoned, clearing the way completely for him to get himself elected consul and military commander, on the strength of his close association with the absentee emperor. He could not aspire to become ruler himself, but, by biding his time for Tiberius's death, Sejanus fancied he would be made regent to the likeliest heir, the child son Gemellus, son of the late Drusus; and that would suit very nicely.

Whether Tiberius went into mental decline on Capreae, or

whether it was simply that, out of sight of all but his intimate friends, he was free at last to indulge a lifetime's pent-up lust and sadism, he seems to have spent his last decade practising debauchery and cruelty in all their forms. He drank more heavily. He surrounded himself with obscene statuary and pictures, played filthy games with women of all ranks and children of both sexes, and imported so-called *spintriae*, youths and girls adept at group sexual exhibitionism, who enacted scenes from manuals of lust to arouse him for his own activities.

He made an entertainment out of torture and execution, inviting unwitting guests from the mainland to furnish himself with victims. Most of the Roman remains on the romantically associated little island in the Bay of Naples are of the dozen villas which Tiberius had built for himself, and in which unspeakable things were done for his gratification; and one must shudder involuntarily at the clifftop from which he had the tortured remains hurled.

An opinion cited by Suetonius had it that Tiberius had always foreseen that some day he would yield to the awful urges within him, which was why he had resisted accepting the title 'Father of His Country', knowing that the shame he would earn would add to the torment he must feel. It is said that he lived in a state of terror in these last unbridled years, with the curses of his victims constantly ringing in his ears with their shrieks.

Perhaps the most unsuspecting victim of all was Sejanus. He had seemed to be getting all he desired. After long reluctance, Tiberius had allowed him to marry his son's widow, Julia Livilla. Sejanus was virtually ruler of Rome, needing only formal election to the position of co-emperor. The awaited summons to the senate duly reached him, and he stood listening smugly to the latest orders from Capreae. The wording was as involved as ever, but as its meaning began to emerge Sejanus's smile faded. Hoping they were doing what they were meant to do, the senators ordered his arrest. Some hesitation followed, but since his allies made no move to save him it seemed safe to assume that the emperor's desire had been correctly interpreted. It would have been treasonable not to accede to it promptly: Sejanus was executed that same evening.

He was declared 'a most ruinous enemy of the Roman people'. So was Tiberius – after he, too, was safely dead, from natural causes, in the year 37. He was seventy-nine. 'To the Tiber with Tiberius!' yelled the mob, when the news reached Rome. Some prayed to the gods to consign him among the eternally damned. From a tight-fisted, uninspired, but diligent ruler, who had once said 'A good shepherd shears his flock; he does not flay them', he had turned into a monster.

Those who rejoiced had seen nothing yet, though: he was to be followed by Caligula.

Claudius

(10 B.C.–A.D. 54)

Having endured Tiberius and then Caligula as their absolute rulers, with their contrived treason trials, their wholesale executions upon a whim, their costly debaucheries, and their deranged unpredictability, the Roman senate had come to the conclusion that enough was enough. It was time they took power back into their own hands, with a re-established republic.

A leader of some sort was needed, nevertheless, not least by the army: soldiers, and especially senior officers, while capable enough of short-term initiative, have always felt the need for a supremo to shoulder ultimate responsibility – 'the buck stops here' mentality.

Even before Caligula's murder, which had to happen sooner or later, the praetorian guard had had their man in mind. He needed to be of the right pedigree, not strongly self-willed, and not a young man of thrusting ambition. Tiberius Claudius Drusus Nero Germanicus – Claudius for short – filled their requirement perfectly.

He was the surviving male heir to the Julian line begun by Julius Caesar: son of Drusus and therefore grandson of Livia, wife of the deified Augustus, and maternal grandson of Mark Antony. His father would have been emperor, had his premature death not let the loathed Caligula in. So far as a claim to the throne went, Claudius was the obvious choice. He was also just turned fifty – he had been born at Lugdunum (Lyons) in 10 B.C. – which made him satisfactorily elderly.

As to any likelihood of his suddenly sloughing off a seemingly innocent skin to reveal a monster's form, as his predecessors had done, that seemed a risk safely worth taking. Claudius was amiably, if misleadingly, dim. He trembled and stammered when addressed. He giggled nervously, drooling from his mouth, and his nose ran. His mother had been in the habit of referring to him as one of Nature's discarded pieces of handiwork, while his august grandmother had seldom the patience to communicate with him except in writing. Augustus himself had preferred the young Claudius not to be present in the imperial box when Games were held, for fear of public ridicule, and termed him *misellus* – little wretch.

In view of these disadvantages the senators hesitated to proclaim Claudius emperor in 41. The army forced their hand. His late brother had been their beloved general, Germanicus. They wanted a leader, but not necessarily one who would be capable or desirous of actually leading. In fact, they misjudged Claudius, as did the senate. He had been despaired of by his forebears, and kept out of the limelight by Tiberius and Caligula; he was a poor specimen of mankind; but he was shrewd, extremely learned, and ready to cut a dash.

One story has it that the circumstances under which he actually became proclaimed emperor were typically abject. Happening to be nearby when Caligula was cut down by his assassins, Claudius hid himself behind a tapestry, leaving his feet sticking out. A soldier spotted them and whisked aside the quivering drape, at which Claudius fell forward on to his knees and seized the man's legs, begging to be spared. He found himself hauled upright and dragged off to the guard room, where he was put into a litter and carried to the praetorian guard's headquarters. There, instead of being executed, as he expected, he was saluted as emperor-to-be. To a large extent it was an army coup, the first Rome had seen, and Claudius, for all his unmilitary aspect, took care to accept the salutes and fanfares, and to tip the guardsmen in gold coin.

He took less trouble to court favour from the senators. Although he was courteous to them personally, he admitted to their ranks men whom they considered unworthy, particularly provincials. He castigated senators for accepting too uncritically measures urged by the more energetic among them – 'nodding through' motions without examining them keenly. With good cause, he suspected many senators of wishing him dead, and of plotting it. Not a few of the vacancies which occurred for him to fill with men of his choice were consequently caused by his having executed ones already in office. The newcomers were, naturally, regarded as his toadies, which no doubt they were; yet he was constantly reminding the senate that it should rouse itself and act independently of the emperor, as in the days of Augustus.

He took an active part in the proceedings, as well as spending much time hearing court cases, to a greater extent and in wider range than any of his predecessors. He did not hesitate to meddle with established laws if his considerable commonsense told him that the letter of the law was making it 'an ass', and if he thought a prescribed sentence for a proven offence was too short or too long, in the light of the evidence, he would vary it.

Such behaviour added to his unpopularity with the more hidebound senators, but must have provoked occasional laughter in court by the absurdity, or shrewdness, of some of his judgements. 'Curb your passions, or at least be more careful in future,' he dismissed one young man, obviously guilty of seducing a considerable number of married women and girls; and he quite nonplussed a woman who refused to acknowledge a youth as her son by ordering her to marry him. But when the spectators at a case of forgery shouted that the convicted criminal ought to have his hands cut off, Claudius agreed that it was a good idea, and sent for the executioner, with his block and chopper.

He determinedly extended the policies of Julius Caesar and Augustus in bringing in senators from far-flung colonies. By conferring citizenship on many more Greeks, Gauls, Spaniards, and, in due course, compliant Britons, he increased the number of those who could call themselves Romans by about one-sixth, to six millions. He wanted the bounds of the Roman Empire to stretch ever further, and himself set the process in action by annexing Mauretania in 43 and embracing the client kingdoms of Judea and Thrace in 44 and 46 as provinces of Rome.

He had an unfortunate habit of dozing in court and in the senate, from which he had to be awakened by pointedly raised voices. The reason for his drowsiness was that he slept so little at night, usually waking before midnight. If he had not the horrid deeds of a Caligula to burden his conscience, he abused his digestion more than enough to keep any man from his rest. No matter where he was, or at what time, he felt in need of a snack. He adjourned one court case because he had smelt cooking in the priests' refectory in the nearby Temple of Mars, and went there uninvited to join in the meal.

It was his custom not to leave table until he could eat and drink no more, and he carried the practice of the *vomitorium* to excess by relapsing into gorged slumber with his mouth wide open, so that his throat could be tickled with a feather and his stomach contents brought up, to make way for the next bout of refreshment. Violent stomach cramps and attacks of heartburn drove him near to suicide at times.

His habits were gross – but many high-placed men's were. He was given to chatting incessantly and telling awful jokes, which amused only himself – a not unknown failing still. With a nervous tic jerking his head violently, he must often have lived up to his mother's description of him as a living abortion. Yet he was well

set up, even handsome, with a fine head of white hair which gave
him considerable dignity when he briefly sat or stood still; and he
was one of the foremost scholars of his day. In fifty years with little
else to occupy him he had made a deep study of history. In Latin
he wrote a study of Augustus's reign, and in Greek, which he loved
especially, he wrote works in many volumes each of Etruscan and
Carthaginian history. The city museum of Alexandria saw fit to
add a new wing, named the Claudian, in which teams of readers
took it in turns to declaim his Carthaginian work from start to
finish each year, while counterparts did the same for his Etruscan
work in the old building.

He made some reforms to the Latin alphabet, wrote his autobiography in eight volumes (Suetonius comments on its lack of
taste), and, in lighter vein, produced a treatise on dicing, his
favourite pastime between his 'snacks': he contrived a special
table for his carriage, with a surface the dice would not roll off.

The other games he enjoyed most were chariot races, combats
with animals, and human blood sports between gladiators and
net-fighters, whose unhelmeted faces showed their death agonies
plainly, which pleased him. He would sometimes sit for hours on
end at such displays, and when the day's supply of trained fighters
ran out he sent inexperienced men into the arena to slaughter one
another. He thoroughly enjoyed an execution, the more painful
the better, and revived some old practices which had been abandoned as too nasty even for Roman tastes.

His contradictory nature, though, permitted many people,
especially in court, to insult him to his face and get only a sheepish
grin back. Whatever physical and mental ailments were in him
seem to have had fluctuating effects, causing cruelty to alternate
with amiability. He was no tyrant; for much of his time he was
troubled with self-doubt and went in constant fear of attack.
Remarkably, his health improved out of all recognition when he
became emperor, suggesting that some psychosomatic influence
had exacerbated his natural defects in the preceding long period of
unemployment; and he had certainly learnt to exaggerate his
symptoms at times when it was prudent to be dismissed as a
harmless idiot.

He was an avid womaniser, not at all diverted by males. He
married four times, twice to women who are remembered in their
own right.

His third wife, whom he married shortly before becoming
Emperor, was Valeria Messalina, grand-niece of Augustus on
both her parents' sides. 'In that lustridden heart, decency did not
exist,' Tacitus wrote of her, and her name has remained synony-

mous with callousness and lack of sexual restraint in a woman – it was applied to Catherine the Great of Russia. Messalina took and discarded lovers by the score: Juvenal pictures her – 'that whore-empress' – sneaking from her snoring husband's bed to disport herself in low brothels. Betrayed at last by the freedman Narcissus, who had once been in league with her, she was killed by a guards officer, and the extra 'husband' she had dared to take on the side, Caius Silius, was executed.

Shattered at having been so comprehensively betrayed, Claudius swore he would remain celibate; but it was not in his nature, and he proved easy prey for his niece Agrippina the younger, whom he had brought back from exile imposed by Caligula. She was twenty-five years Claudius's junior and had a little boy named Nero, whom Messalina had tried unsuccessfully to have murdered, for fear that he might rival her own son by Claudius, Britannicus.

Agrippina was ambitious for power, and a determined organiser, and she made a dominant empress for a timid ruler who was beginning to fail in health and was losing his hold on his empire. The union was incestuous and unprecedented, but a decree was easily pushed through the senate by well-wishers, so persuasively argued that Claudius found himself being positively urged to get on with the marriage. Agrippina was well pleased and began almost at once to assume the power which was before long to be solely hers.

'From this day', wrote Tacitus, 'the country was transformed.' Claudius's days of power were on the wane. He had nothing left to do for Rome. He had extended the empire in the sense of giving Roman citizenship to the people of its widespread territories. He had granted status and power to many of the freedmen who served him, though that was not wholly a good thing, for many resentments arose between senators and knights and these sons of former slaves, who were not backward in vaunting their new status and, with Agrippina, held increasing sway over the emperor.

Claudius's sole but significant military adventure was to take part in the first expedition into Britain since Julius Caesar's time. It was mounted in A.D. 43, partly to enable Claudius to show himself a soldier worthy of his ancestors, though ostensibly to protect south British tribes allied to Rome from the Catuvellauni, the Belgic tribe settled in Hertfordshire who had led the resistance to Caesar. Claudius himself did no fighting, but the captors of Colchester decently waited for him to catch up and lead the triumphant entry into their foes' capital there. Soon afterwards he returned to Rome, leaving Plautius and Vespasian to get on with the conquest. It was the beginning of the long Roman occupation of Britain, and merited a splendid welcome home for him.

Suetonius refers to evidence that Claudius foresaw his approaching end. He reports that, chancing to meet Britannicus, who was twelve years old, he embraced him warmly, saying, 'Grow up quickly, my boy.' He must have been well aware of Agrippina's plans for her Nero, four years older than Britannicus, to succeed in his place.

It is not certain that she decided to ensure Britannicus did not come of age while his father still lived, thus depriving her of regency over him. Claudius may even have died naturally. The general opinion, though, has always been that his wife preferred not to wait for Nature to take its course, and fed him poisoned mushrooms. In view of his habit of vomiting up his food, the story goes, a further dose was administered, both orally and as an enema. He may have been smothered as well, just to make sure.

It happened in October 54, when Claudius was sixty-three. He had reigned for fourteen years. Agrippina's plans could go forward. Claudius's death was not immediately announced; instead, a troupe of actors was summoned to the palace, supposedly to perform for him, while swift arrangements were being made for Nero to succeed. In the brief interim, Rome was to all intents and purposes under a woman's control for the first time ever.

Nero

(A.D. 37–68)

Whether or not Agrippina had had her husband, the Emperor Claudius, murdered, his death in October 54 could not have been more timely for her plans. Nero, her son, was not yet seventeen. Claudius's son, Britannicus, who was only twelve, had been declared out of the running for the succession. For a few months, Agrippina was able to enjoy the heady sensation of personal power over the empire.

The actual business of governing, though, was carried out by the commander of the praetorian guard, Sextus Afranius Burrus, who had been adviser and man of business to Claudius and to

Tiberius before him, and the Stoic philosopher Lucius Annaeus Seneca.

Seneca had been Nero's tutor for a number of years, after being exiled by Claudius but reinstated at Agrippina's insistence. He was widely admired for his published works, and his popularity rubbed off on to his young charge, the emperor-to-be. His influence on Nero was considerable. Sage old observers noted that, unlike his predecessors, all of whom had had edicts and promises of their own to propound to their people, Nero assigned Seneca to compose his accession speech for him. It was none the worse for that, promising to follow the great Augustus's examples, to rule and judge justly without favouritism, and to reduce the taxes whenever the opportunity should arise. It was the sort of professionally crafted speech which has served monarchs and ministers down the ages, except that it had not yet become hackneyed in Nero's time and could be believed as expressing his own sincere sentiments.

Gifts were handed out in the expectant quarters, honour was done to the departed Claudius, and lavish entertainments were mounted. The Roman people were happy to feel that their future was in the hands of a temperate, well-educated youth, wise beyond his years, with a strong-minded mother to give him her loving support, and a distinguished soldier and an eminent scholar working in evident harmony as his chief advisers.

Nero had been born at Antium (Anzio) on 15 December 37. With Agrippina for his mother, and a murdering, swindling, incestuous and sadistic father, Gnaeus Domitius Ahenobarbus, it was little wonder that his natal horoscope bore many bad omens: even his father commented that any child of his and Agrippina's was bound to become a public enemy. Gnaeus managed to cheat murder or execution by dying naturally when his son was three, at which the boy's uncle Caligula seized his inheritance and banished his mother, leaving Nero to be brought up in poor circumstances by an aunt, Domitia Lepida.

It was Claudius who ordered the reinstatement of mother and son. He married Agrippina and adopted Nero, making Seneca his tutor. Under the philosopher's civilising influence the potential savage developed keen interests in music, poetry and the theatre, which kept him out of mischief. He did not play the fiddle, as legend has it – the instrument did not exist until well over a thousand years later. His principal delights were the lute and his own voice, which he never tired of hearing, although it proved a wearisome sound to others.

He performed in private at first, but in later years indulged his vanity by putting on public entertainments which it was compulsory to attend and forbidden to leave, with himself as sole performer. Even had his voice been of better quality (small, rusty and husky are among the terms used of it) it would have required a super-enthusiast (or sycophant) to endure, for example, his solo rendering of entire operas.

'No one' (writes Suetonius) 'was allowed to leave the theatre during his recitals, however pressing the reason. Women in the audience gave birth, and men became so bored that they furtively dropped over the wall at the rear, or feigned death and got themselves carried away for burial.' When Nero entered competitions he pretended to treat the other contestants as equals, but criticised them behind their backs to the judges, whose own 'impartiality' he praised to their faces. He was not above bribing his rivals to let him win, and employed a vociferous *claque*.

His stage presence was unprepossessing, too. Of average height, he was thick-necked, big-bellied, and had spindly legs, with knobbly knees. His blue-eyed features appeared 'pretty, rather than handsome' to Suetonius, who described his body as 'pustular and malodorous'.

From childhood he was extremely fond of horses and aspired to be a chariot-racer. Both in Italy and later in Greece, where he considered his talents to be more finely appreciated, he took part in race meetings, inevitably being declared the winner. Once, at Olympus, he drove a ten-horse team, fell out of the chariot, was helped in again, but had to retire before the end of the race: he still got the prize.

Burrus and Seneca were not a little concerned to note the Emperor's predilection for pleasure before work, and tried to persuade him to confine it to private circles. But he was not to be bridled for long, despite a tendency to stage-fright seemingly unnecessary in one who could not fail to be acclaimed and who made a point of announcing his own competition victories to cheering audiences. In fact, there was little criticism of him from among the people until his latter years; sporting monarchs have always been popular.

Like his predecessors, Nero practised another set of indulgences. They involved boys, girls, married women, men older than himself – even his own mother, if the story is true that whenever they travelled together in a closed litter they whiled away the journey in carnal sport. Agrippina reputedly went out of her way to tempt him, to the dismay of Burrus and Seneca, who wished to limit her influence over him.

Suetonius reports that he raped a Vestal Virgin, 'married' a boy named Sporus, whom he had had castrated and dressed in clothing suited to an empress, and on another occasion ceremonially played the role of 'wife' to his freedman Doryphorus – omitting the castration element. Nero's theory, it appears, was that no one was wholly chaste, therefore it was hypocritical to deny one's sexual proclivities. He encouraged others to follow his example. He possessed a lawful wife as well, Claudius's daughter Octavia, whom he had married shortly before becoming emperor.

He was profligate with money, spending and gambling recklessly and never wearing the same clothes (often effeminate in style) twice. Yet in his early years as ruler he still found time for official duties, though Burrus and Seneca did the real work. More worrying to them than Nero was his formidable and scheming mother. Even if Agrippina had sometimes shared his bed (or travelling litter), there were signs that her influence on him was beginning to wane. What might she get up to in order to restore it?

One thing she could not do was try to displace him with the younger Britannicus. Britannicus had died in the year after Nero's accession, at a palace dinner. It was, of course, rumoured that Nero had had him poisoned, though there is no proof. In fact, he professed to an abhorrence for taking human life: he had wanted to put an end to gladiatorial combats to the death, but was persuaded that this would be unpopular with the people, who preferred blood to ballets any day. When he was compelled to sign a warrant for a justified execution he groaned that he wished he had never learned to write his name.

He was himself a man easily frightened for his life, and readily persuaded to believe in plots against him. Seneca made use of this to widen the growing rift between Nero and his mother. He encouraged the emperor's passion for a beautiful young freedwoman, Acte, which resulted in Agrippina's allying herself with Nero's wife, Octavia. It was enough to cause Nero to banish his mother.

Nero's next and strongest passion was for Poppaea, the newly wed wife of one of his sporting cronies, Otho. Almost certainly on Seneca's advice, Nero posted Otho to the governership of Lusitania (Portugal), a proud appointment for a man only in his mid-twenties, worth leaving his wife behind in Rome for.

Poppaea determined that if Nero was going to have her, she was going to have him – as husband, with no risk of a malignant mother-in-law returning to spoil things. She persuaded him that Agrippina was plotting his downfall. He sent his mother a letter of reconciliation, inviting her to come and celebrate the Feast of

Minerva on the Bay of Naples. When the festivities were over he sent her happily away in a galley which had been artfully designed to collapse at sea.

The plan worked, except that Agrippina managed to save herself from drowning and struggled to her home. Receiving this news after a night of guilty suspense, Nero, according to Tacitus, asked Seneca's and Burrus's advice. The outcome was that two officers were sent to stab his mother to death in her bed.

For some time he remained horrified at what he had done. Suetonius says that for the rest of his life he imagined himself pursued by avenging Furies, with whips and fiery torches, and went so far as to try to have them exorcised. There was the more realistic threat of some public outcry, and especially one from the army, which still revered Agrippina's late father, its great commander Germanicus. But nothing transpired; rather, messages of condolence, thinly veiling congratulations, began to reach Nero.

He breathed more easily; but Tacitus says that he was never again the same man. Vestiges of respect for his mother while she lived had held back his wildest propensities; now they were unleashed.

For a start, the aunt, Domitia Lepida, who had brought him up as a child, was given a lethal dose of laxative, enabling him to tear up her will and seize her property. He plunged into his theatrical excesses and chariot racing. He urged respectable people to join in the revels, which sank to depths of lewd savagery. Burrus and Seneca would perhaps have restrained his worst excesses, but the former had died in 62, and Seneca soon afterwards withdrew from court, to live as a scholarly recluse. He had seen the writing on the wall. A new counsellor, Gaius Ofonius Tigellinus, whose tastes for debauchery and horseracing matched Nero's, had been appointed to command the praetorian guard in Burrus's place. Seneca knew they could never work together.

Poppaea, though, welcomed Tigellinus's appointment and allied herself with him to manipulate the emperor. First, he was encouraged to divorce Octavia, banish her, concur with trumped-up charges of immorality against her, and have her executed. As Poppaea intended, he married her immediately.

This pursuit of lust, excitement and matrimony caused him to pay less and less attention to imperial affairs, losing him senatorial support. Things were not going too well for Rome abroad. The occupation of Britain was suffering setback from Boudicca and her East Anglian Iceni, who captured several important strongholds and massacred tens of thousands of Romans and their

British allies before at last being overcome. There was trouble, too, in Asia Minor, but again it was put down, thanks to the commanders in the field.

If Nero did not literally fiddle while Rome burned, he disported himself while affairs of empire were neglected and morality went to the pack. And Rome did burn. In 64, a week-long conflagration destroyed a major part of the city, making large numbers homeless. Rumour spread that the emperor himself had started the blaze, or rather had ordered it started by his thugs, who beat back all attempts to stop it. Nero had a personal alibi: he was away at Antium. He returned during the later stages of the blaze, and, according to Suetonius, watched from a tower, enraptured by 'the beauty of the flames', while he sang in its entirety the lengthy dirge *The Fall of Ilium*. Then he went looting, and instituted a compulsory relief fund, demanding heavy contributions, which he pocketed.

There were those who believed that the gods had destroyed Rome because of their displeasure with its ruler. Others said that Nero had done it because he wished to rebuild the narrow, congested city into a fine monument to his own glory, dominated by a wonderful golden house in splendid grounds.

Whatever the truth (and the new Rome which was eventually laid out was an immeasurable improvement on the old) the disaster helped bring to a head the growing dissatisfaction with a ruler who did little ruling, preferring to spend lengthy periods away from the city and even from Italy in theatrical posturing. Plots began to be hatched against him, the principal one, in 65, involving members of the supposedly loyal praetorian guard and other hitherto trusted allies, led by one of Nero's best friends, Gaius Calpurnius Piso. Its aim seems to have been to replace Nero with Seneca. There is no evidence that the old man had consented, or was a conspirator himself; but when the plot was discovered, and executions, enforced suicides and banishments prevailed, Seneca, like Piso, was among those to perish.

Poppaea had not fared well. She had borne Nero a girl child, which died in infancy. While she was pregnant again, in 65, he kicked her to death for nagging him. He married once more, Statilia Messalina, whose husband he had driven to suicide.

He was living on borrowed time now. He was only in his thirty-first year, having reigned for nearly fourteen of them, with auspicious beginnings but an accelerating downhill progress since Agrippina's murder. Uprisings in Gaul and Spain, under the local commanders Gaius Julius Vindex and Servius Sulpicius Galba, were not put down as they should have been – Nero was away performing in Greece again – and it took pressing persuasion by the senate to get him back to Rome. The good news was that Vindex had been defeated by a loyal commander; the bad was that other elements of the army had abandoned their duty to the emperor and were supporting Galba to succeed him.

Aware that his assassination was imminent, Nero fled to a freedman's humble villa outside Rome. As he heard the approaching horses of his executioners he acted out his death scene, lamenting what a loss he would be to the arts. He cringed from the act of suicide, but managed it at last, expiring with a horrifying grimace which would have had any audience applauding. So, on 9 June 68, the curtain fell on the Julian line.

Vespasian

(A.D. 9–79)

After the death of Nero, in A.D. 68, extinguishing the royal line, three successive contenders for the emperorship of Rome were urged forward by factions of the army. The rivalries thus caused resulted in each losing his life and many others losing theirs in a year of civil war, culminating in the emergence of a fresh, reforming dynasty.

Servius Sulpicius Galba was already in his seventies and serving as governor and commander in Nearer Spain when he heard of Nero's death and learned that the senate had nominated him to succeed. He had enjoyed the favour of Augustus and held various offices under Tiberius, Caligula and Claudius. His proposers for the throne had been certain of the provincial armies and Marcus Salvius Otho, from whom Nero had stolen his wife Poppaea. Otho accompanied Galba to Rome, for moral support, but was dismayed when the old man, instead of gratefully naming him his heir, adopted another of his own choice. This was Piso Licinianus, a young man without military experience, which offended the praetorian guard. Galba and he added injury to insult by refusing to pay the soldiers the bonuses which were customary on such occasions to reward their loyalty. After an undistinguished reign of only seven months, Galba was cut down in the street by cavalrymen, and Piso was killed also, on 15 January 69.

Into the imperial breach stepped Otho himself; he was in his thirty-third year. He had the support of a majority of the army, but not all of it: the forces in Upper Germany had declared themselves in favour of their governor, Aulus Vitellius. The dispute was settled in battle between the two factions near Cremona. When Otho, who was elsewhere at the time, heard the news, though it was tempered with a report that reinforcements for his own troops were on their way, he committed suicide on 16 April, saying that he would allow no more bloodshed on his behalf.

He had reigned only ninety-five days. Widespread grief affected his soldiers, and blood was spilt after all, though in suicidal sacrifices to the honour of a young man who, it was said, had accepted the throne in an effort to prevent the spread of civil war. Though not of long noble ancestry, he had shown true nobility by giving up his own life to prove his sincerity.

The forces which had defeated Otho's had been mostly German legions from the south. They had marched in the cause of their own candidate for the throne, whom they had proclaimed even before Otho had accepted it. This was Aulus Vitellius, in his early fifties, whose father, Lucius Vitellius, had been the emperor Claudius's closest friend and adviser. Galba had appointed him governor of Lower Germany in 68, but by the time he assumed office Nero was already dead, and Galba a few weeks later. Vitellius was hailed emperor by his own army, but Otho had been appointed by then, hence the march from Germany to overthrow him.

Vitellius's claim was endorsed by the senate on 19 April 69. He did not hasten to Rome, though, and by the time he did arrive it was to find that his men, whose indiscipline and propensities for cruelty matched his own, had pillaged the city and alienated the people. Other units of the army had transferred their allegiance to a more respected commander, Vespasian, who had been campaigning for the emperorship for himself ever since news of Nero's death had reached him in the Middle East, where he had the backing of the army with which he had conquered most of Judaea.

Vitellius paid little attention and settled down to indulging the gluttony for food and torture for which he was equally infamous. Too late, he discovered that pro-Vespasian troops from the Danube, under Antonius Primus, were advancing on Rome. Deserted by most of his forces, Vitellius attempted to abdicate, but was prevented from doing so. He went into hiding as the first invaders entered the city, but was found and dragged before jeering mobs, who humiliated and then lynched him.

Although it had been Primus who had defeated what was left of the Vitellian forces, the commander representing the absent Vespasian in the advance on Rome was Gaius Licinius Mucianus, governor of Syria. When he got there, and saw the results of pillage by the soldiery which Primus should have forbidden, he treated him with such disdain that Primus, an unprincipled character of doubtful loyalty, was forced to step down, leaving Mucianus to restore order in the city and prepare the way for Vespasian's coming, which was late in 70.

Titus Flavius Vespasian had the simplicity of the brave soldier of relatively humble origins. His father had been a tax-collector, though a knight, at Reate (Rieti, in Central Italy), near where Vespasian was born in A.D. 9. He had gone into the army as a young man, serving in Thrace, Crete and Cyrene, his military promotion paralleling a gradual ascent of the ladder of senatorial status. From quaestor, the lowest grade of senator, and aedile, one step up, he had become a praetor, second only in rank to consul as a state official.

He served in Germany in 43 and 44, and then commanded the 2nd Legion in the invasion of Britain, subjugating Vectis (the Isle of Wight) and driving on to the borders of Somersetshire. He was made a consul in 51 and for a time was governor of Africa under Claudius. With the advent of Nero, and more particularly his influential mother Agrippina, Vespasian went into retirement – 'keeping a low profile', living quietly and modestly with his family. He had married Flavia Domitilla, a naturalised Roman of African origin, who had borne him two sons, Titus and Domitian, and a daughter, Domitilla. Both Domitilla and Flavia Domitilla had died, and Vespasian had returned to a former mistress, Caenis, a freedwoman who had been a secretary to Claudius's mother. They never married, even when he became emperor. She died in 75, four years before him, leaving him to turn to a selection of concubines to share his habitual afternoon siesta.

The years in the wilderness were hard ones, for Vespasian had no fortune to subsist upon. He had to mortgage his estates to his brother and become a mule trader, which left him with the nickname 'Mule Driver'. Fortunately, military command and senatorial progression had not taken away any of his innate modesty and preference for a simple style of life. He had been admired by his soldiers for his insistence on sharing their burdens and hardships, and the uniform he chose for his burly form was little different from a private's. He drank little and did not eat to excess. When someone asked him why he didn't broaden the scope of his sexual activities into the more bizarre areas he replied simply, 'I'm quite content just to be a male.' But he was no prude. He liked crude soldierly jokes of a sexual and scatological kind, the latter seeming to reflect itself in the expression on his broad face, which someone likened to that of a man straining to relieve his bowels.

When Nero was free of his mother's dominance and indulging his musical bent, Vespasian went with him on one of his visits to Greece. He quickly lost his imperial favour, though, by noticeably absenting himself from Nero's tedious performances, or falling asleep when he did attend. He was banished from court, though many had fared far harder for such offences.

There was no denying Vespasian's worth as a commander in the field, though, and he was soon recalled. The Jews in Judaea had mounted a strong rebellion against their Roman overlords, a revolt which might easily spread to Egypt, and a strong man was needed to put them down. Vespasian was made governor of Judaea early in 66, to the resentment of Gaius Licinius Mucianus, who, as governor of Syria, had hitherto held jurisdiction over Judaea as well. On the face of it, Mucianus was not Vespasian's type at all: rich, flamboyant, effeminate and cruel; yet he was highly intelligent, a good organiser, and decisive and energetic when action was called for. The two commanders began to appreciate one another's qualities when Nero had died and instability and civil war beset an empire without an established emperor.

With the successive deaths of Galba and Otho, they saw the urgent necessity of electing an emperor who could gain widespread respect. It soon became obvious that Vespasian himself was that man. In his modest way, he demurred; but a crop of omens, some reported from Rome and others manifested to himself, and increasing urging from the armies, removed all but his private doubts.

He had all the attributes. Although he was of humble origins he had proved himself as a commander and provincial ruler. He was popular with a majority of the army. Not least in importance, he had two grown-up sons, Titus and Domitian, for heirs. The stability offered by a dynasty was sorely needed, and he was in the position to found one.

Leaving the completion of the victory in Judaea to Titus, Vespasian took himself to Rome late in 70. With the help of Mucianus, who characteristically boasted much of the credit for himself, he quickly restored law and order. He purged the army of slack and disgruntled elements, reorganised and redeployed the legions and gave them plenty of fighting in Germany to keep them happy, and made it plain to them that, while he was grateful to them for conducting him to the throne, he was going to stand no nonsense.

The senate was given much the same treatment and message. He ensured elections to it on a more democratic basis, making financial grants to new senators who had not the customary family and property qualifications to support them in office. At the same time, he made it plain that the senate was answerable to him, the emperor. He had been urged to rule, and he proposed to do so.

In a practical demonstration of his restorative intentions he collected the first basketful of rubble from the burnt-out ruin of the Capitol, carrying it away on his shoulder. He also took part in the search for several thousand bronze tablets buried in the rubble, forming the ancient archives of Rome. Those which were beyond repair he had copied. He had no reservations about mingling with ordinary people in this sort of activity, without fear of the assassin's knife. His predecessors, hedged about with hatred and jealousies, had kept themselves closely guarded and escorted, with all visitors being searched for weapons. Vespasian rescinded the search order, and throughout his years of rule made a point of spending time in open places, such as the Gardens of Sallust, where anyone might approach him. If they ventured to bandy words with him, he let them, and even accepted insults with a laugh and a disarming quip.

The new Rome began to grow under his régime. Roads were widened and aqueducts repaired. A new forum and the public baths were built, and the Temple of Peace, as well as that most staggering of all Roman remains today, the Colosseum, with accommodation for 50,000 spectators to watch the savage combats in its arena. His influence was potent far from Rome, too. He reorganised the provinces and made their people proud of them. He sent Gnaeus Julius Agricola to extend and consolidate the Roman hold and influence on Britain.

Suetonius says that Vespasian's one serious failing was 'avarice', citing the opinion of some that 'greed was in his very bones'. It is a misjudgement. He raised taxes and controlled public expenditure painfully enough to draw protests from those who were hardest hit; but it was not in order to finance extravagances of his own, which he did not practise, or to waste on pomp and ceremony. The so-called Year of Four Emperors, with its civil war and external disputes, had left the economy in ruins. He needed to rebuild it, just as he was rebuilding Rome, and funds had to be found for both purposes. When he thought it justified he did not hesitate to spend public monies on innovations, such as paying professors of Latin and Greek, establishing prizes for poets and artists, and subsidising performances at the Theatre of Marcellus, which he had given a new stage.

Of course, there were occasional plots to murder or overthrow him. Nothing came of them, and it was unwise bathing in cold water at Reate while recovering from a fever that brought his death on 23 June 79, aged almost seventy. Typically of him in both respects, he joked, 'Dear me, I must be turning into a god!', and tried to get to his feet, which he thought more appropriate to a dying emperor than lying down.

He had reigned well for almost nine years. Each of his sons had his due turn as Caesar in his place. Titus, who immediately replaced Vespasian, had only two years on the throne before a fatal disease took him in 81, aged only forty-one. Domitian fell to the assassin's dagger in 96. Neither had an heir. The Flavian dynasty, whose founder, Vespasian, had proved exactly the right man for the right time, came to an end with them.

Trajan

(A.D. 53–117)

Marcus Ulpius Traianus was born in September A.D. 53 at Italica (the modern Santiponce, near Seville); he was the first Roman emperor to be born in the provinces. His ancestors were certainly Italian, if not perhaps Roman, but probably intermarried with the native inhabitants of the province. His father was apparently the first member of the family to have a career in the imperial service and commanded a legion in Vespasian's Jewish campaign. He rose accordingly with his Flavian patrons and became governor of Syria in 75.

The young Trajan held the traditional magistracies and was a praetor before commanding a legion in Spain in 89. In 91, thanks to the continuing patronage of Vespasian's son, the Emperor Domitian, Trajan was elected consul – still a position of honour under the Empire and one which ennobled his family. However his merit was such that he survived Domitian's assassination and the fall of the Flavian dynasty. The new emperor, the elderly senator Nerva, first made him governor of Upper Germany, then in October 97 adopted him as his successor. On 1 January 98,

Trajan entered on his second consulship as the emperor's colleague. When Nerva died later the same month, Trajan was accepted as his successor by both the senate and the armies. It was a remarkably smooth transition of power, for Trajan had neither extensive family connexions nor great achievements to recommend him; more important perhaps, he had few enemies either.

Trajan followed what was the customary practice when the succession had been smooth of deifying his predecessor. He took the title Imperator Caesar Divi Nervae Filius Nerva Traianus Augustus (Emperor Caesar, Son of the Divine Nerva, Nerva Trajan Augustus). The double tribute to Nerva may have been intended to reassure the senate that their new master, whom they had known as the protégé of the despotic Domitian, intended to be a 'constitutional' emperor and practise that co-operation with the senate which had been the mark of the Augustan principate and the revival of which had been symbolised by Nerva. This may have been the more important because Trajan spent the first year of his reign on the Rhine and Danube frontiers, securing the loyalty of the legions (despite his decision to halve the donative they expected on the accession of a new emperor) and preparing for a campaign into Dacia. He marked the military nature of the Empire by listing after the sequence of traditional republican offices and powers, the title of proconsul, though this form was only used in the provinces. All in all the titles he chose to assume indicate an acute understanding of the dual nature of his position, of the continuing need to satisfy or appease both the traditional senatorial class, from whom the murderers of Domitian had emerged, and the army, whose rebellion had destroyed Nero and brought about the chaos of the Year of the Four Emperors. In this he followed the example of Vespasian rather than Domitian.

Like Domitian, however, Trajan recognised that a Roman emperor had to be first of all a military commander. Subsequent emperors had learned the secret revealed in 69, that, in Tacitus's words, 'an emperor could be made elsewhere than in Rome'. He was to spend a good part of his reign on the frontier, and he abandoned the policy established by Augustus after the loss of Varus's three legions in Germany of regarding the frontier of the Empire as fixed. Not all subsequent emperors had adhered to this policy, for Claudius had invaded Britain and Domitian had himself crossed the Danube into Dacia. It was Trajan however who made expansion imperial policy again and indeed pushed the Roman Empire to its furthest limits.

His main achievements were in Dacia (modern Romania). In

101 he resumed Domitian's war against the Sarmatian king, Decebalus. By 106 he had captured the Dacian capital of Sarmizegethusa, north of the Iron Gate in western Romania, and Decebalus had killed himself to avoid capture. Trajan then created a new province of Dacia north of the Danube, extending to the Black Sea and the Carpathian mountains. Colonies of veterans were established and other settlements made to exploit the silver mines and salt mines of the new province. The advancement of the frontier provided the settled and peaceful provinces on the south side of the Danube with a much deeper buffer zone against barbarian movements from the Russian steppes. The modern Romanians claim descent from Trajan's settlers. Though his success in Dacia may have owed much to Domitian's years of careful preparation, Trajan claimed the glory. Military success of this nature had not been enjoyed by any previous emperor; it redounded to his credit and made the business of government easier.

His second major war was a more doubtful affair. This was fought against the Parthian empire in the east, Rome's old rivals since republican days. The chronology of Trajan's campaigns is uncertain, but in 105–6 one of his generals annexed that part of Arabia south-east of Judaea, then known as the kingdom of Nabataea. That eased problems of supply in the event of open war, which Trajan clearly desired. The traditional cause of war rested in control of Armenia, the kingdom lying between the two empires, destined by its geography to be the client of one or the other. In 110 or 111 the Parthians deposed the pro-Roman king. In 113 Trajan marched to restore him, for Rome had long determined that it was too risky to allow Armenia to become a Parthian dependency.

His campaign was at first successful. In 115 he conquered upper Mesopotamia, and marched down the valley of the Tigris to capture the Parthian capital of Ctesiphon. This was an unprecedented success and the Roman legions found themselves on the shore of the Persian Gulf, where Trajan is said to have wept because he was too old to emulate Alexander and march on to India. The story may be apocryphal, but it shows how a desire for military glory was believed to be Trajan's motivating force. The speed of the conquest precluded thoroughness, however. Within a year revolts had broken out in various parts of the territories he had overrun. Trajan, in poor health, was on his way to Rome when he died at Selenus in Asia Minor, in August 117, aged sixty-three. Just before his death he adopted Hadrian, the husband of his favourite niece; Hadrian, as governor of Syria, had been responsible for the logistical support of the Parthian War.

Trajan's absorption in warfare had made him a distant emperor in Rome, and this may have added to the authority which his successes also enhanced. He had himself been trained in the imperial administrative service, and he was free of the resentments and feuds which had bedevilled the Julio-Claudian emperors. He co-operated willingly with the senate and always showed respect to the traditional institutions; nevertheless his reign showed a development of the military-bureaucratic Empire, away from the senatorial-republican Empire which Augustus had professedly established. Trajan was still willing to pretend that the princeps was an agent of the senate and the Roman people, but there was a wealth of difference between this parvenu military commander ruling through the army and imperial bureaucracy and the early emperors, Augustus and Tiberius; they had, as great Roman nobles, been viewed with resentment by those senators who considered themselves their social equals bound by family ties, and to whom the princeps had been ready to seem to defer on the floor of the senate. In reality the Empire had become a monarchy by the beginning of the second century. Nerva was the last senatorial emperor, Trajan the first monarch.

But if he was a monarch he was a benevolent one. He distributed cash and gifts to the Roman populace; he increased the number of citizens in receipt of free grain. He showed respect to the senate. He cut taxes and set up a public fund (*alimenta*) to support poor children in Italian cities. He took care to send efficient and honest officials to the provinces. One of these was his friend the younger Pliny, who was dispatched as governor to Bithynia-Pontus, a province on the northern coast of Asia Minor. The tenth book of Pliny's *Letters* is devoted to correspondence with the emperor, and offers a detailed picture of Roman administration in action. It also shows the humble tone that even senators of good birth now thought proper to adopt towards the emperors. Pliny, who had earlier known Trajan as an equal, is now capable of the grossest flattery.

Part of the correspondence details with the Christian sect, already persecuted in Rome by Nero and Domitian. Pliny took the view that the Christians were difficult, because they refused to conform to normal religious practices, but otherwise harmless. Trajan advised him to punish only the most obvious cases of insubordination, and not to seek them out or accept unsupported charges.

Like his most capable predecessors, Trajan assumed responsibility for extensive public works throughout the Empire:

roads, bridges, aqueducts, and harbours were all built;
wastelands reclaimed. In emulation of Augustus, but also from a
sense of public need, he redeveloped a great part of central Rome.
He built a new aqueduct and public baths on the Esquiline hill
(which could be used by the inhabitants of the crowded Suburra).
His most ambitious undertaking was however the construction of
a new forum designed by Apollodorus of Damascus, just to the
north of the old forum. This took the form of a porticoed square
with an equestrian statue of the emperor in the middle. The
Capitoline and Quirinale hills were cut back to allow the building
of two half-circular brick complexes. Several storeys high, these
provided streets of shops and warehouses: the Quirinale complex
has been excavated and is known as Trajan's Market. Behind the
square was a basilica, libraries and a temple. The whole was
dominated by the enormous column raised to commemorate the
emperor's Dacian triumphs. The column is encircled by a relief
carving spiralling to the top and portraying scenes from the war,
the most vivid surviving representation of the Roman army in
action that we possess. The statue of Trajan on top of the column
was removed in the Middle Ages and replaced during the counter-
Reformation by one of St Peter. Trajan's ashes were placed within
the base of the column.

These buildings impress one with something of Trajan's
personality. The column and the equestrian statue (no longer
surviving) testify to his pride in his achievement and his love of
glory; they make it easy to believe the story that links him with
Alexander. At the same time there is a decency, sobriety, restraint
and respect for what is useful displayed in the purpose of the
forum and market. Nero had built his Golden House for his own
self-gratification. The Flavians built the Colosseum to entertain
an idle populace and, incidentally, to further their
demoralisation. Trajan's works are intended to serve and
facilitate trade and to encourage learning. They speak of a respect
for civic virtues and the decencies of everyday life. As such they
are themselves worthy of respect, and may by their very nature be
held to represent a more admirable boast than Augustus's claim
to have found Rome of brick and left it of marble.

The Romans were to come to regard Trajan's reign as the
apogee of Empire, though there was in truth little falling off in the
reign of his immediate successors, Hadrian and the Antonines. In
Hadrian's reign the historian Florus considered that Trajan had
rejuvenated the Empire. Certainly the contrast between the
confusion, danger and political uncertainties of the first century
and the serenity of the age of the Antonines is remarkable, and

Trajan, who ruled the Empire for the twenty years that served as the bridge between the two so different ages, must take much of the credit. Already in his lifetime Pliny had published a *Panegyric*, portraying him as the ideal ruler. Later in the fourth century the historian Eutropius said that the highest compliment that the senate could pay an emperor was to declare him 'more fortunate than Augustus, better than Trajan'. He indeed passed into legend as the model emperor. Dante records a medieval legend of how the memory of Trajan's justice had moved Pope Gregory the Great to pray for his admission to paradise.

It is possible to take a less favourable view of Trajan's achievement, to see him as essentially autocratic and ready to sacrifice the true interests of the Empire to his ambition for military glory. Certainly it can be argued that his Parthian war overstrained the imperial resources and served no useful purpose, and his eastern annexations were indeed soon abandoned by Hadrian. But his achievement in Dacia was far more solid. The extension of Roman power there might bring no lasting peace, but the creation of that province brought obvious advantage for the Danube region and the whole eastern half of the Empire. In general it may be fairly said that, whatever his personal limitations, Trajan deserves the coupling with Augustus that he long enjoyed in the popular memory. Without his work the peace and prosperity which the Mediterranean world experienced in the second century would have been far more fragile and precarious.

Hadrian

(A.D. 76–138)

After the aberrations, the cruel and self-centred uses of power, and the generally violent ends of the emperors of the Julian line it is a relief to turn to men of worth and solid achievement such as Trajan and Hadrian.

A good man was certainly needed when Hadrian was appointed in 117, at the age of forty-two. The Roman Empire was unstable within and threatened from without. The soldier-emperor Vespasian had provided the much-needed dynasty, which had for long been lacking. Unfortunately, the first of his sons to succeed him, Titus, in 79, reigned only two hectic years, during which there was strife in Britain, the devastation of Pompeii and Herculaneum by the eruption of Vesuvius, and another great fire in Rome.

He was replaced by his younger brother Domitian, a throwback to the sadistic dictators, feared by all. He met a violent death, in 96, leaving no heir, natural nor adopted. Faced with appointing one, the senate played safe with the elderly and childless Nerva, who survived long enough to reverse his predecessor's harshest decrees, and to nominate as his own heir the first emperor-to-be from outside Italy, the Spanish-born soldier Trajan, already on his way to raising the Roman Empire to its height of military glory.

Trajan hailed from one of those little communities dotted about the Empire, created for disabled soldiers, who tilled the land they were allotted there, married local women, and, if not too disabled, founded families. Trajan came from such a family at Italica, in Spain. He had a young first cousin there, Hadrian, and Trajan was proud to assume his guardianship when the ten-year-old boy's father died in 85 or 86. The co-guardian was a knight named Attianus, who, when Trajan soon went off to serve on the Rhine, took responsibility for their ward's upbringing.

He took him to Rome for five years. Hadrian was not impressed. He was proud to be a 'Roman', but cared nothing for the pretentious and not altogether wholesome life of the capital, with its studied sophistication, its fashions, its poets and sages. Although he had a natural bent for the classic arts, and would show himself an accomplished architect, his was an essentially outdoor nature. He was finely built, handsome, a hard competitor at athletics and a mighty hunter. Attianus had the sense to take him back to Italica and let him get on with developing body and mind together through healthy pursuits.

Hadrian had a much older brother-in-law at Italica who envied him his looks and ardent youth. This Servianus jealously tried to make trouble for him by writing to Trajan, now back in Rome as a distinguished general enjoying the emperor Domitian's favour. Hadrian was reported as idling his time, hunting and running up debts. To his dismay, he was summoned to Rome to account for himself.

He need not have worried. Trajan, little past his mid-thirties, with a born soldier's regard for a well-set-up fellow, not to mention an appreciative eye for a good-looking youth, took immediately to the cousin half his age; and it was mutual. Servianus's spite could not have proved more in vain.

All the same, it was to academic study that Trajan returned this surrogate son. A fellow Spaniard, Quintilian, much favoured by the emperor, had founded the first state college, and it was there that Hadrian was enrolled to concentrate on studying the Greek language and culture essential to anyone hoping for high office. Trajan soon got him a civil service appointment as a minor magistrate, bringing him into contact and friendship with influential officials. It was a simple move from that to the army, as a tribune, or company officer, posted to serve with the 2nd Legion at Buda-Pesth, on the Empire's northern frontier.

This was the beginning of the ranging about in many lands which would result in Hadrian's becoming the most-travelled of emperors and the one most intimate with the nature and state of the vast Empire at its mightiest.

In the following year, 96, Hadrian was in Bulgaria with another legion when Domitian was assassinated in Rome. Nerva reigned his brief reign, watched suspiciously by the armies for his decision about an heir. His choice of Trajan, who had by now added more victories to his name and been appointed governor of Upper Germany, was heard with relief and acclaim. Hadrian, now twenty-one and serving in Germany with the 22nd, was deputed to carry congratulations to his cousin who was at Cologne. The malevolently watchful Servianus sabotaged his carriage, but Hadrian completed the journey on foot. This impressed Trajan even more than the message of praise, and when he went to Rome to assume emperorship he took Hadrian with him. Servianus had been foiled again.

Trajan's childless wife, Plotina, took an almost maternal interest in Hadrian, which extended to providing him with a wife. He had no cause to thank her. His instinctive dislike of the chosen Sabina, a great-niece of Trajan, a silly, ill-tempered young woman, deepened with the years into hatred on both sides. By varying accounts, Hadrian consoled himself with other officers' wives and with youths.

Trajan made an excellent emperor, business-like and courteous, admirably supported by his queen at home and gloriously served by his armies in the campaigns which occupied much of the rest of his life in trying to extend the Empire's boundaries in many directions. Hadrian was with him, learning the arts of war and of command from a great leader and father-figure, who drank with and confided in him during idle hours on campaign.

Promotion came early to him: command of the 1st Legion ('Minerva's Own'), and then the supreme civil rank of consul, at the age of only thirty-two. More importantly still, Trajan presented him with his signet-ring, which he himself had received from Nerva as token of his adoption as emperor-to-be.

Trajan was now in his early sixties, but that did not deter him from starting a new campaign in the east, aiming to cross the Euphrates and conquer Egypt and the other lands beyond. He gained much territory, though with that result so often fatal to over-ambitious generals who stretch their lines of communication too far and too thin, and leave in their rear unsubjugated enemies who can prove more troublesome than those who lie ahead.

The triumphant advantage petered out into a withdrawal, the news of which encouraged uprisings against weakened Roman garrisons in many territories, even as far away as Britain. Now a very sick man, Trajan appointed Hadrian to command the eastern army. He himself made for Rome, but suffered a stroke on the way and died on 8 August 117.

The news reached Hadrian swiftly. The shrewd empress Plotina had arranged for him to succeed, herself signing the documents which her paralysed husband could not.

Hadrian did not hesitate. At this moment of shock the Empire was open to attack on many fronts and by dissidents within. He dashed off a letter to the senate, pledging his service. Then, much helped by one of his generals, Turbo, he proceeded to crush the incipient rebellions and consolidate the army's positions. He ordered complete withdrawal from the newly conquered territories across the Euphrates. Rome did not need them, and could not have held them.

This retrenchment was bitterly resented by some generals and by those enterprising Roman civilians who had hastened to follow the armies into areas where they knew there were rich pickings to be had in the form of gold and other resources. It resulted in a conspiracy against Hadrian by four generals, who were promptly executed, though without Hadrian's order. He voiced his regret, pledging never to punish members of the senate, as the four had been, on his sole authority, and urging those who suspected him of dictatorial intentions to accept that he had none, and bore no grudges against those who opposed his accession.

He distributed money and gifts to the populace, ordered a mass public entertainment (the killing of 200 lions and lionesses), and decreed that the estates of executed persons should be made over to the state, not to himself, as the custom had been. If not kind to animals, he was to children, carrying through a scheme begun by Trajan for poor infants' welfare. As a gesture towards women, he ordered that the public baths be theirs alone for morning use, instead of having to be shared with men. Some were grateful, others were not; but all recognised that their new emperor was striving to please.

Hadrian wanted this to be seen farther afield, too. Not for his own glory, but in the interest of imperial unity, he wished to revive the old Augustan notion of a family of peoples, observing the cult of Rome, where their presiding 'father' dwelt. It was well meant and idealistic, but it was naïve of him to expect that an Empire so vast, incorporating powerful elements as disparate as Christianity, Judaism, paganism, and numerous other creeds and sects, should melt into mutual loving embrace.

The travels which he began in the year 121 and continued for the greater portion of his remaining years were partly aimed at furthering this mission, but had also military and administrative purposes. Before setting off he introduced important reforms of the senate and the civil service, bringing in many more representatives from outside Italy itself. He did this in the army, too, though ensuring the status of the praetorian guard as an exemplary élite, with its senior officers only Italians (or as close as he himself was to being Italian-born). He also raised territorial forces in the respective kingdoms and provinces, imbued, in theory, with local loyalties.

At one end of the scale he reformed the postal services and banned heavy traffic from city centres; at the other, he reorganised the fiscal and legal systems. It was an ambitious undertaking all round, but, by and large, it worked. Hadrian was able to set off to inspect, overhaul and show himself throughout the Empire, confident that things would run smoothly and peaceably while his back was turned.

Most of the rest of his story is of those travels, which are confusedly chronicled. Beginning with the Rhineland, he toured western Europe, crossing in 122 to Britain, still a stubborn province, prone to bloody uprisings and non-co-operation by the surly populace, who did not want to know about the municipal innovations of the occupiers. Hadrian's personality impressed itself on some of them, and by the time he left the island, after not many months, he had breathed enthusiasm for progress and commerce into some of the southern people at least. In the north he had initiated the building of what remains his most impressive monument, the strategically sited Hadrian's Wall, undulating massively for seventy-three miles, from Solway to the Tyne.

He passed through Gaul into Spain, to Asia Minor, the Aegean Islands, and Greece, where he made many reforms and began some of the other great buildings which have endured, in whole or in part, as witness to his constructive reign. At Athens they include the Pantheon, Panhellenion, and the temple of Olympian Zeus.

He was in Rome from 126–128, carrying out more reforms. His building work there included the temple of Venus and Roma, the pantheon of Agrippa, the Basilici Neptuni, and his own splendid mausoleum, upon which later grew the Castel Sant' Angelo. None of his creations was more personal to his emotions, though, than the obelisk to Antinoüs, his golden youth and intimate companion for several years, who had drowned in the Nile. Precisely how close their relationship had been, and whether the boy had died accidentally or had committed suicide from some complex notion of idealism, have been argued about down the centuries, while his beauty, represented in many surviving sculptures, has inspired artists and poets.

Buildings initiated by Hadrian adorn many other places, in Europe and the Middle East, where he ordered the rebuilding of Jerusalem and magnificently restored Pompey's tomb at Pelusium.

From 134, sad, increasingly sick, and childless – his empress had refused to bear any – Hadrian lived in decline, though still struggling with work, in Rome and at the astonishing 'villa' of his own planning at Tibur, fifteen miles away. Covering some 750 acres, it was a microcosm of a city embodying replicas of the finest buildings of Athens and Egypt.

It was at Baiae, on the Bay of Naples, that he died – and was glad to do so – on 10 July 138, aged sixty-two, after nearly twenty-one years' enlightened and constructive reign. Even his death was distinguished by his farewell address to his soul:

> *Anima, blandula, vagula,*
> *Hospes comesque corporis*
> *Quae nunc abidis in loca,*
> *Pallidula, rigida, nudula?*
> *Nec ut soles dabis jocos?*

Little soul, wandering, pleasant guest
and companion of the body, into what places wilt
thou go now, pale, stiff, naked, nor wilt thou
play any longer as thou art wont.

Marcus Aurelius

(A.D. 121–180)

Marcus Aurelius Antoninus was the last of the five good emperors
who, succeeding the turmoils of the first century, gave the Roman
Empire almost a hundred years of stability and conscientious
government. Gibbon's judgement on their achievement is well
known: 'If a man were called to fix the period in the history of the
world during which the condition of the human race was most
happy and prosperous, he would, without hesitation, name that
which elapsed from the death of Domitian to the accession of
Commodus. The vast extent of the Roman Empire was governed
by absolute power, under the guidance of virtue and wisdom. The
armies were restrained by the firm but gentle hand of four
successive emperors, whose characters and authority commanded
involuntary respect. The forms of the civil administration were
carefully preserved by Nerva, Trajan, Hadrian and the
Antonines, who delighted in the image of liberty and were pleased
with considering themselves as the accountable ministers of the
laws. Such princes deserved the honour of restoring the Republic
had the Romans of their day been capable of enjoying a rational
freedom.

Though modern scholarship has called this judgement into
question in detail, it has not impaired its serene authority. The
second century A.D. remains one of the happiest periods of human
history. Marcus Aurelius (as he is generally known) approaches
more closely than any other emperor the Platonic ideal of the
philosopher-king. He was diligent and self-sacrificing, deeply
imbued with the principles of Stoicism, the only philosophy of the
ancient world which provided a moral justification for public life.
Moreover, owing to the happy survival of his *Meditations* and
much of his private correspondence, we are more easily able to
come to a just appreciation of his character and qualities than of
any other Roman except Cicero.

He was born in 121 to one of the most prominent families of the
new political establishment which had succeeded the governing
class of the early Empire. It was an establishment drawn from
outside Rome, from the municipalities of Italy and the provinces,
especially Spain. At the time of the boy's birth, his grandfather

was consul for the second time and prefect of the city; his father's sister was married to Antoninus Pius, who would succeed Hadrian as emperor and adopt Marcus.

There is some confusion as to how Marcus was selected as a future emperor. In 136 Hadrian announced that Lucius Ceionius Commodus would succeed him, and the young Marcus was in the same year betrothed to Commodus's daughter. In 138 however Commodus died, and Hadrian adopted Titus Aurelius Antoninus (Antoninus Pius) as his successor; he ordered him to adopt Marcus and Commodus's son. Marcus was therefore chosen as a future emperor long before he came of age. It seems likely that Hadrian, himself an intellectual of philosophic inclinations, believed in the need for a long period of apprenticeship; he had served such himself, though he had not been selected as an adolescent.

Marcus's education was entrusted to a leading literary figure and teacher of rhetoric, Fronto. Much of the correspondence between them survives; it shows Marcus to have been serious, high-minded, industrious and affectionate. He was drawn as a young man to the variety of Stoicism promulgated by Epictetus in his *Diatribai* ('Discourses').

Meanwhile Marcus learned the business of government in association with the emperor who had adopted him. He was consul in 140, 145 and 161. In 147 the *imperium* and *tribunicia potestas*, which together represented the formal powers held by the emperors, were conferred upon him. Henceforth he served as a sort of junior emperor, standing to Antoninus Pius in the same relation as first Agrippa, and then Tiberius, had stood to Augustus. In 145 he had married the emperor's daughter, his cousin Faustina, his engagement to Commodus's daughter having been broken off at Hadrian's death.

Already possessed of the full powers of the emperor, he succeeded smoothly on his father's death in March 161. By his own decision his adopted brother, Lucius Aurelius Verus, who was ten years younger, was made co-emperor. For the first time the empire had two joint rulers whose status was constitutionally equal, though in fact Marcus was clearly the senior partner. This innovation looked forward to the more elaborate scheme by which, more than a hundred years later, Diocletian hoped to restore stability to the Empire. It was probably intended to secure Rome against a power struggle should Marcus himself die suddenly; it may also have been that he felt himself obliged to carry out Hadrian's wishes which had led to his own elevation. The acceptance of such a duty was in accordance with his philosophical principles.

Marcus's reign (161–180) saw no important innovation in civil policy. There was a quantity of what has been described as 'ameliorating legislation', which removed certain anomalies in civil law, improved the condition of widows, minors and slaves, and clarified the rights of blood-relationship in the law of inheritance. One development in the criminal law has been criticised: a distinction of classes was made explicit. Henceforth there were two tiers of citizenship, the emperor's subjects being divided into *honestiores* and *humiliores*, those with, and those without, property; there were separate scales of punishment, the *humiliores* being treated much more harshly.

In general Marcus was inclined to mercy. After the defeat of a rebellion headed by the governor of Syria, Avidius Cassius, in 175 he resisted pleas that the rebels be put to death, and wrote to his wife Faustina that 'nothing ... endears a Roman emperor to mankind as much as the quality of mercy. This quality caused Caesar and Augustus to be deified; it was this characteristic, more than any other, which earned your father the honour of being named "Pius" '. He seems to have believed that virtue carried its own insurance, and pointed out that in the case of all emperors who had been murdered there had been reasons why they deserved to die, but that no emperor recognised as good had been conquered by a pretender or slain. He ordered that no senator should be subjected to capital punishment in his reign.

He disliked the Christians as any emperor must who was not prepared, like Constantine later, to put himself at their head. There was however no official persecution in his reign. This did not prevent sporadic locally inspired persecution, such as that at Lyon in 177, where forty-eight Christians were tortured and put to death, with the emperor's approval.

Much of his reign was spent in military campaigns on the frontier, particularly on the Danube. In the first year of the reign however, 161, Syria had been invaded by the Parthians. That war was fought nominally under the command of the co-emperor Verus, though its successful outcome, which resulted in the occupation of Armenia and Mesopotamia, was the work of Gaius Avidius Cassius, who later rebelled. This victory had one unhappy consequence; the returning army brought back a plague which raged over the Empire for some years.

In 167 Marcus advanced across the Danube on a punitive expedition which was interrupted when news came that the Germans had crossed the Upper Rhine and even made their way into Italy where they besieged Aquileia. Marcus repulsed them, but this invasion was a foretaste of what the barbarians would inflict on the Empire in the century after his death. He resumed the campaign on the Danube: the column which now stands in Piazza Colonna in Rome records the feats of the Danube campaign of 172–5. These years saw a prolonged campaign in Bohemia which subdued the tribes there and safeguarded the Danube frontier for the moment at least.

The rebellion led by Avidius Cassius took Marcus to the east in 175–6. He visited Alexandria and Athens and, like Hadrian and Augustus before him, was initiated into the Eleusinian Mysteries, though the experience in no way affected his philosophical views.

His wife Faustina died during his campaign. Suggestions that she may have been involved in Cassius's rebellion have no foundation except rumour. Certainly Marcus, in his surviving writings, never wrote of her without admiration.

Marcus then proclaimed his sixteen-year-old son Commodus as co-emperor. He has been criticised for this reversion to the hereditary system after the successful period when the Empire had passed to an adopted son chosen for his suitable qualities. Yet it is hard to see how Marcus could have avoided the choice. If he had rejected his son, he would probably have had to kill him.

With Commodus he embarked on a new campaign beyond the Danube. It seems that he had determined to resume the expansionist policies of Trajan, or at least to create a wide Roman-controlled buffer zone which would allow the Danube to become a fall-back frontier. However, initial successes were cut short by his death at his headquarters in March 180. He had just time to ensure support for the undisputed succession of Commodus, who, however, soon abandoned the expansionist policy.

If Marcus Aurelius has been the best-known emperor between the Julio-Claudians and Constantine, it is because of his writings rather than his deeds. His *Meditations* may be regarded not only as one of the best-known books of antiquity, but as offering a rare opportunity to get to know the mind and character of a Roman man of action. They are fragmentary notes, rather than a coherent statement of his philosophy, often written in camp, in ill-health and exhaustion. It is doubtful if they were intended for publication; the exhortation is addressed to the writer himself rather than to any imagined reader. It is of interest that they were written in Greek; this may be taken as evidence of the extent to which the two cultures had become one, but it also represents the Greek basis of Marcus's thought. For him philosophical concepts most naturally found expression in Greek.

This was all the more so perhaps because Marcus was hardly an original thinker. His ideas are essentially the customary moral tenets of Stoicism as expounded by Epictetus: the world is a unity governed by a divine intelligence of which the human soul forms part. Some of his thinking approached the Neoplatonism into which all pagan philosophies eventually merged, but Marcus's understanding of the soul did not allow for any consciousness persisting after death. His mind could not allow itself the comfort of any future reward; he saw himself tied to the stake of duty; he was bound to a lonely virtue. The demand he made of himself and the standards he set were high; reading the *Meditations* it is easy to see why Stoicism could never be a philosophy with a wide popular appeal.

Modern critics have found something neurotic in Marcus's austerity. They have suggested that his anxieties reflect the strained ethos of the pre-Christian age. This seems a retrospective reading. Marcus had no reason to feel that the pagan world was crumbling, or that the days of the Empire to which he devoted his service were numbered; had he done so he might have been inclined to Christianity. In fact, though the Empire was subject to strains and dangers during his reign, these were capable of being controlled. Too much of general import can be read into Marcus's remorseless self-examination. His achievement was real enough. That there was still vitality in the Empire was revealed by the manner in which it survived the failure of Commodus and the disorders that succeeded him.

Diocletian

(*Ruled* A.D. 284–305)

Diocletian, emperor from 284 to 305, restored efficient government after the disorders of the third century. He reorganised the whole machinery of the Empire. As Augustus shaped the Republic into the Empire, so Diocletian effected the transformation of the Augustan principate into the Byzantine Empire. Moreover his reforms made it possible for the Empire in the West to survive the next century.

He was born in obscurity in Illyria about 245. His father was probably a freedman, and he himself rose in the army. The only certain point of his life before he became emperor is that he was among those army chiefs whom the emperor Carinus gathered to fight against the Persians. To have risen to such heights before the age of forty is evidence of Diocletian's ability and also of the extent to which a career in the Roman Empire was open to men of talent.

Carinus's colleague and brother Numerianus died unexpectedly during the campaign. The praetorian prefect Aper was accused of having murdered him, and Diocletian, acclaimed as emperor by the soldiers, slew Aper with his own hand. The circumstances are obscure, but Diocletian had already been assured by a soothsayer that he would become emperor on the day he killed a boar (Latin: *aper*). The coincidence was so convenient as to suggest premeditation.

At any rate Diocletian was hailed as emperor in November 284, though at that time his authority extended only over Asia Minor and Syria. It was challenged by Carinus. A battle fought at the confluence of the Morava and Danube might have been indecisive if Carinus had not been murdered. By the middle of 285 Diocletian was master of the whole Empire.

It was a precarious inheritance. Every frontier was threatened, and it was impossible to count on the loyalty of the armies. Diocletian set himself to effect the thorough reforms which alone could restore stability. It will be convenient to treat these in systematic detail, though they were not necessarily sequential.

First, he early decided to share authority in the Empire. Such a decision was by no means new; there had been many informal and formal compacts of this kind. Indeed co-emperors had been quite usual. What was remarkable was the formal structure Diocletian created and the attempt he made to ensure continuity. He appointed as his colleague Maximian, a fellow-Illyrian, the son of a shepherd. Maximian's talents were primarily military, as Diocletian's were perhaps for administration. Diocletian delineated their spheres of authority. Rome remained the nominal capital but Maximian's headquarters were to be Milan, Diocletian's Nicomedia in western Anatolia, a point from which he could guard the Persian frontier.

Six years later, two more colleagues were added: Galerius (also of peasant and Illyrian birth) and Constantius Chlorus, a nobleman. These were named as Caesars and each was attached to an Augustus, Constantius to Maximian, and Galerius to Diocletian himself. Constantius's headquarters were to be Trier, Galerius's Sirmium. The Empire was still considered an undivided inheritance, but for administrative purposes it was divided in four parts: Diocletian was responsible for Thrace, Asia and Egypt; Galerius for Illyria, Greece and the Danube provinces;

Maximian for Italy, Sicily and Africa; Constantius for Gaul, Spain and Britain. Marriage alliances also linked the Augusti and their Caesars; Diocletian bound them together by religious oaths. He and Maximian assumed the character and name of gods and surrounded themselves with an unprecedented pomp and ceremony. It was his intention too that this system should guard against pretenders and secure the succession: Caesars would become Augusti and themselves appoint Caesars. This hope was to prove quite unfounded, but in the meanwhile the new stability enabled the Empire to defeat usurpers and invaders and maintain its integrity.

Diocletian's military and administrative reforms were of more lasting importance. First he increased the army from 300,000 to 400,000 men. Then he divided it between frontier troops who were permanently stationed on guard duty, and a mobile field army held in reserve under the direct command of one of the tetrarchs. Soldiers were henceforth exempted from duty after twenty years' service. Constantine would later build the army of the later Roman Empire on the foundations laid by Diocletian.

In keeping with the elevation of the imperial person, Diocletian abolished the last vestiges of the Republic. Senators no longer collaborated in legislation; consuls became imperial nominees. He ended Augustus's division of the Empire into senatorial and imperial provinces. It was now divided into twelve dioceses, six in the east, six in the west. Governors were appointed by the emperor; to reduce the power concentrated in any one governor, each diocese was divided into a hundred provinces. Civil and military powers were separated. The bureaucracy of course multiplied despite vain attempts to check this. Administrative work became more specialised, and the administration relied increasingly on the application of a code of practice. Only fragments of the Gregorian and Hermogenian codes survive, but some 1200 extant imperial rescripts are evidence of Diocletian's social conservatism and eagerness to regulate every aspect of his subjects' lives.

Economically Diocletian's administration was strongly interventionist. He made a thorough and far-reaching reform of the taxation system, abolishing the local variants, often customary in origin, and regularising the special requisitions which had been the necessary recourse of recent governments. In place of the old heterogeneity, he established a homogenous system of land tax and poll tax for the whole Empire including Italy, long excused payment of taxes. Land and manpower were the basis of the new system. The unit on which the basic tax was calculated was that area of cultivable land (*Iugum*) which could theoretically be worked by one man (*caput*) providing him with the means of subsistence. Apparently the taxpayer was required to pay according to the number of *iuga* and *capita* for which he was assessed. Reassessment was to take place every five years. This system replaced the old variable revenues with one of fixed returns. To make that possible the required productive manpower had to be guaranteed. Consequently, Diocletian attempted to make all occupations hereditary, and thus ensure economic stability; in time this led to the economic stagnation of the Byzantine state.

Economic stability depended also on currency reform. In 296 Diocletian introduced a new coinage to replace the old inflated and depreciated currency. The measure, unaccompanied by any reduction of government expenditure, was insufficient to prevent a renewed inflation. Diocletian's response was to try to enforce a prices and wages policy. An edict of maximum prices was published in 301; it is at least testimony to the thoroughness of the imperial bureaucracy. Prices were regulated for food (ranging from wheat to the small birds called figpeckers, and even dormice), wages (from advocates to muleteers, barbers and sewer-cleaners), clothing and the provision of services, including freight charges throughout the Empire. It is obvious that such far-reaching measures would have required supervision by an army of bureaucrats. Altogether more than 1000 articles were enumerated; severe penalties were decreed for black marketeers. Diocletian's successors found this edict unworkable.

If Diocletian was socially conservative, concerned with the preservation of traditional virtues such as would have pleased Cato himself, the Empire he constructed was far from the old Roman ideal. Indeed it took on aspects of a theocracy. The emperor was no longer a First Citizen as Augustus had been; instead he was a god who must be adored. In place of the familiarity with which the first emperors had been treated in Rome, he introduced the magnificence of the Persian court. He assumed the radiate diadem, which the Romans had hated as a mark of monarchy. Access to the imperial person was restricted; when at last obtained, the subject was required to prostrate himself before the being whom he had to address as his 'lord and god' (*dominus et deus*). In Gibbon's words: 'Like the modesty affected by Augustus, the state maintained by Diocletian was a theatrical representation . . . it was the aim of the one to disguise, and the object of the other to display, the unbounded power which the emperors possessed over the Roman world.' The changed approach however marked a change of reality too: henceforth the Empire would be a military bureaucracy, the emperor remote. It is symptomatic that Diocletian did not visit Rome till the twentieth year of his reign, and then stayed only a few weeks.

His reign saw the last major persecution of Christians. Various explanations have been advanced: the Caesar Galerius was violently hostile to the sect; Diocletian may have resented their refusal to participate in emperor-worship and the consequent appearance they gave of constituting a state within the state; it may be that the sharpness of the Christians' own doctrinal disagreements made them appear a danger to public order. Most probably it was a combination of all these things. Diocletian, wishing to impose uniformity on the Empire, could hardly tolerate the existence of so disruptive a religious group. At any rate four edicts were issued in 303–4, commanding the burning of Christian churches and sacred books, and threatening all those who continued to adhere to the banned sect with the loss of civil rights and property. Though Diocletian (members of whose own family and household had themselves adopted Christianity) promised not to spill blood, the persecutions spread throughout the Empire with great violence.

Diocletian's policy was not egotistic. His elevation of the emperor above all other mortals proceeded from his sense of what was necessary for the stability of the Empire. He saw lack of continuity and uniformity as its defects; and he set himself to provide them. It was in keeping with this policy that he decided to abdicate after a reign of twenty years. He compelled his fellow-Augustus Maximian to abdicate at the same time. Lacking Diocletian's sense of public obligation, however, Maximian did so reluctantly, and was never ready to accept his retirement as final; had he done so some of the convulsions of the next two decades might have been avoided.

Diocletian abdicated on 1 May 305, and retired first to Nicomedia, then to his native Illyria, where he had built a magnificent palace at Salona on the shores of the Adriatic, at the site of the modern Split. He appears to have passed the last nine years of his life in contented retirement. When Maximian urged him to reassume the imperial purple, he replied that if Maximian could see the cabbages which he had planted with his own hands at Salona, he would no longer urge him to give up the enjoyment of happiness for the pursuit of power.

If emperors are to be judged by their influence on the future, Diocletian stands with Augustus, Trajan and Constantine as one of the greatest of Rome's rulers. His elaborate system of shared

responsibility for the administration of the Empire proved unworkable, but his reorganisation of finances and of provincial and
military administration fixed the pattern of the Byzantine state.

Theodosius I (The Great)

(A.D. 347–395)

Theodosius I resolutely maintained the unity of the Empire
already threatened with disintegration; he not only strengthened
the position of Christianity as the official religion of the Empire,
but narrowed the definition of what it meant to be Christian, and
turned what had been the faith of martyrs into a persecuting
religion itself.

He was born in Galicia in north-west Spain, probably in 347.
His family was already Christian and his father, Flavius
Theodosius, an imperial general. The future emperor served on
his father's staff in Britain, Gaul and the Danube provinces, but
retired to his Spanish estates when his father lost favour and was
put to death in 375. In 376 he married a fellow-Spaniard, Aelia
Flacilla. Their son, Arcadius, who would eventually succeed to
the eastern half of the Empire, was born in 377.

The following year public catastrophe restored Theodosius's
private fortune. The Emperor Valens was heavily defeated by the
Visigoths at Adrianople and killed in what was the greatest
disaster sustained by Roman arms since Cannae five hundred
years earlier. Valens's colleague Gratian recalled Theodosius,
who defeated the Sarmatians and was then proclaimed co-
emperor in January 379. He was given responsibility for the
eastern part of the Empire, which included the vital frontier
provinces of Dacia and Macedonia, both thoroughly penetrated
by the barbarians.

The task facing him was formidable. The Roman army was not
only demoralised; it was also outdated. Adrianople had been a
battle of vast significance for the future of warfare, for it
represented the first victory of heavy cavalry over infantry.
Moreover, the legions defeated there were no longer the heavily
armed troops of earlier times. They had discarded much of their
defensive armour and were therefore ill-equipped to meet the new
challenge. There were difficulties also in raising sufficient

numbers, for the conscription applied only to certain classes, and was evaded whenever possible.

Theodosius therefore first strengthened the army by directing that Teutons be admitted to it, then sought a political solution to the problem of the Gothic tribes. In 382 he concluded a treaty of alliance (or *foedus*) with the Visigoths. By its terms the Goths were assigned territory within the Empire between the lower Danube and the Balkan mountains in return for a promise of military assistance; the revolutionary feature of this treaty was that the Goths retained their autonomous position and were not incorporated in the political system of the Empire within which they had been granted land. It was a desperate remedy for a desperate situation; but it stabilised the eastern frontier.

From 380 to 387 Theodosius made Constantinople his base. He proclaimed his own greatness and his confidence in the future by extensive development, building the Forum Tauri, the largest public square known in antiquity, on the model of Trajan's Forum in Rome.

This activity however took third place to the military necessities and the Emperor's role in the settling of the theological disputes which divided Christianity. The long struggle between those who subscribed to the Arian heresy and the adherents to the Nicene Creed (which declared Jesus Christ to be of the same substance as God the Father) was not yet ended. Theodosius, however, 'the first of the Emperors baptised in the true faith of the Trinity' (though only after a serious illness in 380) set himself to establish unity of faith in the Empire. That same year he issued a decree prescribing that only those who believed in the consubstantiality of God the Father, God the Son and God the Holy Ghost were to be considered Catholic Christians (a designation here used for the first time). The whole weight of imperial authority was thus cast behind the Nicene Creed. In 381 he summoned the second ecumenical council to Constantinople to confirm what as emperor he had already ordained. The pattern of the Eastern Church in which the bishops would be subordinate to the imperial authority was thus established. Though it cannot be said that the emperor exercised strict control over all church matters, he had by his actions announced himself to be the arbiter in matters of faith, Basileus-Hiereus, king and priest.

A new crisis arose in 383. Maximus, a Spanish general, was proclaimed emperor by the troops in Britain and gained control of the western provinces of the Empire. In 387, four years after the murder of Theodosius's colleague Gratian, who had been succeeded by his half-brother Valentinian II (a minor), Maximus invaded Italy itself. Valentinian's court fled eastwards to Thessalonica. Theodosius, having protected his eastern flank by coming to an agreement with the Persians with regard to the control of Armenia, prepared war against the rebel. Valentinian was sent with a fleet to Italy, while Theodosius confronted Maximus in Pannonia and defeated him completely.

Valentinian was restored to power in Rome, but Theodosius attached the Frankish general Arbogast to Valentinian's staff as his personal representative. Moreover he emphasised his own authority throughout the Empire by basing himself in Milan for the next three years. In 389 he visited Rome itself; the Empire was still one and indivisible.

In 390 came the incident by which, in Gibbon's words, 'the reign of a wise and merciful prince was polluted by an act of cruelty which would stain the annals of Nero or Domitian'. This was the massacre of Thessalonica. The emperor's general there, another barbarian, Botheric, and his principal officers were murdered by the city mob, angered by his imprisonment of their favourite charioteer for having made unwelcome advances to a beautiful slave-boy of the general's. Without investigation Theodosius ordered exemplary punishment. The act of revenge was treacherously accomplished. The people were invited to the celebration of games in the circus. 'As soon as the assembly was complete,' says Gibbon, 'the soldiers, who had been secretly posted round the circus, received the signal, not of the races, but of a general massacre. The promiscuous carnage continued for three hours, without discrimination of strangers or natives, of age or sex, of innocence or guilt; the most moderate accounts state the number of the slain at seven thousand; and it is affirmed by some writers that more than fifteen thousand victims were sacrificed to the manes of Botheric.' Such actions were hardly unknown in antiquity; what followed was unprecedented.

Ambrose, the bishop of Milan, was an old friend and ally of the emperor's. Nevertheless he wrote to Theodosius reproaching him for the crime, and demanding that he repent. Then he denied the emperor communion till he had done so. Theodosius was compelled to do public penance for his sins in the Basilica of Milan before being readmitted to communion at Christmas 390. This public evidence that a Christian emperor was subject to a power greater than his own will made a powerful impression; it was later to be interpreted as showing that the Church had been placed above the temporal power, but Theodosius himself and his successors of Constantinople maintained imperial authority over the bishops and the Church. Nevertheless it showed clearly that a

Christian emperor was accountable for his actions in a way that his pagan predecessors had not been.

Theodosius was the first emperor not to assume the title of *pontifex maximus*, the chief priest of the old state religion of Republican Rome. He had early, supported by Ambrose and the other bishops, made his intention to suppress the old pagan religions clear. Now, in February 391, two months after his public penance, he issued an edict prohibiting sacrifice and the visiting of temples. The age of religious intolerance, a vice from which the ancient world had been free, had now begun. In his very last edict he was to reaffirm his order: 'It is our will and pleasure that none of our subjects, whether magistrates or private citizens, however exalted or however humble their rank be, shall presume in any city or in any place to worship an inanimate idol by the sacrifice of a guiltless victim.' The act of sacrifice and the examination of entrails were declared treasonable. Even those pagan rites which did not involve sacrifice were declared illegal, and offenders subject to confiscation of the property in which the offence was committed or the payment of a heavy fine. In this, as in other ways, Theodosius's reign may be seen as a bridge between the ancient world and its medieval successor.

Not surprisingly this policy provoked reaction. In late 391 Theodosius had moved back to Constantinople, partly perhaps because of the uneasy relations between his son Arcadius and his second wife Galla, the sister of Valentinian II. His departure from Italy, followed in May 392 by Valentinian's death, was the signal for a renewal of conflict within the Empire. The barbarian general, Argobast, though formerly Theodosius's own representative in Rome, now conspired with some of the old pagan aristocracy to proclaim a former teacher of rhetoric called Eugenius as emperor. Theodosius's first response was to issue a final edict completely outlawing paganism and issuing instructions for pagan temples to be demolished. For some months he hesitated before embarking on military action, possibly trying by diplomatic means to break the union of his opponents, possibly hoping that it would disintegrate of its own accord. By the spring of 393 this policy had clearly failed; the rebels, under the command of a Roman nobleman, Nicomachus Falvianus, supported by all those who hoped for the survival of their ancient religion, had occupied all Italy. A war, remarkable in ancient history for having some ideological basis, was inevitable. In May 394 Theodosius marched from Constantinople at the head of a largely barbarian army to defend the legitimate authority of the Roman emperor and the new supremacy of the Christian religion;

among his generals was the Vandal chief, Stilicho, who had married Theodosius's niece, and who would later be the chief defender of the Western Empire against Alaric and the Goths.

The armies met at the River Frigidus on the north-east frontier of Italy. After an initial setback when his Visigothic cavalry were repulsed in an attempt to break the enemy's line, Theodosius was completely victorious; Arbogast, Eugenius and Nicomachus Flavianus were all put to death. Later Christian tradition interpreted the victory as a divine judgement rather than ascribing it to the superior organisation and greater experience of the imperial army.

Theodosius proceeded to Milan where he presented his second son Honorius as Augustus of the West; the elder Arcadius had been left in charge at Constantinople. However, the settlement of the Empire that the victory of the River Frigidus had seemed to assure was short-lived. Theodosius had fallen ill soon after the battle; though he seemed to recover he had a relapse and died suddenly in January 395. On his deathbed he entrusted Stilicho with the care of his sons. His body was carried back to Constantinople and buried in the mausoleum built by Constantius II. 'The genius of Rome', in Gibbon's words, 'expired with Theodosius, the last of the successors of Augustus and Constantine who appeared in the field at the head of their armies and whose authority was recognised throughout the whole extent of the Empire.' After his death Rome and Constantinople became the separate capitals of his sons Honorius and Arcadius, and were never effectively reunited, though in theory the unity of the Empire was never broken.

Nevertheless, if Theodosius had managed to do no more than prolong the integrity of the Empire for his own lifetime, he had still made two lasting contributions to European history. First, he had completed Constantine's work and secured the permanent triumph of Christianity over the old pagan cults; the equation of Europe and Christendom which formed the character of the medieval world dates from his reign and was his achievement. Second, his military reforms, and the use he made of his barbarian allies, who were to be thoroughly incorporated in the imperial army, secured the Eastern Empire even if they failed to do the same for the West. Theodosius was the last emperor to hold real authority over the whole historic Empire; but he may also be regarded as the true founder of the Byzantine Empire which was to survive him by more than a thousand years.

Homer

(? 7th or 8th Century B.C.)

Homer is the first (and some would say the greatest) poet of western literature; but in practical terms all that is attached to the name is the authorship of two epic poems, the *Iliad* and the *Odyssey*. In antiquity some other poems went under his name, notably the *Margites*, the *Battle of the Frogs and Mice* and the Homeric *Hymns* to different gods. But few read these now, while acquaintance with the great epics is still common.

Every statement one might make about Homer is open to dispute. Not even the century of his birth is known. The *Iliad* is the story of the siege of Troy; and the historical Troy was certainly destroyed by invaders in the mid-thirteenth century B.C. Ancient writers made Homer a contemporary of the war or, with specious precision, placed his birth 168 years after its conclusion. But these writers had, after all, no conception of the true date of the fall of Troy. In fact part at least of the *Iliad* cannot be earlier than the eighth century B.C., since references are made to artefacts datable to that period. Some modern scholars would put the composition of the *Iliad* and the *Odyssey* as late as the sixth century B.C.

Scholars would now generally accept that the *Iliad* and the *Odyssey* in their present form were each the work of a single poet, though not necessarily the same one. This was not always so, and in the nineteenth century many argued that the poems were a more or less ill-matched collection of lays, 'stitched together' by rhapsodes (= 'stitchers') in the way that, for example, Sir Thomas Malory compiled the *Morte d'Arthur*. But perception of the artistry of the poems has grown to the point where this is no longer tenable.

The present form of the epics dates substantially from the sixth century B.C., when the Athenian ruler Pisistratus ordered that a canonical text be established for recitation (by rhapsodes) at the annual Panathenaic festival. The poems thus edited were already called by the name of Homer.

Who then was Homer? Born some time between 800 and, say, 575 B.C., he was an oral composer of narrative poetry probably similar in his methods to the Yugoslav goslars of the twentieth century. (It was from studying the practice of oral heroic

composition in Yugoslavia that Milman Parry in the early years of
this century first established that Homer's is a distinctively oral
style of composition, making use of traditional tales that perhaps
go back many centuries and composing with the use of metrical
'formulae'.) Several cities of Ionia, which comprised the western
coast of Asia Minor and its islands, vied for the honour of his birth:
Chios, Smyrna, Colophon, Ios, Salamis; but, said the anonymous
epigrammatist (*Anth. Plan.*, 4.296) diplomatically, 'I say your
home is heaven, and your mother no mortal, but the Muse
Calliope'. Arguments for Chios could be drawn from the self-
description of the poet in the Hymn to Apollo, of

> the sightless man
> Of stony Chios. All whose poems shall
> In all last ages stand for capital.

Arguments for Smyrna depended on an epigram attributed to
Homer which referred to his 'delicate and curious nursery:
Aeolian Smyrna, seated near the sea'. (Chapman's translations.)
In later years a guild of bards calling themselves the 'sons of
Homer' held a distinguished position on Chios.

It is likely that the poet was blind. The lines of the Hymn to
Apollo, taken with the fact that the bards who appear in *Iliad* and
Odyssey are both blind, suggest that this was common: the life of a
singer was one of relatively few that were open to a blind man.

When western culture rediscovered Homer in the eighteenth
century, it was on the basis of his poems that writers tried to
reconstruct his life. Thomas Blackwell's *Enquiry into the Life and
Writings of Homer* (1735) was perhaps the most influential.
Blackwell perceived Homer's life as that of a wandering bard, or
aoidos (the word used of Homer's bards, Phemius and
Demodocus), like that of the Provençal troubadours or the
Highland runers (one must remember that this was the heyday of
the poems of 'Ossian'). 'As this condition is in itself of the utmost
importance to a poet, the consequences of it are almost equally
happy: the *aoidoi*, or bards, were under a necessity of frequent
travelling, and every now and then exercising their vein upon the
greatest subjects. In this situation did Homer begin to wander
over Greece, carrying with him those qualities that procured him
a welcome wherever he came.'

If Blackwell had known the ancient *Life of Homer* that goes
under the name of Herodotus, he would not have been so
confident about that welcome. This composition organised
Homer's supposed biography to include visits to most of the
places of which he appears to show knowledge in the poems, but

also describes a visit to Cyme in South Italy, where he gave a recitation to the old men in the public square.

> When he realised that the Cymeans liked his poetry and found that they enjoyed listening to him, he made the following proposals to them: he said that if they wanted to feed him at public expense, he would make their city very famous. ... But the story is that one of the magistrates opposed his request, using among his arguments that if they thought it right to feed hostages (*homēroi*), they would acquire a large and useless crowd of hangers-on. It was as a result of this event that the name Homer replaced Melesigenes, since the Cymeans call blind men *homēroi*.

The story is obvious invention, not least because of the two explanations for his name (both equally absurd) in as many sentences; it also belongs to a common Greek story-pattern in which poets are rejected by prospective patrons. But the picture of the wandering bard making his painful way to a living is a plausible one. Such a poet would be called in Homer's language a *demiourgos*, literally a 'people's worker'. Many no doubt lived a permanently wandering life. Lucky ones, like Phemius or Demodocus, might be taken up by a wealthy prince or noble and kept as retainers. What was Homer's lot, we do not know.

For the rest we, like Blackwell, must fall back on generalities. For example: his access to great men gave him the opportunity to observe jewellery and fashions such as he describes in his poems. The harshness of his existence gave him fuel for the extensive similes which so often describe humble objects and activities such as potting or beekeeping. A good example is the comparison of the hero Ajax, hard pressed in battle, to a donkey which

> with heavy strength endued
> In some wide field by troops of boys pursued
> Though round his sides a wooden tempest rain,
> Crops the tall harvest, and lays waste the plain;
> Thick in his hide the hollow blows resound,
> The patient animal maintains his ground.
>
> (*Iliad* XI: Pope's translation)

His extensive travels gave him a great knowledge of men which comes out in his marvellous naturalism, not least in the description of the shield made by Hephaestus for Achilles, in Book XVIII of the *Iliad*. The description is too good to excerpt, portraying as it does a whole universe, a world of peace and war, labour and gaiety, sowing and harvest, in the compass of some two hundred lines.

But the ancient tradition abhorred a vacuum. Many stories were attached to Homer's name – of his quarrel with the perhaps contemporary Hesiod; his studies with a bard called Phemius (the bard of the *Odyssey*) and his friendship with one Mentes (another Odyssean character). A curious tale is that of his failure to answer the riddle of the fisherboys on Ios: 'What we catch, we leave behind; what we fail to catch, we take with us.' (The answer: lice). According to *The Contest of Homer and Hesiod*, Homer died of shame at his failure to guess the answer. Herodotus agrees that he died on Ios, but says it was from sickness.

Ultimately Homer is important for what he wrote and not for who he was. Few would dissent from a high estimation of his poems. Where the eighteenth century admired them for their naturalism, present opinion tends to emphasise the marvellous compassion of the martial epic, the *Iliad*: the poetry is in the pity. Homer's claim to absolute veracity, which derives from the direct inspiration of the Muse, has to contain the whole human gamut: the anger of Achilles, the glorious deeds of men, and human wretchedness. As Achilles says to Priam, whose son Hector he has killed and dragged behind his chariot:

> Sit,
> And settle we our woes, though huge, for nothing profits it.
> Cold mourning wastes but our lives' heats. The Gods have destinate
> That wretched mortals must live sad; 'tis the Immortal state
> Of Deity that lives secure.
>
> (*Iliad* XXII: Chapman's translation)

It is often questioned whether in fact 'the world of Odysseus' portrayed in the Homeric poems forms a coherent whole and can be regarded as a picture of the social world of Homer's day. The forceful argument of Sir Moses Finley for its essential coherence and historicity has been challenged, but there can be no doubt that the world of the poems is a convincing one, even if it blends features of different historical epochs with purely imaginary ones. The sum is a profound vision of the world of men, and of their relation with the gods.

Even in antiquity, critics like Xenophanes (sixth century B.C.) mocked Homer's 'ridiculous' gods with their human or sub-human antics and jealousies: 'Homer and Hesiod attributed to the gods everything that is a shame or a mockery among men, theft, fornication and fraud.' Now, scholars would argue that a consistent and serious theodicy can be discerned in the poems. Deathless and ageless, superior in power and honour, they look down on the world of men and pity them. They mingle in the human fray with passion and prejudice, but even Zeus cannot defy necessity to save his half-divine son Sarpedon from death. Gods and men move as unequal partners on the terrestrial stage, and while caprice may rule the gods, men have to strive for heroism as the only way to leave a lasting mark in the world.

Homer has been with us for over two thousand years, and he will not go away. He will continue to move readers and provoke argument. That, and not the vicissitudes of his earthly span, makes his true biography.

Aeschylus

(c. 525–c. 456 B.C.)

Aeschylus, the oldest of the three great Attic tragedians, was born in 525/4, according to the most reliable ancient source. If the date is correct, he came to tragedy late in life, since his first victory took place in 484 (with what play, we are not told). This would fit with what we know of the military distinction of his earlier years. He fought against the Persians at the battle of Marathon in 490, alongside his brother Cynegirus (who was killed), and he may also have fought at the battle of Salamis in 480 B.C. The epitaph which he is supposed to have written for himself stresses these actions rather than his literary achievements:

> This memorial in barley-bearing Gela covers the Athenian Aeschylus, son of Euphorion. The grove of Marathon could tell of his glorious valour, and the flowing-haired Mede knows it well.

His family came from Eleusis, and it was said with some plausibility that he was an initiate of the Eleusinian Mysteries. This may be mere inference from two lines in Aristophanes's *Frogs*, but according to Aristotle he was accused of revealing the secrets of the Mysteries (presumably in one of his plays, most likely *Eleusinians*).

It was probably Aeschylus who gave Attic tragedy the form it maintained for over a century. The origins of the *genre* are shrouded in mystery. Aristotle tells us that it began when the dithyrambic chorus, in the hands of the sixth-century poet Thespis, was given a dramatic role through the introduction of a speaking actor to answer them and present a story. The name tragedy ('goat song') has been thought to be connected with an original performance by a chorus of goat-tailed satyrs, but might equally imply, for example, a song sung in a contest for a goat as prize. In Aeschylus's day tragedy already used two actors as well as the chorus – all of whom wore masks. Tragedies were performed at the two festivals of Dionysus, the Lenaea in January/February and the Dionysia in March/April. Both Aeschylus and his older contemporary Phrynichus generally presented trilogies with a connected theme, followed by a boisterous satyr-play also related in theme.

Aeschylus probably introduced many of the spectacular elements of tragedy – rich costumes, the distinctive actors' boots or *kothournoi*, and the solemn dances. Scenic effects and the use of such devices as the crane (to bring on flying characters) and the *ekkyklema*, a kind of trolley used to wheel from within the stage-house a tableau of the events inside, were probably also his introductions.

We have few details of his career, and only two of his trilogies are dated with certainty: *Persians*, which was the second play of a trilogy which comprised *Phineus* and *Glaucus of Potniae*, plus the satyric *Prometheus the Firekindler*, was presented in 472; and the *Oresteia*, the only trilogy to survive in full, was presented in 458 (with the satyric *Proteus*), two years before his death. He is known to have visited Sicily, where he wrote *Women of Aetna* for a festival to celebrate the foundation of the tyrant Hieron's new city of Aetna, soon after 465. The *Suppliants*, because of its character, used to be regarded as an early play, but it is known now that it was produced in competition with Sophocles, whose first victory was in 468: *Suppliants* may date from 463. In all Aeschylus wrote over seventy plays (even the exact number is uncertain) and they continued to be restaged and to win prizes after his death.

He described his own work as 'slices from Homer's banquet', and many of the known titles draw on the *Iliad* and other epics of the Trojan War (known generically as 'Homer' in his day). One trilogy included *Memnon* and *The Weighing of Souls*, plus no doubt a third focusing on the death of Achilles; another was made up of *Myrmidons* (Achilles's subjects), *Nereids* and *Phrygians* or *The Ransoming of Hector*; yet another the *Judgement of Arms*, *Thracian Women* and *Salaminian Women*. (The plural titles derive from the characters of the choruses.) It was not without reason that

Aristophanes in *Frogs* called his plays 'full of Ares' (the god of war). Aeschylus also wrote at least five plays revolving round the legends of Dionysus at Thebes (a body of legend familiar to us from Euripides's *Bacchae*). It is possible that early tragedy had frequently taken its themes from the legends of the god to whom its festival was dedicated.

Persians of 472 is one of the few tragedies on a historical theme, for it concerns the final defeat of the Persian army at the battle of Plataea (479) and relives the disaster from the Persians' point of view. Without plot or action to speak of, it is a harrowing outpouring of emotion and rich language – the sea at Salamis 'flowers with corpses', to take an example – and may even have been commissioned as part of a regular celebration of the great deliverance from the Persian threat.

Various absurd stories circulated as to Aeschylus's reasons for visiting Sicily. It was said that he was ashamed of a defeat by Sophocles, or by Simonides in the composition of an epitaph on the heroes of Marathon; or that he was embarrassed by the collapse of the stage-building during one of his performances. In fact there need be no other reason than the attraction of a glittering and lavish court and a penchant for imported culture (the lyric poets Pindar and Bacchylides were also lionised by Hieron).

At any rate Aeschylus returned to Athens, and everything we know of him makes it clear that he was passionately committed to the Athenian democracy, and particularly to the reforms introduced by Pericles and Ephialtes in 462 B.C., which 'radicalised' the democracy and in particular turned the court of the Areopagus, which had acquired wide powers, into a court exclusively concerned with the trial of homicide cases. The plot of the *Oresteia* hinges on the series of revenge killings in the family of Agamemnon: the latter, who sacrificed his daughter Iphigeneia in order to gain a fair wind for Troy, was murdered on his return by his wife Clytaemnestra and her paramour Aegisthus; in due time Orestes avenges his father's murder by the murder of Clytaemnestra and Aegisthus, but is pursued by the avenging Furies of his dead mother. Fleeing to the oracle of Apollo who had enjoined the murder, he finds no cleansing of the blood-pollution possible – blood must have blood – until, at a trial before the Areopagus in Athens, the goddess Athena cuts the Gordian knot by declaring the murder of a mother less heinous than that of a father. The Furies are banished to a cave below the Areopagus where they are to become guardians of the city of Athens.

This conclusion in *Eumenides* has often been seen by readers as a

casuistic and humdrum finale to the magnificence and overwhelming horrors of the first two plays, *Agamemnon* and *Libation-
Bearers*. But in performance the effect is reversed. A trial scene can
hardly fail on stage. And the bringing of questions of legend, of
ancestral guilt and religion into the arena of the everyday is the
most powerful endorsement there could be of the new status of the
court of the Areopagus. That said, it is not for Aeschylus's politics
that we enjoy his plays, but for their power of language and
imagination and spectacle – the ghost of Darius rising from the
tomb in *Persians*, the red carpet rolled malevolently from the door
to greet the returning Agamemnon, and the fierce menace of the
Furies in *Eumenides*. So horrific was the appearance of the latter in
the first performance, according to tradition, that several pregnant women in the audience suffered miscarriages through
fright.

The grandiloquence of Aeschylus's poetry was mocked in antiquity, and the feel of some of his more contorted passages is caught
in Robert Browning's extraordinary translation of *Agamemnon*:

> Beacon did beacon send, from the fire the poster,
> Hitherward: Ide to the rock Hermaian
> Of Lemnos: and a third great torch o' the island
> Zeus' seat received in turn, the Athoan summit.
> And, – so upsoaring as to stride sea over,
> The strong lamp-voyager, and all for joyance –
> Did the gold-glorious splendour, any sun like,
> Pass on – the pine tree – to Makistos' watch-place.

What is there to match the plangency of Cassandra's farewell to
life in the same play?

> Ah the fortunes of men! when they go well
> A shadow sketch would match them, and in ill-fortune
> The dab of a wet sponge destroys the drawing.
> It is not myself but the life of man I pity.
> >   (Translated by Louis MacNeice)

The dense theological poetry of the great choruses of the
Agamemnon is also without equal:

> Universal Pan,
> For ever watching at the heart of things,
> And Zeus, the Warden of domestic Right,
> And the perennial sanctity of Kings,
> Let loose the Fury who, though late
> Retarded in the leash of Fate,

Once loosed, after the sinner springs;
Over Ocean's heights and hollows,
Into cave and forest follows,
Into fastest guarded town,
Close on the sinner's heel insists,
And, turn or baffle as he lists,
Drags him inexorably down.

(Translated by Edward Fitzgerald)

The *Prometheus Bound*, a play rich in spectacle – with the hero Prometheus chained to a crag of Caucasus, visited by the daughters of Ocean in a flying carriage, and concluding with an earthquake and thunderstorm that, apparently, plunged all the characters into darkness – has since antiquity been part of the Aeschylean canon. The relative simplicity of its choral language was attributed to its having been perhaps written for a Sicilian audience. But in recent years it has become clear, from close analysis of style, that the play cannot be by Aeschylus. So we know less of Aeschylus than we did, though our admiration for him, and for the *Prometheus Bound*, will hardly be lessened.

He died in 456/5, and was buried in Gela in Sicily. Legend said that according to an oracle Aeschylus would meet death from the sky, and that an eagle, mistaking his bald head for a stone, had dropped a tortoise on it to crack it, and had killed him outright. Such foolishness can be left to refute itself, for quaint deaths are a regular feature of ancient biographies of poets. Presumably Aeschylus had returned to Sicily after the production of the *Oresteia* – why, we do not know. Perhaps Gela was simply a pleasant, prosperous retirement home for the old soldier and democrat.

Pindar

(518–438 B.C.)

While the infant Pindar slept on Mount Helicon, so the legend ran, bees came and settled on his lips. There they built a honeycomb; and the sweetness of the honey of those godlike creatures imbued his words ever after with a lyrical glory.

Pindar's lyric genius was universally recognised in antiquity as unmatched.

Born in 518 B.C. at Cynoscephalae in the territory of Thebes, Pindar's parentage is uncertain: his father was either Daiphantus (probably) or Pagondas: his mother was Cleodice. Other names of members of his family preserved in the tradition are illegitimate inferences from his poetry. It is probable that he belonged to a noble clan of Thebes, the Aegeidae, which claimed semi-Spartan ancestry. In early years he seems to have acquired some musical training from his uncle Scopelinus, who played the *aulos* or double-reed pipe (not an instrument favoured at least by the Athenian upper classes, because of the inelegant grimaces demanded by its embouchure). Developing as a young man a passion for music, Pindar went to Athens to learn his skill, and was instructed by the shadowy figures Apollodorus and Agathocles.

By the age of twenty his talent was already mature, and it is from this year that his earliest known poem dates. This is an ode in praise of Hippocleas of Thessaly (*Pythian* 10), who had won the double-course race at the Pythian Games at Delphi in that year, 498 B.C. Nearly all of Pindar's surviving poems belong to this *genre*, the *epinician*, a sung choral ode which celebrates victory in one or other of the athletic or horse-racing events of the Panhellenic festivals. His works were collected in seventeen books, of which four contain poems known by the names of the Games they were composed for: Pythians, Olympians, Nemeans and Isthmians. The other books included hymns to the gods, maiden-songs, processional songs, paeans, dithyrambs and laments. All except the last and the epinicians are concerned with religious matters and intended for religious occasions: we are lucky that the surviving works show Pindar's genius at its fullest stretch, embracing perennial concerns of man as well as his relation to the gods. For a poem in praise of a victory in the Games is far more than it sounds. To achieve victory, for Pindar, a man cannot rely on training alone; excellence must be in his nature. He believes that excellence is transmitted hereditarily, and that human achievements flourish and decay like the manifestations of the enduring order of nature itself.

> Ancient virtues bring to fruit the strength of man, alternating through the generations: the black fields do not give crops constantly, and trees are not wont to bear their wealth of fruit in every season, but they alternate. (*Nemean* 11)

This uncertainty and vicissitude distinguishes man from the gods whose power is unchanging:

One is the race of gods and men; we have our breath from one
mother; but utterly different powers separate us, so that for the
one there is nothing, for the others the brazen heaven is an
enduring home. (*Nemean* 6)

This belief that blood will out, and that blue blood has the best
chance of success, has not endeared Pindar to modern liberals or
Marxists. His own answer would be that those who achieve
success must proportion their pride and their desires to their
mortal state; for the envy not only of the gods but even more of
men awaits the haughty, who sooner or later can be sure of a fall. A
man who, by contrast, takes a just but modest pride in his
achievements will show up his envious detractor as merely one
who 'rolls his vain thought in darkness, and it falls to the ground'.
(*Nemean* 4)

At some point in the years following his ode for Hippocleas
Pindar must have visited Sicily, then ruled by the great tyrants of
the cities of Acragas and Syracuse. His next commission of
490 B.C. was for Xenocrates of Acragas, winner in the chariot-race
at Delphi – evidently, then, a man of high birth and wealth who
could afford to maintain a stable for chariot-racing. This was
followed by odes for other Sicilians, a man from Orchomenos near
Thebes and two from Attica. By the mid-480s Pindar had
established a connexion with the aristocracy of the island of
Aigina, notably the family of Lampon, for whose sons Pytheas and
Phylacidas he wrote several odes. He seems to have developed a
real fondness for the island and its mythology; figures of
Aeginetan legend occur in every ode for the islanders, and some
like Peleus and Achilles are among his favourite examples of
heroic achievement and mutability (Peleus was entertained to a
banquet by the gods, but died wretched; Achilles was of semi-
divine birth but was doomed to die before Troy). The Aeginetan
odes contain some of his most luminous and satisfying poetry.

In the meantime he had kept up his connexions with Sicily. In
476 B.C. he was commissioned by Hieron, the tyrant of Syracuse,
to celebrate his victory in the horse race at Olympia: the result was
his most famous (though not really his best) poem, *Olympian* 1,
which begins

Water is best, and gold that shines like blazing fire in the night,
more than the wealth of a great man; but if, my heart, you wish
to speak of Games, do not look for a star in the bright waste of
sky that gives more warmth than the sun, nor may we sing a
greater contest than the Olympian.

Clearly now Pindar's fortune was made. But success brought its problems. His style of celebration was designed as a heightened conversation of equals, one aristocrat to another, the poet warning his patron, through the choral song that graced the festal dinner, that man must preserve his modesty, his *sophrosyne*. Yet here he was required to praise an absolute ruler, who if he did not challenge the might of the gods surely claimed a place far above any paid encomiast. Yet praise from an inferior is worthless. Some of Pindar's most complex poems to Hieron are concerned with this problem of elevating the poet's own status sufficiently to be a worthy encomiast without falling victim to the overweening pride he censures in others.

> Little among the little I shall be, great among the great, and will cultivate the divinity that dwells in my heart, giving it honour according to my talent. (*Pythian* 3)

> It is a slippery path to kick against the pricks; let it be enough for me to associate with the good. (*Pythian* 2)

But predictably legends arose that Pindar had been assailed by malicious backbiting. Those who edited Pindar in antiquity believed that a reference to 'chattering jackdaws' in *Olympian* 2 was a swipe at Pindar's fellow-poets, Bacchylides and his uncle Simonides, the former of whom also wrote for Hieron and seems to have supplanted Pindar in his favour – perhaps because of the very simplicity of his style. There is no reason to believe a word of this, but this kind of story was common. The biographical tradition liked to arrange antipathies between poets believed to be contemporary. One story reports that Pindar called the poetess Corinna a 'Boeotian sow'. Unfortunately there is no way of knowing whether this ungentlemanly behaviour is authentic – or even if the date implied for Corinna is correct within a couple of centuries.

It was also said that Pindar had been attacked in his native, aristocratic Thebes for writing in praise of tyrants, and had defended himself in the obscure *Pythian* 2. The first may be the case, but the interpretation of the ode is by no means certain. Pindar could not win: he wrote a poem for an Athenian which praised Athens, and was promptly fined a large sum in Thebes, this time for supporting democracy! Again the story may be apocryphal.

A series of Sicilian commissions followed, for Hieron, for his brother Theron the tyrant of Acragas (who between them were filling Sicily with buildings of unparalleled magnificence – and

size – in the Greek world, and in other ways ostentatiously
cultivating the arts), for Hieron's general Chromius, and for other
Sicilians. *Olympian* 2, for Theron, contains a beautiful description
of the underworld which seems to reflect features of Sicilian
religious belief, and perhaps was designed to flatter the
convictions of Theron himself. The last datable Sicilian ode was
composed in 470 B.C. and celebrated the foundation of Hieron's
new city of Aetna (Aeschylus wrote the *Women of Aetna* for the same
celebrations).

Four years later Hieron was dead. Theron had died in 472 B.C.
Pindar's links with Sicily were broken, and the next commissions
came from still farther afield – from Rhodes (where his one poem
for a Rhodian, *Olympian* 7, was inscribed in letters of gold in the
temple of Athena at Lindos), from Cyrene (for whose king he
produced his longest ode, 300 lines of danced song incorporating
most of the story of the Argonauts) and in his last years again from
Aigina and his native Thebes. He died in 438 B.C., according to
tradition in the arms of Theoxenus, a young man whose beauty he
had praised in one of his informal banquet pieces.

One could not look for a better concluding quotation than the
last lines of Pindar's last poem, *Pythian* 8:

> Creatures of a day. What is a man? What is he not? The dream
> of a shadow. But when the god-given brightness comes, shining
> light is on him and days of sweetness.

Little can be recovered of Pindar's personality, though he seems
to have been noted for personal piety. Various inferences from the
odes suggest a devotion to the Great Mother (or Mother of the
Gods, usually identified as Rhea), whose shrine stood by his
house, and perhaps to Pan. If the latter is the case Pan repaid the
honour, for legend said that he was once caught singing an ode of
Pindar's as he frisked half-hidden through the vales of Arcadia.
Pindar's reputation in later years was of a man with a particular
devotion to the Apolline cult of Delphi. Plutarch, himself a priest
at Delphi, tells us that at certain festivals special honours were set
aside for the descendants of Pindar.

His reputation as the greatest of the lyric poets also lived long,
so that when Alexander the Great sacked Thebes, one hundred
years after Pindar's death, he gave orders that the house of the
poet alone be left standing among the ruins. The scholars of
Alexandria and the critics of antiquity echoed the judgement of
the great conqueror.

Sophocles

(*c.* 496–406 B.C.)

One short day
Inclines the balance of all human things
To sink or rise again. Know that the gods
Love men of steady sense and hate the proud.

Athena's words to Odysseus in Sophocles's *Ajax* seem to encapsulate the central perception of the Greeks in relation to their gods. Suspicion of the man who attempts too much, a firm purpose to keep an even keel in emotion, in temper, in action, are the *leitmotif* of many of the Greek poets and thinkers. No one expressed that view more coherently in his plays than Sophocles, and none, we may believe, adhered to it more consistently in his own long life.

Sophocles was born in 496 B.C., the son of a wealthy weapons manufacturer of the Athenian deme of Colonus, named Sophillus. We are fortunate in having rather more records of his public career than of other Athenian dramatists; the *Life* appended to the ancient editions of his works contains more reliable information and shows more discrimination than most.

He belonged to the Athenian upper classes who, even in the age of the democracy, had a better chance of public office than men of the people. Nevertheless, he had no need to seek fame through politics, and until he was over fifty preferred to cultivate his talent for poetry. His teacher of music was Lamprus, whom ancient sources link with Pindar and Pratinas as an exponent of the old sober style of music; Sophocles himself played the lyre, and at least once played it on stage, in the character of Thamyras.

His first victory was with a play now lost, *Triptolemus*, in 468 B.C., when he was twenty-eight. Four of his seven surviving plays are of uncertain date. This is a small haul from a total output of 123 plays, 24 of which won first prize at the dramatic festivals (he was never placed third). So it would be rash to deduce too much about his development from these few. Nevertheless, we have some external information. He made three innovations in the dramatic technique that had been largely established by Phrynichus and Aeschylus: he increased the number of the chorus from twelve to fifteen, he introduced scene-painting, and – most important – he introduced the third actor. This last innovation made a radical difference to the flexibility of plot and action, since it allowed a dialogue on stage while a third actor was changing masks, so that in practice a number of characters could be introduced into the drama without loss of dramatic momentum. Clearly the official organisers of the dramatic festivals were in agreement with the change, which Sophocles could hardly have instituted without their approval: it suggests that he was well acquainted with the literary coteries of Athens.

He moved indeed in an extensive circle of cultivated people. It is said that he founded a kind of literary club or *thiasos* (religious confraternity) of the Muses. More than one contemporary describes his grace and charm of character. By 452 he had become friendly with another dramatist, Ion of Chios (490-pre 421 B.C.), who was also successful in the Athenian dramatic competitions. Ion was on friendly terms with Cimon, one of the older generation of Athenian politicians who entertained friendly feelings towards Sparta and imitated its fashions, such as long flowing hair. Ion contrasted Cimon's charm of manner with the boorish aloofness of the first citizen of the democracy, Pericles; and we may well imagine that Sophocles could have shared these attitudes so appropriate to his class. (Herodotus was another of his friends.)

Sophocles was also a lover of boys (where Euripides was a lover of women), which again marks him as an adherent to the older and aristocratic fashions of Athenian society. This comes out most clearly in an account Ion wrote of a dinner party at which both he and Sophocles were present, in Chios, 'when Sophocles was sent as general to Lesbos' (see below). Both men clearly enjoyed a drink, and, when merry, Sophocles was not above making suggestive remarks to the boy who poured the wine, causing him to blush deeply. (This led the conversation to a discussion of the use of colour in painting, and whether 'the purple cheeks of youth' should be painted, any more than the 'golden hair' of the gods.) Yet even in his sexuality Sophocles remembered the Greek rule of temperance: on being asked in old age how he regretted the loss of his sexual powers, he replied 'most gladly have I escaped this thing you talk of, as if I had run away from a raging and savage beast of a master'. (The story is in Plato, *Republic* I.)

In common with many artists who flourished in the mid-fifth century, Sophocles wrote a handbook on his art entitled *On the Chorus* (which implies, On Drama). In this he described three stages in his own style, from the Aeschylean bombast of his early period, through a 'sharp and artificial' style to the best and 'most suited to expressing character'. It would seem that all the extant plays belong to the last period, which must therefore have represented an acme achieved fairly soon. The first datable extant play is *Antigone* of 441, though *Ajax* is probably earlier, and *Women of Trachis* may be.

It was said that it was the success of *Antigone* that secured Sophocles the election to the post of general (one of ten) in 440, when he had the task of crushing the revolt of Samos. (No doubt this was when he visited Lesbos, and went to dinner with Ion in Chios.) His public career had begun before this, however, in 443/2 when he was hellenotamias, or treasurer of Athens's imperial revenues. It continued for more than twenty years, though we have few details: he was general again at some time, along with Nicias. Pressure of state business may account for the gaps in the stage record when he is known to have produced no play (in 467, 428, 415, and no doubt others).

Sophocles's art has since Aristotle been seen as the acme of Attic drama, and it was on the model of his most famous play, *Oedipus the King* (post-430) that Aristotle erected many of the 'rules' of tragedy, most notably that of the dominance of plot over character. If we find ourselves puzzled by *Ajax*, where the title character dies halfway through, or by *Women of Trachis*, where the focus of attention seems at one time to be Heracles, at another his long-suffering wife Deianeira (whose tragedy is it?), we are perhaps asking the wrong question. The function of the poet is to tell a story, and to create characters to convey that story. The story of Ajax is not over with his death, but only when burial is secured. The conclusion of *Women of Trachis* is Hercules's death (though nothing is said of his apotheosis) and could not be left out of Deianeira's story. In *Electra* we ask what comes after, knowing of Orestes's pursuit by the Furies in Aeschylus's parallel play: but that is no part of Sophocles's story, which we must perhaps accept as a 'happy' ending.

Sophocles's most famous plays are the three concerned with the saga of Thebes. These do not form a trilogy, for Sophocles never followed the older, Aeschylean pattern of composing connected trilogies, and the three were presented at widely differing dates. The earliest is the *Antigone* (the latest in mythical chronology), which focuses on the political issue of obedience to a law that is immoral or against religion – in this case, whether Antigone may bury her dead brother, the traitor Polynices. The combination of political argument and a central female character keeps the play much in the public eye today, and the legend has been more used by European and American dramatists and poets than any other tale from the Greek canon.

Oedipus the King has always been admired for the detective-story perfection of its plotting, in which Oedipus gradually comes to realise that he is the victim of his own curse: he has brought plague on Thebes by his unwitting murder of his father and marriage to his mother. The horrifying description of the plague in the opening scene has been thought to show the impact of the plague of Athens in 430, graphically described by Thucydides (though the disease is still unidentified). Certainly horror is to the fore in the description of Oedipus's self-blinding with his wife's brooches:

> At each stroke blood spurts from the roots,
> Splashing his beard, a swirl of it, nerves and clots –
> Black hail of blood pulsing, gushing down.
>
> (translated by Robert Fagles)

The lines contradict any view of the serenity of Greek classicism as mere blandness. Nonetheless, despite this and other examples like the description of Philoctetes's filthy and suppurating wound in the play bearing his name, such things are only part of the picture. *Philoctetes* (409) is one of the subtlest of Sophocles's plays, with its contrast of the trickster Odysseus and the innocent nobility of Neoptolemus, who together come to steal Philoctetes's bow, which alone can enable the Greeks to capture Troy. The contrast of the old aristocracy and the new smooth-tongued rhetoric of democracy seems encapsulated here.

Sophocles was famed in antiquity for his piety. We have seen how he founded a fraternity of his own. He also established a shrine to Heracles, who it is alleged led him in a dream to discover a stolen crown. Strangest of all, he entertained the god Asclepius when he came to Athens, until his temple was ready for him, and also wrote a paean for him. If this means anything, it must mean that Sophocles housed the sacred snake of the god while its pit was prepared. For this, it is said, he was honoured after his death as the hero Dexion, the Receiver.

It is just such a deep piety, as well as love of the deme Colonus, expressed in a choral ode beautifully translated by W. B. Yeats, that is at the root of his last play, *Oedipus at Colonus*. This deals with the arrival of the aged, blinded hero at Colonus, his last encounter with his warring sons Eteocles and Polynices, and his mysterious assumption to the gods. In the quarrels with his sons, scholars in antiquity sought to find a reflection of friction between Sophocles and his own Iophon (also a tragedian), who allegedly sued Sophocles for showing excessive favour to Sophocles the younger, son of Sophocles's illegitimate son Ariston. The story seems wildly

implausible, and the connexion with the play no less so; it is probably based on something in the plot of Leucon's comedy *Phratores*.

Various absurd stories describe Sophocles's death, the most
famous being that he choked on a grape-pip – a suitable end for a
bon vivant. He is also said to have died of voice strain while reciting!
Presumably he died of old age. His tomb was on the road to
Decelea, and was crowned by a Siren to symbolise the magic of his
poetry.

It was that poetry that gave us perhaps the greatest document
of Athenian humanism, the choral ode in *Antigone*:

Numberless wonders,
terrible wonders walk the world but none the match for man . . .
speech and thought, quick as the wind
and the mood and mind for law that rules the city –
all these he has taught himself . . .
Only Death, from Death alone he will find no rescue.

(translated by Robert Fagles)

Pheidias

(*c*. 490–*c*. 431 B.C.)

Pheidias the sculptor was the son of Charmides and a citizen of
Athens; the inscription on the base of the statue of Zeus in the
temple at Olympia read 'Pheidias, the son of Charmides, the
Athenian, made me'. The name Charmides was used by several
aristocratic or well-to-do families at Athens, some of them of
political importance and notoriety, but it is not possible to link
Pheidias with them, despite his involvement in the complex
political world of Athens in the fifth century B.C.; it is as a sculptor
that he won his reputation in antiquity.

According to Pliny the Elder (who wrote a ragbag compendium
of general knowledge in the first century A.D., and died while
studying the effects of the eruption of Vesuvius which destroyed
Pompeii in A.D. 69) Pheidias's 'date' was the 83rd Olympiad, that
is, the four-year period 448 to 444 B.C. This is not, of course, a
birth date; it is intended by Pliny to indicate the time at which an
artist reached the peak of his achievement, and it coincides with
the beginning of Pheidias's work on the sculptural decoration of

the Parthenon. His earliest work in fact probably belongs to the 460s and he must have been born towards the beginning of the fifth century, perhaps around 490 B.C. It is impossible to be more precise. He died, in exile, at some time after the outbreak of the war between Athens and Sparta in 431 B.C.

Athens was a very important artistic centre. In the earliest period, in the Dark Ages around 1000 B.C., the evidence of Athenian achievement can be seen in her decorated pottery, which has a coherence, a discipline of shape and form which far surpasses that produced in any other part of the Greek world. This continues till the late eighth century; there is then a period of some quiescence, followed by a revival in the sixth century. This revival is by no means confined to the minor art of pottery decoration (though this is important). Contact with Egypt had stimulated the development of sculpture in the Greek world, and, after a period when the larger statues were made of wood, the Greeks suddenly began to produce stone statues of great competence, many of them over life size, and though in certain respects these echo Egyptian types, from the outset they show an inventiveness and originality which is to create a distinctly Greek achievement.

Athens was in the forefront of this. There are several examples of splendid marble statues dating early in the century, and from this moment the impetus is continuous. The rise to power of the 'tyrant' Peisistratos brought a further stimulus; under his benevolent administration Athens was prosperous, and the wealthy families were able to commission statues to publicise themselves and their achievements, setting them up to commemorate the holding of priestly offices, and to mark their graves when they died. Many of them have been found. Thus we have a good, first-hand knowledge of Athenian sculpture in the golden age before the Persian invasion. Though many statues are by anonymous artists, the personalities of their creators can be seen in their work, and towards the end of the period we can begin to see the work of sculptors whose names are known, such as Antenor.

By 525 B.C. another important development in the art of sculpture had taken place. This was the invention of the technique of moulding statues in bronze by the hollow cast process. Bronze statuettes do occur at a much earlier date, but these are cast in solid bronze, using a great deal of expensive metal. By the hollow cast technique the bronze was reduced to the equivalent of thin sheet; much less metal was needed, and bronze statues could now be cast in life size or even greater (the technique required the casting of a statue to be done in several pieces, which were then fixed together). A chance discovery made a few years ago of a group of bronze statues in Piraeus, which had been gathered together probably at the time when Athens was plundered by the Roman dictator Sulla, has brought to light a bronze statue of Apollo, perhaps by the sculptor Canachus, which would seem to have been made about 525 B.C., and indicates the foundation of a school of bronze sculpture there. At first, however, it was the city of Argos which was particularly famous for its school of bronze sculpture, and the most important sculptor of this School – of whose work we know in reality nothing – was Ageladas.

Pliny says that Pheidias was the pupil of Ageladas. Chronologically this is just about possible. Since there were other bronze sculptors at Athens, such as Myron (who made the famous statue of the discus thrower), in whose work some points of contact with the early style of Pheidias can be seen, Pliny's statement may well rest on nothing more than the chronological suitability.

The earlier statues by Pheidias were certainly of bronze. They included a group set up at Delphi as a thank-offering for the victory over the Persians at Marathon, and depicting Athena and Apollo and one of the commanders, Miltiades, and the heroes who gave their names to Cleisthenes's new tribes. There were two bronze statues of Athena on the Acropolis at Athens. One was regarded as particularly beautiful. Lucian poses the question 'Which of the works of Pheidias do you praise most highly?' and the answer is 'Who but the Lemnian goddess?' This title shows that she was given to Athens by Athenian settlers sent to Lemnos around 450 B.C. The other was a colossal statue of Athena the Champion, again an offering for the victory at Marathon. She was about 30 feet in height, wearing, as well as her dress, the aegis breastplate which is her own attribute, and a helmet with nodding plumes. She could be seen from ships approaching Piraeus, and served as a landmark to guide them into harbour (an exaggerated version of this says she could be seen from Cape Sounion, but this is an impossibility). She was eventually taken to Constantinople.

When the decision was taken to rebuild the Acropolis the colossal Athena was already in position and the realignment of the entrance now meant that she was directly in the line of vision as people went through the new gateway, the Propylaia. Pheidias's contribution to the rebuilt Acropolis was much more than this. He had become a part of the intellectual circle associated with Pericles, and was clearly destined to play a major role in Pericles's reconstruction. Plutarch, indeed, calls him the director and supervisor of the whole enterprise. Where he got this information is uncertain. It is generally agreed that Pheidias was responsible for the sculptural decoration of the Parthenon, and this is reasonable (though, of course, it does not mean that the statues and reliefs were all carved by him personally – there are too many of them to be within the achievement of a single sculptor, even if he worked on them for his entire lifetime). His masterpiece was undoubtedly the great gold and ivory cult statue which was placed in the Parthenon in 436 B.C.

How far he supervised the design and construction of the buildings is another matter. Plutarch himself points out that other great architects and artists were employed on the various buildings – the architects he names for the Parthenon are Callicrates and Ictinos. Both of them were important men, and major artists in their own right. Callicrates is named on an inscription which designates him as the architect responsible for work on the temple and precinct of Victory, at the entrance to the Acropolis, which seems to have been the prelude for the whole enterprise of reconstruction (the building of that temple was postponed for a generation after the inscription, while the other work on the Acropolis was carried out). Callicrates was also responsible for work on the fortification of Athens. He seems to have been older than Ictinos, who may have worked also in the Peloponnese, at the temple of Apollo at Bassae; but Ictinos is not named as architect of any other of the buildings on the Acropolis. Someone brought intellectual powers of a high order to the design of the Parthenon, and it is most unfortunate that we cannot tell which of the architects it was, or whether the ideas embodied in the design were imposed on the architects by Pheidias as the chief inspirer and organiser of the project.

Though the Parthenon reused foundations and material which had been prepared for its predecessor, the unfinished building destroyed by the Persians, the design was altered; it was made slightly wider, which meant that it could have a façade of eight columns rather than the six originally planned, but more importantly made possible the introduction of a ratio, first imposed on the proportion of width to length, of 4:9 (which means $2^2:3^2$) a proportion which is not found in other Greek temples, but has the attraction not only of being mathematically neat, but of introducing a squared relationship which is, of course, appropriate for architectural structures. Mathematical harmony – the relationship of the length of a musical string to the note it produced – exercised the philosophical intellects of the fifth and fourth century. 'Let no one ignorant of geometry enter' was the message over the door of Plato's academy, and the design of the

Parthenon entirely reflects this.

His contribution to the decoration is easier to evaluate. The Parthenon is the most lavishly decorated of all Greek temples, and a large number of craftsmen must have been employed in its execution. The relief slabs of the Doric frieze over the outer colonnade betray this variety of hands: though a coherent sequence of design may be assumed for them, the quality of workmanship is variable (it has been suggested, wrongly, that they had been prepared for an earlier temple). Here we can see the work of a master designer – Pheidias – who has not yet imposed his discipline on his craftsmen, in the first of the sculptural decorations to be executed. The later sculpture is a different matter. Over the porch and along the top of the cella walls comes the great processional frieze, echoing the sacred procession of Athena's festival, but perhaps intended rather to honour the heroes who fell at Marathon. This has a sublimity and a coherence which never falters from one end to the other. By any reckoning, this is one of the greatest masterpieces of sculpture the world has produced; and the genius responsible for it is Pheidias. The same is true of the pedimental groups which decorate the two gable ends, that at the west showing the struggle between Athena and Poseidon for the patronage of Athens, and that at the east the birth of Athena. These are less well preserved than the Frieze, and their design perhaps less in accordance with modern tastes, but of their original genius there is no doubt.

In his own time, however, Pheidias's masterpiece must have been his gold and ivory Athena. This was essentially a wooden statue, to which were affixed plaques of gold and ivory; ivory for the flesh parts, gold for the drapery, the helmet, the shield on which she rested her left hand, the statue of victory which she held in her right. So long as it survived it was universally admired for its majesty and the feeling of religious awe it inspired. Viewed in the half light of the interior of the Parthenon, standing on a base and reaching almost to the ceiling, it is next to impossible for us to conceive its qualities from the shoddy, miniature versions manufactured for Roman tourists that are all we have of it. She was taken, eventually, to Constantinople, and perished in a fire.

Pheidias's association with Pericles was his undoing. He was prosecuted as a form of indirect attack on Pericles, accused of embezzling the gold destined for the statue. He disproved the charge, since the gold plaques could be removed and weighed (they could, indeed, be melted down in an emergency, and remade from the moulds, which were kept). He was also accused of representing himself as one of the figures decorating Athena's shield, though this is improbable, since portraiture was not a developed aspect of sculpture in the fifth century.

Nevertheless Pheidias left Athens shortly before the outbreak of the Peloponnesian war. He went to Olympia, where he was commissioned to outdo his Athena with a great seated gold and ivory statue of Zeus for the temple there (perhaps showing that the Parthenon had itself been intended to outshine that earlier temple). This was made in a building which was called afterwards the 'Workshop of Pheidias'. Recent excavations have revealed some of the moulds in which the gold plaques of the statue were fashioned, as well as other debris which demonstrates conclusively that Pheidias worked there after, not before, he made the Athena for the Parthenon. Like the Athena, the Zeus perished in late Roman times. This was, in all probability, Pheidias's last work. He never returned to Athens, and in later years his gold and ivory statue at Olympia was still cared for by his descendants. We do not know when he died, but it must have been at some time in the struggle between Athens and Sparta.

Until recently Pheidias's work could only be judged properly by the sculpture from the Parthenon. In 1972 a skin-diver, exploring the sea bed near Riace, in Calabria, found two bronze statues. They represent two warriors, of heroic appearance and visage, originally holding hoplite shields and spears, one with a helmet on his head. They are magnificent specimens. Great care has been taken with the details. Their teeth are silver, their lips are made in copper to give a different colour to the bronze. Though there is still controversy about their origin, and, indeed, date, the most convincing argument is that they were taken from the Athenian memorial to the victory of Marathon set up in Delphi – works, then, of Pheidias in his younger days, but already displaying that genius which was his, in the medium in which he first worked, and distinguished himself, bronze.

Herodotus

(c. 485–c. 424 B.C.)

Herodotus, born in the Greek city of Halicarnassus on the coast of Asia Minor between 490 and 480 B.C., was one of the world's great story tellers. He has frequently been described also as 'the Father of History'. Some of the stories he told he had discovered for himself, for he had great curiosity, the first quality of a historian. Many of them he picked up from other people, including Egyptian priests and Greek politicians, in the course of wide-ranging travels. Some were written down and already belonged to recorded literature.

Herodotus must have been a great listener as well as a great writer, and he also had a good eye for sites and monuments, many of them in remote places, which he took pains to describe. He obviously knew Athens well. Halicarnassus was a Dorian settlement, but it used Ionic, the language of Athens, in its official documents. It was close too to the mighty Persian empire, and was controlled by a pro-Persian dynasty until it entered into alliance with Athens before 454 B.C.

Herodotus usually, but not always, identified the sources for his stories, sometimes giving two or more variants of them, and although by later standards there were times when he approached the past uncritically, he was well aware himself of the need to maintain a sceptical frame of mind before forming his own judgements. He asked questions about evidence as well as about events. Thus, when near the beginning of his *Histories* he describes how King Croesus of Lydia, then the most powerful Greek kingdom in Asia Minor, crossed the River Halys, a strategic boundary, he notes that it was 'by the existing bridge', adding that 'such, at any rate, is my own belief in spite of the common Greek story that it was Thales of Miletus who contrived the crossing'.

It was in nearby Miletus, an important cultural centre, that Greek science and philosophy had developed in the generations before Herodotus, and Thales was not the only outstanding figure produced by that city. Hecataeus, like Herodotus, was a traveller and prose writer, who produced a world map suggesting that the world was surrounded by a great ocean. Herodotus himself mentioned Hecataeus four times, on each occasion critically, although Hecataeus's own work is said to have opened with the words 'I write to me what seems probable, for the tales told by the Greeks are both various and absurd'. Towards the end of Herodotus's *Histories* he observed succinctly that his business was 'to record what people say, but I am by no means bound to believe it – and that may be taken to apply to this book as a whole'.

Whatever the sources of Herodotus were – and some of them were certainly Persian – the main texts are missing, and much that we now know of the ancient world in the 6th and 5th centuries B.C. we have derived, therefore, from him. We can claim too that both as a student and as a writer he was a genuine pioneer. As a twentieth-century ancient historian, Professor Momigliano, has concluded, 'there was no Herodotus before Herodotus'.

His long and immensely readable prose work, the *Histories*, his life's work, was a triumph of narrative focused mainly, though not exclusively, on the struggle between Greeks and Persians, culminating in the Persian invasion of Europe in 480 B.C., and their defeat by the Greeks, a crucial defeat which soon passed into legend. The *Histories* were planned by Herodotus as carefully as an epic poem, and they were designed 'to preserve the memory of the past by putting on record the astonishing achievements both of our own and of other peoples and more particularly of how they came into conflict'. Yet 'digressions' were an essential part of the plan of Herodotus, stories within the story or tangential to it, and broad-ranging surveys of society and culture, notably a vivid account of Egypt in Book II.

Herodotus believed that the Egyptians were the first to discover the solar year – through astronomy – and to divide the year into twelve parts. 'Their method of calculation', he wrote, 'is better than the Greek.' Yet to fulfil 'the needs of my story', he turned from mathematics, science and religion to cats and to crocodiles (including how to catch them). He described mummification in detail. He might be troubled by chronology, fitting people, events, and buildings, into precise sequence, but he was confident when he turned to what we would now call sociology, dividing the population of Egypt into seven classes – priests, warriors, cowherds, swineherds, tradesmen, interpreters and pilots. He identified very specifically the feeling in Egypt and elsewhere that 'craftsmen and their descendents are lower in the social scale than people who have no connexion with manual work'. 'All the Greeks', he wrote 'have adopted this attitude.'

Herodotus's interest in birds and animals was almost as great as his interest in people. He could be credulous, as when he described ants bigger than foxes which dug for gold – some of them were said to be kept in the menagerie of the Persian King. Yet he refused to believe in one-eyed men stealing gold from griffins that guarded it, and after describing the phoenix he added 'I myself have not seen this bird except in pictures'. He had a good word for the Tin Islands, of which Britain may have been one. 'It seems to be true,' he wrote, 'that the countries which lie at the circumference of the inhabited world produce the things which we believe to be the most rare and beautiful.'

The division of the *Histories* into nine books was not the work of Herodotus himself: it was made by librarians in Alexandria centuries later. Nevertheless, Herodotus pointed out himself on more than one occasion how he had the whole work in mind when he was dealing with the parts. He was concerned in a fashion which recalls historians of our own times not only with power struggles – particularly great conflicts on land and sea which he had chosen as his main theme – but with comparative and often clashing patterns of thought and behaviour. He moved easily from what has been called in our century, a century as troubled as that which he was describing, 'the history of events' to what would now be called the social structures of his own and other peoples. Indeed, large sections of the *Histories* besides Book II focus on religions, traditions, and attitudes to such subjects as dress, food and medicine; and literature and drama are used as evidence alongside factual survey. During the last decades of our own century, it has been possible more fully to appreciate Herodotus's achievement as a historian than it was half a century ago, when history was usually more narrowly confined to politics and diplomacy. Then and in the nineteenth century, historians of Herodotus were primarily preoccupied with cataloguing mistakes in his information, not all of them obvious or correct, and in scorning his credulity.

Herodotus was capable of examining the role of individual character in the making of decisions both on the Greek and the Persian side. Thus, Croesus figures prominently in the first chapters of the book, the character of Xerxes is explored at the end, and there are revealing pictures of Miltiades, Themistocles and Mardonius. Judgements are made from time to time, like 'this was a wicked thing to do' or 'many things make it plain to me that the hand of God is active in human affairs'. Herodotus could be guilty of anachronism in putting particular words or arguments into particular people's mouths, but he kept his grip on the complex events he was describing, recognising that there were often 'mutually exclusive interpretations of them'. Historical outcomes, he recognised, could be very different from historical intentions, even when these were buttressed by the enigmatic support of the Oracles at Delphi and elsewhere. Omens or 'warning signs could not be dismissed, but there was "wisdom in forethought",' he believed; and he often made an effort when dealing with major historical decisions to look at the psychology of the people who made them or of other people who influenced or contradicted them.

At the same time, Herodotus's contributions to geography and anthropology are just as interesting to contemporary readers as his contributions to psychology or to the 'history of events'. The mysteries of space fascinated him as much as the mysteries of time. His world was not 'the little frog pond' of the Mediterra-

nean, as Socrates once described it, but reached out in the south to
Ethiopia and beyond, in the east to India, in the north to what we
now call Russia, and in the west to the Pillars of Hercules – the
Straits of Gibraltar – and beyond. He devoted several pages to the
River Nile and the problem of its source, and without knowing
about the equator noted how travellers round Africa had found
themselves returning with the sun on their wrong side.

What he says on his travels or imagined on the basis of other
travellers' tales was designed to amuse and to titillate his readers
as well as to inform them. The Ethiopians had 'the tallest men in
the world, the best-looking and the longest-lived'; 'Indian tribes'
dressed in cotton and copulated in the open like cattle; 'no nation
regards the sanctity of a pledge more seriously than the Arabs'; it
was said that every person in Neuria turned once a year into a wolf
for a few days and then back into a man again, although he,
Herodotus, did not believe it. Nor did he believe an anecdote
purporting to explain why when Spartans wanted 'a stronger
drink than usual' – they did not usually drink their wine neat –
they used the phrase 'Scythian fashion'.

Geography received the same treatment as history or folklore
from Herodotus, a treatment often tinged with humour. He was
particularly interested in rivers. When Xerxes moved into
Europe, he writes 'save for the great rivers there was not one
stream his army drank from that was not drunk dry'. The Danube
was the greatest of all rivers – 'that mighty stream which rising
among the Celts, the most westerly after the Cynates of all European nations, traverses the whole length of the continent' – and
those Scythians who lived to the north of it endured 'intolerable
cold' so that 'in order to turn earth into mud what was required
was not water but fire'. Men were never the complete victims of
the environment. Nearer home, the Samians, whom Herodotus
admired, were responsible for three of the greatest building and
engineering feats in the Greek world, including a tunnel nearly a
mile long, eight feet wide and eight feet high, driven through the
base of a hill nine hundred feet in height. There are many
references to what we would now call technology in Herodotus.

The narrative of the Persian wars, proclaimed as the main
theme of the *Histories*, quickens in Book 5. In Book 1 Ionia had
passed into Persian hands. Now its liberation begins, and it was a
process in which Herodotus probably participated and which he
describes at length. Athens comes into the picture, too, a city to
which Herodotus probably migrated in the 450s B.C., but of which
by a law of 451 he failed to become a citizen. His Athenian
sympathies are evident in the narrative. He first tells the story of

how it was 'forced from despotism', adding that while it had been great before, it now, 'her liberty won, grew greater still'. Other Greek states, including Aegina, Corinth and Sparta, often at loggerheads with each other, are described next before turning again to Persian plans. When Miletus fell to them, he writes, a play on the subject produced in Athens reduced the audience to tears and the author was fined a thousand drachmas for reminding them of a disaster which touched them so closely. This is the kind of detail that we do not find in Thucydides, the second best known historian of the ancient Greek world.

The Athenian victory at Marathon in 490 B.C. has passed into most versions, even outline versions, of world history. Yet once again Herodotus introduces what is now quite unfamiliar detail, ceasing conspicuously to say much about Greek history between 489 B.C. and 481 B.C. The story quickens again in Book 7 with the death of Darius, the accession of Xerxes, and the great Persian invasion 'directed nominally against Athens' but in fact 'aimed at the conquest of the whole of Greece'. It was because the Athenians, with their strong sea power, 'stood firm and had the courage to meet the invader' that Xerxes was repelled, though Herodotus bestows praise also on Leonidas of Sparta and many other 'distinguished Spartans' who fell at Thermopylae: in the words of an inscription,

> Four thousand here from Pelops' land
> Against three million once did stand.

'Xerxes', Herodotus adds, 'felt fiercer anger against Leonidas while he was still alive than against any other man, and that is why he cut off his hand after he had been killed and had it fixed on a stake.'

The naval battle of Salamis sealed the Persian fate, yet Herodotus finds time in describing it to include a reference to the outstanding contribution of Queen Artemesia of his own city Halicarnassus to the Persian cause. 'My men have turned into women, and my women into men', Xerxes is reported to have said, as he watched the battle from across the straits. And while saluting the Greek victory, Herodotus also found time to point out that the news of it was conveyed back to Persia with unique speed. 'There is nothing in the world that travels faster than those Persian couriers. The whole idea is a Persian invention.'

It was because Herodotus did not leave the story at that point but went on to deal in Book 9 with further unsuccessful Persian diplomacy and warfare, culminating in decisive Greek victory at Plataea in 479 B.C., that he is able to end the *Histories* not with

Persian withdrawal but with Persian demoralisation. He can even seek to point a moral in his last sentence, which takes him back to King Cyrus of Persia with whom he had begun in Book I. 'Soft countries breed soft men. It is not the property of any one soil to produce fine fruits and good soldiers too.' There were other morals scattered in his pages. 'It is always the great buildings and the tall trees which are struck by lightning. It is God's way to bring the lofty low.' 'The evil of internal strife is worse than united war in the same proportion as war itself is worse than peace.'

Euripides

(*c.* 485–*c.* 406 B.C.)

Euripides has had a mixed press in comparison with the other great Attic tragedians, who have been consistently admired where they have had readers. His reputation was high in antiquity, though many of his plays were more successful after his death than they had been in his lifetime. More than twice as many of his plays were preserved by the ancient compilers of collected editions than those of either Aeschylus or Sophocles, a preference perhaps partly due to a relative simplicity of language that made him suitable for school use.

The earliest translation of a Greek play into English was the *Iphigeneia in Aulis* by Lady Lumley (probably soon after 1549, but not printed until 1909); and in Italy too Euripides was the earliest to be translated. But in the nineteenth century opinion began to swing violently against him. Euripides was a mocker of the gods, who brought religion into disrepute. Aligned with the Sophists whom Plato castigated, he was seen as a mere casuist with no poetry in him. The extreme apologists for Euripides, who saw him as leading a creative revolution against absurd mythology, gave way to the liberal humanism of the interpretation of Gilbert Murray, whose book on the dramatist (1918) was still in print in the late 1960s. More recent criticism has turned towards matters of poetic art and dramaturgy, but Murray's revaluation of the sophistic contribution to art and thought remains valid and powerful.

Euripides was born about 485 B.C. (Some said he was born on the day of the battle of Salamis, the triumph over the Persians of

480 B.C.) He was the son of Mnesarchus or Mnesarchides, a merchant whose home was at Phyla in central Attica. His mother was called Cleito, and many jokes in Aristophanes depend on the statement that she was a greengrocer: it is not known why this canard (as it surely was) was apposite. Mnesarchus was wealthy and the holder of a hereditary priesthood of Apollo.

When Euripides was eight or nine the ruined walls of Athens were rebuilt, and the restoration of the temples of the Acropolis was begun. Over the next ten years Polygnotus was producing the great series of paintings of scenes of Greek mythology in the 'painted stoa' of the agora. Perhaps it was the sight of these that stirred Euripides's early ambition to be a painter. At the same time, an oracle given to his father had said that he would win at contests where crowns were awarded: so he practised his boxing and is said to have won a victory at Athens, before discovering his true métier.

He may have discovered that his real skill was with words through hearing in his early years the lectures of the great wandering philosophers of Greece. Tradition asserts that he was acquainted with Anaxagoras (b. *c.* 500), who was prosecuted for atheism for asserting that the moon is a large rock about the size of the Peloponnese, with Socrates, and with Protagoras, who first read his work *On the Gods* in Euripides's house. Protagoras was about his own age, and Socrates younger, but Anaxagoras was older and representative of the early states of the questioning spirit that had arisen in Ionia. This developed in Athens into an intellectual ferment of which Protagoras's dictum, 'Man is the measure of all things', is perhaps the central statement. Mythology was questioned, speculation about physical nature was pursued, techniques of argument were practised for their own sake, morality was quizzed for absolute values and found to be a matter of mere relativism. Conservatives felt the foundations of their world shaken. Euripides's dramas speak from the centre of this intellectual complex.

He first competed at the Dionysia in 455 B.C., and won his first victory in 441. After this he won only two other victories, with *Hippolytus* in 428 and (probably posthumously) with *Iphigeneia in Aulis* and *Bacchae* together in 405. Eighty titles are known, and we have nineteen of the plays. It is possible to date the extant plays with some confidence as the dates of nine of them are known, and stylistic analysis has shown an uncommonly regular development in Euripides's use of metrical freedoms, so that the remaining plays can be slotted neatly in between them, with a margin of a few years each way.

The first extant play is *Alcestis* of 438 B.C., which won second prize. The other plays presented at the same time included *Telephus* which was to furnish Aristophanes with a subject of parody for years to come. *Alcestis* is an unusual play since it has a happy ending (the restoration of life to Alcestis who consented to die to let her husband live), and it probably filled the slot at the end of the day which was usually allotted to the satyr play.

Euripides's first success was *Hippolytus* of 428 B.C. Most readers would share the high opinion evinced by its original audience of this powerful drama of the chaste Hippolytus's flight from the advances of his stepmother Phaedra. When she is repulsed she writes a false indictment of Hippolytus for attempted rape, and hangs herself. Hippolytus's father, Theseus, curses his son, who flees from the palace to the Troezenian coast. Here, a huge bull emerges from the sea and frightens his horses; his chariot is smashed and Hippolytus is killed. The play ends with Hippolytus's patron goddess Artemis, whose rivalry with Aphrodite has brought the plot about, taking leave of the dying Hippolytus. She will and can do nothing for him, and the gods may not even look on death. Man is left to his fate.

The story presents many of the themes that were to make Euripides notorious in his own time and later. First, there is the showing-up of the gods as amoral operators who will do with men whatever redounds to their own honour, but leave them with the responsibility all the same. The 'double motivation' is as old as Homer, but Euripides first drives home its moral inadequacy. Gods must do better than that to be worthy of worship. Man is the measure of all things.

The ancient *Life* of Euripides said that *Hippolytus* was written when Euripides discovered that his wife Choirile was being unfaithful to him with his own slave Cephisophon. After this he developed a reputation for misogyny. Largely no doubt this was fuelled by Aristophanes, whose *Women at the Thesmophoria* (411) concerns the abduction of Euripides's father-in-law by the women as a hostage for Euripides's speaking better of their sex in future. Clearly Euripides's attitude to women was something new, and noticeable to his public, and this was elevated by later writers into a simple misogyny. Truly to define Euripides's attitude to women is not so simple. A modern woman might sympathise with Medea when she says she had rather fight in battle three times than give birth once; and there are many cases in which Euripides shows an unusual understanding of female psychology and female oppression. But recall the end of *Medea* (431): the foreign enchantress, deserted by her husband Jason for the daughter of the king of Corinth, murders her own children and hurls their bodies at Jason's feet to spite him, before ascending to the sky in the chariot of the Sun. Was the message this, that any woman who showed an awareness of the limitations of her lot was bound to end up as a murderess? No wonder the Athenian women attacked Euripides.

It is of course absurd that the plot of *Women at the Thesmophoria* gets reported as history in the *Life*. Probably no less absurd are the stories of Euripides's general misanthropy, for example his living in a cave at Salamis and writing his dramas there. It may be true however that his lack of success drove him out of Athens – though he claimed to be indifferent to public opinion – and to the court of King Archelaus of Macedonia. But this was late in his life, in 408 B.C., and one cannot see why the king of Macedonia would want a poet universally reviled in his own city. Productions at Athens continued, and on Euripides's death in 406 B.C. Sophocles dressed his own chorus in mourning. The unpopularity of the poet in Athens is a figment. Another absurd legend was that Euripides died by being torn to pieces by some Molossian dogs belonging to Archelaus. Many poets are given deaths in some way appropriate to or derived from their works, but we do not know what Euripides had written to deserve this fictional fate.

But we anticipate. Euripides continued after *Hippolytus* to produce plays regularly, and many of them reflect very evidently the mood of the times as the Peloponnesian War progressed into disaster. *Trojan Women* (415), for example, is a graphic portrayal of the distresses and horrors of war. Since what has reached us from antiquity is the first few plays from an alphabetical order, plus a selection of ten designed for school use, the quality is necessarily uneven. We do not, as with Sophocles and Aeschylus, have a selection of what ancient scholars considered the better plays. Some we find weak in plot, drab in language and unsatisfactory in human interest. Euripides was a variable writer.

In the last fifteen years of the century his style of plotting underwent a change: instead of the savage intensity of plays like *Hippolytus*, *Medea* or *Heracles* we have plays whose plot is almost fantasy. Two in particular, *Helen* and *Iphigeneia in Tauris* are very similar in that each involves a rescue of a marooned heroine, and each is distinguished by long lyric monologues by actors, as distinct from chorus. Music was playing an increasingly important role in drama and becoming more florid and elaborate, and the role of the chorus was less and less bound to the plot. One of the few surviving texts of Greek music is a setting of a monologue from *Orestes* (408), a play almost burlesque in its proliferation of incident and 'peripeteia' (reversal of fortune), culminating in a rooftop chase and the arrival of Apollo to disentangle with a word the inextricable plot.

In these plays Euripides's art looks forward to what we know of fourth-century tragedy, and can guess from the style of fourth-century comedy, in which again the chorus's role has dissolved and 'human interest' predominates. Yet in his last play, *Bacchae* (405), Euripides returned to a more formal plot, a greater integration of the chorus, and a myth of the patron god of tragedy, Dionysus. *Bacchae* remains one of the most admired and often performed of Greek plays. It centres on the opposition of Pentheus, king of Thebes, to the new religion of Dionysus. The god himself appears in disguise and tricks Pentheus into going to watch the orgiastic rites of his female devotees on the mountains, where they tear apart with bare hands and drink the blood of young animals in an access of superhuman strength. Pentheus has the misfortune to be seen, and suffers the same fate as the lions and deer. His own mother, Agave, who is among the Bacchants, drunk with mystic frenzy, bears his head back to the palace as a trophy. The end of the play is lost but centred on Agave's realisation of what she had done.

This plot fits ill with any view of Euripides as a pure rationalist. The play was a stumbling block to the scholar Verrall who, in his work published in the two decades following 1890, wished to see Euripides as a mocker of the gods, and was constrained to argue that half the play was no more than conjuring tricks by the mysterious stranger. One should hardly think of an old man's reversion to conventional religion – rather a recognition of the irrational that is in man and is diagnosed by theorists of the human condition at their peril. This play occasioned the step from scholarly concentration on Gilbert Murray's 'freethinking' Euripides to the re-emphasis on the irrational in Greek culture in the great work of Murray's successor as Regius Professor of Greek at Oxford, E. R. Dodds. Somehow Euripides, with all his unevenness of quality and his problems of interpretation, is central to our experience of the Greek achievement.

Thucydides

(*c.* 471–*c.* 399 B.C.)

Two of the most searching and influential of modern philosophers, David Hume and Emmanuel Kant, described the first
page of Thucydides's *History of the Peloponnesian War*, the great war
between Athens and Sparta and their allies from 431–404 B.C., as
the beginning of real history. It was a war which still lives not only
because of the military and naval action which determined its
outcome but because of the issues which were at stake and the way
people living at the time described them. An earlier seventeenth-
century English philosopher, Thomas Hobbes, a translator of
Thucydides, had already drawn out of the *History* what for him
was an extremely congenial philosophical generalisation relevant
to the study of conflict in all periods of history. 'In the nature
of man, we find three principal causes of quarrel. First, Competition; secondly, Diffidence; thirdly, Glory. The first makes men
invade for Gain, the second for Safety, and the third for Reputation.'

Thucydides himself believed that we can learn directly from
history. He described his book as 'an everlasting possession, not a
prize composition that is heard and forgotten', 'to listen to for the
moment'. Yet it is misleading to cull general philosophical or
political propositions from his pages and turn them into a kind of
anthology of well-reasoned attitudes which transcend time.
Thucydides was above all else a practising historian, describing
circumstances and events which he knew well. He began with
particulars rather than with abstractions, and he knew how
complex particulars can be. He was fully aware also of the
vagaries and irrationalities of the story. The pattern could neither
be fully predicted nor controlled. War, in particular, broke
routine. He spent much of his time therefore describing, for
example, the great plague which struck Athens in 430 B.C. during
the early stages of the long war against Sparta and which left no
scope either for intelligence or courage. All that it could provide
were victims. 'One could either only feel sorry for the ill or become
infested oneself.'

Nor was plague the only uncertain happening in history for
Thucydides. The historical characters who took decisions or who

chose the people who took the decisions often made mistakes from which posterity could learn, Thucydides stressed, but the unfolding of events was never entirely dependent upon them. There was a further element of uncertainty, for example, in revolutionary disturbance, which could be compared – not only imaginatively – with plague. In such circumstances 'men of inferior intellect generally succeeded best'. The operations of 'human nature', which Hobbes was to seek to identify, were reflected for Thucydides in 'ungovernability in passion' and 'uncontrollability by justice'. In the account which he presented of the strife of revolution in Corcyra, modern Corfu, one of the most haunting episodes in the whole of his *History*, we learn of such moral anarchy in the island that intelligence and courage availed for as little as they did in time of plague.

Different generations can learn and have learnt different lessons from Thucydides, who never claimed to be a prophet. His first readers, who were well aware of the outcome of the long protracted war, must have felt a strong sense of the irony of history as Thucydides led them once more through a sequence of very recent events which had surprised and shocked them; and the carefully ordered arrangement of his work, which began with a meticulous reckoning of the great power of Athens at the outset of the war, must have added to the irony. It was Sparta at the end of the day, not Athens, which won the war. Later generations, with the benefit of longer hindsight – more and more days to come – have been able to relate Thucydides's narrative to an extended time span, encompassing the decline both of Athens and Sparta, the rise of Macedon and the victories of Alexander the Great, the fall of Greece before the Romans, and the subsequent destruction of Rome itself.

Thucydides maintained that the war he described – and he broke off abruptly in late 411 B.C. before it ended – was deemed, even before it began, to be 'great and memorable above any previous war'. In the light of two world wars in the twentieth century, the *History* acquired a new significance. During the first of them, also called 'great', it was observed that there were soldiers and sailors, still educated in a classical tradition, who carried copies of Thucydides around with them. During the second, when that tradition was further attenuated, Winston Churchill was more than once compared to the great Athenian statesman, Pericles. In more recent times still, serious classical scholars in the United States, a country with many traditions, did not hesitate to relate the themes of Thucydides to the Vietnam war, and they revised their interpretation of Thucydides in the light of it. What seemed to stand out then was not only the defeat of Athens, with all its resources and all its claims to power, but the terrible sufferings of war. For such late readers, Thucydides seemed to be less of a coolly critical historian or an eloquent protagonist of human freedom than a highly sensitive and deeply involved participant in a complex human process. They turned to his work not only as a historical source, but as a contemporary ratification.

Unlike Herodotus, whom he never named, Thucydides helped to make the history he was telling. Nor did he linger long over the distant past. 'I believe', he wrote briskly in his first chapter, 'that former ages were not great either in their wars or in anything else.' He quite explicitly condemned, therefore, 'the tales of chroniclers who please the ear rather than tell the truth', and when he turned to what we now would call contemporary history, the history that interested him most, he was always anxious above all else to get at the different levels of the truth. This is not to say, however, that he omitted all reference to the more distant past. He began with 'inquiries into the early history of Hellas' before turning to the origins of the war; and there are frequent references throughout his *History* not only to the Persian wars and their impact, but, if usually obliquely, to earlier Greek literature.

Thucydides began his *History* as soon as war broke out, when he was already 'of mature years'. He lived long enough to see the war end twenty-seven years later. A rich man, connected by birth with the Athenian aristocracy, he served as an Athenian general during the war in the unsuccessful defence of Amphipolis, an Athenian colony, in 424 B.C. His failure led to banishment, but the fortunate consequence of this was that he was now able while in exile to secure full intelligence not only about what was being decided in Athens – and why – but about the motives and manoeuvres of the enemies of Athens. He survived its fall in 404 B.C., and although he returned, he did not die there.

Such highly distinctive individual experiences helped to shape both his mode of reporting and his judgements on events. Thucydides did not believe that powerful Athens lost the war because of particular military or naval defeats – including a spectacular defeat in Sicily in 413 B.C. – but from the internal conflict and social disintegration. It was after his narrative broke off in 411 B.C. however, that Persian subsidies enabled the Greek enemies of Athens to build a large fleet, but even then it was possible for the Athenians to defeat it in a bloody battle in 406 B.C. 'They continued to resist', Thucydides wrote in a summary note forecasting the end in Book II (when he is praising Pericles), 'and were at last overthrown only when they were ruined by their own internal dissensions.' They would still have won the war had they remained true to the ideas and spirit of Pericles, as expressed in his remarkable funeral oration, summarised in the same book.

Athenian institutions, Pericles had told his fellow citizens, did not emulate those of other countries. They were not a copy: other people copied them. They were democratic institutions, very different from those of authoritarian Sparta, but they left open a place for excellence. Public business was conducted with a respect for freedom, but there was also a recognition of the need for leadership. Only when the integrity of democratic leadership was lost, Thucydides argued, did Athens succumb.

Thucydides's views on the most effective pattern of politics have often been discussed. Tyranny he ruled out. It is clear also that he had no sympathy either with an oligarchy which was concerned only with the self-interest of its own members or with a democracy which failed to appreciate excellence. Most strongly of all, Thucydides, suspicious of crowd psychology, attacked the mindless 'rabble' in Athens and elsewhere. Yet while Hobbes could claim that Thucydides 'least of all liked democracy' and pointed 'to the desperate actions undertaken upon the flattering advice of such as desired to attain, or to hold what they had attained, of authority and sway among the common people', Thucydides was not looking for Hobbes's Leviathan, a sovereign in complete command. To impose order he defended rather 'a balanced mixture of the few and the many', as others of his contemporaries did, to rule with sense.

Political matters figure prominently in Thucydides, who was deeply concerned also with the relationship between material resources and political and military initiatives, what would now be called the logistics of war. In dealing with Athens, he inevitably devoted much of his attention, therefore, to the 'empire' which it had built up after the Persian wars; and politics and diplomacy were directly relevant as well as economics in this connexion. In 480–479 B.C., at the critical point in those wars, Athens had accepted Spartan leadership. But when the Persians had withdrawn from Europe, it was the Athenians who continued the struggle, creating a League to face the Persians. 'At first', Thucydides writes, 'the Athenians were leaders of others who were autonomous and deliberated in common councils.' Later, however – and he thoroughly approved of the change – they acquired 'a firmer hand' over what soon became an empire. The contributions they collected became 'tribute', which was used not only to build a fleet but also to pay the public office-holders who took decisions in Athens at the centre.

Thucydides went on to note the unpopularity of the imperial system in some of the cities which were bound to Athens, and, above all, the fear of the Spartans as they watched the power of Athens grow. 'The truest explanation' for the Peloponnesian War, he maintained, was 'the growth of the Athenian power which terrified the Lacedaemonians [the Spartans] and put them under the necessity of fighting.' *Their* strength lay traditionally on the land, not at sea, and, while they were 'terrified', for long they 'remained inactive'. They were goaded into action by their allies, who persuaded them to break a thirty-year truce with Athens, made in 446 B.C., while it still had fifteen years to run.

The word 'necessity' figured much in Thucydides's analysis. The power of Athens needed no justification: 'we are contending for a higher prize than those who enjoy no like advantages', said Pericles in his funeral oration. Yet Spartan resentment and counter-action needed no justification either. 'Brave men go to war as soon as they are wronged.' Nonetheless, while there was 'necessity' behind this process, Thucydides identified at every point in the story foolish decisions and equally foolish acts following from them – on both sides – noting carefully how they affected the fortunes of war and its final outcome. Great actions were not necessarily successful ones. Events could confound all plans. When the first great Athenian fleet left Athens for Sicily in 415 B.C. 'the expedition seemed more like a display of power and greatness than a preparation for war'. Yet already there was a sense in some quarters in Athens that Sicily would be no more likely to fall to the Athenians than Athens in the not very distant past had fallen to the Persians.

One of Thucydides's main techniques – though it was more than that – was to put such opinions (and counter-opinions) into the form of speeches. Pericles's funeral oration was one of them, but there were many others. Thucydides did not claim that the speeches had actually been made in the form set out in his pages. 'I put into the mouth of each speaker', he wrote in Book I, 'the views that, in my opinion, they would have been most likely to express, as the particular occasions demanded, while keeping as nearly as I could to the general purport of what was actually said.' The technique was a remarkably successful one, although exegesis of the speeches requires a knowledge of Greek rhetoric, the art of words, as well as of the course of events.

Future historians, including historians writing in this century, have dealt with the origins of the Peloponnesian War at far greater length than Thucydides and have used quite different techniques, but few have matched his ability to make basic points quickly and without fuss. The wisest of them have admired his skills even when they have dissented from his judgements on people or events. Thus, the great nineteenth-century English historian Macaulay thought Book 7 of Thucydides, which dealt with Sicily, 'the *ne plus ultra*' of the historian's art. There is much, however, that we would like to know that Thucydides left out. For example, it is remarkable how little he tells us of the culture of Athens during one of its greatest ages or of the contrasting ways of life of its allies and enemies. He is far narrower in his sense of what history is about than Herodotus had been.

Perhaps the most important and interesting general point he made was that the Spartans were 'the most convenient of enemies' for the Athenians. Since they were 'totally different in disposition – one people swift, the other slow, one aggressive [a virtue], the other lacking in boldness' – they were enemies capable of fighting each other to a stalemate. The people of Syracuse, however, whom the Athenians met in Sicily, were 'similar in disposition' to the Athenians and for this reason 'they fought most effectively against them'.

Almost every episode in the *History* has been subject to detailed scrutiny by historians, ancient and modern. Yet reading about a historian is no substitute for reading him. Thucydides reads well even in translation. His work was divided into books and chapters long after his death, and there are many changes in tempo and judgement as it moves from one episode to another. The reader is inevitably caught up in the experience of war and the politics that went with it. Characters live – among them Pericles, Brasidas, Nicias and Alcibiades – although we are left in the last resort to make our own judgements of them. And we learn much of ruses, tricks, stratagems and plots, not to speak of spies and traitors and 'the appetite for war'.

Whatever our own stance, we can share Thucydides's sense of the suffering that accompanied or followed the sounds of battle. Inevitably military action brought 'brilliance' to the victors and misery to the vanquished. 'By stealing away the means of providing easily for men's daily lives' it offered not diversion, but destruction. It was a 'teacher of violence' and 'assimilated the passions of most men to their circumstances'. It was because Thucydides demonstrated how in all circumstances protracted war carries with it momentous and unforeseen consequences that he can still speak with authority to societies and cultures completely different from his own.

Aristophanes

(*c.* 450–*c.* 383 B.C.)

'Looking for a sanctuary that would not fall, the Graces found the soul of Aristophanes.' So runs an epigram attributed to the philosopher Plato. The emphasis may seem surprising in a description of a poet whose name is usually associated with rollicking and often bawdy comedy. But Plato was right to recognise Aristophanes's lyrical gifts, which are the equal of any of the Greek poets. Aristophanes himself would perhaps most have wished to be remembered for the serious political cutting edge he claimed to have given to comedy.

He was born around the middle of the fifth century B.C., the son of one Philippus of the deme of Cydathenaeum. He first emerges into the light of history with the production of a play, *Banqueters*, in 427 B.C., when he was in his twenties (yet, as we are told, was already bald).

He began his career as a comic dramatist at a time when the institution of Attic comedy was undergoing several changes. Comedies were the distinctive dramatic performances on the final day of two Attic festivals of Dionysus, the Lenaea in January/February and the Dionysia in March/April. Designed to reflect the cheerful and drunken spirit that was part of the god's image, comedy nonetheless adhered to a strict formal scheme in which a situation of conflict was set up, a formal strife or 'agon' of two leading characters was followed by a 'parabasis' in which the chorus (often of animals or other non-human entities, from which many of the plays take their titles), stepped forward to address the audience on behalf of the poet, and the play concluded in more or less riotous festivity. Other regular elements included the *pnigos* or 'choker' (like a Gilbert and Sullivan patter-song). The licentious spirit of the festival was expressed in the freedom with which characters and chorus alike would deliver criticism or abuse, often highly obscene, of prominent citizens. The actors wore grotesquely padded costumes and long leather phalluses which made possible plenty of sexual by-play and outrageous *double entendres* in the dialogue.

Shortly before 427 the number of comedies at each festival had been reduced from five to three. The older generation of comedians which included Cratinus and Eupolis had evidently concentrated on the abusive side of comedy – to such an extent that it was rumoured, later, that Eupolis had been drowned in the Hellespont by an outraged Alcibiades! *Banqueters* is lost and we know little of it except that it was produced for Aristophanes by Callistratus, and won second prize. The next year (426) Callistratus produced Aristophanes's *Babylonians*, which evidently held to the old traditions and contained a virulent attack on the rising politician or 'demagogue' Cleon, who had succeeded Pericles as the chief citizen of the democracy.

Cleon remained the prime butt of Aristophanes in his next two comedies, *Acharnians* of 425 and *Knights* of 424, and also received attention in *Clouds* (423) and *Wasps* (422). His response to *Babylonians* was to prosecute either Aristophanes or Callistratus (which, is not clear) for slandering the magistrates' council and people of Athens, but the charge was dismissed. *Babylonians* probably won the first prize.

However, the first play preserved, *Acharnians*, contains much more than political abuse. The leading character is one Dikaio-polis ('He who sets the city to rights'), and the plot revolves around Dikaiopolis's plan for a private peace with Sparta, with whom Athens had been at war since 431. The audience would have been enlarged by the numbers of farmers from the country-side who took refuge within the city walls during the campaigning season, and the play won first prize. The parabasis of men of the Attic village of Acharnae contains an explicit political lecture on the war and a poetic manifesto as well:

Since first to exhibit his plays he began, our chorus-instructor has never
Come forth to confess in this public address how tactful he is and how clever.
But now that he knows he is slandered by foes before Athens so quick to assent,
Pretending he jeers our City and sneers at the people with evil intent,
He is ready and fain his cause to maintain before Athens so quick to repent.
. . .
For before, when an embassy came from the states intriguing your favour to gain,
And called you the town of the violet crown, so grand and exalted ye grew,
That at once on your tiptails erect ye would sit, those crowns

were so pleasant to you.
And then, if they added the *shiny*, they got whatever they asked
for their praises,
Though apter I ween for an oily sardine than for you and the
City the phrase is.
By this he's a true benefactor to you, and by showing with
humour dramatic
The way that our wise democratic allies are ruled by our State
democratic.

. . .

And therefore the Spartans approach you today with proffers of
Peace and Goodwill,
Just asking indeed that Aegina ye cede; and nought do they care
for the isle,
But you of the Poet who serves you so well they fain would
despoil and beguile.
But be you on your guard nor surrender the bard; for his Art
shall be righteous and true.
Rare blessings and great will he work for the state, rare
happiness shower upon you;
Not fawning, or bribing, or striving to cheat with an empty
unprincipled jest;
Not seeking your favour to curry or nurse, but teaching the
things that are best.

These lines emphasise Aristophanes's claim as a comedian to a
serious political role. Much debate has ensued as to the politics of
Aristophanes the man, who has often been represented as a
laudator temporis acti, a conservative out of sympathy with new
intellectual trends (*Clouds*), with the development of legal practice
and corruption (*Wasps*), with the conduct of the war (*Acharnians*,
Peace) and with women (*Thesmophoriazusae, Lysistrata, Women in
Parliament*). It has however to be remembered that comedy is by
nature a conservative *genre*, since laughter at the absurd depends
on a firm sense of the normal, and that it would be a strange
man who positively preferred war to peace, corruption to rectitude.

A more complex issue is that of Aristophanes's attitude to
'modern' poetry, particularly that of Euripides. Again the issue
rears its head first in *Acharnians*, which contains a lengthy broad
parody of a scene from Euripides's *Telephus*, preceded by a visit by
Dikaiopolis to Euripides to borrow some of his poetic rags and
tatters to cut an appropriate figure when making his big speech.
Again the fun, repeated in *Thesmophoriazusae* and *Frogs*, has been

taken as indicative of a deep disenchantment with the new poetry. But what would one expect from a satirist? Again it seems to have been common for comedy to attack poetry and music; and the most significant piece of evidence is a splendid compound verb coined by Cratinus, to 'euripidaristophanise', which suggests that to contemporaries what the two poets had in common was much more important than their supposed differences.

All we really know of Aristophanes the man comes from the semi-fictional portrait of him in Plato's *Symposium*, which presents him as easy-going, friends with everyone present, always ready for a laugh but with an underlying seriousness. The discourse on Love put into his mouth in this dialogue reflects admirably the blend of the theoretical, the fantastic and the plain absurd which appears, in a different blend, in his plays. The secret of love, he says, is that in origin the human race had three sexes, male, female and hermaphrodite, which were split apart by the gods; since then, each half has been seeking its other half: and hence there are lovers of the same sex and of the other sex in the world.

After *Acharnians*, which Aristophanes produced himself, his career progressed with continuous success. From a career of forty years we know the titles of forty plays. Of these eleven survive in full, and we have fragments of all the others. Many of the plays won first prize at their festivals. *Knights* of 424, in which Cleon was brought on as a sausage-seller of unparalleled vulgarity, landed Aristophanes in more hot water. About this time he was the victim of a lawsuit from Cleon for exercising citizen rights to which he was alleged not to be entitled. The case was dropped when Aristophanes agreed to curb his attacks, but this did not stop him keeping up the pressure in *Clouds* and *Wasps*, where Cleon is presented as a dog on trial for stealing from the kitchen.

Clouds (423) is one of the most popular plays for its memorable – though totally unfair – portrait of Socrates as the unworldly philosopher, measuring the jump of a flea and speculating on the organ with which gnats hum; gaping at the stars and receiving a lizard's excrement in his face; and giving courses alike in good and bad logic.

Birds (414) and *Lysistrata* (411) are both wish-fulfilment plays of very different kinds. In the former, two humans, tiring of the foolish ways of Athens, set off to the realm of the Birds to build the city of Cloud-Cuckoo-Land. The play contains lyrics of surpassing beauty, appropriate for the singing birds of the chorus as they gather to the new city. It has lost none of its satirical bite, for a performance of the 1970s in Athens roused the ire of a minister and resulted in cartoonists showing him ever after in the company of a chicken. *Lysistrata* represents the attempt of the women of Athens to stop the war by going on sexual strike, and has been understandably popular in recent years for its contemporary suggestiveness.

But Aristophanes's triumph was surely *Frogs* of 405, in which the god Dionysus (appearing for the first time in extant comedy) descends to the underworld to obtain political advice from the recently dead Euripides and Aeschylus. A memorable weighing of the contestants' words in their plays is used to establish their credentials: Aeschylus, with his heavy polysyllables, sinks the scale every time. As Euripides says,

'Twas all Scamanders, moated camps, and griffin-eagles flashing
In burnished copper on the shields, chivalric-precipice-high
Expressions, hard to comprehend.

Aeschylus fights back with two brilliant parodies of Euripides's own style, the second a lyric about a stolen cock:

> O Artemis, thou maid divine,
> Dictynna, huntress, fair to see,
> O bring that keen-nosed pack of thine,
> And hunt through all the house with me.
> O Hecate, with flameful brands,
> O Zeus's daughter, arm thine hands,
> Those swiftliest hands, both right and left;
> Thy rays on Glyce's cottage throw
> That I serenely there may go
> And search by moonlight for the theft.

In the end it is Aeschylus whom Dionysus leads back to life, as a reward for his wise advice on how to run the city of Athens – advice surely much needed in the last anguished years of the Peloponnesian War. Aristophanes could not, after all, save Athens single-handed. Nevertheless he was awarded a crown of sacred olive, and the play was ordered to be performed a second time – a rare honour.

His other extant full plays are *Peace* (421), *Thesmophoriazusae* (411), *Women in Parliament* (391) and *Wealth* (388). The last two are markedly different from their predecessors, in particular in the attenuated role of the chorus, and, in *Wealth*, in the greater emphasis on continuity of plot and the melancholy of the message that wealth is blind: if only he could see who really deserved him, man's troubles would be over. Interestingly, this play was the earliest to be translated into English, by Thomas Randolph (1603–35).

But if once Plutus should receive his eyes,
And but discern 'twixt men, the world were changed:
Then goodness and full coffers, wealth and honesty,
Might meet, embrace, and thrive and kiss together;
While vice with all her partners starves and pines,
Rotting to dirt and filth, leaving to hell
Black souls. Who better counsel can devise?
Ergo, 'tis fit Plutus receive his eyes.

Wealth indeed belongs to what is called Middle Comedy, a transitional stage between the ribald Old Comedy and the New Comedy of Menander with its tedious moralism and emphasis on love-stories and plots of mistaken identity. In 387 the comic abuse of individuals was forbidden by law, as good an indication as any of the changed and reduced character of the famed Athenian freedom after the financial exhaustion of the war and the brief savagery of the rule of the Thirty. Aristophanes probably died within a few years of this ban, though his sons Philippus and Araros both followed in his footsteps as comic poets.

The best assessment of the impact of Aristophanes's art comes, again, from Plato. On being asked by Dionysius of Syracuse for information about the nature of Athenian political life, Plato sent him some of Aristophanes's plays to study. That Aristophanes's concerns, though particular, were not parochial, is shown by his continued popularity on the Greek stage and throughout the world.

Praxiteles

(*fl.* 360 B.C.)

The defeat of Athens by Sparta at the end of the fifth century B.C. had a depressing effect. It was felt particularly at Athens, of course, where the city narrowly escaped total destruction. Her fleet was reduced to a token twelve ships, her fortifications destroyed, and the loss of revenue from her dependant allies became permanent. Compared with the confident and expansive age of Pericles, she was but a shadow of her former self. Buildings such as the Propylaia and the Temple of Nemesis at Rhamnous, on which work had stopped at the outbreak of war were left, permanently, in their unfinished state. There were very few new buildings, and these were built in the cheapest manner possible.

Athens was now thrown back on her own resources, her industry, her silver mines, her agriculture and trade, all of which provided a hope of reasonable prosperity. Only one condition was needed, that a period of peace would enable this economic development to take place. About this time a new statue group was set up in the Agora, emphasising this, for it depicted the goddess Eirene – that is, Peace personified – holding in her arms her child Ploutos – that is, Wealth. Compared with the strident confidence, the spirit of success and power which can be seen in Athenian sculpture of the fifth century, this is a subdued and rather sentimental group – mother looking lovingly at her offspring. The original does not survive, and it is not even certain whether it was made in bronze or marble. We have copies and adaptations dating to the Roman period (including one most unsuitably used to depict the monstrous Messalina and her awful child, the future emperor Nero). The appeal of the type was universal, and, modified perhaps by Egyptian iconography of Isis and the infant Horus, forms one of the prototypes for Christian representations of the Madonna and child.

The sculptor was Cephisidotos. We have another statue which is probably his work, a bronze original this time, depicting Athena. This, too, clearly shows the difference in spirit between the fifth and fourth century. The statue shows the goddess in a relaxed pose, rather than that of a vigorous champion. Even the gods have become human, and the old sense of mysterious power has been softened. These attitudes find their best expression in the work of the man who was probably Cephisidotos's son, Praxiteles. Praxiteles was born at about the point of transition from the fifth to the fourth century – as so often we do not have the precise date of his birth. Pliny says he flourished about the time of the 104th Olympiad, that is, 364–60 B.C. There survives the base of a statue dated to about 330 B.C. signed by Praxiteles the Athenian. His life therefore coincides with the declining fortunes of Athens, from the end of the war with Sparta to the years which followed Philip of Macedon's victory at Chaironeia. His work was popular, both in his own lifetime and afterwards; not only do we have several copies of his most famous works made in the Roman period, but he was written about by authors such as Pliny. Whether the stories are historically accurate is another matter.

One statue of Praxiteles is described by Pausanias in his account of the Sanctuary of Zeus at Olympia. It stood in the Temple of Hera, which by the second century A.D. seems to have become a veritable art gallery. It was, says Pausanias, 'a stone [that is, marble] Hermes carrying the infant Dionysus'. When Olympia was excavated in the nineteenth century, the German archaeologists found, in the debris of the temple, a statue which exactly corresponds to Pausanias's description. Until recent years, when several bronze statues of importance, such as those from Riace, were found at the bottom of the sea in shipwrecks, Praxiteles's Hermes was reckoned the only original statue by a known Greek sculptor of the first rank which had survived.

The newly discovered bronzes have altered this position, but even more, the Olympian Hermes has been judged to be not Praxiteles's work, but a copy made in the Hellenistic period. The judgement depends on the techniques employed in the carving and finishing of the statue (the fact that Pausanias tells us it is by Praxiteles is not significant – it is Praxiteles's design, clearly enough, and he is merely repeating what he was told at Olympia). We do not know when it was put in the temple, or why, or where it came from. Pausanias says it is one of the later dedications. Despite this it is a fine statue, highly finished and beautifully carved. In pose, and general sentimentality, it immediately recalls the work of Praxiteles's father – refined, elegant, but endowed, now, with a certain languor. It is completely in the spirit of the fourth century. It was not, however, his most famous statue. It may well be an early work, because of the connexion with Cephisidotos, but even this is not certain, and it has been suggested that it dates rather to the end of Praxiteles's career. There are no other direct copies of it (which is surprising, if one was specially made for Olympia) though there is an echo of it in a wall-painting at Pompeii. One of the objections to its being original is the unsightly prop which runs between Hermes's left thigh and the tree trunk on which he rests the arm holding the infant. Such props are necessary reinforcements in marble statues, but are best avoided or concealed; its prominence here suggests that the original was in bronze.

There seems little doubt, however, that Praxiteles's most famous work was originally carved in marble. This was his statue of Aphrodite, the goddess of love. There is a full account of this in Pliny. Praxiteles seems to have made it of his own volition, rather than as a commissioned work, and then to have offered it for sale. Perhaps this part of the story is suspect, for although statues were undoubtedly made as commercial objects during the Roman period – and Pliny would be familiar with this – it is less likely that this is the way Greek sculptors of the fifth and fourth centuries B.C. operated. If this were not true, then Pliny's whole tale must be an invention. The model for the statue, according to the late Roman author Athenaeus, was Praxiteles's mistress, Phryne ('Toad' – though the name seems to have been intended as a compliment). Pliny remarks on the statue's fame: 'The statue of Aphrodite, to see which many people sailed to Cnidos, is not only Praxiteles's best work, but the finest statue in the whole world.' He had made two versions of Aphrodite, which he offered for sale, one of which was clothed, the other nude. The clothed statue was preferred by the people of Cos (who were given the choice of buying either statue) because it was more chaste and severe. The nude which they rejected was bought instead by the people of Cnidos, and immediately became more famous. King Nicomedes of Bithynia offered (in the third century B.C.) to pay off the whole of Cnidos's debts, if they would sell him the statue, but they refused, rightly, because it was that statue which had made Cnidos famous.

This was, in fact, the first important Greek statue to depict a totally naked female. Nude males are a regular subject for Greek sculpture, from its very origins (the reasons for this are social and historical; men exercised naked in the gymnasium, and competed naked in the athletic contests such as the Olympic games). Females, however, were kept, as it were, under cover; for them to appear naked in public was unthinkable. Nude male statues stand complete and unabashed – not for Greek sculptors the fig-leaves of later prudishness. For the females, however, even when, with Praxiteles's Aphrodite, they take their clothes off, there is always a discreet hand to screen their sex. (When Apuleius's mistress Fotis reveals herself for the first time she stands 'like a living statue, the goddess of love rising from the sea. The hand with which she pretended to screen herself showed she was aware of the comparison.') Praxiteles's statue, then, was made not because convention tolerated, or expected nudity, but the reverse, despite previous conventions. It is his own choice, as an artist; and it emphasises, again, the tendency of the fourth century towards humanism, the appreciation of human nature, the human – female – physical form rather than remote convention of traditional religion and attitudes.

The statue stood not in a temple, but in an open shrine, overlooking the sea on the hill slopes of Cape Triopion, where the city of Cnidos was refounded by Mausollos of Caria, about the middle of the fourth century. Cnidos was excavated for the British Museum in the nineteenth century, and a head of a goddess, one of the finds made then by Sir Charles Newton, was taken to London. It has been suggested recently by Professor Iris Love, who has resumed the excavation of Cnidos, that this comes from

Praxiteles's statue, but this attribution is not generally accepted. It is, however, certain that the original was of marble, not bronze. The popularity of the statue is shown, not only by the copies we have of it, but the later imitations, which begin immediately, and are multiplied in succeeding centuries: Praxiteles, indeed, can be credited with the invention of a universal aspect of European art. How long she remained at Cnidos is uncertain, but it is clear that the Cnidians would not voluntarily part with her. There is a late Roman epigram – the pith of the original is lost in translation – which runs 'The Cypriote goddess, seeing herself at Cnidos, remarked "Dear me, wherever did Praxiteles see me naked?"' – but this is a literary form, and doesn't prove that at the time it was written the statue still stood in its shrine.

The Aphrodite was the most famous of Praxiteles's statues, but there were many others, and he was undoubtedly a very prolific artist. This seems a characteristic of fourth-century sculptors – Lysippus, Praxiteles's younger contemporary, is credited with no fewer than fifteen hundred statues. Such productivity must have been stimulated by demand. Sculptors were never tied to their native cities, but worked on commission wherever and whenever a statue was needed. Even if Athens, in the fourth century, was poorer than she had been in the fifth, clearly there was still money available for commissioning statues (and it must be remembered that these are now individual statues, rather than the great pediment groups and other architectural sculpture of the fifth century). Other parts of the Greek world – particularly those of the eastern side of the Aegean – were perhaps more prosperous in the fourth century than previously.

The known list of Praxiteles's works illustrates the geographical distribution of his sculpture. There was a bronze statue of the young Apollo about to kill a lizard which is climbing up a post. It is shown on coins of Nicopolis in Epirus (a Roman city, but perhaps indicating that the statue was originally set up in that part of Greece). Two famous statues of Eros (Cupid) were made by Praxiteles, one set up at Thespiai in Boiotia, another at Parion in the Asia Minor region of Mysia. He also made statues which were set up in his native Athens. According to Pausanias, he was responsible for a statue of Artemis in her sanctuary on the Acropolis (which is referred to on an inscription of 346 B.C.). He also tells us about a statue of a satyr which was placed at Athens in the 'Street of the Tripods' which ran from the theatre of Dionysus, and was the usual place for monuments commemorating victories in the dramatic festivals. This, it appears, was Praxiteles's own favourite. Pausanias tells us that when Phryne asked which statue he considered to be his most beautiful work, he promised, as a true lover, to give it to her, but refused to tell her which it was (again, the implication is that Praxiteles kept in his studio statues which he had made to please himself, rather than for commission; so this is as dubious as the story about the Aphrodite). Phryne therefore got one of his slaves to rush out and tell him his home was on fire. Praxiteles hurried home, saying that if the satyr and the Eros were destroyed he had worked in vain. This gave the game away; so Phryne told him of the trick, and that there was no fire. Phryne was then allowed to keep the Eros, while the satyr was put in the temple of Dionysus by the Tripod Street.

Another work which survives from Praxiteles's own time is the base at Mantinea from the temple of Leto and her children – again, it is Pausanias who tells us that this supported statues of Leto and her children Artemis and Apollo. The statues have long since disappeared, but the base itself was discovered in the nineteenth century, and slabs carved in relief which decorated it are now in the National Museum at Athens. There are three of these slabs, carrying a series of figures with plenty of space left between them. They depict Apollo playing his lyre, a Scythian slave, Marsyas the satyr playing the pipes and six Muses, exquisitely carved and draped. It is unlikely in the extreme that they were carved by Praxiteles himself, but they show the typical proportions of fourth-century figures, tall, slender bodies and heads proportionately smaller, and so surely reflect the styles and ideas of Praxiteles himself.

It is these softer poses, and elegant proportions, combined with the emotional appeal in Praxiteles's statues, which link this achievement to the taste of the succeeding Hellenistic age, and made him (like his contemporaries) so much more popular to collectors and patrons of the Roman period (though at times, admittedly, more knowledgeable connoisseurs such as Cicero, and those people who formed the artistic tastes of the Emperor Augustus, reverted to a preference for fifth-century sculptors, particularly Polycleitos). Popular taste prevailed, and Praxiteles was fully in line with this.

His style is less appreciated at the present day, when taste prefers, not even the fifth century, but the altogether more formal art of the archaic period, and is much more likely to enthuse over the primitive forms found in the prehistoric figures of Cycladic art than the humanism of the fourth century. There is, it is true, something too facile, too soft, too emotional in Praxiteles's art; but of his greatness and influence the ancient world was never in doubt.

Virgil

(70–19 B.C.)

To those who care to carp about such things – and the study and interpretation of ancient classical literature has bred centuries of carpers – the very name Virgil is a nonsense: there is no Virgilius form from which it could have derived, and all accounts matter-of-factly show that his given names were Publius Vergilius Maro. But those who have pedantically insisted on calling him Vergil have been in the vast minority. As he himself put it, in a different context: *Non nostrum inter vos tantas componere lites* – 'Not ours to decide such high dispute.' We shall swim with the tide.

Not a lot is known about him. Accounts were written in ancient times, but some are lost and others of doubtful factuality. Unlike those many literary figures whose celebrity actually owes more to the details of their lives than to their works, Virgil stands close to the summit of poetic achievement on the strength of his ability to convey, in the most felicitous language, the essence of those two mighty states, Nature, and the Roman Empire at its most aspirant.

He was born on 15 October, 70 B.C., at Andes, a now-lost farming settlement near the small town of Mantua in that part of northern Italy known as Cisalpine Gaul. His father was reasonably prosperous, combining farming with beekeeping, though some place him originally a little lower, as a hired hand who bettered himself by marrying his employer's daughter, Polla Magia, Magia Pollia, or whatever version of her name one cares to use. The Magia part of it was to acquire significance centuries later.

Throughout his life Virgil retained respect for rural folk, whose intimacy with Nature, he felt, assured them harmony of character and inborn virtue and piety. Without doubt it helped him to accord with the Emperor Augustus, who expediently refused to set himself up as a living god – in Italy at least – but acknowledged and encouraged belief in a divinity which watched over himself and his subjects alike.

On reaching the age of twelve Virgil was taken by his father to Cremona, no great distance away, to be educated formally. From there he went for a time to Mediolanum (Milan), and finally, aged seventeen, to Rome. The career to which his education was designed to lead him was political, by way of administrative posts of rising importance, then into the senatorial ranks. It was less important to be capable of drafting a persuasive minute than to be able to get up on one's legs and make a compelling speech, either to one's peers or to some interested part of the populace. Hence the study of rhetoric, of the art and tricks of public speaking, was one of the most important to an ambitious young man with a good mind. Virgil was one such, so rhetoric, mathematics and philosophy were his principal studies.

Literature attracted him increasingly, especially the legends of the gods and Muses, as retailed by Homer and others. This interest began to take a stronger hold when Virgil realised that he was not cut out for public life. He was diffident, modest and shy by nature, and one embarrassing experience of addressing a jury on some matter was enough for him. He returned to his father's farm, to devote himself to agriculture and study.

His deep reading in Latin and Greek led to experiments with writings of his own. Some of the shorter poems attributed to him are said to have been composed during those quiet years of farming and reading. In 41 B.C., however, when he was approaching his thirties, there occurred an upheaval which, catastrophic though it would have seemed at the time, set him on his road to fame.

In the course of his struggle to gain control of the Roman world, Octavian, as the future Emperor Augustus was then known, defeated the forces of Julius Caesar's assassins, Brutus and Cassius, at Philippi. Large numbers of soldiers were released from service and rewarded with grants of land, confiscated from its owners. Cremona and much of the neighbourhood of Mantua suffered in this way, and among the evicted landowners was Virgil.

He and his father found refuge at Naples with his old teacher of philosophy, Spiro the Epicurean, while awaiting the outcome of an application for repossession of their property. This appears to have been granted only to be followed after some time by a further eviction. Virgil spent little more of his lifetime in the north. He returned to Rome for a while, and it was there, in the year 37, that he published the work which was to make him immediately famous.

This was the *Eclogues* (Pastoral Poems), a sequence of ten poems on which he had been working for several years. They were not arranged in order of composition – the first in the sequence, entitled 'The Dispossessed', is a countryman's lament upon being

exiled, an experience which had not come to Virgil until well after
the time when he must have begun to compose:

> Tityrus, while you lie there at ease under the awning of a
> spreading beech and practise country songs on a light
> shepherd's pipe, I have to bid farewell to the home fields and
> the ploughlands that I love. Exile for me, Tityrus – and you lie
> stretched out in the shade, teaching the woods to echo back the
> charms of Amaryllis.

And later:

> Is some blaspheming soldier to own these acres I have broken
> and tilled so well – a foreigner to reap these splendid fields of
> corn? Look at the misery to which we have sunk since Romans
> took to fighting one another.

But the elderly Tityrus, who figures in several of the pieces, is able
to answer:

> Ah, Meliboeus, the man to whom I owe this happy leisure is a
> god. Yes, I shall always treat him as a god. He shall have an
> altar, and I will often stain it with the blood of a young lamb
> from my flock. He gave the word – and my cattle browse at
> large, while I myself can play the tunes of my choice on my
> rustic flute.

He explains that he has achieved this by taking a trip to Rome to
petition the authorities to be allowed to keep his lands, and that
this 'god' had assented. Many commentators have argued that the
episode is not autobiographical at all, merely imaginative, while
others have seen Tityrus and Meliboeus as Virgil's fused
depiction of himself. So it is with a number of other 'clues' in the
Eclogues, from which the sparse details of Virgil's life have been
filled out. It is of little matter; what is of consequence is that the
poem scored an immediate success in Rome, assuring Virgil the
warmest of welcomes among men and women of fashion, as well as
approval from on high.

His old mentor, Spiro, had paved the way for him with
introductions to his many friends in such circles. After years of
war and civil strife, hope was dawning of a golden new age, and
Virgil's songs of an idyllic relationship between shepherds and
shepherdesses, their flocks and Nature's gentle manifestations,
struck just the right note of refreshing optimism. Arcadian
escapism was what he offered, and it was eagerly seized. His

verses were on every cultivated tongue and were recited and sung in theatres.

The 'god' whom he represented Tityrus as acknowledging to be the source of his good fortune and vowing always to venerate was the young Octavian, not yet proclaimed emperor but holder of that position to all intents and purposes. It was to him that Virgil was advised by his new friends to look for patronage, and it was readily given. For all his autocratic ruthlessness and ambition, Octavian had a homely mentality and a preference for a modest style of living, so that Virgil's unspoiled purity must have appealed to him. Also, the voices of this respected poet and of his contemporary and friend, Horace, could be useful instruments to Octavian. Although he was being careful not to proclaim his own divinity, he had no objection to others drawing attention to it. He needed, too, the services of potent propagandists to repair the tarnished image of Julius Caesar, who had adopted Octavian as his heir.

Octavian's closest adviser, Maecenas, rich and powerful, took a keen interest in Virgil. He not only arranged for him to be subsidised from the state coffers, but suggested the theme for his next major work, the *Georgics* (Points of Husbandry). Maecenas's motive was to gain publicity for the government's determination to restore Italy's chief industry, agriculture, from the decline it had suffered due to the civil wars. No subject could have been more suited to Virgil, who seized the opportunity to employ his pastoral genius in proclaiming the dignity of rustic labour and life.

He left Rome and settled in the Campania, for part of the time near Nola, in the shadow of Vesuvius, and then across the bay, at Naples, in a comfortable house which his generous bounty enabled him to buy and furnish to his modest taste. He never married, and there are no accounts of amorous entanglements of any kind.

His task was all-absorbing. He composed painfully slowly, at a rate which has been averaged out at less than one line each day over the seven years it took him to complete the *Georgics*, totalling 2,188 lines. He described himself 'licking his lines into shape, as a bear does her cubs'. The work is in four books, of roughly equal length: 1. The farmer's year and the influence of the weather on his crops; 2. Trees, vines and olives; 3. Rearing animals; 4. Beekeeping. Much of the content is practical, almost a manual, including details of equipment and techniques. Rural observances and festivals are also described, all with love and enthusiasm, as well as a countryman's practical wisdom.

Dryden was to term the *Georgics* 'the best poem of the best poet', which may have been going a little too far, even in the context of Virgil's own work. Nevertheless, it has been acclaimed the most perfect of the works to come out of that great flowering time. It was read out, spread over four days, by Virgil alternating with Maecenas, to the emperor, as he lay suffering from a throat complaint. Augustus, as he was known by then, approved warmly, especially upon hearing such lines as those praying that he should be spared to restore Italy from ruin to prosperity.

Augustus himself had a new theme to offer: an epic of the glory of Rome and Romans, as exemplified by Augustus's victories and projects, fulfilling his destiny as chosen representative of the gods. The *Aeneid* was a labour of love which was to occupy the entire remainder of Virgil's life, and still not reach completion. He did not spin it out in order to live off it: as he lay dying, in the year 19 B.C., he lamented that he was not to be granted the three further years of life which he estimated were needed to revise what it had already taken him eleven years to do. The perfectionist in him wanted the entire draft destroyed. Fortunately, it was forbidden by Augustus himself, who was assuredly not going to allow such an achievement of his sponsoring to go to waste.

In any case, it was found after Virgil's death that the *Aeneid* was as complete as anyone save he would have wished. He had first sketched it in prose, then, in those eleven unremitting years, had translated it into verse, leaving only some lines uncompleted and general revision needed. A little was done by other hands, but the *Aeneid* as published in about 14 B.C. is nothing short of being one of the greatest of all poetic works. Perhaps it does not outstrip the *Iliad* and *Odyssey* of Homer; but it was composed at a different time, in a different language, for a more critical public than Homer's, so comparisons are invidious.

Arma virumque cano, Troiae qui primus ab orbis Italia, fato profugus ...

'Arms I sing, and the man who first from the shores of Troy came, Fate-exiled, to Italy ...'

It is a demonstration of the great part played by Rome in history, from the fall of Troy, which sets Aeneas wandering, divinely instructed to refound Troy in Italy. He passes through many vicissitudes, often arriving at wrong destinations, until he comes at last to the place where Rome is to arise. The poet is enabled to parade, by supernatural projection, a great host of the souls of Aeneas's Roman descendants-to-be awaiting reincarnation – Augustus, of course, prominent among them.

This latter episode takes place, in Book VI of the twelve, in the nether regions, a setting which would add to Dante's inspiration for his vision of the journey through Hell and Purgatory in the *Divina Commedia*, in which he depicts Virgil as his conducting guide.

Dante's choice of him, from among all the ancient sages, was no coincidental fancy. Writers and churchmen in the Middle Ages attributed magical leanings to many of the ancients, partly no doubt because of their beliefs in auguries and visions of the supernatural. It became strongly believed in Naples that Virgil, who had lived so long there, had been a practitioner of the black arts; but what had impressed Dante was the likeness of the *Aeneid* to a sacred allegory of more than mortal inspiration, while in the fourth of the *Eclogues* Virgil discourses on the coming of a Heaven-sent child, who will prove to be the Firstborn of an era of peace and happiness. He had written that passage several decades before the birth of Christ, and to many medieval churchmen it seemed indubitable that he had been a true prophet, a belief confirmed for many by the significance of his mother's name, Magia.

Virgil had intended doing some of his estimated three years' work of revising the *Aeneid* in Greece and Asia Minor, where he could visit some of the places which he had incorporated in it. In Athens he encountered Augustus and was persuaded to go back to Italy with him.

On the way, visiting the ancient Greek town of Megara in great heat, Virgil contracted sunstroke. His condition grew worse as he travelled home, and on 21 September 19 B.C., he died soon after landing at Brundisium (Brindisi). He was buried at Naples, at his chosen spot on the hill of Pausilypon, now Posillipo. His tomb was held in awed reverence for many years, but its genuine site is no longer known.

Horace

(65–8 B.C.)

There is a moving anecdote of that austere, embittered poet and don, A. E. Housman, lecturing at Cambridge in 1914. It was his habit to speak for precisely fifty-five minutes, never once looking at his audience, before closing his notes and marching from the room, as remote as he had entered it.

On this occasion, a May morning when the trees were thick
with blossom, he looked at his hearers for the first time in two
years and said in a changed voice, of the Latin ode which he had
been minutely dissecting, 'I should like to spend the last few
minutes considering this ode simply as poetry'. He read it out, first
in Latin, then in his own English translation, emotion mounting
visibly:

Diffugere nives, redeunt iam gramina campis arboribusque comae;
Mutat terra vices et decrescentia ripas flumina praetereunt;
Gratia cum Nymphis geminisque sororibus audet ducere nuda choros.
Immortalia ne speres monet annus el amum quae rapit hora diem . . .

> The snows are fled away, leaves on the shaws
>   And grasses in the mead renew their birth,
> The river to the river-bed withdraws,
>   And altered is the fashion of the earth.
> The nymphs and Graces three put off their fear
>   And unapparelled in the woodland play.
> The swift hour and the brief prime of the year
>   Say to the soul, *Thou wast not born for aye . . .*

'That', he concluded, 'I regard as the most beautiful poem in
ancient literature'; and walked swiftly from the room. Someone
present likened it to having overhead a secret meant for no one's
ears: 'I was afraid the old fellow was going to cry.'

Arguably, *A Shropshire Lad* and those few other slender volumes
which make up Housman's work strike a swifter and easier
response among people who would claim to know nothing about
poetry, but to know what they like, than almost any other English
poet's work. In his wistful melancholy, we recognise our own
responses to the waxing and waning of the seasons, of love and
youthful ambition, and of the inescapable transience of life. This is
the quality, too, of Quintus Horatius Flaccus – Horace – whose
Ode 7 from the Fourth Book had publicly pierced Housman's
formidable armour on that single occasion. There is much
similarity between the two poets' work; and of all the ancients save
perhaps Homer it is Horace who holds most appeal still.

He was born on 8 December 65 B.C., at Venusia (now Venosa),
a military settlement in southern Italy. His father, a freed slave,
was a retired auctioneer's clerk, making a frugal living from a
small farm which scarcely paid its way. Nevertheless, he was
determined to give his son a better standing in life than his own.
(There is no mention of Horace's mother, who presumably died
while he was an infant.) Local schooling was good enough for

soldiers' sons, but Rome was the place to go for the best of higher education, so to Rome they went together, Horace carrying with him a love of natural beauty deeply assimilated from his native surroundings.

As well as the best teachers in the capital, he had the continuing benefit of his father's company, in the role of *paedagogus*, an extracurricular teacher with a countryman's shrewd cast of mind whose observations on city people and their ways gave his son valuable standards in judging human nature, which he acknowledged later had considerably whetted his sensibilities.

In his late teens Horace went to Athens, alone. His father's death seems to have occurred about this time, and it is gratifying to imagine that the move was made with that worthy man's knowledge that his son was progressing to an even higher education. He had reached the age of twenty there when the sensational news arrived of the assassination of Julius Caesar. Roman students in Athens, republicans almost to a man, were elated. When, six months later, Brutus came there in person, seeking recruits for his army, Horace was one of those who eagerly volunteered, likely motivated less by any clear idealism than by the traditional students' herd instinct.

He went with the army to Macedonia and Asia, attaining the junior command rank of tribune, over a part of a legion. He was no natural warrior, and had a poor physique. When the battle of Philippi, in 42 B.C., was clearly going against Brutus and Cassius, Horace was among those who were glad of the excuse to throw down their shields and run away.

He ran to Rome, 'with wings clipped'. His prospects were bleak. The family farm back in Venusia had been confiscated for the benefit of some more loyal and deserving ex-warrior. He had failed as a soldier, and on the wrong side. He had no occupation, no influential friends. Moreover, he had no father now, to act as counsellor and steadying influence. He slipped for a time into loose and feckless company, among which he underwent some of those amorous experiences which so enhance the poetic imagination.

Having 'fought' on the wrong side did not debar him from getting a lowly Treasury clerkship. The pay was only enough to subsist on. In desperation he started writing poetry, perhaps more out of bitterness than in the hope of income. These earliest pieces were circulated privately among his raffish friends, and if they did not actually make him money, they got him attention for his scathing and witty observations about life as he had so far found it.

It was inevitable that among those who should come to know

this outspoken newcomer were Virgil, his senior by some five years, and the tragic poet Varius, comparatively veteran in years but lesser in artistic stature. They befriended him, and in about 38 B.C. introduced him to the ruler Octavian's close confidant, Maecenas, who was always on the lookout for new protégés whose talents might enhance the new order of government. It was not an immediately salutary meeting, though. Horace was overawed by his influential interviewer, who, for his part, may not have been impressed with the sort of work which the young man hesitantly recited to him. Nothing came of the encounter; yet in time to come Maecenas and Horace were to be the closest of friends.

Horace's first publications were his *Epodes* – short satirical or lyrical poems, characterised by a shorter line following a longer, and the first book of *Satires*. Maecenas seems to have been their patron. Horace kept on his clerkship, though, and with it his independence, free to keep his modest home, lie late in bed of a morning when not required at the office, idle about the bustling capital, taking in the sights and sitting chatting and drinking with his friends. He had no inclination to marry and was too fond of an untroubled life to bother further with the complications of love affairs, though he was darkly handsome until he became prematurely grizzled, balding and corpulent.

His heart remained a countryman's, and his greatest joy came when Maecenas gave him a farm and estate in the Sabine hills, near Tibur (Tivoli), handy to Rome. It was not luxurious, but it provided him with the seclusion he cherished, with slaves to look after him, plenty of wine to hand, and rustic sights and sounds to attune his mind to composing his greatest works, the *Odes*, the *Epistles*, and the rest of the *Satires*.

The *Odes*, upon which Horace's greatness chiefly rests, were composed over the space of seven to ten years. The first three books were published together in 23 B.C., followed later by a fourth. He worked slowly, according to his own dictum of making a poem so perfect that the slowly moving fingernail can detect no flaw in it. What is especially astonishing about his achievement is that he was pioneering a form never before employed satisfactorily by a Latin poet. Catullus, who had died when Horace was a boy, had had the idea of using the metres reputedly originated by Sappho of Lesbos, the female Greek lyrical poet of more than five centuries earlier. It was no straightforward work, however, to make Latin words fit Greek measures, and Catullus's achievement at it had been limited.

Precise selection of vocabulary, use of epithet, irony and humour enabled Horace to use the lyric metres of Greece as a perfectly adapted vehicle for the Latin tongue and the spirit of his time, filtered through the medium of his personal temperament. The fusion was so magnificently achieved that his results have influenced the poets and, to some extent, the prose writers of many nations and ages. He is one of those rare beings who speaks for and to all mankind in the tones of a witty, perceptive, understanding friend, whose musical tongue, once heard, leaves impressions on the memory which recur and recur.

It is as futile to begin quoting his *Odes* for examples as it is to quote Shakespeare or Dickens for theirs; though the temptation is there:

Eheu fugaces, Postume, Postume,
Labuntur anni.

Ah me, Postumus, Postumus, the fleeting years are slipping away.

Dulce et decorum est pro patria mori.

To die for one's native land is sweet and becoming.

Integer vitae scelerisque purus.

The man of upright life unstained by guilt.

Pallida Mors aequo pulsat pede pauperum tabernas Regumque turris.

Pale Death with impartial foot kicks at the doors of poor men's hovels and of kings' palaces.

The sentiments often match those of Omar Khayyám, not to mention Housman and many others who have recognised that time is flying, youth slips away squandered if not lived fully, and that regrets for things undone are a waste of emotion. It seems a pity that, of the countless translations of Horace there have been down the centuries, there is not a full or even substantial one by Housman, whose style, based on Latin models, and showing impeccable feeling for the phrase which tingles the emotion, could almost certainly have given us the perfect English rendering.

After the *Odes* followed the *Epistles*: rib-nudging conversational pieces in which the poet seems to be taking his reader into his confidence as he chats frankly of his views on aspects of life and people encountered in it, revealing much of himself in the process. He discourses also on contemporary literature, the poor state into which the drama has fallen, owing to a general decline in taste, into which, praise be, Augustus's discerning patronage is not likely to allow poetry to lapse.

The last *Epistle* has been labelled by others the *Ars Poetica*, the Art of Poetry. It is a discursive piece, giving the impression in parts of random thoughts jotted down and never worked up into an integrated pattern. It has as much to say about drama as about anything else, its burden being that there is more to writing than technique, but that if any of his readers persists in wanting to write, then there are certain rules which had better be observed, for only the highest standards are a worthwhile aim:

> *Mediocribus esse poetis*
> *Non homines, non di, non concessere columnae.*

To poets to be second-rate is a privilege which neither men, nor gods, nor bookshops ever allowed.

The *Ars Poetica*, incomplete and haphazard though it is, has had great influence on writers, more especially critics, from the Middle Ages onward and has been the starting-point for many other self-appointed exemplars; and, in Horace's view, it all comes back eventually to the Greeks:

> *Grais ingenium, Grais dedit ore rotundo Musa loqui.*

It was the Greeks who had at the Muse's hand the native gift, the Greeks who had the utterance of finished grace.

The *Ars Poetica* and the final *Epistles* had been written at the personal behest of the Emperor Augustus, to whom Horace was established as a virtual poet laureate. In this capacity he also wrote to order, in 17 B.C., the *Carmen Saecularae*, the Song of a Hundred Years, for performance by a choir of boys and girls to celebrate Augustus's revival of the *Ludi Saeculares*, the secular games, that year. Its virtuous, wholesome sentiments and robust metre subsequently proved ideal for musical and verbal adaptation into university, college and school songs, generally of nineteenth-century vintage.

In 8 B.C., Maecenas died. His last exhortation to Augustus, whom he had served so well in fostering the arts, were, 'Remember Horatius Flaccus as you would me'. In an *Ode* addressed to this most assiduous patron of his when he was convalescing from an earlier illness, Horace had written:

> Maecenas. Ah, if half of me,
> The better half, be torn away,
> Why should the other longer stay?
> The day that sees the fall of thee

Shall see the other fall. I swore
No oath in vain; when thou shalt make
The final journey, I shall take
The road, thou going on before.

It had been remarkably prophetic. Within three weeks of
Maecenas's death, Horace expired too, on 27 November, near to
the end of his fifty-seventh year. The two friends were buried side
by side on the Esquiline Hill, in the gardens created there by
Maecenas and bearing his name.

Livy

(c. 64 B.C.–A.D. 12)

If ever an age seemed destined to produce historians, the age in
which Titus Livius grew up was such an age. When he began to
write, in his early thirties, the Empire of which he was a citizen
had been convulsed by more than fifteen years of civil war. Few
cities in Italy had not suffered losses of men and heavy economic
imposts. As the internecine slaughter moved from one generation
to the next, becoming ever more bitter, ancient Roman values – it
was said – were forgotten or deliberately called into question.
Corruption replaced the sober probity of the ancestors, greed their
austerity, vengefulness their upright firmness. All Roman writers
looked back to the past as to a kind of Golden Age. Livy was seized
in his early maturity with a more interesting perspective – to
chronicle the growth of great Rome from an insignificant Italian
city to the ruler of the world, and to draw from it past lessons in
personal behaviour that could influence the present times.

Livy was born in Patavium (modern Padua) probably in 64 B.C.
(A less persuasive tradition makes the date 59 B.C., and that of his
death A.D. 17.) The towns north of the Po (Padus) had suffered
badly from Mark Antony in the civil wars, for they had remained
staunchly on the side of the senate against his high ambition.
Patavium might consider itself to Transpadana what
Transpadana was to Italy: it was a byword for moral rectitude of
the type one associates with the gentry of an ancient shire. When
the historian and general C. Asinius Pollio chaffed Livy, in a
hostile tone, with his *Patavinitas*, it was surely the moral tone of his

writing rather than any provincial phraseology to which he referred.

Little can be recovered of Livy's life. He studied rhetoric as would most Romans destined for education and a public career: His family must have been well-to-do. His career did not however include the customary trip to Athens which others, such as the poet Horace, made. On the whole Livy was a stay-at-home creature, preferring the company of his books to that of the intelligentsia or of politicians. Not surprisingly his studies went deeper than others', and he wrote at some date a treatise on rhetoric in which he put himself firmly in the camp of Cicero in matters of style – a natural stance for one committed also to Ciceronian political ideals. His daughter married a professor of rhetoric named L. Magius.

The lands north of the Po produced a number of the great writers of the late Republic – most notably Virgil, from Mantua. There is no evidence that Livy knew or met Virgil; nor can we say if he was acquainted with the elderly Cornelius Nepos, whose *Lives of Illustrious Men* was published in 35 B.C. The latter's work, indeed, would not have been particularly sympathetic to Livy, whose attitude to history demanded a less than wide-eyed attitude to his heroes.

The exact date at which Livy began to compose his history is uncertain, though the first portion (perhaps Books I–V, covering the first 360 years of Rome's history) was published between 27 and 25 B.C. For a man in his early thirties, it was an ambitious task. Historians rarely started young in Rome. A passage in the preface where he refers to Caesar Augustus by this title, which he had held since 16 January 27 B.C., dates the final version of the books to that period. But it is quite likely that Livy had been at work for two or three years already. The conclusion of the civil wars at the battle of Actium in 31 B.C. had seemed to offer a prospect of peace and to usher in a new age. Virgil's *Georgics* of 29 B.C. were imbued in parts, and in their conception, with optimism about the future of rural Italy.

> O happy, if he knew his happy state,
> The swain, who, free from business and debate,
> Receives his easy food from nature's hand,
> And just returns of cultivated land! . . .
> Without concern he hears, but hears from far,
> Of tumults, and descents, and distant war;
> Nor with a superstitious fear is awed,
> For what befalls at home, or what abroad.
> Nor his own peace disturbs with pity for the poor . . .

Already Augustus was talking of the planned 'restoration of the Republic' which was finally announced on 13 January 27 B.C.; in 28 B.C. he had restored eighty-two temples as a first sign of commitment to the resuscitation of ancient values. The circumstances would warm Livy's heart, and unfreeze his pen.

He planned a history that would stretch from Rome's foundation in 753 B.C. to his own day – perhaps to that very battle of Actium as a fitting conclusion to the turbulent story of how Rome reached its present eminence, on the threshold of new concord and prosperity. The writing of history had by this time a long tradition at Rome, and Livy had some scope to choose his models. The earliest chroniclers of *Res Romanae* (Roman affairs) had compiled simple *Annales*, yearly records of major events. The first true historian of Rome, Fabius Pictor (*fl. c.* 200 B.C.), wrote fine if colourful history, in Greek; in his successors' hands the style degenerated into romance. In 133 B.C. the publication of the *Annales Maximi* of the Roman state put Roman historiography permanently on a new footing. The chronological record was no longer a matter of dispute, and the historian could arrange his material with greater art in confidence of the periodic articulation of those records.

Yet Livy chose, to begin with, to lay out his history on largely annalistic lines. His method was generally to use one or two sources for a particular period, changing from one to the other as its coverage dictated but with little attempt to evaluate their biases. For the Punic Wars he used Valerius Antias and Claudius Quadrigarius, for the Sullan period he balanced Sulla's own memoirs and the work of the pro-senatorial Sisenna; the 'truth-loving, censorious and embittered' Rutilius Rufus was his source for the period before 92. And so on. Often the *acta senatus* were his only records.

Naturally the variety of sources affected the picture he drew, but the strong moralism of the man ensured that his tale was internally consistent. Military affairs interested him but little – though he is better on ships – and his lack of political experience inhibited his judgements. Predominantly his is a story of great men in testing moral situations. He has been compared with Sir Walter Scott, and indeed his narrative gifts and his generous if stern heart do recall that great author. It is sometimes difficult for modern readers, trained in the scrupulous discipline of source criticism and alert to Livy's bland chopping and changing of sources (Macaulay regarded his value as exclusively literary) to understand the judgement of Dante on 'Livy who never errs'. Yet in one sense you always know where you are with Livy.

Machiavelli, shocked at his contemporaries' propensity to admire and imitate the plastic arts of antiquity rather than its arts of life and moral examples, composed the *Discourses* on Livy to emphasise the value of the historian as a mentor in the ethics of effective political behaviour.

It was the indissolubility of politics from morality in Livy's outlook that placed him firmly against such predecessors as Sallust, 'the comfortable author of a pessimistic history' (Ronald Syme), whose Thucydidean amoralism could look like pure censoriousness. C. Asinius Pollio, one of Augustus's literary mentors, was himself the author of a history of his own times, from 60 B.C., which was probably published by the time Livy began work. Livy will not have had much time for this author. And Pollio briefly dismissed Livy as a 'Pompeian', which meant a supporter of Republican values, of the 'concord of the orders', not deeply in tune with the autocracy of Augustus or the increasingly aristocratic tone of the ruling clique. No wonder that Livy never enjoyed the patronage of the emperor's court: but clearly he did not need it. His closest contact came in A.D. 8, by which time he had perhaps been living in Rome for ten years, when he gave the young future Emperor Claudius (aged eighteen) instruction in rhetoric. When Augustus supplied him with information on historical evidence, he coolly accepted it with the double-edged remark that 'it would be sacrilege to disbelieve it'.

A further parallel with Livy's contemporary Virgil is in the message on the duties of empire he draws from the triumph of Scipio Africanus over Antiochus the Great in 189 B.C. The envoys plead with Scipio 'to cease from strife with mortals and the gods, tend and spare the human race'. Scipio replies: 'From things in the power of the gods we have what the gods grant us: our spirit remains the same in every fortune.' How closely that plea, and Scipio's implicit acceptance of its imperative, recalls the words Virgil puts in the mouth of the prophetic Anchises in *Aeneid* VI:

> But, Rome! tis thine alone, with awful sway,
> To rule mankind, and make the world obey:
> Disposing peace and war thy own majestic way.
> To tame the proud, the fettered slave to free,
> These are imperial arts, and worthy thee.

The attitude has been well compared with that of Kipling's *Recessional* for Queen Victoria's Diamond Jubilee in 1897, invoking the 'God of our Fathers ... Beneath whose awful hand we hold / Dominion over palm and pine'. Alas for Livy, the centuries that followed, whatever benefits they brought to the peoples of the empire, were scarcely to bear out the hopes he and Virgil shared for a renewal of Rome's ancient piety.

Livy's history was eventually completed in 142 books, which in the end took the story up to the death of Augustus in A.D. 14. The last twenty books were – prudently – only published after Augustus's death. The fate of Livy's work was not a happy one: of those 142 books we have 1–10, 21–45, plus part of 91. The outline of the story is preserved in the *Epitomes* found at Oxyrhynchus (books 37–40, 48–55) and the 'Periochae'. No doubt all too many Roman men of letters were glad to have the abridged version only: the poet Martial wrote (14.190)

> In a small parchment see great Livy rolled,
> Whom all my study was too small to hold.

We know that Dio Cassius made use of Livy for his work on the late Republic; to possess his work alone only makes us regret Livy the more, for despite his shortcomings (and despite the increasing abandonment of the annalistic framework in later books) he provides for the periods he covers an incomparably more reliable account of events than can be derived from any other source. He is the indispensable text, not only for those who, like Machiavelli, seek precepts in statecraft from lucidly narrated events, but for all those whose interest is engaged by Livy's celebration (in the Preface) of his own nation, which 'if any nation deserves the privilege of claiming a divine ancestry, that nation is our own; and so great is the glory won by the Roman people in their wars that, when they declare that Mars himself was their first parent and father of the man who founded their city, all the nations of the world might allow the claim as readily as they accept Rome's imperial dominion'.

Ovid

(43 B.C.–A.D. 18)

Publius Ovidius Naso was born in the year following Julius Caesar's assassination, on 20 March 43 B.C. It was a dangerous time to be born in Italy. Civil war raged on land and sea. Starvation was a widespread threat; fear and confusion reigned almost everywhere, as Mark Antony and Octavian battled for supremacy, with the serpent-like Cleopatra waiting to throw in her lot with whichever won.

Ovid was lucky enough to be born and spend his boyhood in a region untouched by strife, its exceptional natural beauty left unsullied. The small town of Sulmo stood a little under a hundred miles inland from Rome, looked down upon by the peaks of the Abruzzi, with deep valleys, sparkling streams, and fertile slopes for the vine. He loved these surroundings, which impressed themselves on his mind and would colour his poetry, especially in the *Amores* and in parts of the *Tristia*.

His family was comfortably off, belonging to an old landowning line of equestrian status, fortunately not one of those marked down for the confiscation of wealth and property which brought disaster to so many in those ruinous years. By the time the boy of twelve was ready to go with his brother to be educated in Rome the wars were over, with Antony defeated at Actium, and Cleopatra, who had failed to work her charm on the victorious Octavian, dead of the asp's bite. The armies were being disbanded, civil administration was being put in order and badly needed public works begun, and people began to enjoy themselves.

Ovid was well taught by the two leading professors of rhetoric of the time, Arellius Fuscus and Porcius Latro, who rounded off his general education and left him with an ambition to be a poet, to the annoyance of his father, who wanted him to take up law. Then, as ever since, poetry did not pay: 'Even Homer didn't make anything out of it,' his father argued.

It was the required thing for a young man to do a year's national service in the infantry or cavalry after leaving school. Ovid managed to evade it, opting for the permissible alternative in the case of youths with artistic talents, which was to tour abroad and cultivate their sensibilities. His travelling companion when he set off in 25 B.C. was another aspiring poet, Pompeius Macer, from Verona, whom he knew as 'Iliacus' for his interest in pre-Trojan War legends. They wandered in Greece, Asia Minor and Sicily for some two years, soaking up impressions of scenery and ways of life for the best part of that time.

Doubtless they gained experience of another kind, too, for Ovid was already experimenting with the erotic elegiac verse which would soon make him a favoured darling of Rome society. He found on his return that his brother had died, and his father was even more determined that he should uphold the family's respectable standing by practising the law. He did make the attempt to come to terms with this situation, briefly serving without success in two departments of justice.

He may also by now have had a wife to consider, as well, as a result of an early arranged marriage. He did not consider her for long, however, describing her later as 'unworthy of me, and no good'. No good at what, he does not specify, but the experience did not deter him from soon marrying again. This wife gave him a daughter – some have said the future poetess Perilla, though it is unlikely. It was again a brief union: 'I have no charge to bring against her, but she did not stay with me for long' was his lofty summing up of it.

Perhaps it would have needed a more complaisant sort of wife to put up with his current ways. The bright, smart young set of Rome had taken Ovid to their bosoms – literally, in the case of many of the girls. The experience they gave him, added to that acquired in his travels, enabled him to publish in 14 B.C. his first work, *Amores*. This was a collection of forty-nine poems, ranging from about sixty to several hundred lines long, detailing for the most part his love adventures with an enthusiastic mistress, 'Corinna'. She was not a real person. She was the mistress of his mind, a fusion of many girls he had known or fantasised upon. Some ten years later he rearranged the poems, added a few more, and had them published again in the three-volume form in which they have endured in their freshness for two thousand years.

Some of the poems are unrestrainedly lascivious. Others deal with themes of a non-amorous nature, for example a deeply felt dirge for that sweet singer of the remembered pleasures and pains of love, Albius Tibullus, with whom Ovid, Gallus and Propertius are bracketed as Rome's greatest elegiac poets. The elegiac, an already existing form, was refined to perfection by these four as the vehicle for expressing to young lovers those very pangs and delights which they themselves were experiencing.

Ovid proceeded further, however, with a more explicit work on love. The *Ars Amatoria* (Art of Love) has been termed, among other things, 'perhaps the most immoral poem ever written'. Its atmosphere has been likened to 'a reckless pursuit of the voluptuous in a society amid which the *demi-monde* reached a pitch of polished luxury unsurpassed in history'. Yet it has been praised for its perceptive observation of that society, and for its ironic humour and zestful style: a sort of ancient equivalent of Byron's *Don Juan*, without the narrative line.

It is in two books, one addressed to men, the other to women. Its message to both is that since love is what everyone is after, it will be the more easily gained by following certain precepts, which he proceeds to detail from personal experience. In their observance

or non-observance can be recognised the stuff of countless plots of
novels, plays and operas down the ages: faint heart never won fair
lady; flattery will get you everywhere; never trust a male friend
with the girl you are wooing; food and drink are mellowing aids;
praise a clever woman for her looks, and a pretty one for her
intelligence; and so on, not least:

> Let girls to poets always yield,
>   For poets have a place in heaven;
> God finds in them a fertile field
>   And fruitful seed to us is given.
> And Muses too delight to bless us;
> You please them much when you caress us.

Among society girls in Ovid's time there was a new spirit of
freedom, and a convenient form of free marriage, *usus*, in contrast
with the more rigid types of union. There were also plenty of
available women who had formerly been slaves or daughters of
slaves. These and young bloods of his own sort had taught him all
he knew about the arts of love, and he was passing on the
instruction for others of their kind, with much insight into male
and female psychology, and sly humour, a mixture certainly not
intended to corrupt anyone, nor even capable of it. All the same, it
was to help get him into dire trouble later, and blight his life.

The precise chronology of Ovid's life in Rome in relation to his
works is difficult to determine. Some of the works themselves no
longer exist, among them a tragedy, *Medea*, which seems to have
been popular in its time, and a possibly uncompleted *Wars of the
Gods and Giants*, which may have been intended to flatter the
Emperor Augustus (as the former Octavian was now called) by
depicting him in the role of Jupiter. A more important work which
has survived is the *Heroidum Epistulae*, better known as the *Heroides*
('Heroines'), a series of dramatic monologues, twenty-one in
number in modern editions, although some half-dozen may not
have been Ovid's own work. They portray, in letter-form as
though written by the notable ladies, their feelings for the men
they love during their absence at war or for other reasons. The
emotions are various: amorous longings, wistful affection,
loneliness of body and spirit, resentment, jealousy, and cynical
awareness that they are being betrayed, or, in at least two cases,
are themselves betraying their absent menfolk.

Again, Ovid's penetrative awareness of the female psyche
makes his verse vivid with feeling which can strike chords with
readers today, as in his own time, although he was writing of
women long dead or legendary even by then:

> Oft with your flocks we slept beneath a tree,
> The leaves and grass a couch for you and me;
> Or in some humble cot on beds of hay
> Waited until the frost should pass away . . .
> The trees you cut still show their marking clear,
> And all can read 'Oenonë' carven there.
> As the trunks grow, so grows my name withal:
> Grow on, preserve it for my funeral.

For the work of his which was to influence generations of poets and painters of many nationalities more profoundly than any, Ovid turned again to ancient history – to the very beginnings, in fact. *Metamorphoses* ('The Changeling Shapes') transports us from the time of the world's creation to his own day, in fifteen books of 250 wonderful stories based on Greek and Roman legends. It goes far beyond stories of the transformations of its title – of men and women changed, for one reason or another, into animals, trees, stones, or (in Julius Caesar's case) a star. It retells the great stories of myth and legend, gods and heroes, tragedy and comedy, mingling charm and beauty, full of thought-inspiring scenes and passing comments.

Metamorphoses makes up a third of Ovid's entire output; but he was aware that it was not only in bulk that it would stand forth for all time:

> Now I have done: and lo, this work of mine
> Nor fire, nor sword, nor wrath of Jove divine,
> Nor tooth of time shall make to pass away.
> Come when you will, grim Death; for now your sway
> Has only power to quench my mortal frame
> And end this life; it cannot touch my fame . . .

A lesser work was the *Fasti* ('Festivals'), a kind of almanac of religious and other anniversaries and occasions, detailing their origins, development, astronomical conjunction and observances, month by month of the year. This was a more derivative exercise, which had been done before in various forms, though he included many lively observations of his own, while his retelling in verse of old tales, including some risqué ones, keeps it far from being a ploddingly worthy catalogue.

There were to have been twelve books of the *Fasti*, one for each month. Only six survive, though it is evident that Ovid at least worked on the others, if perhaps he never completed them. This is most likely due to the dramatic upheaval which happened to his life and work in the first few years following the birth of Christ.

Like the Judge in Gilbert and Sullivan's *Trial by Jury*, the Emperor Augustus had been a lively rip in his time – 'a shocking young scamp of a rover' – but had been forced to mend his ways and outwardly set a good moral example. In 2 B.C., Augustus had found it necessary to send his daughter Julia and her various lovers into exile. Ten years later, in A.D. 8, he had to do the same to yet another Julia, his granddaughter, also an adulteress.

On the first of these occasions, Ovid, by then middle-aged, had thought it diplomatic to become respectable himself, by marrying for a third time. His new bride, named Fabia, was related to a highly respected patron of the poet's, Paullus Fabius Maximus, which would no doubt elevate him in imperial eyes. He may have undertaken the *Fasti* as a demonstration that he was at heart a serious writer, wishing to produce something of national value. He had certainly taken the step of trying to retrieve some of the moral reputation which the *Ars Amatoria* had cost him by publishing the *Remedia Amoris*, a necessarily dull short poem instructing how the fires of love kindled by his earlier advice might be extinguished.

These steps were not enough, however. Both Julias had been members of that smart set for which Ovid had been spokesman in his advocacy of the pleasures of free love. Although Augustus was considerably under the thumb of his empress, Livia, who had personally influenced the passing of a spate of anti-adultery laws, he could not legally act against Ovid unless he committed some specific offence. Evidently that was what Ovid at last did. It was in all probability something relatively trivial; but whatever it was, together with the Empress Livia's belief that Ovid's filthy ditties had helped erode her daughter's and granddaughter's morals, was enough excuse for Augustus to banish him.

As banishment went, it was the mildest form, *relegatio*, enabling him to keep his property and civic rights. He had to leave his wife and home, however, and go to Tomi, a half-Greek, half-barbarian town on the Black Sea, there to remain for an unspecified period. It was a shattering blow for a poet and society favourite in his prime.

> Ah! when I think of that last fatal eve
> When all the joys of Rome I had to leave,
> When I recall that cruel, cruel hour,
> E'en now adown my cheek the teardrops pour . . .

The journey, in A.D. 8, took nearly a year, by land and sea. Tomi (close to what is now the busy industrial port and holiday resort of Constanta, in Romania) was dreary and unhealthy, with a climate which Ovid likened to perpetual winter, and a constant threat of incursions by barbarian raiders. He had no literary company to stimulate him, no civilised playmates, male or female. The rough people even spoke alien languages, Getic and Sarmatic, which he took the trouble to learn out of sheer boredom. He wrote home that he had virtually forgotten Latin.

Nevertheless, he went on composing in it. The five books which make up the *Tristia* and the four which comprise the *Epistulae ex Ponto* are poetic lamentations, addressed to his wife and friends and any well-wishers who might help to get his sentence remitted. They are inevitably melancholy and sometimes bitter, foreshadowing, in their introspective and confessional passages, Oscar Wilde's *De Profundis*.

These and a very few other pieces were the product of ten weary years in exile. Before that time was out the news reached him of Augustus's death, in 14, bringing him hope of a reprieve at last. But none was forthcoming from that harsh moralist Tiberius, who succeeded. In Tomi, the last great representative of the golden age of Roman literature died, four years later, just into his sixties.

Subsequent literature's debt to him is enormous, from the French medieval romances, and Chaucer, to the Elizabethans, and Shakespeare himself, from his own studies and through one of his principal sources, Arthur Golding's translation of *Metamorphoses*, published in 1567, which the bard of Avon obviously knew almost backwards.

Even the puritanical Milton knew his Ovid and derived things from him, hastily averting his eyes from others. A livelier spirit, Dryden, translated some of the works, finding them in tune with that joyful time of Restoration release, which corresponded to an extent with the time in which the young Ovid had sung on behalf of all lovers.

In his preface to the *Epistles from Pontus*, Dryden writes: 'If the imitation of Nature be the business of a Poet, I know no Author who can justly be compared with this, especially in the Description of the passions ... Now I will appeal to any man, who has read this Poet, whether he find not the natural Emotion of the same Passion in himself...'

It is as high a tribute as almost any literary creator could hope to receive.

Seneca

(4 B.C.–A.D. 65)

Lucius Annaeus Seneca was the leading intellectual figure in Rome in the middle of the first century A.D.; his writings were to have an enduring influence throughout the Middle Ages and the Renaissance. He was also politically active; having been tutor to the young Nero, he acted as chief minister for the first years of his reign, years which were later praised by Trajan as excelling the government of all other emperors. Despite this however his reputation has been uneasy, scholars being divided on his merits as a writer and as a man.

He was born at Corduba (Cordoba) in Spain in 4 B.C. The province of his birth was highly Romanised; his father, also Lucius Annaeus Seneca, was famous in Rome as a teacher of rhetoric. The family was indeed highly capable. The eldest son was that Gallio before whom St Paul was tried in 52; the youngest was the father of the poet Lucan.

Lucius himself was educated at Rome, training as an orator and studying philosophy in the school of the Sextii where Stoicism was blended with neo-Pythagorean ideas. After spending some time in Egypt, where his uncle by marriage, Gaius Galerius, was prefect, he entered public life around the year 31.

His life was reputedly in danger under Caligula and in 41 Claudius banished him to Corsica on a charge of having committed adultery with Caligula's sister Julia Livilla. He spent eight years in exile on the island, studying science and philosophy and writing the three treatises known as the *Consolations*. Some of his other philosophical works and some of his tragedies probably date from this period of exile.

He was recalled through the influence of the emperor's third wife Agrippina in 49. The following year he became praetor and married the wealthy Pompeia Paulina. He was made tutor to Nero and cultivated the friendship of the Praetorian prefect Sextus Afranius Burrus.

The murder of Claudius in 54 opened their way to power. Seneca drafted Nero's first speech to the senate in which he proclaimed that *clementia* (clemency) would be the theme of his reign, and boasted that he was the first emperor to have come to power without the guilt of civil war or blood feud. For a time Nero was content to leave affairs of state in the hands of Seneca and Burrus. Both provincials (Burrus came from Gaul), they had a wider understanding of the needs of the Empire than most of the Roman nobility or the freedmen by whom Claudius had generally been controlled. They introduced fiscal and judicial reforms and encouraged a more enlightened attitude towards slaves. Corbulo, a general of their choice, defeated the Parthians in Armenia. Boudicca's rebellion in Britain was suppressed, and the administration made more sensitive to native interests. The food supply of Rome was safeguarded by the completion of Claudius's harbour works at Ostia. To check the depopulation of Italy a number of colonies of veterans were established, at Capua and Noceria (57) and at Puteoli, Tarentum and Antium (60).

Nevertheless neither Seneca nor Burrus could escape involvement in the struggle for power that soon developed between Nero and his mother Agrippina. Though both owed their rise to her, they were as eager as Nero to deprive her of power. First, they contrived to dismiss her supporter, the financial secretary Pallas, who was accused of malpractice. Then, when Agrippina began to show a new affection for her stepson Britannicus, they acquiesced in his murder by the emperor. The extent of their complicity cannot be known. They promoted the interest of the freedwoman Acte, who might exercise over Nero the influence formerly wielded by his mother. When Agrippina, realising how her power was slipping away, took up the cause of Nero's neglected wife, Octavia (the sister of the murdered Britannicus), Nero seized the opportunity to order her from the court, and Seneca and Burrus had achieved their aim.

In 59 Nero murdered his mother. There is no evidence that Seneca was privy to the plot. Nevertheless he helped to make Nero's return to Rome six months later easier than it might have been. He wrote a speech for him to deliver in the senate explaining his version of his mother's death. However, Nero was escaping any control. When Burrus died in 62 and was replaced as praetorian prefect by the disreputable Ofonius Tigellinus, Seneca found himself unable to continue in office. He received permission to retire, and devote himself to writing. In 65 however he was accused of being a party to the conspiracy of Piso; if he was not guilty, he must certainly have sympathised with its alleged aims. He was ordered to commit suicide, and met death with the fortitude appropriate to his philosophy.

Seneca's political career would hardly have made him memorable if it had not been buttressed by his reputation as a writer. His works fall into two principal groups: philosophical essays and tragedies. There is also the *Apocolocyntosis divi Claudii – The Pumpkinification of the Divine Claudius*, a political skit dealing with the deification of the Emperor Claudius, who had sent him into exile and only reluctantly consented to his recall. It is evidence of his wit and capacity for resentment.

The philosophical works expound a version of what is known as 'middle' Stoicism, of a type adapted to suit the Roman temperament by Panaetius of Rhodes in the second century before Christ, and developed by Poseidonius, also from Rhodes, a hundred years later. His influence lies behind Seneca's eight books on physical science, the *Naturales Quaestiones*. These achieved great popularity which survived into the Middle Ages, though there is little either original or profound in them. Ten books survived of what are inaccurately called Dialogues. They are in fact ethical essays on general subjects such as anger, constancy and tranquillity of mind. Three of them are *consolationes* to the bereaved: to a lady on the loss of a son; to his mother on his own exile; to Claudius's freedman Polybius on the death of his brother. This last is full of flattery of both Polybius and the emperor, whom he hoped to persuade by this means to end his exile. In the circumstances the gross flattery may be considered venial.

Early in Nero's reign Seneca presented an essay to him, *De Clementia*, from which Shakespeare may have drawn some of the arguments employed by Portia in her great speech on the quality of mercy in *The Merchant of Venice*. *De Beneficiis* (in seven books) discussed benefits as seen by giver and recipient. It was addressed to his friend C. Lucilius, as were the *Epistulae Morales* (Moral Letters), of which one hundred and twenty-four survive. These essays, some of which may have been real letters but which give the impression of having been intended for publication from the first, discuss a whole range of moral problems, not capable of being reduced to a single formula.

Seneca wrote nine tragedies on themes from Greek mythology: these are thought to have been intended for private reading or recital rather than stage performance. They are forceful, rhetorical and exaggerated. There is a ready resort to the supernatural as a dramatic device. Ghosts, witches, tyrants make frequent appearance; revenge is a dominating theme. Despite this they tend to the static, and must often appear insincere. They were however to be of considerable importance in the history of the theatre, for they were the only examples of classical tragedy known to the Renaissance. Plays like Shakespeare's *Titus*

Andronicus, Webster's *Duchess of Malfi* and the Revenge tragedies of Tourneur and Middleton owe much to Seneca.

His moral writings gained the respect of early Christians, who appreciated his denunciation of the delusory pleasures of wealth, the stupidity of much official religion and the cruelty of the Games. The respect was such that before 40 A.D. a correspondence between Seneca and St Paul had been forged. Yet, though Seneca was in many ways more human than his age, his character reveals considerable discrepancies. He preached the Stoic virtues of moderation but acquired a vast fortune himself, and the profits of his estates were employed in usury. He warned against the tyranny of princes, yet flattered Claudius grossly (till it was safe to abuse him) and condoned Nero's murder of his mother.

He is now seen as not having been a philosopher of any real originality, but his writings contributed immeasurably to the transmission of classical culture to Christian Europe. Dante and Chaucer both knew his work; Erasmus edited it. Whatever his limitations he remains an important figure in the history of western culture.

Pliny the Elder   Pliny the Younger

(A.D. 23–79)   (A.D. 61–113)

Gaius Plinius Secundus, known as Pliny the Elder to distinguish him from his nephew Gaius Plinius Caecilius Secundus, was born in A.D. 23 (some authorities say 24) at Novum Comum (near the modern Lake Como) in northern Italy, although Verona has also been suggested as a possible birthplace. He was born into a noble and prosperous family with equestrian traditions and was sent early to be educated in Rome, possibly under Pomponius Secundus, a Roman statesman whose biography he was later to write.

As a young man he entered the army and served with a cavalry regiment, distinguishing himself in the field. He spent many years in Germany, some of them with the future emperor Vespasian, eventually becoming colonel of his regiment. Whilst he enjoyed the active life he was by education and temperament curious, inquiring, and scholarly, and after writing a treatise on throwing missiles from horseback began a history of the Germanic Wars which ran to twenty volumes. Later he went on scientific expeditions searching for the sources of the Danube. 'Man is by nature fond of novelty', he said later.

Returning to Rome in A.D. 52 he studied law, but before being called to the bar went home to Comum to devote himself to writing and study. There his studious disposition and fecund imagination came into their own, and he often spent twenty hours a day at his self-appointed tasks. He read the Greek authors avidly and made copious notes and comments which filled many volumes. Such was his lust for knowledge and his awareness of the value of time that he was read to by his servants during meals and ablutions.

Appointed procurator (or governor) of Gaul, Africa, and Spain successively by Nero towards the end of his reign, he discharged these duties, according to Suetonius, with *'summa integritate'* (great integrity). When his old friend Vespasian became emperor in A.D. 70 Pliny was recalled to Rome to enjoy court favour, despite which he again took up his studies.

The following year, in A.D. 71, on his brother-in-law's death, he became the guardian of his eleven-year-old nephew Plinius Caecilius Secundus, whom he adopted and for whose guidance he subsequently wrote the *Studiosus*, a treatise on oratory in six volumes, and the *Dubius Sermo* in eight volumes on grammar and linguistics. He further extended Aufidius Bassus's history of Rome by 31 books to include his own time, then began his monumental encyclopaedic work *Historia Naturalis* (Natural History), in 37 *'libri'*, or books. The Romans from Cicero's time had shown a veritable genius for composing manuals of all kinds, and Pliny the Elder was to become, with Varro, one of the two most famous and influential compilers.

In his preface Pliny the Elder stated that his *Historia Naturalis* was a study of 'the nature of things, that is, life'. It contained an extraordinarily comprehensive range of subjects, including: cosmology and astronomy; physical and historical geography; zoology; botany; agriculture; medicine and drugs; metallurgy; architecture; and an incidental history of fine art. He quotes over a hundred source books, many of them Greek, including Aristotle and Theophrastus. Although credulous in sometimes uncritically accepting fantasy or myth as fact, Pliny's *magnum opus* is still a great source of information about Roman life and thought. An erudite rather than an elegant writer, he sacrificed style to substance. Like Seneca he believed in a benevolent God, admired nature and castigated contemporary man for his inhumanity, folly, and love of luxury. Although he gave no explanatory commentary and made little attempt at systematic classification, his philosophical asides are very pertinent:

> It is not possible to determine whether Nature is a kind mother or a harsh stepmother to man.

> Other animals live affectionately with their like, fighting only other species; but many calamities come to man from his fellow men.

> The power and majesty of nature fails to be fully perceived if one merely looks at the parts and not at the vast whole.

The whole work was dictated to a team of shorthand writers, and finally finished in A.D. 77. It is the only one of his works to survive, and most of it was published posthumously. After its completion the active life called him again as Vespasian created him admiral of the fleet, and it was this which led indirectly to his death. In A.D. 79 he was in charge of the Roman fleet at Misenum when Mount Vesuvius was erupting nearby. As his nephew graphically described in a letter to Tacitus later, Pliny the Elder's attention was drawn to the great column of smoke and ashes rising into the sky and he, full of scientific curiosity, hastened to investigate. Landing on the beach, he dictated his observations under a hail of stones and debris; then went again the following day, this time using a pillow to protect his head. Unfortunately, in the confusion, he was suffocated by the noxious fumes. He was fifty-six, and as he died unmarried his nephew was his only heir. He had saluted death as 'the best thing God has bestowed upon man amidst the many calamities of life', and it is perhaps befitting that, in however bizarre a fashion, he died in the pursuit of knowledge.

His nephew, Pliny the Younger, took the forename Gaius after being adopted under his uncle's will. He was born at Comum in A.D. 61 or 62, the son of Caecilius and Plinia (the elder Pliny's sister). They were a high-ranking wealthy family and he was later to inherit a number of estates in different parts of Italy. During the period of his uncle's care he studied in Rome under Quintilian, then later under the Stoic philospher Musonius. As passionately devoted to literature as his uncle was to the acquisition of knowledge, Pliny the Younger began his literary career by writing a Greek tragedy at the age of fourteen. At eighteen he began to practise law and quickly became very successful, owing to his remarkable powers of oratory and rhetoric. He was often involved in the prosecution of officials, but whatever the case he refused all fees from rich and poor alike, to the amazement of both fellow-orators and clients. He regarded himself as employed to protect the innocent and detect vice wherever it might be found, and was proud of his powers.

'Eloquence is indeed the talent of very few,' he wrote later, 'but that faculty which Candidus calls loquacity is common to numbers' (*Letters*, vol. V). He and Tacitus were considered by many to be the two greatest orators of their age. The successful barrister is clearly detectable in another of his later writings:

> Besides, as is usually the case, we are much more affected by words which we hear, for though what you read in books may be more pointed, yet there is something in the voice, the look, the carriage, and even the gesture of the speaker, that makes a deeper impression upon the mind (*Letters*, vol. II).

Many of his harangues and orations were published, but, like his history of his own times and his poetry, these have been subsequently lost. He delivered many important speeches in the Forum, including one with Tacitus, impeaching on behalf of the Africans Marius Priscus, who had been proconsul of Africa. Pliny managed to avoid Domitian's persecution of the Stoic opposition despite his sympathy with their views, and some authorities state that he later served as a military tribune in Syria.

Despite a busy and successful public life he found time to administer his various estates and to introduce reforms and innovations. He was unusually kind and generous to his slaves and servants; established a school at Comum for any children who would be able to benefit from it; and founded a great library there also, and other charitable bequests. He patronised Suetonius and Martial, amongst others. He wrote in *Letters*, vol. VII:

> ... a man of true generosity will study in what manner to render his benefaction most advantageous, rather than how he may bestow it with least expense.

If his philanthropy had any ulterior motive it was the desire for immortality, as he explained:

> Nothing, I avow, excites me so much as the desire of having my name handed down to posterity; a passion highly worthy of the human breast, especially of his who, not being conscious of any crime, fears not to be known to future generations (*Letters*, vol. V).

He married three times and it is tempting to wonder if a sentence in his *Letters*, vol. II, bears any relation to this fact:

An object in possession seldom retains the same charm which it had when it was longed for.

Be that as it may, it is clear that his last marriage, to Calpurnia, was a happy one, as there are many affectionate references to her in his letters. It seems that none of his marriages produced any children. His strong sense of morally apt behaviour is evident elsewhere:

> I hold it particularly worthy of a man of honour to be governed by the principles of strict equity in his domestic as well as public conduct; in small, as in great affairs; in his own concerns, as well as those of others: and if every deviation from rectitude is equally criminal, every approach to it must be equally laudable (*Letters*, vol. VIII).

His public career continued with imperial service: in A.D. 100 he was made a prefect of the state treasury (*consul suffectus*) under Trajan shortly after his accession as emperor. In answer to this honour Pliny composed his celebrated 'Panegyricus', a eulogy on the new emperor, which many held to be basically quite sincere. After this first office Pliny was appointed a curator of the Tiber and its banks, for the prevention of floods. In A.D. 111 he was made proconsul of Asia, then governor of Bithynia, where he remained until his death in 113, aged fifty-two, though the circumstances of his death are not known.

Pliny's claim to fame rests on his *Letters*, which have been compared to those of Cicero and Marcus Aurelius, in giving the flavour of their particular period, often through small details of social life. These letters comprise 10 volumes, 9 of which had already been published before he was sent to Bithynia: Books I–II between A.D. 97–8, Books III–VI between A.D. 99–107, and Books VII–IX between A.D. 108–9. The tenth volume, consisting largely of Pliny's official correspondence with Trajan about the province of Bithynia, was published posthumously.

Amongst the most famous of these letters are his eye-witness account of the destruction of Pompeii (vol. VI); his description of the eruption of Vesuvius and his uncle's death (vol. VI); and in A.D. 112 his letter to Trajan asking advice about the persecution of Christians, as to whether 'the name [i.e. Christian] was punishable or only crimes attached to the name?' He added that the Christians were meek, inoffensive men who tried to be peaceable and virtuous, but would not take part in emperor-worship or public sacrifices. Trajan's answer was that they must not be officially hunted down but only brought to court by private informers, which in effect greatly reduced persecution. Other letters dealt with public affairs, literature, boar-hunting, descriptions of villas or scenery, and particular problems such as the absence of a fire brigade.

Only the 'Panegyricus' and the *Letters* survive. It is clear that the *Letters* were written with publication in mind, which accounts for their relative impersonality and premeditated quality: nevertheless, he reveals himself as a master of the epistolatory style.

His attitude to death was almost diametrically opposed to that of his uncle:

> Death is ever bitter and premature to those who are engaged on some immortal work ... who look forward to posterity and endeavour by their exertions to hand down their name to future generations ... as it ever carries them off from the midst of some unfinished design.

Premature or not, enough of his 'design' was finished to ensure him the lasting fame which he so assiduously cultivated.

Plutarch

(A.D. 46–c. 119)

Plutarch is a writer whose chief importance may be held to lie in his influence on the development of European civilisation, particularly in the period that runs from the Renaissance to the Romantic era and the modern industrial world. His *Parallel Lives* of Greeks and Romans not only provided the popular images of the great historical figures of ancient history; they were also used as models for morality and conduct, and they influenced the development of the art of biography and history. His other writings had a comparable influence on the development of the essay as a characteristic Renaissance form.

Born in A.D. 46 at Chaeronea in Boeotia, his life was comparatively uneventful. His father, Aristobulus, was himself a historian and philospher; the young Plutarch studied mathematics and philosophy at Athens under Ammonius. He lectured on philosophy at Rome, where he may have enjoyed the friendship of the emperors Trajan and Hadrian. According to the Suda lexicon (a Greek dictionary dating from about A.D. 1000)

Trajan honoured him with consular rank. There is no other evidence of this, nor of the report of the Christian historian Eusebius that Hadrian made him governor of Greece. He was however certainly a Roman citizen; this fact is recorded in an inscription found at Delphi, where from 95 he held a priesthood.

He travelled widely, visiting Alexandria as well as Rome and most cities in Greece. However, he normally lived at his birthplace, where he held the chief magistracy and directed a school. Little is known about his family, though in a letter to his wife Timoxena he mentions four sons. He died about 119.

A catalogue of his works, reputedly made by his son, lists 227 titles, not all authentic. There are, however, omissions.

The most famous of his works were his *Lives*, dedicated to Trajan's friend Sosius Senecio. They were designed to encourage mutual respect between Greeks and Romans, and to provide model patterns of behaviour. For this reason they tend to concentrate on what was admirable in their subjects' lives.

Many have been lost; twenty-two pairs survive. Plutarch's plan was to publish biographies of Greeks and Romans in pairs which were chosen for their similarity of character, career and achievement, each pair being followed by a formal comparison. They display wide research, many authorities being quoted, though Plutarch was handicapped by an inadequate knowledge of Latin which, despite his stay in Rome, he seems only to have learned late in life. Of the *Lives* it may first be said that there had been nothing like them in either Greek or Roman literature before; Plutarch therefore deserves the credit due to an innovator. In general he gives the birth, youth and character, achievements and circumstances of death; there are frequent ethical reflections, for his aim was to edify as well as to please. He distinguishes between history and biography, and the weight of the *Lives* varies according to the authorities he used – some of whom were more given to scandalous gossip than others. He is admittedly partisan; there is for instance a bias towards Sparta and against Athens. Perhaps the fullest tribute that can be paid him is to say that almost two thousand years after they were written, the *Lives* can still be read for enjoyment and instruction.

His other surviving works, about 60 essays on ethical, philosophical, scientific, literary and political subjects, are collectively known as *Ethica* (Latin: *Moralia*); many are in dialogue form. Their range may be gathered from a list of some of the titles: 'How a Young Man Ought to Hear Poetry'; 'On the Education of Children'; 'How to Recognise Progress in Virtue'; 'On the Fortune of Alexander'; 'On the Fortune of the Romans';

'Whether the Athenians Were More Famous in War or in Wisdom'; 'On Eating Flesh'; 'Do Animals Reason?' (a dialogue set on Circe's island, in which a pig, one of Odysseus's transformed companions, attacks the Stoic doctrine which denied the faculty of reason to animals, and goes on to convince Odysseus that many animals are morally superior to men); 'On the Creation of the Soul in the Timaeus' (one of Plato's dialogues); 'Precepts of Health'; 'On Primary Cold'; 'Precepts of Politics'; 'On the Love of One's Offspring'.

Plutarch's interest in religion and antiquarian problems is revealed by a number of essays, including one on the Egyptian gods Isis and Osiris and one 'On the Great E at Delphi' which offers an interpretation of the word EI carved at the entrance to the temple there. His work 'Greek and Roman Questions' represents a large collection of antiquarian lore.

Plutarch is not an original thinker. He is frequently superficial. Yet all his work has charm and interest; he is invariably fertile in anecdote. He wrote Attic Greek, though influenced by the demotic that he spoke. His philosophy is eclectic, borrowing from the Stoics, Pythagoreans and Peripatetics; its core is Platonic. As a Platonist he believed in the immortality of the soul; he had himself been initiated into the Dionysian mysteries which also taught immortality. He believed in the superior achievement of Greek culture and the virtue and necessity of the Roman Empire. As for himself, despite his time in Rome and acquaintance with two emperors, he seems to have preferred a quiet life in his home town in Boeotia.

Plutarch is one of those writers whose posthumous reputation has far surpassed any fame gained in life. Even so he enjoyed a contemporary acclaim also. He had an immediate influence on the art of biography, and the Emperor Marcus Aurelius took a copy of the Lives on his campaigns. As with most Greek authors, his reputation faded in the west with the fall of the Roman Empire, though he remained popular in Byzantium.

With the revival of Greek learning in Italy in the fifteenth century Plutarch was rediscovered by the West. His works were translated into both Latin and Italian. The Greek text of the Lives was published in Florence in 1517. In 1559 the French bishop Jacques Amyot translated them into French; his translation of Moralia appeared in 1572. Amyot's versions permeated French literature. Both Rabelais and Montaigne quote him frequently, and Montaigne formed the style of his Essays on the model of Plutarch's.

An English version of Amyot's French text was made in 1579 by

Sir Thomas North. The Elizabethan was the great age of translation, and North's Plutarch achieved classic status. It continued to be read even when it had been superseded by more accurate translations done from the Greek, and Shakespeare used North as his source for his Roman plays. The greatest tribute to the quality of North's work is that many of the speeches in *Julius Caesar*, *Antony and Cleopatra*, and (especially) *Coriolanus* are essentially versified North.

Plutarch was not only suited to the Renaissance spirit; he helped to form it. His fondness for the illustrative anecdote, his identification of characters as exemplary patterns of vice or virtue, his emphasis on the part played by vicissitudes of fortune in bringing about the downfall of great men, all contributed to the formation of Renaissance ideas of the heroic and the tragic hero.

He continued to be read and to exercise influence at least until the early Romantic period. When Gulliver compared the contemptible stature of politicians in Lilliput and in England to the heroes of the Roman Republic, it was to Plutarch that he owed that conception. His influence on the classical French theatre of Corneille and Racine was at least as great as on Shakespeare. Dryden edited a new version of the *Lives* in 1683; new editions appeared throughout the following century. The *Moralia* were also translated again at the end of the seventeenth century. His influence could find practical expression also. Charlotte Corday spent the night before her assassination of the revolutionary leader Marat in reading Plutarch; there she could find justification for the virtuous murder of tyrants.

Though the development of scientific historical methods in the nineteenth century cast doubt on his authority, and the Romantic ideas of personality (even more, the psychological studies of the early twentieth century) made his treatment and understanding of character seem schematic and artificial, so that Plutarch lost the influential position he had so long held, he remained the principal source for popular ideas of famous Greeks and Romans. He can never regain that authority he has lost; but at the same time he can never fail to please and interest those who wish to know about the ancient world. Few writers have left posterity so heavily in their debt.

Josephus

(A.D. 37–96)

Josephus was a learned Jew who lived in the first century A.D. in a period critical both for the relations between the Jews and Rome and the background of the earliest stage of the Christian Church. Though circumstances made him at different periods a diplomatist and a military leader, his main enduring importance lies in his work as an historian.

He left four works written in Greek: *The Jewish War*, an account of the revolt of the Jews against Rome in A.D. 66–70; *The Jewish Antiquities*, a history of the Jews from the Creation to his own time; *Against Apion*, a defence of Jewish traditions against Gentile criticism; and a *Life*, a very unbalanced autobiography which devotes to six months of his activities in the Jewish revolt more than twenty times the space it gives to his first twenty-seven years. He also mentions an earlier Aramaic account of the Jewish war, but this has not survived, although some argue that a medieval Slavonic translation of *The Jewish War*, with significant variants from the Greek version, reflects traces of this.

All we know of the background and early life of Josephus comes from his autobiography. He was born in A.D. 37 to a family of hereditary priests of the highest rank in Jerusalem, with royal blood through his paternal great-great-grandmother. He had one brother, Matthias, and was educated with him, apparently by their parents. Josephus claimed that by the time he was fourteen he was such a prodigy that the chief priests and leading citizens of Jerusalem used to consult him on Jewish law; one wonders whether Josephus really was treated as gravely as he suggests, or whether the reality was that his father's aristocratic friends amused themselves by trying to catch out a bright but conceited boy.

Jewish society at the time of Josephus was divided into the sects of the Sadducees and Pharisees, known from the New Testament, and the Essenes, a movement of puritanical and communistic tendencies, now better known from the Dead Sea Scrolls. At the age of sixteen, Josephus attached himself to each in turn, and then tried out (for three years, he says) the discipline of a hermit who lived the primitive life in the wilderness. At the age of nineteen he finally decided to live by the precepts of the Pharisees.

Of his following seven years Josephus tells us nothing, but the sequel indicates that his aristocratic and priestly descent, and his Pharisaic connexions, made him of consequence in the ruling Jerusalem establishment. We next hear of him in A.D. 64, when he undertook a mission to Rome to seek the release of some priestly colleagues of his who had been arrested and sent to Nero by the Roman procurator; although his account does not say so, he may have been acting on behalf of the Jewish authorities. He claimed to have suffered shipwreck on his journey, and if this was more than a traveller's tale, the details he gives show him to have been a first-class swimmer; some later incidents indicate that he was a strong, athletic man. In Rome, he achieved his objective through the mediation of a court favourite, a Jewish actor.

On his return to Palestine, he found revolutionary anti-Roman movements afoot, the immediate cause being the tyranny of the Roman procurator, although widespread disturbances elsewhere in the Roman Empire must have contributed. In his different works, Josephus gives overlapping accounts of what followed. *The Jewish War* brings out the strong opposition of the Jewish establishment to action against Rome, and in the *Life* Josephus emphasises that he himself played a major role in the attempt to dissuade the agitators from active revolt, pointing out the disastrous consequences that would ensue from opposing the Romans by force of arms. In A.D. 65 the differences between agitators and moderates erupted into civil war in Jerusalem. Assassinations followed, and Josephus felt himself in danger of being murdered as a suspected Roman agent because of his repeated anti-war advice. The Jewish authorities could do no more than await the expected arrival of the governor of Syria, Cestius, to put down the disturbances. But such restraint did Cestius use on reaching Jerusalem, that the insurgents were able to seize the initiative and defeat his forces, in November A.D. 66. Josephus summed up the dismay of the Jewish moderates by saying that 'the defeat of Cestius was fatal for our whole nation'. The deceptive impression it created of the insurgents' chances of success brought them total ascendancy, so that a full-scale rebellion broke out. Some prominent members of the Jerusalem peace party managed to desert to the Romans, others were murdered by the insurgents, and the remainder, who included Josephus, had no alternative, other than death as suspected traitors, to joining the revolt, however reluctantly.

What follows is narrated both in *The Jewish War* and in the *Life*, and the two accounts are so different that some critics allege deliberate falsification. *The Jewish War* states that the revolutionaries, joined by former moderates, met in the Temple to appoint commanders for defence. Ten were chosen, amongst them Josephus, who was put in charge of Galilee. The picture is very different in the *Life*. There the leading moderates in Jerusalem, learning that part of Galilee was still quiet and hoping that this might prove a lever for moderation, sent Josephus with two other priests to persuade the disaffected there to lay down their arms. Are these two accounts irreconcilable? Perhaps not. Josephus shows throughout his writings that he was the sort of man who liked to emphasise the regard in which he was held. In *The Jewish War*, written to inform Greek-speaking readers of the background and course of a major upheaval, it was appropriate for him to stress that in a crisis his nation's leaders chose him as one of the senior generals. But in the *Life*, another issue arose. Here he devoted some space and much venom to a counter-attack on another aristocratic Jew, Justus of Tiberias in Galilee, who had written a Jewish history, now lost, in which he had evidently branded Josephus as a warmonger directly responsible for the anti-Roman insurrection in Galilee. Josephus, living in Rome as a client of the emperor, would not wish such an accusation to pass unchallenged, and so the details of his mission of pacification may have been intended to put the record straight vis-à-vis Justus. Thus the apparent stark difference between the two accounts may be a mere matter of omission. In the *Life*, Josephus mentions writing to Jerusalem for further instructions when the other members of his mission left Galilee, and it may have been only then that he was given his military command, which in *The Jewish War* he recounted without any mention of his initial unsuccessful peace mission.

Josephus set about organising the defence of Galilee, fortifying important positions and attempting to train an army on Roman lines. His choice of places to fortify has been criticised for poor strategic judgement, and the subsequent behaviour of his forces did not indicate much success for his training programme. But Josephus was working against time, and faced a difficult task. As commonly in revolutions, numerous factions emerged. One local leader, John of Gischala, at first an energetic lieutenant of Josephus, later joined the extremists and organised opposition to Josephus, going to the length of attempted assassination.

Such were the divisions in Galilee, between city and city, between moderates and extremists, between rich and poor, that the country was near to anarchy. The Jerusalem authorities blamed Josephus, and sent a commission of two priests and two lay

Pharisees with strong military support to remove him from command. Josephus alleged that John of Gischala was behind this. In the *Life*, he gave a long account of how he managed to outwit the emissaries, who variously tried to charge him publicly, arrest him, and kill him in ambush. Josephus, though he had a keen sense of the value of his own skin, was no coward, and one gets the impression that he enjoyed this battle of wits, which he won. He still had considerable public support, despite the factions opposed to him, and when he eventually met the commission, they could do no other than promise to take a report to Jerusalem on the situation in Galilee. Josephus did not expect the promise to be kept, but the delay gave him time to send his own delegation to the capital, which returned with an order confirming his appointment.

Meanwhile, the Romans were preparing to avenge the defeat of the governor of Syria. The Emperor Nero appointed the veteran general Vespasian, who with his son Titus assembled a large army in Syria. Vespasian moved south and entered Galilee. Despite the training Josephus claimed to have given his army, it suffered an immediate collapse of morale and large-scale desertion, and Josephus himself took refuge in Tiberias. Throughout he had held (or so he claimed) that war could only end in disaster for the Jews, and he now sent a report to Jerusalem, giving the authorities there the alternatives of suing for peace at once or sending him adequate forces for defence. It does not appear that they did either.

Though Josephus had little heart for the war, he did not shirk his duty, and on learning that Vespasian was preparing to attack Jotapata, one of his strongholds, he quickly went there to direct the defence. He gives a graphic account of the siege, which lasted forty-seven days, ending in a massacre. Josephus managed to escape by jumping into a deep pit communicating with a concealed cave, where he found forty other Jews already in hiding. When the hiding-place was discovered, Vespasian sent messengers offering Josephus, as commander, safe-conduct for surrender. He was ready to agree, but the other fugitives were fanatics who forcibly prevented him and urged mass suicide. Josephus, with (as he himself put it) a resourcefulness which did not fail him, argued that suicide was sinful and proposed an alternative form of death pact, in which they would kill each other in sequence, in order decided by lot. This was agreed, and, according to the ancient Slavonic version of *The Jewish War*, Josephus manipulated the lots so that he remained as one of the last two survivors. He then surrendered and was led to Vespasian. Some of the Roman soldiers gave him a hostile reception, but Titus persuaded his father against summary execution. Josephus then requested a private interview with Vespasian and Titus, which was granted. He thereupon prophesied that Vespasian would become emperor. The veteran general was at first not impressed, but on hearing of other predictions by Josephus which had come true, he decided to keep Josephus as his own prisoner instead of sending him to Nero, as he had originally intended. The prophecy could have been a clever ploy by Josephus to prevent his being sent prisoner to Rome; it would have been dangerous for Vespasian to allow Nero to learn that Vespasian had been spoken of as soon to succeed him.

After clearing up remaining stubborn resistance in Galilee, Vespasian moved southwards. He was about to march on Jerusalem when he heard of the death of Nero in June A.D. 68 by suicide. In the resulting power struggle, the Roman armies in the east and in Egypt backed Vespasian, and that summer he went to Alexandria, where he was proclaimed emperor. In view of the fulfilled prophecy, Vespasian now ordered the freedom of Josephus, who had remained with Titus. Titus effected the emancipation by a ritual which left Josephus a free man without stigma from his former bondage.

Vespasian had left the problem of Jerusalem to Titus, who now put the city under siege. Inside it there was the same factional strife that Josephus had encountered in Galilee, with the extremists perpetrating the foulest excesses of robbery, murder and rape. Aware that there was a substantial peace party in the city, Titus used Josephus, speaking in Aramaic, to invite surrender. His duties also included the interrogating of deserters. He was thus an obvious target for the extremists whilst making his proclamations within earshot of the city walls, and once he was knocked unconscious by a stone and only saved from capture by troops sent to his help by Titus. Josephus gives a gruesome account of the siege, in which famine culminated in cannibalism. The city was finally taken after desperate resistance, with appalling slaughter and the burning of the Temple. Josephus repeatedly emphasises that the latter was not the fault of Titus; it was set on fire against orders by a common soldier, and the troops which Titus sent in to extinguish it were out of hand and added to the blaze.

Josephus accompanied Titus on his return to Rome, where Vespasian gave him a house, a pension, and Roman citizenship; he took his patron's family name and became Flavius Josephus.

He spent the remainder of his life in Rome, where he published *The Jewish War* between A.D. 75 and the death of Vespasian in A.D. 79. He continued to enjoy the favour of both Titus and

Domitian, the two sons who in 79–81 and 81–96 respectively succeeded Vespasian as emperor, and in 93 or 94 published *The Jewish Antiquities*, with the *Life* following, as in effect an appendix to a revised edition. The work *Against Apion* was also written towards the end of his life. He probably died at about the same time as Domitian, the last emperor he mentioned, in A.D. 96.

Josephus was married three times, each time to a woman of his own race. His first wife was a prisoner with him under Vespasian; she bore him three children, of whom one son survived to manhood. After her death he married a lady from Alexandria, but divorced her after settling in Rome, to marry a Cretan Jewess of good birth, who bore him two sons.

It is clear that there were strenuous attempts to discredit Josephus in his own lifetime, by fellow-Jews who regarded him as a self-seeking traitor, and this attitude has carried over into modern scholarship, where writing about Josephus is liberally sprinkled with such terms as 'lick-spittle', 'cowardice', 'duplicity'. But in fact he retained to the end a strong sense of the virtues of Jewish institutions and culture, which he explained to non-Jews in the *Antiquities* and strongly defended in *Against Apion*. The fact was that he was a man with loyalties to two cultures in tension, Jewish and Hellenistic-Roman, and it was this which exposed him to the accusations that he was a traitor to the Jews and a sycophant to the Romans.

The reliability of what he wrote is another problem. In some passages Josephus was manifestly on the defensive, and there are frequently grounds for concluding that he was slanting his presentation of material to show himself in the most favourable light.

Difficulties of another kind arise in assessing the relevance of his writings to early Christianity. Indisputably he provides the most important account of the fall of Jerusalem, which was very significant for the early history of Christianity. But in addition to this there are in the *Antiquities* three direct references to Christian origins, one mentioning John the Baptist, one referring to James the brother of Jesus, and the third giving a brief account of Jesus, which in the existing Greek text (although some critics argue that this was altered by later Christian copyists) speaks of the Resurrection. The Slavonic version of *The Jewish War* gives some longer and markedly more pro-Christian narratives about John the Baptist and Jesus, and these would be of the highest importance if they could be proved to be the genuine work of Josephus. Most authorities consider that they are not. There is, however, an alternative view that the Slavonic version represents the first form of Josephus's work, and that the existing Greek text is a revision in which Josephus, always anxious to be on the right side of his patron, had, late in his life, removed pro-Christian sentiments in deference to the anti-Christian Domitian.

REFORMERS

Hammurabi

(*Reigned* 1792–1750 B.C.)

Hammurabi was the king who raised the minor city of Babylon to a world-renowned capital; he also produced an important collection of laws. It has been suggested that a memory of his name is preserved in the Bible, in the Amraphel king of Shinar recorded as clashing with Abraham in Genesis 14:1 and 9.

He was the sixth ruler of a dynasty of Amorites, a nomadic people from the Syrian desert who entered south Iraq (then known as Sumer and Akkad, afterwards as Babylonia) and other parts of the Near East from the late third millennium B.C. onwards and gradually established kingdoms on the basis of the old Sumerian city-states. A cuneiform text shows that Hammurabi could claim to trace his ancestry back through twenty-four generations, although the earliest names in the list were really tribes rather than persons.

When Hammurabi came to the throne, Babylon controlled an area of about fifty miles radius. Within seven years he had conquered cities 120 miles from Babylon, and by the end of his reign his sway held over territory which stretched from the Persian Gulf in the south to Nineveh (perhaps even 200 miles further to Diyarbakir) in the north, and from the Balikh tributary of the Euphrates to the Zagros, that is, at least 500 miles by 350, larger than modern Iraq without its desert area. He owed his success as a ruler to a combination of military ability, skill in diplomacy, painstaking attention to administrative detail, and genuine care for the well-being of his land.

The position at Hammurabi's accession was an unstable balance between many petty dynasts in the region from Babylonia to Syria, whose alliances formed the basis of more powerful groupings which were beginning to arise. Kings kept in close touch through ambassadors and exchange of letters, and in case of need would request and receive from their allies assistance in the form of shipping and men to the order of 10,000 troops or even more.

Although Babylon was already solidly established at the accession of Hammurabi, it was not able successfully to stand alone, and for his first decade Hammurabi was in the orbit of a more powerful Amorite ruler further north, Shamshi-Adad of Assyria, who headed a loose coalition of states. With the death of Shamshi-Adad, the leadership of this coalition fell to Hammurabi. His recognised status as the head of one of several competing coalitions is made explicit in a letter of the period: 'There is no king who is strong by himself. Ten or fifteen kings follow Hammurabi of Babylon, the same number follow Rim-Sin of Larsa, the same number Ibalpiel of Eshnunna, the same number Amutpiel of Qatana, and twenty kings follow Yarim-Lim of Yamhad.'

In his thirty-first year this balance shifted decisively in Hammurabi's favour with his defeat of Rim-Sin of Larsa, which gave the whole of southern Babylonia into his hands. That his concerns were not limited to military conquest is shown by his then creating a major canal to give 'a permanent abundant water supply for Nippur, Eridu, Ur, Larsa, Uruk and Isin', that is, to all the ancient southern cities. The name of the canal – 'Hammurabi is the prosperity of the people' – shows that he recognised the importance of canal-digging as a basis of the prosperity and strength of his kingdom, and indeed much of his activities throughout his reign were devoted to the digging of canals.

The culminating stage of Hammurabi's expansion came in his thirty-third year, when he attacked and occupied Mari, a powerful and wealthy city 250 miles upstream on the Euphrates, controlling the trade routes to Syria. Subsequent action against areas east of the Tigris left Hammurabi indisputably the most powerful king of his time, with his capital enjoying a supremacy which endured as long as Babylonian civilisation lasted.

It is not possible to give more than an impressionistic picture of the man Hammurabi. Some passages in his texts, in which he speaks of his reverence for the gods and service to their temples, have sometimes been interpreted as implying personal piety, but they may be no more than conventional phrases. Yet there is a hint that he took a more austere approach to life than some of his royal contemporaries. His erstwhile ally Zimri-Lim of Mari built himself a huge luxurious palace covering more than six acres, but we hear nothing of such indulgence from Hammurabi, whose building activities chiefly concerned canals, temples and city walls.

Of other sides of Hammurabi, texts supply details here and there, but leave us in ignorance of many things we would like to know. His military activities are a case in point. Since they were successful, we assume that he was an able general, but we have little to tell us wherein his ability lay, since the information is mostly limited to bald statements of conquests in date-formulae (lists in which years were identified for calendary purposes by mention of significant events, often military). But for one entry there is a formula which lights up the nature of Hammurabi's military skill: it shows a capacity for imaginative use of technology instead of sole reliance on standard siege warfare. The entry in question reads: 'By the vision given to him by the god Marduk, he destroyed (a certain city) with a great mass of water', that is, he devised a method of engineering an artificial flood to breach the city's walls.

The considerable diplomatic activity between Hammurabi and other kings involved correspondence between ambassadors and their masters, and some dispatches of ambassadors at Hammurabi's court have survived. These enable us to see something of Hammurabi as he appeared to the eyes of his contemporaries. It becomes very clear that he was a hard-working man in personal day-to-day control of all state affairs. He dictated dispatches to other rulers, interviewed foreign ambassadors and instructed his own representatives, inspected his forces, made decisions about troop movements, and arranged to borrow troops when necessary. The sequel to the latter in one case illuminates another facet of Hammurabi's character: when the foreign ruler wanted his troops returned, after they had completed the period for which they were lent, Hammurabi used delaying tactics, despite strenuous efforts by the foreign ruler's ambassador.

State and administrative decisions were all made directly by Hammurabi, and he seems to have had no ministers to advise him or to act on their own responsibility. This shows a strong man, but it may in the long run have been a source of weakness to his kingdom; after his death his kingdom declined rapidly, and a factor in this may have been the lack of ministers experienced in decision-making and government, resulting from Hammurabi's reluctance to delegate responsibility. He was very accessible, both to foreign ambassadors and to his own subjects, and anyone with a grievance could complain to him directly, over the heads of his officials – perhaps a survival from the practice of the nomadic sheikhs from whom he was descended. He was, however, a proud man, and one could not take liberties with him. When a foreign ambassador's criticism of an action of his came to his ears, he dispatched a sharp rebuke telling the offender that he would do as he pleased.

We obtain further details of Hammurabi's personal involvement in the running of his land from about 150 letters of correspondence between the king and his local officials. Predominately these letters are concerned with grants of land for feudal services, and with the remedying of complaints brought to him, particularly about land allocations and water rights. These make it abundantly clear that Hammurabi was concerned with just government and the protection of his subjects from oppression. Another aspect of this is that from the time of Hammurabi we hear of royal judges appointed by the king, whereas previously the usual system had been that judges were local officials with courts associated with the temples.

This concern of Hammurabi for justice ties in with his most important memorial. At the beginning of this century French excavations in south-west Iran revealed a monument of black diorite, seven and a half feet high, bearing a long cuneiform text which proved to contain laws promulgated by Hammurabi late in his reign. The laws proper are sandwiched between a prologue and an epilogue, and in the epilogue Hammurabi gives a clear statement of why he produced the laws, and had them carved on stone and set up in a public place. It was 'that the strong may not oppress the weak, to see that justice is done for the orphan and widow'. Hammurabi tells how he intended his monument to be used in the interests of justice: 'Let the oppressed man who has a cause go and have the inscription on my monument read out and hear my precious words, and let my monument make his cause clear to him. Let him see what his verdict is and let his heart be easy.'

These were not the first written laws of the ancient Near East. They were, however, the best organised up to that time and the most extensive, although they are far from covering all aspects of life. Hammurabi refers to his laws as 'the judgements I have judged and the decisions I have decided'. This explains their origin and their form. They were not abstract decrees but verdicts in particular cases, as for example: 'If a man has kidnapped the infant son of a free man, he shall be put to death.' Some of the verdicts must relate to actual cases which had come before Hammurabi himself, whilst the nature and interrelationship of others suggests that they were decisions for parallel cases with variant circumstances which could be foreseen as likely to arise. For

Statue of Buddha at Sarnath, to the north of Benares, where he
preached his first sermon.

Sassanian rock carving at Taq-i-Bustan, near Kermanshah, depicts a royal investiture. The figure on the left, standing on a lotus flower, is thought to be Zoroaster. *Below:* Lao Tzu (from the original drawing by Hohusai).

example, there is a law that if a builder has built a house so badly that it collapses and kills the householder, the builder shall be put to death. Then there follow laws to the effect that if the householder's son is killed, the builder's son shall be put to death, if a slave of the householder is killed the builder shall give a slave in replacement, if the collapsing house destroys property the builder shall make good the property and rebuild the house, and if a wall bulges the builder shall put the fault right. Even such a conscientious ruler as Hammurabi could hardly have been called upon to decide separately in every one of these cases, and this group must represent an attempt to provide in advance for all possible consequences of a collapsing house. Behind Hammurabi's own decisions was traditional practice, incorporated in such a form as to take account of changes in the social pattern and to replace the formerly diverse customary law of different cities by a single standard.

All the laws are in the 'If..., plus verdict' form of the law about kidnapping quoted above, although most are longer. The subject matter of the principal laws (with some omissions) may be summarised as follows:

False accusation of sorcery (death for accuser); false witness (death in capital cases, a fine in others); looting of a burning house (death); land grants for royal service (many provisions in different circumstances); agriculture; mortgage of land; loan transactions; trading partnerships; debt (members of a debtor's family could be taken into servitude but this was limited to three years; another law provides exemption of wife from seizure for debt); sale of a slave-girl (not permitted if she had borne sons to her master); custody of goods; slander; adultery; rape; divorce (divorced wife was protected by husband having to surrender property sufficient to maintain her; wife might divorce husband if she had been chaste and he a runabout; husband must maintain and might not divorce wife who had become incurably ill); rights of a widow (property protected against her sons); incest (of man with daughter, punished by banishment; with daughter-in-law, drowning; with mother, burning); bride-price and dowry; inheritance (disinheritance of a son only permitted after a second grave offence; rights of sons of a slave-girl by her owner; rights of a priestess to income from her father's estate and to a dowry in event of marriage); assault (literally an eye for an eye for an injured freeman, but a fine if the injured man was of a lower class); fees for surgeons, builders and shipwrights; rates of hire and wages.

The long-term importance of these laws was once over-estimated, when they were wrongly thought to be the basis of the biblical laws, which correspond at some points. More recently there has been a reaction denying them any long-term importance, but this is ill-founded. The laws are significant as a record of the concern for economic and social justice of a major ruler of the early second millennium. Hammurabi regarded it as his duty to give protection against oppression; in his prologue he claimed that he was divinely appointed 'to proclaim justice in the land, to destroy the evil and the wicked, that the strong might not oppress the weak'. Many of his laws do serve to do just this. Some indeed, such as the laws governing land grants for royal service, directly protect the interests of the state, and others are concerned with the regulation of commerce. But there are many other laws which, although they have an economic aspect, are primarily of social concern. The provision made for a divorced or incurably ill wife, the guarding of the rights of a widow or priestess, the limitation of the period for which a debtor's family might be held in servitude, the prohibition against selling a slave-girl who had borne sons to her master, are all instances of the protection of socially disadvantaged persons, making good the noble claim of Hammurabi in his prologue.

Moses

(? Thirteenth Century B.C.)

Moses is a dominating figure in early biblical tradition. The first half of the book of Exodus and parts of Numbers consist largely of narratives related to him, and the laws which make up much of the remainder of Exodus, of Leviticus and Deuteronomy and some of Numbers are traditionally ascribed to him. Yet his very existence has been doubted, and even if he was a real man, the powerful personality which gave origin to these traditions remains shrouded in mist, the period in which he lived is open to question, and his historical connexion with some of the most striking traditions linked to him has been disputed.

The biblical tradition

It is represented that Israel already existed as twelve tribes, all in slavery in Egypt, and that Moses was born there to a family of the tribe of Levi. A decree of the pharaoh for the killing of all male Hebrew babies led to his being hidden in a rush cradle in reeds by the Nile, where, watched over by a sister, he was found by a princess who then brought him up in the palace as an Egyptian. His murder of a tyrannical Egyptian overseer led to his flight into the Sinai desert, where he joined a tribe of Midianites and married the daughter of their priest. Serving as a shepherd for his father-in-law, he experienced a theophany in the wilderness, when the god Yahweh identified himself to Moses as the god whom Abraham, Isaac and Jacob had worshipped without knowing his name.

Yahweh instructed Moses to return to Egypt and lead out the Hebrews. With reluctance Moses, after experiencing several miracles, obeyed. Assisted by his brother Aaron as spokesman, he put miraculous pressure on the pharaoh to allow the Hebrews to leave; a series of ten plagues culminated in the death of all the Egyptian firstborn, which finally forced the pharaoh's consent. The circumstances of the departure of the Hebrew slaves gave rise to the institution of the Passover. Subsequent change of heart by the pharaoh led to pursuit by the Egyptian army; the Hebrews were saved by the miracle of a sea in front of them opening to allow their passage and then closing to engulf the pursuers. Moses then led the Hebrews into the wilderness of Sinai to a holy mountain wrapped in smoke and fire; there Moses received another theophany and promulgated laws for the Hebrew people. The migration continued, with hardships leading to several attempted rebellions against Moses's authority, each settled in Moses's favour by miraculous means. There was an initial attempt to enter Palestine from the south (Numbers 13) and finally Moses led the Hebrews to somewhere in Transjordan, from where the promised land of Palestine was visible, and died there.

Problems in the biblical tradition

The intense research to which this material has been subject has revealed literary, historical and geographical problems which complicate the quest for the historical Moses.

Literary analysis of the Old Testament indicates that many of its books grew up gradually from smaller units. Some Old Testament scholars holding this view argue that the Exodus traditions and the Sinai traditions were originally distinct and unrelated. One of the main grounds for this conclusion is that although many Old Testament texts refer to the sequence of divine interventions which led the Israelites from bondage in

Egypt to settlement in Palestine, in none, until a late passage in
Nehemiah, is there any reference to Mount Sinai. For example,
Joshua 24:5–13 lists a whole series of incidents from Egypt to
Palestine without mentioning Sinai. This is taken to prove that the
Exodus and Sinai traditions originally had no connexion, in which
case Moses could not have been historically associated with both
series of events. But the basic assumption in this argument may be
wrong. The intention of such passages as Joshua 24:5–13 may not
have been to list divine interventions as such, but rather to list
those divine interventions which saved Israel from perils, and the
Sinai event, important as it was, did not come into that category.

There is another indication of two originally distinct groups of
traditions. This is the fact that although Exodus 6:3 specifically
states that God was not known by the name Yahweh until He
revealed Himself to Moses in the Midianite desert, other biblical
passages say that worship of Yahweh under that name began as
early as the third generation of mankind (Genesis 4:26). The
simultaneous existence of these contradictory traditions is
explicable only if the later Israelites contained at least two groups
with different antecedents, one having worshipped Yahweh by
that name since prehistoric times and the other only coming to
know Yahweh under Moses. But this need prove no more than
that these two groups were not united before the time of Moses;
they could have come together under Moses.

What was the time of Moses? 1 Kings 6:1 places the Exodus 480
years (or 440 years, according to the Greek version) before
Solomon, and even the lower figure would date it not later than
1400 B.C. But Ruth 4:20, which allows only five generations
between Moses and Solomon, would require Moses to be at least a
century later. A later date for Moses is also indicated by Exodus
1:11, which mentions the building of the Egyptian city of
Raamses. As this city was built by the pharaoh Ramesses II,
whose reign began in 1290 B.C., this places Moses in the thirteenth
century B.C.

The very existence of Moses as a real man has been denied in
one hypothesis, which makes him the de-mythologised vestige of an
old bull-god. But this is more incredible than any of the traditions
it attempts to explain. Other scholars, though willing to accept
that there was an early charismatic leader bearing the name
Moses, see the traditions about him as derived not from actual
events affecting a real man, but from claims made by certain later
Israelite groups to show in the most favourable light those who
were thought of as their ancestors. For example, incidents in
which Aaron acted as Moses's spokesman were introduced to

exalt the status of the priesthood.

The geographical problem centres on the site of the sacred mountain associated with Moses, Mount Sinai, otherwise called Horeb. The traditions identifying it with one of several peaks in the south of the Sinai peninsula do not go back further than the early Christian period. Others have looked for it in north Sinai, on the view that it must have been near to Kadesh-barnea, the scene of much of the desert sojourn, which was certainly there. Yet others, concluding that the mention in Exodus 19:18 of fire and smoke coming from the mountain must relate it to volcanic phenomena, look for it in the formerly volcanic region south-east of the Gulf of Aqaba. There is also the possibility that the names Mount Sinai and Mount Horeb originally denoted different places. One specific suggestion on this basis is that Mount Sinai, somewhere in the Sinai peninsula, belonged to a southern group of tribes, whilst Mount Horeb, associated with a northern group, lay south-east of the Dead Sea.

Moses and Egypt

There is proof, independent of the claims of the biblical traditions, that Moses was linked with Egypt. Exodus 2:10 treats the name 'Moses' as of Hebrew origin, but that is philologically unacceptable, and the name is actually Egyptian. This fact was used in a hypothesis, most fully developed by Sigmund Freud, that Moses was in origin an Egyptian, whom the legend, about his being hidden as a baby and then found by a princess, was designed to turn into a Jew. He was probably an aristocrat, a suggestion which agrees with the biblical implication that Moses was brought up as a grandson of the pharaoh and even, according to Josephus (q.v.) in his *Antiquities*, as his heir. Certainly there was nothing impossible about an Egyptian aristocrat, in trouble with his authorities, joining a desert tribe and becoming its leader; there is an Egyptian story of a courtier, Sinuhe, who did just that in the twentieth century B.C. Freud went on to argue that the religion revealed to the Israelites by Moses was also of Egyptian origin. He linked it to a monotheistic reform associated with the fourteenth-century pharaoh Akhenaton. But this is untenable. Even in Egypt itself, Akhenaton's monotheism vanished with his death, and moreover the religion of Moses was so different from that of Akhenaton, which was based on sun-worship, that it cannot possibly have derived from it. For other details, the plain biblical narrative is at least as credible as Freud's interpretation of it.

A possible historical reconstruction

The miraculous elements in the Moses tradition are not susceptible to historical investigation, and must be evaluated according to the reader's view of whether God does or does not suspend natural laws for particular individuals or groups. Leaving this question on one side, it is possible to offer an outline of Moses's life which conflicts neither with the main biblical tradition nor with other data.

In the late second millennium B.C. the ancestors of the people we later meet as the Israelites of the Bible were still separate groups of tribes, some probably already in Palestine, others scattered over the desert to the south, others on the borders of Egypt. The tribes were all of desert origin and so had their basic cultural and religious background in common, though within this each group had its own distinct historical and religious traditions. The southern group contained Midianites, of whom one clan was the Kenites (supposed descendants of Cain), who formed part of the later Israelites (1 Chronicles 2:55 and 2 Kings 10:15*ff*.). This Kenite group already worshipped God under the name Yahweh, and knew a mountain sacred to him to which pilgrimages were made.

Moses was born to a tribe of the Egyptian group, which the Egyptians were attempting to settle and use as slave labour. He was already prominent, as a tribal leader appointed by the Egyptians to act for them (implied by Exodus 2:14), when he came into conflict with the authorities and fled to the desert. There he joined a Kenite clan, and realised that the god they worshipped as Yahweh was the nameless god of his own tribe's tradition. A religious experience at the sacred mountain gave him a blinding new vision of the nature of God, with the realisation that beyond the old idea that each clan or tribe had its own particular god was the reality that there was one God who was over all. Under the stimulus of this he returned to Egypt, from where he led his group of tribes to the sacred mountain in the desert. There, in an atmosphere of awe heightened by the storms playing around the peak of the mountain, or possibly by volcanic phenomena, Moses disappeared into the mountain to meditate. He had the problem of bringing his own vision of God into a form his followers could grasp. He needed to communicate, on the one hand the nature of God, and on the other His concern for each individual of the group. He himself saw that God was unique, too great to be represented in any form, and His revealed name too sacred to be uttered. Totally dependent upon God, man must set apart some of his time wholly for God. God had concern for each member of the group, and this required individuals of the group to have concern for each other.

Moses returned from the mountain to promulgate his new revelation of God. He did it by means of a set of ordinances independent of time or cultural background, in brief and memorable form, the basic elements of what we know as the Ten Commandments. The impact of Moses's revelation was such that some of the southern tribes joined those who had come from Egypt, so that henceforward the combined group had certain traditions about their antecedents which were incompatible. From the sacred mountain Moses led his tribes to Kadesh-barnea, south of Beer-sheba, with the intention of eventual settlement in Palestine. Some clans attempted to enter that country from the south, but with limited success, and Moses then led the main body south of the Dead Sea to enter from east of the Jordan, but died before this was achieved.

Moses and the biblical Laws

A substantial part of the laws of the biblical books from Exodus to Deuteronomy are in the context of a settled agricultural life of a period later than Moses; for example, a law about the burning of growing or stacked corn (Exodus 22:6). Such laws cannot be accepted as genuinely Mosaic unless one attributes to Moses a miraculous ability to foresee the future. But the central group of laws, the Ten Commandments, are another matter; they are not circumscribed by a particular social context. That they received later explanatory elaborations is put beyond doubt by the fact that in the two forms of these laws occurring in Exodus 20 and Deuteronomy 5, different reasons are given for the prohibition against working on the Sabbath Day. But there is nothing in the basic elements of these laws ('You shall not take the name of the Lord your God in vain', 'Remember the Sabbath Day, to keep it holy', 'Honour your father and your mother', etc.) which could not be genuinely from the time of Moses, and everything against deriving them from any other ancient Near Eastern laws. Almost all ancient Near Eastern laws, like most of those in the Bible except the Ten Commandments, were in the conditional form, *i.e.*, of the type 'If a man kills a man, he shall be put to death'. The direct prohibitions of the Ten Commandments are, as laws, unique. The only parallel to their form is in certain ancient treaties between overlords and vassals, where the overlord included prohibitions against the vassal doing certain things.

Attempts have been made to relate the form (but not the content) of the Ten Commandments to such treaty terms, but this remains an unproven hypothesis.

No other person in the second millennium B.C. approached Moses in his importance for later generations. Still today, hundreds of millions of people live by religions, Judaism and Christianity, which derive directly from his revelation, or by a third, Islam, which owes to Moses its basic concept of the unity of God.

Akhenaton

(*Ruled c.* 1380–*c.* 1364 B.C.)

From the nineteenth century excavations in rock tombs at Tell el-Amarna in Middle Egypt have revealed many hymns and prayers to the god Aton, or to Aton as king, and one great hymn is often attributed to the pharaoh Akhenaton himself.

Amenhotep IV, who changed his name to Akh-en-Aton, introduced or strengthened the Aton religion and he has been called the first religious reformer, or the first monotheist, believer in only one God. A long and beautiful hymn to Aton is engraved at Amarna in the tomb of a priest named Eye or Ai, and there are shorter hymns and prayers which seem to have been based on or abridged from this long hymn.

Amenhotep IV came to the throne of Egypt about 1380 B.C. when he was about ten years of age and he reigned sixteen years, dying when he was about twenty-six. He was the son of Amenhotep III and husband of the famous and glamorous Nefertiti, who is known from a beautiful sculptured head found at Amarna in 1912 and now in the Berlin museum. She may have been a second wife, or known under a foreign name.

The chief state god of Egypt during the period of the New Kingdom (1580–1100) was Amun, 'the hidden one', often identified with the sun god Re as Amun-Re. Symbolised by a ram, Amun-Re was usually represented as a man with a beard wearing a cap with two tall plumes, and holding a sceptre and a cross or ankh. The power of the priests of Amun at Thebes became so great that it provoked a reaction which sought to break their influence by substituting Aton for Amun as state deity. The movement probably began at Heliopolis, the home of sun-worship in Egypt.

On the death of Amenhotep III his son came to the throne. In statues and pictures he appears as a delicate man, perhaps a cripple, and with a deformed head. Although he died at the age of twenty-six he had six daughters, who are seen in pictures. About the fifth or sixth year of his reign he changed his name to Akh-en-Aton, or Ikhnaten, 'it is well with Aton', or 'he in whom Aton is satisfied'.

The name of the god Aton or Aten came from an old word for the sun, its brilliance and heat which reached all parts with its rays. Aton was the sun, especially the disc or globe of the sun with its rays which are depicted as reaching out with hands at the end of each. In early times Aton was represented as a man with a falcon's head bearing a great red disc adorned with a uraeus or cobra. Later the head and body disappeared and the disc remained with long fanlike rays. By identification of Aton with the sun-god Re, the reform movement of Akhenaton joined with the powerful ancient worship of the sun and gave it new interpretations.

Already in the reign of Amenhotep III Aton had been placed alongside Amun, and a hymn to them both anticipates the ideas of the later Hymn to Aton. Great temples were built for Amun, but also for Aton, in the capital Thebes, which was called 'the city of the brightest of Aton'. There may have been a co-regency of the two pharaohs, but whereas Amenhotep III was a diplomatic and conciliating ruler, his son became a radical reformer who opposed the cult and priests of Amun as obstacles to his plans. He built a new temple to Aton in Thebes and attacked Amun, but opposition was so great from the priests of Amun, who accused the royal ruler of heresy, that he not only abandoned the worship of Amun but decided to leave Thebes and build a new royal city further north.

This was on the eastern bank of the river Nile, where a barren site was made into a garden city of temples, palaces and small houses, all surrounded by gardens. The pharaoh called this place Akhet-Aton, 'the horizon of Aton'. Today it is known as Tell el-Amarna, from the tribe of the Beni Amran who lived in the region. Fourteen great steles, upright pillars, marked the boundaries of the new capital, and on them Akhenaton vowed never to go beyond 'this pure place'. He proposed to have tombs built for himself and Nefertiti in the eastern mountains, which reversed the ancient Egyptian custom of building tombs on the west bank of the Nile, where the sun went down with the dead (who were believed to be reborn with the rising sun).

Akhenaton had already attacked traditional art forms and expressions. The spoken language, which previously had been forbidden in official documents, was now adopted for them in spite of opposition. Paintings and reliefs were changed from classical formality to realistic expression, which appears in portraits of the pharaoh on pillars and temple walls, showing him enthroned or offering sacrifice. A simpler theology revealed that the sun shone impartially on all people and indicated the unity of all life, and magic was condemned as hindering moral progress. Religion, politics, literature and art were removed from the static Egyptian traditions, in attempts to broaden people's vision.

The great Hymn to Aton, attributed to Akhenaton, begins with the praise of Re who is in the Aton disc or globe, the great living Aton, lord of heaven and earth, king of Upper and Lower Egypt, who encircles all things and lives on truth. When Aton rises life begins and every land is filled with his beauty. As Re he reaches the end of the lands and subdues them for his son, the pharaoh. When he sets in the western horizon the land is in darkness like death, the lions come forth and creeping things that sting, but at daybreak Aton drives away the darkness, men go to their work, and beasts and plants flourish (see Psalm 104).

Aton, it continues, creates seed in man and nurses children in the wombs of women, like chicks in their shells. How manifold are the things which he has made, the only God, who has no other like him. In the lands of Syria, Nubia and Egypt men are set in their places and everyone has his food. Their languages are different, as are their natures and colours, and foreign people are different again, but Aton makes their life also. He is in the heart of Akhenaton, and there is no other that knows him, for he has been well versed in the divine plans. Everything is made to flourish for the king, the divine son who came forth from his body, 'the king of Upper and Lower Egypt, Akh-en-Aton, and the chief wife of the king, Nefert-iti, living and youthful for ever and ever.'

Akhenaton has been hailed as the first monotheist in history, before Moses or Zoroaster, but this is much disputed. In favour of his monotheism it is emphasised that he attacked the worship of other gods, especially Amun, and caused the names of other gods to be chiselled out of inscriptions all over the land. He abolished the human and divine representations of the god. He adopted the old symbol of the disc or globe, but gave it a new form by adding hands to its rays. He abolished the use of magical formulas in funerary inscriptions. He used natural expressions in art and language, and by comparative simplicity of worship he justified the claim that Aton was the only God.

On the other hand, all the ideas in the hymns to Aton can be paralleled in hymns to Re and Amun. Even if Aton is called the 'sole God', such a phrase was applied to many gods, and worshippers hailed the particular deities on which they were concentrating at the moment with praises that might later be applied to other gods.

It was Amun and his priests that were particularly attacked. The names and figures of Amun were erased systematically, whereas the name of Re was left untouched. There is little moral teaching in connexion with Aton, in contrast to the ethical monotheism of the later Hebrew prophets. Akhenaton praised beauty rather than righteousness, and in a typical Egyptian manner he considered himself to be a god. Akhenaton was the official interpreter of the god to the people, regarded as a god himself, son of Aton and son of Re, with priests of his own cult who worshipped him. He was more poetical and pantheistic than many, and he has been called a henotheist, a worshipper of one God in rituals while recognising that there are other deities.

It has been said that Akhenaton was centuries ahead of his time and he completely failed to attract the people. His courtiers aped the king, but the masses held to the traditional beliefs in popular gods and in funeral ceremonies. The worship of Aton was that of the sun by day, but it said little about the future life or the underworld, in which Egyptians had been interested since time immemorial. It did not replace the great god Osiris, with the mythology of his death and restoration to live and reign as king in the world beyond. The religion of Akhenaton was simple and beautiful, a refinement of much in old cults and a concentration upon unity, but it did not last beyond his time.

Akhenaton and Nefertiti personified the royal reform and they appeared in many pictures. But from the fifteenth year of the pharaoh's reign Nefertiti is omitted, and it has been speculated that she joined a party of reaction by withdrawing to the northern end of the capital, but it is not known how long she lived or where she died. In the seventeenth or eighteenth year of his reign Akhenaton died, but nobody knows where. Fragments of a great sarcophagus in a tomb that he was building for himself in the necropolis at Akhetaton bear images of the queen and reliefs of the globe of Aton sending forth its rays. Akhenaton therefore probably died and was buried at Amana, the city that he had sworn he would never leave.

The last surviving son of the previous pharaoh, Amenhotep III, was Tutankhaton, 'living image of Aton', who has become better known to the modern world than his artistic and reforming predecessor. In 1922 Lord Carnavon and Howard Carter discovered his magnificent tomb in the Valley of the Kings at

Thebes. Unlike most Egyptian royal tombs it had not been destroyed by grave-robbers, and the splendid furniture that it contained caused universal wonder. This is now in the state museum in Cairo, but exhibitions of the treasures have been made with loans in many cities of the world, as the gold of Tutankhamun.

Tutankhaton was only nine years of age when he succeeded to the throne and he died at the age of eighteen. But he was adopted by the army and the priests of Amun and married to a royal princess to confirm his position. His name was changed to Tutankh-Amun, he was crowned at the traditional capital of Thebes, and he was said to have spent his life 'making images of the gods'. The reforms of Akhenaton were overthrown and in its turn the name of Aton was erased from inscriptions. The capital of Akhetaton was ruined and it remained unknown until modern excavations revealed something of its glory and the religious beliefs and reforms of the monotheist or henotheist Akhenaton.

Solon

(c. 630–561 B.C.)

Solon of Athens was probably born between 630 and 625 B.C.; he died some time after 561. His father was Exekestides, and he belonged to a distinguished family, reputedly the descendants of the kings who, it was remembered, had ruled Athens in the remote past.

Our knowledge of early Greek history, before the fifth century B.C., is fragmentary. Nothing was recorded at the time, so that we depend largely on the often random information preserved by later writers. Solon, however, is the first Greek of historical importance (and so, by definition, the first European) who speaks to us direct. He lived at a time of economic turmoil, which threatened upheaval in the established political order; his own political views and programme he publicised by writing verse, the easiest way to circulate opinions in an age when the art of writing was a recent development, and writing materials either cumbersome or costly. Much of his verse has survived, quoted by later writers, and this gives us a fascinating insight into the problems which he tried to solve, and into the character of the man himself.

To understand him, we have to understand the situation in the Greek world in the sixth century B.C. After a prolonged period of isolation and impoverishment, the more progressive – and favourably placed – Greek cities had during the course of the eighth century B.C. resumed contact with the wealthier, older civilisation of the Near East, particularly the cities of Phoenicia and Syria. Trade between Greece and these cities had developed as a result, and the archaeological record begins to detect the influence of Near Eastern ideas in Greek art, together with the influx of expensive luxuries. Little is known for certain about this, but it seems that trade, from the Greek end, was controlled by the wealthier landowning families – and certainly organised for their benefit.

Solon himself, we are told, engaged in trade, and had travelled overseas to Egypt in pursuit of this. Many such families had grown greedy as a result, acquiring additional land, impoverishing former owners and forcing them either to leave home to settle overseas, or to work for their wealthier masters virtually (or even actually) as slaves. These aristocrats, by custom and tradition, dominated the state; they controlled the law, because they alone knew the law; and when the laws were first written down they obviously benefited the well-to-do. The ordinary inhabitants were practically powerless. At times their dissatisfaction led to outright rebellion, particularly in those cities, such as Corinth, which had taken the lead in developing overseas trade. Such rebellion had to be led, and the leadership emerged, inevitably, from within the aristocratic families themselves, in the person of ambitious individuals seeking to harness popular dissatisfaction to advance their own political authority, or motivated by genuine concern for the well-being of the poorer citizens. Such revolutions could be violent; the aristocrats would be expelled, and their land confiscated for redistribution among the poor.

Athens was slow to experience these pressures. There are signs of considerable prosperity in the eighth century B.C., and there may have been a fair degree of political harmony as a result. The outlying communities were assimilated into the political organisation, and their leading families retained their station in the enlarged state. There was plenty of agricultural land, supporting in particular olive groves; olive oil was a desirable product for the export trade.

In the seventh century it appears that this settled and prosperous existence was under threat, and a young aristocrat,

Cylon, made an abortive attempt at a revolution, with external support. This failed; the Athenian people rallied round their aristocratic leaders, particularly Megacles of the Alcmaeonid family, and the supporters of Cylon were trapped on the Acropolis. Here they sought refuge at the altar, but despite this they were seized by Megacles and put to death, an act of sacrilege which continued to reverberate in later Athenian history. Soon after this Athenian law was codified for the first time by Dracon. These laws were hard, 'written in blood', said the fourth-century politician Demades, and hence our term 'draconian' – but there is no accurate record of them, and the reform of the constitution attributed to him is the work of a fourth-century political pamphleteer, and totally anachronistic in detail.

Whether or not as a consequence of these laws, the economic situation at Athens grew worse. The aristocracy came to control more and more of the land, and used its products as objects of exchange to heighten their own standard of living. Athenian citizens who previously had been free men were taken into bondage; their land was taken over for the benefit of the wealthy, and they were obliged to make over a proportion of their crops each year to their masters. Marker posts were put up on the land, signifying this bondage. Failure to make due payment meant that they could be seized and sold into slavery.

The causes of this situation are uncertain. Later Greeks, such as Plutarch (writing in the second century A.D.), thought in terms of the developed societies in which they lived. The bondsmen were enslaved because of debt, and in later society debt meant they had borrowed money at interest (which in the Roman Empire could reach as high as 48 per cent) and had been unable to repay, perhaps because of crop failure. By Plutarch's time coined money had been the medium of exchange and borrowing for centuries, but it is now known that coined money had not developed – certainly not at Athens – before the sixth century B.C. The obligation, and indebtedness, was one of service; an obligation to work land originally belonging to themselves for the benefit of the rich who used their produce as a medium of exchange.

During the early sixth century the problem at Athens became serious; where Cylon had failed there were fresh rumblings of revolution, calling for the confiscation and redistribution of land. Some at least of the aristocrats were worried and called upon Solon to solve the problems. Plutarch tells us this was because he himself was not involved in extortion, nor had he shared in privation; but this, perhaps, is part of later interpretation, which saw Solon simply as a moderate. The real reason is more likely to be the arguments he put forward in his poetry. Enough survives to show what his attitude was. 'My mind within me grieves, seeing the most ancient land of Ionia oppressed.' He upbraided the rich for their greed, and the harm that this did to the city. He argued for justice and fairness; but he did not preach revolution or confiscation. 'I stood as a stout shield protecting both – I did not allow either side unjust victory.' The Athenian aristocracy was, in fact, dividing into faction politics; different groups were forming round various leading families, reflecting, almost certainly, geographical divisions. If one group were particularly aggressive and self-seeking, they could dominate Athenian affairs; Solon would be the candidate of the others.

He was elected to the archonship, the chief office under the aristocratic Athenian system. This he would hold for one year, which would be given his name (Athenian years being counted by the sequence of Archons, not by any numerical era). This was recorded, and can be translated into a precise date according to the Christian system: it was 594 B.C. By the fifth century Athenians believed this was also the year in which he produced his reforms as a solution to the city's difficulties, but this may be an assumption. The archonship and the reforms are more likely to be separate, the reforms coming at a later date. Solon was the 'mediator' between the wealthy and the poor; Plutarch tells us that he himself said (so this is based on his poetry) that he was reluctant to be involved in politics, fearing the greed of the rich and the arrogance of the poor.

His reforms were part economic, to put right the grievances and the injustices, and part political, to confirm the rights of Athenian citizens. He cancelled obligations, 'debts on the security of the person', whereby Athenians might be enslaved; those already enslaved he now set free. He removed the marker posts; 'I uprooted the marker posts which were set up everywhere', he says. He brought back from foreign lands people who had even forgotten their native dialect. The harsh laws of Dracon, which must have exacerbated the situation, were repealed.

The political reforms were aimed at giving Athenians a recognised role in the state, in accordance with their status. They were divided into four property classes, according to the amount of corn produced on their estates (a form of assessment which shows clearly that we are here still seeing the workings of a pre-monetary society). The three lower classes have traditional names. The lowest (who should be equated with the liberated bondsmen) were called 'thetes' (the word used to describe the labourers hired by a farmer in Hesiod's poem 'Works and Days').

Their lands – but notice that they are assumed to own land – produced less than two hundred measures (bushels) of corn a day. Next came the 'yoke fellows' or 'zeugites', peasants whose land produced between two and three hundred measures. Their class surely included the bulk of the Athenian population. Above them were the aristocracy; first the cavalry, 'hippeis', the term used in many ancient Indo-European societies to denote the most powerful. They produced three to five hundred measures. But above them Solon placed a supreme class, the 'five hundred measurers'; an invented term for a newly defined group.

Each group had its role in the state marked out. The richest fulfilled the financial offices of state, and so forth. Even the lowest class, however, had their rights guaranteed. They were to be members of the democratic citizen assembly, even if office was denied them; and they had the right, through their citizenship, to sit on the newly established jury courts. Other reforms are attributed, by the later authors, to Solon. Some are disputed by modern scholars, since they are not attested in Solon's own words, and may include further anachronisms. This does not matter. The great achievement of Solon is clear. He prevented oppression, redressed wrongs, tried to reconcile the different groups in the state, and prevented bloodshed and violent revolution. He was clearly not a revolutionary, and in many ways seems rather to have confirmed, or restored, ancient principles and institutions in the state which were withering under the pressures of economic growth. He himself emphasises that he gives the people 'as much power as was their traditional right': he did not hand over authority to those unsuited by their ancestry to exercise power. The political rights of the aristocrats he strengthened; but these were duties, not licence.

After his reforms he left Athens, we are told, for ten years, to give them an opportunity to work. In a sense, he failed. He had put right the economic evils, but his political system was too fragile to withstand the pressures, feuds and alliances of the powerful families. In the end, revolution, of a sort, was inevitable, and we are told that Solon lived to see it. His kinsman Peisistratos, who had been on excellent terms with Solon, seized power for himself in 561. Even so, Solon's principles and precepts had effect. There was no violence, and there were no mass expulsions of his rivals, or confiscation of land to divide amongst the poor. Peisistratos kept affairs under his control, and thus, on the basis of Solon's economic work, enabled the Athenian state to grow to new heights of prosperity. In the longer term, Solon was successful; above all he confirmed Athens as a state that did not normally go to extremes in political matters, and which was, essentially, a model of stability rather than endemic upheaval.

In this way Solon was the 'father of the Athenian democracy' (though it is unlikely that he would himself have appreciated this soubriquet). Further development of the constitution was necessary before it became really democratic; that was largely the work of Cleisthenes, after Peisistratos's son had been driven from power, and long after Solon's death. Perhaps, though, the greatest testimonial to Solon came more than two centuries after his own time; when the independence of the Athenian democracy had been overrun by the Macedonian military machine, first in the time of Philip, then again by Alexander. The Athenian leaders refought their political battles in the courts, especially the two orators Demosthenes the patriot, and his rival Aischines. In his great speech in his own defence Demosthenes eulogises the city and its institutions; and he quotes, at length, what must have been the most famous, and most powerful, of Solon's poems to make his point.

The achievement of Athens depended on its political system, and the reasonableness of its politicians, during most of its history. It is the triumph of the consensus; and that, in essence, is what Solon represents.

Asoka

(*Ruled* 269–232 B.C.)

Hailed as one of the six greatest rulers of history, Asoka was certainly one of the most benevolent and humane. He is important also in helping to date early Indian history, both by the contacts of his family with the Greeks and by the monuments which Asoka had made and of which a good number remain to this day.

The Greek warrior Alexander the Great defeated the Persian empire in 330 B.C. and continued his conquests further east into India. He reached the Indus river, fought his way down to the coast, turned west but died after a banquet in Babylon in 323. Alexander had intended to retain his Indian conquests and appointed governors for the regions, but Indian revolts made their position untenable. However, Greeks and Indians remained in contact and Greek envoys visited Indian courts, writing admiring accounts of Indian culture.

Soon after Alexander's invasion the Indian dynasty of the Mauryas was founded, led by Chandragupta, who ruled at Pataliputra, the modern Patna, in the state of Magadha or south Bihar. Chandragupta Maurya built a great palace and ruled firmly for twenty-four years, administering justice personally. According to a tradition of the Jain religion Chandragupta abdicated his throne and became a Jain monk, but this is uncertain. He was succeeded by his son Bindusara, of whom little is known except that he exchanged gifts with the Greek ruler of Syria, Antiochus I. Bindusara died in 272 and after a short interval he was succeeded by his son Asoka (pronounced Ashoka or Ashok).

Asoka ruled over the greatest Indian empire so far, from the Himalaya mountains down to the south, and his inscriptions have been found over a very wide area. These were edicts, rather like those of ancient Persia, inscribed on rocks and stone or metal pillars, but in contrast to the Persian they do not glorify conquests but give details of policy and instructions to the people. Many are still to be seen, and in the city of Delhi are an iron and a stone pillar bearing edicts of Asoka. The writing of the decrees is in the ancient Brahmi script; this, together with the memory of Asoka himself, had been forgotten in India for many centuries until the writing was deciphered in 1837 by James Prinsep, an English civil servant and scholar working in Bengal. With this decipherment the times and words of Asoka became known again.

Some Buddhist sources suggest that Asoka began as a tyrant, killing all his rivals, but a major rock edict puts it differently. When 'the Beloved of the Gods' had been consecrated eight years he made war on Kalinga, on the eastern coast of India. A hundred thousand people were killed, it says, and a hundred and fifty thousand deported. But at this slaughter and destruction Asoka 'felt remorse'. Families, men, women, servants and slaves had suffered violence, murder and separation from their loved ones; this weighed heavily on the king, and he had a complete change of heart.

Asoka now declared that victory should not be won by force of arms but by Dharma, a pregnant Indian word for virtue, truth, religion and justice, here perhaps best rendered as righteousness. The Beloved of the Gods considered that those who do wrong should be forgiven and all beings should be unharmed, self-controlled, calm in mind and gentle. By Dharma he had conciliated the forest tribes in his kingdom, and in all his frontiers up to the lands ruled by Antiochus and other Greeks. Even where his envoys had not gone people heard of his conduct according to

Dharma, so they would follow it.

The humane rules and actions of Asoka are revealed in other rock edicts. Medical services were provided of two kinds, for human beings and for animals. Medicinal herbs were planted, other useful roots and trees brought to where they did not grow before, wells dug by the roads and shade trees planted for the use of men and beasts. Another edict promoted the welfare of prisoners, releasing them if they had children or were sick or old.

Killing animals for human purposes, which was forbidden in the Jain and Buddhist religions, was also prohibited by Asokan edicts. Formerly in the royal kitchens thousands of animals had been killed daily for meat but now only three a day were killed, and this was to cease. Even for religious rituals, sacrificing animals to the gods would no longer be allowed. There was much evil in festivals, though some were approved, and the sound of the drum should become the sound of Dharma.

Several edicts teach religious toleration and that all sects should be honoured. To disparage another religion out of devotion to one's own would really harm one's own sect more seriously. But giving honour and presents to religious teachers was not as important as following their essential doctrines and seeking to increase the glory of Dharma.

It is clear that after his change of heart, if not before, Asoka had become a Buddhist. He taught respect for Hindu Brahmin priests, and gave help to other sects, and some of his teachings were common Indian ideas, while he regularly called himself the Beloved of the Gods. But Buddhism received his special help, and he tells of his deep respect for a faith in the Buddha, the Dharma and the Sangha, the threefold Buddhist creed of the Buddha, the Doctrine and the Order of monks. Some scholars think that Asoka became a Buddhist monk, while others doubt it, but he certainly did much to help the Buddhist cause. He praised the sermons of the Buddha on Dharma and enjoined monks and nuns, and lay men and women, to meditate upon them often.

After he had been consecrated ten years Asoka went to the tree of enlightenment, the Bo-Tree at Buddh-Gaya on the middle Ganges (see 'Buddha'), and he arranged tours to other sacred places. After twenty years he went to Lumbini where the Buddha had been born and caused a pillar to be erected and a stone enclosure to be made. Some of these monuments remain to this day.

Asoka told the order of monks and nuns to study special passages of scripture and keep a copy of his instructions in their meeting hall. On every day of monkish confession and penance the laity should also come to see that the rules were observed. Any monk or nun who caused a schism in the order was to be dressed in white garments and expelled. According to tradition, Asoka convened a council at Pataliputra to fix the canon of Buddhist scripture, and afterwards missions were sent throughout India and beyond.

Asoka was a missionary ruler, who has been compared with the Christian Emperor Constantine, though he was more humane. It is said that he sent one of his sons, Mahendra or Mahinda, to Ceylon (Sri Lanka), where the slab of rock under which this missionary slept is still shown. There was a demand in Sri Lanka for visible relics of the Buddha, so his collarbone was brought there and later one of his teeth, said still to be preserved in the Temple of the Tooth in the town of Kandy. Mahendra's sister, a nun, is said to have brought a branch of the tree under which the Buddha had been enlightened, the Bo-tree, and an ancient rambling tree in the ruins of a great monastery at Anuradhapura in Sri Lanka is claimed to be the oldest tree in the world.

Asoka's empire was difficult to hold together and in his last years he seems to have lost control over some of the provinces. Although Mauryan kings continued to rule for some fifty years after Asoka's death there was gradual disintegration. There were minor revolts in different parts of the kingdom during his lifetime, perhaps partly from the weakness of central control, but perhaps also from popular unrest at the strict regulations against festivals, 'displays of heavenly chariots, elephants, and balls of fire', as the edicts indicate.

In the twenty-ninth year of Asoka's reign his chief wife died, and he raised another wife to the chief position. It is said that the new wife was jealous of the king's devotion to the Bo-tree and pierced it with a poisonous thorn so that it withered, but Asoka nurtured the tree back to life. Perhaps the queen was less sympathetic to Buddhism and to Asoka's benevolent ideas and actions than her predecessor. Another story said that when Asoka was ill his new queen cured him, so that he promised to give her whatever she asked. She obtained permission to send a rival prince to suppress a revolt, and ordered the officials there to blind him. The blind prince wandered about singing till he reached the capital, where Asoka recognised his voice, and had the wicked queen burnt to death. Scholars regard this as a monkish legend, which may reveal the rivalry of the queen and the order.

Another legend says that Asoka gave all his treasure to a Buddhist monastery, so that when a monk came begging for alms Asoka had only half a mango left to give him. Again this is unlikely, but it may be that the king's power weakened in his later years and that there were struggles between rulers and monks. He died in the thirty-seventh year of his reign, about 232 B.C.

Asoka was a humanitarian who relaxed the stern rule of his predecessors. He supported the Jain and Buddhist ideal of 'not-killing', or non-violence (*ahimsa*), and substituted pilgrimages to holy places for the hunting expeditions in which so many monarchs have delighted, in India and elsewhere. But some of the populace may have preferred festivals and the chase to pilgrimages and visits to monasteries.

Asoka was not a complete pacifist. While he sought to conciliate the forest tribes he also warned them in an edict that he still had power and if they revolted they would be killed. He maintained an army, which was essential for the order of a large and disparate empire. It is said that he abolished torture but upheld the death penalty, simply allowing condemned men after trial three days to put their affairs in order and prepare themselves for the next world.

Asoka wrote that in the past there had been no officials to put the Dharma into practice, so he instituted 'officers of righteousness' to attend to everything relating to Dharma, investigate public affairs, and administer charities. This created a centralised system which lasted throughout his reign. Although he became a Buddhist, Asoka said little about specific Buddhist doctrines and was most concerned with its moral teachings, which led to peace and goodwill. He never mentioned the Buddhist doctrine of Nirvana, the state of indescribable peace, but he often spoke of heaven and the gods according to general Indian belief.

Asoka stands out above other rulers of India, and his successors are known by little more than their names. He has been called an idealist, but he was an active man who tried, sometimes perhaps imperiously, to put into practice the compassionate ideals of his religion. Today he is revered as the greatest ruler in Indian history, and a copy of one of his columns figures on the state seal of the republic of India. To his officers and city magistrates he said, in his edicts: 'You are in charge of many thousands of living beings. You should gain the affection of men. All men are my children, and just as I desire for my children that they should obtain welfare and happiness both in this world and the next, the same do I desire for all men.'

Tiberius Gracchus

(163–133 B.C.)

Tiberius Gracchus was the elder of two brothers whose attempt to solve the social and economic problems of the second century B.C. exposed the fragility of Rome's traditional political structure. His father, also Tiberius Sempronius Gracchus, was a member of the richest plebeian aristocracy. Consul in 177 (and again in 163) and censor in 169, he was described by Mommsen as 'the true model of a Roman aristocrat', proud, conservative, energetic and brave. The boy's mother, Cornelia, was the daughter of Publius Cornelius Scipio Africanus, Hannibal's conqueror. She was famous beyond Rome; Ptolemy VIII asked her to marry him and become queen of Egypt. She replied that she preferred to raise her three children (two sons and a daughter, who was to marry her cousin Scipio Aemilianus) as Roman citizens. Herself highly educated, influenced by the Greek culture which the Scipionic circle brought to Rome, she saw to it that her sons combined the high morality and public spirit that had actuated the best of Rome with the lucid rationalism of the Greeks. The result was of great consequence to the Republic.

The crisis which disturbed Roman life in the second half of the second century B.C. and to the attempted resolution of which both Tiberius and Caius Gracchus devoted themselves, had its origins in the growth of slavery and changing practices of land tenure. The Roman Republic had been created and made great by the exertions of independent peasant smallholders. All traditionalist Romans were agreed on this; Cato said 'it is from the farming class that the bravest men and sturdiest soldiers come'. They had provided the conscript legions which had conquered Italy for Rome and defeated Hannibal. However, the dislocation caused by the Punic Wars, the opening of Rome to world markets, and the growth in the number of citizens (from about 200,000 in 200 B.C. to well over 300,000 by the middle of the next century and almost 400,000 by its end) had brought about a great change. Smallholders were dispossessed and replaced by great landowners running huge estates with slave labour; an agricultural proletariat was created; many of the dispossessed flocked to the city.

The problem of Roman agriculture was serious because it was also a military and political problem. The disappearance of smallholders led inevitably to a professional army and to the emergence of an unemployed urban mob. The social class of Rome that stood between the comparatively few rich men and a mass of paupers and slaves was in danger of disappearance. No doubt this was an unavoidable consequence of the growth of empire. It was not however a course that seemed irreversible to men at the time. Tiberius Gracchus set himself to reverse it. In this intention he was at one with many of the best minds of the day: his father-in-law Appius Claudius (consul in 143), Publius Crassus Mucianus (the *pontifex maximus* or head of the state religion), and Quintus Metellus (the conqueror of Macedonia) were all in general agreement with his aims.

Tiberius Gracchus was invested with the tribunate on 10 December 134. His whole political career was to be crammed into the next twelve months. Though he was concerned almost entirely with the land question, his attempts to resolve this provoked a constitutional crisis which led directly to his death. In order to make the course of events clear, it is necessary first to outline the powers, responsibility and position of a tribune.

The office of tribune of the people had been created in the early days of the Republic. The ten tribunes were not magistrates and could not take the auspices; they possessed however a peculiar authority to intervene in the interest of the people against executive action proposed by the magistrates or senate. Their persons were inviolable. They could convene the popular assembly. They were empowered to initiate legislation, and, often of more importance, the veto of a single tribune was sufficient to prevent any law being passed. The office was restricted to plebeians, having been originally created to protect their interests against the patrician families who monopolised the magistracies in the early Republic. By the time of Gracchus, however, there was also a large plebeian aristocracy, to which indeed he belonged on his father's side. It was therefore possible for the son of a consul, like Gracchus, to become a tribune.

Immediately on entering office he proposed an agrarian law. He could do so with some confidence for, thanks to his family connexions, he had been able to discuss matters with many of the most experienced statesmen of the time, and had also assured himself of the support of the celebrated jurist Publius Mucius Scaevola, who had been elected consul for that same year, 133.

Gracchus's intention was simple. He believed that the land problem could be resolved if the leases on public lands which had been acquired after the second war with Carthage and subsequently let in large holdings could be cancelled, and the estates thus made available be let out again, subdivided into small farms. A large number of free peasant farmers would in this way replace the great landowners whose estates were worked by slave labour.

In outline at least this was a re-enactment of the Licinian-Sextian law of 368–7. That had fixed the amount of public land that any one man could lease and farm at 500 *iugera* (about 312 acres); it had also provided a precedent for the resumption of land held by custom but without prescriptive legal authority. Tiberius Gracchus was in fact more generous to the possessors than the old law had been, for in addition to the 500 *iugera* it permitted, he also proposed that if the landholder had two sons he might retain an additional 250 *iugera* for each, thus bringing the maximum holding of public land in the hands of one family up to 1,000 *iugera* (about 625 acres), a substantial farm. This estate was offered free of all dues, and in the original proposal at least he offered compensation for any improvements effected on the land resumed by the state.

The domain-land thus resumed was to be broken up into lots of 30 *iugera*, which were to be distributed partly to Roman citizens, partly to their Italian allies, as inalienable heritable leaseholds for which their occupiers would pay a rent to the state. A commission (*collegium*) of three men was to be established to handle the resumption and distribution, its members to be elected annually like other magistrates; they would also be required to decide what was domain land and what was properly private property. The commissioners were to be regarded as a permanent feature of the state machinery. This suggests that further measures were contemplated when the initial redistribution had been completed. These may have included the purchase by the state of other lands; they must certainly have included the continuing supervision of the public lands and the prevention of their reacquisition by great landowners. The absence of such a regulatory body had been one reason for the failure of the old Licinian-Sextian law.

These proposals were moderate and disarming in their intention. They were more generous in their treatment of the existing landholders than the previous law had been. Moreover, unlike an earlier reformer, Caius Flaminius (a tribune who gave his name to the Via Flaminia, the great north road from Rome, and to the Circus Flaminius in the city), who had had some public land taken from the Gauls in 232 divided into small freehold lots, Tiberius Gracchus's scheme envisaged the state as retaining ultimate ownership of the land. He did not propose a charitable gift, but a businesslike measure.

Nevertheless it aroused the opposition of the great landowners, who had long been accustomed to regard the public lands as their private property. When it was obvious that Tiberius would obtain a majority for his proposals in the popular assembly, they found another tribune, Marcus Octavius, to interpose his veto. Gracchus responded by suspending the business of the state and the administration of justice, and placing his tribune's seal on the public treasury. In effect this made it impossible for the business of government to be carried on.

The senatorial opposition could wait, however; Gracchus could not. He brought his proposal forward again; again his colleague vetoed it. The senate invited Gracchus to discuss the matter in the senate house, an offer which he seems, mistakenly, to have thought implied acceptance of the principle of redistribution. He was soon disillusioned.

At this point his former moderation deserted him. When Octavius continued his obstruction, Gracchus took the unprecedented and unconstitutional step of demanding that the assembly dismiss his colleague, on the grounds that a tribune who acted in opposition to the will of the people had forfeited all right to hold the office. The assembly carried the measure; Octavius was forcibly removed from the tribunes' bench, Gracchus's law was carried by the assembly, and the first allotment-commissioners were elected. The appointment of Tiberius, his brother Caius and his father-in-law Appius Claudius to this powerful position did nothing to appease his opponents in the senate. Their response was to deny the new commissioners supply to establish their office.

The rift between Gracchus and his opponents grew daily sharper and wider. For the moment his enemies were compelled to acquiesce in the measure, but they let it be known that Gracchus himself would suffer. One, Quintus Pompeius, announced that he would impeach Gracchus on the day his tribunate expired, when he would lose the protection the office gave him. Even now Gracchus believed his life to be in danger, and hardly dared to appear in public without an escorting mob. He realised he depended entirely on the continuing favour of the people. So when the king of the Attalids (a tribe in Asia Minor) died, bequeathing his kingdom and treasure to Rome, Gracchus proposed that this treasure should be distributed among the new landholders he was creating, to enable them to equip and stock their farms.

Then, in defiance of constitutional practice, he announced that he would offer himself for re-election for the following year, promising a number of other popular reforms, such as shortening the period of military service and abolishing the exclusive privilege of senators to act as jurymen in civil trials. His enemies interpreted his intentions as subversive of all constitutional practice. They hinted that Gracchus was aiming to make himself king. Nevertheless he was twice chosen by the elective assembly, but on each occasion another tribune interposed his veto to nullify the election. It was then said that Gracchus proposed to continue in office without further formality.

His opponents in the senate urged the consul Scaevola to have him put to death as a public enemy. When Scaevola refused, the ex-consul Publius Scipio Nasica called on his supporters to arm themselves. They pursued Gracchus to the slopes of the Capitol and beat him to death. Three hundred of his followers were also killed, and their bodies thrown in the Tiber. It was a day of unprecedented violence in the city, and inaugurated a century of party-strife that would spiral into civil war.

Tiberius Gracchus's agrarian legislation survived his death. It has been estimated that, as a result of his work, some 70,000 citizens became landowners. Yet, inasmuch as the economic forces which encouraged the concentration of land in the hands of comparatively few large landowners continued to operate, Gracchus had failed to effect any durable reform.

Of far greater significance was his political legacy. However personally admirable and idealistic he had been, he had, in F. R. Cowell's words (*Cicero and the Roman Republic*), 'served notice that the age-old supremacy of the Roman senate and the almost immemorial constitutional practice of the Republic were henceforward liable to be challenged by any ambitious man who was able to speak in the name of the Roman people'. Some of these men, like his brother Caius, would destroy themselves in their assault on the Establishment; their continuing attacks, and the measures found necessary to resist them, would in time destroy that Establishment itself and render the old Republican constitution unworkable.

Constantine the Great

(c. A.D. 288–337)

Of all the Roman emperors Constantine the Great may be considered to have influenced the course of European History most decisively, for it was he who made it possible for the pagan Empire of antiquity to evolve into a Christian Empire; yet it must also be said that his own attachment to Christianity was more ambiguous than early Christian historians admitted. He was certainly interested in religious affairs, to the point of himself delivering sermons to his court; but, though his edicts of toleration and his addresses to Church councils testify to his commitment to the promulgation of Christianity, he also continued not only to tolerate paganism but to honour its gods; he was not baptised into the Christian faith till he was on his deathbed.

Constantine was born in the late 280s in the Danube province of Moesia. His grandfather Claudius Gothicus, an Illyrian, whose victory over the Goths at Nissa in modern Serbia had reprieved the ancient world for at least a hundred years, was himself briefly emperor (268–70). Claudius's son, Flavius Valerius Constantius Chlorus, was a distinguished member of that new military nobility stemming from Illyria which in the second half of the third century brought new stability and energy to the Empire.

It is probable that Constantius Chlorus was not married to the boy's mother (the future Saint Helena) at the time of Constantine's birth. As the hereditary element was to be again important in determining the imperial succession, this caused some embarrassment; his biographer, the Christian apologist Eumenius, denied his illegitimacy. No doubt the Christian respect for the institution of marriage encouraged this dishonesty.

In 293 Constantius Chlorus was named Caesar by Diocletian. He was thus appointed to the second rank in the Empire to play his part in the curious and (as it turned out) impractical division of power and responsibility by means of which Diocletian hoped to secure an orderly transfer of the Empire. He was allocated the north-western provinces of Gaul and Britain as his sphere of responsibility. The young Constantine was however brought up in the eastern part of the Empire, mostly at Diocletian's court. The language spoken there was still Latin, and throughout his life

Constantine used that language more happily than Greek; his speeches and sermons in the Greek-speaking provinces were composed in Latin and translated into Greek by secretaries. He was still attached to the imperial court when persecution of Christianity again became public policy in 303. This may have caused some embarrassment, for it is believed that some members of his family were already Christian: the name of one of his half-sisters, Anastasia, is thought to show Christian influence. However, the persecutions revealed the strength of Christianity, and this may have had more influence on Constantine than any family attachments.

In 305 the two Augusti, Diocletian and Maximian, retired, Maximian doing so with extreme reluctance to comply with Diocletian's plans for the succession; they were replaced by their Caesars, Galerius and Constantius Chlorus. Two new Caesars were appointed, Maximinius Daia in the east and Severus in the west. Constantine was therefore passed over, though as one aim of Diocletian's scheme was to substitute merit, ability and experience for hereditary claims, this was not surprising. Indeed, since Constantius Chlorus had divorced Helena (whom he had married after Constantine's birth) in order to marry a stepdaughter of Maximian's, it would have been more surprising if Constantine had been named as Caesar.

Nevertheless his father now summoned him. Galerius was reluctant to let him go, and Constantine left Nicomedia secretly, even laming the horses of the imperial post after the first stage in order to delay any pursuit. It is impossible to determine the facts of this episode, but it seems clear that Constantine thought himself in danger at Galerius's court.

He joined Constantius Chlorus in Britain, and took part with him in a campaign against the Picts. On returning from this Constantius died at York (July 306). According to Diocletian's scheme, Galerius, as the surviving Augustus, should now have nominated a colleague and provided him with a Caesar. The army however had different ideas: they acclaimed Constantine as Augustus. His principal sponsor was Erocus, a chief of the Alemanni whom Constantius had recruited for his Pictish war. It was therefore a barbarian voice that made him emperor, though there is no reason to suppose that Erocus acted spontaneously.

The support of the army in Britain for Constantine was a fact which Galerius could not ignore. He therefore compromised, for it would have taken a dangerous war to impose his will. He accepted Constantine's elevation, but only as Caesar, and named Severus as his fellow-Augustus. Constantine's action soon inspired emulation, for Maxentius, son of Maximian, saw no reason why he should be denied what the son of another Augustus had obtained. The empire was therefore again embroiled in civil war. Maxentius, with the help of his father, who still regretted his unwilling abdication, soon dealt with Severus, who, hardly daring to use his troops because they were mostly Maximian's veterans, surrendered to the usurper, and was murdered. Galerius called on the retired Diocletian for help; Maximian, who had quarrelled with his son, was again persuaded to retire, and the Illyrian general Licinius, an old comrade of Galerius, was made Augustus. But Maximian regretted this abdication too, and now turned to Constantine. He bestowed on him his daughter Fausta and the title of Augustus. Yet the old man was now quite unbalanced. He soon quarrelled with the son-in-law he had elevated. When Constantine was campaigning against the Franks, Maximian yet again proclaimed himself Augustus. Constantine turned his army against his wife's turbulent father, drove him out of Arletum (Arles), pursued him to Massilia (Marseilles), and allowed him to choose his own manner of death.

Galerius died in 311. The Caesar Maximian Daia proclaimed himself Augustus, but in fact he and Licinius divided the eastern half of the Empire between them; even though Licinius had been named Augustus of the west, he had no authority there. Real power was divided between Constantine and Maxentius, each of whom had seized it for himself. Constantine marched against his brother-in-law, invaded Italy, and defeated him at the Milvian Bridge just outside Rome. This victory made him master of the Western Empire. It was commemorated by the Arch of Constantine, hastily built on the approach to the Colosseum from the fragments of an arch built in honour of Trajan. The inferior workmanship on Constantine's arch is evidence of the cultural decline of the Western Empire. The inscription to be read on the arch states that Constantine had defeated the tyrant 'by the inspiration of the divine' (*Instinctu divinitatis*). Yet the arch does not represent the emperor as a Christian, for it also shows sacrifices to Apollo, Mars and Diana. On the other hand, it was subsequently related that Constantine had had a vision before the battle in which the Cross appeared in the sky with the legend 'In this sign, conquer'. Another version says that he received instructions in a dream to have a Christian monogram painted on his soldiers' shields.

After the defeat of Maxentius, Constantine met Licinius at Milan to arrange the administration of the Empire. The principal result of this conference was the Edict of Milan, which granted toleration to the Christians and restored the property which they had forfeited during the years of persecution. Constantine had indeed anticipated the decree: in 313 he had already donated the Lateran to the Bishop of Rome; the Basilica Constantiana (now S. Giovanni in Laterano) was built there.

From this time his commitment to Christianity grew steadily. His views were stated in a series of letters, written between 313 and the early 320s, on the subject of the Donatist schism in Africa. He deplored the harshness of those Donatists who refused to readmit lapsed Christians to the Church. Such an attitude, Constantine insisted, could lead only to a divided Church, which was 'insane and futile'. Those who contributed to such division were agents of the Devil, acting contrary to the clemency of Christ.

Between 312 and 324 Constantine and Licinius shared power in the Empire, though their agreement was never easy. In 316 they fell out, and Licinius had to cede territory in the Balkans to his fellow Augustus. The tension between the two did not slacken, and in 324 Constantine attacked his colleague. Licinius was defeated at Adrianople and Chrysopolis. Constantine became sole emperor, a position he held till his death in 337.

The period of his single rule was marked by three achievements. The first was the progress of Christianity to the point where it became the official state religion. Paganism was not outlawed; indeed much of Constantine's legislation seemed contradictory. For instance, certain measures were taken against pagan priests and soothsayers; on the other hand, a law of 320 called for the recital of prayer 'in the manner of ancient observance' if the imperial palace or any public building should be struck by lightning. References to pagan gods appeared on Constantine's coinage for at least ten years after the Milvian Bridge. No attempt was made to interfere with traditional rural cults; classical culture continued to enjoy prestige and imperial encouragement.

Yet the trend was running in the other direction. In 325 the Council of Nicaea was summoned to try to resolve the disputes within the Christian Churches which had arisen principally because of what was to be known as the Arian heresy. The doubts about the nature of the Trinity advanced by Arius, Bishop of Alexandria, were not of a nature likely to appeal to Constantine's severe intelligence or his authoritarian temper. This did not prevent him from interfering personally. He addressed the opening meeting of the Council, and argued that the dispute concerned a matter of trivial detail. He was unsuccessful in convincing the subtle disputants.

His commitment to Christianity may be seen in the programme

of church building which he encouraged. In the late 320s his mother Helena visited Palestine as a pilgrim in search of the True Cross. She founded churches at the Mount of Olives and the Cave of the Nativity at Bethlehem. Constantine's mother-in-law, Eutropia, matched her with a foundation at Mamre where, as Constantine believed, Christ had shown himself to men in God's appearance to Abraham. Then, when the Holy Sepulchre was discovered, the emperor himself instructed the bishop of Jerusalem to build a basilica on the spot, and even suggested its design. In Constantinople too he was responsible for the building of the original church of Santa Sophia and the church of the Apostles; in Rome he endowed St Peter's, begun in the late 320s, with property and plate; he interested himself in churches built in Trier, Nicomedia, Antioch, Gaza, Alexandria and other cities. Augustus had boasted in his *Res Gestae* of having built more than a dozen temples in Rome itself. Constantine's contribution to the building of Christian churches was in no way inferior.

His second lasting achievement was to complete the administrative reorganisation begun by Diocletian. He made a more exact definition of the powers of his officials; and, most important, he separated the military and civil powers, depriving imperial prefects of the military powers they had possessed and restricting them to purely civil functions. He also reformed the military system. He reduced the importance and strength of frontier garrisons, and replaced them by local militias commanded by duces (dukes) and comites (counts). In their stead he based the defence of the Empire primarily on mobile field armies under the direct command of himself and his deputies. He initiated the development which would see cavalry replace infantry as his main military arm, though it was not till the lessons of the catastrophic defeat of the Roman armies by the Goths at Adrianople in 378 had been absorbed that this became the rule. The effectiveness of his reforms has been questioned. The Greek historian Zosimus, writing in the fifth century, considered that Constantine had destroyed the security of the Empire by these measures: 'he first sowed the seeds of the ruinous state of affairs that still endures'.

Constantine's third achievement was Constantinople itself. He was not of course the first emperor to abandon Rome; indeed it was a long time since the emperors had been accustomed to reside there. Milan and Nicomedia had both been the seat of government. Yet the establishment of Constantinople as the imperial capital was to be of crucial and lasting importance. It contributed to the decline of the West; Constantine did not visit Rome after 326 (when he offended Romans by his refusal to take part in a pagan procession). But it also made possible the long survival of the Roman Empire in the East.

Constantine's true character is impossible to determine. His life was written by Christian panegyrists. We do not know by what stages he moved from adherence to a syncretic solar cult to acceptance of the Christian religion. He was a powerful and ruthless ruler: during that visit to Rome in 326 he had his wife Fausta and his eldest son and deputy emperor Crispus put to death in Constantinople. But despite the faction which he had encouraged and from which he emerged, despite his different religious policy, he was essentially Diocletian's heir. He continued his work of re-establishing imperial authority by moving towards an autocratic rule. His adoption of Christianity pointed towards the basileus-hiereus (king and priest) role of the Byzantine Emperors. He founded the Second Rome as surely as Augustus had created the First Empire from the rubble of the Republic.

Obverse of a coin of Philip II of Macedon, showing the head of Zeus. The father of Alexander the Great had a high respect for Athenian culture – an outstanding representative of which was the philosopher Plato, seen in the mosaic giving his pupils a lesson in geometry.

Details from a mosaic at Pompeii showing Alexander the Great on horseback (*above*) fighting Darius III in his chariot (*below*). Alexander's armour is very similar to the actual armour discovered recently in the tomb of Philip II.

Queen Hatshepsut

(*fl.* 1500 B.C.)

In heaven Queen she is among the spheres,
  In earth she Mistress-like Makes all things pure,
Eternity in her oft change she bears,
  She beauty is, by her the fair endure.
• Time wears her not, she doth his chariot guide,
  Mortality below her orb is placed,
By her the virtue of the stars down slide,
  In her is Virtue's perfect image cast.

More than three thousand years separate those lines, written in fulsome praise of Queen Elizabeth I, from the equally fulsome ones proclaiming the ascension to the throne of Egypt of Queen Hatshepsut.

King of the North and South, Ka-Ma-Ra, Son of the Sun, Khnum-Amun-Hatshepsut. The Horus of Gold: bestower of years: Goddess of risings: Conqueror of all Lands: Lady of both Lands: Vivifier of hearts: Chief Spouse of Amun: the Mighty One.

Yet the two women, so far apart in region and time, have remarkable similarities of character. Unlike Elizabeth, Hatshepsut did not have to fight for her throne, but she seems to have been so forceful in personality that her father, Thothmose I of the XVIIIth Dynasty, made her unofficial co-ruler of his kingdom while she was only about fourteen. Soon afterwards he died. Hatshepsut was then married, according to custom, to her half-brother Thothmose II, and they were crowned together.

But there was no question, from the beginning, of who was to be the dominant partner. Thothmose II seems to have made little impression on history beyond fathering Hatshepsut's two daughters, Neferu-Ra and Meryt-Ra. When he died, thirteen years after the marriage, the difference to his kingdom must have been scarcely felt, since his wife had been virtually ruling all the time.

It was said by some (much later, for nobody would have ventured to say it publicly at the time) that Hatshepsut usurped the throne. There was a male heir-apparent, a slightly mysterious youth, also a Thothmose; he may just possibly have been a brother or half-brother of Hatshepsut, but more probably he was her husband's son by a slave mother. Although he was duly installed as Thothmose III, his youth allowed his dominant stepmother soon to exercise the real power of the State as co-regent. She also made it clear that by virtue of descent she was the true heiress of Egypt.

To Hatshepsut blood was of great importance. She herself was of pure descent on her mother's side, from Amen-hotep I, Aah-hetep II, and Queen Nefertari, but her father's mother, Senseneb, had been of inferior origin. Hatshepsut did not care to think of herself as the granddaughter of a commoner, and set about righting matters by organising no less than a miracle – or what her credulous people would believe to be a miracle.

She declared that a divine revelation had shown her that Amun, who had at first been the god of Thebes, then, with the rise of the Theban dynasty, principal god of all Egypt, had been her celestial father. Dissatisfied at the introduction of base blood into the veins of the Egyptian monarchy, he decided to restore the balance by siring a child of his own on Queen Aahmes. This product of an immaculate conception was Hatshepsut herself. To make things absolutely clear she had the whole story depicted in sculptures on her great temple of Deir el-Bahri.

They showed the god Amun, in the likeness of Thothmose I, appearing to Queen Aahmes 'in a cloud of glorious light and sweet perfumes'. Then came the birth of the heavenly daughter and the bestowal on her of several spiritual doubles, or Kas, by the gods. Formally presented to Amun and the great falcon-headed god Horus, she was baptised by them with water, told 'Thou art as pure as thy double', and given the emblems of monarchy.

As the young princess grows, she is shown travelling with her father to various shrines, symbolising her assuming ownership of her kingdom. Like Elizabeth Tudor, Hatshepsut believed in going on progresses which would keep her well in the eyes of her people. And her description of herself at the time is not at all unlike the image which the Virgin Queen liked to disseminate.

> Her Majesty was increased above all things, fair to behold above all things, her speech godlike, her form godlike ... and Her Majesty was a beautiful maiden.

Both queens were their own best publicity agents. Hatshepsut, however, went further than Elizabeth in having herself portrayed in some sculptures as a male figure, with a false beard, and referred to as 'he'. Thus, in one of the Deir el-Bahri carvings, she appears as a young man standing before her earthly father Thothmose, who addresses her:

> Come, O blessed one, whom I embrace in my arms, that thou mayest see thy orders fulfilled in the palace; thy Kas are most precious. Thou hast received the investiture of the double crown, thou art blest by thy magic power, thou art mighty by thy valour, thou art powerful in the two lands ...

He bids all at his court listen to her words, obey her commands – 'for whoever adores her, he shall live, but he who speaks evil of her shall die'.

At the time of her crowning as pharaoh she must have been a dazzling figure. If she was not strictly beautiful, she gave the impression of beauty, as did Elizabeth. Sculptured portraits of royalty were sometimes mere conventions, but more often were accurate likenesses: even as an enormous sphinx, Hatshepsut's face on top of the great lion-body is the face of her statues as a woman: she has high cheek-bones, long eyes, a shapely nose, full, smiling lips. It is a pleasing face, but one to respect, even fear, rather than admire for its charm. Allied to a blaze of jewels and golden ornament it must have been overpowering, leaving no doubt in the minds of her subjects that she was the true daughter of the Sun God.

Very soon in her reign she began the building of Deir el-Bahri. It was built into the cliffs on the eastern side of the Nile, almost appearing to grow out of them, and commanded a wide view of the Theban plain. Much of it still stands, a triumph of architecture, more Greek than Egyptian in feeling, its colonnades of white limestone rising, tier after tier, until they reach the living rock behind them. They are richly carved with figures, hieroglyphs and scenes defined in gold. An avenue led up to the entrance of the temple, guarded with sphinxes, and each sphinx was a portrait of Hatshepsut. All the great building was a detailed record of the queen-king, her living memorial, guardian of her immortality after death. Among its sculptures were representations of the obelisks she erected before the temple of Amun at Karnak, in honour of her celestial father.

> I sat in the palace and thought on him who created me, and my heart moved me to raise to him two obelisks of electrum [an alloy of gold and silver] whose peaks should pierce the heavens ... that my name may remain and live on in this temple for ever and ever.

The larger of these obelisks still stands, the most brilliant ornament even of Karnak.

As Elizabeth Tudor was to do, Hatshepsut reinforced her own strength with strong advisers, efficient men such as Hapu-Seneb, her vizier-priest, a sort of prime minister, and Neshi, her treasurer. One of the most notable was Senmut, the architect of Deir el-Bahri. He it was who designed the obelisks, and he seems to have been an intimate of the royal family, Hatshepsut's seal-bearer and head tutor to her two daughters. A monument describes him as 'the companion greatly beloved, keeper of the palace, keeper of the heart of the queen, making content the lady of both lands, making all things come to pass for the spirits of Her Majesty'. Elsewhere he was shown holding the elder child, Neferu-Ra, in his arms.

One of the highest officials in the land, he was of humble birth. His relationship with the queen can only be guessed. Yet, perhaps in his lifetime, the tomb he had built for himself near hers was attacked and partly destroyed, and the many portraits of him on the walls of Deir el-Bahri were defaced. He had offended someone very gravely.

The most famous carving on the great temple was the story of the expedition to Punt, or Puoni, made in the eighth year of Hatshepsut's reign. Punt is now thought to have been on the coast of Somaliland, north-east Africa, a region hardly known to the ancient Egyptians, though there was a legend that from it many gods had come into Egypt. It was known to be rich in the scented gum from which was made the incense burnt in honour of Amun, and it was (according to Hatshepsut) Amun's own prophecy that he would lead her ships, 'by land and water, on strange shores which join the harbours of incense to "a secret land, in truth a place of delight".'

Obedient to his wishes, the queen fitted out five huge galleys, stocked with things which could be used for barter. The voyage was completely successful. They reached the coast of Punt without accident, and there were the incense trees, the trees of myrrh, *commiphora*, and many other strange trees and plants quite new to the Egyptians, besides 'gold, ivory and curious beasts'. Because of the danger from prowling wild animals the natives lived in huts raised above the ground; they were a light-skinned people of friendly aspect and manners, happy to welcome the voyagers and trade with them. The expedition must, one feels, have been under some kind of divine protection.

Within two years the galleys were back in the harbour of Thebes, unloading their treasures, even more than Hatshepsut had hoped for, and, best of all, the myrrh trees for Deir el-Bahri, carefully packed and still living. Like Queen Elizabeth, the Egyptian queen thanked and praised the sailors who had gone venturing for her, then gave thanks to Amun for all he had done. Thebes was enriched by gold and ivory, rare animal skins, apes and leopards, all kinds of fine things. On the walls of her temple Hatshepsut ordered a carving to be executed of the ibis-headed god Thoth making an inventory of all the treasures.

Hatshepsut was good at enriching her country, and furthering its prosperity. Though shown in one wall-picture as a lion-headed goddess engaged in warfare, she seems not to have been interested in war. Under her Egypt prospered, as never before. Derelict buildings were repaired, new ones went up. The obelisks of Karnak were erected, to be a wonder of the world for thousands of years to come. She reopened the ancient mines of Sinai, from which came copper and turquoise. The district had a guardian, the goddess Hathor, one of whose titles was the Lady of Turquoise, and another Mistress of the Land of Punt. Perhaps Hatshepsut had a special devotion to her – after all, they were divinely related through Amun, and Hathor was the protectress of women and of the art of make-up. A temple to her was restored in Sinai, by Hatshepsut's command.

Throughout the queen's long reign, something like twenty years, her young relative Thothmose had been kept in the shadows. It would have been strange if he had not resented it. She died at last, and he came into his kingdom as a ruler so forceful and aggressive that he has been termed 'the Alexander the Great of Egyptian history'.

We do not know how Hatshepsut died, but there has been speculation that Thothmose had her murdered. After her death her name and images were ruthlessly defaced on the walls of Deir el-Bahri, perhaps so that Thothmose should be able to forget she ever existed. Happily, the work of destruction was not so complete that some of it could be repaired in modern times.

Her actual tomb escaped destruction, at the time. It was not within her temple, but on the opposite side of the mountain from it, and was discovered in 1904. Thieves had been there, and had taken everything but small valueless objects. A fine sarcophagus of red sandstone had held her body, but the mummy itself had gone, and has never been found, or at least identified. It would have been a richly clad one, adorned with gold and jewels worthy of her own splendour.

But the frank and touchingly proud eulogy she wrote of herself was inscribed on the walls of her temple, a joyous affirmation of her immortality.

> ... I bear the white crown, I am diademed with the red crown
> ... I rule over this land like the son of Isis, I am mighty like the
> son of Nu ... I shall be for ever like the star which changeth not.

Sappho

(612–post 550 B.C.)

> Come to me from Crete, to this holy temple, where is your
> pleasant grove of apple trees, and altars fragrant with
> frankincense; there, cold water babbles among apple branches,
> all the place is shaded with roses, sleep comes down from the
> trembling leaves. There is a meadow for horses, blossoming
> with spring flowers, and gentle breezes blow ... There,
> Cyprian goddess, take the nectar mixed in golden cups and
> pour a libation for the feast....

This fragmentary poem, copied on a potsherd in the third century
B.C. and discovered in the 1930s, is one of the earliest surviving
texts of Sappho. It invokes the goddess of Love, Aphrodite, and
invites her to join Sappho in a pleasance on her native island of
Lesbos or Mytilene, where a festival is taking place.

One might think that the green and fertile isle of Lesbos was
particularly rich in lovers' haunts. Longus, the second-century
author of the romance *Daphnis and Chloë* describes a similar
garden of love:

> In the spring there are roses, and lilies, the hyacinths, and both
> the forms of violets. In the summer poppies, pears, and all sorts
> of apples. And now in the autumn vines, and fig trees,
> pomegranates, oranges, lemons and the green myrtles. Into
> this garden, flocks of birds come every morning; some to feed,
> some to sing. For it is thick, green and shady; and watered all by
> three fountains; and if you took the wall away, you would think
> you saw a wood. As I went in there yesterday about noon, a boy
> appeared ... naked he was, alone he was ... therefore I ran at
> him as fast as I could, thinking to get him in my clutches.

In fact it was due to Sappho's poetry that such a location had
become the accepted setting for amorous dalliance. Sappho the
celebrant of Aphrodite and the pleasance was also the first poet of
personal passion in western literature. To understand how these

roles fit together requires a little exploration. The biographical tradition is not much help. Sappho was born in 612 B.C., the daughter of Scamandronymus and Cleis of the little seaside town of Eresos on Lesbos. She was born at a time of political turmoil, when power had been seized by Pittacus (later to be canonised as one of the Seven Sages of Greece) by his murder of the tyrant Melanchrus. He maintained his position by ruthless trimming, abandoning his political allies to support the seizure of power by a new tyrant, Myrsilus. Myrsilus exiled a number of aristocratic families, among them that of Sappho, who at six was already an orphan, though she had a brother Charaxus. They spent some years in exile in Sicily. A resistance against Myrsilus continued, whose members included Alcaeus, one of the aristocrats Pittacus had abandoned; and it is one of Alcaeus's poems which vividly brings to life the delight of this faction when Myrsilus died, about 590:

> Now is the time to get drunk,
> now is the time for vigorous drinking,
> since Myrsilus is dead.

Pittacus now assumed sole power as *aisymnetes* or 'moderator', and about this time Sappho was able to return from exile. This may have been as late as 586–5. Sappho was in her late twenties, married to one Cercylas and the mother of a daughter, named Cleis like her grandmother. Cleis was already old enough to be interested in clothes, for a fragmentary poem seems to condole with Cleis for Sappho's inability to procure her a gay headband from Sardis; such things are indeed obtainable in Mytilene, but the exile imposed by the sons of Cleanax (meaning Myrsilus) makes this impossible.

Back in Lesbos, in calmer times, Sappho's gift for poetry could flourish. Her work was admired by Alcaeus, a line of whose addresses her as 'violet-tressed, chaste, sweetly-smiling Sappho'. Rather later, the Athenian statesman Solon heard one of her songs performed, and instantly demanded that the singer teach it to him. When someone asked why he was so eager, Solon replied, 'So that I may die knowing it'.

As we have seen, the subjects of her poetry included aspects of the cult of Aphrodite, and several are direct prayers, including one of the two complete poems known to western literature before the recovery of papyri at the beginning of the twentieth century. Ambrose Philips wrote a pretty translation of one:

O Venus, beauty of the skies
To whom a thousand temples rise,
Gaily false in gentle smiles,
Full of love-perplexing wiles,
O goddess! from my heart remove
The wasting cares and pains of love ...

Any reconstruction of the occasions of her poetry can only be speculation, but most scholars would accept that Sappho was the leading figure of some kind of *thiasos* or sorority which cultivated Aphrodite through religious observance and song. A papyrus published in 1974 states that 'she educated in tranquil circumstances the upper-class girls not only of the island towns but also of Ionia; and was in such favour among the citizens that ...' (the rest of the text is unfortunately lost). In the next generation a 'pupil' of Sappho's, a Pamphylian woman called Damophila, is supposed to have had disciples of her own in this way.

Though one can only speculate, one is constrained to remember the maiden-songs of the contemporary Spartan poet Alcman and their enigmatic references to one Aenesimbrota, apparently the head of a kind of academy for elegant young ladies, among whom are the performers of these religious hymns. Another parallel might be what little we know of the sanctuary of Artemis at Brauron in Attica, where young girls retired, as to a junior nunnery for a period before the onset of puberty and readiness for marriage. They were known, mysteriously, as 'bears'; and they had certain religious duties in the Panathenaic Festival. Many states also contained peer-groups of adolescent males in more or less cloistered circumstances perhaps analogous to those of these girls. In these groups homosexual practices were pursued and encouraged.

Such parallels would go some way to explaining and providing an occasion for what is surely the most famous or notorious feature of Sappho's poetry, its repeated expression of erotic passion for a series of young girls. The very name of 'Lesbian' has become attached to the female homosexual tendency, though this usage is not found in ancient Greek, where the verb *lesbiazein*, to play the Lesbian, means 'to engage in fellatio'. (The modern use does not seem to be attested before 1896.) Sappho's attachment to her own sex was familiar in antiquity, but attracted no disapproval, any more than did male homosexuality. Nevertheless, by a paradox, the biographical tradition recorded that she ended her life by leaping from the promontory of Leucas (in the Ionian Islands; then a peninsula) through unrequited love for a ferryman called

Phaon. Ovid in his fictional 'Letter of Sappho to Phaon' struggled
to reconcile the paradox:

> No more the Lesbian dames my passion move,
> Once the dear objects of my tender love;
> All other loves are lost in only thine,
> Ah youth, ungrateful to a flame like mine!
>
> (translated by Alexander Pope)

Such fancies aside, Sappho repeatedly wrote of her love and
longing for 'her' girls who went away. It is natural to assume that
they went away to get married. The Greek word *nymphe* means
both 'nymph' and 'bride', and the paradise garden of poem 2 is the
traditional haunt of nymphs as well as the site of the celebrations
of her brides-to-be. Many of Sappho's poems are wedding songs,
and they bring the contemporary wedding in relation to a
legendary one just as the traditional wedding songs of Sparta
always recounted the wedding of Helen and Menelaus. One of
Sappho's poems included a long description of the wedding of
Hector and Andromache: though the part we have does not refer
to a contemporary situation, it is highly likely it was part of a
wedding song.

> The sweet music of the flute was mingled with the clash
> of castanets and the young women sang a sacred song
> so clearly that their wondrous echo reached the sky . . .
> and in the streets, the mingled scents of myrrh and cassia and
>   frankincense;
> with one voice the elder women shouted
> for joy and with a clear cry all the men called on Paean,
> the noble archer, the skilled lyre player, and they all sang
> in praise of Hector and Andromache who were like gods.
>
> (translated by Josephine Balmer)

And here Sappho is much smitten with the loss of one of her
girls:

> Frankly I wish I were dead. She was weeping
> as she took her leave from me
> and many times she told me this:
> 'Oh what sadness we have suffered, Sappho, for
> I'm leaving you against my will.'

The prayer to Aphrodite translated by Ambrose Philips continued with a plea to the goddess for the return of a so-far-
unrequited love (though Philips changed the feminine pronouns
in Aphrodite's reply to masculine ones):

Tho' now he shuns thy longing arms
He soon shall court thy slighted charms;
Tho' now thy off'rings he despise,
He soon to thee shall sacrifice.

But the poem on which interpreters of Sappho have built most
is the other poem preserved in the literary tradition, translated in
1760 by Francis Fawkes.

More happy than the gods is he,
Who, soft-reclining, sits by thee;
His ears thy pleasing tale beguiles,
His eyes thy sweetly-dimpled smiles.

This, this, alas! alarm'd my breast,
And robb'd me of my golden rest:
While gazing on thy charms I hung,
My voice died faltering on my tongue.

With subtle flames my bosom glows,
Quick through each vein the poison flows:
Dark, dimming mists my eyes surround;
My ears with hollow murmurs sound.

My limbs with dewy chillness freeze,
On my whole frame pale tremblings seize,
And, losing colour, sense, and breath,
I seem quite languishing in death.

Who is the man whom Sappho describes as (literally) 'equal to the
gods'? (Fawkes's translation begs an important question.) For
Ulrich von Wilamowitz he was the girl's bridegroom, and the
poem an analysis of Sappho's jealousy. In recent years George
Devereux has gone further in explaining Sappho's symptoms as
the classic expression of an anxiety attack of a type characteristic
of homosexuals. Mary Lefkowitz points out that the symptoms
may rather be those which in ancient poetry characterise the
madness of love, not jealousy; the man's 'godlikeness' is in his
superior power over the girl, or his power of resistance to the
charms which Sappho finds irresistible.

Argument over the precise interpretation of this striking poem
will continue. We might understand it better if we could be more
sure of the circumstances of its composition and performance, and
knew more of the nature of Sappho's relations with her *thiasos*. The
sands of Egypt may yet yield up papyri with the answers. All we
have is the poetry.

Olympias

(*d.* 316 B.C.)

Greek noble families had always used their womenfolk for political purposes. It was usual for political alliances between leading families to be cemented by matrimony, daughters being given in marriage purely to secure an advantage for their fathers. This seemed neither unusual, nor reprehensible. Marriage served a variety of interests but that of the woman involved was usually of no moment. Families – and their estates – had to be maintained, and women had a duty and a function in this. At the highest level this was true of the most powerful families, and dynastic marriages were part of the diplomatic arsenal, of which Philip II of Macedon took full advantage.

Philip's marriages were listed by the historian Satyrus, a younger contemporary of Aristotle who wrote a series of 'Great Lives'. His reliability has been doubted, and the account of Philip's marriages survives only as a quotation in the author Athenaeus, but recent studies have argued for the reliability of the information preserved, and especially the order of the marriages in which Satyrus presents them. It is emphasised by Athenaeus that the early marriages, at least, were contracted in the course of war; that is, they were part of the settlement enforced by Philip after victory to secure future peace and co-operation from the defeated enemy.

First he married Andata the Illyrian – presumably as part of the settlement with Bardylis after Philip's first great victory – and had by her a daughter Cynna. She was eventually married to Philip's nephew, Amyntas, son of Perdiccas, a potential successor. Then he married Phila, sister of the ruler of Elimaea, a marriage made to reassert the unity of the Macedonian state. Philip's third and fourth wives were Thessalian, and seem to represent different stages of his campaigning to incorporate that part of Greece into his kingdom. The first of them was Nikesipolis of Pherae, niece of the former ruler of that town, Jason, who had built up a substantial power for himself in the 370s, and had even proposed himself as the leader of a Greek crusade against Persia. She produced a daughter, Thessalonike, and seems to have died shortly afterwards. The second was Philinna of Larissa. She bore a son, Arrhidaeus. Her status is, perhaps, uncertain. One historian, Justin, calls her a dancing girl and prostitute, and if so there was no political significance in the liaison. Satyrus, however, ranks her as a full wife, and Arrhidaeus was acknowledged as a royal prince and brought up at court. By a strange twist of fate he was to become the successor of Alexander the Great.

The fifth wife was Olympias. She was the granddaughter of Alketas I, king of the Molossi, the principal tribal group in north-west Greece, the district known as Epirus. Her father was King Neoptolemus, who had died; she was the niece of the present king, Arybbas. The marriage took place perhaps eighteen months after the victory over Bardylis, in 357; dynastic marriages with Illyrian princesses were no longer necessary to support Philip's foreign policy, but an alliance with the Greek peoples on the other side of the Pindus mountains, themselves subject to constant Illyrian attack, was a sensible move. Epirus and Macedon were similar areas, and one district, Orestis, had gone over from Macedonia to Molossian control; it was now returned, perhaps as the dowry that Olympias brought with her. From Philip's point of view, as king of Macedon, this was a much more serious marriage.

At this time, Olympias is only a name, a young girl of no significance except as the daughter of a king. She was politically useful, both to Philip and to Arybbas. That she and Philip married as a result of young love is hinted at by Plutarch, but, though romantic, this seems less likely historically. Nevertheless, this marriage outlasted the political circumstances which caused it. Olympias was still recognised by Philip as his wife as late as 337, twenty years – and several more wives – after the marriage. She had a status much more significant than that of a political expediency, and her own character undoubtedly will have contributed to that.

In the following year she bore Philip his first son, Alexander. Even if, in an emergency, the immediate successor would have been Amyntas, Alexander – if he lived long enough – would be the successor in Philip's maturity, and undoubtedly this was Philip's own choice. Olympias's position therefore was enhanced, as the mother of the destined heir, and linked with that of Alexander. Subsequently she bore another child, a daughter called Cleopatra.

After this, the next wife was Meda, daughter of Cothelas king of the Getae, a tribe of eastern Thrace, and, in effect, given to Philip by her father, anxious to make a favourable peace. Meda was brought to Macedon, and, according to Satyrus, introduced to Olympias. The circumstances of this marriage make it unlikely that the senior queen would have regarded it as any threat to her own position. Even so, Plutarch suggests that after a while Philip had ceased to sleep with her, though the reason he gives is that the king feared her 'spells and enchantments'.

It was the final wife, Cleopatra, who supplanted Olympias. She was a Macedonian, not a foreigner. It was not, apparently, a marriage contracted for reasons of state. Satyrus tells us this was a marriage for love, Philip's own personal choice. Cleopatra was introduced to Olympias, as Meda had been, but this marriage could not possibly be tolerated by her. Cleopatra's uncle had intimated that the Macedonians should now hope for a legitimate heir to the throne. The position of Olympias and Alexander was undermined; their lives, almost certainly, threatened. They sought refuge with Alexander of Epirus. Soon Philip persuaded his son to return. Olympias did not.

After Philip was murdered, in the following year, suspicion naturally fell on Olympias of organising the plot. It was unnecessary; there were enough other Macedonians who had quarrelled with Philip; the murderer, Pausanias, had a personal (and sordid) grudge against Philip, and Olympias is unlikely to have been involved. Her hatred for Cleopatra was another matter, and she took her vengeance. The child Cleopatra had borne to Philip was slaughtered on its mother's lap; and Cleopatra was then forced to hang herself with her own belt. Despite this, Alexander allowed her remains to be buried with Philip, in a gold casket, but placed in the anteroom, not in the actual burial chamber of the tomb.

There can be no doubt that Alexander had been placed at grave risk when his mother was supplanted by Cleopatra, though Philip appears to have been anxious for a reconciliation. Equally, after Philip's death, Alexander's position continued to be insecure. Olympias was obviously dedicated to promoting his interest, and no doubt would have had no compunction in murdering Philip to secure this. This was known, and led to stories that she was in fact implicated in the assassination. The vengeance on Cleopatra was another matter. Alexander could not completely condone this, and his act of piety had to be to his father, whatever his mother may have thought of the burial arrangements.

When he set out on his campaign in the Near East, Olympias, of course, was left at home. The governor of Macedon was Antipater, one of Philip's generals, and a trusted supporter of Alexander. It was, clearly, an awkward situation. Despite the distances and difficulties, Alexander had an efficient secretariat, and there are numerous references to letters passing between him and Macedon, both to Olympias and Antipater. Details are sparse –

the historians are concerned more with the achievements of Alexander in the Near East – but it is clear that Olympias and Antipater quarrelled violently. It is not unlikely that Olympias exaggerated her position as the queen mother, and attempted to interfere with Antipater's administration. At the end, both were writing to Alexander accusing the other, and when, shortly before his death, Alexander sent orders to Antipater recalling him from his office, and summoning him to Babylon, it appeared to be a triumph for Olympias. Probably there were other reasons. Alexander is said to have expressed himself forcefully about his mother and her interference. 'She is charging too high a rent for accommodating me for ten months in her womb.'

While Alexander lived, Olympias's position and status were assured. After his death, all was confusion. No effective heir existed, and a struggle for power developed among Alexander's commanders. Alexander's widow, Roxane, or rather the child she was expecting, and Alexander's half-brother Arrhidaeus, the son of Philip and Philinna, were the actual inheritors of the kingdom. Arrhidaeus was medically incapable; the son of Roxane (who took his father's name) would remain incapable of ruling in his own name for at least eighteen years. Both would obviously be figureheads; the struggle would evolve round them, but would not be directed by them. Another factor was the sympathies to be expected from Alexander's soldiers, which were far from unified. The army itself was divided. The main force had been with Alexander at Babylon, but there was also the contingent of veterans sent home to Macedon, and there must have been other units, garrisons and so forth, stationed in many critical parts of the empire, or still engaged in the conduct of 'mopping-up' wars. Alexander's son, Alexander IV, had the advantage of being the child of the revered dead king, but he had, from the point of view of the ordinary Macedonian, that is, the infantry, the disadvantage of being the son of a foreign mother, not, in the real sense, a true Macedonian. Arrhidaeus was the son of Philip, whose reputation was surely as high as Alexander's, and though his mother was Thessalian, not Macedonian, Thessaly to all intents and purposes had been incorporated into the Macedonian state. The difference, compared with the Bactrian Roxane, was significant.

Arrhidaeus's status was further enhanced by renaming him; he now became Philip, emphasising the fact that he was Philip's son. Moreover, since the succession obviously passed at the moment of Alexander the Great's death, it was Philip Arrhidaeus who was the direct successor, rather than Alexander IV, born subsequently, and Philip's name alone is used for dating the regnal years in, for example, Egyptian documents. The joint kingship, even if little better than titular, was uneasy.

Effective power as regent was, at first, wielded by the Macedonian general Perdiccas; but this was disputed by his rivals, and, from Olympias's point of view, the danger was that he would depose (and assassinate) the legitimate kings to take the title for himself.

In the summer of 322 Perdiccas approached Antipater, who was still in charge of Macedon and, as one of Philip's generals, a man respected by the younger generation of Macedonian leaders. He asked for the hand of Antipater's daughter, Nicaea, in marriage. Such an alliance would have strengthened Perdiccas's position, and pointed him in the direction of monarchy; it posed a potential threat to the legitimate kings. Olympias had to prevent this and offered her own daughter, Cleopatra, instead, only to find she would have nothing to do with him. But the damage had been done. Antipater was offended, and the other Macedonian generals used the proposed marriage with Cleopatra as proof that Perdiccas was aiming at the kingship for himself. He died, assassinated by his own Macedonian officers, in the ensuing civil war. The remaining generals then disposed of Alexander's empire to their own advantage. Antipater was recognised as regent, since he belonged to an older generation, was respected by the rivals, and could be relied on to remain in Macedon without interfering too directly in the ambitions of the others.

This was a severe blow to Olympias, in view of the old enmity which existed between her and Antipater. It is noticeable – and to be expected, of course – that she was not taken into account at all in the wheeling and dealing that followed Alexander's death. If she had been in Macedon at the time, it was now prudent for her to return to her own family, in Epirus. It is in these confused and difficult circumstances that she now began to play an active role in politics, in her own right.

Antipater died in 319, bequeathing his position as regent to one of Alexander's generals, Polyperchon, who had not shown any personal ambition for himself. The choice was a strange one, and seemed particularly strange to Antipater's son, Cassander, but the regency was not a hereditary office, and Antipater probably did not want to undermine the legitimate monarchy. Cassander found an ally in Eurydice, a granddaughter of Philip II who had married Philip Arrhidaeus, and was showing herself to be as dominant as Olympias herself. Philip Arrhidaeus was persuaded to depose Polyperchon and give the regency instead to Cassander. Polyperchon fled to Epirus, and to Olympias, bringing with him her infant grandson, Alexander IV.

For Olympias, the situation and choice was very clear; if Cassander, the son of her old enemy Antipater, prevailed, Eurydice would use his success to promote, through her husband Philip Arrhidaeus, her own position, while Olympias's grandson, the other king, would be vulnerable in the extreme. Alternatively, Olympias had to support Polyperchon, and defeat Cassander and Eurydice, in order to ensure that the kingdom eventually passed to the young Alexander. Olympias gathered together an army, the troops of Polyperchon and a contingent from her homeland, and with it invaded Macedon in the summer of 317.

Olympias was acting with regal authority. In the previous year she had sent an order to Nicanor, who had been appointed by his brother Cassander as commander of the Macedonian garrison at Piraeus, the harbour of Athens, to hand over both the harbour and the fort to the Athenian people. Nicanor had hesitated, and in fact Athens was secured by Cassander. Now Cassander's base in Macedon itself was under threat. The crisis came swiftly. Eurydice heard of Olympias's preparations for invasion and sent urgent messages to Cassander, operating in southern Greece, to come to her aid. She gave gifts to the leading Macedonians, to keep them on her side. The army of Olympias and Polyperchon caught up with her at Euioia, in Macedonia, and the two forces drew up their battle lines. The mere presence of Olympias was decisive, for the Macedonians, mindful of her reputation, changed sides. Philip Arrhidaeus was captured immediately. Eurydice fled to Amphipolis, but was captured on the way.

'In this way', says the historian Diodorus, 'Olympias gained possession of the kings themselves, and, without the risk of battle, took over the kingdom. However, she did not use her good fortune in a humane fashion but, having cast Eurydice and her husband Philip into captivity, attempted to maltreat them. She walled them up in a narrow space, supplying them with the necessities of life only through a small opening. She treated them in this way for many days, so that the Macedonians, pitying the sufferers, began to turn against her. So she ordered Thracian soldiers to stab Philip to death.' It was a merciful end. Olympias's main hatred was directed towards Eurydice, her real rival, 'who expressed herself without restraint, claiming that the kingdom belonged to her rather than Olympias'. Olympias therefore 'sent her a sword, a noose and some hemlock, and ordered her to choose for herself the means by which she could commit suicide'. Eurydice prayed that a similar fate might befall Olympias. She laid out for burial the body of her husband as best she could, and then ended her own life by hanging herself with her own girdle. Even then Olympias's rage was unabated. She put Nicanor to death, and destroyed the tomb of another of Cassander's brothers, Iollas. Thus, she said, she avenged the death of Alexander, since she believed that Antipater had had him poisoned. She selected a hundred of Cassander's Macedonian supporters and had them slaughtered. The Macedonians hated her for her ruthlessness, and, says Diodorus, all of them remembered the words of Antipater, uttered as though in prophecy on his deathbed: 'never entrust the first position in the kingdom to a woman'.

As soon as he heard the news Cassander hurried back from southern Greece. Olympias appointed a general to fight Cassander, and herself withdrew to the coastal city of Pydna, taking with her the young Alexander, his mother Roxane, and her stepdaughter Thessalonike. Cassander put the city under siege. The Macedonians went over again to Cassander, and Polyperchon's troops deserted as he marched to Olympias's rescue. The siege lasted all winter, and those in Pydna were starving. Olympias's soldiers deserted, and were well received by Cassander. She tried to escape by sea, but when Cassander captured the ship, Olympias surrendered to him, having exacted a guarantee of her personal safety. Despite this, he now had her put on trial by the relatives of those she had killed, and she was condemned to death. Cassander tried to arrange for her to escape to Athens, but she refused to go. She appealed to the Macedonians, using her prestige and rank and reputation for the last time. Cassander, afraid she would be successful, sent two hundred soldiers to kill her, but they, even then overawed by her, withdrew with their task unfulfilled. It was left to the relatives of her victims to murder her.

Such, says Diodorus, was the end of Olympias, who had attained to the highest dignity of the women of her own time, wife of Philip, the mightiest of those who in his time had ruled in Europe, and mother of Alexander the Great.

Aspasia of Miletus

(*fl.* 440 B.C.)

Ancient Greek cities depended on the strength of their armies, and at a time when all the prosperous Greek cities employed the same tactics, clothed their soldiers in the same type of body armour, and equipped them with identical weapons, this meant numbers.

The principal role of women in the Greek cities was, therefore, to ensure the maintenance of the population. This had to be within the established social structure, which grew up to serve this essential function. The community was made up, not so much of individuals, but of families, and the family was not the so-called 'nuclear family' with which we are familiar – father, mother and children – but all living relatives – grandparents, parents, cousins, nephews and nieces as well as sons and daughters. Each family owned land, and social organisation was directed towards the preservation of the family as a unit, both in human and economic terms. The ancestors were buried on the family lands, in the family burial plots, and continued to be part of the family, receiving offerings from the living members. The family was organised as a religious unit as well.

As a result there were, therefore, complex rules of marriage and inheritance. These varied from city to city, but all served the same purpose, the maintenance of the social system on which the city depended. At Athens, even in the classical period, if no son survived the death of a father, and property therefore passed to a daughter, she was obliged to marry her nearest male relative to ensure that the property stayed with the family; and if the nearest male relative was already married, he was obliged to divorce in order to marry the heiress.

Marriages, therefore, were contracted for the obligations of political and social circumstances, not for personal love or choice. This does not mean they were invariably cold and unhappy; a large number of elaborate gravestones which have survived from Athens, particularly from the fourth century B.C., depict scenes of tenderness and affection where a bereaved husband says farewell to his wife, and though there is an element of ostentation, the general impression is one of sincerity. On the other hand, Athenian women were forced by convention to live a restricted life. Their responsibilities centred on the home and their children. They went out of doors mainly for religious functions, and normally under close supervision. Such restrictions, of course, applied particularly to the well-to-do. The poorer farmers could not afford to segregate their womenfolk in this way (the poor man's ox, said Aristotle, is his wife).

Aspasia has to be understood in this context. Wives had a very restricted social existence. The normal private social gathering was the male dinner party. Athenian houses (like those in other Greek cities) of all but the humblest type had special rooms for these parties, the *androcs*, or 'men's room'. These rooms were arranged with couches placed round the walls, with low tables in front of them. The diners reclined on these couches, rather than sat up to table. There are innumerable representations of dinner-party scenes painted on the vases produced by the potters of fifth-century Athens for use in these feasts, and there are also literary descriptions. The most famous of these is the dialogue called the *Symposium* or 'drinking party' written by Plato. At these parties, which often lasted all night, and frequently degenerated into drinking bouts, it is clear that the respectable women – the wives and daughters of the household – were totally excluded, banished to the 'women's quarters'. At times, the men might exclude all women – they do so, for example, in Plato's *Symposium* so that they are not distracted from the pleasures of philosophy: but normally the pleasures were of a less esoteric nature, and women were essential.

Such women, of course, were not at all respectable. Their activities are also depicted on countless Athenian vases of the fifth century. They were entertainers; trained as musicians, they are shown playing the flute, accompanying the songs of the men (we have the words, if not the music; many are political – but not all of them). They also, inevitably, provided the men with sexual solaces that were, perhaps, not expected from their wives. In origin such girls were slaves, bought from overseas, and hired out by their owners for the evening. There was, however, an inter-mediate status between the flute girl and the respectable wife; the bought companion who became the permanent mistress. The purchase does not imply slavery. Unmarried women were essentially subordinate in law to a *kyrios* – the word means master, but the *kyrios* was invariably a male member of her own family, and normally her father. For a financial consideration the *kyrios* would transfer her into the possession of another man. She did not have the status of a wife, and in this respect was probably freer; and certainly, her man would have chosen her for her own sake, and for company, not for family or dynastic purposes. Aspasia was such a woman; her distinction was that she became the mistress of the leading Athenian of her day, the statesman Pericles.

She was not Athenian, but came from the east Greek city of Miletus. Her father's name was Axiochos, which suggests that she was a free-born Greek. Many inhabitants of Miletus were not Greek but Carians, the neighbouring non-Greek people, and there is a version of her origin which says she was a Carian prisoner-of-war, but this is a confusion.

The best account of her is given by Plutarch in his biography of

Pericles; but, as always with Plutarch's writings, we cannot rely completely on his version, which may be distorted by his distance from the people whose lives he is writing (Pericles and Aspasia lived almost six hundred years before Plutarch), and his lack of direct knowledge of the circumstances. He is, of course, dependent on earlier written accounts which are now lost, so that we cannot test their reliability. As the dominant politician in Athens, Pericles was subject to the jokes and innuendoes contained in the comedies performed as part of the religious dramatic festivals at Athens; and, as we have seen, one favourite way of attacking Pericles was to attack those associated with him. It is these 'comic' statements, made to hurt rather than with a view to truth, which can distort the later historians, and though Plutarch tells us when he is copying a statement made by one of the comic playwrights, there may well be other occasions when he is ignorant of the real origin for the statement he gives.

Aspasia's relationship with Pericles seems to have begun in the 440s (we cannot be more precise) when Pericles was in his late forties or early fifties. Pericles had married, probably in the late 460s, a relative whose name we do not know. By her he had had two sons. He divorced her in about 455 B.C., 'having found each other incompatible', according to Plutarch, who goes on to say that he legally handed her over to another man with her own consent, and himself lived with Aspasia 'whom he loved dearly'. But Plutarch is muddled – he obviously thought that Pericles left his wife because of Aspasia. The 'other man' is, in fact, Hipponikos, whom Plutarch thinks was the first husband of Pericles's wife – but her children by Hipponikos were born after those by Pericles and the divorce must have antedated Aspasia's arrival by many years.

Aspasia's attraction was not merely her beauty. According to some writers, says Plutarch, Pericles was attracted to her because of her political acumen. He adds that the philosopher Socrates visited her, and brought his followers to listen to her, despite the fact that at that time she made her living by running a brothel. Plato in the *Menexenus* in fact attributes to Socrates a statement that she taught oratory, and that Pericles himself learnt this art from her – she even wrote speeches for him. Socrates then recites a speech which she wrote, but Plato elsewhere uses the literary device of manufacturing his own compositions in the style of others and it is hardly likely that here we have Aspasia's own words. Nevertheless, it demonstrates the reputation enjoyed by Aspasia in the following century.

Elsewhere, the reputation is much lower, particularly amongst the writers of comedy. Cratinus, who also made bitter attacks on Pericles himself, calls her, bluntly, a prostitute, a 'shameless bitch'. In a play by Eupolis called *The Villages*, Pericles appears as a character, asking whether his son is alive, and is answered by Myronides (a general who died earlier: the feeling here is that these characters are ghosts reappearing after death, so this is not contemporary with Pericles's own lifetime). Myronides replies that the son is alive, and would have had citizen status long ago if it had not been for the fact that his mother was a whore.

Plutarch probably takes all this too seriously; the aim is as much to belittle Pericles as to ridicule and insult Aspasia, and for the Athenians of the fifth century this was all fair game. Similarly, the accusation that she induced Pericles to pass a decree against the island of Samos (which had, in fact, revolted against Athenian domination) because Samos was embroiled in a quarrel with her own city, Miletus, is an attack on Pericles. The quarrel with Miletus was real, but the attack on Samos was made because of the anti-Athenian government which then prevailed there.

Her real status may well have been different. In 451 B.C. the Athenians passed a law, on the proposal of Pericles, that only people both of whose parents were Athenian would be entitled to Athenian citizenship. Previously Athenians had been able to marry non-Athenian women. This was particularly noticeable amongst leading Athenian families (which of course is where we have the most information). Pericles was himself descended on his mother's side from Agariste, daughter of the tyrant of Sikyon. Themistocles's mother was Thracian, and the family of Cimon, Pericles's rival until he died in 449, having landed property in Thrace, also often took Thracian women as wives. Pericles's new law may, in fact, have been aimed at Cimon's family, rather than resulting from any need for a general tightening up of Athenian citizen laws. (The figures for disqualified citizens given by Plutarch are suspiciously large.) At this time he had not yet met Aspasia. The irony is that when he did, he was prevented by his own law from legally marrying her, in the sense that his children by her could not hold Athenian citizenship. It is this element of technical, rather than moral, illegitimacy in the relationship that led to the comic poets' distortions.

At the end of his life, weakened by the plague and on the point of death, Pericles asked the Athenian people that his son by Aspasia, the younger Pericles, should be given citizenship. As a favour to the dying man, this was granted, but it does also suggest that, although not legitimately married to Pericles, Aspasia was by status a free woman, not a bought slave; a mistress, rather than a mere concubine.

Plutarch emphasises Pericles's love for her – every day, he says, when Pericles left for the meeting place in Athens, the Agora, and when he returned he would greet Aspasia with a kiss (that this was considered worthy of note says much about the usual relationships between Athenian husbands and wives). When she was prosecuted, Plutarch says, Pericles begged her off by bursting into floods of tears during her trial.

So, at the end, she remains an enigma; one of the most famous women of the fifth century B.C., but – as is inevitable in Greek society of the time, particularly Athenian – famous only because of her association with the great man who was her lover.

Artemisia of Halicarnassus

(*fl.* 480 B.C.)

Artemisia, queen of Halicarnassus (the present-day Bodrum in Turkey) in the fifth century B.C., could reasonably have claimed to be the first woman admiral. Though she did not win a victory, she probably saved a fleet from total annihilation. Ever a realist, she could see when a cause was lost. Unlike many of her male colleagues, she had no particular wish to die a hero's death. If prudence suggested battle were best avoided, she would eloquently counsel disengagement.

We have the word of her brother, a minor poet, that she was tall and beautiful. We have the evidence of her near-contemporary, the historian Herodotus, that she was far-sighted, forthright, and occasionally devious. Hippolyte has become a legend as queen of the Amazons. Artemisia's name enjoys no similar distinction, which is a pity. Despite her reluctance to succumb to the fool's enticement of glory, she was courageous. Despite her ruthlessness, she was capable of love. Despite her loyalty to her sovereign emperor, King Xerxes, she was honoured by her enemies. Unquestionably, she deserves greater recognition.

During her reign, two superpowers confronted each other from either side of the Aegean. One was Greece, a collection of loosely federated states given military muscle by the Spartans and naval punch by the Athenians. The other was Persia: an empire that stretched from the Indus to Asia Minor, from Syria to southern

Egypt. Artemisia's fragment of this realm, which covered nearly two million square miles, lay on the coast of Asia Minor near Samos and Rhodes.

Racially, Artemisia and her subjects had more in common with the Greeks than with the Persians. Most of them were settlers who had sailed across from the Peloponnese. Her father, Lygdamis, was descended from these colonists, and her mother came from Crete. When Lygdamis died, he named her as his successor. It is a sign of her wilful – tempestuous, perhaps – character, that neither of her two brothers disputed her inheritance.

In 480 B.C. Xerxes, having stretched himself to the limits in the east, turned his attention to Greece. He assembled an army that, when camp followers, women, and other non-combatants were taken into consideration, numbered about five million. His navy was on an equally imposing scale. Among the ships were five triremes contributed by Artemisia. A trireme might be described as the capital ship of its day. A large sail provided some of the power, though its real thrust and nearly all its manoeuvrability came from three banks of oars. The Greek version had a powerful ram jutting out from its bows. The Persian vessels were intended for boarding tactics and hand-to-hand combat.

By the time Xerxes had planned his invasion, Artemisia was approaching middle age and had a grown-up son. In any case, being a woman, she would have been exempt from military service. But this was not her attitude. If the Halicarnassians were going to be involved in a war, she, unquestionably, would lead them.

Xerxes's preparations for the campaign were painfully slow. Assembling such a multitude from all parts of the empire took time. So did the building of a bridge of boats across the Hellespont (the Dardanelles) to make the journey easier, and so did his almost obsessive concern with inspecting his soldiers and reviewing his fleet. Whether the sight of their leader engendered confidence in his men is doubtful; but the sheer immensity of this display of military might will have improved his own. When one considers that many of his warriors had Greek ancestors, and that the only generals with any real authority were Persians, it is not surprising that desertions were frequent. Nor is it remarkable that the progress of Xerxes, his soldiers and his sailors, was reported to the enemy – yard almost by yard.

Consequently, the Greeks had ample time to make preparations. The army's advance was held up for several days at the pass of Thermopylae, where three hundred Spartans held out against impossible odds. They were overwhelmed eventually, after their leader, King Leonidas, had been killed. Nevertheless, Xerxes's initial optimism had received its first setback.

At sea, events were not faring very much better. The Persian navy's first target was Euboea, an island to the north of Athens. The idea was to split the force into two. One half was to remain off Artemisium on the south-eastern corner. The other was to sail round Euboea in an anti-clockwise direction. If everything went well, the Greek ships would be crushed between the two. Fate was clearly on the side of the enemy. The two hundred ships that should have encircled the island ran into a storm and were lost without exception. This calamity reduced the Persian strength to approximately that of the Greeks. In the battle that began at noon three days later, there were heavy losses on both sides. As Herodotus describes it, '. . . the armament of Xerxes injured itself by its own greatness, the vessels falling into disorder, and oft-times running foul of one another; yet still they did not give way, but made a stout fight. . . . The Greeks therefore suffered much, both in ships and men; but the barbarians experienced a far larger loss of each.'

So far, Artemisia's contribution to the Persian cause seems to have attracted little attention. Had she been fighting for the Greeks, it would doubtless have been better recorded, for few things escaped the pens of the zealous Athenian scribes. However, we have her own word for it that 'I was not the least brave of those who fought at Euboea'. As she survived, we must assume that she was with the squadron off Artemisium. She made the statement in front of Xerxes; but since the emperor was elsewhere at the time of the engagement, he could neither deny nor agree with it. Probably she was speaking the truth, for her five ships were regarded as among the best in the fleet.

After the action, the two navies separated. The army, now recovered from its mauling at Thermoplyae, took Athens and set the city ablaze. At sea, the warships had yet to gain control. The point at issue at this juncture was: should they be committed to another battle, this time off Salamis, an island just to the west of Piraeus? Xerxes, despot though he was, liked to put important matters before his commanders and to abide by a majority decision.

Resplendent on a throne, with his kings, his solitary queen-admiral, his generals and his captains seated before him in strict order of precedence, he sought their opinions. Sensing his mood, and fearful for their futures if they said the wrong thing, all but one insisted that a naval engagement should take place. The exception was Artemisia. 'Spare your ships', she told him. The Greeks had already shown themselves to be better seamen; and, in any case, there was no need for such action. All that was required could be done by the soldiers. But 'if you are hasty to fight', she said, 'I tremble lest the defeat of your sea force bring harm likewise to your land army'. Her argument was supported by facts that showed how good her intelligence sources were, and how well she understood the situation within the Greek forces. Nevertheless, there was an awed silence. Such outspokenness, it was generally thought, could cost the queen her life.

In the vote that followed, she was the only abstainer. The matter was settled; but, as Xerxes made plain, he was by no means displeased with Artemisia's candour. There was much to be said for her argument. However, all the others wanted a battle, and a battle they should have.

The outcome was a fiasco. As Artemisia had said, the Greeks demonstrated their superiority in seamanship, and also their skill in naval architecture. The rams inflicted a terrible slaughter on the Persian vessels, made the worse by the fact that, unlike the opposition, none of their crews could swim. Artemisia was fortunate. The Greeks' attitude to the role of a woman in warfare was curiously ambivalent. After all, their own goddess Minerva included armed combat among her other responsibilities. Furthermore, at the height of this particular battle, the spirit of a woman is said to have appeared before the Attic fleet, urging the captains, from one end of the line to the other, to greater efforts.

Nevertheless, apparently resentful that Artemisia should be allowed to participate, a prize of 10,000 drachmas had been offered for her capture. At one point, it seemed probable that it would be won. Her trireme, well out in front, was heading back for the main body of the fleet with a Greek ship in hot pursuit. Suddenly, her path was blocked by the flagship of Damasithymus the Calyndian king. There could be no question of turning back. With single-minded resolution she rammed the petty princeling's boat, dispatching it and all aboard it to the bottom of the sea. The Greek captain, assuming that he was mistaken and that Artemisia's vessel must be one of his own, hauled off and went in search of other prey. The Persians, for their part, concluded that the sunken ship must be Greek, and applauded Artemisia's courage and initiative. Xerxes was particularly impressed. As he said afterwards: 'All my men fought like women; all my women like men.'

The survivors of the thrashed Persian fleet eventually reassembled. Once again, Xerxes wanted another opinion; and on this occasion, he did not summon all his other commanders. Artemisia's verdict would be enough. Should he, he wondered, follow the advice of his best general, Mardonius, and make one more attempt, or should he abandon the campaign? His counsellor was quick in her reply. Give Mardonius 300,000 troops, she said, and let him do what he likes. As for the rest of us, let us go home.

It was an ignominious retreat for Xerxes, though he fared better than Mardonius and his men, who were all wiped out. The bridge across the Hellespont had been destroyed by a storm. He who had so recently crossed over in triumph made the return trip in a small fishing-boat. Artemisia travelled in better style, taking with her some of the emperor's children whom he had asked her to escort to Ephesus.

It would be pleasing to report that Artemisia settled down into a comfortable old age, telling the tales of battles fought long ago. But this was not to be; she made the mistake of falling in love. Not surprisingly, the young man in question could find no attraction in her now sadly faded beauty. For the queen who had slept with kings and princes, this was too much. The heart that could not return her passion might survive, but the eyes that could not communicate desire must be robbed of their sight. As an act of compassion, perhaps, she waited until the youth was asleep before carrying out the deed. Afterwards, resigned at last to the ravages of age, she travelled to an island many miles away, where she threw herself off a promontory into the sea.

Strangely enough, it was her old enemies, the Greeks, who honoured her. The Spartans built a memorial to her, Aristophanes wrote a play about her, and a small town in the Peloponnese is named after her.

Cleopatra

(69–30 B.C.)

In legend, she is a beautiful seductress, wanton, lustful and treacherous – 'the serpent of old Nile'. Shakespeare, dramatising her life and loves fifteen hundred years after her death, gave her this image through the words of companions of Mark Antony who resented her influence over him. But Shakespeare saw too the historical truth about Cleopatra – that she was a great queen, a patriot, and a woman of enormous character and courage.

She was born in 69 B.C., the last of the Greek Ptolemaic dynasty.

It had deteriorated since the fourth century, when Ptolemy I had chosen rich, fertile Egypt to rule over. His son Ptolemy II turned it into the greatest naval power in the eastern Mediterranean, created a magnificent, glittering court in his seaport city of Alexandria, and added thousands of volumes to the immense library his father had founded.

The Ptolemies intermarried, as was the dynastic custom. Perhaps the stock produced by the union of brother and sister suffered from lack of fresh blood, for by the time of Ptolemy IV the family had become corrupt, weak and cruel, their kingdom in decline, while the Roman Empire rose in power and threat. Ptolemy XI, who had been an adherent of Sulla, the Roman dictator, left his kingdom to the Roman Republic, but it had been declined by the senate. An amiable, weak man, he was not equipped to combat the might of Rome, only to placate it by bribery. This was not unwelcome to the always impoverished Julius Caesar, or to his consuls Crassus and Pompey, the powerful First Triumvirate of Rome. Ptolemy's enormous gifts of money and produce kept his throne secure but impoverished his people, who rebelled at the increased taxes they had to endure.

He fled to Rome, and his daughter Berenice, Cleopatra's elder sister, promptly seized his throne. Bribery again did its work, and an army was sent against Berenice. Ptolemy was given a polite escort back to his kingdom, where he lost no time in having Berenice and her supporters executed.

Now the heir to Ptolemy's throne was the fourteen-year-old Cleopatra. No authentic portrait of her exists, but her appearance can be guessed at from a copper coin which shows her in youth. She was not, of course, Egyptian in feature, or even as dark as she is usually portrayed on the stage. 'I . . ., that am with Phoebus's amorous pinches black', Shakespeare makes her say of herself, and the suns of Egypt would perhaps have darkened her skin, in spite of the elaborate beauty aids used by Egyptian ladies. Her features are strong, her chin determined, with full lips and a high brow: her luxurious hair is gathered at the nape of a long neck. Her voice is said to have been sweet and seductive, and her brain was certainly far better than that of her father. She spoke Greek and Latin fluently, and seems to have been a natural linguist. By the age of fourteen she would be fully mature physically, and very attractive.

One man who must have thought her so was Mark Antony, the young general who had led the Roman army against Berenice, and stayed in Alexandria. He was handsome and lusty, fond of life's pleasures, a fine soldier popular with his troops. It would have been strange if he had not found the brilliant girl who was to be queen of Egypt in her own right fascinating, and legend says that he did.

Queenship came when she was eighteen. Her brother Ptolemy XIII was only ten, not old enough to rule, and in the hands of three so-called regents, politicians who wanted the deposition of Cleopatra and power for themselves. Brother and sister were now formally married, though not in fact. They disliked each other, and were soon to be at war.

The boy may have been malleable: the girl was not. She had grown up surrounded by intrigues and danger. In 48 B.C., when she was twenty-one, she fled Egypt for Syria and raised an army there, with which to return and defeat her brother's protectors.

At this point fate took a hand. Julius Caesar arrived in Alexandria resolved to end the war between sister and brother, and incidentally to collect the money their father had owed him.

Imperiously he summoned Cleopatra to join him so that peace terms might be talked. She obeyed – not openly, for her brother's troops would have killed her on sight, but, with typical wit and resource, rolled up in a carpet carried on the shoulder of a faithful servant. At Caesar's feet, the bundle was untied, and out crawled or rolled the slender girl who had been inside it.

From that moment of surprise he was infatuated with her, and her cause was won, her throne protected by Caesar. For her sake the usually cautious Caesar embarked on the Alexandrian war against Ptolemy and a younger sister, while Cleopatra remained at his side, his adored mistress. Perhaps there was a marriage ceremony. In the summer of 47 B.C. their son, known as Caesarion, was born. This unfortunate boy was put to death by Octavian after Cleopatra's suicide; she had been unwise enough to make him assume the *toga virilis* at the age of seventeen, thus establishing him as an adult and a possible heir to Egypt.

Caesar now had a year of triumphs, during which he restored Roman rule throughout the East. Through him the Roman Republic was virtually abolished, the Roman Empire established. Back in Rome, he sent for Cleopatra and his son, set her up in a villa by the Tiber, had a golden statue of her placed next to that of Venus the Great Mother, and celebrated his victory over Cleopatra's Egyptian enemies. What he failed to do was to divorce his wife and marry her officially. At the fertility Festival of the Lupercalia in February 44 B.C., Mark Antony offered Caesar the crown which would have made him king of Rome and enabled him to found a dynasty by Cleopatra. Caesar refused, sensing the disapproval of the citizens. They were not the only ones to rebel against the power he held. On 15 March he was assassinated by a band of conspirators.

For Cleopatra it was the end of her Roman hopes. Nobody was going to support any claim she might have. She may have turned now to Mark Antony who, though allied with Caesar's heir, Octavian, was still her friend, and the hero of the moment. To him she and her rich country must have seemed a double lure; he appointed a meeting with her at Tarsus.

The fateful meeting, immortalised by Shakespeare – 'The barge she sat in, like a burnish'd throne ...' – began the partnership which would link their names for ever. Now aged twenty-nine, Cleopatra was at the height of her beauty, a witty, sophisticated woman who had shown her fitness to occupy the highest of ranks. Her lavish entertainment and costly gifts must have impressed the somewhat simple-minded Antony, and persuaded him that she was inviting him to take Caesar's place at her side. Perceiving that he was, compared with Caesar, a soldier, bluff-mannered and earthy, she subtly changed her own ways to fit in with his. Only a clever woman could have achieved this, and she was a very clever woman indeed. Soon they were lovers.

That first winter together in Alexandria was one of sensual pleasures – banquets, drinking parties, gaming, hunting and high-spirited public pranks. It was wholly to the hedonistic Antony's taste. But in February of 40 B.C. came tidings of a quarrel between his family and Octavian. He went to Italy, to fight or attempt a reconciliation; but the necessity was removed by the sudden death of his wife Fulvia. Unscrupulously, Antony agreed to patch things up by marrying Octavian's widowed sister, Octavia.

To Cleopatra it was a bitter blow. She was newly the mother of twins, a boy and a girl, who would have made her marriage with Antony almost a certainty. Now she could do nothing but grieve, and wait. She waited three years. Then Antony returned to her, not so much for love as for a political alliance which would give him control of the East – possibly the world. This time they were married, Octavia set aside; and now, their heads shown together on coins, they were joint rulers of the East, he as autocrator, or absolute monarch, and she as queen.

In March 36 B.C. they set out together on Antony's campaign against Parthia, but Cleopatra, knowing that she was again pregnant, turned back to Alexandria. The child was another son, Ptolemy Philadelphus. Antony was marching through Armenia with the major part of his troops, the rest taking an easier way. Somehow, perhaps because of bad generalship on his part, the two sections of the army failed to coalesce, his siege-engines were taken and destroyed, and, as winter drew on, he found himself in a desperate situation, with 24,000 of his infantry and cavalry gone. His only remaining hope lay in help from Cleopatra.

She came to him, in his winter refuge at Sidon, and gave him what she could in the way of clothing and food for his men. Octavian, however, was wily enough to try to tempt Antony away from Cleopatra by sending Octavia to Athens, causing Antony to suffer a certain conflict of loyalties between his two spouses and to provide him with a chance to ill-treat or neglect her, thus giving her brother an excuse to make war. This partially succeeded. Antony refused to leave Cleopatra's side, and Octavia returned to Rome, where she was regarded as a wronged wife and Antony as a villain. He withdrew from his Syrian campaign, but in the spring of the next year marched into Armenia, captured its king, and brought home a vast quantity of looted treasure. He held a magnificent triumph in Alexandria, attended by Cleopatra and her children in splendour.

Rivalry between the increasingly powerful Antony and the resentful Octavian smouldered. It was bound to come to war, and war at sea; both Rome and Egypt had fine fleets. Waiting in Athens, Antony's reputation grew worse and worse; he was a slave not only to Cleopatra but to drink. Rumours went back to Octavian, who late in 32 B.C. declared war not on him but on Cleopatra, the foreign head of state who was threatening Rome.

In the summer of 31 B.C. the two camps were set up, Antony's on the southern peninsula at Actium, Octavian's to the north in Gomaros Bay. For weeks it was stalemate, Octavian refusing to leave his post and engage in open battle, Antony's ships blockaded. Later historians were to blame Cleopatra for the action which Antony eventually took, when he broke out of the gulf and challenged Octavian at sea. Cleopatra's ships were ranged behind Antony's, ready to sail back to Egypt if disaster threatened.

On 2 September the two fleets engaged. From the first Octavian's seemed the stronger; after two hours the Egyptian ships hoisted their purple sails and swiftly headed south. Antony lost no time in following: he knew when he was beaten. Taken aboard Cleopatra's flagship, he sat down 'in silence, his head in his hands'.

Cleopatra returned to Alexandria; Antony lingered behind at Paraetonium, meditating suicide, but then drifted back to Alexandria, disheartened and despairing. There he lived like an exile in a dwelling he had built near Pharos, comparing himself to the disillusioned misanthrope Timon of Athens. Cleopatra coaxed him out of hiding and cheered and encouraged him, knowing very well that her days as well as his were numbered. Octavian was merciless. A final short, sharp naval engagement took place, and Antony fled inland, crying that Cleopatra had betrayed him, since her ships had not taken action against Octavian's.

From the mausoleum of the Temple of Isis Cleopatra sent him a message that she had killed herself. This may well have been to prompt him to suicide, knowing his weakness and irresolution as she did. She herself had no intention of surviving to walk in chains in a Roman triumph, as her sister Berenice had done, and Antony must be brave enough to follow her proud example.

When he received it he begged his slave Eros to kill him, as he had promised if defeat was inevitable. But Eros slew himself, and Antony, ashamed, fell upon his sword. He only succeeded in wounding himself gravely, and was still alive when Cleopatra's servants came to find him. At the mausoleum of Isis she waited with her women, Charmian and Iras, to draw her dying warrior-husband up to the high window above the door that was bolted against Octavian's troops. Straining every muscle, they pulled the heavy limp body inside; then Cleopatra gave way to wild grief. He rallied slightly, enough to speak to her in words which are recorded history, immortally rendered by Shakespeare.

> I am dying, Egypt, dying:
> Give me some wine, and let me speak a little . . .
> The miserable change now at my end
> Lament nor sorrow at; but please your thoughts
> In feeding them with those my former fortunes
> Wherein I liv'd, the greatest prince o' the world . . .

Antony was dead and buried, Cleopatra's younger children in Octavian's hands, herself a prisoner. To prevent her committing suicide Octavian sent a message that if she continued to starve herself, as she was doing, her children would be killed. She knew well that it was his intention to have her led through Rome's streets in celebration of his triumph.

Even now she could, by a subtle ruse, defeat him. Summoned by one of her women, a countryman bearing a basket of figs was admitted to her prison. The fruit was fine and ripe, but underneath lay coiled a small viper. Seated on her throne, wearing her royal robes as the incarnation of Isis, Cleopatra put the serpent to her breast.

> Methinks I hear
> Antony call; I see him rouse himself
> To praise my noble act . . . husband, I come.

When Octavian's soldiers burst in they found the queen of Egypt dead, serenely smiling, Iras dead beside her, Charmian dying. Octavian was cheated of his triumph, and Cleopatra had won immortality. She was thirty-nine years old.

Livia

(58 B.C.–A.D. 29)

Livia Drusilla, wife for fifty-two years of the Emperor Augustus, was by birth a member of one of the greatest aristocratic families of Rome. Her father, M. Livius Drusus Claudianus, was a member of the Claudian *gens*, who was adopted by the tribune Livius Drusus. As a Claudian he possessed an extensive and influential set of relations, belonging to the proudest and most wayward of Rome's old patrician houses.

Claudians had been conspicuous in the service of the Republic. Some were notable for their virtue and high sense of duty. One, Claudias Claudex, had expelled the Carthaginians from Sicily; another, Tiberius Nero Claudius, defeated Hannibal's brother Hasdrubal; Appius Claudius Pulcher acquired a reputation for sagacity by advising the senate against an alliance with King Pyrrhus of Epirus. But, if they had done the state service, they had also been distinguished for pride, self-will and vice: another Claudius Pulcher had lost a battle after publicly ridiculing the auspices; Cicero's enemy Publius Clodius was a violent and degenerate member of the family. All the evidence suggests that Livia belonged to the former type; her virtue and sense of duty were to be exemplary for the greater part of her life.

Born in 58 B.C., she married a cousin, Tiberius Claudius Nero, when hardly more than a child. Both her father and husband fought against Caesar, her father later being killed at Philippi. Her husband had reconciled himself to the dictator, yet proposed, after his murder, that the senate reward those responsible. He then made his peace with Antony, but was soon found fighting against Caesar Octavianus (the future Augustus). Both he and Livia were among those besieged by Octavian in Perusia (Perugia) in 41 B.C. Their elder son, the future Emperor Tiberius, had already been born, probably in 42. After the fall of Perusia, Tiberius Nero refused to submit to Octavian, and fled instead to the south, taking Livia and their child with him. He attempted, unsuccessfully, to raise an army in Campania. He then made overtures to Sextus Pompeius, who held Sicily against the Triumvirs. Eventually however he made peace with Octavian in 39.

Livia and Octavian met in the autumn of that year, probably in October. They fell in love almost at once, even though Livia was already six months pregnant. Octavian divorced his middle-aged wife Scribonia (whom he had married for political reasons), and Nero agreed to divorce Livia. Then Livia and Octavian married, on 17 January 38. Her second son Drusus was born just three days before the marriage. It was rumoured that Octavian was his father, but there is no evidence that he and Livia met before the autumn.

It was undoubtedly a love match – Octavian had shaved his beard to make himself more attractive; but it was also one of great political value and significance. By his marriage, Octavian acquired a network of influential connexions. His party now attracted ambitious aristocrats like Appius Claudius Pulcher, that year's consul. As for Livia, she had exchanged an erratic and unsuccessful husband for the coming man in the state. Both she and her new husband had reason to be satisfied.

Nevertheless all the evidence supports the view that the marriage, which in its origins was not without scandal, was, unlike Octavian's two previous ventures into matrimony, very much more than a political convenience. In an age when divorce was easy and frequent it endured till Augustus's death, and did so despite there being no children. Both had children by previous marriages, Livia's two sons and Augustus's daughter Julia. Their failure to produce another child meant that there would be two rival strains in the imperial family (as it soon became) – the Julians and the Claudians. This gave rise to some tension and many rumours. It became a fixed idea that Livia devoted herself to plotting the advancement of her own sons and the destruction of those members of Augustus's family who were not related to her. Both Tacitus and Dio Cassius would give the authority of history to such rumours. She was in time to be accused of the murder of Augustus's nephew Marcellus, of Julia's sons Gaius, Lucius and Agrippa Postumus, even (absurdly) of Augustus himself. The investigations of modern historians have found no substance in these scandals. On the contrary, whatever is known of Livia shows her to have been a pattern of virtue.

As a Roman lady of the old school she played no part in politics; nevertheless there is ample evidence that Augustus greatly valued her counsel. He had such respect for her judgement that he made a practice of setting down his thoughts on paper before discussing a question with her. The nature of her advice can however only be conjectured. Though some historians, like Sir Ronald Syme in *The Roman Revolution*, have seen Livia's hand in the constitutional settlement of 23, when Augustus abandoned the practice of holding one of the consulships every year and took instead the *tribunicia potestas* (the power of a tribune), at the same time associating Marcus Vipsanius Agrippa with him in his *imperium* (authority), such judgements must, for lack of firm evidence, remain intelligent guesswork. Certainly Livia had at the very least acquiesced in the marriage of her son Tiberius to Agrippa's daughter Vipsania, and could not have been distressed to see the formal elevation of her son's father-in-law; it is possible that she saw it as balancing the influence of Augustus's nephew Marcellus, who in 25 had been married to the princeps's daughter Julia. Yet too much may be read into the presumed tensions within the imperial family: Livia's other son Drusus would be married to Antonia minor, Marcellus's half-sister and Augustus's niece, being the daughter of his sister Octavia and Mark Antony. In time two of the children of this marriage between Drusus and Antonia would be interlocked with Augustus's own descendants, Germanicus being married to Agrippina, Julia Livilla to Gaius Caesar, both Agrippina and Gaius being Julia's children by her marriage to Agrippa. The fact was that Livia's descendants were to be found throughout the imperial family. It took the strains that developed in Tiberius's reign to create the impression of a family feud that cannot actually be identified in Augustus's lifetime.

Moreover, when Agrippa died in 12, Livia either acquiesced in Augustus's decision that Tiberius should divorce Vipsania in order to marry Julia and become the stepfather of her sons; or may even have encouraged it. Tiberius obeyed, even though he resented the scheme, for he had loved Vipsania. His later estrangement from Livia may have had its origins in her complicity in this heartless reordering of his life.

Livia's younger son Drusus was killed fighting on the northern frontier in 9 B.C., regretted by all. He left five children. There is no evidence that Livia was particularly close to these grandchildren, though she and Augustus consulted each other about their development and their future, as surviving correspondence relating to the problem child, the future Emperor Claudius, indicates.

In 6 B.C. Tiberius, unhappy in his marriage to Julia and perhaps resenting the growing importance of his stepsons Gaius and Lucius, whom Augustus had adopted, asked leave to retire from public life to the island of Rhodes. Augustus was strongly opposed to this request. Tiberius had to go on hunger strike before Livia obtained permission for him to go. A few years later, when Tiberius wished to return to Rome, the position had changed. Augustus preferred him to remain in exile. Livia's pleas were unavailing. All she could obtain for him was an appointment as Augustus's legate, to show that he was not in complete disgrace. It was only the deaths of the young princes Gaius and Lucius that made Tiberius's recall expedient. Then, with no other successor in view, Augustus turned to him, adopted him, and made him his partner in government. This course was enjoined on him by the course of events and the needs of the Empire; it required no scheming on Livia's part to recommend it.

Before then however the scandal of Julia's immoral and politically dangerous behaviour had broken. It is said that Livia herself informed Augustus of his daughter's immorality and association with members of the dissident aristocracy such as Iullus Antonius, a grandson of the Triumvir. It is quite probable that no one but Livia would have dared tell the princeps of his daughter's disgrace. She and Julia can never have been close; their characters and outlook were too different, and Livia may have resented Julia's failure to be a good wife to Tiberius. When however the younger Julia (no blood relation of Livia's) followed her mother's course and was exiled in A.D. 9 it was Livia who paid her an allowance from her own income.

This was a private example of her public charity. Livia established homes for orphans and made herself responsible for the payment of dowries for poor brides. She was ready with assistance for the parents of large families and for the provision of tombs for slaves. She was a model of chastity and may have influenced Augustus's attempt to improve morality by legislation. Yet she was not easily shocked: when she encountered some nudists in the street she saved their lives by saying that to a woman like herself a naked man was no different from a statue. In the antique Roman fashion, she spun her own wool and made her own clothes, and the emperor's too.

There can be no doubt of Augustus's love for her. He would tolerate scandal about himself happily enough, but, according to Seneca, would suffer no insult to Livia. She inspired his respect; he may have been a little in awe of her. When Augustus told the senate that they should admonish and command their wives, they replied that they would like to know how he admonished and commanded Livia. She herself accounted for her influence over him by saying it depended on 'her doing gladly whatever pleased him, not meddling with any of his affairs, and, especially, pretending to be blind to the favourites with whom he fell in love'.

Augustus died in A.D. 14 in Livia's arms, trying to kiss her and saying, 'Farewell, Livia, live mindful of our marriage'. She personally supervised his funeral, remaining by his funeral pyre for five days. He left her one-third of his estate, having applied to the senate for permission to do so, since the Voconian Law of 169 B.C. restricted a woman's inheritance to 100,000 sesterces. Livia was also admitted by the will to the Julian *gens*, and took the name of Julia Augusta. When the senate deified Augustus, she was named as a priestess of the new cult. With Tiberius she built a temple to him, and she gave a million sesterces to a certain Numerius Atticus because he swore he had seen Augustus ascending to heaven. She conducted a private festival lasting three days on the anniversaries of his birthday.

She had still fifteen years left to live. Her influence declined owing to age and the gradual estrangement of Tiberius. She was blamed by the people for not attending the funeral of her grandson Germanicus, whom Tiberius's friend Piso was accused of murdering. She may have been in poor health, or she may have declined to go in protest at the rumours of Tiberius's responsibility which Germanicus's widow Agrippina was eagerly spreading. Others indeed said Livia had instigated the murder herself, but there is no evidence of this, as there is none that Germanicus was in fact murdered. In contradiction, Livia is also represented as having exercised a restraining influence on Tiberius, but there is no evidence for this beyond rumour.

Livia died in 29 at the age of eighty-six. Tiberius, who had withdrawn to Capri three years before, did not attend his mother's funeral. If she had indeed schemed to make him emperor, their estrangement had taken place long before her death.

Boudicca

(*d.* A.D. 62)

The first heroine to take her place in British history was born about A.D. 20, into a Britain which as yet had not come under the domination of Rome. In 54 B.C. Julius Caesar had landed on the coast of Kent, and reached the Thames, but had been chased out by the war-chariots of the British prince Cassivellaunus, after imposing a monetary tribute to Rome which was never paid. He had not returned.

Boudicca (often wrongly called Boadicea) was, in fact, a Celt. She came of one of the many Celtic tribes who inhabited Britain, perhaps the Trinovantes or the Coritani, since their territory neighboured that of the Iceni, whose king she was to marry. The Iceni tribe occupied what is now Norfolk; southward, the present-day Essex was the land of the Catuvellauni, whose chief was Cunobelinus, the great leader whom Shakespeare was to immortalise as Cymbeline. He had held his court in the town which would become the Roman Verulamium and the Christian St Albans, but after capturing Camulodunum (Colchester) set up his headquarters there. In company with his brother, Epaticcus, he expanded his territory in all directions, including the eastern area bordering on Iceni country.

Boudicca's youth is unchronicled, though she is said to have been of royal blood. She must have lived in one of the Celtic settlements which was their nearest approximation to a town, a small collection of round-shaped houses made of wood and wicker, with thatched roofs; the walls would have wattle and daub in-filling. The furnishings would be crude and the life-style primitive, but the Celts were expert craftsmen in metal-work, functional and ornamental, minted their own golden coins, drove chariots, built ships, and made pottery which was often elaborately decorated. Their women spun and wove on looms, and wore beautifully wrought jewellery of gold or bronze. Archaeological digs have revealed rings, torques (heavy neck ornaments), bracelets, brooches, circlets for the head and magnificent helmets and weapons. Clothing was of linen, wool, and animal skins and furs. Trousers were worn by both men and women on occasion. The Celts were good farmers, and traded their products with the Roman Empire.

Boudicca would have had no formal education, but as Roman chroniclers of her rebellion remembered her as being an inspiring orator when haranguing her troops she may have had natural skill with words. Her religion would be Druidism, which prevailed all over Britain. The Druid priests taught the doctrine of immortality, believing that at death the soul passed into another body; this gave them no fear of death in battle, and probably contributed to Boudicca's own extraordinary bravery.

The Celts worshipped many gods and nature-spirits, rulers of earth and air, wind and storm, rivers, wells and trees, which demanded to be placated by human blood-sacrifices. This horrified the Romans, themselves noted for the savagery of their sports. Children had to be brought up to be strong and ruthless, in a country where danger always threatened. Though Cunobelinus was growing old, his thirst for land was unabated, and he had two sons with the same ambition. It was important for other tribal leaders to keep up their unity with others whose support they might need, and the best way to do this was to intermarry, choosing for their king or prince a high-born girl from a friendly tribe.

Such a girl was Boudicca. No description of her in youth exists, but her appearance at the time of her revolt evidently impressed spectators enough for a Roman scribe, a century later, to write it down from their memories. She was then about forty; tall, massively built, 'terrifying of aspect', with a loud, carrying voice. Her mantle of red hair fell to her knees and must have blown about her like a banner when she rode, standing up, in her chariot. A great gold necklet encircled her throat, and her cloak was fastened by a brooch, also of gold. She had probably put on a good deal of weight in her maturity, with the birth of two daughters, but in girlhood she may well have been strikingly beautiful.

She was about twenty-three when Rome again invaded Britain, this time successfully. There were various reasons. Roman merchants wanted direct access to British goods, but were not prepared to come over and barter without the protection of Roman soldiery. The Emperor Claudius, by no means a warlike figure or a leader of men, needed some military success to win respect for himself from the Roman citizens and his legions.

Therefore, in the year 43, an invasion force of four legions, with cavalry and auxiliaries (and, rather curiously, a train of elephants) landed on the coast of Kent at Richborough, or Rutupiae. British resistance fell before them, and when Claudius arrived in person he found his army in possession of Camulodunum, of which Cunobelinus's son Caractacus was now king. After Claudius's satisfied departure Camulodunum became the main Roman base in Britain – in effect, the capital – though it later gave way to the more accessible Londinium.

The south-east of Britain was a fairly easy conquest, but other areas were more stubborn. The new governor, Ostorius Scapula, who took over in 47, was annoyed to find revolts still being stirred up by Caractacus. These he suppressed, and followed up his action by demanding the disarmament of the tribes, including the Iceni. It was a humiliating experience for a proud tribe to have their houses, even their persons, searched for weapons. They revolted, and were quickly disciplined; but the resentment remained, and Boudicca was one of those who must have felt it most. It is not known whether Prasutagus had been king of the Iceni when he married her, but by now he and she were king and queen. He was probably older than his wife, and in the year 60 he died.

Roman administrators had from the beginning extracted all the taxes they could from Britain. There was a land-tax imposed on owners of property, customs dues, a corn tax, and levies to pay for the support of garrisons and the building of such expensive edifices as the great temple of Claudius at Camulodunum. This last tax was bitterly resented.

At the time of Prasutagus's death the procurator (chief inspector of taxes) was an unscrupulous man called Catus Decianus. Prasutagus had had a 'client-king' relationship with Rome, amicable enough, ruling his kingdom autonomously and presumably being taxed not too heavily. In his will he left the Roman emperor, Nero, a share of his kingdom, the rest being apportioned to his two daughters – possibly to safeguard the Iceni and particularly his own family after his death.

But things fell out otherwise. When Claudius had acknowledged the existence of these 'client-kings', they had each received money as a form of grant. Catus Decianus now came forward and declared that it had been not a grant but a loan. He demanded not only that, but the whole of the dead king's wealth, to be paid over to the emperor, no doubt with the object of taking a sizeable cut himself. The whole territory of the Iceni was taken over, the king's estates were plundered and looted. The royal palace, which was probably near Norwich, was overrun with pilfering soldiers and clerks making inventories.

Boudicca protested angrily. The Romans retaliated by tying her to a stake and flogging her. When her young daughters shrieked, they were seized by soldiers and raped.

It was an outrage which would cost thousands of lives. Boudicca was respected, even revered. Her own fury spread through her kingdom. It was known that now their king was dead they would no longer be ruled separately, but be amalgamated with the hated Romans. They looked to their queen for leadership, and got it.

The moment was ripe for rebellion. The governor, Suetonius Paulinus, was busy with a campaign in North Wales to put down the refractory Druids in Anglesey. He had a daunting prospect. Wrote a Roman historian: 'The enemy lined the shore in a dense armed mass. Among them were women robed in black, with wild hair like Furies, brandishing torches. By them stood Druids, shaking their fists to Heaven and shrieking dreadful curses. The strange sight terrified the Roman soldiers so that they could hardly move ...'

They did move, however, at the terse orders of their officers, and the Druids were mown down, their tents burned, their priests slaughtered at the spot where they would have made their human sacrifices. Suetonius's campaign had been successful.

But at this moment, a messenger arrived with disturbing news – the Iceni, under Boudicca, had rebelled, and other tribes, including the Trinobantes, had joined them. There was nothing Suetonius could do, so far away from East Anglia, and Catus Decianus, in London, could spare only a handful of men to stem the tide of the Icenian advance. It was heading for Camulodunum, where Boudicca had infiltrated a kind of fifth column to keep the authorities quiet while spreading rumours of impending disaster. The usual phenomena were reported – the statue of Victory in the temple of Claudius was said to have fallen with its face to the ground, strange and frightful howlings were heard in the theatre, and it was bruited that, most improbably, a picture of the town in ruins had been seen floating down the Thames.

The old legionaries manned the Claudian temple, prepared to put up a fight, and some simple defences were set up. But all was in vain. Camulodunum was suddenly filled with the enemy troops, armed and ruthless. The garrison struggled gamely, but within two days their fortress fell and they were destroyed. The Iceni thought of Camulodunum as a centre of oppression, tyranny and taxation, and they had always hated that temple. The city itself was set on fire, and its wooden houses were soon ashes. The inhabitants were put to the sword, no one being spared, from old age to infancy. Nor were they only killed outright: every kind of barbarity was practised on the wretched ones who tried to escape. All this was done easily and quickly, the victors entertaining themselves with 'sacrifices, feasts and licence'. The marks of fire can be seen on objects preserved today in Colchester Museum, and on the tombstone of a cavalry officer, Longinus, which had been there before the massacre, his horse's hooves treading on a naked British rebel.

A relief force had been dispatched from Lindum (Lincoln) to come to the aid of Camulodunum. It was ambushed at the edge of the Fen country, its infantry massacred.

Londinium lay ahead. Within it was Catus Decianus, whose behaviour towards Boudicca and her family had started all the trouble. He did the wise if cowardly thing and fled to Gaul, probably taking with him his highest staff officers. Nobody was left to defend Londinium, a city of merchants, and all Catus Decianus could do was to allow the able-bodied among its citizens to follow his retreat, leaving the old and the weak to the mercy of the Britons.

They had no mercy. The inhabitants of Londinium were of their own kind, but they were looked on as enemies – as collaborators, in the same way as those who fraternised with the enemy in occupied countries during the Second World War. Tacitus the historian wrote: 'They would neither take the vanquished prisoners, sell them, nor ransom their lives and liberties; but hastened to massacre, torture and crucify them.'

Suetonius had recruited forces, and managed to get to the outskirts of Londinium, but he knew very well that Boudicca's army would be too much for his troops. There was nothing he could do at that moment. The Britons were killing everyone they could find, in the most brutal manner, as they had done in Camulodunum. Exact figures are impossible to obtain, but an estimated 70,000 has been guessed at. The original city of London was burnt to the ground, nothing at all remaining of it. Such was the revenge exacted for a flogging and two rapes.

Suetonius knew that an open confrontation in battle was his only hope of subduing the Britons. Boudicca marched her army north-westwards from London and laid waste the city of Verulamium, the only one to which the Romans gave the high rank of Municipium. Suetonius was on her heels, with 10,000 men and supplies. As she retreated northwards, to the Midlands, he followed, and caught up with her at some spot which has never been defined – possibly between High Cross and Mancetter in Leicestershire. Aware of his presence, she drew up her own lines, with the wives and children of her soldiers in chariots behind them. Then, with her two daughters, she drove round the field, cheering and encouraging her fighting men in words Tacitus recorded:

> The Britons are used to fighting under a woman's command. There is no question now of avenging my ancestors, my kingdom, or my plundered treasure. Avenge *me* – a simple woman, one of you. Avenge my outraged liberty, my beaten body, my ravished daughters! ... the day has arrived to vanquish or die. Such shall be the fate of *one* woman – let men live slaves if they will.

Her troops cheered, and fought bravely. But nothing they were trained for could withstand the Roman charge with lance and sword, though they fought all day. Some 80,000 Britons died, including those women and children who had come to watch, and even their animals. Boudicca's cause was finished.

She must have escaped from the battlefield, but she had no hope left, and she preferred to die rather than fall captive. 'Boudicca ended her life with poison', says Tacitus. Her burial-place is not known. One legend sites her grave beneath Parliament Hill, on Hampstead Heath. But her lasting memorial stands high above Westminster Bridge, the statue designed by Thornycroft in 1902, showing her driving her war-chariot, her daughters crouching beside her. Beneath are lines from Cowper's poem:

> Regions Caesar never knew
> Thy posterity shall sway ...

Zenobia

(*fl.* A.D. 270)

Zenobia, queen of Palmyra in the second half of the third century A.D., was politically one of the most able women of the ancient world, who made a briefly successful challenge to the might of the Roman Empire.

In the desert north-east of Damascus lies the oasis of Palmyra (Tadmor), which since the time of Solomon had been important for trade between Syria and regions further east. Caravans from China, India, Iran and Arabia passed through it laden with silks, precious stones, rare woods and spices, and the city there became both rich and widely influential, controlling merchant colonies on the Euphrates and as far away as the Persian Gulf. From the early second century A.D. there had been a Roman garrison there, although the city remained autonomous. By the third century Palmyra was, in its organisation, a typical Graeco-Roman city, with a senate and an assembly and some 30,000 inhabitants. Its architecture was magnificent. There was a colonnaded street nearly 1,000 yards long, with columns in four rows 40–50 feet high, and many fine buildings, of which the most impressive was a temple about 200 yards square on a raised terrace. Palmyra's position as a major entrepôt resulted in its being culturally very mixed. This is shown in its frescoes, which combine oriental influences with Graeco-Roman motifs; and in the sculptures, where one may represent a man in Parthian dress, a second a youth wearing a Roman toga, and a third an Arab scene. The same mixed influences are seen in religion, which shows a pantheon combining eastern, desert and western elements; and in the personal names.

Because of its strategic importance as a bulwark on Rome's frontier against Iran, Palmyra was in about A.D. 200 granted the title of Roman colony, and its leading family given Roman citizenship. In A.D. 226 a new Persian dynasty, the Sassanians, began a more vigorous thrust westwards. This made Palmyra, in a key position, even more important to Rome, and its rulers used this situation to win for Palmyra power and a brief empire. The most notable of its rulers was known to the west as Zenobia, the Roman form of her native name Bath-Zabbai.

In A.D. 232 the Roman emperor used Palmyra as a base to drive the advancing Persians back to Iran, but gradually the advantage turned in favour of the Persians. In A.D. 259–60 their king Shapur (Sapor) I defeated the Emperor Valerian and took him prisoner, and broke through north Syria into Asia Minor. At this point there comes into prominence the family to which Zenobia belonged.

Zenobia claimed to be connected with the Ptolemies, the Egyptian dynasty to which Cleopatra, whom she greatly admired, belonged. This can be neither proved nor disproved, but since her native name was Aramaic, it is probable that her immediate stock was from Palmyra or Syria. She was the wife of Odaenathus (the Roman form of the Semitic name Udaynath), who was current head of the leading Palmyrene family which had earlier received Roman citizenship. In A.D. 258, Valerian, on a visit to Palmyra, had raised Odaenathus to consular rank. Odaenathus now showed his gratitude. A Roman officer had checked the Persian advance, and he now attempted to proclaim his own sons as joint emperors. Odaenathus, however, supported the son of Valerian, Gallienus, and the usurpers were killed. He attacked the Persians, and in campaigns from A.D. 262 to 264 he drove the Sassanian king right back to his capital, Ctesiphon on the Tigris. We say that Odaenathus did this, but according to the specific statement of the later Emperor Aurelian, the driving force behind Odaenathus was Zenobia. Gallienus (emperor A.D. 260–68) rewarded Odaenathus with the titles Corrector Orientis (Regulator of the East), Dux Romanorum (Roman Commander), and Imperator (Ruler). These titles made him viceroy over Rome's eastern territories, and he was in effect king, with only nominal overlordship by Rome, of an empire stretching from Armenia to Arabia. But he did not identify himself exclusively with Rome, for he adopted the title King of Kings which the defeated Shapur had borne.

Odaenathus did not enjoy his glory for long, for in A.D. 266 or 267 he, together with his heir (a son by an earlier wife, not by Zenobia), was murdered by a cousin. It was at this point that Zenobia, earlier the driving force behind the ruler, came into open prominence. She seized the reins of government, executed the assassin, and reigned in the name of her son Wahballat, in Latin form Vaballathus, or, translated into Greek, Athenodorus. Inscriptions found at Palmyra describe Zenobia as 'the most illustrious and pious queen'. She proved herself a remarkably able ruler, and Roman writers enthused about her, one of them saying that 'she surpassed in courage and skill many an emperor'. They also give a romantic portrayal of her person. One may perhaps discount the great beauty attributed to her, as an inevitable ingredient in the story of any queen who becomes the subject of legend. One may also wonder how anyone other than her husband could have known, if it were more than tittle-tattle, that, as Gibbon neatly put it, 'she never admitted her husband's embraces but for the sake of posterity. If her hopes were baffled, in the ensuing *month* she reiterated the experiment'. But credence may be given to more sober statements about her. She was dark and had a clear masculine voice. She was a keen hunter and preferred to ride horseback rather than travel by coach. She was physically tough and would march several miles with her infantry, and in drinking, although not given to drunkenness, she could keep up with her generals. In court ceremonial she followed Persian custom, which involved prostration by the person receiving audience, but she went to public assemblies in the manner of a Roman ruler, wearing a helmet and a purple robe fringed with gems, with one arm bare.

Zenobia was a well-educated woman, and besides Aramaic, the local language of Palmyra and of much of the rest of the Near East, she spoke Egyptian very well and also Greek. Her Latin was less good but she made the effort to speak it and insisted that her sons (the Roman authors mention others beside Vaballathus) should learn it. She was well versed in oriental history and even wrote a short work on this herself. Such was her interest in Greek and Roman thought and literature that she welcomed to her court Longinus, the most distinguished philosopher of his day, who had studied at Athens, Rome and Alexandria, and made him her instructor, secretary and counsellor. She also gave her protection to Jews, both those settled in Palmyrene territory and (when she came to control Egypt) those in Alexandria, and is mentioned in the Talmud on this account. She may even have involved herself in the affairs of the Christian Church. Paul of Samosata, patriarch of Antioch, was regarded by other Christian leaders as heretical and was deposed in A.D. 269. The fact that he nevertheless remained in his post until A.D. 272, the year of the downfall of Zenobia herself, suggests that she was shielding him. But she was not only concerned with thinkers; she gave attention to such mundane but vital details as the maintenance of the roads on which Palmyra's trade and wealth depended, as we learn from extant inscriptions.

When she seized rule, Zenobia seems at first to have thought of herself as acting to protect Roman interests, as an aspect of the titles bestowed upon her late husband and now assumed by their son. The new Roman emperor Claudius Gothicus (A.D. 268–70) was occupied against the Goths, Teutonic invaders in Europe, and was glad for Zenobia to exercise authority in the east, nominally on behalf of Rome. An opportunity soon arose for her to make a major extension of her area of rule. With Rome too involved elsewhere to protect Egypt, a usurper seized that country. A leading Egyptian thereupon called upon Zenobia to occupy Egypt and eject the usurper. This she did in A.D. 269, sending her commander-in-chief, Zabda, with 70,000 men. That Zenobia was subsequently able to withdraw the greater part of her army, leaving only a garrison of 5,000 men – a small number to hold Egypt – was an indication of widespread acceptance of her rule. Although her occupation of Egypt was nominally on behalf of Rome, she proceeded to rule the country as part of the kingdom of Palmyra. Claudius Gothicus was succeeded in A.D. 270 by the Emperor Aurelian. At first, coins struck by Zenobia in Alexandria bore effigies both of her son Vaballathus and of Aurelian, with the title 'Augustus' (implying 'Emperor') given only to the latter. But shortly afterwards, Aurelian, continuing the fight against the Gothic invaders, suffered a defeat. Zenobia now saw the possibility of an independent empire; in early A.D. 271 Aurelian's head was dropped from the coins, which now designated Vaballathus as Augustus and Zenobia as Augusta, that is, Emperor and Empress.

Odaenathus had, with Roman approval, exercised some authority over parts of Asia Minor. Zenobia now determined to use this to add that region to her empire, and in A.D. 271 she sent her forces there; they established garrisons as far west as Ankara, and even reached Chalcedon on the Bosphorus, although without taking it. Zenobia briefly ruled an empire extending from Egypt and Arabia to western Asia Minor.

By A.D. 272 Aurelian had stabilised the invading Goths, and was able to move to settle the problems in the east. Already a Roman general, who had been operating against pirates in the Mediterranean, had taken his forces into Egypt and, after a hard struggle, expelled the Palmyrene garrison. Aurelian now moved against Asia Minor, forcing the Palmyrene forces to withdraw towards Antioch in north Syria.

Meanwhile Zenobia in Palmyra was enlarging her own army. For a long period Palmyra had furnished cohorts for the Roman army, commanded by Roman officers, and so there was no shortage of well-trained veterans. Zenobia also sent out a general call to the desert Arabs, who flocked to her. She set up training camps, which she visited daily, dressed as a general, helmeted and bare-armed. Because of the wealth of Palmyra, there was no shortage of weapons, and the city was famous for its archers. As the units – cavalry, camel-troops armed with swords, and archers – were equipped, Zenobia sent them off to the Orontes valley.

The Roman and Palmyrene armies met near Antioch. The Palmyrene troops were by no means inferior to the Roman. In particular, the Palmyrenians had a dangerously powerful force of armoured heavy cavalry, which Aurelian knew would cut up his own less well-trained light cavalry, if they succeeded in engaging them. He therefore ordered his own cavalry to draw attacks from the Palmyrene cavalry, but to make repeated feints of flight, until the Palmyrenians were exhausted from the heat and the weight of their armour. As soon as the Romans saw that the Palmyrene cavalry had ridden themselves almost to a standstill, they turned and made a massacre, those who were not cut down being crushed to death in the jam of maddened horses. Zenobia rode out to exhort her troops to make a last stand, but the Roman stratagem had broken their morale and they fell back on Emesa (Homs), north of Damascus.

Zenobia received fresh levies and re-formed her forces for a second battle. The remnant of the Palmyrene cavalry were not to be caught by the same ruse a second time, and with their superiority in horsemanship broke the formation of the Roman cavalry and almost annihilated them. But Aurelian had a very mixed infantry, including Palestinians using heavy clubs. These troops stood their ground and went for the cavalrymen and their horses with their clubs. This was a form of fighting against which the heavy cavalry had had no training and so had no ready defence, and the infantry won the day. Zenobia, who had previously used Emesa as a base, had to withdraw rapidly to her capital, leaving a considerable treasury for Aurelian to capture.

It was no easy task for Aurelian to mount an attack on Palmyra. It stood in the desert seventy miles from Emesa, and on the way the Roman troops were continuously subject to attack by what the Roman authors called Syrian brigands, who were in fact fighters organised by Zenobia to employ guerrilla tactics. When Aurelian reached Palmyra, he found that the queen had set up a formidable system of defence. Aurelian himself described it: 'What a store of arrows is here, what great preparations for war! There is no section of the wall that is not held by two or three siege-engines, and their machines can even hurl fire.' Aurelian sent Zenobia a letter inviting surrender, with a safe-conduct for herself and her children, and a promise that the rights of the Palmyrenians would be respected. She returned a defiant reply, dictated by her in Aramaic but translated into Greek in recognition of diplomatic niceties. She referred to the example of Cleopatra, with whom she claimed kinship, who had preferred death to surrender. She pointed to the difficulties Aurelian had already had from her Syrian guerrillas, and rejected surrender because she still had the desert Arabs and the Armenians as allies, and was imminently expecting reinforcements from the Persians.

Unfortunately for Zenobia, the Sassanian king Shapur died that very year, and the expected Persian reinforcements did not arrive. The queen succeeded in escaping from her besieged capital by night, and rode by camel across the desert to appeal to the Persians to send urgent assistance against the common Roman enemy. But Aurelian heard of her flight and sent horsemen in pursuit. She was caught when almost at her goal, crossing the Euphrates, and was brought back to Aurelian. With Zenobia captured, there was a split in Palmyra between those who wanted to continue the fight and those who sought honourable surrender. The latter won the day, and Aurelian, having become master of the city and seized its vast treasure, withdrew with his prisoners to Emesa, leaving a small garrison in Palmyra.

Aurelian took Zenobia and Vaballathus as prisoners to Rome, and made the deposed queen take part in his triumphal procession in A.D. 274. This was a humiliating experience for a proud woman; she had to walk before her own splendid processional chariot, with gold fetters on her hands, feet and neck, and adorned with such a weight of her jewellery that she had to make frequent stops to rest. Aurelian did not go uncriticised for the unmanly deed of leading a woman in his procession. He defended himself vigorously, saying that Zenobia was equal to any man. 'Those people who blame me now would praise me highly, if only they realised what kind of woman she is, how sound in counsel, how firm in purpose, how stern when severity is demanded.' He even went further, and said that it was she who deserved the credit for the deeds attributed to her husband.

Subsequently, Aurelian presented Zenobia with an estate at Tibur (Tivoli). There are conflicting traditions as to what happened then. One Greek author – and he is in many respects the most reliable in his facts – says that Zenobia was so broken by the collapse of all her hopes that she pined and died. But other classical authors claim that she lived on to bring up her children (whether younger children by Odaenathus or those born from a second marriage to a Roman nobleman not being clear), and that a century later her descendants were to be found as men of senatorial rank in Rome.

Hypatia of Alexandria

(*c*. A.D. 370–415)

The philosopher Hypatia of Alexandria is important on two main counts: she was the first female mathematician of any note whose name has survived; and she was one of the outstanding teachers of the Neoplatonist school at Alexandria.

According to tradition, which may or may not be reliable, she was a woman of considerable beauty, intelligence and virtue. Certainly this is the impression given by the Church historian Socrates in his *Ecclesiastical History*, and it is confirmed with little subtlety in Charles Kingsley's 1851 novel *Hypatia*:

> ... most probably, had any of us entered that room that morning, we should not have been able to spare a look either for the furniture, or the general effect, or the Museum gardens, or the sparkling Mediterranean beyond; but we should have agreed that the room was quite rich enough for human eyes, for the sake of one treasure which it possessed, and, beside which, nothing was worth a moment's glance. For in the light arm-chair, reading a manuscript which lay on the table, sat a woman, of some five-and-twenty years, evidently the tutelary goddess of that little shrine, dressed in perfect keeping with the archaism of the chamber, in a simple old snow-white Ionic

robe, falling to the feet and reaching to the throat, and of that peculiarly severe and graceful fashion in which the upper part of the dress falls downward again from the neck to the waist in a sort of cape, entirely hiding the outline of the bust, while it leaves the arms and the point of the shoulders bare. Her dress was entirely without ornament, except the two narrow purple stripes down the front, which marked her rank as a Roman citizen, the gold embroidered shoes upon her feet, and the gold net, which looped back, from her forehead to her neck, hair the colour and gloss of which were hardly distinguishable from that of the metal itself, such as Athene herself might have envied for tint, and mass, and ripple. Her features, arms, and hands were of the severest and grandest type of old Greek beauty, at once showing everywhere the high development of the bones, and covering them with that firm, round, ripe outline, and waxy morbidezza of skin, which the old Greeks owed to their continual use not only of the bath and muscular exercise, but also of daily unguents. There might have seemed to us too much sadness in that clear gray eye; too much self-conscious restraint in those sharp curved lips; too much affectation in the studied severity of her posture.... But the glorious grace and beauty of every line of face and figure would have excused, even hidden those defects, and we should have only recognised the marked resemblance to the ideal portraits of Athene which adorned every panel of the walls.

We should be careful about mocking Kingsley's highly romanticised description too much: he was, after all, merely carrying on the tradition of Hypatia's beauty and 'seemliness'. Even the editors of the *Catholic Encyclopedia* (Charles Herbermann *et al.*, 1913), whose purpose was more to bury Hypatia than to praise her, reluctantly conceded that she was 'a highly respected teacher ... and (it is said) of many virtues'.

She was the daughter of the mathematician and mathematical astronomer Theon of Alexandria, whose contribution to scientific progress was negligible but who is nevertheless a rather important figure in the history of science. He it was who produced an edition of Euclid's *Elements* which was so successful that it was not until the nineteenth century that a version faithful to the original surfaced. Theon's version, which he probably prepared for his students, included many alterations of a trivial nature, a few genuine corrections of Euclid's errors and many 'corrections' in areas where Theon had simply been incapable of understanding the original, and a single novel proposition (book 6, no. 33), which is in essence that the area of a sector of a circle is governed by the angle between the two radii which define it (and, trivially, the circle's radius). He produced editions also of Ptolemy's *Almagest* and *Handy Tables*, again almost certainly for the benefit of his students: in both cases his commentaries are of little interest. However, in his commentary on *Handy Tables* there is a brief discussion of an idea which was of some significance until about the end of the sixteenth century: 'trepidation'.

Owing to the phenomenon known as precession, the point on the heavenly sphere where the celestial equator (the projection of the terrestrial equator onto the sphere of 'fixed stars') intersects with the ecliptic (the apparent circle traced out by the sun during the course of the year) slowly moves. For example, at the time of the vernal equinox the sun crosses the celestial equator at what is by tradition called the first point of Aries: this point now lies in the constellation Pisces and, according to some, has moved into the constellation Aquarius (it depends upon where you draw the boundary line between Pisces and Aquarius). That this movement of the intersection occurred was known to the ancients, and Ptolemy calculated that it was at a rate of about one degree per century, thereby completing a full circle in 36,000 years. In his commentary on *Handy Tables*, however, Theon mentioned the theory that the point of intersection vibrated, as it were, back and forth along the ecliptic over a range of eight degrees.

Theon's version of *Handy Tables* was adopted by the Arabic scientists; and when, in the ninth century, it was realised by them that Ptolemy's calculation of the rate of precession was wrong (only 26,000 years are required for a complete circle to be executed) many of them preferred to believe, not that the great Ptolemy could have made a blunder, but that the rate of precession was not constant, varying in cyclical fashion. It is indisputable that this notion came from Theon's comment.

Hypatia helped her father with parts of his edition of the *Almagest* and possibly of *Elements*, and is believed to have herself prepared commentaries on Apollonius's *Conics* and Diophantus's *Arithmetica*; she may have prepared her own edition of the *Almagest* after her father's death. None of her works, however, survives: book-burning was a popular pastime in Alexandria in those days.

We know very little of the detail of her teachings; simply that she was a celebrated Neoplatonist and lecturer in the natural sciences. Neoplatonism is a school of religious philosophy which originated in Alexandria in the third century A.D. and found its basis and inspiration in the Platonic theory of ideas or forms, developed by Aristotle, with which was combined the ethical teaching of the

Stoics and the doctrine of emanation derived from oriental mysticism. Its real founder was Plotinus, who was followed by his pupil Porphyry, and he in turn by his disciple Iamblichus. Hypatia became head of the school about 400, and was one of its most famous preachers.

As a natural philosopher – what today we would call a scientist – the details of her teachings are equally scant. The little we do know comes from the few surviving letters to her of the astronomer and physicist Synesius of Cyrene, later to become bishop of Ptolemais. In one letter he asks her how to construct an astrolabe (astrolabes were a pet topic of her father's) and a hydroscope; so it is evident that she was a practical rather than a purely theoretical scientist.

However, she had the very considerable misfortune to be in the wrong place at the wrong time. She was labelled as a pagan by the increasingly fanatical Christians of Alexandria – not merely because of her Neoplatonism but also, it seems, because the fanatics distrusted the whole area of learning and knowledge as being in some way pagan.

Matters were not helped by the appointment of one Cyril as patriarch of Alexandria, in 412. Cyril was the nephew of Theophilus, likewise patriarch of Alexandria; this was the Theophilus who treated St John Chrysostom most shamefully in Constantinople in 403. On Theophilus's death in 412 there was a riot between Cyril's supporters and those of a rival called Timotheus, from which Cyril emerged the victor. Cyril's activities thereafter make it astonishing that he was subsequently canonised. He immediately plundered and closed the churches of the Novitians, and he expelled all the Jews from Alexandria. Such actions aroused the enmity of Orestes, the prefect of Egypt, and Cyril, who had in the past used carefully controlled mobs to further his own ends, imported to the city an army of five hundred monks from Nitria 'in self-defence'.

This, then, was the man responsible for promoting peaceful coexistence between the Christians and the other religious adherents in Alexandria at a time when public unruliness was far from infrequent. And Hypatia must have known, from the day of his appointment, that her time could not be long in coming. Apologists for Cyril claim that it was widely believed that she was preventing a reconciliation between him and Orestes, who, it is said, was a friend of hers. There is no evidence to suggest that she was preventing such a reconciliation, little that such a rumour ever existed.

Again, Cyril's apologists claim that he knew nothing of her

murder until after the event, and that certainly he could have done nothing to stop it. This may indeed have been the case, but there is no evidence to support it, and the circumstances would suggest a high probability that Cyril was only too well aware of plans to kill her, and quietly approved of them.

According to Socrates and others, in March 415 a mob led by a lector called Peter rampaged through the streets of Alexandria until they found Hypatia, by this time a middle-aged woman. They seized her and dragged her into a church, where they set about tearing pieces of flesh from her body with potsherds. Eventually she succumbed to this rather crude form of flaying: her murder was a brutal one, carried out in the name of the Prince of Peace.

It is difficult to determine exactly what position Hypatia might have held in the history of scientific philosophy had she not met this untimely end and had not all her works been destroyed by pious vandals. Certainly she was extremely highly esteemed by her contemporaries, but it seems probable that – like her father but to a more important degree – her chief contributions were as an interpreter, commentator and developer rather than as an original theorist in her own right. This is not intended in any way as a denigration of her abilities: without people such as Theon and Hypatia there is a very considerable danger that – as indeed happened – the works of the great authorities of the past become somehow immutable, regarded as absolute truths with which it is heresy to disagree. To take a modern analogy, Einstein himself said that he had merely built upon Newton's work in developing his theories of Relativity. (Einstein was perhaps being rather over-modest, but the point remains.) So it is perfectly possible that, but for that mob of bloodthirsty fanatics, we might now speak of Hypatia in the same breath as Ptolemy or Euclid.

One can however claim with some confidence that had it not been for Hypatia and other distinguished teachers in Alexandria, Neoplatonism would not have survived to influence medieval philosophy and Christian mysticism in our own day.

Thales

(*c.* 624–*c.* 546 B.C.)

In the seventh century B.C. the Greek world had emerged from a period of isolation and poverty which had accompanied the collapse of the Late Bronze Age kingdoms. Greek traders had resumed contacts with the coastal regions of the eastern Mediterranean, at the latest during the previous century; the Greeks were becoming increasingly involved in the affairs of that region, which was then dominated by the Assyrians and incorporated into their empire. At its height, at the middle of the century, that empire included Babylon and Egypt, both proud peoples with long traditions of their own, eager to resume their independence. They rose in rebellion; and in 612 the Assyrian might was shattered with the capture of Nineveh by an army of Babylonians, and peoples from the mountain areas to east and north, the Medes of Iran and the Scythians of South Russia. The Greeks benefited from this: they served the Egyptians and Babylonians as mercenary soldiers.

Many of these came from the Greek communities on the eastern side of the Aegean, and from their neighbours, the Carians. The Greek cities of the region, including Miletus on the mainland coast, established trading posts and flourished considerably – recent studies of the extent of Miletus in the seventh and sixth centuries have shown that it was then in all probability the largest of all the Greek cities, a position it maintained until it was destroyed by the Persian King Darius in 494 B.C.

It was at Miletus that Thales was born, probably in 624 B.C. His father was called Examyes, which is a Carian, not a Greek name, though his mother was Greek. This does not mean he was not a real Milesian: the city was created by Ionian Greek settlers who intermarried and amalgamated with the local inhabitants, and the expansion of Miletus at this time can only have been achieved through the successful integration of the Carian population.

Though the Greeks had adopted the Phoenician alphabet perhaps a hundred years or so before Thales's birth, it was at this stage not used for the recording or writing of what we would term history and so the earliest written references we have to Thales are in the fifth-century historian Herodotus. He tells us that Thales predicted an eclipse of the sun which occurred in 585 B.C. during a battle between Alyattes, King of Lydia (who at that time had established himself as overlord of the Greek cities of Asia, including Miletus) and Cyaxares the Mede; that some Greeks said Thales diverted the course of the river Halys, so that the last Lydian king, Croesus, could cross it to give battle with the Persian King, Cyrus (though Herodotus does not believe them); and later he remarks that Thales, who he says was Phoenician by descent, proposed a federal government for the Ionian Greeks based in the city of Teos.

By the fourth century B.C., at the very latest, Thales was regarded as one of the seven sages. Why this was so is less certain, though there is no doubt of his reputation. We have no writings of Thales himself or even quotations from his writings – indeed he is expressly stated not to have committed his wisdom to writing, which is not surprising given the date at which he lived; it is, indeed, unlikely that he was the author of any form of systematic treatise. His ideas may well have been passed on verbally, by instructing a younger generation, who in turn would instruct others, sometimes acknowledging Thales's authorship, at other times assimilating his ideas with their own. Even when it became normal to write treatises, this process of passing on and assimilation into the works of a later generation was normal practice: plagiarism, even without acknowledgement, was not a matter for reproach. The writings which survive intact are those, generally, of the last generation of scholars (for example: the Hellenistic doctors whose achievements are described later in this book, Erasistratus and Herophilus, are known largely through the writings of the last great medical authority in the ancient world, Galen). In this sense, Thales's work (whatever form it took) was immediately supplanted by that of his successor.

Thus it is very difficult to attribute with any hope of certainty specific ideas and discoveries to Thales. In a sense this does not matter, for his importance and contribution to scholarship do not depend on what exactly they were. Of his importance, there is no doubt. To Aristotle and later generations Thales was the first philosopher, the instigator of the Greek tradition of the logical and rational pursuit of wisdom, passed on through the generations to the time of Plato and Aristotle, and in turn passed on by them. The terminology is significant. Thales is one of the seven sages, or wise men (*sophoi* in Greek). The term philosopher – lover of wisdom – is coined by Plato, who uses it to distinguish his own beloved master, Socrates, from his contemporaries who gave instruction in wisdom for payment, the sophists (*sophistai*). Thus 'philosopher' is not a term used by Thales, or those who succeed him, down to the time of Plato.

The early philosophers (Pre-Socratics), whose writings do not in general survive, studied a variety of subjects which include matter which we would term science and mathematics (it is worth remembering that an alternative term for physics is natural philosophy). Particularly important is their interest in the nature of the universe, and their attempts to find a rational explanation for it. Traditional belief, in Greece and other countries in the Near East, attributed the creation of the universe, and all the specific aspects contained in it, to the supernatural powers of the gods recorded in myth, consonant with the belief, general in Greek religion, that every single object or aspect of life had its own particular protecting divinity. The great achievement of the philosophers was to turn from this belief for the creation of the universe – cosmogony – to attempt to elucidate the reality – cosmology. Even though later philosophers, following the tradition of Socrates and Plato, became more concerned with the study of human behaviour, the scientific aspect was never totally lacking in their work, and in some ways the division of Greek thinkers into philosophers or scientists is artificial.

The starting point for Thales must have been the context in which he lived and worked. The Greek world of his day was beginning to emerge, not only from the isolation of the so-called 'Dark Age' but from a primitive world in which traditional patterns of belief about the gods and the world they created and controlled were unchallengeable. Miletus, as a city, was in the forefront of developing relations, largely commercial rather than political, with the other countries and peoples of the Mediterranean. Greek traders found here different traditions, different beliefs. One way to adapt to this was to seek parallels between eastern and Greek religions, accepting different names for the gods purely as aspects of the perceived phenomenon of linguistic difference: thus the Phoenician god Melkart to many Greeks (including Herodotus) is the Greek Heracles. To others, the differences presented a challenge – was it possible that all such beliefs were, in fact, erroneous? The possibility for scepticism and, therefore, rationalising was present, at least to the percipient few (religious scepticism, in all probability never extended to more than a minority, even though, eventually, the religious views of the majority might change). To say that Thales was responsible for the scepticism is, of course, a gross exaggeration: that he took the first, tentative steps towards the rational explanation of the universe, however, is certainly what later philosophers, especially

Aristotle, believed.

These inquiries and ideas were not confined to speculation about the nature of the universe. Mathematics, whether theoretical or practical, was equally important. This fact points, perhaps less surely and directly than was once thought, in the direction of Babylon. Babylonian mathematics already had a long and influential tradition of achievement. (Its influence can still be seen in the survival of its sexagesimal system, counting in 60s instead of 100s: it is for this reason that there are sixty seconds in a minute, sixty minutes in an hour, and 360 degrees in a circle.) Babylonian mathematical knowledge was considerable – it has been suggested by one of the very few modern scholars who is both a mathematician and who can read the Babylonian texts that the Babylonian mathematicians had already made thoroughly familiar for centuries the mathematical concepts which form the basis of Euclid's *Elements* – and that where Euclid's mathematics diverge from Babylonian, the change in quality is immediately noticeable.

How far Thales was familiar with Babylonian mathematics and science cannot be accurately assessed, because of our uncertain knowledge of what Thales actually achieved. He is credited by later Greek authorities with the discovery of several mathematical theorems, including 'Thales's Theorem', that the angle inscribed in a semi-circle is a right angle, which was certainly familiar to Babylonian mathematics (in the same way that the more elaborate 'Pythagoras's Theorem' was already familiar). What is meant by this attribution is another matter. Assuming that later accounts are correct, and that Thales did 'teach' his theorem, it does not necessarily mean that he was familiar with the whole of Babylonian mathematics (or, even more, that he could read and knew Babylonian mathematical texts, compiled in their cuneiform system of syllabic writing). However, there is a strong tradition that Thales visited eastern Mediterranean regions, including Egypt, at the time when the neo-Babylonian empire flourished, and that he acquired knowledge, perhaps of Babylonian mathematical techniques, is not in itself inherently improbable. His prediction of the eclipse is more problematical. Again, the Babylonians had kept precise and full records of astronomical phenomena, which would undoubtedly include eclipses. In theory this should have made it possible for them to predict when eclipses would happen, but even if this were so, their knowledge of astronomy, and the practical limitations of their mathematics, would not make it possible for them (or Thales, using information gathered from them) to predict where the eclipse would occur.

Though stories such as the prediction of the eclipse illustrate Thales's reputation as a wise man, his standing, to Aristotle, as the originator of philosophy does not depend on them. Aristotle's views are summed up in his *Metaphysics*. 'Most of the earliest philosophers thought that the principles which were in the nature of matter were the only principles of all things, that of which all things that are consist, and from which they first came to be and into which they are resolved as a final state.... There is always some permanent substance or nature (*physis*) either one or more, which is conserved in the generation of the rest from it.' The ideas about this propounded by some of Thales's successors can be seen elsewhere in this book, in the account of Democritus. 'Thales,' says Aristotle 'who led the way in this kind of philosophy, says that the principle is water, and for this reason declared that the earth rests on water. His supposition may have arisen from the observation that the nourishment of all creatures is moist, and that warmth itself is generated from moisture and lives by it; and that from which all things came to be is their first principle.'

Aristotle's phraseology is important. While he is quite definite that Thales believed that the first principle, or basic element from which everything is created, was water, he can only guess as to the reasons why Thales chose this. This in turn suggests that only the conclusion of Thales's thought still survived in the fourth century, the reasoning behind it being all lost.

Thus it is quite unprofitable to restore Thales's philosophy. How long his reasoning, as well as his ideas, survived is uncertain – perhaps only for a short while. What is important is the process he started. From his time there is a continuous line of descent, through his pupil Anaximander to the later generations of Greek scholarship, to the Hellenistic age and, ultimately, to the present day. It is no small achievement.

Democritus

(*c.* 460–*c.* 361 B.C.)

The natural philosopher Democritus was largely responsible for the development and promulgation of the atomic theory among the Greeks. In addition, he did less well known works in the fields of mathematics, cosmology, medicine, biology and ethics; in each case, his ideas reflected the materialism inherent in the atomic theory.

He was almost certainly born in Abdera, although it is sometimes suggested that he came from Miletus. According to Diogenes Laërtius, a third-century A.D. author who wrote the *Lives of the Philosophers*, Democritus wrote 72 works, the titles of some 60 of which survive in a catalogue which may have been that of the Library at Alexandria. None of the works, however, survives, and so our knowledge of Democritus's ideas is based on what other writers said about them and on about 300 quotations ostensibly from his works, although it is believed that many of these are spurious. Indeed, as with so many of the great thinkers of the ancient world, fable and fabrication surround much of the reports of his life.

However, two features of Democritus's biography seem to be genuine: that he travelled extensively, to Egypt, Chaldea, Athens and the Red Sea; and that one of his teachers was Leucippus, who was born in Miletus in about 490 B.C. and who was probably the true originator of Greek atomism. Quite how great a contribution Democritus made to the theory which he expounded is uncertain: it may well be that the relation of Democritus to Leucippus was rather like that between T. H. Huxley and Charles Darwin in the nineteenth century – that Democritus was, in effect, Leucippus's bulldog. However, such an extreme view is hard to defend, since by all accounts Democritus had a lively, speculative mind, and would certainly have embellished and expanded upon the original. It is not too much to say that he was the Aristotle of his day.

Atomism, as put forward by Democritus, claimed that all of reality was made up of atoms and void – thereby flying in the face of the then-popular opinion that void could not be 'real' and therefore could not exist. In fact, the existence of the void was as fundamental to the atomic theory as was the existence of atoms, for atomism depicted a universe in which there was never-ending change, with all atoms being in a state of constant motion; without the void, quite simply, the atoms would not have the space to move around in. Such dynamic ideas were at odds with the widely held Eleatic view that there were no such things as change and movement in the universe, and that, when our senses told us that change was occurring, they were deluding us. (The Eleatic school of philosophy owed its name to the fact that its two leading advocates, Parmenides and Zeno, both came from Elea.)

Democritus's atoms came in all shapes and sizes; in fact, some later thinkers speculated about atoms as large as worlds, although

Democritus himself seems to have believed that all atoms were, almost by definition, invisibly small. Certainly they were indivisible: the very word 'atom', *atomon*, implies exactly this. They were in a state of permanent motion (Aristotle, among others, pointed out that neither Leucippus nor Democritus had explained where this motion originally came from), and were all made of the same 'stuff'. The very evident variances in the properties of different substances therefore came about not through any difference in the 'composition' of the atoms of which those substances were made, but through differences in the shape, arrangement and position of the constituent atoms. To use a common illustration, their shapes could differ as do those of A and N, their arrangements in the same way as AN and NA, and their positions as Z and N (which is like a Z on its side).

This is a comparatively simple idea, but its ramifications were enormous: with the use of a little – or, in some cases, quite a lot of – imagination, *everything* could be explained in terms of these assumed properties of atoms. For example, water could flow because its atoms were spherical and so were unable to 'snag on-to' each other, while stone was solid because its atoms were jagged and hooked, so that they locked together like a tangle of barbed wire. Hot peppery spices had rough atoms, too, which was why they had such a potent effect on the tastebuds; and fire was made up of fast-moving spherical atoms which caused considerable pain as they impinged upon the skin.

Even the soul was made up of atoms; these were spherical, like the atoms of fire (in fact, on occasion it seems that Democritus made little distinction between fire and soul). Spherical atoms were of course highly capable of penetrating barriers, and indeed the ambient atmospheric pressure caused the human body to exude soul atoms at all times. Fortunately, however, the body was able to replenish its supplies of soul by taking in soul atoms from the air by breathing. Should there be a minor disparity between the number of soul atoms being inhaled and the number being lost, the person would fall asleep until a balance was regained; a major disparity resulted in death. The 'proof' of this idea was that it was obvious that, after death, it took the soul some little while to ooze completely out of the body: hair and fingernails continued to grow and, on very rare occasions, it was possible for a dead person to be resuscitated.

One consequence of this materialistic vision of the soul was that it precluded any idea of an after-life: the atoms of the deceased soul were dissipated to all quarters – and were, anyway, indistinguishable from all the other soul atoms.

The atomic theory had applications in the field of the senses, too. For example, what is happening when we see an object? At first, an atomist might offer the simplistic explanation that the object was emitting streams of atoms which entered the eyes and altered the configurations, in some way, of the atoms therein. But this notion had one very serious flaw: however small the individual atoms were, in due course the object would run out of atoms to emit. Since most objects manifestly did not just slowly melt away, a more sophisticated explanation was called for. Leucippus had suggested that objects in some way 'imprinted' the air around them, and that these 'imprinted' images (*eidola*) fled from their source – rather like the ripples from a pebble dropped in a pond – until, by chance, they encountered the eye. Democritus took this one stage further. He suggested that not only the object but also the eye was 'imprinting' the air in this way: the two sets of images collided and interacted in the air in front of the observer, forming a final image which he or she saw. (We should not place too much weight on the fact that this process is not too dissimilar from the way that a hologram works.)

Atomism had a very similar explanation for the way in which we hear sounds – and in this, of course, the atomists were more or less right. Touch and taste were much simpler senses to explain: they involved direct contacts between the object being sensed and the relevant organ. Smell, however, was believed to involve a mechanism very like those connected with sight and sound: it seems churlish to remark that smell really does come about thanks to the 'simplistic' process whereby the object emits atoms which interact with the sensors in the nose.

Like smell, sight and sound, thought was a product of the interaction between *eidola* from without the body and the atoms of the soul. Unfortunately, Democritus's full explanation of the process involved does not survive, but it seems that he believed that thought could arise only in the aftermath of sensation: the sensation disturbed the configuration of the body's soul atoms, which then returned to form a new balance, this process being what we call thought. Thanks to this idea, there could be no such thing as 'pure' thought, no way in which images from without could interact directly with the mind: the disturbing influences had first to pass through the medium of the senses. (Epicurus, 341–270 B.C., that other great champion of atomism, disagreed.)

Knowledge gained by the senses he described as 'bastard' knowledge, in contrast to 'legitimate' or 'genuine' knowledge, which involved objects which were simply too small for the senses to perceive. 'Legitimate' knowledge, then, related to the only things which were real – atoms and void – whereas 'bastard' knowledge was a far less definite affair: convention was the main governor of the knowledge which came from the senses; none of it was absolute. (We have all wondered if the colour which we see and call 'red' is the same as the colour other people see and call 'red'.) Yet how could one acquire 'legitimate' knowledge if one could not draw upon the evidence of the senses? Democritus's prescription was to take the evidence of the senses and submit it to rigorous critical reflection. Put in a rather different way, the mind takes the senses' evidence and does its best to overthrow it; it succeeds but, like a clumsy wrestler, likewise falls to the canvas – its pre-existing pattern of conceptions is changed.

It would be wrong to let our consideration of Democritus's atomism swamp all the other aspects of his thinking – although, as noted, they too are almost always related back in some way to atomism. His opinions on theology are a case in point.

He did not believe in gods or other such spiritual entities, claiming that they had been born out of humanity's desire to explain in some way the abrupt, unexpected and sometimes catastrophic eruptions of volcanoes, tremors of the earth, uprisings of violent storms, and so forth. If you have no knowledge of microbes, it seems quite obvious that you are dying because it is the will of the gods that you should do so, rather than because you have been invaded by plague bacilli. Yet, while he thought that belief in superhuman agencies was a product of sheer ignorance, Democritus was not prepared to dismiss all of what we might call the 'supernatural' out of hand. He held that people's minds could be entered (*via* the usual circuitous route, no doubt) by *eidola*, or effluences, rather like the 'imprints' involved in the sense of sight. Not all of these *eidola* were beneficial; but all had the properties of audibility and visibility, and the potential to forecast the future.

Atomism entered his mathematical speculations, too. He seems, for example, to have believed that a sphere is in reality a regular polyhedron, composed of a colossal number of imperceptibly small faces – a view which is not ridiculous, since of course a *real* sphere, rather than a mathematical ideal, is more or less exactly that. Another surviving discussion of his is strongly reminiscent of the four paradoxes presented to the ancient world by Zeno of Elea. Democritus considered what happens when you slice horizontally through a cone. On the one hand it seems self-evident that the two faces thereby exposed must be exactly congruent – because they would completely cover each other if you reassembled the cone. But, if this is the case, how does the cone ever manage to taper? Surely a succession of congruent faces would produce a cylinder? If, on the other hand, one agrees that one of the faces is fractionally smaller than the other, then one has a similar dilemma: a smooth cone becomes impossible, and all cones must be rather like circle-based versions of the step pyramids. The interesting thing here is that the puzzle involves mathematically ideal cones as much as real ones. No real solution could be produced until millennia later, with the onset of the idea of the infinitesimally small (which was to usher in the age of calculus); one of the most appealing proposed solutions, in the light of modern 'doublethink' in frontier physics, was the idea that the two surfaces are both equal and unequal, a notion not too far removed from that of the infinitesimally small.

Democritus's cosmology was exceptionally elegant – and, as is the case with so many of his ideas, has a certain chilling similarity with current beliefs. In order to understand it, we have to draw upon yet a further property of atoms, that like atoms attract other like atoms: you rarely find objects made out of a mixture of chalk and cheese.

We have seen that atoms were believed to be in a state of perpetual motion; in fact, this motion had been in existence since long before the universe was born. Picture, then, a time when all of space was filled with atoms moving at high speed in random directions. Obviously such randomness could not last: collisions galore occurred between atoms and, where these collisions occurred between like atoms, they tended to stay together. Moreover, there was an overall swirling motion, or *dine*, set up: heavier atoms, being more resistant to the rotation, tended to move towards the rotation's centre; agglomerates of lighter atoms were squeezed out towards the edges of the vortex, where their speed of revolution was in some cases so great that they caught fire, becoming stars.

The important point about this model of the universe was that it depended not upon pure chance but *upon the properties of the atoms themselves*. The atomists were challenged at the time, and over the succeeding centuries, to explain why it was that atoms should just chance to have the appropriate properties – and this is precisely the dilemma which faces modern cosmology. Had the properties of matter, energy and space-time been just a little different, then the universe would be a complete chaos or might never have come into existence at all. One popular suggestion is that it was God who, as it were, put the right figures into the relevant equations – but it is a suggestion which Democritus would have abhorred.

There was a further cosmological consequence of the fact that like atoms attracted each other. Since the void was infinite, and since there was an infinite number of atoms, an infinite number of separate universes must have formed. We cannot see the other universes because our own is surrounded by a 'skin' of linked like atoms: our universe is but one bubble among an infinite number. We have no knowledge of what conditions are like in the other 'bubble universes': the central world of some may have no sun or no moon, or even no people. In modern parlance, the physical laws may be quite different.

These ideas are so like some of the ones floating around the edges of late twentieth-century cosmology that one is seriously tempted to wonder if perhaps Democritus's mind really *was* invaded by *eidola*, which spoke to him of the future. That, of course, is nothing but a fancy: what seems certain is that Democritus was possessed of one of the most brilliantly intuitive minds of his – or any other – age.

Hippocrates

(*c.* 460–*c.* 370 B.C.)

Hippocrates was almost certainly born on the island of Cos, and belonged to 'the family of the Asclepiadae', a corporation of doctors who claimed descent from Asclepios, the great physician. He taught at Cos, enjoyed wide fame during his lifetime, travelled to many parts of the Greek world, and contributed to an extremely important corpus of Greek medical writings which are known as the *Hippocratic Collection*. There is still some controversy as to exactly which of these writings he was responsible for, and it is unlikely that a definitive answer will ever be available. One of the collection, the famous oath, is thought to date from just before Hippocrates's time.

Since no one can do more than make informed guesses as to exactly which of the *Hippocratic Collection* were written by Hippocrates himself, we have to base our reconstruction of his ideas on the collection as a whole. In fact, in so doing we probably diverge little from the reality, since not only were his ideas certainly moulded by others prevalent at the medical school on Cos, but also they in turn moulded the ideas of his immediate successors.

The medical schools of Cos and Cnidas (at the south-western

tip of Asia Minor) were constantly squabbling over perceived differences in their medical beliefs. For example, the school at Cnidos believed that the four 'humours' or chief fluids of the body, which determined a person's mental and physical characteristics, were phlegm, blood, bile and water, whereas that at Cos held they were phlegm, blood, choler (yellow bile) and melancholy (black bile). Such a disagreement is trivial in light of the fact that both schools subscribed to the doctrine of the four humours. (By way of analogy, modern physicists disagree about the details of Relativity, but few of them fail to accept its general truth.) So the Cnidian writings can help us gain a general picture of Hippocrates's medicine.

The most important point of similarity between the two schools was that both held it as a central tenet that medicine was a rational science. Diseases were not inspired as punishments or rewards by the gods. Earlier physicians had accepted this in part, but in the face of some ailments had been forced to fall back on the activities of supernatural influences. The prime example was epilepsy, the 'sacred disease', sufferers from which malady were believed to be being possessed by gods or demons. The Cnidians and the Coans alike rejected such transrational explanations, and took it as axiomatic that diseases were produced solely by physical causes – a term which, to them, included also what we would describe as psychological causes. Likewise, they were suspicious of any medical practice or theory whose origins could be traced directly to philosophical preconceptions (although in practice it was of course impossible for them to divorce themselves entirely from the philosophical ambience of their time).

In short, both schools sought to base their medicine solely on direct observation, on the evidence presented to them by the senses of touch, smell, sight, hearing and taste, as interpreted by intellect. Their ideas are, therefore, generally regarded as being the direct ancestors of modern medicine. There was an important difference though in emphasis between the two schools. The Cnidian practitioners adopted a more empirical approach than the Coans; they set great store by observation and classification, and this fidelity to facts tended to limit their horizon. The Coans, on the other hand, were always attempting to interpret their findings, searching for underlying causes of symptoms.

However, we must not for a moment think that either the Coans or the Cnidians were able by virtue of their rational approach to make any startling medical discoveries. As we have noted, they accepted the doctrine of the four humours, as advanced by Empedocles (*c*. 490–*c*. 430 B.C.). Disease was a result of

On a wall of the Luxor temple, Alexander the Great is depicted as divine Pharaoh pouring water, the symbol of life, before the sun god, Amun-Re, the giver of life. *Below:* The Edict of Asoka and Lion Column during excavation at Sarnath.

Above: Bust of Julius Caesar in the Naples Museum, and the only known life bust of Cleopatra. *Below:* Wall-carving at Dendera showing Cleopatra introducing her son Caesarion to the gods of Upper Egypt.

disturbances either of the balance between the humours or of the humours themselves, so that they became indigestible; the disease waned as the body 'restored order' by slowly 'cooking' the affected humours until they returned to normal. The waning of the disease was not a steady, gradual process: there was always at least one crisis, or turning point, during the disease's course. At the crisis there would be a great many changes taking place simultaneously, matched by an equal plurality of symptoms; the crisis having been survived, the disease would then abate at its natural rate.

Clearly the Hippocratic idea of the crisis was based on good, objective observation. The same can be said of the notion of the 'deposit'. A disease could be either preceded or succeeded by the 'deposit', a disability or symptom confined to one part of the body. From this area the 'deposit' could transport itself to other localised areas of the body in the process known as metastasis. Thanks to appropriate metastasis of a 'deposit', one disease might turn into another. In fact, this is exactly what appears to happen in many diseases, although modern medicine reveals that sometimes what is really happening is the reverse of what it seems. The first sign of lung cancer, for example, may be a spontaneous fracture of the leg due to bone cancer there; this 'deposit' might then seem to migrate to the lung (and elsewhere). In fact, of course, the metastasis (the term still in use) is from the lung to the leg, rather than the other way around, and is a spread rather than a migration.

But understanding of the underlying mechanisms for various phenomena is not always essential for successful medical treatment, assuming that one's model – however far removed from the truth – is consistent and in accordance with observed events; should the events follow the same pattern from case to case, then very often something can be done to cure the sufferers. This is especially so if physicians preserve their observations of different cases, so that they can learn by their failures.

This the Coan physicians did – as did the Cnidians – and consequently they were able to effect cures rather more frequently than their contemporaries. In order to appreciate their success-rate, however, we have to think a little harder about exactly what we mean by the term 'cure'. Even today, physicians cure the vast majority of their patients by what is called the 'placebo effect'. In some instances, of course, diseases simply run their courses and go away, but in many others a cure is effected not directly by any treatment which the physician may prescribe but by the very fact that *any* treatment *is* being prescribed. And, obviously, the greatest success-rates are achieved when the patient trusts the therapist implicitly.

The placebo effect must not be underestimated. However, the Coan and Cnidian physicians, with their rationalistic approach to medicine, must have been able to effect cures in some cases where other physicians were powerless. This cannot but have increased the regard in which patients held these therapists, and consequently the rate of cures made by the placebo effect must have increased, too. The 'great leap forward' for which the Coan and Cnidian medical schools were responsible derived directly, therefore, only in small part from any actual medical advances which they made.

Dangerous diseases were rife and little understood; the process of learning how to cure them through knowledge of past failures could take generations – perhaps many generations. Moreover, owing largely to an inability to understand the nature of disease, but partly to a lack of technology, the physician had only a very limited number of possible therapies to hand. This was inevitable when there was virtually no knowledge of anatomy (dissection of human corpses was forbidden), and physiology had not emerged as a science.

As with many modern herbals, therefore, some diseases were regarded as treatable by virtually every potion in the pharmacopoeia, while some potions were regarded as beneficial to virtually every ailment – rather like today's popular view of aspirin. The Hippocratic physicians must have been only too aware that their pharmacopoeia was severely limited; in short, and rather more bluntly, that their 'cures' didn't very often do much good.

But sometimes their lack of success was due to failure to adhere to their own doctrine. Where the doctrine stressed the vital importance of accurate, rigorous observation – something which was indeed carried out in many cases – it is clear from the writings of the *Hippocratic Collection* that the observations were very often 'flawed'. And they were 'flawed' because the physicians were breaking one of their own rules: they were allowing philosophical theories and preconceptions to overrule the evidence of their senses.

However, Hippocrates and his associates made one startling breakthrough. This was their insistence that much could be done by way of both curative and preventive medicine through concentration on diet, environment (both locational and seasonal) and everyday regimen. In today's terms, if you eat the right things, do the right amount of appropriate exercise and don't live in the middle of a city you will keep better health than if the reverse applies. This may seem obvious, but before the era of Hippocrates it was not. The treatise on *Airs, Waters, Places* in the *Collection* is of the highest interest on the correlation of health and environmental factors. In the *Epidemics*, Book V, we have a clear recognition of the regenerative powers of nature: 'Nature is the physician of diseases.'

The Coans and Cnidians sometimes took the matter of diet, season, location and regimen to ridiculous extremes. Nose-bleeds, for example, were supposed to be more prevalent and more copious in the earlier than in the later part of the year, because the hot red blood matched the hot red weather. But this overemphasis on these matters was not, in medical terms, very important: if a particular medicine is good for you, it doesn't really matter when your physician insists that you should drink it

These physicians, working at the very dawn of medicine, had, therefore, little success in either theoretical or practical terms. Their medical theories were underlaid by the general ignorance of the times, their therapies were limited and haphazard; and, while they succeeded in formulating an excellent set of rules for the practice of medical research and treatment, they were constrained in this practice by their lack of knowledge.

Why then is Hippocrates regarded as the 'Father of Medicine'? Simply for the formulation of that set of rules, for the realisation that medicine is a rational science – that diseases have objective causes – and for the championing of these ideas.

But one must ask oneself a further question: did the Hippocratics have any effect on the development of medical science? The answer is, almost certainly, very little. If the schools of Cos and Cnidas had never existed, medicine would probably have discovered the beneficial Hippocratic ideas at much the same time that it in fact did rediscover them. Nevertheless the Hippocratic influence with its devouring quest for knowledge, its recognition of the primacy of the patient even if he were a slave, its strict and lofty rules by which a physician conducted his practice, and the disinterested friendship it offered all men without distinction, was an example of fifth-century humanism at its best and has provided a practical ethic for the medical profession to the present day.

Euclid

(c. 325–c. 270 B.C.)

Almost nothing is known about Euclid's life: the dates for his birth
and death given above are far from generally accepted, and are
based purely on evidence which suggests somewhat hazily that he
was born some time after the death of Plato (c. 347 B.C.) and died
some time after the birth of Archimedes (c. 287 B.C.). It is possible
that he studied at Athens and virtually certain that he thereafter
moved to Alexandria where, like so many others, he did all his
useful work. Tradition, which is probably valueless, has it that he
was a henpecked husband.

It is impossible to evaluate the veracity or otherwise of two
anecdotes which are told about him. The first concerns a student
who is supposed to have asked him what he gained from his
geometrical knowledge, to which Euclid responded by beckoning
a slave and telling him to give the student some money, 'because
he must make a profit out of what he learns'. The other, more
famous, tale is given to us by Proclus, who was writing in the fifth
century A.D. Euclid's patron Ptolemy I, finding geometry hard
work, asked if there were not any quicker way of going about it:
Euclid replied that there was no 'royal road to geometry'.

Yet about Euclid's ideas we know a very great deal – especially
about his ideas on geometry. Two of his books on geometry
survive, *Elements* and *Data*, of which the former is overwhelmingly
the more important – so important, in fact, that it has often been
described as having had a more profound effect upon western
consciousness than any other work save the Bible, a claim which
must be regarded as dubious. Less partisan is the claim that
Elements is the best-selling textbook of all time: it has gone through
well over a thousand editions since the invention of printing.

Aside from *Elements* and *Data*, Euclid is known to have written
several other works on geometry which are no longer extant: *Conic
Sections, Division of Figures, Porisms* (porisms are thought to have
been propositions that conditions existed such that certain
problems were incapable of determinate solution), *Pseudo-
graphemata* (or *The Book of Fallacies*) and *Surface Loci*. Allied to
his work on geometry is his book *Optics*, in which he considers rays
of light to be straight lines and examines their behaviour using the
tools of geometry. He wrote also a surviving work on astronomy,

Phenomena, and is thought to have been the author of several extant fragments, including one on density. *On Mirrors*, which is occasionally attributed to him on the evidence of Proclus, is almost certainly not his. Similarly, he was responsible for at most parts of a work called *Elements of Music*, although again this is sometimes attributed to him in its entirety.

Of all these works, *Elements* is by far the most noteworthy. We shall return to it shortly.

Euclid's astronomy, as given to us in *Phenomena*, was descriptive rather than theoretical. He believed that the universe was spherical, and explored its geometry, while concerning himself also with the rising and setting times of the fixed stars. His one significant contribution was his introduction of the observer's horizon as a specific, meaningful entity in astronomy.

His *Optics* concerns itself not so much with optics as with perspective – in fact, as a scientific rather than a geometrical text it leaves a lot to be desired. It accepts Plato's erroneous notion that vision comes about through rays of light being emitted from the eyes: these rays travel in straight lines and, taken together, form a cone whose point is at the observer's eye. In fact, the geometry of the situation is not affected by getting the reality back to front in this way, and so the text was of some value at the time – especially since in it one or two useful geometrical conclusions are drawn.

The nature of Euclid's contribution to geometry is hard to assess. Certainly he was a masterly expositor, which is why *Elements* has survived and was used virtually unchanged for so long; but there is no way of telling quite how many of the proofs contained in it were his own, and to what extent he was merely setting out the theorems of others in a logical, rigorously schematic way. Probably the truth of the matter was that he was less concerned with the originality or otherwise of the various proofs, and more with the way in which, taken all together, they gave a complete and consistent view of the universe in terms of geometry. Just as one theorem flowed from those which had gone before it, so could knowledge of the workings of the universe advance by logical reasoning from what was already known.

In fact, of course, not all of the theorems could be derived from earlier ones – Euclid had to start somewhere. He began by setting out five postulates and five axioms. The axioms need not concern us here, but the postulates deserve some attention. Stated simply, they were:

1. A straight line can be drawn between any two points.
2. A straight line can be extended in either direction.

3. Using any centre and any radius, a circle can be drawn.
4. All right angles are equal.
5. Should two straight lines be cut by a third, and should the internal angles on one side of the third line add up to less than two right angles (i.e., to less than 180°), then the two lines will meet on that side of the third line.

Postulates *1* to *4* are apparently self-evident, although they have certain interesting implications. For example, the absolute terms of postulates *2* and *3* suggest that Euclid thought in terms of infinite space, since there is no notion that a line cannot be extended indefinitely or a circle constructed of however great a radius one might choose. Moreover, postulate *3* implies an infinitely divisible space, since equally the radius of the circle may be as small as one wishes.

Postulate *5* likewise implies that space is infinite. In fact, postulate *5* is very much the odd one out. Its assertion may not at first seem 'self-evident' until one looks at the pair of diagrams. In *a* we see that the two lines AB and CD will indeed always meet on the side of EF on which the internal angles (θ and ϕ) add up to less than 180°. In *b*, however, the internal angle of any line cutting AB and CD add up to 180° exactly on both sides, and therefore it must be assumed that AB and CD never meet, even if they are infinitely extended. By extrapolation, one can say that the distance between two parallel lines will remain the same, no matter how far they are extended in either direction.

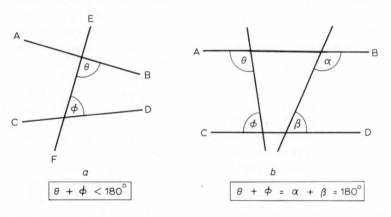

$$\boxed{\theta + \phi < 180°}$$

a

$$\boxed{\theta + \phi = \alpha + \beta = 180°}$$

b

So much appears to be 'self-evident', and was regarded as such until the nineteenth century, when J. K. F. Gauss (1777–1855) questioned it. As he pointed out, while the proposition that parallel lines will never meet is 'self-evident', no one had yet succeeded in *proving* it – and over the millennia people had frequently tried. The matter was taken further by Bolyai Farkas (1775–1856), who spent a lifetime trying to prove the postulate, and especially by his son, Bolyai János (1802–60), who investigated one of the forms of geometry which would emerge should it be that the postulate was actually wrong. A little later the Russian mathematician Nikolai Ivanovich Lobachevski (1792–1856) independently investigated this branch of non-Euclidean geometry, which is now known as Lobachevskian or hyperbolic geometry.

It follows directly from postulate 5 that, if you have a straight line L and a point P which does not lie on L, only a single line can be drawn through P which will never, no matter how far extended, meet L. Bolyai and Lobachevski suggested that in fact more than one such line could be drawn through P (and therefore, necessarily, an infinite number). If such a geometry were a genuine reflection of reality, then space would have a hypervboloid shape: if you can imagine two post-horns joined at their infinitely large flares, and with their infinitely long shafts tapering away forever, you are imagining something close to a hyperboloid. Neither Bolyai nor Lobachevski assumed that their new geometry actually *meant* anything, in real terms: it was just a different way of looking at things. Still, it rocked the scientific boat, since the unquestionable truth of Euclidean geometry had been accepted for over two millennia, and so Lobachevski was in due course fired from his post at the University of Kazan.

An alternative form of non-Euclidean geometry was investigated by Georg Friedrich Riemann (1826–66), who suggested instead that through the point P *no* line could be drawn which would never intersect with L. Immediate consequences include the notion that a straight line is not the shortest distance between two points, that a straight line cannot be extended indefinitely, and that more than one straight line can be drawn between any two points. If this geometry reflected reality, then the universe would be ellipsoidal – hence the term 'elliptical geometry'. (An ellipsoid is the solid shape you generate if you take an ellipse and spin it about one of its axes.) There is no reason to believe that Riemann believed that his geometry was any more 'real' than Lobachevskian geometry – except for the fact that it applies on the surface of a sphere. For example, no 'straight line' drawn on a spherical surface is of infinite length (if you start running in any direction you will eventually end up in the same place at which you started). Albert Einstein was, however, to find that Riemannian geometry was closer to the reality than

Euclidean geometry. The difference is subtle enough that, for example, no compensations had to be made when the Viking probes were sent to land with pinpoint accuracy on Mars.

To explore the non-Euclidean geometries at such length may seem to be getting away from the subject of Euclidean geometry, and Euclid himself; but this is not the case. As we have mentioned, postulate 5 was very much the odd one out: Euclid had the astonishing power of insight to realise that it could not be proved from other, more 'self-evident' postulates. In a sense, by including it in his list of five postulates, he was himself laying the foundations for non-Euclidean geometry.

Elements strayed beyond the boundaries of geometry into other areas of mathematics, notably number theory: the proofs it contains that there are an infinite number of prime numbers (numbers without integral factors other than themselves and 1), which had not been proven before, and that the square root of 2 is an irrational number (i.e., one which cannot be expressed as a ratio), which had been proven before but not nearly so concisely or well, seem likely to have been Euclid's own. In the realm of geometry, tradition has it that the proof in *Elements* of the Pythagorean theorem (see page 498) was likewise devised by Euclid himself.

The way in which the theorems and problems of *Elements* are set out was to provide a blueprint for scientists for many centuries. Although sometimes one or more of the stages are omitted, the pattern is that there is first a general statement of the theorem or problem, followed by a more detailed statement of it, usually related to a diagram. This is followed by a definition, and then by a constructive stage, in which, for example, extensions may be made to the diagram. Finally comes either the detailed proof of the theorem or the solution of the problem, followed by a more colloquial concluding discussion, which points out that the original statement has been proven. The conclusions, in the case of the theorems, contained the expression 'which had to be proven'; similarly, the concluding stages of problems used the words 'which had to be done'. The Latin versions of these expressions are *quod erat demonstrandum* and *quod erat faciendum*, whose abbreviations are QED and QEF.

While this scheme of presentation was influential, so too was the pattern of his logic. In his day there were two methods of providing logical proof. One was analysis, whereby a hypothesis would be presented and deductions made from it until it was shown that some self-evident or already proven proposition was a necessary consequence of the initial hypothesis. The other, which

Euclid used throughout *Elements* (although not always in his other works), was synthesis, in which known truths were built upon until previously unknown truths became evident. We use both tools (as well as such elegances as lateral thinking) today, but for many centuries, thanks to Euclid, synthesis was dominant.

Whether he was a pioneer or a mere reporter – a textbook writer – is, then, largely unimportant: Euclid almost single-handedly shaped the whole future of mathematics. His influence is still felt strongly today.

Herophilus

(*b. c.* 320 B.C.)

The practice of dissection of the human body had not been tolerated in Greece of the fifth and fourth centuries B.C. for religious and traditional reasons. The researches of Hippocrates and Aristotle had been severely restricted for this reason, the latter having to content himself with experimentation on animals and attempts to translate by analogy to the human organism what he had discovered. This hardly made for accurate medicine.

However, when the Ptolemies attracted Greek scientists to Egypt, the ban on the use of human corpses for medical purposes ceased. For millennia the Egyptians had mummified their dead, a procedure involving ritual dissection. In this ambience there could be no objection to the learned men of Alexandria demonstrating their anatomical lectures with corpses; and the lectures of Herophilus became celebrated far and wide.

Herophilus was born, according to Galen, at Chalcedon, in Bithynia, a Greek city which is now one of the suburbs of Istanbul, on the Asiatic side of the straits. Very little else is known about his life – for example, we have no notion of how or when he died – except that he studied under Praxagoras of Cos, and later practised medicine and taught at Alexandria. He wrote a number of books, principally the *Anatomica*, but all have been lost. What we know of his theories, discoveries and teachings we know only from second-hand sources, the most distinguished of them being the later writings of Galen. Even so, it is obvious that Herophilus was one of the giants of ancient medicine, not only in achievement but in reputation.

Clearly it is impossible to determine the exact order in which he made his various discoveries or even to hypothesise about how he might have been led from one field of operations to the next, but it is possible that his work on the human brain followed from his study of the eye. Through dissection he discovered the nerves and their origins in the brain – thereby, incidentally, demolishing any idea that they could be, as it were, modified arteries. However, he was able to go very much further than this, distinguishing between the sensory nerves and the efferent nerves (the former bring information to the brain while the latter carry information from it and, when they lead to muscles, are called motor nerves). In particular, he traced the optic nerve from the eye to the brain; however, since dissection suggested to him that this nerve at least was hollow, he believed that its function was the transportation of *pneuma*. It is tempting to equate *pneuma* with electricity and thereby claim that Herophilus had discovered the workings of the peripheral nervous system all in one fell swoop, but that would be stretching matters too far.

His work on the brain had one immediate and important result: it showed that this organ, and not the heart, is responsible for both the intellectual processes and the experiencing of sensations. This was by no means a proof of the obvious. We can liken Herophilus's discovery, and its consequences, to a sort of small-scale version of the Copernican revolution. It is 'perfectly obvious' to *us* that the earth goes around the sun, but for centuries before Copernicus it was 'perfectly obvious' that the converse was true. Most people of Herophilus's time must have found the notion that the brain was the seat of human intellect rather fanciful; and we still talk about 'feeling in our heart of hearts' that something is the case.

While this simple feat was perhaps the most important of his achievements in his study of the brain, it should be recognised that he also did some startlingly sophisticated work on the brain's anatomy, in particular being able to distinguish the cerebellum (which is responsible for things like balance and posture) from the cerebrum (which is responsible for most of the brain's obvious activities including, probably, intellectual thought). Other discoveries are reflected in such technical terms connected with the brain as *torcular Herophili* and *calamus Herophili* – terms which are still in use today.

Few major areas of the body or organs failed to receive his attention, and often the results of his research showed a sophistication of practice and thought which was to be unsurpassed for as long as two millennia. He did important work in the field of gynaecology, dissecting and describing accurately the female generative organs, and noting incidentally the Fallopian tubes, which were to be rediscovered by Gabriel Fallopius (1523–62). He investigated the causes of problematical births, such as breech deliveries, although it is unclear whether or not he suggested any ways of preventing such difficulties; and he examined menstruation's effect on health and psychological well-being.

However, it must not be thought that his was a success story in every field. He seems, like many a modern general practitioner, to have relied excessively on the use of drugs, often to the detriment of the patient, although in many other ways he was positively naturopathic in his emphasis on such practices as exercise and attention to diet as prophylactic medical measures. He also seems to have enthusiastically espoused the use of bleeding as a means of treatment, something which must have been regretted by countless patients in their terminal moments until well after the end of the Middle Ages.

That his theory of respiration so nearly misses the mark is also surprising, in view of the fact that he had shown that, contrary to much contemporary medical belief, the arteries carried blood. (Later, Erasistratus, who believed that the arteries did *not* carry blood, came out with a theory much closer to the reality!) According to Herophilus's scheme, the act of inhalation brought new air to the lungs (obviously); from the lungs the air was – somehow – spread to the far corners of the body. In the next stage of the process old, used air was brought from the various parts of the body; and finally, in the act of exhalation, the old air was expelled. It is tempting, as with so many of Herophilus's ideas, to say that this is more or less exactly what really does happen; but Herophilus himself would have demurred had someone tried to explain to him the true nature of respiration. His postulated process involved the four distinct phases which I have listed.

He had a similar near miss in his work on the pulse. His mentor, Praxagoras, had used the pulse to help in diagnoses, but he seems to have used it in no more sophisticated a way than that in which one feels the forehead of a child to see if it is hot. Herophilus, by contrast, had the idea of timing the pulse – which he did by use of a clepsydra (water clock), a practice which must have been far from simple. In addition to the rate of the pulse, he noted also its magnitude, its rhythm and its vigour. He certainly realised that the pulse was a reflection of the beating of the heart, but he was barred from going on to such heady heights as the discovery of the circulation of the blood by one trivial error.

When a pulse of blood passes down an artery, the artery wall is temporarily stretched; it then returns to its 'normal' position until the next pulse of blood arrives. Herophilus, however, got this the wrong way round: he believed that the 'normal' condition of the arteries was the dilated one. He was therefore, as it were, in the position of trying to find an explanation for the troughs rather than for the wave-crests. While the error is understandable, it does seem strange that he was incapable of making the tiny conceptual leap necessary merely to wonder if perhaps things might be the other way round.

Herophilus's achievements were, however, remarkable. He converted dissection into a genuinely scientific means of discovery, and his anatomical findings – still enshrined in the terminology of the subject – entitle him to be considered the father of the science.

Aristarchus of Samos

(*c.* 310–*c.* 230 B.C.)

Aristarchus of Samos flourished around 270 B.C. We know nothing whatsoever about his character or career, and we are not even certain about his dates; he was probably born in or about 310 B.C. and died about 230 B.C. He was an older contemporary of the famous Archimedes, who has in fact left us the only real account of his most important discovery; the original book by Aristarchus has been lost, though part of another, *On the Sizes and Distances of the Sun and Moon*, has come down to us.

Aristarchus is famous on two counts. Firstly, he was one of the first – if not the very first – to maintain that the earth is in orbit round the sun rather than being the centre of the universe. Secondly, he made a noble attempt to estimate the distance-scale of the sun and moon. His method was perfectly sound in theory, and gave poor results only because the measurements could not be made with sufficient precision.

Before the time of Aristarchus, it had always been assumed that the earth is the central body of the universe, remaining motionless with the heavens turning round it. There were, of course, several variations on the main theme, but there had never been any question of the earth being a mere planet, even though it had long been realised that the world is a globe rather than a flat plane. Aristotle, the great philosopher, certainly believed in a central earth, and his authority was so great that it was in the main unchallenged – and remained so for many centuries after his death, with only a few dissentients. In fact, the geocentric or earth-centred theory was by no means unreasonable, and with enough care it could even be made to represent the movements of the planets with reasonable accuracy, as Ptolemy, last of the great astronomers of classical times, proved later. There were also religious considerations. Anaxagoras of Clazomenae, who lived long before Aristarchus (he was born around 500 B.C.) had even been accused of impiety by claiming that the sun was a red-hot stone larger than the Peloponnesus, and only his friendship with Pericles, the most powerful man in the Athens of the time, saved him from serious persecution.

Just why Aristarchus came to the conclusions he did is not known, but they seem to have been quite definite. Fortunately, his ideas are given in the famous *Sand-Reckoner* (or *Psammites*) of Archimedes, who wrote as follows:

> But Aristarchus of Samos brought out a book consisting of certain hypotheses, in which the premises lead to the conclusion that the universe is many times greater than that now so called. His hypotheses are that the fixed stars and the sun remain motionless, that the earth revolves round the sun in the circumference of a circle, the sun lying in the middle of the orbit, and that the sphere of the fixed stars, situated about the same centre as the sun, is so great that the circle in which he supposes the earth to revolve bears such a proportion to the distances of the fixed stars as the centre of the sphere bears to its surface.

Nothing could be clearer than that. Yet Aristarchus found few followers, and one critic, Cleanthes the Stoic, even suggested that he should be accused of impiety – though so far as we know nothing came of it.

The real troubles were twofold. First, Aristarchus could give no definite proof of the correctness of his ideas, and to the Greeks of that period they seemed far-fetched. Secondly, the bold step of removing the earth from its proud central position and putting the sun there instead appeared to solve nothing at all. To the best of our knowledge his only real supporter was Seleucus of Seleucia, a Chaldaean who lived about a century after Aristarchus and has left us a treatise on the subject of the tides. Later Greek scientists, notably Hipparchus, reverted to the idea of a central earth. And Ptolemy, who lived from about A.D. 120 to 180, brought the geocentric theory to a high state of perfection. Admittedly it was cumbersome and artificial; but it did fit the facts as they were then known, and it was not until the fifteenth century that it was challenged. Nikolaus Krebs (Nicholas of Cusa), who lived from 1401 to 1464, considered the possibility that the earth might move round the sun, but the real change came with the publication of the famous book by Copernicus in 1543. Even then the 'great revolution' was a slow process, and it was not really completed until the work of Sir Isaac Newton.

Incidentally, it seems that Copernicus did know of Aristarchus's beliefs. He even mentioned them in one of his works, though he deleted all reference to Aristarchus later.

It is a tremendous pity that we do not have Aristarchus's original book, and have to rely upon the second-hand account left to us by Archimedes. We do not even know how far Aristarchus was prepared to go. Presumably he believed that the planets, like the earth, move round the sun; he must have believed in perfectly circular orbits (as indeed did everyone else up to the time of Johannes Kepler in the early seventeenth century), but whether or not he accepted the clumsy epicycles described by other philosophers, including Ptolemy in later years, is not known. Unless an ancient manuscript turns up, which is very unlikely, we will never be able to tell.

Now let us turn to Aristarchus's other major contribution: his attempt to determine the relative distances of the moon and sun.

His method was straightforward enough. He was well aware of the cause of the regular phases of the moon from new to full; and he also knew that when the moon appears as an exact half, the earth, sun and moon must be arranged in a triangle, with the angle at the moon equal to 90 degrees. He measured the second angle, that at the earth, and gave a value for it of 87 degrees, from which it followed that the sharpest angle – that at the sun – must be 3 degrees. The triangle could then be solved, and the relative distances found. Here we are on firmer ground, because we have Aristarchus's own description of the results:

We are now in a position to prove that the distance of the sun from the earth is greater than 18 times, but less than 20 times, the distance of the moon, and the diametter of the sun also has the same ratio to the diameter of the moon; this follows from the hypothesis about the halved moon. Again, we can prove that the diameter of the sun is to the diameter of the earth in a greater ratio than that which 19 has to 3, but in a lesser ratio than that which 43 has to 6; this follows from the ratio thus discovered as regards the distances, from the hypothesis about the shadow, and from the hypothesis that the moon subtends 1/15 part of a sign of the zodiac.

There is nothing wrong with this reasoning – but in fact the real distance of the sun is 400 times that of the moon. The trouble stemmed from the fact that it is extremely difficult to determine the precise moment of half-moon, particularly when all the estimates have to be made with the naked eye alone. The lunar surface is not smooth; it is very uneven, with mountains, valleys and plains, to say nothing of the huge craters. This means that the terminator, or line between the daylit and night hemispheres, is jagged and uneven. It is not surprising that Aristarchus arrived at the wrong result. The angle at the sun, at the time of half-moon, is not 3 degrees; it is only about 10 minutes of arc, and the error is large enough to wreck the accuracy of the whole method. To make matters worse, Aristarchus gave the apparent diameter of the moon as 2 degrees, whereas a careful check should have established that the real figure is only about half a degree.

All the same, it was a serious attempt, and it showed that useful measurements could be made. Moreover, Aristarchus was well aware that the sun is considerably larger than the earth – a great improvement on the opinion of the earlier philosopher Heraclitus of Ephesus, who was born about 544 B.C. and who believed that the diameter of the sun was about twelve inches!

It has often been said that the Greeks were the first to turn astronomy into a true science. This is probably justified. There were two major steps to be taken. One was to abandon the old idea of a flat earth, and this was taken at a comparatively early stage; Pythagoras, who lived from about 580 to 500 B.C., certainly knew that the world is a globe, and Eratosthenes of Cyrene, a younger contemporary of Archimedes, even managed to measure its size with surprising accuracy. The other step was to relegate the earth to the status of an ordinary planet moving round the sun. Had this been achieved, the progress of astronomical science would have been a great deal quicker than it actually was, but of the really major philosophers only Aristarchus seems to have had the courage to maintain it.

Hipparchus of Nicaea, whose career extended from about 160 to 126 B.C. (we are unsure of his precise dates), is generally regarded as the greatest observer of antiquity. He drew up a star catalogue which was later elaborated by Ptolemy, and he improved upon Aristarchus's estimates of the sizes and distances of the sun and moon. He also discovered the phenomenon of precession, which shows that he was capable of making very accurate measurements. Yet he returned to the geocentric theory, and so far as we know neither he nor Ptolemy seriously considered any alternative. Aristarchus's revolutionary views were to all intents and purposes forgotten. One of the last mentions of him in the classical period is due to Plutarch, who died in or about A.D. 120. In his fascinating work *De facie in orbe lunae* (On the Face in the Orb of the Moon) we read:

> Do not, my good fellow, enter an action against me for impiety in the style of Cleanthes, who thought it was the duty of the Greeks to indict Aristarchus of Samos on the charge of impiety for putting in motion the Hearth of the Universe, this being the effect of his attempt to save the phenomena by supposing the heaven to remain at rest, and the earth to revolve in an oblique circle, while it rotates, at the same time, about its own axis.

After that – silence on the subject, until its revival well over a thousand years later. It is therefore not easy to decide how much influence Aristarchus really had. On the whole it seems that this influence was not really very great; the Greeks in general were simply not ready to accept such a radical change in outlook. But this in no way diminishes the magnitude of Aristarchus's achievement. He was many centuries ahead of his time, and the fact that he was almost totally ignored was no fault of his.

Erasistratus

(*c.* 304–*c.* 250 B.C.)

Erasistratus, born on the island of Chios in the Aegean, seems to have come from medical stock. As with most of his scientific contemporaries, few details of his early life are known for certain. It seems likely that he studied medicine in Athens under a son-in-law of Aristotle's, Metrodoros, although another tradition has it that Erasistratus's connexion with Aristotle was more direct, Aristotle being his grandfather. Of course, both may be correct.

From Athens Erasistratus went to Cos, where he was strongly influenced by the ideas of Praxagoras, which ideas had earlier profoundly affected those of Herophilus (*q.v.*). Other influences on Erasistratus at this time appear to have included that of Chrysippos the Younger, who was physician to Ptolemy Philadelphus; possibly for this reason, Erasistratus turned in the later years of his life to the medical school at Alexandria, which operated under the patronage of the Ptolemies.

At Alexandria Herophilus had pioneered the science of

dissection; his techniques and his deductions were of a modernity which was not to be equalled for nearly two millennia. Erasistratus proved that he was a worthy companion of Herophilus, also performing extensive dissections of dead human beings, and at the same time carrying out vivisections on animals.

The fact that he experimented on living animals makes one of his cardinal blunders all the more astonishing. Praxagoras had concluded, from his labours in dissection, that arteries did not carry blood – because the arteries of the dead are generally empty. Herophilus had shown that this was false, and might easily have hit upon the notion of the circulation of the blood (see page 449). Erasistratus, for reasons which we can only imagine were of principle rather than of observation, reverted to Praxagoras's view. He maintained that the arteries carried invisible *pneuma* ('vital spirit').

But, owing to his practice of vivisection, there was a difficulty in maintaining this. If you cut the artery of a living creature it spurts blood. Erasistratus had to explain this harsh fact in terms of his theory, and so he constructed the improbable theory that, on the cutting of the artery, the *pneuma* escaped instantly, leaving a vacuum; since nature was even then well known to abhor a vacuum, blood rushed from nearby veins through capillaries in a desperate attempt to fill the space vacated by the *pneuma*. Nearly five hundred years were to pass before Galen proved this to be nonsense.

Otherwise, however, Erasistratus showed little inclination to be tempted into the follies of preceding generations. Had it not been for this single blind spot – the belief that the arteries carried not blood but *pneuma* – he too would probably have hit upon the idea of the circulation of the blood; indeed, despite the blind spot, he came even closer to it than had Herophilus.

In order to understand Erasistratus's notions of the functions of heart, arteries, veins and nerves, we have to realise that there were, as he and many of his predecessors, contemporaries and successors saw it, two distinct types of *pneuma*. There was the 'animal' *pneuma*, which was carried along the arteries, and the 'psychic' *pneuma*, which travelled along the nerves (Erasistratus believed that the nerves were hollow). He held that *pneuma* was not a material which was innate to the body – like, say, blood – but something which the body drew in from the exterior and, in due course, expelled again. In the act of inhalation, *pneuma* was drawn from the surrounding atmosphere into the lungs, whence some of it was sent to the brain and some to the other parts of the body along the arteries. The *pneuma* that was sent to the brain was there converted into 'psychic' *pneuma*. This 'psychic' *pneuma* was sent from the brain along the various nerves to affect the activities of the body's muscles and organs.

If one substitutes the word 'oxygen' for '*pneuma*' in this explanation of the respiratory process, one comes up with something astonishingly close to the reality. However, it is only too obvious why Erasistratus was unable to make the final conceptual leap necessary in order to describe and explain the dynamics and *raison d'être* of the circulation of the blood.

From the foregoing description it might seem that Erasistratus was a vitalist who believed in the existence of some force independent of matter. Such was not the case. He was as thorough-going an atomist and materialist as Democritus (*q.v.*) before him. To him *pneuma* was not some arcane, metaphysical principle, but a real fluid of some kind, albeit undetectable to the human senses.

Erasistratus's mechanistic beliefs held sway in his ideas about digestion. Food, on its arrival in the stomach, was ground down by the mechanical action of the stomach muscles – a notion which was to resurface much later, during the seventeenth century, in the work of the Italian scientist Giovanni Borelli (1608–79). Both men, separated as they were by some two thousand years, failed to recognise the role of chemistry in the body's breakdown of foodstuffs. Before Erasistratus it had been variously thought that digestion was a process akin to cooking, or to fermentation: Erasistratus, seeking proof of his mechanical explanation of the process, was able to discover and describe the stomach muscles responsible for the squeezing and kneading which do indeed take place. To the food in the stomach was added necessary *pneuma*, moreover, brought there by the appropriate arteries. This idea allowed him to put forward a perfectly logical explanation for the fact that digestion is poor during illness: the arteries, since they were bearing less *pneuma* than usual, were open to invasion by blood from the veins, so that even less *pneuma* was able to make its way to the stomach.

The role of the liver, as he saw it, was to create blood. Some of the food being mechanically ground in the stomach was sent to the liver, where it was transformed by some unknown process into blood. (In fact, blood cells are formed in the bone-marrow, in lymphoid tissue, and in certain cells which play their part in the immune system.) Impurities were sent off to the gall-bladder; the pure blood from the liver was sent to the heart, from there to be sent *via* the veins to the extremities of the body.

Thanks to his vivisection, Erasistratus was able to draw some useful conclusions about the brain; if we are to believe Galen, then

Erasistratus's explorations of the brain were even more detailed, sophisticated and subtle than were those of Herophilus. In addition to distinguishing the cerebrum from the cerebellum, as Herophilus had done, he was able to describe the meninges (the three membranes which surround the brain). Moreover, it appears that he put forward the significant hypothesis that there was a relation between a creature's intelligence and the degree of convolution on the surface of its brain (obviously, we are here talking about genera and species rather than about individuals). This is of course a true relation – and one which has in more recent times given researchers into the neurology of the dolphins some food for thought. It would be tempting to suggest that Erasistratus came to this conclusion for theoretical reasons, but it seems more likely that he derived it solely from his observations.

Just before we chastise him for not having made a deduction in the third century B.C. which was left to be made until the twentieth century A.D., we should remember that there is nothing wrong, *per se*, with deductions made from experimental observation: if a consistent pattern emerges from your experiments, then it is reasonable to hazard that this pattern extends beyond the scope of your experiments and possibly betrays an underlying truth. Certainly, Erasistratus was a fine experimenter, and one of his known experiments was two thousand years later to be repeated and be regarded as the seminal experiment in the modern study of human metabolism.

The experiment is a simple if rather cruel one. If you put an animal in a sealed (but obviously not airtight) container – for example, a bird in a cage – and weigh it you will obtain a value for the combined weight. If you keep the beast in the cage for some considerable while, giving it nothing to eat, and then weigh the cage, creature and droppings, you will obtain a new value for the weight considerably lower than the first one you took. Now, while you have added nothing to the system in the form of food, you have similarly taken away nothing: how then does the loss of weight come about?

In order to explain this, Erasistratus seems to have turned the argument on its head: what invisible material was responsible for maintaining the weight of an organism which *was* receiving adequate food? The answer was, of course, *pneuma*. As we have seen, in some way *pneuma* was incorporated into the food which was being ground in the stomach. While the *pneuma* was transported around the body in the arteries or, in the case of the 'psychic' *pneuma*, the nerves, the food-product from the stomach was carried by the veins. Assisted by the driving force of the *pneuma*, food could be absorbed into the various organs through fine pores in the local veins. He suggested that, in the natural way of things, the organs lost material in the form of *pneuma*, but 'sucked in' new material, in the form of food, from the veins through these pores. He likened the process to the making of a rope: while the rope may fray and disintegrate at one end, the same materials can be used at the other to generate new rope. (This is a vastly simplified explanation.)

The two schools of Herophilus and Erasistratus survived into the second century A.D., and did much to influence the thinking and practice of later generations. Greek control of medicine continued throughout the Roman period. Indeed, medicine was one of the few sciences that survived the Roman period, and most of the good practitioners of the Middle Ages continued to look back to Greek models.

Archimedes

(*c.* 287–212 B.C.)

In 212 B.C. the Roman general Marcellus captured Syracuse, and the usual scenes of mindless slaughter by his soldiers ensued. Despite the fact that Marcellus had given strict instructions that Archimedes's home and person should in no way be violated, a Roman soldier who came across the sage (reputedly drawing a geometrical figure in the sand, oblivious of the massacre going on around him) simply stabbed him to death. Later Marcellus expressed considerable remorse, arranging for an impressive funeral for the philosopher and giving all sorts of material assistance to his surviving relatives. Marcellus no doubt considered himself a civilised fellow for acting thus, but butchery is butchery, whether the victims are peasants or philosophers.

As Archimedes himself had requested some while before, the grave was marked by the figure of a sphere inscribed in a cylinder: the philosopher believed that his single greatest achievement was the establishment of the relationship between the surface and volume of a sphere and its circumscribing cylinder.

His most *famous* achievement, on the other hand, according to schoolchild lore, was of course to run naked and dripping through the streets of Syracuse shouting 'Eureka!'. He had been commissioned by King Hieron II of Syracuse to find out if a crown which had been made for him was of solid gold or if the jeweller had crookedly incorporated a certain amount of silver. While Archimedes knew that silver was less dense than gold, he had little clue as to how to go about determining the volume of metal used in making the crown in order to establish its average density. According to persistent legend, the solution to the problem eluded him until one day, as he stepped into his bath, he noticed that the water spilled over the edges because of the introduction of his body: in other words, his body was displacing the same amount of water as its own volume. Instantly his problem was solved. It was easy enough to obtain quantities of silver and gold equal in weight to Hieron's crown and to discover their volume by measuring the amount of water they displaced. If the crown was then discovered to displace more water than the solid gold, it could be deduced that the crown was made not of pure gold but of gold alloyed with silver – and, indeed, to calculate how much silver was present in the alloy.

The repercussions of this elegant solution were vastly more important than the possible exposure of a criminal jeweller. Whether it was Archimedes himself who worked out the next step we do not know, but the rule concerning buoyancy is now known as Archimedes's Principle: an object floating in water displaces a quantity of water equivalent to its own weight; moreover, an object which is too dense to float will nevertheless display a 'weight-loss' equivalent to the weight of water it displaces.

His name is attached also to the so-called Archimedes's screw, a device which is still in use for irrigation in Egypt. It consists of a cylinder with, inside it, a close-fitting screw. One end of the cylinder is placed in water and, when the screw is turned, the water is brought up to the top of the cylinder. There is good evidence that the Egyptians had invented the device long before the time of Archimedes, and hence there is some doubt as to exactly why his name should be associated with it. However, he certainly did define the curve which is now known as the Archimedean spiral: $r = a\,\theta$, where a is a constant and r the distance of the line from its point of origin at angle θ. In loose terms, the line is twice as far away from the origin at the 180 degree mark than at the 90 degree mark, and so on.

The principle of flotation and the water-lifting screw are very practical matters, and it was almost certainly as a practical scientist that Archimedes achieved his greatest fame in his own age and those immediately succeeding it. That this was so can be gathered from the frequently repeated tale of the defence of Syracuse, which tale was taken perfectly seriously by the ancients. As a result of a diplomatic blunder on the part of the new king of Syracuse, Hieronymus, during Rome's war with Carthage (Hieronymus picked Carthage to win), the Romans under Marcellus, as we have seen, put the city to siege; but it was to be three years before they succeeded in taking the city. So much is historical fact; and it is virtually certain, too, that Archimedes did invent various weapons of war with which to help in the defence of his native city. But it is unlikely that he succeeded in building an apparatus of concave mirrors with which he could reflect the sun's rays in such a way as to burn up the Roman fleet; or that the Romans became so terrified of Archimedes's death-dealing gadgets that eventually all the defenders had to do was to show *anything* unidentifiable at the top of the city's walls to cause large-scale Roman panic and temporary retreat.

In somewhat less dramatic vein, an extremely important practical discovery of his was that of the principles of the lever. Of course, people have been using levers since the dawn of time (some animals use them), but before Archimedes no one had taken the trouble to work out rigorously the mathematics of the device. He discovered that the amount of effort you need to use to move an object using a lever is in inverse proportion to the distance you are from the fulcrum, and that the *precise* amount of effort needed can be calculated by consideration of the distances between the fulcrum and the object and the fulcrum and you: if you are trying to move a 50 kg object, and you are twice as far from the fulcrum as is the object, then you need exert only 25 kg of effort. (We are talking, of course, in terms of a first-class lever, where the fulcrum is between the effort and the load.)

When explaining about the lever to King Hieron, Archimedes is popularly supposed to have said: 'Give me a place to stand on and I will move the world.' In other words, given a long and rigid enough lever, you can move anything. According to Plutarch, though, he said something rather more interesting: '*If there were* another world, and I could go to it, I could move this one [my italics].' In the brilliant glare of Archimedes's genius, it is easy to forget that he belonged to an ignorant age, and that he shared much of that ignorance.

In many ways Archimedes was millennia ahead of his time. This can be seen in the way in which he worked out a very accurate value of π, the relationship between the lengths of the circumference and the diameter of a circle. His value was that it lay between $3\frac{10}{70}$ and $3\frac{10}{71}$; translated into decimals, this means that it lay between $3 \cdot 14286$ and $3 \cdot 14085$, whereas its real value is

3·14159. (These figures are approximate: π is an irrational number, and therefore cannot be expressed exactly in any system. The Babylonians said it was 3·0; in 1897 a move by the Indiana state legislature to declare π equal to 3·2 was defeated by only two votes.) But the impressive thing is not the accuracy of Archimedes's estimate but the way in which he arrived at it. He considered the case of a circle with a polygon circumscribed about it and another polygon inscribed within it. Clearly, the greater the number of sides in each of these polygons, the closer both of them would approximate to a circle – and the closer would be the lengths of their circumferences to that of the circle. (Indeed, a circle can be thought of as a polygon with an infinite number of sides.) This way of approaching the problem indicates that Archimedes was very close indeed to inventing the calculus – a feat which had to wait some two millennia until Newton and Leibniz 'discovered' calculus more or less simultaneously. Archimedes would almost certainly have made the final step had it not been for the fact that the 'Arabic' system of numerals had yet to be introduced to Europe.

This was not the only respect in which Archimedes was two millennia ahead of his time. The 'science explosion' from the mid-sixteenth century onwards can be attributed not only to the publication in 1543 of Copernicus's *De revolutionibus orbium coelestium* ('Concerning the revolutions of the celestial spheres'), but also to the translation into Latin, in 1544, of the works of Archimedes. That Roman soldier had a lot to answer for.

Archimedes used the technique of 'proto-calculus' for various other geometrical purposes – for example, to find the areas of segments of a parabola and, as we have seen in connexion with his tombstone, for the surface area and volume of a sphere.

While Archimedes is best remembered in the lay mind for his practical achievements, it is generally supposed that he was himself less concerned with these than with his theoretical work, especially in the field of mathematics. Of his 17 known works, 10 survive (although in addition there are several works in Arabic which are occasionally ascribed to him); all are concerned with theoretical rather than practical science apart from a lost work on the calendar and another lost work on the construction of a working planetarium. This planetarium Archimedes almost certainly did build, since Cicero tells us that he was lucky enough to be given a demonstration of it.

Perhaps his most appealing work is a small volume called *The Sand-Reckoner*, in which he makes an attempt to calculate the number of grains of sand which could in theory be contained in a sphere the size of the universe (as it was then conceived). He arrived at the figure 10^{63} – a number which is so staggeringly huge that it hardly bears thinking about. But this is one of the reasons why this little work is of such interest: Archimedes was trying to point out that there is nothing so big, no number so large, that it cannot be quantified – at least in a 'thought experiment'. But what was even more fascinating was that, in order to execute the calculations, Archimedes invented a system of notation rather similar to the exponential one which we use: he did not actually write 10^{63}, but he came very close to it. Once again, had he had access to the much more efficient 'Arabic' system of numerals, he would have made a mathematical leap which, in the event, had to wait a couple of millennia. He may even have made the leap: his book *Principles*, in which he expanded the system, is lost.

Because Archimedes wrote almost exclusively about his theoretical, rather than his practical, scientific feats it became fashionable to be contemptuous about the very thought of 'getting one's hands dirty'. Useful machines were rather beyond the pale: let the engineers, who had no theoretical scientific knowledge (it was assumed), build the bridges and the catapults – the 'scientists' had better things to do. Yet, while in some ways Archimedes undervalued his practical achievements, this idea of 'not getting one's hands dirty' was totally alien, a complete anathema, to him: he believed that pure reason alone could do only so much. Here are some comments which he addressed to Eratosthenes, who was at the time generally regarded as being the second best in the world at everything, and consequently nicknamed Beta. (He was in fact the first best at several things, producing an estimate of the earth's size which was astonishingly accurate.)

Seeing moreover in you ... an earnest student ... I thought fit to write out for you and explain in detail ... the peculiarity of a certain method through which you will be able to start to investigate some of the problems in mathematics by means of mechanics. This procedure is ... useful even for the proofs of the theorems themselves, for certain things first became clear to me by a mechanical method, even though they had to be demonstrated by geometry afterwards because their investigation by the said method did not furnish an actual demonstration. But it is of course easier to supply the proof when we have previously acquired by the method some knowledge of the questions. This is a reason why, in the case of the theorems whose proof Eudoxus was the first to discover ... no small share of the credit should be given to Democritus, who was the first to make the assertion ... though he did not prove it ...

Archimedes, then, was not an ivory-tower scientist who believed in keeping his hands clean at all costs; he was quite the opposite. His achievements were so numerous that we have been able to look at only a small percentage of them, yet the greatest of all was probably his realisation that science is of little value if it cannot relate in some direct way to the real world.

Eratosthenes

(c. 284–c. 202 B.C.)

Eratosthenes, son of Aglaos, was born in the North African Greek city of Cyrene, perhaps in 284 B.C. Cyrene had been founded by colonists from the Aegean island of Thera in the seventh century, and had a long history of independence until its incorporation into the kingdom of Ptolemy I. Greeks from Cyrene migrated to Alexandria, and some of them became famous and important.

Eratosthenes, however, went first to Athens in order to study at the philosophical schools there. Later accounts of him state that he was the pupil of the philosopher Ariston, who came from Chios, as well as of his fellow Cyreneans Lysanias the grammarian, and the poet Callimachus. After settling in Athens he was at last tempted, shortly after 246, to follow his fellow countrymen to Alexandria, being invited by Ptolemy III, who had just succeeded to the throne, to be tutor to his son, and head of the great library.

There are clear precedents for this. The tradition in the Greek world that powerful political figures added to their prestige by patronage of the arts and learning goes back at least to the sixth century B.C. (and, in a sense, even further, for the poems of Homer were put together for the kings of the East Greek cities in the remoter Dark Age). In the fifth century Pericles, as the dominant politician in Athens, included in his circle men like the sculptor Pheidias, and the natural philosopher Anaxagoras, from the Ionian city of Clazomenai. At the end of the fifth century the backward frontier kingdom of Macedon was ruled by Archelaus, who sought to make it more fully a part of the contemporary Greek world; amongst his other actions, he attracted to his court leading artists, such as Apelles the painter (who decorated his palace) and the Athenian playwright Euripides.

In the 360s, when the future Macedonian king Philip was held hostage at Thebes, he was introduced not only to the latest developments in fighting methods, but to Greek philosophy. Having become king, he secured the services of Aristotle (who in many ways is the greatest of the all-round Greek philosophers, and who included in his learning the old Ionic tradition of studying natural science) as tutor to his son Alexander. Alexander, in turn, saw his conquests of the Near East as a means of extending not only his own kingdom, but the frontiers of Greek knowledge.

After Alexander's death the empire was fought over by his Macedonian generals, seeking to establish themselves as rulers of it in its entirety, or at least of fragments. When Ptolemy established himself in control of Egypt he was, in a sense, a usurper; but he was also a Macedonian king, and he understood that his position depended not only on his possession of a Macedonian army, but his patronage of the arts. This centred on the 'palace' at Alexandria – the royal quarter of the city, rather than a single building as we understand the term. It included not only the residence of the king, and the banqueting-halls where he held his official feasts, but also the area set aside for learning, the sanctuary of the Muses (the Museum) and its library. To this the Ptolemies attracted learned men, scientists, doctors and poets. For the library they collected texts – buying from the city of Athens, for example, the official copies of the plays produced for the dramatic festivals of Dionysus by Aeschylus, Sophocles and Euripides. Copies of the poems of Homer were obtained, and the variant readings they contained were studied in order to produce a standard and definitive version.

The men in charge of the great library of Alexandria were scholars of the highest rank. The library seems to have been organised for Ptolemy originally by the Athenian philosopher Demetrius of Phalerum, who based it on the library in the philosophical school founded by Aristotle – the Lyceum. Aristotle's interests, as we learn from his works, were universal, and the Alexandrian library obviously followed in this tradition. It was greatly enlarged in the third century B.C. The first 'head of the library' was a man called Zenodotus, who was an authority on Greek literature, particularly the epic and lyric poetry. His office seems to have been established in 284 with the expansion of the library under Ptolemy II. He was succeeded by the poet

Callimachus. Eratosthenes himself was next in succession, and he held the office apparently until he died around the end of the third century B.C. – possibly in 202, possibly some eight years later. The next librarian was Aristophanes of Byzantium, a grammarian. It is important to notice that the other librarians (excluding for the moment Eratosthenes) were essentially scholars with literary interests.

Eratosthenes was a polymath, rather than a scientist purely and simply, following in the Aristotelian tradition. He composed an epic poem entitled *Hermes*, dealing with astronomy, and other poetic works (it is interesting to recall that those scientific works which Aristotle published in his own lifetime, now all lost, were admired in antiquity as much for their literary merit). He wrote treatises of literary criticism, twelve books on ancient comedy, studying all aspects of the plays whose texts had been collected in the library. It is these interests which suggest why he was appointed librarian, and his work is essentially a continuation of that undertaken by his predecessors.

Eratosthenes also wrote an influential study of historical chronology, which succeeded for the first time in putting the dating of historical and literary events on a properly organised basis; the problem here, of course, is that there was no universally recognised Greek calendar – each city having its own system – or universally accepted starting date as the essential reference (as we use the supposed date of the birth of Christ). As part of this work, he compiled a list of those who won victories in the Olympic games. Again, it is cataloguing and categorising work of this type which is typical of the Heads of the Alexandrian Library. Eratosthenes wrote a geography – he has been described as the first systematic geographer – and an astronomy, a description of the constellations: significantly, to this he attached an account of the mythology behind their naming, as well as a purely scientific description. He wrote on philosophy (mainly, it would seem, on ethics), on mathematical problems and definitions, on geometry (especially, in the literal sense, the measurement of the earth) and on music.

It is not surprising, when one considers this list, that his fellow scholars referred to him as the pentathlete – the all-rounder, in sporting parlance – in his attempt to maintain the Aristotelian tradition. It is also not altogether surprising that another nickname he earned was Beta, the runner-up who was always second but never first (though this doesn't mean he was ever regarded as second-rate). He was indeed a respected scholar and his work is not without significance to the present day. He seems to have made the first true map of the world, based on the system still employed now, of locating places by reference to lines of latitude and longitude.

Even so, all the books he wrote have been lost, either super-seded by later scholars (for example, the geographers who have survived are Strabo, who wrote in the first century B.C., and the later Ptolemy, whose life is described elsewhere in this book) or else simplified by later compilers and condensers, who select matter which, for whatever reason, they consider important and reject the rest. His chronological system obviously required up-dating. His use of the four-yearly sequence of the Olympic games (whether or not he actually invented it) continued, though it was cumbersome, and an annual cycle was obviously preferable, if a generally accepted era could be found. Hellenistic eras, such as that dating from the foundation of Antioch (the Seleucid era) could not find favour in areas such as Ptolemaic Egypt, which were political rivals; not even the foundation of Rome would be satisfactory to all as the basis for yearly calculations. Eratosthenes's work eventually led to the Christian chronology of Bishop Eusebius (composed about A.D. 300) which, translated into Latin by St Jerome, became the basis of Western chronological knowledge.

It is difficult to judge his mathematical works, and his achieve-ment in geography, solely from the fragments and excerpts which survive. Two of these, however, are of considerable interest and may be taken to indicate the quality of his writing and investiga-tion. Most spectacular is his calculation of the circumference of the earth. Greek scholars before Aristotle knew that the earth was a sphere (traditional cosmogony thought of it as a flat disc). Aristotle, in his work on the Heavens (*De Caelo*) demonstrates this from observations of the earth's shadow cast in eclipses of the moon, and from the varying positions of the stars. He had even estimated its circumference, a measurement he gives as 400,000 stades, though he does not say how he arrived at this figure, and since the 'stade' is a variable measurement, we cannot say exactly what this figure means.

Eratosthenes was more precise. The fullest account of his cal-culation is given by a second-century A.D. writer of a treatise on the circular motion of the heavenly bodies, Cleomedes, but there is also a reference to it in Strabo's *Geography*. Eratosthenes's calculations were carried out, naturally, in Egypt. Five assumptions, says Cleomedes, are necessary for this: that Alexandria and Syene (Aswan, in upper Egypt) are on the same meridian; secondly, that the distance between them is 5,000 stades; thirdly, that rays of the sun, wherever in the world they fall, are parallel; fourthly, that straight lines cutting parallel lines do so at the same angle; and fifthly, that the circumferences which pertain to equal angles are the same. It is then not difficult to understand Eratosthenes's method (see the diagram).

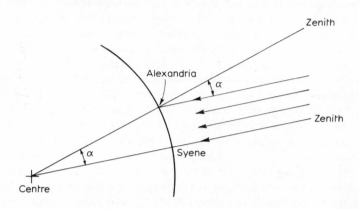

He says that Syene and Alexandria are on the same meridian. As Syene is on the tropic of Cancer, the pointers of sundials at the solstice necessarily do not throw a shadow (because then the sun is directly overhead). At Alexandria, however, at the same time, the sun does cast a shadow from the pointers of sundials. By measuring the angle of the shadow we can calculate what fraction of the earth's circumference is constituted by the distance between Syene and Alexandria. This Eratosthenes found to be one-fiftieth of a circle. The total circumference of the earth is therefore 50 × 5,000, that is 250,000 stades. What this represents in modern measurement is uncertain, since it would seem the length called a stade by the Greeks varies and we do not know which length Eratosthenes used, any more than we know Aristotle's. Strabo gives a variant figure of 252,000 stades, which may (or may not) be a more accurate record of what Eratosthenes calculated (in any case Alexandria is $7\frac{1}{2}$° north of the tropic of Cancer, which is 1/48, not 1/50 of a circle). But even allowing for this and other difficulties (such as measuring the exact angle of the shadow and the exact distance between Alexandria and Syene, coupled with the fact which we know but Eratosthenes did not, that the two places are not on exactly the same meridian), it is clear that this figure approximates to the real circumference of the earth. If Eratosthenes was using a stade equal to 300 royal cubits, or 157·5 m., his calculation gives the diameter of the earth as 7,850 miles. This is only 50 miles short of the true polar diameter, though he was perhaps lucky to get so close.

Equally ingenious is his 'sieve', a method for finding out which numbers are prime. This also illustrates the difficulties encountered by Greeks in calculations involving multiplication and division which seem so straightforward to us (the reason of course being the lack of a simple symbolic system in Greek for representing numbers). Again, we do not have Eratosthenes's own account of this, but it is preserved in the mathematical text-book of Nicomachus, a first-century A.D. Pythagoran. This involves selecting out the odd numbers from three onwards in sequence, and writing them in an extended line. The unwanted numbers are then 'sieved' out by a regular system of counting; starting with three one goes past the next two numbers (5 and 7) which are primes, and thus arrives at the third, 9, which is not: this, therefore, is 'sieved' out. The process is then continued, passing over the next two numbers and crossing out every third number (i.e. 15, 21, 27, etc.). This is then repeated, but starting with the next prime number 5, and sieving out every fifth number (i.e. 15, 25, 35, etc.); then back to 7, deleting every seventh – and so on 'as far as you like'.

Even if Eratosthenes is not the profoundest of the Greek mathematicians (a title which should probably go to Apollonius of Perge), the contribution he made in his own lifetime, and to those who followed (and, perhaps, superseded him) makes him a worthy member of the scientists who worked at Alexandria.

Pytheas

(*fl.* 240 B.C.)

In the seventh century B.C. fast, fifty-oared sailing galleys from Phocaea, a Greek colony on the coast of Asia Minor, linked the western with the eastern Mediterranean for the first time, and broke out through the Pillars of Hercules into the Atlantic, to trade wine, olive oil and textiles for the silver and copper of the river Tartessos (Guadalquivir) region of Iberia (Spain).

On their way along the European coasts and the islands of the western basin they established trading posts and colonies. About 600 B.C. on a magnificent harbour just east of the mouth of the river Rhodanus (Rhone) Phocaeans founded the town of Massalia (Marseilles). It was here in or very close to the year 280 B.C. that

Pytheas, the greatest of the Greek maritime venturers, was born.

From the early decades of the fifth century B.C. the Carthaginians, who had established control over southern Spain, blocked the Gibraltar straits to Greek shipping, cutting off their trade with Tartessos, but in 241 B.C. the new power of Rome defeated Carthage and destroyed her fleets. Massalia seized the opportunity to send a single ship under Pytheas through the straits to revive their old trade in precious metals with Tartessos and probe the unknown lands beyond for gold, for tin, the catalyst which turned copper into the harder bronze, and for amber, which had not been seen in the Mediterranean for centuries.

Little is known of Pytheas the man. He was certainly one of the first scientific geographers, and possibly a master mariner. The account he wrote of his voyage was ultimately lost, though it was quoted by later geographers. Before the voyage he had become well known for fixing the latitude of his native town by sighting on the North Star, Polaris, and determining the angle at which it stands above the level horizon. This voyage was intended as a purely commercial venture, but Pytheas was to broaden its scope.

He sailed from Massalia some time between 240 and 238 B.C., probably in one of the large, 400- to 500-ton Massalian merchantmen, with its big cargo capacity and good sea-keeping qualities, rather than a narrow, cramped military galley. Navigation of the Mediterranean was usually suspended in the winter and early spring, and he would have departed in April, skirting the coast westward, past the small Greek settlements of Agathé ('The Good') and Emporion ('The Trading Post') in Iberia, until the great rock of Gibraltar rose to starboard and behind it the Jebel Musa in Morocco – the twin Pillars of Hercules.

Pytheas sailed between them unmolested by Punic ships, the first Greek to do so in nearly three hundred years. Then it was seventy miles to Cadiz, the Phoenician Gadir, past the cape later known as Trafalgar, navigating head currents, high tides, reefs and hidden sandbanks, once familiar to Greek mariners but now unknown, then half a day's sail to the mouth of the Tartessos. Having established contact with the Celtic silver merchants he continued west, calling at the copper town at the mouth of the Rio Tinto. This was as far into the unknown 'Outer Ocean' as any Mediterranean mariner had ever been known to sail.

He followed the rocky Iberian coast north, reached Biscay but did not cross the Bay. As a navigator without charts or compass, able to approximate latitude by observing the positions of the sun and stars but unable to fix longitude, he followed ancient practice

and hugged the coast of northern Iberia until he reached the coast
of Gaul. Here he knew he was on the same latitude as Massalia,
and reported that 'the northern part of Iberia is more readily
accessible by way of the Celtic land than in sailing by way of the
Atlantic'.

He continued along the Biscay coast, past the estuary of the
Gironde and the mouth of the Loire, and put in at Celtic Corbilo,
then, after three days' sailing, reached Uxisame (Ushant). Off the
grim granite cliffs Pytheas and his ship's company saw thick
Atlantic fog for the first time. They were, he recorded, 'at the very
ends of the habitable world'.

The safest course onwards was still along the coast – east to the
Straits of Dover – but Pytheas headed north across the empty sea.
He was steering for Belerion (Cornwall), the land of tin.

With the help of advice from the natives of Brittany, and
possibly with a pilot, he made his landfall just east of Land's End
and ran his ship up stern-first on the sands near the site of
Penzance. Ashore he watched the friendly Celts dig out the raw tin
from veins under the earth, smelt it and refine it, hammer it into
ingots and transport it across to Iktis (St Michael's Mount) when
the ebb tide made the causeway passable, ready for transport by
coracle across to Brittany.

Gold and amber were also Pytheas's commercial targets. From
Iktis he rounded Land's End and sailed right up the western coast
of England, exploring inlets and estuaries all the way, landing to
study the Celtic natives. He found no towns, only small tribal
farming communities scattered round the country, often fighting
one another, using bronze armour and war chariots. The British
Celts lived in rough shelters of turf and twigs or in small round
stone huts. Even in summer the Mediterranean sailors found the
climate cold. There is no record of a landing in Ireland, where
gold was to be found at that time.

Threading the Hebrides and the Minches he reached the
Pentland Firth. Here, where the Atlantic and North Sea currents
clash head-on, he recorded 120-foot tides. This sounds like a tall
story, until one reads that in 1862 a sea climbed 200 feet up the
cliffs of Stroma Island. He also recorded the local name Orka for
the island across the Firth.

As he sailed northward he noticed that the summer days grew
longer, and noted their length at five different places, realising
that he had found another method of estimating latitude. He
described an island, six days' voyage further to the north of Orka,
which later Roman writers, notably Tacitus, called 'ultima Thule'
and regarded as truly the end of the world. This was almost

Statue of Augustus Caesar
in the Vatican Museum,
from Livia's villa at Prima
Porta. Mosaic of Virgil from
a Roman villa at Carthage
with the manuscript of the
Aeneid on his knee. The poet
owed much to the patronage
of Augustus. Beside him
stands Clio, the muse of
history; whilst Melpomone,
tragic mask in hand, leans
on his chair.

Two of the emperors who in the judgement of Gibbon gave the Roman Empire its period of greatest prosperity and happiness are commemorated on the Arch of Constantine. *Above:* Trajan at a boar hunt, and (*left*) Marcus Aurelius addressing troops. (Original reliefs revised by Constantine for his Arch, the emperors' heads reworked as portraits of Constantine)

certainly Shetland. Pytheas was here at the time of the summer solstice, 21 June, when he measured twenty hours of daylight. Lacking a mechanical clock or chronometer to measure time in hours of fixed duration, he may have used an hour-glass regulated to run for an equinoctial hour. This was an hour of constant value, which some think Pytheas himself introduced, based on the equality of day and night at the equinox, the point at which the sun crosses the equator, and replaced the older measurement of an 'hour' as the twelfth part of the time between sunrise and sunset, which produced far too variable a unit. By modern time-keeping Pytheas overestimated the length of daylight at Thule by about one hour. Beyond the island, the natives told him, was a region where the sun was permanently above the horizon in summer but slept all winter.

Pytheas also described the 'Frozen Sea' which lay a day's sailing north from Thule. This cannot have been solid Arctic pack ice. The explorer Nansen thought that 'what Pytheas saw may have been the ice sludge in the sea which is formed over a great extent along the edge of the drift ice, when this has been ground to a pulp by the action of the waves'. Pytheas recorded, according to geographer Strabo's commentary, a region 'in which there was neither land properly so called nor sea nor sky, but a sort of mixture of all three, like a jellyfish, in which (he says) earth and sea and everything are held suspended in a sort of compound of all the elements, upon which one can neither walk nor sail'. This again, Nansen thought, aptly described the ice sludge when it is shrouded in thick fog.

Pytheas voyaged no further north, but turned south-east into the North Sea to carry out the final part of his commercial mission, the search for the source of amber, which the ancient Greeks called electron. This hardened fossil tree-resin of flora buried for 50 million years was found in abundance along the southern shores of the Baltic, particularly under the beaches of the modern Gulf of Danzig, between Polish Gdansk and Russian Kaliningrad, still called today the Amber Coast.

In his search for the yellow semi-gem, with its nuances of orange, brown and rare red, Pytheas crossed the North Sea, sailed through the Kattegat and discovered a passage through the Danish islands. For the first time in history a Mediterranean ship sailed the Baltic. Pytheas reached the Amber Coast, which he found inhabited by the Gutones, later identified as the Goths, who burned the precious amber for fuel.

It would now be approximately late September, and with his commercial mission complete, Pytheas must have been anxious to quit the Outer Ocean for home before its savage winter weather began. How much more of the coast of continental Europe he traversed we do not know, but he apparently returned to Britain and explored the eastern shore. The Roman historian Pliny describes him as having recorded the perimeter of Britain as 3,875 miles, a reasonably accurate figure covering all the major indentations, which Pytheas must have penetrated. At some point he crossed over to the Gallic shore, to follow the coast back to the Pillars of Hercules.

When he reached Massalia he had sailed more than 7,000 miles. He and his men had seen lands which no other Mediterranean mariners had ever seen and which no Greek or Roman was to look on again for several hundred years, of such little interest were his geographical discoveries to his contemporaries, many of whom were sceptical. His intellectual curiosity and explorer's itch had led him well beyond his original commission, and he himself apparently considered his exploration of Britain his most important achievement. Certainly no deep-sea sailor, Mediterranean or otherwise, had ever navigated those rocky coasts before.

Pytheas was a pioneer in the calculation of latitude, for which he used both the solstitial measurement of the sun in equinoctial hours and the more reliable method of taking a sight of the sun by day or the North Star on cloudless nights and determining the angle which it made with the level horizon, which, with the help of a simple apparatus like a simplified sextant, could have achieved reasonable accuracy. He had no method of fixing his east–west position, longitude, except by crude dead reckoning of distance travelled. In the Atlantic he studied the ebb and flow of the ocean tides, so insignificant in the Mediterranean, and was probably the first man in the classical world to make the connexion between the rise and fall of the tide and the position of the moon in the sky.

The advances in geophysics achieved as results of Pytheas's voyage far outweighed the benefits which accrued to trade, though he did establish that the tin trade with Brittany and Britain could be conducted far more directly across Gaul than by sea. The distance from Marseilles round the coasts of France and Spain to the Bay of Biscay is roughly 1,700 miles. The same journey overland is no more than 300 miles, from Narbonne to Bordeaux even less, and the overland route was smooth, with no obstacles. To carry amber from the Baltic by sea was particularly impractical. In later Roman times tin was shipped by coracle from Cornwall across to Corbilo on the Loire estuary, thence direct to Massalia across Gaul. Amber was carried overland from Denmark. Following the end of the first Punic War, after Pytheas's voyage, Carthage re-established her naval power in the western Mediterranean and her blockade of the Straits of Gibraltar, cutting off once more all trade with ports in the Outer Ocean, including the supply of silver and copper from Tartessos.

Rome finally crushed Carthage in 146 B.C., Massalia became part of a Roman province and shared in her commercial monopoly. Britain was also absorbed, and ships sailed freely within the Roman Empire, but none rivalled the extent and variety of Pytheas's voyage, which remained one of the most outstanding and astonishing maritime achievements of the ancient world.

Hero of Alexandria

(*fl.* A.D. 62)

Until very recently it was widely believed that Hero belonged to the second century B.C., but it now seems almost certain that an eclipse referred to in his writings, and of which it is assumed he was an observer, occurred in the year A.D. 62. So we can tentatively suggest that he was born around 20 or 30.

Little is known about his life. We do think however that he was the head of the engineering school at Alexandria. In addition to the general courses of mathematics, geometry, astronomy and physics, there were practical courses in carpentry, metal-work, surveying and architecture. The practical aspect of the curricula reflected the displacement of Athens in favour of Alexandria as the centre of Greek scientific activity. Plato had deplored the use of geometry to invent machines – 'moving' geometry – regarding this as a degradation of the ideal principles which the science enshrined. In Alexandria there were no such inhibitions; rather, the ages-old empirical methods of the Egyptians encouraged a more practical approach.

Hero's own bent was very much towards the practical aspects of the subjects he taught, and much of his mathematics reflected this. He was not so much concerned with absolute exactitude as with a sufficiently good approximation for working purposes. If we look at the formula Hero gave for calculating the area of an equilateral triangle in terms of the length of one of its sides, s, we find

$$\text{area} = \frac{13}{30} s^2$$

which, assuming s to be of unit length, gives the result 0·4333333, whereas the more accurate answer given by Hero's formula, which he did not originate though it is attributed to him, is 0·4330127. This formula was:

$$\text{area} = \sqrt{s(s-a)\ (s-b)\ (s-c)},$$

where s is half the total length of the triangle's sides (its semiperimeter), and a, b, and c the lengths of each of its sides. The formula applies to the area of *all* triangles.

However, he could also be very accurate when he wished to be. He reported and possibly invented a formula for the algorithmic calculation of square roots which is still used by modern computers. Indeed, if you press the square-root button on your pocket calculator and the machine seems to think for a moment before displaying the answer, this is probably because it is using Hero's iterative formula.

In another area, optics, he was able by intuition to arrive at the deduction that a ray of light which hits a mirror at an angle x bounces off the mirror at the same angle x.

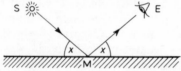

He simply adhered to the assumption that nature always takes the easiest way out: to use the terminology of the diagram, SME is the shortest route for the light to travel from its source *via* the mirror to reach the observer's eye. The pragmatic Hero assumed that economical nature would necessarily opt for this shortest-route rule. In this instance he was right.

But, as already indicated, Hero's real fascination for us concerns his invention of ingenious machines. Of greatest fame is the 'aeolipile', a primitive form of steam-jet engine. In essence this was a hollow sphere JK mounted on a cauldron of water AB (see diagram). A bent tube EFG pierces the lid, CD, and hollow sphere, whilst diametrically opposite to it another bent tube HI rests on the lid and forms a pivot at H. Two further tubes bent at right angles, diametrically opposite one another, and at right angles to the line GH, are inserted into the sphere. A fire is lit under the cauldron and when the water boils steam enters the sphere through the tube EFG. As the steam leaves the sphere through the bent pipes and enters the atmosphere it will cause the sphere to rotate.

This was a quite incredible invention for the first century A.D., but neither Hero himself nor any other scientist of the ancient

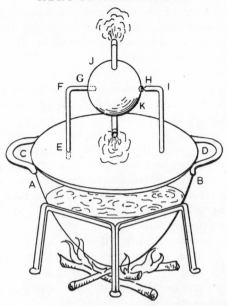

world seems to have thought it worth developing. This is a great pity: from Hero's model it would have been easy enough to extrapolate the steam engine, the jet engine, and even (with a little imagination) the electrical generator. As it was, the most obvious application of the principle, the steam engine, was not to be developed until 1698, when Thomas Savery (*c.* 1650 – 1715) produced the first commercially successful model.

One of Hero's other inventions was a dioptra, a sort of theodolite, useful in land-surveying. The details of its construction need not concern us here, but it is worth noting that it is no coincidence that Hero should devise such an instrument. He was more of a mensurationist than a geometer, and while the very word 'geometry' refers to the discipline's origins in the field of land-surveying, by Hero's time geometry was a theoretical science while its humble sister, mensuration, was very much concerned with practical matters. Unlike the aeolipile the dioptra was widely used, its value in day-to-day terms being obvious to all.

Some of his other inventions must have seemed much more dramatic to his first-century audiences. There was, for example, his hodometer (mileometer) for chariots, which worked on the same principle as that on many modern bicycles, with a pin on one of the wheels knocking a toothed gear each time it went by.

Useless but interesting was his 'automatic theatre', or 'theatre of apotheosis'. This device consisted of two elements: a small stage that appeared before the viewer, was home to a puppet-play, and then disappeared again; and a larger stationary stage on which was played a more complicated puppet-show. At first sight the device seems to be as ingenious as any of the products of the automata-makers some 1,500 years later, but in fact Hero's toy was even more clever, for nowhere in it appeared a cog-wheel (gear): all the effects were achieved by the use of drums, strings and, of all things, mustard-seed.

The 'motor' which drove the device had some similarity to that which drives many grandfather clocks: a weight is allowed to fall only slowly; to the weight is attached a cord which starts off wound around an axle; the turning of the axle instigates the other events. In fact, Hero used a plurality of axles whose actions were governed not only by uncoiling string but by, for example, the slipping of pins from holes; but the overall principle was the same. The weight in question was housed within a punctured container which started off filled with mustard-seed. As the seeds fell out of the hole or holes in the container, the weight slowly settled, at a rate which Hero could calculate with reasonable ease or, more probably, deduce empirically.

The 'automatic theatre' was only the most splendid of an astonishing number of toys which he invented. There were a water-powered organ, a working model of the geocentric universe, a vacuum-powered cupping glass, a fire-powered hissing model serpent, a tableau of bacchanalian dancing figures, a machine for quenching fires, a model triton which blew on a horn, and so on. One of the trickiest devices was a model bull whose head could be cut off: defying all logic, however, the head somehow remained attached to the model animal's body, and immediately after the apparent decapitation seemed to take a drink from a suitably placed bowl.

To list all of Hero's mechanical inventions would demand several pages. His gadgets were extremely clever, but all of them (with the exception of his precursor of the theodolite) were characterised by one thing: they had no practical purpose. It might be said that he built all his models in order to demonstrate various physical principles and, much more importantly, to show that certain everyday physical effects could be put to useful purpose. But it may equally be true that he built nothing more important than executive toys because those represented the limits of his imagination: clever and ingenious he was, but he failed to grasp that any human invention could have the effect of fundamentally altering the human condition, as the steam engine was to do during the Industrial Revolution. More likely than either of these two hypotheses is that the essential *raison d'être* to harness his inventions for industrial purposes did not exist in the first century A.D. When slavery was an established part of every society and provided an abundant and ever-available supply of labour, what practical purpose would be served by economising in its use? Sixteen centuries would elapse before a more highly developed economic system and the rise of the bourgeoisie in Europe brought about the conditions which would favour the commercial development of the engines of Savery, Newcomen and Watt.

Ptolemy

(*c.* A.D. 100–*c.* 180)

Ptolemy is widely regarded as the most significant figure in ancient astronomy, holding much the same position as does Euclid in mathematics. In their two separate fields, however, neither man seems to have been a great original theorist: both were, in essence, scientific popularisers who gathered together an eclectic mixture of other people's deductions. Their original contribution to knowledge lies, then, solely in the selection process whereby they discarded some ideas and promoted others – a task at which Euclid was very much more successful than Ptolemy.

We know very little indeed about the biographical details of Ptolemy's life. He is said to have been Egyptian, but the evidence for this is not wholly convincing; moreover, since the only place mentioned by name in his records of astronomical observations is Alexandria, it seems likely that he spent all of his working life there, and it was quite probably also the place of his birth. Similarly, we can deduce approximate birth- and death-dates for him only from his writings: his earliest recorded observation is from A.D. 127 and his latest from A.D. 141. These observations appeared in his *Almagest* and, since he wrote several major works after that, it seems reasonable to assume that he lived on well into the reign of the Emperor Marcus Aurelius, which ended in A.D. 180. However, some historians suggest that he was born as early as A.D. 75 and died some time around A.D. 150, producing his major works in something of a flurry towards the end of his life.

Ancient astronomy was in a curious state by Ptolemy's time, progressive (and correct) ideas jostling shoulders with very primitive ones. Several centuries before, Aristarchus had propounded the revolutionary suggestion that the earth went round the sun, rather than *vice versa*, but his ideas were largely ignored. Instead, most astronomers believed that the earth lay at the centre of the universe, and that all the heavenly bodies went around it: various 'mechanisms' had been proposed to explain this, the most famous being that of the crystal spheres. There were considerable difficulties with this scheme of things, the most important being that, while the 'fixed' stars behaved exactly as one might expect were they to be revolving around the earth in a circle (the perfect shape, and hence the only one which the Greeks, and many after them, would accept as a possible 'orbital' path), the planets – from *planētēs*, 'wanderer' – did not. In particular, what we know to be the outer planets had the disconcerting habit of, every now and then, reversing the apparent direction of their motion before continuing in the same direction as before – they 'looped the loop', as it were. In order to explain such aberrations, it was necessary to invent a curious scheme involving epicycles: each planet performed a circle around a centre which moved in a circle around the earth. When even this complicated 'mechanism' failed to predict accurately the positions in the sky of the planets, it was necessary to bring in further epicycles as well as other equally artificial concepts.

The need was, therefore, to produce some sort of a scheme whereby the positions of the planets could be predicted with a degree of precision at least as good as that of the naked-eye observational instruments then available. And this was not merely an academic exercise: navigators really *needed* accurate tables of the planetary positions, because sometimes their lives and frequently their incomes depended upon such information.

In seeking to provide such a set of tables, Ptolemy had to choose between two completely different models of the universe: the heliocentric (sun-centred) universe of Aristarchus, or the much more popular geocentric (earth-centred) universe of the great astronomer Hipparchus (*c.* 190–*c.* 120 B.C.). Unfortunately Ptolemy chose the latter. However, it was not particularly his fault that he did so: the cycles and epicycles, etc., of the geocentric theories were becoming hopelessly elaborate, true, but because Aristarchus had like everybody else insisted that the circle was a perfect shape, and hence the only one involved in planetary motions, his system, too, had to rely upon additional epicycles in order to predict the planetary positions accurately. Indeed, many centuries later, when Copernicus resurrected or rediscovered Aristarchus's system, still adhering to the idea of circular paths, his version – according to Arthur Koestler in *The Sleepwalkers*

(1959) – required a full 48 epicycles, whereas the most sophisticated version of the Ptolemaic system then available required a 'mere' 40.

Ptolemy made a number of other wrong choices. While rejecting Aristarchus's heliocentrism he nevertheless adopted the same astronomer's estimate of the distance of the sun, between 18 and 20 times the distance of the moon. Since he accepted Hipparchus's correct estimate of the distance of the moon – roughly 30 times the diameter of the earth – his calculation of the distance of the sun was a fairly typical mixture of good and bad data. Another wrong choice of Ptolemy's was to accept and elaborate upon the astrological beliefs of Poseidonius (c. 135–c. 50 B.C.), despite the fact that many astronomers (e.g. Eudoxus) had spoken out against them: once again, to be fair to Ptolemy, we should remember that it is easy enough with hindsight to realise that he made the wrong choice, but that he opted for the system that, in his own terms and his own times, seemed to make the most sense. He was, after all, merely reporting on the state of the art at his time. Countless eminent scientists have similarly made the wrong choice in more recent ages between conflicting theories – one thinks immediately of the truly great scientist Ernest Rutherford, who in an unguarded moment wrote: 'The energy produced by the breaking down of the atom is a very poor kind of thing. Anyone who looks for a source of power in the transformation of the atom is talking moonshine.' That was in 1933: just over a decade later it was proved rather dramatically that Rutherford himself had been 'talking moonshine'.

Such blunders are not uncommon in the history of science. The reason that they are so important in Ptolemy's case is that, for over a millennium, Ptolemy's great work was taken as a definitive statement on the structure and nature of the universe: Rutherford's statement was disproved within a decade or so, and therefore hardly disrupted the advance of human knowledge. But this ossification of the human thought processes was most certainly not Ptolemy's fault: he had written a major work on the subject of astronomy/cosmology, as it appeared to be in his own time. Succeeding generations, on the other hand, viewed his synthesis in ridiculously favourable lights: his great work on astronomy (and it *was* a great work) was titled by his successors as *Megale mathematike syntaxis*, which means roughly that it was a 'great mathematical work'. Frequently his 'disciples' called it the *Megiste* ('Greatest') *mathematike syntaxis*: as far as they were concerned, it was the standard work. It was forgotten by the Greeks for a while, and preserved only among the Arabs, who took the word '*Megiste*' and translated it into '*Almagest*', 'the Greatest', a title which it retained when, some time in the twelfth century, it reappeared on the occidental scene. Presumably because of its title, it came to be regarded as the last word on all matters cosmological and astronomical. It was adopted as such by, among others, the Christian Church, which was able with startling ingenuity to discover justification of the system in various parts of the Bible.

However, if Ptolemy had an unhappy knack for adopting the wrong theory, one should say in his favour that the *Almagest* was nonetheless an impressive work. He assumed in the reader a mathematical knowledge no greater than that obtainable from a perusal of Euclid, and from that stage led on to prove various astronomical equations in a way to which one cannot take exception. His underlying assumptions may have been disastrously wrong, but one would be hard pressed to fault his deductions from those assumptions. Moreover, the *Almagest* at least kept alive one important astronomical/cosmological/geophysical idea: that the earth was not flat but spherical. While we find this today a very obvious idea, during the centuries when the *Almagest* was lost to western culture, being faithfully preserved only by the Arabs, the notion was far from obvious. Christian theologians took references from the Bible such as 'the four corners of the world' and deduced therefrom that the world was not only flat but rectangular; others maintained that the sun was only a short distance away. Voices in support of biblical literalism have continued down to our own day.

One additional point about the *Almagest* must be noted: it is almost our sole source for the ideas of the astronomers before Ptolemy. He deserves his renown therefore, if for nothing else, as a historian of science.

Two others of his works are of some note. First is his *Geography*, which like the *Almagest* spent some centuries 'in exile' among the Arabs, to be returned to the West from the twelfth century onwards retranslated into Latin from the Arabic. Ptolemy accepts from Posedonius an estimate of the earth's size of about 5,725 miles in diameter while rejecting the earlier and rather more accurate calculation of Eratosthenes (about 7,960 miles, although the exact figure is debatable). Ptolemy's world-view therefore incorporated a world which was really quite a lot smaller than the world actually is; but, once again, the important notion here is that the world was assumed to be spherical. Thanks to Ptolemy's underestimate of the world's size, in conjunction with his acceptance of the spherical shape of the world, Christopher Columbus was to set off in the late fifteenth century in the confident expectation that he would be able to sail westward to the Orient: accepting Ptolemy's figure for the earth's size, Columbus 'knew' that there was no room for another continent to get in the way.

His book *Optics* was to inspire much of the work of the great Islamic scientist Ibn al-Haytham in the early part of the eleventh century; the rewritten version of *Optics*, which owes far more to the Arabic than to the Alexandrian scientist, was to have a profound effect on medieval ideas on the subject of light.

We can therefore say that Ptolemy was – with the possible exception of Euclid – the foremost scientific populariser in the ancient world; at least in so far as we can judge the effects of his books. To describe him as anything more is, in a curious kind of a way, to undervalue him. He was a synthesist, and such people have been of value down all the long ages. We can say with hindsight that his influence on our culture would have been more beneficial had he chosen the *right* elements of Greek science – especially astronomy – to promote, but it was certainly not his fault that later thinkers came to the consensus that the *Almagest* should be interpreted literally, and only literally, as a complete and final cosmology.

PHILOSOPHERS AND RELIGIOUS LEADERS

Zoroaster

(*c.* 628–*c.* 551 B.C.)

Iran has a long tradition of religious thought and activity, related to that of India but also influencing western religion and so providing a meeting-place of Indian and Semitic thought. Ancient Media, in the north-west of Iran, and Persia, in the south, were united by Cyrus the Great in 549 B.C. to form a Persian empire which with its successor was in contact and conflict with the Greeks.

The prophet Zarathushtra, called Zoroaster by the Greeks, was a man of deep religious experiences and leader of a reform which came to revolutionise Iranian religion. His dates are still much debated. Some Zoroastrian and western scholars date the success of his mission '258 years before Alexander the Great'. Alexander sacked Persepolis in 330 B.C., when Zoroaster would be forty years of age, and as he lived to be seventy-seven, his dates on this calculation would be 628–551 B.C. But other scholars disagree strongly, disputing the calculation from Alexander, and pointing out the many similarities of ancient Iranian with Indian Vedic religion, which is agreed to have flourished at least between 2000 and 1000 B.C. Zoroaster has been dated a thousand years earlier than on the other theory, to times ranging from 1700 to 1200 B.C., and his religion has therefore been claimed as 'the oldest of the revealed world-religions'. However, Indians also claim revelation for their ancient Vedic hymns, and the religion of ancient Israel with the law revealed to Moses is also believed to have flourished in the second millennium B.C.

Zoroaster was a priest as well as a prophet, trained from boyhood in the doctrines and rituals of traditional Iranian religion. Part of this training consisted of learning by heart verses (*manthra*, Indian *mantra*) in praise of the many gods worshipped at that time. The training was oral, since writing was not known and, as in India, religious verses were passed down by memorisation for generations.

It is said that Zoroaster was dissatisfied with the traditional religion of his country and wandered about for years seeking the truth. He was discontented with the violence and brigandage of his time, and longed for justice and a life of peace. He complained of persecution: 'I am thrust out of my family and my tribe. I have no favour from my village or from the wicked rulers of the land. To what country shall I flee? Where shall I turn my steps?'

When he was about thirty years of age Zoroaster went to a river to draw water for a spring festival gathering. Coming out in a state of purity, he had a vision of a shining being who led him into the presence of the supreme God. This was Ahura Mazda, the wise Lord, later called Ohrmazd. Zoroaster was made a prophet and given the vocation of teaching righteousness and justice, in obedience to the one uncreated and eternal God, Ahura Mazda. 'Zarathushtra, the only one who has heard our teaching, he will make known our purpose and that of righteousness.'

Zoroaster's own beliefs and teachings, as distinct from later developments, are known primarily from hymns he composed, which were preserved by his followers. Seventeen of these hymns, or Gathas (Indian *Gita*), are considered to be original to Zoroaster himself. They were passed down orally by Zoroastrian communities and put into writing shortly before the Christian era. The Gathas are inspired utterances, like some other prophecies, which reveal Zoroaster's own experiences, since many of his words were addressed directly to God. They are in ancient forms of verse, as used by priestly seers, which were valuable for memorising. They were not originally works of doctrine or morals, but Zoroaster believed that God had given him messages for all people, and he probably preached in plainer words which were developed by his followers.

Zoroaster's teaching of only one God, and his claim to personal revelations, were rejected by most of his contemporaries, and for several years he had only one convert, his cousin. So he left his homeland, Rhages or Ray, part of modern Tehran, and went to Bactria in the east, where King Vishtaspa was converted and established the teachings of Zoroaster in his country. It is said that Zoroaster lived many years after Vishtaspa's conversion, but few details are known of his life. Like priests in many religions, Zoroaster was married; he had three wives who bore him three sons and three daughters. His enemies were still active, and the prophet is said to have been attacked while at prayer and to have died in defence of a fire-temple.

The ancient religion of Iran involved the worship of many gods; it was a polytheism like that of ancient India. There were gods of sky and earth, sun and moon, wind and storm. Especially important, from the times of nomadic life in central Asia, were fire and water. Fire, essential for warmth and cooking, was always kept alight in the hearth and received ritual offerings of fuel, animal fat and incense. Fire rituals were retained by Zoroaster and have been passed down the ages to be observed today. The spirits of water also received ritual offerings, and worshippers drank a fermented liquid called Haoma (Indian *Soma*). The temples of the modern Parsis (Persians), descendants of the Zoroastrians who are now found chiefly in India, are popularly called 'fire-temples', because the sacred fire always burns within them, and Haoma is still used in rituals.

Zoroaster rejected most of the ancient Iranian gods and proclaimed that Ahura Mazda was the one God, creator of all that is good. However, the great problem of the evil that exists in the world, which troubles most religions, led Zoroaster to a vision of an adversary to the good God called the 'hostile spirit', Angra Mainyu or Ahriman. Indeed, good and evil were two primal spirits, twins, but always in conflict. Zoroaster said, 'in the beginning the twin spirits declared their nature, the better and the evil, in thought, word and deed. Wise people choose well between the two, but foolish ones do not ... and the false gods did not choose rightly between them.'

It was later said by some Zoroastrians that the twin spirits came from an original unity, Zurvan, infinite time, but others opposed this notion as a heresy. Unlike the dualism of Manicheism (see 'Mani'), Zoroaster did not believe that spirit was good and matter was evil. All the creations of Ahura Mazda, matter and spirit, are good, but evil has come into the good creation and corrupted it. It is the duty of all beings to join with Ahura Mazda in fighting evil, and at the end of all things he will be victorious and evil will be destroyed or rendered impotent.

Dualism, the opposition of good and evil, may have provided an answer to the sufferings of the world, but Zoroastrians believed firmly that good would finally triumph and so dualism would not be perpetual. They called the faith 'the religion of the good life', because right and moral behaviour were essential to those who worked with Ahura Mazda for the establishment of righteousness and the overthrow of evil.

Some of the ancient Iranian gods were rejected completely by Zoroastrians, and others were regarded as emanations of Ahura Mazda, appointed by him to various tasks. One of them was Mithra (Indian Mitra), forms of whose worship were later adopted by other peoples and spread across the Roman Empire, with temples that were built even as far away as northern Britain. In Zoroastrian teachings Mithra survived attacks on the gods by being considered as a judge of the dead, and Parsi temples are called 'Door of Mithra'.

Like Job and other religious questioners, Zoroaster in his Gathas addressed queries to Ahura Mazda. 'Who was the first father of righteousness? Who appointed their path to the sun and the stars? Who set the earth in its place and the clouds in the sky? Who made the waters and the plants? Who made the morning, noon and night? Who among those to whom I speak is righteous? How shall we rid ourselves of evil? All these problems are addressed to the Wise Lord, that I may become one with him and that my word may have power.'

Further important teachings of Zoroaster were about death, judgement and a future life. Belief in some kind of survival of death is found in most, perhaps in all, religions but the conceptions of the kind of life after death vary widely. Indian beliefs in reincarnation or transmigration, which have affected much of Asia, are different from Zoroastrian beliefs in resurrection and judgement, which are more akin to those of Christianity. In this and similar beliefs Iran stood between India and western religions.

Zoroaster believed that when a spirit, male or female, leaves this world it is judged by the extent to which it has lived the good life and helped the cause of Ahura Mazda. The soul appears before the judge Mithra and its good and bad thoughts and deeds are weighed in scales. If good outweighs the bad, the soul is led by a beautiful maiden across the Bridge of the Separator and enters Paradise, the English word coming from the Persian for a park or heavenly garden. If the scales go down on the bad side, a horrid hag seizes the soul and takes it to a bridge which shrinks to the width of the edge of a blade, and they plunge together down into hell. Hell is ruled by the evil Angra Mainyu and is a place of darkness and suffering; though, in later belief at least, the damned would be finally released.

Even for the righteous Paradise was not the end, since there would be a final judgement, a great battle between good and evil, leading to the ultimate destruction of wickedness. After that men and women will live like the immortals, in perfection, in a world where mountains and valleys will be levelled out and every place will be like gardens in spring.

In later Zoroastrianism belief developed in an eschatological figure, a coming Saviour. This was Saoshyant, 'one who brings benefit', thought by some to be the last of the sons of Zoroaster, born of the prophet's seed miraculously preserved. Belief in the salvation to be brought by this coming Saviour strengthened Zoroastrians during times of struggle, and it went along with a glorification of Zoroaster himself. He was praised as the greatest priest, the master and judge of the world, at whose birth all creation rejoiced and the evil spirit fled away.

Zoroaster himself looked forward to the final struggle of good and evil, with the establishment of righteousness on earth after the great victory. His teachings of faith in one God who was entirely good and opposed to evil, doctrines of the immortality of the soul, of life after death, judgement and resurrection, and the final triumph of goodness, represented great advances in religious thought.

In due course Zoroastrianism became the established religion of later Persian empires, and its teachings are considered to have influenced late Judaism and early Christianity; this may be seen by comparing the teachings of the Old Testament with those of the inter-testamental Jewish books and with the New Testament, where beliefs in life after death and the struggles of good and evil are more pointed than in the earlier biblical periods.

Zoroastrians are now very few in number, though the influence of Zoroastrianism has been great, and it has survived for some three thousand years. After dominating Iran and influencing neighbouring lands, it was crushed by Islamic invasions of Iran from the seventh century A.D. Most of its surviving adherents migrated to India, especially the region round Bombay, where they became known as Parsis. Today there are some 120,000 people in India and 25,000 in Iran who treasure and follow the religion inaugurated by Zoroaster, and some tiny groups in Europe and America.

Lao Tzu

(? *b*. 604 B.C.)

Lao is pronounced like the *lou* in 'louse'. Tzu, sometimes rendered Tse, is sounded like 'adze' without the 'a'. The Jesuit missionaries in China Latinised the name to Laocius (see 'Confucius'). He is usually regarded as the founder of one of the world's great religions, author of a mysterious and fascinating book, the *Tao Tê Ching*.

However, many scholars, Chinese and western, consider either that Lao Tzu never existed or that virtually nothing can be known about him. The great English sinologist, Arthur Waley, from the evidence of vocabulary, grammar and rhyme structure, and especially from its particular ideas, held that the *Tao Tê Ching* was written by 'an anonymous quietist', about 240 B.C.

In the first century B.C. a great Chinese historian, Ssu-ma Ch'ien, tried to write a life of Lao Tzu, whom he considered to be the author of the *Tao Tê Ching*. He admitted that he was faced with masses of conflicting legends and could not entirely disentangle them. A few of the chief legends and possible connexions are as follows.

On 14 September, 604 B.C. (the Chinese like to be precise in dating), a woman in the kingdom of Ch'u, leaning against a plum tree, gave birth to a child. Buddhist legend, well known in China, had said that the Buddha's mother gave birth standing under a tree (see 'Buddha'). Legends further say that this Chinese infant had been sixty-two years (sometimes eighty-one) in his mother's womb, so that when he was born his hair was already snow white, and he was nicknamed Lao Tzu, Old Master, because of his white hair. The extraordinary child spoke as soon as he was born, as did the Buddha in legend. Later he was called Lao Tan, Old Long Ears, because long ears were held to be signs of sanctity, again as in Buddhist legend.

This legend may be confused with tales of at least two other people, P'eng Tzu and Lao Tan. Grandfather P'eng was the Chinese Methusaleh, who is said to have prolonged his life to some eight hundred years by feeding on powdered mother of pearl. Then there was a certain Lao Tan, a historical figure who was treasurer of the state of Chou in 374 B.C., but of course he would not fit in with a claim to birth in 604, or to a further claim that Lao Tzu or Lao Tan met with and discomfited Confucius, who died in 479. To add to the confusion, there was a different sage called Lao Lai Tzu, about whom similar stories are told, and who wrote a book on Taoist practices which has not survived.

The story of the meeting with Confucius was clearly a piece of anti-Confucian propaganda by the Taoists, who differed from their rivals on many points of doctrine. This legend said that Confucius was fifty-three years younger than Lao Tzu (the dates cannot be reconciled) and in one or more meetings with the rival sage Confucius did not acquit himself very well. At the end of the encounter Lao Tzu is said to have rebuked Confucius by saying: 'Abandon your arrogant ways and countless desires. They do not promote your welfare.' This was hard on Confucius who, although he aspired after governmental office, put virtue and truth above all things and taught the middle way between extremes. The legend continued that Confucius went away shaking his head and confessing to his disciples, 'Today I have seen Lao Tzu, and can only liken him to a dragon.'

Another story says that Lao Tzu became disgusted at the decline of the Chou dynasty. When he was a hundred and sixty years old – some say two hundred – he resolved to leave the world and retire to the mountains in the west of China, rather like the Buddhist Western Paradise, roughly in the direction of Tibet, and identified with the heavens. He rode in a chariot drawn by a black ox, and the sage is often shown in pictures with such an ox. When he came to a pass which leads westward, the keeper of the pass pleaded with the sage to leave some tangible remains of his passing and his wisdom. This pass-keeper was another famous Taoist worthy, and it was said that he had been expecting the arrival of Lao Tzu from the troubled state of the weather. At his request Lao Tzu promptly sat down and wrote the book, running to little more than five thousand characters, which embodied his ideas about Tao and Tê, the famous *Tao Tê Ching*.

A later Taoist book, the *Lieh Tzu*, says that when Lao Tzu was setting out on his journey to the west he dismissed his attendants, and told a chosen disciple that all that has the breath of life, all that possesses bodily form, is mere illusion: a Buddhist notion. Legend continues that having written his book Lao Tzu left for the mysterious west, and a late story, also influenced by Buddhism, describes temptations that came to him in the first three nights beyond the pass. Lying under a tree he was tempted by the Evil One and by beautiful women, as the Buddha in legend was tempted by Death and his daughters. But to Lao Tzu these women were only 'skin bags full of blood', and he resisted their blandishments easily. Nothing further is known about his death, or where it occurred, if indeed he ever existed.

The historian Ssu-ma Ch'ien was aware that Lao Tan and Lao Lai Tzu were confused in the stories about Confucius. He records the great age attributed to Lao Tan, but also refers to the Lao Tan who was a treasurer in 374, remarking that some thought him to be identical with the Taoist philosopher, though others said that he was not the same. The effect of his biography on modern readers is usually to persuade them that no solid facts about the life of Lao Tzu exist.

If Lao Tzu never existed it was nevertheless, as Waley remarked, a Chinese custom for books to 'shelter themselves', as it was called, under the names of well-known men. Similar practices existed in other parts of the ancient world, in Indian, Hebrew and Greek literature. The 'sheltering' of a book removed its anonymity, but could easily lead to confusion when one or more ancients were connected with it.

The only solid material that we possess is the *Tao Tê Ching*, often called the *Lao Tzu*. Some scholars think it was written by several teachers; others insist that it is the work of one man, even if nothing else is known about him. Traditionally it was dated to the sixth century B.C., and some modern writers cling to this date. Others find such an early date for it impossible, and since the book attacks the ideas and practices of the Confucians it seems more probable that it must belong to the fourth or third centuries B.C.

Tao Tê Ching means Way-Power-Classic, or, as Waley interprets it, 'The Way and its Power'. Tao (pronounced *dow*) means Way, as will be expounded. Tê (pronounced *dir*) means virtue in the sense of power. Ching (pronounced *jing*) is a title given to Chinese classical writings.

The *Tao Tê Ching* is in eighty-one short chapters, an auspicious number, nine times nine. It opens with a dramatic statement, or non-statement, about Tao. The way that can be told of is not an unvarying Way, not the eternal Way. Names or terms that can be named or defined are not eternal or unvarying, for Heaven and Earth sprang from the Nameless, whereas the Named is the mother of the ten thousand creatures of earth.

The word Tao was used in the general sense of a way or path in earlier Chinese works, to mean the way in which anything was done. 'When Tao prevailed' meant 'when a good government was exercised on earth'. Confucius spoke of this Way, and of his own Way, and the Way of good people who followed traditional paths. But for the Quietists who sought out the inner meaning of things, Tao was the way to achieve something without doing anything. It was the ultimate reality, the unity underlying the many individual things, and those who sought for this unchanging unity with Tao came to be called Taoists.

Such people sought harmony with the laws of the universe, and they worked without working. The second chapter of the *Lao Tzu* says that the sage relies on 'actionless activity', yet by wordless teaching he influences the myriads of creatures. The Way is like an empty vessel which is never filled, yet can be drawn from; it is a deep pool that never dries up; it is the mysterious female from which heaven and earth sprang; it is the uncarved block which has received no marks. The Way is like water, a favourite Taoist image, which does not fight, takes the lowest ground, but finally prevails and benefits all mankind.

To be in harmony with the universe, and not in rebellion against it, is the first step on the Way. The infant is nearest to Tao because of its simplicity; weakness and softness are symbols of Tao, showing that to yield is to conquer but to grasp is to lose.

Against Confucian scholarship, which easily became formal, the *Lao Tzu* exhorts men to 'banish wisdom' and discard knowledge, whereupon the people will benefit a hundredfold. Both the culture and the morality of the Confucians was considered here to go against the natural order of things and the inborn virtues. So 'banish human kindness, and reject morality, abolish skill and reject profit'. If this Way was followed people would be naturally dutiful and compassionate, and thieves and robbers would disappear. People should be given simplicity to look at and the uncarved block to hold; they should have few desires and be unselfish.

The Taoist should push towards the void, as in Buddhist philosophy, hold on to quietness and return to the root from which he grew. Such a person is truly royal, truly of heaven, which is synonymous with Tao. It was when Tao declined that morality appeared, and knowledge brought artificiality or hypocrisy. The all-pervading Power or Virtue (Tê) can only act through the Way, which is intangible and immeasurable.

This idea led to teachings on warfare. Chapter thirty of the *Tao Tê Ching* says that he who wishes to help a ruler by the Way will oppose conquest by arms, for such things rebound. Thorns and brambles will grow where armies have been, and years of famine follow great campaigns. The next chapter continues that weapons are evil and the Quietist does not think them lovely, for that means to delight in them and so in the slaughter of men. An army that has killed men receives lamentations, and the victor in battle is welcomed with rites of mourning.

Such pacific teachings expressed old strains in Chinese thought, and alongside the social occupations of Confucians Taoism offered visions and mysticism. In later times there grew up exercises of breathing, and forms of yoga, which led to living on herbs and dew, and seeking immortality through alchemy. In popular religion Taoism adopted organisation like Buddhism, with priests and temples, and it absorbed superstitions and magical practices which made it ridiculous to the educated. Taoism also formed secret societies which in many ages worried governments, like the notorious Boxers, or Harmonious Fist society, which led the revolts in 1900.

But there have always been educated men who have studied the *Tao Tê Ching* and other Taoist classics, keeping them by their bedside. Chinese Communists have shown interest in Lao Tzu, as representing opposition to feudal Confucianism. The Taoist search for unity with nature is now interpreted as conformable with dialectical materialism, though its quietism and pacifism are difficult to adapt.

Confucius

(551–479 B.C.)

Jesuit missionaries who worked in China from the sixteenth century onwards Latinised the name of its greatest sage as Confucius. This was their version of K'ung Fu-tzu or Master K'ung, which was the common title used by the Chinese. His personal name was Ch'iu and K'ung was the family name. He was born in 551 B.C. and died in 479 at the age of seventy-two, and down the succeeding ages has been hailed as 'the Teacher of Ten Thousand Generations'.

Confucius was born in the town of Tsou in the small feudal state of Lu, in the modern province of Shantung in north-east China. His mother and father are not named in early records, but it seems that the father died when Confucius was very young, leaving him to struggle to get an education and make his way in the world. He himself said that when young he was in humble circumstances, and that was why he had many practical accomplishments in everyday affairs, the lack of help having made him very handy. Later traditions gave him all the advantages of a gentleman, and attributed to him the words: 'At fifteen I set my heart upon learning, at thirty I stood firm, at forty I was free from doubts, at fifty I understood the biddings of Heaven, at sixty my ear was docile, at seventy I could follow the dictates of my own heart without transgressing the right.'

It is known that Confucius had an elder brother and a niece, and that he was married, though early sources say nothing about his wife. He had a son and daughter, but the son died while Confucius was still alive. Although Confucius apparently did not own much property, he seems to have acted as head of the family; later tradition said that his elder brother was a cripple. Tradition again makes him a man of aristocratic ancestry, but it does appear likely that his forebears could have belonged to the lesser aristocracy yet had fallen to the humble status to which he confessed.

In modern times Confucius has been called both a reactionary feudal teacher, and a man of the people. But he was educated, and had the leisure for archery and music. How he gained his education is not known, and it is said that he had no regular teacher. His later follower, Mencius, said that the Master had been a storekeeper and kept correct accounts; he was in charge of sheep and oxen and made it his duty to see that they were strong and well-grown. With such early struggles to get education and work, Confucius had sympathy with working people, and this ensured that he would later be popular with all classes of society. He encouraged able young disciples, however poor, and declared that from the poorest upwards nobody had ever come to him without receiving help.

Confucius became a learned man, but not through reading many books. Some of the classical works later associated with him had in fact not yet been written, and of others few copies existed. Books were written on strips of bamboo tied together by cords; they were clumsy to hold and bulky to store. Confucius probably knew some historical works and learnt traditional poems by heart. He studied religious and ancestral rituals, but questioned both past and present practices.

Confucius has been called the first private teacher in China. In many ways he resembled Socrates in Greece, who lived about a century later (see 'Plato'). What became the 'Confucian school' may have begun as a group of friends forming a debating society. Some of these friends were about the same age as Confucius, but his pre-eminence is evident from the surviving dialogues. Twenty-two men are mentioned by name in these dialogues, and no doubt there were others, most of them coming from Lu and neighbouring states. These dialogues are the *Analects*, to use the traditional English term for the *Lun Yü*, 'Selected Sayings', a compilation of twenty books or short chapters, with some 500 verses, in which chapters three to nine are recognised as the oldest, and some of the other parts seem to be hardly Confucian at all. As with Socrates, the *Analects* present sayings by and about the Master, rather than work from his own hand.

China in the time of Confucius was divided into small states that were always quarrelling among themselves, while barbarian tribes pressed in on all sides. The central court of the Chou dynasty, which had once united the country, had become weak and there were powerful feudal lords who deposed or assassinated rulers. Among violence and disorder there seemed to be no power that would bring peace.

Confucius believed that government should seek the good of the people, and he sought to bring order and peace into the world. Only if government were administered by men of the highest integrity, trained for public service, could general welfare be guaranteed. Confucius saw himself as a reformer, not primarily a scholar, and he believed his place was in the world of politics, but, like Plato, he was not very successful in his practical efforts. For a time he was employed in the government of the state of Lu, and later tradition said that he held high office and was minister of crime. But the *Analects* say nothing of this, and many Chinese scholars reject the story. The political career of Confucius was not a success. He would not compromise with those in charge of government, and it seems that they hesitated to give power to one who held reforming ideas and would put them into practice. So Confucius turned his attention more and more to teaching his ideals to young men, several of whom held posts in government.

When he was near sixty Confucius, like Plato, set off on his travels to seek a ruler who would give him the desired opportunity to practise his ideals. The details of his travels are sketchy. He went to states where he was respected but was not given administrative posts, and probably had several travelling companions, though tradition credited him with a great retinue. After wandering around for about a decade Confucius was invited back to Lu, where friends and disciples awaited him. In the closing years of his life he devoted himself to arranging manuscripts, according to tradition editing five so-called Confucian Classics. He may have edited the *Spring and Autumn Annals*, a chronicle of events in the state of Lu, though this has been much questioned.

The deaths of his son and of several of his closest friends were blows to Confucius, and he may have been disappointed that he had achieved so little; 'nobody understands me', he complained. When he was ill, some of his disciples dressed up like ministers attending a high dignitary, but Confucius rebuked them for imposture. Who would he deceive in pretending to have retainers when he had none? 'Do I deceive Heaven?' He said he would rather die in the arms of his disciples than receive a state funeral, and he could trust them to give him decent burial. When a disciple asked permission to pray for him the Master said, 'My praying began long ago'.

After the death of Confucius his disciples drop out of sight, but later ages said that they revered him as the greatest man who had ever lived, and one even compared him to the sun and moon. Although he was a simple teacher, Confucianism became official doctrine in due course and imperial recognition was given to him and his school to strengthen the power of the throne. Confucian scholars became the guardians of tradition, both of political officialdom and of ancient literature. Confucianism was established as the state philosophy, and down to this present century government posts were filled by means of examinations in the Confucian classics.

Furthermore, ritual veneration was accorded to Confucius; from early centuries sacrifices were offered to him in schools, and in some temples he was worshipped alongside Lao Tzu and the Buddha. Confucian halls were built in which scholars and town officials directed rituals, and carved tablets proclaimed his praises. These halls usually included school buildings and libraries and were surrounded by trees and courtyards. There were elaborate ceremonies on the sage's birthday, with drums booming, torches shining, and altars blazing with lights. A modern scholar described the impressive rituals with lights gleaming in the darkness and silk-robed officials gliding through the hall. 'The celebrant entered, and the vessels were presented towards the silent statue of the Sage, the "Teacher of Ten Thousand Generations".'

This writer thought that Confucius would have been shocked at this ceremonial, and considered that the modern attacks on halls and temples would not have disappointed him, because they might show that only certain aspects of Confucianism had been rejected and not Confucius himself. However, in the revolutions of this century Confucius has been burnt in effigy, and Chairman Mao once said, 'I hated Confucius from the age of eight'. On the other hand, the first President of the Chinese Republic, Sun Yat-sen, declared that 'both Confucius and Mencius were exponents of democracy'.

The tomb of Confucius is still to be seen at Ch'ü-fu in Shantung, and has been neglected or repaired according to the temper of the times. It has recently been repaired and redecorated. It is a simple building, with a bell and drums, and at the end stands a grey-brown stone tablet, about six feet high, bearing the inscription, 'Confucius, the Primal Sage'.

Confucius taught the ideal of the gentleman (*chün-tzu*, literally 'son of a ruler'), a term that came to be applied to a man of serious character and behaviour. Of one such man he said in the *Analects*: 'In his personal conduct he was serious, in duty to his superior he was punctilious, in providing for the people he was beneficent, in directing them he was just.' The gentleman, like Aristotle's high-minded man (see 'Aristotle'), abstained from extremes, and was moderate in conduct and opinion. He would keep his head in success, and would not be embittered by adversity or feel resentment when neglected.

It is said that Confucius rarely discoursed upon goodness, and refused to define it or apply it to his contemporaries. He spoke of what was right, not of what would pay the best. He spoke of Tao (pronounced *dow*), the path or way, as the way in which things should be done or kingdoms ruled, but not in the mystical and indefinable sense of the Taoists (see 'Lao Tzu'). He taught a negative version of the Golden Rule: 'what I do not want others to do to me, I have no desire to do to them'.

Confucius had great concern for social order, and for him the model began at the top. If the rulers were immoral the whole state would decline, and he compared an oppressive ruler to a tiger. Each man should perform the duties of his station, children should obey parents, pupils obey masters, and subjects obey rulers, but, as has been said, the example began at the top. The Chinese emphasis upon filial piety to ancestors and to living parents does not appear in the earliest parts of the *Analects*, and seems to be a later development.

Like Socrates, Confucius had a sense of Heaven (T'ien) which inspired and directed him. Among his sayings were 'Heaven begat the virtue that is in me', 'If I have done wrong may Heaven reject me', and 'He who sins against Heaven has nowhere left for prayer.' He said that respect for the spirits should keep them at a distance. This has been interpreted as indicating that he was an agnostic, but on the other hand it may suggest a proper concern that spirits should not turn against human beings because of neglect. Similarly when he was asked how the dead should be served, Confucius replied that until you know about and serve the living you cannot know about the dead.

Although Confucius did not enjoy political success or widespread renown in his lifetime, he and his followers were responsible for the ideal of the scholar–gentleman which profoundly influenced Chinese society. Belief in the perfectibility of man through learning and the practice of goodness, with an emphasis upon virtue and kindness, became accepted ideals, treasured down the centuries.

Pythagoras

(*c*. 560– *c*. 480 B.C.)

The details of the life and teachings of Pythagoras are obscured by the fact that he was the founder of a community – part scientific, part mystic – which became widespread throughout the Greek-speaking world of antiquity. Subsequent philosophers referred to the teachings of 'the Pythagoreans', and it is difficult to determine how much of these were directly attributable to Pythagoras. It seems likely that many of the mystical observances were generated by his followers.

However, we can trace the major events of his life, at least in outline. He was born on the island of Samos, and as a young man travelled extensively in Egypt and Babylon; it is widely believed that, in the course of his travels, he learnt of the mathematics used in those lands. Back on Samos, he found himself in vehement opposition to the policies of the tyrant Polycrates, and so at some time in the period 530 – 520 B.C. he emigrated to the Greek city of Croton, in southern Italy, where he set up a school devoted to religion, philosophy and politics.

Once again, it was to be his political ideas which were to lead to a change of scene. Initially his school, which came to have a considerable influence in the Greek cities of the area, was welcomed by the aristocrats, because Pythagoras's politics seemed to them to be a breakwater against the inrushing tide of democracy. However, over a couple of decades, the relationship turned sour; and in about 500 B.C. an attack, led by one Cylon, was launched against the school, leaving many of the leading Pythagoreans dead. Pythagoras himself retired to Metapontum, where he died some twenty years later.

It seems that Pythagoreans taught by the use of *akousmata* ('things heard'), which were little more than cryptic hints. The *akousmatikoi* or 'listeners', were permitted to hear these hints from the teacher's lips, but were required to do so in silence: no debate or questioning was allowed. Those disciples who underwent a considerable period of training and who reached a very advanced level could, however, qualify as *mathematikoi*; that is, they were allowed to ask questions and occasionally put forward ideas of their own. (The term *mathematikoi* has given us our word 'mathematics', but at the time it simply implied that those described by it were at a certain high level of understanding.) This method of teaching was therefore one which our modern rationalist society would regard as thoroughly inefficient; it seems certain that the Pythagoreans were relying upon that deeper form of awareness which is more commonly associated with some of the Eastern religions, notably Zen Buddhism.

This is no coincidence, for Pythagoras's concerns were, at the most fundamental level, religious. He seems to have believed that he himself was semi-divine, and was thereby able to remember his earlier incarnations in this world; it was because he could draw on the memories and experiences of several lifetimes, not just the one, that he was so understanding and wise. Moreover, the very fact that he could remember his past lives was a powerful proof that reincarnation really did occur; and this was a strong incentive to would-be disciples to join his school, since the spiritual development they gained would serve them well in the next life. In order to achieve higher incarnations, they had, they were told, to strive to be more like Pythagoras himself, for he, being on a higher spiritual plane, was clearly much closer to the gods than they were. To this end they should purify their spirits by such measures as listening to music and the disinterested pursuit of knowledge – as well as procedures which can only be described as taboos, such as not eating beans, not picking up what had fallen down, and taking care to erase the body's impress on the bed when rising in the morning.

It was through music that Pythagoras lit upon the field of thought which allowed his school to make its most important donation to our civilisation.

It seemed obvious to the Pythagoreans that music was merely

the most accessible manifestation of the harmony which permeated the entire universe, study of music would, therefore, perhaps
lead them closer to the divine cosmos. Examination of music's
'consonant intervals' showed that there are simple numerical
relationships between them: if you halve the length of a vibrating
string, the new note is an octave higher than the old (i.e., the
relationship is 1:2). Moreover, all the numerical relationships
involved in the consonant intervals used only the numbers one to
four, which seemed to prove to the Pythagoreans that they were on
the right track: the sum 1+2+3+4 adds up to 10, and 10 was to
them a sacred number, being the base of our counting system. If
these numerical relationships were fundamental to music, then
they must be fundamental also to the universe. He and his school
came to look upon numbers with a mystical rapture: 'all things are
numbers', he is reputed to have said.

Everywhere they looked, they found confirmation that numbers
were the 'language' of the universe. One point defined a point (of
course), 2 a line, 3 a triangle (the simplest plane figure) and 4 a
tetrahedron (the simplest solid figure); hence another reason for
the importance of the numbers one to four (they did not conceive
of a fourth-dimensional object defined by 5 points). Naturally
occurring crystals recognised the numerical basis of things by
appearing in the form of regular polyhedra. Even the human body
had 1 head, 2 eyes, 3 joints to a finger, 4 limbs, 5 digits per hand,
and so on.

Inevitably the Pythagoreans were led on to consider sequences
– 'inevitably' because sequences can be viewed as linking abstract
numbers with geometrical forms. Take, for example, the sequence
of 'triangular' numbers, 1, 3, 6, 10, 15 and so on. The reason for
calling them the 'triangular' numbers becomes obvious on consideration of this diagram:

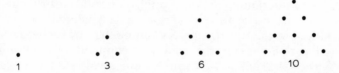

One could develop from here to get the 'pyramidal' numbers, by
considering stacks of these triangles: 1, 4 (=3+1), 10 (=6+3+1),
20 (=10+6+3+1), and so on. In fact, the 'pyramidal' sequence
represents the partial sums of the series formed by the 'triangular'
numbers: 1+3+6+10 ...

Of more significance was the sequence of 'square' numbers, 1,

4, 9, 16, 25, and so on (and hence also the 'cubic' numbers 1, 8, 27, 64, 125 . . .). By considering the *gnomon* for the 'square' number 25 the Pythagoreans came across something curious:

On one side of the line are 16 (4^2) dots and on the other 9 (3^2) dots. In other words, $3^2+4^2=5^2$. And there were other trios of 'square' numbers for which this relationship worked: for example, $5^2+12^2=13^2$ and $7^2+24^2=25^2$. All of this related rather neatly to the fact that the square on the hypotenuse of a right-angled triangle is equal to the sums of the squares on the other two sides, a geometrical relationship long associated with the name of Pythagoras. (Certainly the Egyptians had discovered the relationship empirically; whether they had proved that it was always so is questionable, at best.)

Proclus (410–485) claimed that Pythagoras deduced the general formula for sums of 'square' numbers such as these:

$$n^2+\left(\frac{n^2-1}{2}\right)^2 = \left(\frac{n^2-1}{2}+1\right)^2$$

where *n* is an odd number, but this is very unlikely. Even if Pythagoras did give the formula to the Greeks, it is much more probable that he had picked it up among the Babylonians, who knew it, than that he deduced it.

But consideration of right-angled triangles brought the Pythagoreans up against a very serious problem indeed: the isosceles right-angled triangle. Assuming that the two equal sides are of length 1 (in fact, the argument is unaffected by the units used), then the sum of their squares must be $1^2+1^2=1+1=2$. So the length of the hypotenuse must be the number which, when multiplied by itself, gives the product 2. But this number, $\sqrt{2}$, cannot be expressed as a fraction: whatever the system you use, it is impossible to give an exact numerical value to $\sqrt{2}$ (it is about 1·414213562). There was another naturally occurring number close to home which displayed this irritating characteristic – π, the ratio between a circle's circumference and its diameter. It was extremely difficult to fit such 'incommensurables' into the Pythagorean number-based universe (one member of the school is said to have been drowned because he laid great stress on the irrational numbers, so sensitive was the issue). Eventually the Pythagoreans were forced to develop the idea of 'fluxion'; the difference between any two numbers can be infinitely subdivided until eventually, in theory, numbers like $\sqrt{2}$ and π can be expressed as the ratio between two integers. (Archimedes was to develop a similar sort of idea some while afterwards.) Of course, this idea of infinite subdivision and *flowing* from one number through an infinity of subdivisions to the next comes close to the notion of the calculus; in this respect, it is interesting to note that Newton was to call his newly discovered calculus 'fluxions'.

The Pythagoreans were interested also in pairs of 'amicable' numbers – that is, numbers where the factors of one member of the pair add up to the other, and *vice versa*. Only one such pair was known to the ancients, 220 and 284. To spell this out:

The factors of 220 are 1, 2, 4, 5, 10, 11, 20, 22, 44, 55, 110
1+2+4+5+10+11+20+22+44+55+110=284
The factors of 284 are 1, 2, 4, 71, 142
1+2+4+71+142=220

In the search for 'amicable' numbers they developed the idea of 'abundant' and 'deficient' numbers, the former being numbers whose factors added up to a sum greater than the original, the latter those whose factors summed less than the original. For example, 18 is 'abundant' because 1+2+3+6+9=21, and 15 is 'deficient' because 1+3+5=9. The concepts of 'abundance' and 'deficiency' are of little relevance or interest except in so far as they set the Pythagoreans off in quest of 'perfect' numbers.

The Pythagoreans turned their eyes to the skies to seek proof of their idea that all the universe is numbers, and 'proof' they found in the music of the spheres. Pythagoras himself seems to have thought that there were only three celestial spheres in which the heavenly bodies moved – those of the moon, sun and stars (including the planets) – to go with the three discovered musical relationships – the octave, fourth and fifth. It was not thought that the spheres were actually playing beautiful music, more that the relationships between them *were* music. In physical terms, of course, the whole idea was nonsense, but it is interesting to note that Kepler's important laws of the seventeenth century and the completely empirical Bode's Law of the eighteenth, both of which describe the planets' orbital movements, are based on similar ideas of numerical 'resonance'.

The idea of the music of the spheres shows how the Pythagoreans were capable of taking the hard edge of science – numbers – and turning it into an elusive mystical cloud (though a beautiful cloud). Nowhere is this more evident than in the cosmology produced (it is thought) by the Pythagorean Philolaus. The earth, moon, sun and stars all circle a central fire, which we can never see because we are on the wrong side of the earth; always on the other side of the central fire from us there is a counter-earth. The sun's light is reflected from the central fire.

Now this may sound like an early stumble towards a heliocentric cosmology, but in fact its whole basis was mystical and arbitrary. Fire was regarded as a superior type of stuff to earth because it was held in religious awe (for obvious primitive reasons), and so fire had to be situated at some 'better' part of the universe than was the earth – why not at the centre of the universe? The counter-earth came into the scheme only because when you added up the spheres circling the central fire – those of earth, moon, sun, Mercury, Venus, Mars, Jupiter, Saturn and the fixed stars – you got a total of only 9, whereas 10 was of supreme mystical importance to the Pythagoreans. Since it would be stretching credulity to invent an extra sphere without any corresponding celestial object, it was necessary to invent a celestial object which *by definition* could never be seen. There is as much of the scientific approach in this cosmology as there is in most of those dictated through spirit mediums by the denizens of 'astral planes'. And yet the cosmology is of great importance: it was the first in which the idea was put forth that the earth itself might move. Copernicus claimed that it was this cosmology which sparked off a certain idea in his head . . .

Pythagoras and the Pythagoreans were, then, as much a religious cult as a scientific brotherhood. Bertrand Russell has described Pythagoras as 'a combination of Einstein and Mrs Mary Baker Eddy'. The legacy which he and his school have donated to our civilisation is the dominance which numbers exercise over so much of our thinking. It was that and the stress on asceticism and the immortality of the soul which impressed Plato and through him influenced much of subsequent philosophy.

Buddha

(? *c.* 563–*c.* 483 B.C.)

The man who is often called *the* Buddha is believed by Buddhists to have been one of a long succession of Buddhas, 'enlightened ones'. In Buddhist scriptures legends name several previous Buddhas, though dating them back hundreds of thousands of years, and events in their lives are sketched on the common model of the historical Buddha. Further, while there have been Buddhas in the distant past, and will be others to come in the far future, it is often said that there is only one Buddha in this present world aeon of thousands of years.

A dialogue of the Theravada tradition of southern Asia, 'the doctrine of the elders', asks whether there could be two Buddhas here at once and declares that this could not happen. First, the earth would not be able to support the weight of two enlightened beings at once and it would sink. Secondly, if there were two Buddhas now their followers would disagree and rival each other. So for all practical purposes there is only one Buddha in our world and this makes him central in devotion. In the Mahayana tradition, the 'great vehicle' of northern Asia, however, there are many Buddhas and celestial beings and Gautama almost disappears.

In the foothills of the Himalaya mountains, along the borders of India and Nepal, was the country of the Shakyas of which, according to Buddhist texts, the capital was Kapilavastu. About the sixth or fifth century B.C., seemingly, the ruler of this state was Suddhodana and his queen was named Maya. The surname of the family was Gautama or Gotama. There are many legends of the birth of the Buddha-to-be of these parents, but clearly they were married and it was not a virgin birth or virginal conception. In one ancient story Queen Maya had a dream in which a white elephant touched her side and entered her womb. The dream was interpreted to indicate that a Buddha had decided to come to earth and had chosen the queen for his vessel. In other stories the Buddha-embryo sat cross-legged in his mother's womb, 'mindful and conscious', while four gods protected him from any dangers from the four quarters of the world.

It is said that the child was born in a grove of trees in the

Lumbini park and that birth pangs came on the queen as she held on to the branches. As the baby was delivered the four great gods received it in a golden net and streams of water came from the sky to wash away impurities. As the child was born he stood on his feet, took seven steps, surveyed the four quarters, and proclaimed in a lion-like voice, 'I am the chief in the world. This is my last birth.'

These are legends, but they are taught in public schools in Buddhist countries to this day, and they express the devotion that Buddhists feel to the founder of their religion. It may be noted that the Buddha is believed to have had many previous lives upon earth, and a popular collection of stories, Jatakas or 'birth tales', recounts some 550 previous lives of this Buddha in human and animal form. It fits into the general Indian belief in transmigration or rebirth into many different lives.

When the child was born, a sage named Asita, dwelling in the Himalayas, heard of the event and came to see him. He observed that the child bore the thirty-two marks of a great man, and prophesied that he would become either a universal monarch or a fully enlightened Buddha. The baby was given the personal name of Siddhartha, but he is often known by the family name of Gautama, or called, after the clan, Shakya-muni, 'the sage of the Shakyas'.

According to tradition, which says the same about previous Buddhas, the young man was brought up in luxury and ignorance of the sufferings of the world, until he saw the Four Signs and made a great renunciation. He had been married to Princess Yasodhara and they had a son Rahula, but not till Gautama was twenty-nine did the gods make the signs appear to him. Riding in the palace park Gautama saw an old man, bent, grey-haired and trembling, and when he asked his charioteer what was the matter with the old man Gautama discovered that old age could come to him also. On following days he saw a sick man, a corpse, and finally a monk who had abandoned the world. In each case Gautama was agitated at such sights.

Behind these legends there may have been a growing concern with the transitory and suffering nature of the world, and an early text expresses this: 'Being myself subject to birth, I sought out the nature of birth. Being myself subject to age, I sought out the nature of old age, sickness, death, sorrow and impurity . . . what if I were to seek the supreme peace of Nirvana?' So Gautama decided to renounce the world and become a wandering ascetic, an old version putting it that when he was still a black-haired youth, while his father and mother wept, he cut off his hair and beard and went forth from home to the homeless life. Legends make him set out in a chariot, leaving his sleeping wife and son and dancing girls, and his very horse died of a broken heart as he abandoned it.

The young man was still a Buddha-to-be, a Bodhisattva or 'being destined for enlightenment' but who had not yet achieved it. He went to various teachers to seek the solution to his problems but found them unsatisfactory. Then for six years he practised extreme austerities until he was almost a skeleton, and statues depict him in this state. Five disciples watched to see if he would die, but Gautama finally decided that he could not be saved by self-torture, and he adopted the Middle Way between the extremes of sensuality and asceticism. He took food and drink and the five other monks went away in disgust.

Gautama went to Gaya near a religious shrine on a tributary of the river Ganges. He sat under a tree which came to be known as the Bodhi-tree or Bo-tree, 'the tree of enlightenment' (see 'Asoka'), and vowed to remain there till enlightenment came to him. With concentrated mind he directed his thoughts to many former existences, many cycles of dissolution of the universe. Then he considered present beings rising and passing away, according to their karma, 'deeds', their good or bad lives. Then he sought the truth of suffering, the fact, the cause, and the destruction. His mind was freed from desires and ignorance, darkness was dispelled, knowledge and light arose. Like a god he saw all beings, past, present and future. He had full enlightenment, and became a Buddha.

Now having all-knowledge, should he teach it? He was tempted not to do so by Mara, death itself, and to proceed at once to Nirvana, 'blowing out', an ethereal state of peace. But a chief god came down from heaven and besought the Buddha to preach for the benefit of mankind, even if only a few would listen. The story shows how Buddhism went beyond being one of the ways of self-salvation and world denial, to become an international religion.

The Buddha thereupon set out for the great religious centre of Benares (Varanasi), and the five monks who had left him saw him coming. They decided neither to greet nor to listen to him, but his presence was so impressive that they gave the Buddha an honoured place, listened to his teaching of deliverance and peace, and became his first monkish disciples. Then two merchants came and brought food and they confessed the Refuge: 'We go to the Buddha for refuge. We go to the Doctrine for refuge.' They became the first lay disciples, and when the Order of monks was formed a third Refuge was added; this triple formula was a primitive confession or creed, and it is recited by countless Buddhists down to this day.

The Buddha went on to Benares and in a park at Sarnath to the north of the city he preached his first sermon, at a place still marked by a great monument erected by the emperor Asoka over two thousand years ago. The sermon is entitled, 'Turning the Wheel of the Doctrine', and it teaches fundamental doctrines of Buddhism: the Four Noble Truths and the Noble Eightfold Path. The truths give a simple analysis of pain or suffering in four steps: the fact of suffering, its cause, its cure, and the path. The Noble (Aryan) Eightfold Path is in three stages, each step called 'right': right views and intention; right speech, action and livelihood; right effort, mindfulness and concentration.

A second sermon was on 'the marks of not-self' or non-soul. The soul or self is not the body, for if it were it would not be subject to sickness. Similarly the soul or self is not feeling, perception, impressions or consciousness. It is not denied that there is a soul, but it cannot be located or comprehended.

Two women became the first lay female disciples, and later an order of nuns was instituted, though with some reluctance. Today there are no Buddhist nuns in southern Asia, though orders of them exist in Japan and Korea. Many men became monks, cutting off their hair and taking the yellow robe, and the Order became the inner church of Buddhism. But the large number of converts aroused hostility from people who saw that they broke up families and produced childlessness.

The Buddha went about northern and middle India for over forty years, and many stories are told of his encounters with kings and merchants, women and ascetics. His father Suddhodana was converted to Buddhism, and his son Rahula became a monk, though after that a rule was made that a son might not be ordained without the permission of his mother and father. The Buddha's chief disciple was Ananda, and his chief opponent among the monks was his cousin Devadatta. The Buddha is said to have taught Five Precepts, Pancha-shila or Pansil, as rules of moral conduct for monks and laity: non-injury, not stealing, chastity, not lying, and temperance. He taught the goal of Nirvana, indescribable peace beyond the heavens, as the goal of the Noble Eightfold Path.

There are several accounts of the last days of the Buddha. He was given a meal of pork by a smith, Chunda, and ate it because it was a gift, though it was infected. Racked with dysentery, he came to a little wattle and daub village in the forest called Kusinara. There, as Ananda and the village elders wept, the Buddha spoke of his passing away and exhorted his followers in these last words, 'All composite things are decaying. Work out your own salvation with diligence.'

A cairn was prepared for the cremated remains of the Buddha, which were divided into eight portions for eight towns. This was the beginning of the relic-holders, stupas, which as dagobas and pagodas in Sri Lanka and Burma are the most notable Buddhist buildings, all claiming to have relics.

According to the Chronicle of Ceylon, the Mahavamsa, '218 years had passed from the Nirvana of the Master unto the consecration of Asoka'. If that consecration took place in 265 B.C. (see 'Asoka') that would place the Buddha's death at eighty years of age in 483 and his birth in 563. But the dates may not be as precise as this suggests, and in other traditions the Buddha's death was only a century or so before Asoka, in the fourth century B.C.

Mahayana or northern Buddhism has many Buddhas and Bodhisattvas. Popular Great Buddhas to this day are Buddha Roshana at Nara and Amida at Kamakura in Japan, where they are represented by the greatest bronze statues in the world, which are both hundreds of years old. The 'historical' Buddha, Shakyamuni, often takes a lower place or disappears among crowds of celestial beings, yet people claim to be his followers and try to practise his teachings.

Plato

(*c.* 428–347 B.C.)

Having repelled attacks from the Persian Empire in the fifth century B.C., the city-states of Greece were involved in struggles among themselves, the city of Athens being defeated by Sparta and further conflicts ensuing. Yet this was the time of the greatest Greek philosophers, led by Socrates, Plato and Aristotle. The art of writing prose was brought to perfection at Athens, distinguishing the literature of this period from previous products of dramatic poetry. Socrates left no written works, but Plato and Aristotle wrote many books, Plato's *Republic*, for example, extending to 370 pages in a standard English translation.

Plato was born in Athens about 428 B.C. and died at the age of eighty-one in 347. He came from a wealthy family, the son of

Ariston and Perictione, was well educated and enjoyed good health. In his *Seventh Letter* Plato wrote that he had been interested in politics and was invited by his relatives to take part in public affairs, but the sight of discord and corruption, and finally the trial and execution of Socrates, repelled him from practical politics in Athens. After the death of Socrates in 399 Plato and other Socratics left Athens for a time, and he is said to have travelled to Egypt and Italy. In Sicily he met the ruler Dionysius and became the lifelong friend of his son-in-law, Dion of Syracuse, teaching him the ideal of a philosopher-king.

Later, when Dionysius died and was succeeded by his son, Plato was recalled to Sicily by Dion to try to put his ideals into practice. But the second Dionysius was suspicious, banished Dion from his court, and Plato returned to Athens. He paid a third and last visit to Sicily in 368, but was kept a virtual prisoner until friends helped him to return home. Ten years later Dion went back to Syracuse and expelled Dionysius II, but was himself assassinated a few years after. Plato was disappointed and saddened by his experiences in Sicily, and his *Seventh Letter* was written to Dion's party after his death to justify Plato's actions in these complicated affairs. Plato died at a wedding feast.

As a young man Plato was a close disciple of Socrates and in his writings his ideas were put into the mouth of Socrates, so that it is often difficult to distinguish Socratic and Platonic teachings. But Socrates declared that he had no positive doctrines to teach; his method was to question the assumptions on which beliefs and conduct were based, laying the foundations of philosophy by examining its presuppositions. He emphasised the importance of the definition of terms used in discussion, examining both logic and morality. Devotion to truth, and determination to face criticism by open discussion brought Socrates great influence. He insisted on the supremacy of the intellect, by which external authority must be judged, and this brought him into conflict with the politicians of Athens. In 399 Socrates was accused of impiety, as not believing in the gods recognised by the city, and corrupting its youth. The penalty proposed was death, and it was assumed that Socrates would leave Athens, but he surprised everyone by remaining.

The defence of Socrates is preserved in the *Apology* by Plato, an outstanding work in world literature. It presents the general outline of the arguments put forward by Socrates, worked into an artistic form. Socrates explained his life and motives and had no difficulty in showing that the accusations against him were false. Yet Socrates did criticise some of the official gods and claimed himself to be guided by a divine voice, and he had taught young men to judge both public and private morality by the light of reason. He offered to pay a derisory fine, but was condemned to death. His words to the court, according to Plato, were: 'Now the time has come, and we must go hence; I to die, and you to live. Whether life or death is better is known to God, and to God alone.'

In two further dialogues Plato describes the last days of his master. In *Crito* Socrates insists that we ought not to repay wrong with wrong, or do harm to any man, and that he is willing to die for his convictions. In *Phaedo* he speaks of the soul as immortal, of judgement after death according to actions in this world, and of fairer dwellings in heaven for the just. As his friends gather round him Socrates drinks the fatal hemlock poison that has been given him and prays for a peaceful journey to the world beyond. He asks Crito to sacrifice a cock to the god of healing, as a thanksgiving for recovery from illness. As his master dies Plato concludes that he was 'the wisest and justest, and the best man that I have ever known'.

After his first visit to Sicily Plato settled down in Athens, and with only two interruptions he gave formal instruction in philosophy for some forty years. He founded his Academy in a park sacred to a hero, Academus, on the outskirts of Athens, with the aim of training young men for public service. A thorough education was provided in science and philosophy, and important work was done in mathematics and astronomy. In later centuries the Academy was devoted more narrowly to philosophy, and in the Christian era to the mystical doctrines of the Neo-Platonists, until, along with other philosophical schools, it was closed down by the Christian emperor Justinian in A.D. 529. Like Socrates, Plato received no fees for his instructions and taught chiefly through dialogue and discussion. He gathered round him many pupils, of whom the most famous was his great rival in philosophy, Aristotle (see 'Aristotle').

Copies of all Plato's publications have been preserved down the ages, an unusual record for ancient documents, and they consist of twenty-five dialogues and the *Apology*. In the early dialogues Socrates is most clearly portrayed. His conversation at first appears to be simple, but its moral earnestness is impressive. He teaches that virtue is knowledge, which seems to mean knowledge of individual happiness or good. No one does wrong willingly, thought Socrates, and so doing wrong is ignorance. The question and answer method led his followers or adversaries into difficulties, but the revelation of their contradictions was essential to the acquisition of true knowledge and virtue. In the early, most truly Socratic, dialogues the main interest is in definition, of courage, piety, virtue, and self-knowledge.

In his middle period Plato developed his own characteristic doctrines, still under the guise of Socratic dialogue. Most notable is the *Republic*, which is the first plan of a Utopia or ideal state in history. The nature of justice is examined, beyond the individual to the state. The three principal classes of the ideal state would consist of the guardians, the military and the workers, corresponding to a threefold division of the soul into wisdom, courage and passion, rather like some Indian conceptions of threefold elements in the soul. The ideal state, according to Plato, would be a closed society, with fixed classes. The guardians at the top would have to be carefully trained in a communalism in which women would share all the men's tasks that were possible for them. Marriages would be arranged according to the best principles, and the children would be brought up anonymously by the state. Such an aristocratic government, Plato saw, could decline into timocracy or government by honour if the military took over, then into oligarchy or government by wealth, and after revolution by the masses it would decline into democracy, which was the least desirable form of government and would be followed by tyranny.

Plato devoted great attention to the education of the guardians, and this brought him in the *Republic* to his famous theory of ideas or forms, discussed also in the *Phaedo* and attributed to Socrates, though scholars consider that Plato invented the doctrine. Plato distinguished between transient and finite particulars or objects, discerned by the senses, and the timeless and universal forms. The form is the very thing itself, which is indicated by its name. For example, there is a universal form of 'table', which includes all particular tables and which is grasped by thought and not by sense impressions. These forms, Plato thought, are more real than the changing objects, things or animals, around us. There is a form of the Good, distinct from all good actions and objects, and it is unique among forms, being even beyond essence.

The forms, in Plato's view, are distinct from particular things, which imitate them, so that love of a beautiful person can give us some apprehension of the form of beauty itself. The theory of forms implies that the soul is immortal, since we may recollect the forms that we saw before we were imprisoned in the body. In the *Phaedo* Plato elaborates his belief in the transmigration of the soul from one body to another. This belief is illustrated also in a remarkable myth at the end of the *Republic*, in which a man who almost died on a battlefield beheld the souls of those who had been killed being rewarded or punished according to their good or evil deeds, in a world beyond death, and then choosing their next life on earth according to the wisdom or folly that they had attained. The *Republic* closes with the belief that the soul is 'immortal, and possesses the power of entertaining all evil, as well as all good', and so we should 'ever hold fast the upward road, and devotedly cultivate justice combined with wisdom', in order that both in this life and in the journey to the world beyond 'we may never cease to prosper'.

In Plato's ideal city a few enlightened souls would understand the form of the Good and would have the duty of governing the others. They would be separated from the rest of the soldiers and workers, live together without family ties or private property, and perpetuate their class by careful procreation. Sometimes they would enlist exceptional soldiers to their ranks, and give them education in mathematics and dialectic. Government in this Utopia would not be the rule of the masses, which as we have seen would be a low democracy, but it would be a science that demands expert knowledge which is given to the few. This kind of communism has had many imitations, though few of them have attached the importance to mathematics that Plato did.

In later writings Plato largely rejects the method of dialogue and sometimes Socrates becomes a secondary character. In the *Statesman* Plato repeats that government is a matter for experts, like medicine. In the *Laws*, the longest and perhaps the last dialogue, the ideal city is again sketched with much detail of public and private life. The citizens would be only about five thousand persons, supporting their families by agriculture, while trade and teaching would be in the hands of foreigners. The duties of the rulers are minutely indicated, and they would be guided by the divine will revealed through the stars, so that everyone should study astronomy. The *Timaeus* develops the religious view of life, showing from natural science that the creator made the world as a living thing, with both soul and body, peopled with gods and men.

Plato's works are both philosophy and literature. His style is easy at times and heavy at others, there are flashes of humour and passages of religious mysticism. His influence has been immense all down the ages, and for many people Plato is *the* philosopher, who raises all the great problems of human experience, and to whose works later writers have only added notes.

From the third to the sixth centuries A.D. a Neoplatonism flourished, which was a mixture of the thoughts of Plato, Aristotle, Pythagoras and the Stoics. Fashionable among non-Christians, it became influential among Christian thinkers from the time of

Augustine of Hippo in the fifth century. In the Dark Ages many Greek philosophical and scientific works were unknown to Europe, but they were preserved by Muslim scholars, translated first from Greek into Arabic and later into Latin. In Dante's *Divine Comedy*, of the fourteenth century, Socrates, Plato, Aristotle and other notables of antiquity appear, along with the Muslims Avicenna and Averroes who made Platonism and Aristotelianism known to the West. They were placed by Dante in Limbo, because they had not been baptised, yet he said that since they had not sinned they did not suffer.

Aristotle

(384–322 B.C.)

Disciple and then rival of Plato (see 'Plato'), Aristotle was born in 384 B.C. at Stagira in Thrace, in a northern peninsula that is now part of Greece. His father was Nicomachus, physician and friend of the king of Macedonia, and in his father's surgery Aristotle probably began his lifelong interest in physical science. When he was seventeen Aristotle left Stagira for Athens and soon entered Plato's Academy, where he remained for some twenty years until Plato's death in 347. Aristotle prepared some of his dialogues, such as *Eudemus*, which shows that at that time he was a strong disciple of Plato, but he also worked independently, doing new work in zoology.

On the death of Plato Aristotle left Athens, perhaps disappointed that he had not been appointed head of the Academy, and disagreeing also with the new head who was said to turn philosophy into mathematics. With another Academy student, Hermeias, a small Platonic circle was formed and Aristotle married Hermeias's niece Pythias. After the death of Hermeias Aristotle went to the island of Lesbos and continued his researches into zoology, referring to the island lagoon in his work *Historia Animalium*.

A further reason for leaving Athens may have been political feuds between Athens and Macedonia. In 342 Philip of Macedon invited Aristotle to become the tutor of his son Alexander, later known as Alexander the Great. Aristotle probably instructed him in Greek poetry and drama, but also in political science, writing for Alexander a work on *Colonists* and another on *Monarchy*. This teaching ended when Alexander became regent for his father. Before long he was king and set out on his famous conquest of the Persian Empire, going with his army as far as India.

In 335 Aristotle returned to Athens and founded his own school in the covered walking area (Peripatos) of the Lyceum, so called from a name of the god Apollo whose temple was nearby. Its members were known as Peripatetics, either from the place or from Aristotle's habit of walking up and down in the garden during his lectures. Here Aristotle founded a library of manuscripts and maps, and a museum with objects to illustrate his lectures on natural science; these provided models for other ancient libraries and museums. It is said that Alexander gave Aristotle money to buy objects for his museum and ordered hunters and fishermen in his empire to report to Aristotle any strange and interesting animals and fishes that they met. Aristotle was thus one of the founders of scientific research and method. His school was organised into a community where members took their meals in common and held a monthly symposium or discussion. His students did research into many fields, including botany, music, and the history of philosophy.

After Aristotle's wife Pythias died he married again and had a son named, after his father, Nicomachus. According to some scholars Aristotle dedicated to his son his work *Nicomachean Ethics*, but others consider that the title came from the son's having edited his father's book. When Alexander died in 323 there was an outburst of feeling against the Macedonians in Athens and Aristotle, like Socrates before him, was accused of impiety towards the ancient gods. So that the Athenians should not 'sin twice against philosophy' by killing him as they had done Socrates, Aristotle handed over his school to his leading pupil. He left Athens and retired to Chalcis in the island of Euboea where he died in 322 at the age of sixty-two, of a disease of the digestive organs.

According to tradition Aristotle, like St Paul, was bald and thin-legged, but he was particularly well dressed. He was of a critical disposition, as is revealed in his writings. In his will Aristotle made provision for his relatives and his slaves, freeing some of the latter and providing security for others, showing a considerate and affectionate nature.

Many of the writings of Aristotle, and his collections of scientific and historical facts, have been lost or preserved only in fragments. The works that remain were not prepared for publication and may give the impression of being lecture notes because of their unequal style and irregular sequence, but their elaborate and concentrated arguments suggest that his writings were intended to help students and to record the substance of his lectures.

It is said that Aristotle's manuscripts were hidden in a cellar for two hundred years to protect them from royal book-collectors. They were taken to Rome in 84 B.C. and published just before the Christian era. Until that time the names of works by Aristotle had been known but not their substance, but now commentators began to expound them. Aristotle had been almost forgotten, but the later Peripatetics framed a system of Aristotelian philosophy, with commentaries on his difficult writings, though they wrote from the mystical viewpoint of Neoplatonism (see 'Plato'). During the Dark Ages in Europe only Aristotle's logic was known, but his works were preserved by Islamic scholars who translated them into Arabic. Eventually they came to the medieval European scholastic philosophers from Arabic versions which in turn were translated into Latin, and they became the dominant influence in the philosophy of the Middle Ages.

Aristotle began by following the teachings of Plato and writing dialogues on the master's model, but in time he differed from Plato, especially in rejecting Platonic belief in the separate existence of forms or ideas. Trained as a physician, and with a respect for the facts of the natural world, he was unable to follow Plato in some of his theories.

In his *Metaphysics* Aristotle distinguished three kinds of substances, the perishable ones which include plants and animals, the sensible ones which include heavenly bodies, and those which are neither sensible nor perishable, including God and the rational soul in man. Aristotle argued for the existence of God as the First Cause of all things. There must be something which originates motion but is itself unmoved, and God is unmoved and eternal: 'God is a living being, eternal, most good, so that life and duration continuous and eternal belong to God; for this *is* God.'

In *On the Soul*, Aristotle ridiculed the theory of transmigration from one life to another which had been propounded by Plato and Pythagoras, but his ideas on immortality are confusing. He says that 'the soul is inseparable from its body', which suggests that it perishes at death, but he immediately adds, 'or at least certain parts of it are'. He says further that the mind is 'an independent substance implanted within the soul and incapable of being destroyed'.

Three works on ethics have been attributed to Aristotle, but the *Nicomachean Ethics* are mostly regarded as authentic. Differently from Plato, his ethics are not religious or mystical, but they are rather dull, if not repressive. Aristotle taught the Golden Mean, or the middle way between extremes, rather like the Buddha and even more like Confucius (see 'Confucius'). He taught that every virtue is a mean or middle between two extremes; thus courage is a mean between cowardice and rashness, liberality between prodigality and meanness, proper pride between vanity and humility, and modesty between bashfulness and shamelessness. The best individual is the high-minded or magnanimous man, not unlike the Confucian gentleman. He should have proper pride and not underestimate himself, yet he should despise those who deserve to be despised. Aristotle described this individual in these terms: 'The high-minded man, since he deserves most, must be good, in the highest degree; for the better man always deserves more, and the best man most ... He is the sort of man to confer benefits, but he is ashamed of receiving them; for the one is the mark of the superior, the other of an inferior ... A slow step is thought proper to the high-minded man, a deep voice, and a level utterance.'

It is difficult to fit all virtues into Aristotle's scheme; for example, truthfulness is said to be a mean between boastfulness and mock-modesty, but this applies merely to truthfulness about oneself and does not fit wider senses. Differently from Stoicism and Christianity, Aristotle considers that the best things should be confined to the few, and he teaches an aristocratic morality where the majority have to be content with the second-best. There is nothing in common between a slave and his master and they cannot be friends, though a master might share in an agreement with a slave, as a man but not as a slave.

Since Aristotle praised pride, and thought that humility was a vice, it is not surprising that he considered that monarchy was the best form of government, followed by aristocracy. He saw ethics as a branch of politics; monarchs and aristocrats should be magnanimous or high-souled (like Indian *mah-atmas*), but ordinary citizens could not hope to live up to such a pattern. Virtue was for the few, and so there could not be many high-minded men in a community. The aim of the state should be to produce cultured gentlemen, loving learning and the arts, as the best of the upper classes did in the palmiest days of Athens in the fifth century B.C. But political power declined, the populace revolted, and the rich defended themselves by illegal means. However, in a more pragmatic manner than Plato, Aristotle recognises the corruptions of aristocracy, and defends democracy in a qualified way, since among actual governments democracies were often the best. In his *Politics*, which reveal the prejudices of educated Greeks of his time, he criticises Plato's *Republic* for giving too much unity to the state and making it into an individual.

Aristotle recognised the error of Plato-Socrates in assuming that if men saw the good they must do it, and therefore that evil was simply ignorance. He realised the overwhelming power of passion, by which a man might go against his own true good; and his emphasis upon the mean was intended to correct such exaggeration, but he did not go on to consider sin or corruption in the way that Christian thinkers treated this problem.

For many centuries Aristotle's greatest influence in Europe was in logic, and he was not regarded as supreme in metaphysics until the Middle Ages. His importance for logic may be illustrated by the syllogism, an argument in three parts: a major premiss, a minor premiss, and a conclusion. The most familiar example is: All men are mortal, Socrates is a man, therefore Socrates is mortal.

Aristotle developed terms which have been used in philosophy ever since: premiss and conclusion, subject and attribute, universal and particular, form and matter. He had a love of tidiness and order, classifying the sciences into theoretical, practical and productive. Whereas Plato mixed together metaphysics, ethics, psychology and politics, Aristotle devoted one or more works to each, although his writings were not arranged or revised for publication.

The rediscovery of the writings of the Greek philosophers in western Europe came in the later Middle Ages, through Arabic translations made by Muslims and Jews. At first the Church regarded these works with suspicion, as not being revelations, but Christian thinkers like Albertus Magnus and Thomas Aquinas in the thirteenth century accepted them wholeheartedly. Although some thinkers of the Renaissance favoured Plato, it was Aristotle who was adopted as the basis for Roman Catholic philosophical theology, and in his *Divine Comedy* in the fourteenth century Dante saw Aristotle as 'the master of those that know, honoured by all around him'.

Saint Paul

(A.D. 10–67)

Christianity as a religious belief and as a living institution must be regarded as one of the most important phenomena in any reputable history book. It is as inseparable from our human story as we record it today as when it was first told two thousand years ago. Moreover, these two claims are not only the dogmatic assertions of those who profess the Christian religion. Those who deny it, or are agnostic or hostile as regards its theology, are at one with those who subscribe to it in acknowledging its significance even if they deplore its existence.

Therefore its beginnings and its development must remain among the most influential elements that go to make up not only our life-style today, but more broadly the life of the world itself. Christianity, unlike some religions, is rooted in history and therefore its emergence can be dated. It began with somebody who came from a discernible background, lived in a particular place, behaved in a certain way and when his earthly life was over (as Christians believe upon a cross) and his resurrection was accomplished (as Christians believe in the Easter message) left behind him disciples who carried on his ministry and founded a Church as the vehicle of his ongoing gospel. In untheological terms, Christianity began 1985 years ago with somebody called Jesus of Nazareth, and second to Jesus in the actual story of Christianity was another man called Saul.

Saul was born about A.D. 10 at Tarsus in Cilicia. His Roman name was Paul. He suffered with a permanent ailment, perhaps 'petit mal'. Like every Jew, he had a handicraft; he made tents. He never married and he was executed by the Romans in A.D. 67. Facts like these locate him in the history-book but do nothing to explain the attributions of 'saint' and 'apostle' to his name. The clue to his greatness, and indeed to his goodness, lies in the claim that he was the 'first Christian', and one of the two principal architects (with Peter) of the Christian Church. The evidence to support these claims is derived mainly from documents in the New Testament such as the Book of Acts and the various Epistles, including those written or dictated by Paul himself.

We first hear of him as a zealous protagonist of the

contemporary Hebrew faith, reacting violently against the Christian heresy as he believed it to be. The fierceness of his persecution of Christians was obviously a reflection of the challenge of it that was beginning to be present in his thinking. This process intensified and culminated in a dramatic conversion to the Christian faith in a vision, or audition, of Jesus on the road to Damascus. Thereafter this man transferred his massive intellectual gifts and his religious commitment into discipleship and apostleship in the name of Jesus. Yet from the beginning of his ministry he invested Jesus with a theological uniqueness as both the fulfilment of his erstwhile Jewish faith, and the metaphysical second person of a divine trinity. The 'man approved of God' in Peter's Pentecostal sermon becomes for Paul the incarnate word of God.

It is with this message that the converted Saul of Tarsus becomes the missionary apostle St Paul, and commits himself, as his letters show, to an evangelism to all mankind – Jew and Gentile. Salvation from sin and death, in the name of the Christ of God (and identified with the Cross, as both the instrument of the death of Jesus, and the symbol of the Church conflict between good and evil), constituted the religion which through the missionary journeys of this tremendous evangelist spread throughout the Mediterranean area. The three main missionary travels recorded in the Acts of the Apostles form an amazing record of trenchant argument, brilliant advocacy, indomitable courage in times of persecution, imprisonment and torture, and administrative ability in guiding the Christian groups which sprang up as the outcome of his preaching. St Peter represented in the early Christian communities the closest attachment to Judaistic practices among the Jews who became converted to Christianity. Paul left Christian groups springing up in the paths of his missionary journeys which were not Jewish but Gentile or pagan in origin. The wider the area of Paul's evangelism the more urgent became the question as to whether Judaism was a necessary apprenticeship for those who were to enjoy the blessings attendant upon conversion. St Paul won the right of any and all to become Christians whatever their cultural or religious background. The differences between the twelve apostles, led by Peter who had known Jesus, on the one hand, and Paul with his disciples like Timothy and Barnabas who had not, were acute; but in the Book of Acts the story is clearly told of the conferences which were held at Jerusalem and Antioch in which a settlement was reached that effectively released the Christian believer from necessary subscription to Judaism as well.

St Paul is entitled to the claim that he was the founder of the Christian Church as a world organisation. His greatness lies in the contribution he made to the emergence and characteristics of this expanding Christian institution of which he was so much the architect and builder. He set the gospel of Jesus within a framework of what today would be called ideology as well as theology. The Christian faith could be argued as well as accepted. It could hold its own in Athens as effectively as in Jerusalem or in Rome. The dynamism and fervour of the conversion experience became harnessed to a close-knit, and practical, intelligent fellowship and institution which was soon to challenge the Roman Empire itself and in many respects to supplant it.

His literary contribution to this developing institution deserves especial mention in any attempt to understand the extraordinary expansion of Christianity in the first century A.D. The Epistles in the New Testament which are indubitably his (though not all which bear his name are written or dictated by him) contain masterpieces of writing and reach sublime heights of spirituality as well as towering moral insights. No one who has read the great paean of love in his letters to the Corinthian Church can fail to recognise Paul's genius. These epistles are masterpieces of counsel, advice, exhortation, explanation, comfort and reassurance to the group of converts left behind after his missionary journeys. Moreover, the impact of his message and the power of his leadership on the primitive Church reflected the moral and spiritual quality of the man himself. If anyone is likely to be called a saint Paul can claim such a title (though he was at pains to disclaim such a dignity, calling himself the 'chief of sinners'). He lived by the power of grace which he proclaimed to be the gift of God. He practised what he preached. In his working life as in his martyr's death he bore the cross which was the banner of his faith.

Nonetheless no article, however brief, about this saint can avoid certain questions that become the more relevant as Paul's 'curriculum vitae' is seen against the backcloth not only of his lifetime but of the centuries that have passed since he died. Did he continue the proclamation of the Gospel as set forth in the life and teaching and death and resurrection of Jesus, or did he adapt and alter and indeed pervert the faith 'once and for all given to the saints'? Was the Pauline Church the 'residuary legatee' of the risen Christ, or was it essentially a creation of Paul's own thinking, using parts of the Gospel but setting them in a framework that was his rather than that of his Lord?

There are a number of hard facts which demand attention if

these questions are to be faced, let alone answered. To begin with, Paul has little or nothing to say about the earthly ministry of Jesus. Not only has he no personal experience of Jesus of Nazareth, he appears to have little interest, if any, in the everyday events which play such a vital part in the four gospels. Paul is concerned with the eternal Christ rather than the human Jesus. Paul was a Roman citizen anxious to preserve the 'Pax Romana', rather than a revolutionary looking towards Jesus and a new kingdom of God to take its place. Moreover, the difference is all the more marked in the respects by which the evil in the world was to be overcome. For Jesus non-violence was explicit (e.g., in the Sermon on the Mount) and the resistance to the occupying power of Rome was to be by the taking up of a cross rather than by the methods of violent insurrection. For Jesus the freedom fighters were to refuse the way of armed resistance. The primitive Christian community was pacifist, according to the best evidence from Roman as well as apostolic sources. This pacifist case is absent from the teaching of Paul and was fairly quickly abandoned by the churchmanship for which he was responsible. This in no way denigrates the heroism and faith of those who were martyred and persecuted by the Romans. Paul himself set an example of such heroism and fortitude. What did happen was that the way was already being paved by Paul for a concordat between the Empire and the Church in which the evidence of war could be justified in the presentation of a 'Holy Roman Empire'.

A martial Christendom came into being and stayed there through the crusades. It is still the official Christianity in the nation state and capitalist systems, even with the apocalyptic threat that is posed at the present day by the destructive capability of nuclear weapons. The decision, for which Paul was so largely responsible, to renounce or to ignore the pacifism of Jesus has reached awesome proportions not only for the Church but for the world itself. It is a fascinating speculation that had Paul met Jesus, whom he worshipped as the Christ and enthroned as the Son of God, he might have been instrumental in the creation of a world-wide Christianity which repudiated mass violence for any cause and in any human activity. Nevertheless, the present world emergency has quickened the issue as never before. In practical terms, did Paul miss the essential point of the gospel of his professed Lord? There would appear to be a growing conviction that he did, and that in that respect Pauline Christianity was morally an aberration. Certainly there is evidence in his epistles that in many particulars this great man was a child of his time rather than a prophet for a time to come.

Paul's attitude to women was that of his own age and was unaffected by the spirit of Jesus. He believed in the God-given superiority of the male, and says so in many of his letters. In these matters, to say nothing of Paul's acceptance of slavery, he insisted that the powers that be are ordained of God and therefore to oppose them is impermissible. As a profession of faith and a way of life, Pauline Christianity was conservative, whereas the ministry of Jesus was revolutionary.

Such strictures would be impudent if they were not blended with an emphasis upon the redeeming work of God through Jesus Christ, which is the glory of the Christian faith and binds together in an unbroken chain the work of Paul and that of his Lord and Master.

Paul believed that Jesus was the saviour of the world and that through penitence and faith in him all things would work together for good. In his avowed intention 'to know Christ and him crucified' and in making that the dominant theme of his ministry and the all-important *raison d'être* of religious practice, he must be acknowledged as one of the principal founders of the Christian Church.

Mani

(*d. c.* 276)

About A.D. 200, at Hamadan in Iran, there lived a Parthian prince named Patik, married to a woman with the Jewish-Christian name of Mariam who was also of noble Parthian blood. Patik was devoutly religious; he heard voices telling him to leave idols and abstain from wine, meat and women. He retired from the imperial capital and attached himself to a small religious group that practised ritual washings. Later Mariam gave birth to a son whom she named Mani.

Legends said that Mariam had dreams of her son's coming fame and heard prophecies about his call to a religious life. She saw him lifted up to heaven and coming down again, an anticipation of a later tradition that when Mani was a man he rose to the heavens and returned with a tablet bearing drawings and paintings. His own testimony about his birth, according to an Arab scholar, was that he was born in northern Babylonia: 'I am a thankful disciple, risen from the land of Babel.'

Patik sent for his son and brought him up in his religion, though it is not clear what that was. The religion may have been that of the Mandaeans, a small group that still exists in the south of Iraq and Iran, claiming descent from John the Baptist, though it has been decimated in recent Iraqi–Iranian conflicts. The Mandaeans believe in a saviour called 'the Knowledge of Life', Manda d'Hayye, and the name of their sect comes from this title. But one of their earliest names was Nasoraeans, meaning 'observants' or adepts in the mysteries of religion, though it is not unlike the name Nasara, Nazarenes, which Muslims apply to Christians. The Mandaeans distinguished themselves from orthodox Christians, criticising them for practising baptism in non-flowing water, but their religion is a mixture of beliefs from various sources.

The Mandaeans practise baptisms or ritual washings in rivers, but they do not forbid wine, meat and women. However, they do condemn gluttony, drunkenness and lust, and it may be that Patik joined a community whose members led ascetic lives and that Mani was brought up in this environment.

Mani received his first revelation when he was twelve years old. A heavenly being told him, 'Leave this congregation. The guidance of morals and restraint of appetites are your task. But the time has not yet come to stand out openly, because of your youth.' The angel was a 'twin', a heavenly double of the prophet-to-be. So Mani left the baptist community to which his father had led him; some reports say that he was expelled.

Mani went into seclusion, and in the next few years was probably studying the teachings of various religions in Iran and neighbouring lands. There were many religious groups, Zoroastrian, Mithraic, Mandaean, Jewish, Christian, even Buddhist and Hindu, and eventually Mani proclaimed himself as the fulfilment of the work of Zoroaster, of Buddha and of Christ.

In the year 240 the angel brought a message from the Lord to Mani saying that the time had come to call the peoples to the truth, and that he should stand forth openly and proclaim his message. He was now called an apostle, or messenger, indicating one who had received a divine revelation in written form and was entrusted with its promulgation. Mani therefore described his revelation to his father and other members of his family, and they were converted, giving him influential support.

Mani then went on a journey to what was called India, perhaps the north-western provinces of what is now Pakistan, which had been under Zoroastrian influences and where Buddhism was also strong. The Parthian language was understood there by the

higher circles of society. After staying there about a year, Mani
returned to southern Iran and Iraq. Tales are recounted about his
success in converting hostile people by miracles and visions.
Accompanied by his father, Mani was received by King Shapur
and allowed to preach freely through the late Persian or Sassanian
empire. It is said that he reorganised the fire-temples of the
Iranian cult, but it is not clear whether this refers to the
Zoroastrian fire-temples or to general ritual in which fire played a
part (see 'Zoroaster').

For a number of years Mani was attached to the court, and it
seems that he wanted his teaching to become the state religion.
This did not happen, though his doctrine was especially favoured.
On the contrary, Zoroastrianism was established as the state
Church, with its priests the Magi, the 'wise men' of the New
Testament. They sought to check the spread of other religions and
established tribunals against Buddhists, Christians, Manichees
and other religious minorities.

Mani then developed a missionary strategy and is said to have
spent many years in Persia, the land of the Parthians, and the
frontiers of the Roman Empire. He also sent disciples on other
missionary journeys where they expounded dogmas, worked
wonders and, by going as far as Alexandria, obtained a foothold in
Egypt during Mani's lifetime.

Critical accounts of Mani describe him as dressed in a green
and blue cloak and yellow and green trousers, and carrying a book
under his arm. Similar dress is depicted on surviving paintings
which represent priests of the mysteries of Mithra, with whom
Mani had connexions.

When Mani's royal patron Shapur died in 273, his troubles
began. Shapur's son lived only a year after coming to the throne,
and was succeeded by his brother Bahram, who curbed Mani's
activities. Mani was forbidden to go to what is now Afghanistan,
and on returning to Iraq was ordered to proceed to the royal court.
There he was kept waiting till the king had washed his hands, and
was then told, 'You are not welcome'. King Bahram had sworn an
oath not to leave Mani alive in the land, demanding to know why
the revelations had come to Mani and not to the king. Mani could
only say it was the will of God.

The king ordered Mani to be put in chains, on his neck, hands
and ankles, and he was taken to prison. For a month the aged
prophet was shackled, though he was able to see his friends and
give them instructions for his larger following. Weakened by
suffering and fasting, Mani could no longer bear the chains and in
February 276 or 277 he collapsed and died: 'he ascended out of his

body to the dwellings of greatness on high'. When the news spread abroad great crowds gathered. The king ordered a burning torch to be thrust through Mani's body, to make sure he was fully dead, and it was then cut into pieces and his head stuck on the gate of the city. Later his followers gathered the remains together and gave them decent burial.

The teachings of Mani were largely Iranian, with some references to Buddhism and Christianity. According to Mani the name of the supreme God was Zurvan, 'infinite time', which some Zoroastrians had postulated as the father of the twins Ahura Mazda and Ahriman (see 'Zoroaster'). The adoption of this name suggests that the Zurvanites were powerful in the Sassanian Empire under Shapur, but the Magi opposed the heresy of Zurvan and formed part of the opposition to Mani which led to his death.

Mani conceived of God sitting on a throne, surrounded by light, power and wisdom, and having three aspects and a fourth totality; or else God was thought to have four faces, like Brahma and some other Indian gods, or like four-faced images of the Buddha. The four faces looked to the four cardinal points of the compass, showing the all-seeing and all-present nature of deity. For Zurvanism also God was four-faced, with sons who stood before him and ruled over four celestial regions.

For Mani the First Man was Ohrmazd, a later Zoroastrian rendering of the name of the supreme God, Ahura Mazda. He taught that Ohrmazd was the son of the four-faced Zurvan, called into being from the Mother of Life, a female divine figure who stood next to Zurvan. Thus there was a triad, the Father of Greatness, the Mother of Life, and the First Man.

Mani, like Zoroaster and many other religious teachers, faced the problem of the suffering and evil in the world, and he adopted the Iranian solution of dualism, a struggle between two opposed forces. However, differently from the Zoroastrians, the Manichees regarded the world and matter as almost wholly evil. This evoked a pessimistic attitude in which the best course for believers was to renounce the world, as far as possible, and lead an ascetic celibate life so that the soul might go to heaven and have no part in perpetuating this miserable life on earth. This was quite different from the Zoroastrian attitude of fighting evil by living a good life on earth.

In Manichaean myths Primeval Man put on his armour and set out to fight the powers of matter, of darkness and evil. His armour consisted of light and its elements were the sons of Ohrmazd. But he was defeated by the prince of darkness, and his armour was taken away, or else his sons were devoured by evil demons.

Ohrmazd had come down into the world of evil matter of his own free will, and lay in a dark ditch, stunned and unarmed. He prayed seven times to the Father of Greatness, Zurvan, who extended his right hand and drew him up out of darkness into the paradise of light, his heavenly home. Thus the principal theme in Manichaean legend was the suffering of man and his redemption out of this world into paradise.

The world, according to Manichaean myths, was created from the bodies of the demonic rulers of darkness, the Archons, who begat the first two human beings, Adam and Eve, by a mixture of sexual and cannibalistic performances. In matter there were sparks of life, fragments of the First Man, but they were imprisoned by the demons. The souls that sought release from this evil material world had to practise ascetic world-denial and study the true nature of the soul, so as to be delivered by Ohrmazd when he defeats the demons.

Manicheism was formed into a community or church, whose members were divided into two grades. The 'elect' followed an ascetic life and hoped for speedy redemption from the evil world, while the 'hearers', who were allowed to marry, provided the necessities of life. Idols were forbidden in temples, but the ritual provided music and psalms, and books of sacred writings were beautifully illustrated.

Mani believed that the great religions which he encountered had all been one true faith in origin, but they had been distorted by misunderstandings and he was sent to restore the true religion. He tried to establish links with Buddhism and Christianity, especially Mahayana or northern Buddhism with its heavenly saviours. With Christianity, Manichees associated the suffering Jesus with the cosmic drama of passion and redemption. Trees, which they thought to contain a large portion of light, symbolised the cross of Jesus who was hanged on every tree. Manicheism appealed to some Christians; the theologian Augustine of Hippo was a Manichee for nine years, and even after he became a Christian he retained some of the anti-material and anti-sexual attitudes of Mani. For centuries the Christian Church was infected by world-denying views that have been called Manichaean. Much later Christian heresies, Catharist and Albigensian, have been called Manichaean, but may have had no connexion with that faith.

While the Buddhist and Christian expressions of the Manichees may have been trimmings, designed to attract people of other faiths, their basic themes were Iranian. God and the devil, heaven and hell, judgement at death and last judgement, and everlasting life for the blessed were both Zoroastrian and Manichaean tenets. Mani respected the older Zoroastrian faith, even though he gave it a Zurvanite form. His scriptures were translated into Parthian, from Syriac originals, and his missionaries took the faith far and wide. By the sixteenth century, however, Manicheism had died out as a practised religion while the other religions survived.

Saint Augustine of Hippo

(A.D. 354–430)

Aurelius Augustinus was born at Tagaste in north Africa in A.D. 354 and died as bishop of Hippo Regius in 430, being known as St Augustine of Hippo to distinguish him from the later St Augustine of Canterbury.

Augustine's father, Patricius, was a pagan, though he received some Christian influences from his mother Monica. However, pagan thought and morality dominated his early life, and at the university of Carthage, where he studied rhetoric, Augustine gave himself up to sensual pleasures, abandoning what little Christianity he possessed. He took a mistress, remaining faithful to her for fifteen years, but a more serious direction to his life came through a passionate interest in the writings of the Roman philosopher Cicero.

When he was twenty Augustine joined the Manichaean religion, which was strong in Africa and claimed to supply 'a satisfactory solution to all things human and divine'. It had been founded by Mani (see 'Mani') about a hundred years before Augustine, and taught a dualism of the conflict of light against darkness, spirit against flesh. This did not accord with Augustine's immoral life and caused him some inner turmoil, but even when he became a Christian teacher later the opposition of flesh and spirit remained basic to his beliefs and influenced much other Church teaching.

A celebrated Manichee, Faustus, claimed to be able to solve philosophical problems which puzzled Augustine, but the latter was not convinced, and after nine years he left the Manichees in disillusionment and disgust. He would have become a complete sceptic but for the study of Plato and Neoplatonism (see 'Plato') which gradually drew him nearer to Christianity. He left

Carthage, going to Rome to teach rhetoric and then to a professorship in the university of Milan.

At Milan Augustine came under the influence of the Christian bishop Ambrose, whose sermons were of a high literary quality and also answered some of the difficulties Augustine had found in the study of the Bible, though he still faced many struggles. His mother Monica had followed her son, having been distressed by his way of life and by his following strange doctrines. An African Christian bishop, himself a former Manichee, had comforted Monica by assuring her that 'it is not possible that the son of these tears should perish'. In Milan Monica was helped by bishop Ambrose, seeing in him an angel of God who was leading her son from doubt to faith, and she distributed gifts of food at churches of the early Christian martyrs.

Augustine's state of confusion is well revealed in his famous book of *Confessions* where, among many prayers and lengthy discourses, he describes the spiritual progress of his early years. He admits frankly that he had long prayed to God to make him pure, saying, 'Give me chastity and continence, but not yet.' He sent his mistress away, then took another, and put her away when he decided to renounce the flesh and become celibate, 'so that I neither sought a wife nor any of this world's hopes'. His first mistress seems to have loved him, and gave him a son, Adeodatus, 'the gift of God', but he did not assuage her feelings by marriage.

Augustine stayed in Milan with a friend, Alypius, and they discussed the joys and vanities of life. After long talking, while Alypius sat silent, Augustine rushed into the garden and threw himself down under a fig-tree, praying in floods of tears. He heard a voice of a boy or girl in a neighbouring house chanting in Latin *tolle lege*, 'take up and read'. Augustine interpreted this as a sign from God to read the first passage that he would find in the Bible. Entering the house, he opened the book at Paul's epistle to the Romans 13:13. 'Not in rioting and drunkenness, not in debauchery and wantonness, not in strife and envying; but put on the Lord Jesus Christ, and make no provision for the flesh.'

Doubt fled away, light and serenity came. Augustine and Alypius decided to become Christians, and they went to Monica who rejoiced with them. Augustine was baptised at Easter 387 by Ambrose, along with Alypius and Adeodatus, who died not long afterwards. Monica also died soon at Ostia near Rome, and in the *Confessions* her son describes a mystical experience that they had together at Ostia shortly before her death, being raised up and 'passing through all things bodily, even the very heaven', musing on and admiring the works of God.

In 388 Augustine returned to the family estate at Tagaste and established a small monastery there. But during a visit to the town of Hippo in 391 he was seized by the people, taken to the bishop Valerius and forcibly ordained priest. He became a colleague of the aged bishop, and from 396 till his death Augustine was Bishop of Hippo. He died on 28 August 430, when the armies of the Vandals who had captured Rome and overrun Italy had invaded Africa and were besieging Hippo itself.

His long bishopric was the most brilliant period of Augustine's career, when he became one of the leading 'doctors of the church', regarded as the greatest of the Latin fathers, and the centre of the theological life of the western world. He was a prolific writer in Latin, but he knew little Greek and no Hebrew and this affected his expositions of the Bible. He plunged into controversy, especially against the Donatists, the Pelagians, and his former Manichee teacher Faustus.

Donatism was a schism in the north African churches named after a bishop Donatus. It began during the persecutions, when some Christians had escaped by surrendering their scriptures and were called traditors or traitors by the faithful. Donatus and his followers were rigorists, who refused to accept the traditors back after the persecutions had ceased. They were also nationalists who objected to the rule of Rome, thus dividing the churches on two counts. They were so influential at one stage that at a conference in Carthage in 411 there were 279 Donatist and 286 Catholic or orthodox bishops. Augustine plunged into the debate, claiming that the church was 'one' and must not be divided, and 'holy' even when not all its members were holy. He believed in peaceful persuasion, though he admitted that force might be used against the recalcitrant. In 414 the emperor declared that the Donatists had forfeited all civil rights in their rebellion. The Vandal invasion, which persecuted Catholics and Donatists alike, helped towards some reconciliation, but the African churches were greatly weakened and finally collapsed before the Islamic invasions in the seventh century.

Pelagius was a British monk who attacked the views of Augustine on original sin and predestination. Augustine taught that man has a hereditary moral disease and a legal liability for the sin of Adam, and he could only be saved if God chose him by his grace. He held that God had elected some souls for salvation and others for damnation, in his inscrutable wisdom. Pelagius said that every man is born without sin and without virtue, just as God had created the first man. Man can decide freely for good or evil, though the grace of God is also necessary. Although

Pelagianism was condemned by Church councils through the influence of Augustine, some other theologians were not easy with his rigid doctrines, though Calvin and his followers in the sixteenth century followed him in teaching total depravity and predestination.

Augustine's most famous writing was *The City of God* (*De Civitate Dei*), in 22 sections. This was written in answer to non-Christian teachers who claimed that the success of the Vandal armies in destroying the Roman Empire was due to the weakening influence of Christianity and the abolition of pagan worship. Rome had fallen to the Visigoth Alaric in 410, though he was a Christian of the Arian heresy which denied the full divinity of Christ. Augustine refuted the pagan arguments by showing how the Roman Empire itself provided the seeds of its decay by its immorality and selfishness. Then he depicted the corruption of heathen religions and the inadequacy of their philosophies. Finally he contrasted the two cities, the city of Earth and the city of God, which persist in interaction and rivalry with one another. The goal of life is the peace of the heavenly city, in the union of hearts 'in God and in one another'. The present conflict is between the love of self and the love of God and, whether Augustine meant it or not, this was often taken in the Middle Ages to justify rejection of this world for the sake of the world to come.

Augustine wrote theological, philosophical and ethical treatises. His theology of sin and the fall of man, his early life and his Manichaean background, led him to teach the enslavement of the spirit to the flesh, of which he saw the most glaring proof in sexual desire. Instead of regarding sex as given by the Creator, as the Bible does, Augustine's experiences of uncontrollable passion led him to regard sex as an evil. It should not be enjoyed and could only be employed for good when it aimed at the procreation of children. He admitted the value of marriage, but regarded celibacy as a higher step to holiness.

The doctrines of original sin and the superiority of virginity were not Augustine's inventions, for there was a strong ascetic trend in the early Church. But his notion of 'concupiscence', the lusting of the flesh against the spirit, has been recognised nowadays by leading scholars as having had 'a most disastrous influence upon much of traditional Christian ethics'. For all his great intellect, extensive writings, and widespread and lasting influence, Augustine had profound flaws in both his life and teaching.

Index

Aeschylus 253–7; birth 253; at Battle of Marathon 253; *Eleusinians* 253; *Persians* 125, 254, 255, 256; works 254; patronised by Hieron 254, 255; *Oresteia* 254, 255, 256, 264; *Eumenides* 255–6; *Agamemnon* 256; *Libation-Bearers* 256; death 256; Aristotle on 253, 254

Akhenaton (Amenhotep IV) 350–54; comes to throne 350, 351; wife (Nefertiti) 350, 352, 353; replaces Amun by Aton 350–51, 353; Hymn to Aton 351, 352–3; builds Akhet-Aton 351; imposes political/religious reforms 2, 351–3; belief in own divinity 353; death 353; reforms overthrown 354; analysis of mummy 5–6

Alexander (III) the Great 139–46; birth 140, 386; under Aristotle's tutelage 140, 145, 464, 510–11; at battle of Chaironeia 137; succeeds to throne 140, 387; destroys Thebes 141, 261; conquest of Persia 139, 141–3, 144, 359; takes Halicarnassus 142, 143; defeats Darius III by Issus 142–3; besieges Tyre 143; welcomed as new pharaoh in Egypt 143; founds Alexandria 143; defeats Darius at Gaugamela 143; campaigns into India 143–4, 359–60; defeats Porus 143, 145; destruction of Persepolis 94, 107, 111, 144, 481; death 20, 66, 146, 388, 391; struggle for succession 20, 66–9, 146, 147, 388–90, 464

Antiochus III 71–7; comes to throne 72; troubles with Asia Minor 72, 73–4; Achaeus supports 72; conquests in Iran 73, 75; executes Achaeus 74, 150; campaigns against Egypt in Palestine 74, 76; reconquers much of Alexander's empire 74–6; receives Hannibal 76; war with Rome 76–7; defeat at battle of Magnesia 77, 151, 162–3, 313; death 77; Arrian on 77; Josephus on 76

Archimedes 458–63; 'Eureka!' story 458–9; Principle 459; screw 459; spiral 459; and siege of Syracuse 458, 459–60; work on lever 460; work on value of π 460–61; mathematics 461; *Sand-Reckoner* 451, 461–2; number science 461–2; *Principles* 462; murder 458; Plutarch on 460

Aristarchus of Samos 450–54; estimates relative sun/moon distances 450, 452–3, 479; heliocentric theory 450–52, 453, 477–9; contradicted by Hipparchus 451, 453, 478; Archimedes on 450, 451, 452; Plutarch on 454

Aristophanes 288–93; birth 288; *Banqueters* 288, 289; *Babylonians* 289; *Acharnians* 289–90, 291; attacks on Cleon 289, 291;

Knights 289, 291; *Clouds* 289, 290, 291; *Wasps* 289, 290, 292; *Peace* 290, 292; *Thesmophoriazusae* 279, 280, 290, 292; *Lysistrata* 290, 291, 292; *Women in Parliament* 290, 292; *Frogs* 253, 255, 290, 292; *Birds* 291–2; *Wealth* 292–3; death 293; sons 293; Plato on 288, 291, 293

Aristotle 510–14; birth 510; enters Academy 510; disciple of Plato 507, 510, 512; *Eudemus* 510; *Historia Animalium* 510; tutor to Alexander 140, 145, 464, 510–11; *Colonists* 510; *Monarchy* 510; founds Lyceum 464, 511; Peripatetics 511, 512; *Nicomachean Ethics* 511, 512–13; accused of impiety 511; death 511; writings 511–12; logic 512, 514; *Metaphysics* 431, 512; *On the Soul* 512; theology 512; ethics 512–13; Golden Mean 513; *Politics* 513–14; geocentrism 450–51; estimate of earth's size 466, 467; *De Caelo* 466; Dante on 514

Artemisia of Halicarnassus 396–400; becomes queen 397; at battle of Euboea 398; at battle of Salamis 399; advises Xerxes 398–400; suicide 400; Herodotus on 276, 396

Ashurbanipal 54–9; succeeds to throne 54–5; conquests in Egypt 55; war with Elam 56–7; war with brother, king of Babylon 57–8; devastates Elam 58; creates library at Nineveh 59; death 59

Asoka 359–63; succession 360; edicts 360–61, 362, 363; reliance on Dharma 360–61, 363; religious toleration 361; Buddhism 361–3; visits Bo-Tree 361; pilgrimages 363; death 362, 363

Aspasia of Miletus 391–6; origins 393; relationship with Pericles 132, 393, 394–6; mixed reputation 394–5; son by Pericles 395; legal status 395–6; Plutarch on 393–4, 395, 396

Attalos of Pergamon 147–53; becomes dynast 148; war with Antiochus Hierax 148–9, 150; defeats Galatians 149; takes title 'king' 149; builds at Delphi 150, 153; alliance with Rome 151; alliance with Greeks 152; death 152

Augustine of Hippo, Saint 524–8; birth 524; mother (Monica) 524, 525; as Manichee 523, 524; influence of Neoplatonism 510, 524; influence of Ambrose 525; *Confessions* 525; on celibacy 525, 527; baptised 525; opposes Donatism and Pelagianism 526–7; *City of God* 527; 'concupiscence' idea 527; 'Rule of St Augustine' 527; Augustinian Canons 527; death 524, 526

Augustus (Gaius Octavius Thurinus; Octavian) 197–202; birth 197; adopted by Julius Caesar as heir 197; defeats Brutus and Cassius 198, 202, 300; seizes power 198; uses Cicero against Antony 181–2, 198; forms Second Triumvirate with Antony and Lepidus 198; demobilises and settles army 199–200; War of Perusia 199; sister (Octavia) marries Antony 199, 493; war with Cleopatra and Antony 25, 91, 199, 202, 402, 404–405; *Res Gestae* 200; becomes emperor 191, 200, 312; beautifies Rome 200–201; marriages 201 (*see also* Livia Drusilla); exiles Julia 201, 319, 409; exiles Ovid 319; death 202, 314, 410; Senate deifies 202, 203, 410; Seneca on 409; Tacitus on 200

Boudicca 410–16; marriage to Prasutagus 411, 412, 413; death of Prasutagus 413; flogged by Romans and daughters raped 413; rebels 413–14; massacres at Camulodunum, Londinium and Verulamium 415; last battle 415–16; suicide 416; Tacitus on 415–16

Buddha (Gautama Siddhartha) 501–505; birth 486, 501–502; previous lives 502; Asita visits 502; revelation 502; renounces the world 502–503; adopts Middle Way 503; under Bo-Tree 503; exhorted by a god to preach 503; first disciples 503–504; 'Turning the Wheel of the Doctrine' 504; Four Noble Truths, Noble Eightfold Path 504; chief disciple (Ananda) 504; Five Precepts 504; death 505

Caesar, (Gaius) Julius 182–97; birth and family 182; spared by Sulla 182; defeats Lusitanians but declines triumph 183; early moves with Crassus foiled by Cicero 178; forms First Triumvirate with Crassus and Pompey 179, 183, 401; daughter marries Pompey 184; first consulship 183–4; campaigns in Gaul 184–6; massacres in Britain 185, 410–11; defeats Vercingetorix 185–6; reaffirms Triumvirate 186; death of Crassus 187; crosses Rubicon 188, 194; civil war with Pompey 88, 180, 188; death of Pompey 188; pardons Cicero 180–81; affair with Cleopatra VII 188, 402–403; named dictator 188; refuses crown of kingship 189, 194, 402; murdered 88, 181, 189, 197, 403; Montgomery on 186; Plutarch on 190–96 *passim*, 332; Shakespeare on 189–97, 332

Cambyses 99–103; made king of Babylon 99; conquest of Egypt 100–102, 103;

takes Libya and Cyprus 100, 103; 'lost army' 101; murder of brother 102–103; struggle with Gaumata 102–103; death 103; Darius on 103; Herodotus on 99, 100–102, 103

Cicero, Marcus Tullius 176–82; birth 176; quaestor, praetor, consul 177; counters Caesar and Crassus 178; has Catilinarian conspirators killed 178, 179, 183; flees to Greece 179; supports Pompey against Caesar 180; pardoned by Caesar 180–81; minor works 181; *Republic, Laws, On Duty* 181; works with Octavian against Antony 182; killed 182, 198

Claudius 208–13; descent 208; instructed by Livy 313; declared emperor 209; autobiography 211; discovers cuckoldry 212; marries Agrippina 212, 214; expedition to Britain 212–13, 225, 412; murder 213, 321; Augustus on 209, 408; Suetonius on 211, 213; Tacitus on 212

Cleisthenes 113–20; family 113–15; archon 115; opposes Hippias 115; and Temple of Apollo at Delphi 115–16, 132; takes control of Athens 116–17; reforms 117–19, 121, 122, 359; Herodotus on 116, 117

Cleopatra VII 400–406; birth 400; queenship 402; marries brother 402; flees to Syria 402; defeats brother 402; affair with Caesar 188, 402–403; brought to Rome by Caesar 402–403; son by Caesar 402; relationship with Antony 199, 401–402, 403–405; son by Antony 403; defeat by Octavian 25, 91, 199, 202, 402, 404–405; Antony's death 405; suicide 151, 402, 405–406; Shakespeare on 400, 401

Confucius 490–95; birth 490–91; as teacher 491–2; *Analects* 492, 494; travels 492; *Spring and Autumn Annals* 493; Taoism 494; legendary meeting with Lao Tzu 487; on the Way 489, 494; teaching 494–5; death 493; ritual veneration and worship of 493; later influence 493–4; Mao on 494; Mencius on 491; Sun Yat-sen on 494

Constantine the Great 369–74; birth 369; father (Constantius) 369, 370; in Britain 370; acclaimed Augustus by army 370; becomes Caesar 370; defeats Maxentius at Milvian Bridge 371, 372; Edict of Milan 371–2; donates Lateran to Bishop of Rome 372; commitment to Christianity 369, 372–3, 374; becomes sole emperor 372; Christianity becomes state religion 372; and Arian heresy 372; Church buildings 373; administrative reforms 373; makes Constantinople capital 373–4; baptism 369; death 369; Eumenius on 369; Zosimus on 369

Cyrus the Great 94–9; birth 95; comes to throne 95, 96; takes Sardis and defeats Croesus 96, 98; builds Pasargadae 96–7; takes Babylon and defeats Nabonidus 97–8, 99; rebuilding of Temple in Jerusalem 98; death 98–9; tomb 99; Herodotus on 95, 96, 98, 277; Plutarch on 95; Rich on 99; Xenophon on 95

Darius the Great 103–108; seizes throne 103, 104; campaign in India 104; war against Scythians 104–105; building of Persepolis 106–107; war with Greece 107–108, 427; Ionian revolt 107, 111; sack of Sardis 107, 109, 111; army defeated at Marathon 107–108, 109, 120, 253, 276; death 108, 122; tomb 108; Herodotus on 104, 105, 108, 276

David 78–84; anointed by Samuel 78; kills Goliath 79; marries Saul's daughter (Michal) 79; friendship with Jonathan 79; spares Saul 80; Psalms 80; death of Jonathan and Saul 80–81; proclaimed king of Judah, Israel 81; takes Jerusalem 81; fetches Ark to Jerusalem 81; defeats Philistines 81; adultery with Bath-sheba 82; sends Uriah to death 82, 83; war with Absalom 82; death 82

Democritus 431–7; birth 432; atomism 431–5, 436–7, 456; materialism 432, 433, 456; mentor (Leucippus) 432, 433, 434; on soul 433; on senses 434; eidola 434, 435; on thought, knowledge 434–5; theology 435; mathematics 435–6; cosmology 436–7; Archimedes on 462; Aristotle on 433; Diogenes Laërtius on 432

Diocletian 239–44; birth 239; becomes sole emperor 240; joint-emperorship scheme 236, 240–41, 243–4; military and administrative reforms 241–2; assumes own virtual godhood 242–3; abdicates 243, 370; Gibbon on 242

Erasistratus 454–8; birth 454; pneuma 455–6, 457–8; vivisection 455, 456; dissection 455; on nerves 455; on respiration 449, 456; on digestion 456; on brain 456–7; Galen on 456–7

Eratosthenes 463–8; birth 463; head of Alexandria Library 463, 465; Hermes 465; astronomy, geography, philosophy, geometry 465; writings 465; chronology 465, 466; mathematics 465, 466; estimate of earth's size 453, 462, 466–8, 480; 'sieve' 468; Cleomedes on 466–7; Nicomachus on 468; Strabo on 466, 467

Euclid 442–7; Elements 423–4, 430, 442, 443–7; Data 442; minor works 442, 443; Optics 442–3; Phenomena 443; five postulates 443–6; number science 446; logic 446–7; Proclus on 442, 443

Euripides 277–81; birth 277; first victory 278; Hippolytus 278, 279, 280; Iphigeneia in Aulis 277, 278; Telephus 279, 290; Life 279, 280; mocked by Aristophanes 278, 279, 290–91, 292; attitude to women 279–80; Medea 279–80; Trojan Women, Helen, Heracles, Iphigeneia in Tauris 280; Orestes 280–81; Bacchae 255, 278, 281; Dodds on 281; Murray on 277, 281

Gracchus, Tiberius 364–8; becomes tribune 365; agrarian law 365–7; brother (Caius) 364, 367, 368; re-election vetoed 368; death 164, 368; Cowell on 368; Mommsen on 364

Hadrian 229–34; consul 231; adopted by Trajan as successor 226–7, 230, 232; succeeds 232; travels to Britain 233; starts Wall 233; founds Pantheon 234; adopts Antoninus Pius as successor 236; death 234; Gibbon on 235

Hammurabi 339–44; comes to throne 339; scale of conquests 339; defeats Rim-Sin 340; occupies Mari 340; austerity 340–41; style of kingship 341–2; laws 342–4

Hannibal 153–9; father (Hamilcar Barca) 153, 154; besieges Saguntum 155; crosses Ebro 155, 160; crosses Alps 150, 155; defeats Sempronius 155; defeats Flaminius by Lake Trasimene 155–6; battle of Cannae 156, 166; marches to walls of Rome 157–8; returns to Carthage 158, 161–2; defeated by Scipio at Zama 158, 159, 162; flees into exile 159; received by Antiochus III 76, 159; suicide 159; Livy on 158, 159, 162

Hatshepsut 375–80; co-ruler with Thothmose I 375; crowned pharaoh 7, 375, 377; as co-regent with Thothmose III 7–8, 376–9; temple of Deir el-Bahri 376, 377–8; on own magnificence 376–7, 379–80; relationship with Senmut 378; disappearance 7–8, 379

Hero of Alexandria 473–7; position at Alexandria 473; mathematics 473–4; Formula 474; optics 474; 'aeolipile' 474–5; dioptra 475, 476; hodometer 475; 'automatic theatre' 475–6

Herod I (the Great) 87–94; summoned before Sanhedrin 88; marriage to Mariamme 89–90; made king of Judaea 89; takes Jerusalem 90; murder of Hyrcanus 91; execution of Mariamme 91; execution of mother-in-law (Alexandra) 91–2; rebuilds Temple of Solomon 92; builds Sebaste, Caesarea, Masada, Jericho 92; death 94; Josephus on 90, 91, 93, 94

Herodotus 271–7; birth 271; critical judgement 272, 274; credulity 272, 273,

274; sources 272; *Histories* 273–4, 275–7; geography 274–5; anthropology 274–5; on Artemisia 396; on Cambyses 99, 100–102, 103; on Cleisthenes 116, 117; on Croesus 272, 274; on Cyrus 95, 96, 98, 277; on Darius 104, 105, 108, 276; on Thales 427–8; on Xerxes 108, 109, 112, 274, 275, 276, 398

Herophilus 447–50; birth 447; dissection 447, 454–5; mentor (Praxagoras) 447, 449; teaches at Alexandria 447, 454–5; *Anatomica* 447; on brain, eye, nerves 448, 457; *pneuma* 448; on gynaecology 448–9; on respiration 449; on pulse 449–50; Galen on 447

Hippocrates of Cos 437–41; birth 437; *Collection* 437, 440, 441; Oath 437; humours 438–9; medicine as rational science 438, 441; stress on observation 438, 439, 440; preventive medicine 440–41; *Airs, Waters, Places* 441; *Epidemics* 441

Homer 249–53; birth 249–50; blindness 250; *Iliad* 249, 251–2, 254; *Odyssey* 249; wanderings 250–52; poetic vision 251–3; death 252; influence on Virgil 300; Blackwell on 250–51; Finlay on 252; 'Herodotus' on 250–51, 252

Horace 304–10; birth 305; friendship with Virgil 302, 307; patronised by Augustus 201, 302, 307, 308, 309; *Epodes, Satires* 307; *Odes* 307, 308, 309–10; *Epistles* 307, 308–309; *Ars Poetica, Carmen Saecularae* 309; death 310; Housman on 304–305

Hypatia of Alexandria 422–6; Neoplatonism 422, 424–5, 426; father (Theon) 423–4; work on Ptolemy, Euclid, Apollonius, Diophantus 423–4; correspondence with Synesius 425; murdered 426; Kingsley on 422–3; Socrates on 422, 426

Josephus 333–9; birth 333; *Jewish War* 333, 334–5, 336, 337, 338–9; *Jewish Antiquities* 333, 338, 347; *Against Apion* 333, 338; *Life* 333, 334, 336, 338; in Jewish revolt 333, 334–7; opposes John of Gischala 335, 336; siege of Jerusalem 337, 338; death 338; on Antiochus III 76; on Herod 90, 91, 93, 94; on Moses 347

Lao Tzu 486–90; *Tao Tê Ching* 486, 487, 488–90; birth 486; legends of 487, 488; legendary meeting with Confucius 487; death 488; Taoism 488–9; Quietism 489, 490; on war 489–90; Ssu-ma Ch'ien on 486, 488; Waley on 486, 488

Livia 406–10; birth 406; first husband 406; bears Tiberius 406; flight from Octavian 406–407; marriage to Octavian 201, 203,

406, 407–408, 409–410; Ovid's banishment 319; death of Augustus 410; death 410; Dio Cassius on 407; Seneca on 409; Syme on 408; Tacitus on 407

Livy 310–14; birth 310; sources 312; instructs Claudius 313; *Epitomes* 314; 'Periochae' 314; Dante on 312; Macaulay on 312; Machiavelli on 313, 314; Martial on 314; Pollio on 310–11, 313

Mani 519–24; birth and youth 519–20; first revelation 520; miracles 521; death of patron (Shapur) 521; death 521–2; monotheism 522; Zurvan 522, 523; debt to Zoroastrianism 522, 524; dualism 484, 522–3; Creation ideas 523

Marcus Aurelius 235–9; birth 235; family background 235–6; uncle (Antoninus Pius) 236; consul 236; succeeds 236; haphazard persecution of Christians 237; campaigns in Danube region 237–8; rebellion of Avidius Cassius 237, 238; sets Commodus (son) as co-emperor 238; *Meditations* 238–9; death 238; Gibbon on 235

Marius 164–9; birth 164; tribune 165; Spanish governorship 165; marries Julia 165, 182; command in Africa 165–6; defeats and humiliates Jugurtha 166, 170; re-elected consul 166; militarises society and reforms army 167; defeats Teutones 168; routs Cimbri 168; retires into exile 168; flees from Sulla 168–9, 171–2; with Cinna, takes Rome and institutes bloodbath 169; death 169, 173

Moses 344–50; birth 344–5, 348; theophany 345; leads Hebrews from Egypt 345; death 345, 349; dating of life 346; historical considerations 348–9; Ten Commandments 349–50; Freud on 347; Josephus on 347

Nebuchadnezzar 59–65; birth 60; campaigns in Palestine 60, 61–3; campaigns against Egypt 60, 61, 62–3; comes to throne 60; failed invasion of Egypt 61; siege of Jerusalem 61–2; reconstruction of Babylon 63–4; 'Hanging Gardens' 64

Nero 213–19; birth 214; becomes Claudius's stepson 212, 214; Seneca and Burrus govern Rome 214, 215, 216, 321; concerts 214–15; sexual excesses 215–16; likely incest with Agrippina 215, 216; banishes Agrippina 216, 322; has Agrippina murdered 217, 218, 322, 324; burning of Rome 218; kicks Poppaea to death 218; forced to suicide 219; Suetonius on 215–16, 217, 218; Tacitus on 217

Octavian *see* Augustus

Olympias 385–91; marriage to Philip 386; bears Alexander 140, 386; banishment 138, 140, 387; enmity with Antipater 387–8, 389; and Alexander's death 388, 391; rivalry with Eurydice 389–90; invades Macedon 390; and murder of Philip Arrhidaeus 390; and Eurydice's suicide 390–91; puts Nicanor to death 391; murdered 391; Alexander on 388; Diodorus on 390, 391; Plutarch on 386, 387

Ovid 314–20; birth 315; *Amores, Tristia* 315; marriages 316, 319; *Ars Amatoria* 316–17, 319; *Wars of the Gods and Giants* 317; *Heroides* 317–18; *Metamorphoses* 318, 320; *Fasti* 318, 319; *Remedia Amoris* 319; 'Letter of Sappho to Phaon' 383; banished to Tomi 319–20; death 320

Paul, Saint 515–19; birth 515; execution 515, 517; *Acts* 515, 516; persecutes Christians 516; revelatory conversion 516; missions 516; correspondence with Seneca 324; epistle to Galatians 148; epistle to Corinthians 517; attitude to women 519

Pericles 126–32; birth, family, youth 126, 395; alliance with Themistocles 127; opposition to Cimon 127; given supreme power 127; accepts treaty with Sparta 128; and Athenian buildings 128, 129; encourages great leap forward in arts 128–9; increasing ruthlessness 129; and building of Parthenon 129; prepares for war with Sparta 129–30; plague 130–31; relationship with Aspasia 132 (*see also* Aspasia); son 395; death 131; Plutarch on 131–2, 394, 395, 396; Thucydides on 120–21, 126–7, 128, 132, 284–5

Pheidias 266–71; parentage 266; work on Parthenon 266–7, 268–71; early statues 268, 271; statue of Athena in Parthenon 129, 268, 269, 270–71; statue of Athena at Piraeus 268; association with Pericles 131, 132, 268, 270; processional frieze in Parthenon 270; charged with embezzlement 131, 270; goes to Olympia 271; death 267, 271; discovery (1972) of two statues 271; Lucian on 268; Pliny on 266, 268; Plutarch on 268–9

Philip II of Macedon 133–9; birth 134; comes to throne 134; routs Illyrians 135; takes Amphipolis 135; loss of right eye 136, 139; destroys Olynthus 136, 141; enmity of Demosthenes 136, 137, 138; routs Athenians at Chaironeia 137–8, 173, 294; marriages 138, 385–7; banishment of Olympias 138, 140, 387; murder 138, 140, 387; tomb 138–9;

Alexander on 133; Athenaeus on 385; Satyrus on 385, 386, 387

Pindar 257–61; birth 258; *Pythians* 258, 260, 261; *Olympians* 258, 259, 260, 261; *Nemeans* 258–9; *Isthmians* 258; Sicilian odes 259–61; attacks on 260; death 261; house spared by Alexander 141, 261; Plutarch on 261

Plato 505–10; birth, family 505–506; *Seventh Letter* 506; death of Socrates 506, 507; friendship with Dion 506; death 506, 510; as disciple of Socrates 506; defence of Socrates 506; portrayal of Socrates 507–508, 509; *Apology* 506–507; *Crito* 507; *Phaedo* 507, 508; founds Academy 507; Aristotle as pupil 507, 510; *Republic* 263, 505, 508–509, 514; *Laws, Statesman, Timaeus* 509; influence 509, 514; *Symposium* 291, 393; *Menexenus* 394; Aristotle on 514; on Aristophanes 288, 291, 293; on Aspasia 394; on Sophocles 263

Pliny the Elder 324–9; birth 324; history of Germanic Wars 325; procuratorships 325; adopts Pliny the Younger 325, 326; *Studiosus, Dubius Sermo* 325; *Historia Naturalis* 325–6; death 326, 328; Suetonius on 325; on Pheidias 266, 268; on Praxiteles 295–6; on Pytheas 472

Pliny the Younger 324–9; birth 326; adopted 325, 326; patronises Suetonius and Martial 327; *Letters* 227, 327–8, 329; relations with Trajan 227, 328–9; *Panegyricus* 229, 328, 329; death 328

Plutarch 329–32; birth 329; *Parallel Lives* 329, 330, 332; (*Ethica Moralia*) 330–31, 332; *De facie in orbe lunae* 454; death 330; Montaigne's debt to 331; Shakespeare's debt to 190–96 *passim*, 332; on Archimedes 460; on Aristarchus 454; on Aspasia 393–4, 395, 396; on Caesar 190–96 *passim*; on Cyrus 95; on Olympias and Philip 386, 387; on Pericles 131–2, 394, 395, 396; on Pheidias 268–9; on Pindar 261; on Solon 356, 357; on Sulla 176; on Themistocles 121, 125, 126

Praxiteles 293–8; birth 294; father (Cephisidotos) 294, 295; statue in Temple of Hera, Olympia 294–5; statue of Aphrodite 295–7, 298; Phryne 296, 297–8; Athenaeus on 296; Pausanias on 294–5, 297–8; Pliny on 295–6

Ptolemy (Claudius Ptolemaeus) 477–81; astronomy 477–80, 481; *Almagest* 424, 477, 479–80; geocentrism 451–2, 453, 478–9; *Geography* 480–81; estimate of earth's size 480–81; *Optics* 481; *Handy Tables* 424

Ptolemy I (Soter) 20–25; with Alexander in Asia 21; made satrap of Egypt 21, 67;

causes downfall of Cleomenes 21–2; takes Alexander's body 22, 23; defeats Perdiccas 22; 'Wars of the Successors' 22–3, 67–9; assumes royal titles 22–3, 140; founds Ptolemais 23; Pharos 23; founds Museum, Library at Alexandria 24, 464; patron of Euclid 442; cult of Serapis 24–5; death and deification 25

Ptolemy II (Philadelphus) 26–31; birth 25, 26; becomes sole ruler 26; deifies Ptolemy I 25, 27; marries sister (Arsinoe II) 27; deifies Arsinoe after her death 27; establishes cult of himself and Arsinoe 28; Strato as tutor 30; develops Alexandria Library 24, 29–30, 31, 464; reclaims Fayûm 30–31; death 31; Diodorus Siculus on 30

Pythagoras of Samos 495–500; birth 495; political ideas 495–6; death 496; teaching methods 496; belief in own semi-divinity 496; music 496–7; numerology 497; number science 497–9, 500; on irrational numbers 498–9; on perfect numbers 499; music of the spheres 499–500; Philolaus's cosmology 508; Proclus on 498; Russell on 500

Pytheas 468–73; birth 469; latitude-fixing methods 469, 470, 472; reaches Gaul coast 470; visits Cornwall 470; describes 'ultima Thule' 470–71; reaches Baltic 471; returns home via Britain 472; work on tides 472; Nansen on 471; Pliny on 472; Strabo on 471

Ramesses II (Ozymandias) 11–15; birth 11; joint sovereign 11; building at Karnak 12, 14; campaign in Syria 12–13; treaty with Hittites 13–14; jubilees 15; death 15; analysis of mummy 4–5

Sappho 380–84; birth 381; temporary exile 381; worship of Aphrodite 382; homosexuality 382–3, 384; reputed suicide 382–3; wedding songs 383; influence on Catullus 307; Alcaeus on 381; Devereux on 384; Lefkowitz on 384; Ovid on 383; Solon on 381; von Wilamowitz on 384

Sargon II 42–7; comes to throne 42; Merodach-baladan rebels 42–3, 46, 47; crushes revolt in Hamath 43; relations with Egypt 43–4; crushes Urartu 44–5; conquest of Babylonia 46; new capital (Dur-Sharrukin) 46; fights Cimmerians 46; deportation policy 47; death 46

Scipio 160–64; birth 160; consul 161; clears Carthaginians from Spain 158, 160–61; attacks North Africa 158, 161; defeats Hannibal at Zama 158, 159, 160,

162; against Antiochus III 162–3, 313; castigated by Cato 163; withdraws from Rome 163; death 163; Livy on 162

Seleucus I (Nicator) 65–71; birth 66; campaigns with Alexander 66; death of Perdiccas 67; relations with Antigonus 67–8; satrapy of Babylonia 67, 68; campaigns in Iran 68; becomes king 69; builds Seleucia, Antioch 69–70; struggle with Demetrius 70; struggle with Lysimachus 27, 70–71, 147; murder 27, 71; Arrian on 71

Seneca 321–4; birth 321; banishment Consolations 321; rules with Burrus under Nero 214, 215, 216, 321–2; and Agrippina's murder 217, 322; retirement 322; suicide 218, 322, 324; writings 323–4; on Augustus and Livia 409

Sennacherib 48–53; innovations 48–9; builds Nineveh 49–50; canal-building 50; attacks Jerusalem 51, 53; campaigns against Elam 51–2; destroys Babylon 52, 53; murder 52, 53

Shoshenk I 15–20; descent 15–16; takes throne 16–17; campaigns in Palestine 18–19; takes Jerusalem 18; builds at Memphis, Tanis, Karnak 19

Solomon 83–7; birth 82, 83; murders of Adonijah and Joab 83; comes to throne 83; foreign gods 84, 85, 87; builds in Jerusalem 84–5; struggles with Jeroboam 85–6; death 85; reputed wisdom 86–7; supposed writings 86

Solon 354–9; birth 354; verse 354–5, 357; elected archon 357; economic and political reforms 357–8; retires 358; results of reforms 358–9; death 354; influence on Peisistratos 114–15; Plutarch on 356, 357

Sophocles 262–6; birth 262; Ajax 262, 264; Life 262; defeats Aeschylus 254, 255; first victory 262; friendship with Herodotus 263; homosexuality 263; On the Chorus 263–4; Antigone 264–5, 266; Women of Trachis 264; Oedipus the King 264, 265; Electra 264; Philoctetes 265; Oedipus at Colonus 265–6; death 266; Plato on 263

Sulla 170–76; birth 170; assists Marius against Jugurtha 166, 170; praetor 170; diplomatic contact with Parthians 171; victorious in Social War 171; marches on Rome 168, 171–2; defeats Mithridates 172–3, plunders Delphi, Olympia, Athens 172–3, 268; wins at Chaironeia 173; makes war against Rome 173–4; institutes terror 174, 175, 182; reforms Senate 175, 177; retires 175–6; death 176; Caesar on 175; Sallust on 170; Scullard on 174

Thales of Miletus 427–31; birth 427;
legendary achievements 428; one of
'seven sages' 428; debt of Aristotle, Plato,
Socrates to 428–30; cosmology 429;
mathematics 430; 'Theorem' 430;
reputed eclipse prediction 428, 430–31;
Anaximander as pupil 431; Aristotle on
431; Herodotus on 272, 427–8

Themistocles 120–26; birth 121; archon
121; creates Piraeus 121, 123, 125; and
Persian invasion 123–4; and rebuilding of
Athens 125; alliance with Pericles 125;
impeached 125; flees 125–6; death 126;
Herodotus on 274; Plutarch on 121, 125,
126; Thucydides on 120–21

Theodosius I (the Great) 244–8; birth 244;
elder son (Arcadius) 244, 247, 248;
defeats Sarmatians 244; treaty with
Visigoths 245; makes Constantinople
base 245; outlaws Arian heresy 245;
crushes revolt of Maximus 245–6;
massacre of Thessalonica 246; does
public penance 246; crushes pagan revolt
247–8; death 248; Gibbon on 246, 248

Thothmose III 6–10; succession 7;
Hatshepsut as co-regent 7–8, 376–9; sole
ruler 7, 379; siege of Megiddo 8;
campaign against Mitanni 8–9; subdues
Palestine, Syria 9, 12; campaign in Nubia 9;
builds at Karnak 9–10; tomb 10; death 10

Thucydides 282–7; *History of the
Peloponnesian War* 282–7; account of
plague of Athens 130–31; account of
revolution in Corcyra 283; banished 284;
death 284; political ideas 284–5; Hobbes
on 282, 283, 285; Hume on 282; Kant on
282; Macaulay on 287; on Pericles 120–
21, 126–7, 128, 132, 284–5; on
Themistocles 120–21

Tiberius 202–208; birth 406; marriage of
mother (Livia) to Octavian 203; forced to
marry Julia 201, 203, 408; self-exile in
Rhodes 201, 203, 408–409; becomes
emperor 203, 310; austerity 205–206;
self-exile on Capreae 206–207; sadism
and debauchery 207; death 207; Dio
Cassius on 204; Suetonius on 205, 207

Tiglath-Pileser I 31–6; comes to throne 32;
institutes Annals 32; fights off Mushki 32;
land-settlement policy 33; takes Babylon
34; founds library at Ashur 35–6; laws
36; death 36

Tiglath-Pileser III (Pul) 37–42; comes to
throne 37–8; defeats Urartu 38; new
Assyrian provinces 38–40; deportation
policy 40; defeats Babylonia and becomes
king 40–41; death 41

Trajan 224–9; birth 224; consul 224;
becomes Nerva's successor 224, 231;
succeeds 225, 231; on Rhine, Danube
frontiers 225; campaigns in Dacia 225–6,
229; war against Parthians 226, 229;
adopts Hadrian as successor 226–7, 230;
toleration of Christians 227, 328–9;
redevelopment of Rome 228; death 226,
232; Eutropius on 229; Florus on 228;
Gibbon on 235; Pliny on 228

Vespasian 219–24; campaigns in Britain
213, 221; consul 221; governor of Africa
221; marriage 221; relationship with
Caenis 221; banished by Nero 222;
governor of Judaea 66, 336–7; becomes
emperor 221, 222–3, 336; rebuilds Rome
223; death 224, 337; sons (Titus,
Domitian) 224, 229–30, 231, 337–8;
Suetonius on 223

Virgil 299–304; birth 299, 311; *Eclogues*
300–301, 304; 'The Dispossessed' 300–
301; patronised by Augustus 201, 299,
302, 303, 304; friendship with Horace
302; *Georgics* 302–303, 311; *Aeneid* 201,
303–304, 313; death 304; Dante's debt to
304; Dryden on 302–303

Xerxes 108–13; comes to throne 109;
crushes revolts in Egypt and Babylonia
109, 112; invasion of Greece 108–12, 122,
397–8; battle at Thermopylae 110, 124,
276, 397–8; routed at Salamis 110, 112,
124, 125, 126, 128, 253, 276, 398–9;
destroys Athens 111, 123, 398; routed on
plain of Plataea 111, 124, 129; routed at
Mykale 111, 124; influence of Artemisia
398–400; builds at Persepolis 113; Hall of
the Hundred Columns 106; possible
marriage to Esther 113; murder 113;
Herodotus on 108, 109, 112, 274, 275,
276, 398

Zenobia 416–22; husband (Odaenathus)
417–18, 419; and succession of Gallienus
417–18; death of Odaenathus 418; seizes
power 418, 419; son (Vaballathus) 418,
419, 421–2; religious tolerance 419;
occupies Egypt 419; takes title 'Augusta'
419; rebels against Aurelian 419–21;
defeated by Aurelian and brought to
Rome 421–2; death 422; Gibbon on 418

Zoroaster (Zarathustra) 481–6; dating of
life 481–2; monotheism 482, 483;
revelations 482, 483; Gathas (*Gitas*) 482–3,
484; converts Vishtaspu in Bactria
483; marriages 483; dualism 483–5; on
life after death 484–5; influence 485–6